The Daily Office —
Benedictine and Episcopal
Vol. 2
Lent & Easter

Copyright © 2018
The quotations from the bible
as found in the Canticles, Responsories and biblical antiphons
are taken from the New Revised Standard Version of the Bible
The Psalms in the psalter are taken from The Book of Common Prayer.
The Collects are taken from the Book of Common Prayer unless
otherwise cited in sources at the rear of this book.

ISBN 9798690351113

Table of Contents

Table of Contents — *3*

Dedication — *5*

Introduction — *7*

The Calendar of the Church Year — *13*

Seasons of the Church Year — *25*

The Season of Lent — *25*
    Holy Week — 65
    The Easter Triduum — 83
    Compline for the Triduum — 96

The Easter Season — *125*
    Easter Day — 127
    Easter Season — 131
    Ascension Day — 169
    Pentecost — 179

The Ordinary Of The Daily Office — *185*
    Morning Prayer — 186
    Noonday Prayer — 203
    Evening Prayer — 206
    Compline — 213

The Four Week Psalter — *223*
    Week 1 — 223
    Week 2 — 289
    Week 3 — 359
    Week 4 — 429

The Proper of the Saints — *495*
    February — 496
    March — 509
    April — 531
    May — 537
    June — 548

Common of the Saints — *553*
    Common of the Dedication of a Church — 554
    Common of the Founding of the Community — 563
    Common of the Blessed Virgin Mary — 569
    Common of the Blessed Virgin Mary on Saturday — 578
    Common of the Apostles — 579
    Common of Evangelists — 587
    Common of Martyrs — 597
    Common of Pastors — 601
    Common of Theologians and Teachers — 605
    Common of Teacher of the Faith — 608

Common of Missionaries	612
Common of Prophetic Witnesses	616
Common of Monastics	620
Common of Professed Religious	624
Common of Holy Persons	628
Common of Ember Days	632
Common of Rogation Days	636
Common of National Holidays	640
Common of the Faithful Departed	644

Daily Office Lectionary — Error! Bookmark not defined.

Devotional Prayers — 670

Acknowledgements — 673

Canticles for Daily or Weekly Use — 674

Canticle You are God *Te Deum laudamus*	674
A Song of Creation *Benedicite omnia opera Domini*	675
The Song of Zechariah *Benedictus Dominus Deus*	677
The Song of Mary *Magnificat*	678

Dedication

With gratitude to the Bishops who ordained me
to the deaconate and the priesthood

The Rt. Rev. John Palmer Croneberger
"God did not give us a spirit of cowardice, but rather a spirit of power
and of love and of self-discipline." (2 Timothy 1:7)

The Rt. Rev. Rufus T. Brome
"So he shepherded them with a faithful and true heart
and guided them with the skillfulness of his hands." (Psalm 78:72)

With thanks to the people who helped make this project happen
Angelina Respoli,
Bro. Anthony Maggiore, OSCO of St. Joseph's Abbey,
Bro. Michael Morotti, OSB of Conception Abbey.

With gratitude to the following persons
who graciously reviewed the manuscript
The Rev. Brother Robert Sevensky, OHC,
The Rev. Robert Solon,
The Rev. Diana Wilcox.

Introduction

The Daily Office Benedictine and Episcopal is offered for those who are looking for a form of daily prayer that emerges from the Benedictine and Episcopal traditions. It draws on the fourfold structure of the Daily Office as found in the Book of Common Prayer integrated with material from the Sarum Offices, and the Thesaurus Liturgiae Horarum Monasticae developed by the Benedictine Order in response to the reform of the Liturgy called for by the Second Vatican Council. Howard Massey's Prayer Book Office provided inspiration for this work

The Anglican Tradition places the main hinges of the office on the hours of Morning Prayer and Evening Prayer. In that tradition, the office of Morning Prayer incorporates elements of the monastic office of Vigils and so it should be the more contemplative office. The contemplative nature of this office can be enhanced with silence after the psalms and the readings. In personal use, a period of Lectio Divina can be included after either reading with the conclusion of the office as the end of personal prayer. To incorporate a more Benedictine character of Vigils, a third reading from a Patristic Source can be included after the Second Biblical Reading. Lectionaries of Patristic Readings are readily available.

The Calendar

Since this book is intended for persons who are looking to celebrate a Benedictine and Anglican cycle of saints, the Anglican saints are mostly drawn from Lesser Feasts and Fasts 2006 of the Episcopal Church, the Benedictine saints are taken from the Calendars of the Swiss American Benedictine Congregation and the Cistercians of the Strict Observance, and the Calendar of the Roman Church for those Benedictine saints included in the universal calendar. Women saints from the Apostolic era and presented in Holy Women Holy Men, A Great Cloud of Witnesses and Lesser Feasts and Fasts 2018 are included to provide a gender balance to the traditional twelve apostles. Founders of Religious Communities in the Episcopal Church are included. Finally, this Calendar incorporates some new saints who are significance for New Monastics. The inclusion of these new Monastic Saints marks the beginning of their local cult as a prelude for their submission in the calendar of the Episcopal Church. Saints not included in Lesser Feasts and Fasts 2006 are printed in italic in the Calendar. Saints from the Benedictine Calendar and other saints not in Lesser Feasts and Fasts 2006 are printed in the calendar in italic.

Three Benedictine feasts are ranked as Principal Feasts: St. Scholastica, the Transitus of St. Benedict and St. Benedict. This calendar retains the traditional dates for the Principal and Major feasts of St. Scholastica, the Transitus of St. Benedict, St. Joseph and the Annunciation of Our Lord Jesus Christ to the Blessed Virgin Mary. When these feasts fall in Holy Week, they are transferred to the week following the Second Sunday of Easter with the following order: The Annunciation, St. Joseph and the Transitus of St. Benedict. All the feasts would begin with Morning Prayer.

Following the classifications of the Episcopal Church, the feasts have three ranks: Principal Feasts and Feasts of Our Lord, Major Feasts and Lesser Feasts. Principal Feasts and Feasts of Our Lord are designated in the Calendar in Bold print. They begin with Evening Prayer I and conclude with Evening Prayer II. The Magnificat Antiphon should be used for both Evening Prayer I and Evening Prayer II. Major feasts begin with Morning Prayer, use proper or common antiphons on the psalms and the Sunday or proper psalmody. Major feasts, such as the Apostles and Evangelists, St. Mary the Virgin and Mary Magdalene may also be celebrated with Evening Prayer I which is provided in either the Proper or the Common of the Saints. Lesser Feasts begin with Morning Prayer and conclude with Compline. Lesser feasts may use the common antiphons for the daily psalter or antiphons taken from the common of the saint but a proper or common antiphon should be used with the Benedictus and Magnificat.

The Psalter

While the Rule of St. Benedict requires that the entire Psalter be recited in one week, this office accommodates itself to those persons living a more active life style and so uses a four week psalter. While ever effort was made to retain the assignment of psalms to the offices suggested in the Rule of St. Benedict, such an arrangement could not be scrupulously followed. The present Psalter is structured around the following themes: Sunday, the Resurrection; Monday, Creation; Tuesday, Zion and the Incarnation; Wednesday, Salvation History; Thursday, the Holy Eucharist; Friday, the Cross, and Saturday, Wisdom and the Burial of Christ. Not all the psalms fit into these categories and some psalms could fit into more than one place. Every effort was made to integrate the major themes of the psalms with the corresponding areas of Christian life and thought.

In an effort to integrate the psalms, classic Jewish prayers, into the Christian tradition, a short passage from the Christian Scripture is offered before the psalm to direct the prayer of that psalm toward the mystery of Christ. These phrases can be alternately used as antiphons.

The assigned antiphons are usually taken from the psalms to show how the major themes of the liturgical year can be found in the psalter. Other antiphons are drawn from the Benedictine Thesaurus. the pages of Scripture, the ancient life of the saint or the Rule of St. Benedict.

How To Use This Work

In using this resource, the reader should use a bible as the source for the readings from the Daily Office Lectionary of the Episcopal Church which is included as a resource at the end of this book. If the reader would like to integrate music into the office, as happens in the best parts of the Benedictine Tradition, suggested hymns are taken from the Hymnal 1982.

This book emerges from the Benedictine Tradition and works well with persons who are engaged in a daily practice of Lectio Divina and contemplative prayer. The Verses and Responses as well as the Responsories are structured into the office as a way to integrate Lectio Divina into the Daily Office as well as to take from the offices those short prayers that are used in the course of the day to practice continual prayer. When the offices are prayed in community, the first line of the Responsory would be said by the officiant and the community would reply. This printing of the office prints the first line of the Responsory in the bold print intended for individual recitation of the office. The lectionary could be used as the basis for daily Lectio Divina and the responsories assist in that practice.

The use of this book requires that the user understand some parts of the liturgical cycle of the church. The Revised Common Lectionary uses a three year cycle: Year A, Year B and Year C. During Year A, the readings from the Gospel are taken mostly from Matthew, during Year B mostly from Mark, with an extended passage from the Gospel according to John, and Year C from Luke. Accordingly, the antiphons for the Gospel Canticles on Sunday are taken from the Gospel used for that year. The Episcopal Daily Office Lectionary uses a two year cycle. Advent of the odd numbered years use Year Two and Advent of the even numbered years use Year One.

This Daily Office is structured around a Four Week Psalter. The current week of the Psalter is found in the proper of the Seasons. Week One of the Psalter always begins on the first week of a new liturgical season. The First Week of Advent uses Week 1 of the Psalter. For the Season after Epiphany and the season after Pentecost, the Week of the Psalter is found with the corresponding week of the Season.

The structure of the four offices is found in the Ordinary of the Daily Office found on pages 181 through 201. To use this book, a person should mark the Ordinary of the Daily Office since the structure of the

Hours is laid out in the Ordinary. The other mark should designate the Week of the Psalter. If a saint's day is being celebrated, the third mark should be placed on the page for that saint's day. If you enjoy a more complete office for a saint with a lesser feast, you can also use the common of that saint with antiphons on the psalms of the day, responsories, a canticle after the first reading for Morning Prayer, antiphons on the Gospel Canticle and a litany.. If a day celebrates a season, a mark should be placed on that day for the season along with a mark on the particular week or day which is being celebrated.

The Common Office for the Dedication of a Church would be used by individual members to celebrate the Dedication of their home church.

The Common of the Founding of the Community would be used by religious communities on their Founding Day. Communities which use this resource should consider adapting at least the Antiphons on the Benedictus and Magnificat with passages which reflect the charism of that community.

The Saturday Common Office of the Blessed Virgin Mary can be used on those Saturdays which do not celebrate a particular saint. This Saturday Common Office of the Blessed Virgin Mary is offered as a devotional office. It includes an Invitatory Antiphon, a Hymn, Antiphons for the Benedictus and a concluding Litany and Collect. While the full office should not be used during the Seasons of Advent, Christmas, Lent and Easter, a person can include the Benedictus antiphon provided for those seasons.

The Office of the Dead is included for use on the Commemoration of All Faithful Departed, for the Faithful Departed of the Benedictine Order and for personal use to pray for a person who has died on the day of their death or the anniversary of their death. The Office for the Dead should never be used on Sundays, the Easter Triduum, or Principle or Major Feasts.

Unique Qualities of The Office in this Work

This Daily Office attempts to bring a greater simplicity to the office, respecting the structure of the office as presented by St. Benedict. A single collect concludes each office and devotional elements, such as the General Thanksgiving, are not included. A collect from the Book of Common Prayer is provided as an alternative to the ferial offices for the Seasons after Epiphany and Pentecost. In this volume, the collect would be taken from the day of the season or of the saint of the day.

This office follows the Benedictine practice of including an intercessory litany with the threefold Kyrie at Morning and Evening Prayer which replaces the Suffrages.

The traditional conclusion of the Offices from the Book of Common Prayer is provided as an alternate structure for the hours. This pattern includes the Apostles' Creed, the Lord's Prayer, three collects, the General Thanksgiving and the Prayer of St. Chrysostom.

Many people engage in a practice of intercessory prayer and the Noonday Office is structured to provide opportunity for prayer for the needs of the World, the Church and personal concerns. These needs can be included in a litany which provides a place for these needs to be raised in spontaneous prayer. Since this office traditionally remembers the hour of the Descent of the Holy Spirit and the Crucifixion of our Lord, the collects and hymns reflect that remembrance.

Compline follows the pattern of the Sarum Office. Proper parts are included for the Gospel Canticle.

While an older tradition would celebrate the offices of the Triduum of Easter with a unique pattern for the office, this book follows the current Benedictine tradition which uses the same structure for the Triduum Offices.

A number of people helped in the production of this series. I am most grateful to Angelina Respoli for her initial reading of the text and her insightful conversations on liturgy, to Bro. Steven Joseph Olderr, O.S.B., for his technical insights on publishing, to Bro. Anthony Maggiore, O.S.C.O., for his assistance in identifying liturgical resources from the Trappists, and to Bro. Michael Morotti, O.S.B. for his help on Benedictine materials. I am thankful to the following persons who graciously reviewed the initial manuscript: the Rev. Brother Robert Sevensky, O.H.C., the Rev. Robert Solon and the Rev. Diana Wilcox.

I deeply regret that this work does not include inclusive language about God. Since the core of the book is the translation of the Psalms from the Book of Common Prayer, I followed the pattern of the language on God as found in that book. The structure of the calendar moves toward a more inclusive monastic calendar.

St. Benedict urges us to prefer nothing to the work of God. (RB 43) This book is offered as a means of integrating the Benedictine culture with the Anglican Tradition as received by the Episcopal Church. As countless Christians, lay, monastic and ordained, found in the Daily Office a source for the sanctification of the day and an entry into the Mystery of Christ, this book is presented with the prayer that its users may continue to discover the richness of the Daily Office as an integral part of the Benedictine and Episcopal Traditions.

February 10, 2020
St. Scholastica
Peter De Franco

The Calendar of the Church Year

January
1 A **THE HOLY NAME OF OUR LORD JESUS CHRIST**
2 b
3 c
4 d *Elizabeth Seton, Professed Religious and Founder of the American Sisters of Charity, 1821*
5 e *Sarah, Theodora, and Syncletica of Egypt, Desert Mothers, 4th-5th century*
6 F **THE EPIPHANY OF OUR LORD JESUS CHRIST**
7 g
8 A Harriet Bedell, Deaconess and Missionary, 1969
9 b Julia Chester Emery, 1922
10 c William Laud, Archbishop of Canterbury, 1645
11 d
12 e Aelred, Cistercian Monk, Abbot of Rievaulx, 1167
13 f Hilary, Bishop of Poitiers and Teacher of the Faith, 367
14 g *Richard Meux Benson, Religious and Founder of the Society of St. John the Evangelist, 1915 and Charles Gore, Founder of the Community of the Resurrection, Bishop of Worcester, of Birmingham, and of Oxford,1932*
15 A *Maur and Placid, Disciples of St. Benedict*
16 b
17 c Antony, Abbot in Egypt, 356
18 d **The Confession of Saint Peter the Apostle**
19 e Wulfstan, Bishop of Worcester, 1095
20 f Fabian, Bishop and Martyr of Rome, 250
21 g Agnes, Martyr at Rome, 304
22 A Vincent, Deacon of Saragossa, Martyr, 304
23 b Phillips Brooks, Bishop of Massachusetts, 1893
24 c Florence Li Tim-Oi, First Woman Priest in the Anglican Communion, 1944
25 d **The Conversion of Saint Paul the Apostle**
26 e Timothy and Titus, Companions of Saint Paul
26 e *Robert of Molesme, Alberic and Stephen Harding, Abbots and Founders of the Cistercian Order*
27 f John Chrysostom, Bishop of Constantinople and Teacher of the Faith, 407
28 g Thomas Aquinas, Friar, Priest and Teacher of the Faith 1274
29 A
30 b
31 c *Marcella of Rome, Urban Monastic and Scholar, 410*

February

1 d Brigid (Bride), 523
2 e **THE PRESENTATION OF OUR LORD JESUS CHRIST IN THE TEMPLE**
3 f Anskar, Archbishop of Hamburg and Missionary to Denmark and Sweden, 865
4 g Cornelius the Centurion
5 A *Agatha of Sicily, Martyr c. 251*
6 b The Martyrs of Japan, 1597
7 c
8 d
9 e *Anne Ayers, Religious and Founder of the Sisterhood of the Holy Communion, 1896*
10 F ***SCHOLASTICA, NUN AND SISTER OF BENEDICT, 542***
11 g *Benedict of Aniane, Abbot, 821*
12 A
13 b Absalom Jones, Priest, 1818
14 c Cyril, Monk, and Methodius, Bishop, Missionaries to the Slavs, 869, 885
15 d Thomas Bray, Priest and Missionary, 1730
16 e
17 f Janani Luwum, Archbishop of Uganda and Martyr, 1977
18 g Martin Luther, Reformer, 1546
19 A
20 b
21 c
22 d **Saint Matthias the Apostle**
23 e Polycarp, Bishop and Martyr of Smyrna, 156
24 f
25 g *Walburga, Benedictine Abbess of Double Monastery of Heidenheim, c 777*
26 A *Photini, The Samaritan Woman, Equal to the Apostles*
27 b George Herbert, Priest, 1633
28 c
29

March

1 d David, Bishop of Menevia, Wales, c. 544
2 e Chad, Bishop of Lichfield, 672
3 f John and Charles Wesley, Priests, 1791, 1788
4 g
5 A
6 b
7 c Perpetua, Felicity and their Companions, Martyrs at Carthage, 202
8 d
9e Gregory, Bishop of Nyssa, c. 394
9 e *Frances of Rome, Married Woman, Founder of the Olivetan Oblates of Mary and Benedictine Oblate, 1440*
10 f
11 g
12 A Gregory the Great, Monk, Bishop of Rome and Teacher of the Faith, 604
13 b James Theodore Holly, Bishop of Haiti and of the Dominican Republic, 1911
14 c
15 d
16 e
17 f Patrick, Bishop and Missionary of Ireland, 461
18 g Cyril, Bishop of Jerusalem and Teacher of the Faith, 386
19 A **Saint Joseph**
20 b Cuthbert, Monk and Bishop of Lindisfarne, 687
21 C ***TRANSITUS OF OUR HOLY FATHER SAINT BENEDICT***
22 d James De Koven, Priest, 1879
23 e Gregory the Illuminator, Bishop and Missionary of Armenia, c. 332
24 f Óscar Romero, Archbishop of San Salvador, and the Martyrs of San Salvador, 1980
25 G **THE ANNUNCIATION OF OUR LORD JESUS CHRIST TO THE BLESSED VIRGIN MARY**
26 A *Harriet Monsell, Professed Religious, Founder of the Community of St. John Baptist, 1883*
27 b Charles Henry Brent, Bishop of the Philippines, and of Western New York, 1929
28 c
29 d John Keble, Priest, 1866
30 e
31 f John Donne, Priest, 1631

April

1 g Frederick Denison Maurice, Priest, 1872
2 A James Lloyd Breck, Priest, 1876
3 b Richard, Bishop of Chichester, 1253
3 b *Mary of Egypt, Monastic c. 421*
4 c Martin Luther King, Jr., Pastor and Civil Rights Leader, 1968
5 d *Harriet Starr Cannon and her companions, Professed Religious, and Founders of the Community of St. Mary, 1896*
6 e
7 f Tikhon, Patriarch of Russia, Confessor and Ecumenist, 1925
8 g William Augustus Muhlenberg, Priest, 1877
9 A Dietrich Bonhoeffer, Theologian and Martyr 1945
10 b William Law, Priest, 1761
11 c George Augustus Selwyn, Bishop of New Zealand, and of Lichfield, 1878
12 d
13 e
14 f
15 g
16 A
17 b
18 c
19 d Alphege, Archbishop of Canterbury, and Martyr, 1012
20 e
21 f Anselm, Monk, Archbishop of Canterbury, and Teacher of the Faith, 1109
22 g *Hadewijch of Brabant, Beguine, Poet and Mystic, 13th Century*
23 A
24 b
25 c **Saint Mark the Evangelist**
26 d
27 e
28 f
29 g Catherine of Siena, Dominican Tertiary, Teacher of the Faith, 1380
30 A

May

1 b ***Saint Philip and Saint James, Apostles***
2 c Athanasius, Bishop of Alexandria, and Teacher of the Faith, 373
3 d
4 e Monnica, Mother of Augustine of Hippo, 387
5 f
6 g
7 A
8 b Dame Julian of Norwich, Hermit, and Mystic, c. 1417
9 c Gregory of Nazianzus, Bishop of Constantinople, and Teacher of the Faith, 389
10 d
11 e *The Holy Abbots of Cluny: Odo, Mayeul, Odilo, Hugh, and Peter the Venerable*
12 f
13 g *Bede Griffiths, Benedictine Monk, Yogi, Priest 1993*
14 A
15 b *Junia and Andronicus, Coworkers of the Apostle Paul*
15 b *Pachomius, Abbot, 348*
16 c *The Martyrs of the Sudan 1983-2011*
17 d
18 e
19 f Dunstan, Monk, Restorer of the Monastic Life and Archbishop of Canterbury, 988
20 g Alcuin, Deacon, and Abbot of Tours, 804
21 A
22 b *Lydia of Thyatira, Coworker of the Apostle Paul*
23 c
24 d Jackson Kemper, First Missionary Bishop in the United States, 1870
25 e Bede, the Venerable, Priest, Monk of Jarrow and Teacher of the Faith, 735
26 f Augustine, Monk and First Archbishop of Canterbury, 605
27 g
28 A *Mechthild of Magdeburg, Mystic, Beguine, Benedictine Nun c.1282*
29 b
30 c
31 D **THE VISITATION OF THE BLESSED VIRGIN MARY**

The First Book of Common Prayer, 1549, is appropriately observed on a weekday following the Day of Pentecost.

June

1 e Justin, Martyr at Rome, c. 167
2 f Blandina and her Companions, Martyrs of Lyons, 173
3 g The Martyrs of Uganda, 1886
4 A
5 b Boniface, Monk, Archbishop of Mainz, Missionary to Germany and Martyr, 754
6 c *Ini Kopuria, Professed Religious, Founder of the Melanesian Brotherhood, 1945*
7 d
8 e *Melania the Elder, Monastic, 410*
9 f Columba, Abbot of Iona, 597
10 g Ephrem of Edessa, Syria, Deacon and Teacher of the Faith 373
11 A **Saint Barnabas the Apostle**
12 b Enmegahbowh, Priest and Missionary, 1902
12 b *Alice of Schaerbeek, Cistercian Nun and Leper, 1250*
13 c
14 d Basil the Great, Monk, Author of a Monastic Rule, Bishop of Caesarea and Teacher of the Faith, 379
15 e Evelyn Underhill, Mystic and Theologian, 1941
16 f Joseph Butler, Bishop of Durham, 1752
16 f *Lutgard, Cistercian Nun, 1246*
17 g
18 A Bernard Mizeki, Catechist and Martyr in Rhodesia, 1896
18 A *Elisabeth of Schönau, Benedictine Abbess and Mystic, 1164*
19 b *Romuald, Abbot and Founder of the Camaldolese Order, 1027*
20 c
21 d
22 e Alban, First Martyr of Britain, c. 304
23 f *Etheldreda, Benedictine Abbess of Double Monastery at Ely, 697*
24 g **THE NATIVITY OF SAINT JOHN THE BAPTIST**
25 A
26 b
27 c
28 d Irenaeus, Bishop of Lyons, c. 202
29 e **Saint Peter and Saint Paul, Apostles**
30 f

July

1 g
2 A
3 b
4 c *Independence Day*
5 d
6 e *Eva Lee Matthews, Professed Religious, Founder of the Sisters of the Transfiguration, 1928*
7 f
8 g *Priscilla and Aquila, Coworkers of the Apostle Paul*
9 A
10 b
11 c **OUR HOLY FATHER SAINT BENEDICT OF NURSIA, ABBOT OF MONTE CASSINO, C. 540**
12 d *John Gualbert, Abbot, Founder of the Vallumbrosan Order*
13 e *Henry, Holy Roman Emperor and Benedictine Oblate, 1023*
14 f
15 g
16 A
17 b William White, Bishop of Pennsylvania, 1836
18 c
19 d Macrina, Monastic and Teacher, 379
20 e Elizabeth Cady Stanton, Amelia Bloomer, Sojourner Truth, and Harriet Ross Tubman
20 e *Maria Skobtsoba, Monastic and Martyr, 1945*

21 f
22 g ***Saint Mary Magdalene***
23 A *John Cassian, Abbot at Marseilles, 433*
24 b Thomas a Kempis, Priest, 1471
25 c ***Saint James the Apostle***
26 d Joachim and Anne, The Parents of the Blessed Virgin Mary
27 e William Reed Huntington, Priest, 1909
28 f
29 g Mary, Martha and Lazarus of Bethany, Hosts and Friends of our Lord
30 A William Wilberforce, 1833
31 b Ignatius of Loyola, Religious, Priest and Founder of the Society of Jesus, 1556

August

1 c Joseph of Arimathaea
2 d
3 e *Joanna, Mary, and Salome, Myrrh-bearing Women*
4 f
5 g
6 A **THE TRANSFIGURATION OF OUR LORD JESUS CHRIST**
7 b John Mason Neale, Priest, 1866
8 c Dominic, Friar, Priest and Founder of the Order of Preachers, 1221
9 d *Teresa Benedicta of the Cross, Scholar, Carmelite Nun and Martyr, 1942*
10 e Laurence, Deacon, and Martyr at Rome, 258
11 f Clare, Abbess at Assisi and Founder of the Poor Clares, 1253
12 g Florence Nightingale, Nurse and Social Reformer, 1910
13 A Jeremy Taylor, Bishop of Down, Connor, and Dromore, 1667
14 b Jonathan Myrick Daniels, Seminarian, Martyr and Witness for Civil Rights, 1965
15 c **SAINT MARY THE VIRGIN, MOTHER OF OUR LORD JESUS CHRIST**
16 d *Roger Schutz, Monk and Founder of Taizé, 2005*
17 e
18 f William Porcher DuBose, Priest, 1918
19 g
20 A Bernard, Abbot of Clairvaux and Teacher of the Faith, 1153
21 b
22 c
23 d
24 e Saint Bartholomew the Apostle
25 f Louis, King of France, 1270
26 g *Raimon Panikkar, Priest and Theologian of the New Monasticism, 2010*
27 A Thomas Gallaudet, 1902 with Henry Winter Syle, 1890
28 b Augustine, Bishop of Hippo and Teacher of the Faith, 430
29 c
30 d
31 e Aidan, Monk and Bishop of Lindisfarne, 651

September

1 f David Pendleton Oakerhater, Deacon and Missionary, 1931
2 g The Martyrs of New Guinea, 1942
3 A *Phoebe, Deacon*
4 b Paul Jones, Bishop and Prophetic Witness, 1941
5 c
6 d
7 e
8 f *The Nativity of the Blessed Virgin Mary*
9 g Constance, Nun, and her Companions, Martyrs 1878
10 A Alexander Crummell, Priest, Prophetic Witness and Founder of the Union of Black Episcopalians 1898
11 b
12 c John Henry Hobart, Bishop of New York, 1830
13 d Cyprian, Bishop and Martyr of Carthage, 258
14 E **HOLY CROSS DAY**
15 f
16 g Ninian, Bishop in Galloway, c. 430
17 A Hildegard, Abbess and Teacher of the Faith, 1179
18 b Edward Bouverie Pusey, Priest, 1882
19 c Theodore of Tarsus, Archbishop of Canterbury, 690
20 d John Coleridge Patteson, Bishop of Melanesia, and his Companions, Martyrs, 1871
21 e **Saint Matthew, Apostle and Evangelist**
22 f Philander Chase, Bishop of Ohio, and of Illinois, 1852
23 g
24 A
25 b Sergius, Abbot of Holy Trinity, Moscow, 1392
26 c Lancelot Andrewes, Bishop of Winchester, 1626
27 d
28 e *Richard Rolle, 1349, Walter Hilton, 1396, and Margery Kempe, c. 1440, Mystics*
28 e *Lioba, Benedictine Abbess of Bischofsheim and Companion of St Boniface, 782*
29 f **Saint Michael and All Angels**
30 g Jerome, Monk of Bethlehem, Priest and Teacher of the Faith, 420

October

1 A Remigius, Bishop of Rheims, c. 530
1 A *Therese of the Child Jesus and the Holy Face, Discalced Carmelite Nun and Teacher of the Faith, 1897*
2 b
3 c
4 d Francis of Assisi, Friar, Deacon and Founder of the Friars Minor, 1226
5 e
6 f *Bruno, Hermit, Founder of the Carthusian Order 1101*
7 g William Tyndale, Priest, 1536
8 A
9 b Robert Grosseteste, Bishop of Lincoln, 1253
10 c Vida Dutton Scudder, Educator and Witness for Peace, 1954
11 d Philip, Deacon and Evangelist
11 d *Ethelburga, Benedictine Abbess of double monastery at Barking, 675*
12 e
13 f
14 g Samuel Isaac Joseph Schereschewsky, Bishop of Shanghai, 1906
15 A Teresa of Jesus, Discalced Carmelite Nun, Founder of the Discalced Carmelites, Mystic and Teacher of the Faith, 1582
16 b Hugh Latimer and Nicholas Ridley, Bishops, 1555 and Thomas Cranmer, Archbishop of Canterbury, 1556, Martyrs
17 c Ignatius, Bishop of Antioch, and Martyr, c. 115
18 d **Saint Luke the Evangelist**
19 e Henry Martyn, Priest, and Missionary to India and Persia, 1812
20 f
21 g
22 A
23 b **Saint James of Jerusalem, Brother of Our Lord Jesus Christ, and Martyr, c. 62**
24 c
25 d *Tabitha (Dorcas) of Joppa*
26 e Alfred the Great, King of the West Saxons, 899
27 f
28 g **Saint Simon and Saint Jude, Apostles**
29 A James Hannington, Bishop of Eastern Equatorial Africa, and his Companions, Martyrs, 1885
29 A *Maryam of Qidun, Monastic, 4th century*
30 b
31 c

November
1 D **ALL SAINTS**
2 e Commemoration of All Faithful Departed
3 f Richard Hooker, Priest, 1600
4 g
5 A
6 b William Temple, Archbishop of Canterbury, 1944
7 c Willibrord, Monk, Archbishop of Utrecht and Missionary to Frisia, 739
8 d
9 e
10 f Leo the Great, Bishop of Rome and Teacher of the Faith, 461
11 g Martin, Monk, Bishop of Tours, 397
12 A Charles Simeon, Priest, 1836
13 b *All Saints of the Benedictine Order*
14 c *All the Faithful Departed of the Benedictine Order*
14 c Consecration of Samuel Seabury, First American Bishop, 1784
15 d
16 e Margaret, Queen of Scotland, 1093
16 e *Gertrude the Great, Benedictine Nun of Helfta, Mystic and Theologian, 1302*
17 f Hugh, Carthusian Monk and Bishop of Lincoln, 1200
18 g Hilda, Abbess of Whitby, 680
19 A *Mechtilde of Hackeborn, Benedictine Nun of Helfta, Mystic and Theologian, 1298*
19 A Elizabeth, Princess of Hungary, 1231
20 b Edmund, King of East Anglia, 870
21 c
22 d *Cecelia, Martyr, 230*
22 d Clive Staples Lewis, Apologist and Spiritual Writer, 1963
23 e Clement, Bishop of Rome, c. 100
24 f
25 g James Otis Sargent Huntington, Priest and Monk, Founder of the Order of the Holy Cross, 1935
26 A
27 b
28 c Kamehameha and Emma, King and Queen of Hawaii, 1864, 1885
29 d *Dorothy Day, Founder of Catholic Worker, Benedictine Oblate and Prophetic Witness 1980*
30 e **Saint Andrew the Apostle**

December

1 f Nicholas Ferrar, Deacon and Founder of Little Gidding, 1637
2 g Channing Moore Williams, Missionary Bishop in China and Japan, 1910
3 A
4 b John of Damascus, Priest, c. 760
5 c Clement of Alexandria, Priest and Teacher of the Faith, c. 210
6 d Nicholas, Bishop of Myra, c. 342
7 e Ambrose, Bishop of Milan and Teacher of the Faith, 397
8 f
9 g
10 A *Thomas Merton, Trappist Monk, Priest and Contemplative Writer, 1968*
11 b
12 c
13 d *Lucy, Martyr, 304*
14 e *John of the Cross, Carmelite Friar, Priest, Mystic and Teacher of the Faith, 1591*
15 f
16 g O Sapientia
17 A O Adonai
18 b O Radix
19 c O Clavis
20 d O Oriens
21 e **Saint Thomas the Apostle**
21 e O Rex
22 f O Emmanuel
23 g O Virgo virginum
24 A
25 B **THE NATIVITY OF OUR LORD JESUS CHRIST**
26 c **Saint Stephen, Deacon and Martyr**
27 d **Saint John, Apostle and Evangelist**
28 e **The Holy Innocents**
29 f Thomas Becket, Archbishop of Canterbury and Martyr, 1170
30 g Frances Joseph Gaudet, Educator and Prison Reformer, 1934
31 A

Seasons of the Church Year

The Season of Lent

The Lenten Season Psalter Schedule

The First Sunday in Lent begins with Sunday 1 Evening Prayer I.
The Second Sunday in Lent begins with Sunday 2 Evening Prayer I.
The Third Sunday in Lent begins with Sunday 3 Evening Prayer I.
The Fourth Sunday in Lent begins with Sunday 4 Evening Prayer I.
The Fifth Sunday in Lent begins with Sunday 1 Evening Prayer I.

The Season of Lent begins with Ash Wednesday. The Psalmody for Ash Wednesday is taken from Wednesday Week 4. The Alleluia is not said during Lent. The Te Deum is not used. When Lesser Feasts are observed, only the Antiphons on the Benedictus and the Antiphons are used. The Antiphons for the psalms, the responsories and the antiphon and canticle after the first reading at Morning Prayer are taken from the Lenten Propers. This practice maintains the integrity of the Lenten Season while acknowledging the Lesser Feast. There are proper liturgical celebrations for the days of Holy Week and the Easter Triduum.

Lent Sunday Evening Prayer I

Hymn Kind Maker of the world *Hymnal 152*

Responsory (Ps. 41:4)
Lord, be merciful to us
   − for we have sinned against you.
Hear, O Christ, our prayer of penitence.
   − for we have sinned against you.
Glory to the Father and to the Son and to the Holy Spirit.
Lord, be merciful to us
   − for we have sinned against you.

Magnificat Antiphon
Year A
First Sunday in Lent
Antiphon Jesus was led up by the Spirit into the wilderness to be tempted by the devil. He fasted forty days and forty nights, and afterwards he was famished.
Second Sunday in Lent
Antiphon No one can enter the kingdom of God without being born of water and Spirit. What is born of the flesh is flesh, and what is born of the Spirit is spirit..
Third Sunday in Lent
Antiphon Those who drink of the water that I will give them will never be thirsty. The water that I will give will become in them a spring of water gushing up to eternal life.

Fourth Sunday in Lent
Antiphon I must work the works of him who sent me while it is day; night is coming when no one can work.
Fifth Sunday in Lent
Antiphon Now a certain man was ill, Lazarus of Bethany, the village of Mary and her sister Martha. Mary was the one who anointed the Lord with perfume and wiped his feet with her hair; her brother Lazarus was ill.

Year B
First Sunday in Lent
Antiphon You are my Son, the Beloved; with you I am well pleased.
Second Sunday in Lent
Antiphon Jesus began to teach them that the Son of Man must undergo great suffering, and be rejected by the elders, and be killed, and after three days rise again.
Third Sunday in Lent
Antiphon Making a whip of cords, Jesus drove all of them out of the temple, both the sheep and the cattle and poured out the coins of the money changers.
Fourth Sunday in Lent
Antiphon Just as Moses lifted up the serpent in the wilderness, so must the Son of Man be lifted up, that whoever believes in him may have eternal life.
Fifth Sunday in Lent
Antiphon Very truly, I tell you, unless a grain of wheat falls into the earth and dies, it remains just a single grain; but if it dies, it bears much fruit.

Year C
First Sunday in Lent
Antiphon Jesus, full of the Holy Spirit, returned from the Jordan and was led by the Spirit in the wilderness, where for forty days he was tempted by the devil.
Second Sunday in Lent
Antiphon I am casting out demons and performing cures today and tomorrow, and on the third day I finish my work.
Third Sunday in Lent
Antiphon Unless you repent, you will all perish as the Galileans whose blood Pilate had mingled with their sacrifices.
Fourth Sunday in Lent
Antiphon Father, give me the share of the property that will belong to me. So he divided his property between them.

Fifth Sunday in Lent
Antiphon Six days before the Passover Jesus came to Bethany, the home of Lazarus, whom he had raised from the dead. There they gave a dinner for him. Martha served, and Lazarus was one of those at the table with him.

Litany
Nourish us with the true bread from heaven that we may ever abide in you as you abide in us.
Lord, have mercy.
Grant us to love what you command and to desire what you promise that our hearts may be firmly fixed on you.
Christ, have mercy.
Strengthen our faith in your death on the cross by which you open the gates of heaven to all people.
Lord, have mercy.

Invitation to the Lord's Prayer
Christ continues to draw us ever deeper into the mystery of his saving love and so with Christ we seek the Father.

Collect
First Sunday in Lent
Almighty God, whose blessed Son was led by the Spirit to be tempted by Satan; Come quickly to help us who are assaulted by many temptations; and, as you know the weaknesses of each of us, let each one find you mighty to save; through Jesus Christ your Son our Lord, who lives and reigns with you and the Holy Spirit, one God, now and for ever. Amen.

Second Sunday in Lent
O God, whose glory it is always to have mercy: Be gracious to all who have gone astray from your ways, and bring them again with penitent hearts and steadfast faith to embrace and hold fast the unchangeable truth of your Word, Jesus Christ your Son; who with you and the Holy Spirit lives and reigns, one God, for ever and ever. Amen.

Third Sunday in Lent
Almighty God, you know that we have no power in ourselves to help ourselves: Keep us both outwardly in our bodies and inwardly in our souls, that we may be defended from all adversities which may happen to the body, and from all evil thoughts which may assault and hurt the soul; through Jesus Christ our Lord, who lives and reigns with you and the Holy Spirit, one God, for ever and ever. Amen.

Fourth Sunday in Lent
Gracious Father, whose blessed Son Jesus Christ came down from heaven to be the true bread which gives life to the world: Evermore give

us this bread, that he may live in us, and we in him; who lives and reigns with you and the Holy Spirit, one God, now and for ever. Amen.

Fifth Sunday in Lent
Almighty God, you alone can bring into order the unruly wills and affections of sinners: Grant your people grace to love what you command and desire what you promise; that, among the swift and varied changes of the world, our hearts may surely there be fixed where true joys are to be found; through Jesus Christ our Lord, who lives and reigns with you and the Holy Spirit, one God, now and for ever. Amen.

The Blessing
May our way of acting differ from the way of the world and may the love of Christ come before all else. **Amen.**

Lent Sunday Morning Prayer

Invitatory The Lord is full of compassion and mercy: Come let us adore him.

Hymn Lord who throughout these forty days *Hymnal 142*

Responsory One (Ps. 91:3)
God shall deliver you
    —from the snare of the hunter.
From the deadly pestilence
    —from the snare of the hunter.
Glory to the Father and to the Son and to the Holy Spirit.
God shall deliver you
    —from the snare of the hunter.

Canticle of the Suffering Servant I *Ecce servus meus*
(Isaiah 42: 1-4)

Antiphon My servant will faithfully bring forth justice.

Here is my servant, whom I uphold, *
    my chosen, in whom my soul delights.

I have put my spirit upon him; *
    he will bring forth justice to the nations.

He will not cry or lift up his voice, *
    or make it heard in the street.

A bruised reed he will not break, *
    and a dimly burning wick he will not quench.
    He will faithfully bring forth justice.

He will not grow faint or be crushed *
   until he has established justice in the earth;
   and the coastlands wait for his teaching.

Antiphon My servant will faithfully bring forth justice.

Responsory Two (Ps. 123:4; Ps. 41:40
I say to the Lord
   — **have mercy on me.**
Heal my soul, for I have sinned.
   — **have mercy on me.**
Glory to the Father and to the Son and to the Holy Spirit.
I say to the Lord
   — **have mercy on me.**

Benedictus Antiphon
Year A
First Sunday in Lent
Antiphon One does not live by bread alone, but by every word that comes from the mouth of God.
Second Sunday in Lent
Antiphon Just as Moses lifted up the serpent in the wilderness, so must the Son of Man be lifted up, that whoever believes in him may have eternal life.
Third Sunday in Lent
Antiphon The hour is coming when the true worshipers will worship the Father in spirit and truth.
Fourth Sunday in Lent
Antiphon The man called Jesus made mud, spread it on my eyes, and said to me, 'Go to Siloam and wash.' Then I received my sight.
Fifth Sunday in Lent
Antiphon I am the resurrection and the life. Those who believe in me, even though they die, will live, [26]and everyone who lives and believes in me will never die.

Year B
First Sunday in Lent
Antiphon Jesus was in the wilderness forty days, tempted by Satan; and he was with the wild beasts; and the angels waited on him.
Second Sunday in Lent
Antiphon If any want to become my followers, let them deny themselves and take up their cross and follow me.
Third Sunday in Lent
Antiphon Destroy this temple, and in three days I will raise it up.

Fourth Sunday in Lent
Antiphon God so loved the world that he gave his only Son, so that everyone who believes in him may not perish but may have eternal life.
Fifth Sunday in Lent
Antiphon Those who love their life lose it, and those who hate their life in this world will keep it for eternal life.

Year C
First Sunday in Lent
Antiphon Jesus ate nothing at all during those days, and when they were over, he was famished.
Second Sunday in Lent
Antiphon O Jerusalem! How often have I desired to gather your children together as a hen gathers her brood under her wings, and you were not willing.
Third Sunday in Lent
Antiphon For three years I have come looking for fruit on this fig tree, and still I find none. Cut it down!
Fourth Sunday in Lent
Antiphon He came to himself he said, "I will get up and go to my father, and I will say to him, "Father, I have sinned against heaven and before you."
Fifth Sunday in Lent
Antiphon Mary took a pound of costly perfume made of pure nard, anointed Jesus' feet, and wiped them with her hair. The house was filled with the fragrance of the perfume.

Litany
Come quickly to help us who are assaulted by many temptations and show us the might of your saving power.
Lord, have mercy.
Be gracious to us who have gone astray from your way and bring us to embrace you with penitent hearts and steadfast faith.
Christ, have mercy.
Keep us both outwardly in our bodies and inwardly in our souls that we may be defended from all adversities.
Lord, have mercy.

Invitation to the Lord's Prayer
Your Spirit comes to us as a strong defense in our Lenten discipline; moved by that Spirit we join in the prayer of Christ.

Collect *From Evening Prayer I*

The Blessing
May we, who are God's new creation, do all to reconcile ourselves to God. **Amen.**

Lent Sunday Noonday Prayer

Hymn Wilt Thou forgive that sin *Hymnal 140*

Reading Isaiah 1: 14-16
Your new moons and your appointed festivals my soul hates; they have become a burden to me, I am weary of bearing them. When you stretch out your hands, I will hide my eyes from you; even though you make many prayers, I will not listen; your hands are full of blood. Wash yourselves; make yourselves clean; remove the evil of your doings from before my eyes; cease to do evil, learn to do good; seek justice, rescue the oppressed, defend the orphan, plead for the widow.

Verse & Response
Now is the acceptable time.
Now is the day of salvation.

Collect *From Evening Prayer I*

Lent Sunday Evening Prayer II

Hymn Eternal Lord of love behold your church *Hymnal 149*

Responsory (Ps. 41:4)
Lord, be merciful to us
   − for we have sinned against you.
Hear, O Christ, our prayer of penitence.
   − for we have sinned against you.
Glory to the Father and to the Son and to the Holy Spirit.
Lord, be merciful to us
   − for we have sinned against you.

Magnificat Antiphon
Year A Evening Prayer II
First Sunday in Lent
Antiphon Worship the Lord your God, and serve only him. Then the devil left him, and suddenly angels came and waited on him.
Second Sunday in Lent
Antiphon God so loved the world that he gave his only Son, so that everyone who believes in him may not perish but may have eternal life.
Third Sunday in Lent
Antiphon My food is to do the will of him who sent me and to complete his work.

Fourth Sunday in Lent
Antiphon I came into this world for judgment so that those who do not see may see, and those who do see may become blind.

Fifth Sunday in Lent
Antiphon Jesus cried with a loud voice, "Lazarus, come out!" The dead man came out, his hands and feet bound with strips of cloth, and his face wrapped in a cloth. Jesus said to them, "Unbind him, and let him go."

Year B Evening Prayer II
First Sunday in Lent
Antiphon The time is fulfilled, and the kingdom of God has come near; repent, and believe in the good news.

Second Sunday in Lent
Antiphon Those who want to save their life will lose it, and those who lose their life for my sake, and for the sake of the gospel, will save it.

Third Sunday in Lent
Antiphon After Jesus was raised from the dead, his disciples remembered that he had said this; and they believed the scripture and the word that Jesus had spoken.

Fourth Sunday in Lent
Antiphon Those who do what is true come to the light, so that it may be clearly seen that their deeds have been done in God.

Fifth Sunday in Lent
Antiphon I, when I am lifted up from the earth, will draw all people to myself.

Year C Evening Prayer II
First Sunday in Lent
Antiphon When the devil had finished every test, he departed from Jesus until an opportune time.

Second Sunday in Lent
Antiphon I tell you, you will not see me until the time comes when you say, 'Blessed is the one who comes in the name of the Lord.'

Third Sunday in Lent
Antiphon I will dig around the fig tree and put manure on it. If it bears fruit next year, well and good; but if not, you can cut it down.

Fourth Sunday in Lent
Antiphon While he was still far off, his father saw him and was filled with compassion; he ran and put his arms around him and kissed him.

Fifth Sunday in Lent
Antiphon Leave her alone. She bought it so that she might keep it for the day of my burial. You always have the poor with you, but you do not always have me.

Litany
You nourished us this day with the true bread from heaven; may we ever abide in you as you abide in us.
Lord, have mercy.
Grant us to love what you command and to desire what you promise that our hearts may be firmly fixed on you.
Christ, have mercy.
Since you endured death on the cross to open the gates of heaven to all people, bring all the departed to share in the light of your glory.
Lord, have mercy.

Invitation to the Lord's Prayer Christ continues to draw us ever deeper into the mystery of his saving love and so with Christ we seek the Father as we pray.

Collect *From Evening Prayer I*

The Blessing
May we, through patience, share in the sufferings of Christ that we may deserve also to share in his kingdom. **Amen.**

Lent Monday Morning Prayer
Invitatory Come let us worship Christ Crucified who is the power and the wisdom of God.

Hymn From deepest woe I cry to thee *Hymnal 151*

Responsory One (Ps. 6:4; Az. 16)
Turn, O Lord, and deliver us
  — **save us for your mercy's sake.**
With a contrite heart may we be accepted.
  — **save us for your mercy's sake.**
Glory to the Father and to the Son and to the Holy Spirit.
Turn, O Lord, and deliver us
  — **save us for your mercy's sake.**

Weeks 1 & 3
Canticle of Hezekiah *Ego dixi*
(Isaiah 38: 10-14.17-20)
Antiphon O Lord, I am oppressed; be my security!

I said: In the noontide of my days I must depart. *
   I am consigned to the gates of Sheol
   for the rest of my years.

I said, I shall not see the Lord in the land of the living; *
   I shall look upon mortals no more
   among the inhabitants of the world.

My dwelling is plucked up and removed from me
like a shepherd's tent; *
   Like a weaver I have rolled up my life;
   he cuts me off from the loom.

From day to night you bring me to an end; *
   I cry for help until morning.

Like a lion he breaks all my bones; *
   from day to night you bring me to an end.

Like a swallow or a crane I clamor, *
   I moan like a dove.

My eyes are weary with looking upward. *
   O Lord, I am oppressed; be my security!
   Surely it was for my welfare that I had great bitterness.

But you have held back my life from the pit of destruction. *
   You have cast all my sins behind your back.

For Sheol cannot thank you, death cannot praise you. *
   Those who go down to the Pit
   cannot hope for your faithfulness.

The living, the living, they thank you, as I do this day. *
   Fathers make known to children your faithfulness.

The Lord will save me, and we will sing to stringed instruments *
   All the days of our lives, at the house of the Lord.

Antiphon O Lord, I am oppressed; be my security!

Weeks 2 & 4
Lamentation Over Loss *Recordare Domine*
(Lamentations 5: 1-7.15-17.19-21)

Antiphon Restore us to yourself, O Lord, that we may be restored.

Remember, O Lord, what has befallen us; *
   look, and see our disgrace!

Our inheritance has been turned over to strangers, *
>   our homes to aliens.

We have become orphans, fatherless; *
>   our mothers are like widows.

We must pay for the water we drink; *
>   the wood we get must be bought.

With a yoke on our necks we are hard driven; *
>   we are weary, we are given no rest.

We have made a pact with Egypt and Assyria, *
>   to get enough bread.

Our ancestors sinned; they are no more, *
>   and we bear their iniquities.

The joy of our hearts has ceased; *
>   our dancing has been turned to mourning.

The crown has fallen from our head; *
>   woe to us, for we have sinned!

Because of this our hearts are sick, *
>   because of these things our eyes have grown dim:

But you, O Lord, reign forever; *
>   your throne endures to all generations.

Why have you forgotten us completely? *
>   Why have you forsaken us these many days?

Restore us to yourself, O Lord, that we may be restored; *
>   renew our days as of old.

Antiphon Restore us to yourself, O Lord, that we may be restored.

Responsory Two (Ps. 6:2; Ps. 90:13)
Have pity on me, Lord, for I am weak
>   **– heal me, Lord, for my bones are racked.**

O Lord, be gracious to me
>   **– heal me, Lord, for my bones are racked.**

Glory to the Father and to the Son and to the Holy Spirit.
Have pity on me, Lord, for I am weak
>   **– heal me, Lord, for my bones are racked.**

Benedictus Antiphon
Lent 1-4 Speak to all the congregation of the people of Israel and say to them: You shall be holy, for I the Lord your God am holy.
Lent 5 As the time approached when Jesus was to be taken up to heaven, he set his face resolutely toward Jerusalem.

Litany
Strengthen us in our practice of almsgiving, prayer and fasting.
Lord, have mercy.
Purify us by our Lenten discipline to draw closer to you.
Christ, have mercy.
Return our hearts to a more faithful reception of your Sacraments and a consistent reading of your Word.
Lord, have mercy.

Invitation to the Lord's Prayer We know that we are powerless to change our lives so we ask for the grace of repentance as we pray with you, O Christ.

Collect
Monday of First Week in Lent
Almighty and everlasting God, mercifully increase in us your gifts of holy discipline, in almsgiving, prayer, and fasting; that our lives may be directed to the fulfilling of your most gracious will; through Jesus Christ our Lord, who lives and reigns with you and the Holy Spirit, one God, for ever and ever. Amen.
Monday of Second Week in Lent
Let your Spirit, O Lord, come into the midst of us to wash us with the pure water of repentance, and prepare us to be always a living sacrifice to you; through Jesus Christ our Lord, who lives and reigns with you and the Holy Spirit, one God, for ever and ever. Amen.
Monday of Third Week in Lent
Look upon the heart-felt desires of your humble servants, Almighty God, and stretch forth the right hand of your majesty to be our defense against all our enemies; through Jesus Christ our Lord, who lives and reigns with you and the Holy Spirit, one God, for ever and ever. Amen.
Monday of Fourth Week in Lent O Lord, our God, in your holy Sacraments you have given us a foretaste of the good things of your kingdom: Direct us, we pray, in the way that leads to eternal life, that we may come to appear before you in that place of light where you dwell for ever with your saints; through Jesus Christ our Lord, who lives and reigns with you and the Holy Spirit, one God, for ever and ever. Amen.

Monday of Fifth Week in Lent
Be gracious to your people, we entreat you, O Lord, that they, repenting day by day of the things that displease you, may be more and more filled with love of you and of your commandments; and, being supported by your grace in this life, may come to the full enjoyment of eternal life in your everlasting kingdom; through Jesus Christ our Lord, who lives and reigns with you and the Holy Spirit, one God, for ever and ever. Amen.

The Blessing
May we guard ourselves from sins and vices of thought or tongue, of hand or foot, of self-will or bodily desire since we are always seen by God in heaven. **Amen.**

Lent Monday Noonday Prayer
Hymn Glory be to Jesus, who in bitter pain *Hymnal 479*

Reading Isaiah 30: 15, 18
For thus said the Lord God, the Holy One of Israel: In returning and rest you shall be saved; in quietness and in trust shall be your strength. Therefore the Lord waits to be gracious to you; therefore he will rise up to show mercy to you. For the Lord is a God of justice; blessed are all those who wait for him.

Verse & Response
Repent and believe in the Gospel.
The kingdom of God has come near.

Collect *From Morning Prayer*

Lent Monday Evening Prayer
Hymn Now quit your care *Hymnal 145*

Responsory (Ps. 32:1; Mt. 5:8)
Blessed are they whose transgressions are forgiven
— **whose sin is put away.**
Blessed are the pure of heart.
— **whose sin is put away.**
Glory to the Father and to the Son and to the Holy Spirit.
Blessed are they whose transgressions are forgiven
— **whose sin is put away.**

Magnificat Antiphon
Lent 1-4 You must be made new in mind and spirit, and put on the new nature of God's creating, which shows itself in a just and devout life.

Lent 5: Jesus knew that his hour had come to depart from this world and go to the Father.

Litany
Kindle in our hearts an active love for our communities that with you we may build a world of justice and peace.
Lord, have mercy.
Visit the sick, comfort the sorrowful and strengthen the weak through the ministry of holy women and men.
Christ, have mercy.
Give light to those who have died in the faith of the church and bring all the dead to their dwelling place.
Lord, have mercy.

Invitation to the Lord's Prayer
Through Baptism we have become sharers of the divine nature, so we draw near to God with Christ and call out in the Spirit.

Collect *From Morning Prayer*

The Blessing
May we keep our manner of life most pure and add to the usual measure of our service so that each of us will have something to offer God with the joy of the Holy Spirit. **Amen.**

Lent Tuesday Morning Prayer

Invitatory The Lord is full of compassion and mercy: Come let us adore him.

Hymn Lord Jesus, Sun of Righteousness *Hymnal 144*

Responsory One (Ps. 32:6; Jn. 8:11)
I will confess my transgressions to the Lord
　　　− you forgave me the guilt of my sin.
Go and sin no more.
　　　− you forgave me the guilt of my sin.
Glory to the Father and to the Son and to the Holy Spirit.
I will confess my transgressions to the Lord
　　　− you forgave me the guilt of my sin.

Weeks 1 & 3
Canticle of God's Judgment *Audite verbum omnis Iuda*
(Jeremiah 7: 2-7)

Antiphon Amend your ways and your doings, and let me dwell with you in this place.

Hear the word of the Lord, *
　all you people of Judah.

You that enter these gates *
　to worship the Lord.

Thus says the Lord of hosts, *
　the God of Israel:

Amend your ways and your doings, *
　and let me dwell with you in this place.

Do not trust in these deceptive words: *
　"This is the temple of the Lord,
　the temple of the Lord,
　the temple of the Lord."

For if you truly amend your ways and your doings, *
　if you truly act justly one with another.

If you do not oppress the alien, the orphan, and the widow, *
　or shed innocent blood in this place.

If you do not go after other gods *
　to your own hurt.

Then I will dwell with you in this place, *
　in the land that I gave of old to your ancestors forever and ever.

Antiphon Amend your ways and your doings, and let me dwell with you in this place.

Weeks 2 & 4
Plea for Mercy *Deducant oculi mei*
(Jeremiah 14: 17-21)

Antiphon We acknowledge our wickedness, O Lord, for we have sinned against you.

Let my eyes run down with tears night and day, *
　and let them not cease.

The virgin daughter, my people, is struck down with a crushing blow, *
　with a very grievous wound.

If I go out into the field, *
　Look, those killed by the sword!

And if I enter the city, *
　Look, those sick with famine!

For both prophet and priest ply their trade throughout the land, *
   and have no knowledge.

Have you completely rejected Judah? *
   Does your heart loathe Zion?

Why have you struck us down *
   so that there is no healing for us?

We look for peace, but find no good; *
   for a time of healing, but there is terror instead.

We acknowledge our wickedness, O Lord, *
   the iniquity of our ancestors,
   for we have sinned against you.

Do not spurn us, for your name's sake; *
   do not dishonor your glorious throne;
   remember and do not break your covenant with us.

Antiphon We acknowledge our wickedness, O Lord, for we have sinned against you.

Responsory Two (Ps. 32:9; Eph. 4:23)
I will instruct you and teach you
   — in the way that you should go.
Be renewed in the spirit of your minds
   — in the way that you should go.
Glory to the Father and to the Son and to the Holy Spirit.
I will instruct you and teach you
   — in the way that you should go.

Benedictus Antiphon
Lent 1-4 Cease to do evil, learn to do good; seek justice, rescue the oppressed, defend the orphan, plead for the widow.
Lent 5 Jesus must be lifted up as the serpent was lifted up by Moses in the wilderness.

Litany
Children are suffering from deprivation and want; feed their bodies, souls and spirits with your riches.
Lord, have mercy.
Parents lament their inability to adequately provide for their families; create new opportunities for all people to earn a just wage.
Christ, have mercy.

The poor endure deprived living conditions in places of pollution and natural disasters; raise up businesses that build up the city of God among us.
Lord, have mercy.

Invitation to the Lord's Prayer You take the side of the poor and disadvantaged so we stand with our brothers and sisters in need as we pray.

Collect
Tuesday of the First Week in Lent
Grant to your people, Lord, grace to withstand the temptations of the world, the flesh, and the devil, and with pure hearts and minds to follow you, the only true God; through Jesus Christ your Son our Lord, who lives and reigns with you and the Holy Spirit, one God, for ever and ever. Amen.

Tuesday of the Second Week in Lent
O God, you willed to redeem us from all iniquity by your Son: Deliver us when we are tempted to regard sin without abhorrence, and let the virtue of his passion come between us and our mortal enemy; through Jesus Christ our Lord, who lives and reigns with you and the Holy Spirit, one God, for ever and ever. Amen.

Tuesday of the Third Week in Lent
O Lord, we beseech you mercifully to hear us; and grant that we, to whom you have given a fervent desire to pray, may, by your mighty aid, be defended and comforted in all dangers and adversities; through Jesus Christ our Lord, who lives and reigns with you and the Holy Spirit, one God, for ever and ever. Amen.

Tuesday of the Fourth Week in Lent
O God, with you is the well of life, and in your light we see light: Quench our thirst with living water, and flood our darkened minds with heavenly light; through Jesus Christ our Lord, who lives and reigns with you and the Holy Spirit, one God, for ever and ever. Amen.

Tuesday of the Fifth Week in Lent
Almighty God, through the incarnate Word you have caused us to be born anew of an imperishable and eternal seed: Look with compassion upon those who are being prepared for Holy Baptism, and grant that they may be built as living stones into a spiritual temple acceptable to you; through Jesus Christ our Lord, who lives and reigns with you and the Holy Spirit, one God, for ever and ever. Amen.

The Blessing
May we humble ourselves under the mighty hand of God, so that he may exalt us in due time. Let us cast all our anxiety on him, because he cares for us. **Amen.**

Lent Tuesday Noonday Prayer

Hymn Rock Of Ages *Hymnal 685*

Reading Deuteronomy 4:29-31
You will seek the Lord your God, and you will find him if you search after him with all your heart and soul. In your distress, when all these things have happened to you in time to come, you will return to the Lord your God and heed him. Because the Lord your God is a merciful God, he will neither abandon you nor destroy you; he will not forget the covenant with your ancestors that he swore to them.

Verse & Response
I treasure your promise in my heart.
Let me not sin against you.

Collect *From Morning Prayer*

Lent Tuesday Evening Prayer

Hymn Now Let Us All With One Accord *Hymnal 146*

Responsory (Ps. 41:4)
Lord, be merciful to us
　　− **for we have sinned against you.**
Hear, O Christ, our prayer of penitence.
　　− **for we have sinned against you.**
Glory to the Father and to the Son and to the Holy Spirit.
Lord, be merciful to us
　　− **for we have sinned against you.**

Magnificat Antiphon
Lent 1-4 Forgetting what is behind, and reaching out for that which lies ahead, press toward the goal to win the prize in Christ Jesus.
Lent 5 Having loved his own who were in the world he loved them to the end.

Litany
Turn our hearts to the needs of women and girls, men and boys who endure exploitation and bring an end to human trafficking.
Lord, have mercy.

Support police, firefighters, and emergency responders who come to the aid of people in dire conditions.
Christ, have mercy.
Lead the dying to behold the light of your glory and comfort them with faith in your presence.
Lord, have mercy.

Invitation to the Lord's Prayer
We implore you to turn our hearts to you again, to renew our baptismal fervor and to draw us closer to you as we pray.

Collect *From Morning Prayer*

The Blessing
May we celebrate and rejoice, because our brothers and sisters were dead and have come to life; they were lost and have been found.
Amen.

Lent Wednesday Morning Prayer
The Ember Days, traditionally observed on the Wednesday, Friday, and Saturday after the First Sunday in Lent. On those days use the daily office of the day with proper parts taken from the Common of Ember Days

Invitatory Come let us worship Christ who calls us to carry the cross.

Hymn The glory of these forty days *Hymnal 143*

Responsory One (Col. 3:13; Mt. 8:35)
Forgive one another
— **as God in Christ has forgiven you.**
Forgive your brother or sister from your heart
— **as God in Christ has forgiven you.**
Glory to the Father and to the Son and to the Holy Spirit.
Forgive one another
— **as God in Christ has forgiven you.**

Weeks 1 & 3
Canticle for Mercy *Miserere plebi tuae*
(Sirach 36: 17-22)

Antiphon Have pity on the city of your sanctuary, Jerusalem, the place of your dwelling.

Have mercy, O Lord, on the people called by your name, *
   on Israel, whom you have named your firstborn,

Have pity on the city of your sanctuary, *
   Jerusalem, the place of your dwelling.

Fill Zion with your majesty, *
   and your temple with your glory.

Bear witness to those whom you created in the beginning, *
   and fulfill the prophecies spoken in your name.

Reward those who wait for you *
   and let your prophets be found trustworthy.

Hear, O Lord, the prayer of your servants, *
   according to your goodwill toward your people.

All who are on the earth will know *
   that you are the Lord, the God of the ages.

Antiphon Have pity on the city of your sanctuary, Jerusalem, the place of your dwelling.

Weeks 2 & 4
Canticle of Jonah *Clamavi de tribulation*
(Jonah 2: 2-9)

Antiphon You brought up my life from the Pit, O Lord my God.

I called to the Lord out of my distress, and he answered me. *
   Out of the belly of Sheol I cried, and you heard my voice.

You cast me into the deep, into the heart of the seas,
and the flood surrounded me. *
   All your waves and your billows passed over me.

Then I said, 'I am driven away from your sight; *
   how shall I look again upon your holy temple?'

The waters closed in over me; the deep surrounded me. *
   Weeds were wrapped around my head
   at the roots of the mountains.

I went down to the land whose bars closed upon me forever. *
   You brought up my life from the Pit, O Lord my God.

As my life was ebbing away, I remembered the Lord. *
   My prayer came to you, into your holy temple.

Those who worship vain idols forsake their true loyalty. *
   But I with the voice of thanksgiving will sacrifice to you.

What I have vowed I will pay. *
   Deliverance belongs to the Lord!"

Antiphon You brought up my life from the Pit, O Lord my God.

Responsory Two (Eph. 4:24; Eph. 5:8)
Clothe yourselves with the new self
> — **created according to the likeness of God.**

Live as children of the light
> — **created according to the likeness of God.**

Glory to the Father and to the Son and to the Holy Spirit.
Clothe yourselves with the new self
> — **created according to the likeness of God.**

Benedictus Antiphon
Ash Wednesday When you fast, put oil on your head and wash your face, so that your fasting may be seen not by others but by your Father who is in secret.

Lent 1-4 Take care and watch yourselves closely, so as neither to forget the things that your eyes have seen nor to let them slip from your mind all the days of your life.

Lent 5 Christ died for us while we were yet sinners, and this is God's own proof of love toward us.

Litany
Turn our hearts from seeking our own gain and attract our hearts to you in prayer.
Lord, have mercy.
Turn our minds from planning our own schemes and lead us to you through the study of your Word.
Christ, have mercy.
Turn our hands from selfish activity and sustain our service for our needy brothers and sisters.
Lord, have mercy.

Invitation to the Lord's Prayer Draw near to us, O Christ, in our Lenten discipline and deepen the practice of our faith through prayer with you.

Collect
Ash Wednesday
Almighty and everlasting God, you hate nothing you have made and forgive the sins of all who are penitent: Create and make in us new and contrite hearts, that we, worthily lamenting our sins and acknowledging our wretchedness, may obtain of you, the God of all mercy, perfect remission and forgiveness; through Jesus Christ our Lord, who lives and reigns with you and the Holy Spirit, one God, for ever and ever. Amen.

Wednesday of the First Week of Lent
Bless us, O God, in this holy season, in which our hearts seek your help and healing; and so purify us by your discipline that we may grow in grace and in the knowledge of our Lord and Savior Jesus Christ; who lives and reigns with you and the Holy Spirit, one God, for ever and ever. Amen.

Wednesday of the Second Week of Lent
O God, you so loved the world that you gave your only-begotten Son to reconcile earth with heaven: Grant that we, loving you above all things, may love our friends in you, and our enemies for your sake; through Jesus Christ our Lord, who lives and reigns with you and the Holy Spirit, one God, for ever and ever. Amen.

Wednesday of the Third Week of Lent
Give ear to our prayers, O Lord, and direct the way of your servants in safety under your protection, that, amid all the changes of our earthly pilgrimage, we may be guarded by your mighty aid; through Jesus Christ our Lord, who lives and reigns with you and the Holy Spirit, one God, for ever and ever. Amen.

Wednesday of the Fourth Week of Lent
O Lord our God, you sustained your ancient people in the wilderness with bread from heaven: Feed now your pilgrim flock with the food that endures to everlasting life; through Jesus Christ your Son our Lord, who lives and reigns with you and the Holy Spirit, one God, for ever and ever. Amen.

Wednesday of the Fifth Week of Lent
Almighty God our heavenly Father, renew in us the gifts of your mercy; increase our faith, strengthen our hope, enlighten our understanding, widen our charity, and make us ready to serve you; through Jesus Christ our Lord, who lives and reigns with you and the Holy Spirit, one God, for ever and ever. Amen.

The Blessing
May we work for mutual reconciliation for we are reconciled to God in one body through the cross. **Amen.**

Lent Wednesday Noonday Prayer
Hymn In your mercy Lord you called me *Hymnal 706*

Reading Exodus 19: 4-6
I bore you on eagles' wings and brought you to myself. Now therefore, if you obey my voice and keep my covenant, you shall be my treasured possession out of all the peoples. Indeed, the whole earth is mine, but you shall be for me a priestly kingdom and a holy nation.

Verse and Response
The Lord shall cover you with his pinions.
You shall find refuge under his wings.

Collect *From Morning Prayer*

Lent Wednesday Evening Prayer

Hymn Forty days and forty nights *Hymnal 150*

Responsory (Mt. 6:14; Lk. 6:36)
If you forgive others their trespasses
  — **your heavenly Father will also forgive you.**
Be merciful as you Father is merciful
  — **your heavenly Father will also forgive you.**
Glory to the Father and to the Son and to the Holy Spirit.
If you forgive others their trespasses
  — **your heavenly Father will also forgive you.**

Magnificat Antiphon
Lent 1-4 Stand firm and unmovable, and work for God always, since you know that in God your labor cannot be lost.
Lent 5 If the world hates you, be aware that it hated me before it hated you.

Litany
Aware of our fragile grasp on life, help us live with an awareness of judgment and yearn for you with holy desire.
Lord, have mercy.
Mindful of your ever-watchful eye, assist us to be aware of our thoughts and to moderate our speech.
Christ, have mercy.
Conscious of our mortality, lead us to hope for heaven and to dwell with you and all who have gone before us in death.
Lord, have mercy.

Invitation to the Lord's Prayer
Praying for our enemies out of love for Christ, let us ask God's forgiveness as we forgive saying with Christ.

Collect *From Morning Prayer*

The Blessing

May we look to Jesus the pioneer and perfecter of our faith, who for the sake of the joy that was set before him endured the cross, disregarding its shame, and has taken his seat at the right hand of the throne of God. **Amen.**

Lent Thursday Morning Prayer

Invitatory The Lord is full of compassion and mercy: Come let us adore him.

Responsory One (Ex. 6:14; Mt. 6:11)
I am going to rain bread from heaven for you
  – each day you shall go out and gather it for that day.
Give us today our daily bread
  – each day you shall go out and gather it for that day.
Glory to the Father and to the Son and to the Holy Spirit.
I am going to rain bread from heaven for you
  – each day you shall go out and gather it for that day.

Weeks 1 & 3
Canticle of the Vineyard *Cantabo dilecto mea*
(Isaiah 5: 1-7)

Antiphon What more was there to do for my vineyard that I have not done in it?

Let me sing for my beloved *
  my love-song concerning his vineyard:

My beloved had a vineyard *
  on a very fertile hill.

He dug it and cleared it of stones, *
  and planted it with choice vines.

He built a watchtower in the midst of it, *
  and hewed out a wine vat in it.

He expected it to yield grapes, *
  but it yielded wild grapes.

And now, inhabitants of Jerusalem and people of Judah, *
  judge between me and my vineyard.

What more was there to do for my vineyard *
  that I have not done in it?

When I expected it to yield grapes, *
  why did it yield wild grapes?

And now I will tell you *
>> what I will do to my vineyard.

I will remove its hedge, *
>> and it shall be devoured;

I will break down its wall, *
>> and it shall be trampled down.

I will make it a waste; *
>> it shall not be pruned or hoed,
>> and it shall be overgrown with briers and thorns;

I will also command the clouds *
>> that they rain no rain upon it.

For the vineyard of the Lord of hosts *
>> is the house of Israel.

The people of Judah *
>> are his pleasant planting.

He expected justice, but saw bloodshed; *
>> righteousness, but heard a cry!

Antiphon What more was there to do for my vineyard that I have not done in it?

Weeks 2 & 4
Canticle of the Exiles *Magnus es Domine*
(Tobit 13: 1-6)

Antiphon If you turn to God with all your heart and with all your soul, then God will turn to you.

Blessed be God who lives forever, *
>> because his kingdom lasts throughout all ages.

For he afflicts, and he shows mercy; *
>> he leads down to Hades in the lowest regions of the earth,

He brings up from the great abyss. *
>> and there is nothing that can escape his hand.

Acknowledge him before the nations, O children of Israel; *
>> for he has scattered you among them.
>> He has shown you his greatness even there.

Exalt him in the presence of every living being,
because he is our Lord and he is our God; *
>> he is our Father and he is God forever.

He will afflict you for your iniquities, *
>> but he will again show mercy on all of you.

He will gather you from all the nations *
>> among whom you have been scattered.

If you turn to him with all your heart and with all your soul, *
>> to do what is true before him,

Then he will turn to you *
>> and will no longer hide his face from you.

So now see what he has done for you; *
>> acknowledge him at the top of your voice.

Bless the Lord of righteousness, *
>> and exalt the King of the ages.

Antiphon If you turn to God with all your heart and with all your soul, then God will turn to you.

Responsory Two (Dt. 8:3; Jn. 6:27)
One does not live by bread alone
>> **– but by every word from the mouth of the Lord.**

Do not live by the bread that perishes
>> **– but by every word from the mouth of the Lord.**

Glory to the Father and to the Son and to the Holy Spirit.
One does not live by bread alone
>> **– but by every word from the mouth of the Lord.**

Benedictus Antiphon
Lent 1-4 O Lord, why does your wrath burn hot against your people, whom you brought out of the land of Egypt with great power and with a mighty hand?
Lent 5 If any want to become my followers, let them deny themselves and take up their cross and follow me.

Litany
As our fasting brings our bodies to yearn for you, let our hearts be fed by every word that comes from your mouth.
Lord, have mercy.

As our self-denial purifies our wayward desires, let our souls cling to you alone.
Christ, have mercy.
As our almsgiving supports those in need, let our eyes see you in our suffering sisters and brothers.
Lord, have mercy.

Invitation to the Lord's Prayer We join you, O Christ, in your fasting and hunger and with you desire a deeper communion with the Father.

Collect
Thursday After Ash Wednesday
Direct us, O Lord, in all our doings with your most gracious favor, and further us with your continual help; that in all our works begun continued, and ended in you, we may glorify your holy Name, and finally, by your mercy, obtain everlasting life; through Jesus Christ our Lord, who lives and reigns with you and the Holy Spirit, one God, for ever and ever. Amen.

Thursday of the First Week in Lent
Strengthen us, O Lord, by your grace, that in your might we may overcome all spiritual enemies, and with pure hearts serve you; through Jesus Christ our Lord, who lives and reigns with you and the Holy Spirit, one God, for ever and ever. Amen.

Thursday of the Second Week in Lent
O Lord, strong and mighty, Lord of hosts and King of glory: Cleanse our hearts from sin, keep our hands pure, and turn our minds from what is passing away; so that at the last we may stand in your holy place and receive your blessing; through Jesus Christ our Lord, who lives and reigns with you and the Holy Spirit, one God, for ever and ever. Amen.

Thursday of the Third Week in Lent
Keep watch over your Church, O Lord, with your unfailing love; and, since it is grounded in human weakness and cannot maintain itself without your aid, protect it from all danger, and keep it in the way of salvation; through Jesus Christ your Son our Lord, who lives and reigns with you and the Holy Spirit, one God, for ever and ever. Amen.

Thursday of the Fourth Week in Lent
Almighty and most merciful God, drive from us all weakness of body, mind, and spirit; that, being restored to wholeness, we may with free hearts become what you intend us to be and accomplish what you want us to do; through Jesus Christ our Lord, who lives and reigns with you and the Holy Spirit, one God, for ever and ever. Amen.

Thursday of the Fifth Week in Lent
O God, you have called us to be your children, and have promised that those who suffer with Christ will be heirs with him of your glory: Arm us with such trust in him that we may ask no rest from his demands and have no fear in his service; through Jesus Christ our Lord, who lives and reigns with you and the Holy Spirit, one God, for ever and ever. Amen.

The Blessing
May we imitate Jesus who when he was abused, did not return abuse; when he suffered, he did not threaten; but he entrusted himself to the one who judges justly. **Amen.**

Lent Thursday Noonday Prayer
Hymn Lead us Heavenly Father lead us *Hymnal 559*

Reading Romans 12: 1-2
I appeal to you therefore, brothers and sisters, by the mercies of God, to present your bodies as a living sacrifice, holy and acceptable to God, which is your spiritual worship. Do not be conformed to this world, but be transformed by the renewing of your minds, so that you may discern what is the will of God—what is good and acceptable and perfect.

Verse and Response
We offer and present to you, O Lord.
Our selves, our souls and bodies, to be a sacrifice to you.

Collect *From Morning Prayer*

Lent Thursday Evening Prayer
Hymn Let thy blood in mercy poured *Hymnal 313*

Responsory (Prv. 22:9; Mt. 25:35)
Those who are generous are blessed
   — **they share their bread with the poor.**
I was hungry and you gave me food
   — **they share their bread with the poor.**
Glory to the Father and to the Son and to the Holy Spirit.
Those who are generous are blessed
   — **they share their bread with the poor.**

Magnificat Antiphon
Lent 1-4 God is always looking at you from heaven, that your actions are everywhere visible to the divine eyes and are constantly being reported to God by the Angels.

Lent 5 A little while and you will no longer see me, and again a little while you will see me.

Litany
Help us to guard ourselves constantly from sin and vices of thought or tongue, of hand or foot, or self-will or sinful desires that separate us from you.
Lord, have mercy.
Shift our focus and action away from love of our own disordered willfulness and lead us to love the will of the Father.
Christ, have mercy.
Grant to all the departed an entrance into the land of light and joy in the fellowship of Blessed Mary, (St. N.) and all your holy ones.
Lord, have mercy.

Invitation to the Lord's Prayer We know how deeply sin has infected our hearts and our wills so we ask you to purify our souls as with Christ we pray.

Collect *From Morning Prayer*

The Blessing
May we boast in our sufferings, knowing that suffering produces endurance, and endurance produces character, and character produces hope, and hope does not disappoint us, because God's love has been poured into our hearts through the Holy Spirit. **Amen.**

Lent Friday Morning Prayer
Invitatory Christ, the Son of God, has redeemed us with his blood: Come let us adore.

Hymn O sacred head, sore wounded *Hymnal 168*

Responsory One (Ex. 34:28; Lk. 4:1)
Moses was with the Lord forty days and forty nights
    – he neither ate bread nor drank water.
Jesus was led by the Spirit in the wilderness
    – he neither ate bread nor drank water.
Glory to the Father and to the Son and to the Holy Spirit.
Moses was with the Lord forty days and forty nights
    – he neither ate bread nor drank water.

Weeks 1 & 3
Song of Penitence *Kyrie Pantokrator*
(Prayer of Manasseh, 1-2, 4, 6-7, 11-15)

Antiphon O Lord, I bend the knee of my heart, and make my appeal, sure of your gracious goodness.

O Lord and Ruler of the hosts of heaven, *
    God of Abraham, Isaac, and Jacob,
    and of all their righteous offspring:

You made the heavens and the earth, *
    with all their vast array.

All things quake with fear at your presence; *
    they tremble because of your power.

But your merciful promise is beyond all measure; *
    it surpasses all that our minds can fathom.

O Lord, you are full of compassion, *
    long-suffering, and abounding in mercy.

You hold back your hand; *
    you do not punish as we deserve.

In your great goodness, Lord,
you have promised forgiveness to sinners, *
    that they may repent of their sin and be saved.

And now, O Lord, I bend the knee of my heart, *
    and make my appeal, sure of your gracious goodness.

I have sinned, O Lord, I have sinned, *
    and I know my wickedness only too well.

Therefore I make this prayer to you: *
    Forgive me, Lord, forgive me.

Do not let me perish in my sin, *
    nor condemn me to the depths of the earth.

For you, O Lord, are the God of those who repent, *
    and in me you will show forth your goodness.

Unworthy as I am, you will save me,
in accordance with your great mercy, *
    and I will praise you without ceasing all the days of my life.

For all the powers of heaven sing your praises, *
    and yours is the glory to ages of ages. Amen.

Antiphon O Lord, I bend the knee of my heart, and make my appeal, sure of your gracious goodness.

Weeks 2 & 4
Canticle of the Suffering Servant II *Audite insulae*
(Isaiah 49: 1-6)

Antiphon You are my servant, Israel, in whom I will be glorified.

Listen to me, O coastlands, *
  pay attention, you peoples from far away!

The Lord called me before I was born, *
  while I was in my mother's womb he named me.

He made my mouth like a sharp sword, *
  in the shadow of his hand he hid me.

He made me a polished arrow, *
  in his quiver he hid me away.

He said to me, "You are my servant, Israel, *
  in whom I will be glorified."

But I said, "I have labored in vain, *
  I have spent my strength for nothing and vanity.

"Yet surely my cause is with the Lord, *
  and my reward with my God."

And now the Lord says, who formed me in the womb
to be his servant, *
  to bring Jacob back to him,
  and that Israel might be gathered to him,

For I am honored in the sight of the Lord, *
  and my God has become my strength.

He says, "It is too light a thing that you should be my servant *
  to raise up the tribes of Jacob
  and to restore the survivors of Israel.

I will give you as a light to the nations, *
  that my salvation may reach to the end of the earth."

Antiphon You are my servant, Israel, in whom I will be glorified.

Responsory Two (Lk. 9:23; Jn. 12: 26)
If you would be my followers
  – take up your cross daily and follow me.

Where the Lord is there also will his servant be
> — **take up your cross daily and follow me.**

Glory to the Father and to the Son and to the Holy Spirit.
If you would be my followers
> — **take up your cross daily and follow me.**

Benedictus Antiphon
Lent 1-4 Surely he has borne our infirmities and carried our diseases. He was wounded for our transgressions, crushed for our iniquities.
Lent 5 The Son of Man must undergo great suffering, and be rejected by the elders, the chief priests, and the scribes and be killed and after three day rise again.

Litany
Let the power of the cross sustain all who lost loved ones through violence and civil strife.
Lord, have mercy.
Let the reconciliation of the cross bring together enemies and all who are estranged.
Christ, have mercy.
Let the love of the cross draw us to a deeper love for God and for one another.
Lord, have mercy.

Invitation to the Lord's Prayer As we contemplate the mystery of the cross let us pray with the Crucified and Risen Christ with whom we are mystically united.

Collect
Friday After Ash Wednesday
Support us, O Lord, with your gracious favor through the fast we have begun; that as we observe it by bodily self-denial, so we may fulfill it with inner sincerity of heart; through Jesus Christ our Lord, who lives and reigns with you and the Holy Spirit, one God, for ever and ever. Amen.

Friday of the First Week in Lent
Lord Christ, our eternal Redeemer, grant us such fellowship in your sufferings, that, filled with your Holy Spirit, we may subdue the flesh to the spirit, and the spirit to you, and at the last attain to the glory of your resurrection; who lives and reign with the Father and the Holy Spirit, one God, for ever and ever. Amen.

Friday of the Second Week in Lent
Grant, O Lord, that as your Son Jesus Christ prayed for his enemies on the cross, so we may have grace to forgive those who wrongfully or scornfully use us, that we ourselves may be able to receive your

forgiveness; through Jesus Christ our Lord, who lives and reigns with you and the Holy Spirit, one God, for ever and ever. Amen.

Friday of the Third Week in Lent
Grant us, O Lord our Strength, a true love of your holy Name; so that, trusting in your grace, we may fear no earthly evil, nor fix our hearts on earthly goods, but may rejoice in your full salvation; through Jesus Christ our Lord, who lives and reigns with you and the Holy Spirit, one God, for ever and ever. Amen.

Friday of the Fourth Week in Lent
O God, you have given us the Good News of your abounding love in your Son Jesus Christ: So fill our hearts with thankfulness that we may rejoice to proclaim the good tidings we have received; through Jesus Christ our Lord, who lives and reigns with you and the Holy Spirit, one God, for ever and ever. Amen.

Friday of the Fifth Week in Lent
O Lord, you relieve our necessity out of the abundance of your great riches: Grant that we may accept with joy the salvation you bestow, and manifest it to all the world by the quality of our lives; through Jesus Christ our Lord, who lives and reigns with you and the Holy Spirit, one God, now and for ever. Amen.

The Blessing
May we rejoice in God who has graciously granted us the privilege not only of believing in Christ, but of suffering for him. **Amen.**

Lent Friday Noonday Prayer

Hymn Alone thou goest forth *Hymnal 164*

Reading Joel 2: 12-13
Yet even now, says the Lord, return to me with all your heart, with fasting, with weeping, and with mourning; rend your hearts and not your clothing. Return to the Lord, your God, for he is gracious and merciful, slow to anger, and abounding in steadfast love, and relents from punishing.

Verse & Response
I will never forget your commandments.
By them you give me life.

Collect *From Morning Prayer*

Lent Friday Evening Prayer

Hymn Take up your cross *Hymnal 675*

Responsory (Mk. 10:45; 1 Tim. 2:5)
The Son of Man came not to be served but to serve
  — to give his life a ransom for many.
Christ Jesus came as a mediator between God and us
  — to give his life a ransom for many.
Glory to the Father and to the Son and to the Holy Spirit.
The Son of Man came not to be served but to serve
  — to give his life a ransom for many.

Magnificat Antiphon
Lent 1-4 All we like sheep have gone astray; we have all turned to our own way, and the Lord has laid on him the iniquity of us all.
Lent 5 Servants are not greater than their masters. If they persecuted me, they will persecute you.

Litany
O Christ, you endured rejection and humiliation, may we, with you, transform the negative energy that enters our lives.
Lord, have mercy.
O Christ, you suffered pain and anguish, may we, with you, bear physical ailments and emotional trials.
Christ, have mercy.
O Christ, you surrendered yourself on the cross, may we, with you, and all the departed, find a place where there is neither tears nor sighing.
Lord, have mercy.

Invitation to the Lord's Prayer We are mystically united with Christ in his death and burial so may the Spirit unite us with the mind of Christ to share in the resurrection as we pray.

Collect *From Morning Prayer*

The Blessing
May we never boast of anything except the cross of our Lord Jesus Christ, by which the world has been crucified to us, and we to the world. **Amen.**

Lent Saturday Morning Prayer

Invitatory Christ suffered death on a cross and was buried for us: Come let us adore.

Hymn Creator of the earth and sky *Hymnal 148*

Responsory One (Ps. 102:13; Hos. 6:2)
You will arise and have compassion on Zion
　　− **for it is time to have mercy upon her.**
You will raise her up on the third day
　　− **for it is time to have mercy upon her.**
Glory to the Father and to the Son and to the Holy Spirit.
You will arise and have compassion on Zion
　　− **for it is time to have mercy upon her.**

Weeks 1 & 3
Lament of Jerusalem *O vos omnes*
(Lamentations 1:12,16; 3:19,22-24,26)

Antiphon Look and see if there is any sorrow like my sorrow.

Is it nothing to you, all you who pass by? *
　　Look and see if there is any sorrow like my sorrow,

Which was brought upon me, *
　　inflicted by God's fierce anger.

For these things I weep; my eyes flow with tears, *
　　for a comforter is far from me, one to revive my courage.

Remember my affliction and my bitterness, *
　　wormwood and gall!

The steadfast love of God never ceases, *
　　God's mercies never end.

They are new every morning; *
　　great is your faithfulness.

"God is my portion," says my soul, *
　　"therefore will I hope in God."

It is good that we should wait quietly *
　　for the coming of God's salvation.

Antiphon Look and see if there is any sorrow like my sorrow.

Weeks 2 & 4
Canticle of the Purified *Audite qui lange estis*
(Isaiah 33: 13-16)

Antiphon They will live on the heights; their refuge will be the fortresses of rocks.

Hear, you who are far away, what I have done;*
    and you who are near, acknowledge my might.

The sinners in Zion are afraid;*
    trembling has seized the godless:

"Who among us can live with the devouring fire? *
    Who among us can live with everlasting flames?"

Those who walk righteously and speak uprightly, *
    who despise the gain of oppression.

Those who wave away a bribe instead of accepting it, *
    who stop their ears from hearing of bloodshed
    and shut their eyes from looking on evil.

They will live on the heights; *
    their refuge will be the fortresses of rocks;
    their food will be supplied, their water assured.

Antiphon They will live on the heights; their refuge will be the fortresses of rocks.

Responsory (Ps. 130:7; Is. 52:9)
With the Lord there is plenteous redemption
    − God shall redeem Israel from all their sins.
The Lord has redeemed daughter Jerusalem
    − God shall redeem Israel from all their sins.
Glory to the Father and to the Son and to the Holy Spirit.
With the Lord there is plenteous redemption
    − God shall redeem Israel from all their sins

Benedictus Antiphon
Lent 1-4 We proclaim Christ crucified, the power of God and the wisdom of God.
Lent 5 God is the source of your life in Christ Jesus, who became for us wisdom from God, and righteousness and sanctification and redemption

Litany
Teach us, O Christ, to renounce ourselves and to follow you, not pampering ourselves but living into the discipline of Lent.
Lord, have mercy.
Train us, O Teacher, to act differently from the way of the world so that for love of you, O Christ, you may come before all else.
Christ, have mercy.
Keep us, O Suffering One, from injuring others as we patiently endure persecution.
Lord, have mercy.

Invitation to the Lord's Prayer Since we know that God is the source of all the good we do, we place all our hope in God and we pray with Christ.

Collect
Saturday after Ash Wednesday
O God, by your Word you marvelously carry out the work of reconciliation: Grant that in our Lenten fast we may be devoted to you with all our hearts, and united with one another in prayer and holy love; through Jesus Christ our Lord, who lives and reigns with you and the Holy Spirit, one God, for ever and ever. Amen.
Saturday of the First Week in Lent
O God, by your Word you marvelously carry out the work of reconciliation: Grant that in our Lenten fast we may be devoted to you with all our hearts, and united with one another in prayer and holy love; through Jesus Christ our Lord, who lives and reigns with you and the Holy Spirit, one God, for ever and ever. Amen.
Saturday of the Second Week in Lent
Grant, most merciful Lord, to your faithful people pardon and peace, that they may be cleansed from all their sins, and serve you with a quiet mind; through Jesus Christ our Lord, who lives and reigns with you and the Holy Spirit, one God, for ever and ever. Amen.
Saturday of the Third Week in Lent
O God, you know us to be set in the midst of so many and great dangers, that by reason of the frailty of our nature we cannot always stand upright: Grant us such strength and protection as may support us in all dangers, and carry us through all temptations; through Jesus Christ our Lord, who lives and reigns with you and the Holy Spirit, one God, for ever and ever. Amen.
Saturday of the Fourth Week in Lent
Mercifully hear our prayers, O Lord, and spare all those who confess their sins to you; that those whose consciences are accused by sin may by your

merciful pardon be absolved; through Jesus Christ your Son our Lord, who lives and reigns with you and the Holy Spirit, one God, for ever and ever. Amen.

Saturday of the Fifth Week in Lent
O Lord, in your goodness you bestow abundant graces on your elect: Look with favor, we entreat you, upon those who in these Lenten days are being prepared for Holy Baptism, and grant them the help of your protection; through Jesus Christ your Son our Lord, who lives and reigns with you and the Holy Spirit, one God, for ever and ever. Amen.

The Blessing
May we renounce ourselves in order to follow Christ and discipline our bodies and relieve the lot of the poor. **Amen.**

Lent Saturday Noonday Prayer

Hymn Sing my tongue his wondrous love *Hymnal 467*

Reading Isaiah 1: 14-16
Your new moons and your appointed festivals my soul hates; they have become a burden to me, I am weary of bearing them. When you stretch out your hands, I will hide my eyes from you; even though you make many prayers, I will not listen; your hands are full of blood. Wash yourselves; make yourselves clean; remove the evil of your doings from before my eyes; cease to do evil, learn to do good; seek justice, rescue the oppressed, defend the orphan, plead for the widow.

Verse & Response
My delight is in your statutes.
I will not forget your word.

Collect *From Morning Prayer*

Holy Week

The Psalms for Sunday, Monday, Tuesday and Wednesday are taken from Week 2 of the Psalter. The Psalms for Maundy Thursday, Good Friday and Holy Saturday are appointed for the day.
Compline is found in the ordinary form of Compline from Sunday through Wednesday on page 209. Compline for the Triduum is found on page 93.

Assist us mercifully with your help, O Lord God of our salvation, that we may enter with joy upon the contemplation of those mighty acts, whereby you have given us life and immortality; through Jesus Christ our Lord. Amen.

Palm Sunday Evening Prayer I

Psalter, Week 2

Hymn All glory, laud, and honor *Hymnal 154*

Antiphon 1 They brought the colt to Jesus; and after throwing their cloaks on it, they set Jesus on it.
Antiphon 2 Blessed is the king who comes in the name of the Lord! Peace in heaven, and glory in the highest heaven!
Antiphon 3 "Teacher, order your disciples to stop." He answered, "I tell you, if these were silent, the stones would shout out."

Responsory
We adore you O Christ
    – **and we bless you.**
By your cross you redeemed the world.
    – **and we bless you.**
Glory to the Father and to the Son and to the Holy Spirit.
We adore you O Christ
    – **and we bless you.**

Magnificat Antiphon Hosanna to the Son of David, the Redeemer of the world. The Prophets foretold the redemption you bring to us. Hosanna in the highest!

Litany
Christ, like a mother hen, you desired to draw your scattered ones together; draw us nearer to you and each other in our meditation on your passion.
Lord, have mercy.
Christ, like a slave, you washed the feet of your disciples; teach us deep humility.
Christ, have mercy.
Christ, like a Passover lamb, by your blood brought us to new life; lead our departed ones to that life you opened through your pierced side.
Lord, have mercy.

Invitation to the Lord's Prayer As we enter into the contemplation of those mighty acts by which God accomplished our redemption, let us draw closer to the Father.

Collect Almighty and everliving God, in your tender love for the human race you sent your Son our Savior Jesus Christ to take upon him our nature, and to suffer death upon the cross, giving us the example of his great humility: Mercifully grant that we may walk in the way of his suffering, and also share in his resurrection; through Jesus Christ our

Lord, who lives and reigns with you and the Holy Spirit, one God, for ever and ever. Amen.

The Blessing
May we trust the word of Christ who said: You will weep and mourn, but the world will rejoice; you will have pain, but your pain will turn into joy. **Amen.**

Palm Sunday Morning Prayer

Invitatory The Lord is reigning from the tree: Come let us adore.

Hymn Ride on! Ride on in majesty! *Hymnal 156*

Antiphon 1 The crowd took branches of palm trees and went out to meet him, shouting, "Hosanna! Blessed is the one who comes in the name of the Lord, the King of Israel!"
Antiphon 2 Jesus found a young donkey and sat on it
Antiphon 3 Do not be afraid, daughter of Zion. Look, your king is coming, sitting on a donkey's colt.

Responsory One (Rev. 5:9)
You have redeemed us O Lord
    − in your blood.
From every tribe, language, people and nation
    − in your blood.
Glory to the Father and to the Son and to the Holy Spirit.
You have redeemed us O Lord
    − in your blood.

Canticle − Canticle of the Suffering Servant I *Ecce servus meus*
(Isaiah 42: 1-4)

Antiphon O glorious cross, O precious wood, O admirable sign. On you, Christ triumphed over evil and redeemed the world by his blood.

Here is my servant, whom I uphold, *
    my chosen, in whom my soul delights.

I have put my spirit upon him; *
    he will bring forth justice to the nations.

He will not cry or lift up his voice, *
    or make it heard in the street.

A bruised reed he will not break, *
    and a dimly burning wick he will not quench.
    He will faithfully bring forth justice.

He will not grow faint or be crushed *
> until he has established justice in the earth;
> and the coastlands wait for his teaching.

Antiphon O glorious cross, O precious wood, O admirable sign. On you, Christ triumphed over evil and redeemed the world by his blood.

Responsory Two (Ps. 41:4)
I say to the Lord
> — **have mercy on me.**

Heal my soul, for I have sinned.
> — **have mercy on me.**

Glory to the Father and to the Son and to the Holy Spirit.
I say to the Lord
> — **have mercy on me.**

Benedictus Antiphon With palms, hymns and canticles, let us greet the Lord as he comes to us. Let us raise our voices and cry out: Hosanna! Blessed is the Lord who comes to us. Hosanna.

Litany
Christ, humble ruler, let us walk with you on the path of humble love.
Lord, have mercy.
Christ, Son of David, let us discover with you the dignity of serving love.
Christ, have mercy.
Christ, Suffering Servant, let us share with you the way of sacrificial love.
Lord, have mercy.

Invitation to the Lord's Prayer As we celebrate Christ as the Son of David, let us walk with him on his journey to the cross.

Collect Assist us mercifully with your help, O Lord God of our salvation, that we may enter with joy upon the contemplation of those mighty acts, whereby you have given us life and immortality; through Jesus Christ our Lord. Amen.

The Blessing
May we trust the word of Christ who said: You will weep and mourn, but the world will rejoice; you will have pain, but your pain will turn into joy. **Amen.**

Palm Sunday Noonday Prayer

Hymn In The Cross Of Christ I Glory *Hymnal 441*

Antiphon He humbled himself and became obedient to the point of death, even death on a cross.

Reading Hebrews 9: 12-14
Christ entered once for all into the Holy Place, not with the blood of goats and calves, but with his own blood, thus obtaining eternal redemption. For if the blood of goats and bulls, with the sprinkling of the ashes of a heifer, sanctifies those who have been defiled so that their flesh is purified, how much more will the blood of Christ, who through the eternal Spirit offered himself without blemish to God, purify our conscience from dead works to worship the living God!

Verse and Response
I am a worm and no man.
Scorned by all and despised by the people.

Collect Almighty God, whose most dear Son went not up to joy but first he suffered pain, and entered not into glory before he was crucified: Mercifully grant that we, walking in the way of the cross, may find it none other than the way of life and peace; through Jesus Christ our Lord. Amen.

Palm Sunday Evening Prayer II

Hymn The Flaming Banners Of Our King *Hymnal 161*

Antiphon 1 Let the same mind be in you that was in Christ Jesus, who, though he was in the form of God, he emptied himself.
Antiphon 2 The message about the cross is foolishness to those who are perishing, but to us who are being saved it is the power of God.
Antiphon 3 May I never boast of anything except the cross of our Lord Jesus Christ, by which the world has been crucified to me, and I to the world.

Responsory
We adore you O Christ
  − and we bless you.
By your cross you redeemed the world.
  − and we bless you.
Glory to the Father and to the Son and to the Holy Spirit.
We adore you O Christ
  − and we bless you.

Magnificat Antiphon
Year A It is written, 'I will strike the shepherd, and the sheep of the flock will be scattered.' But after I am raised up, I will go ahead of you to Galilee.
Year B A woman came with an alabaster jar of very costly ointment of nard, and she broke open the jar and poured the ointment on his head.
Year C An angel from heaven appeared to him and gave him strength. In his anguish he prayed more earnestly, and his sweat became like great drops of blood falling down on the ground.

Litany
Christ, like a mother hen, you desired to draw your scattered ones together; draw us nearer to you and each other in our meditation on your passion.
Lord, have mercy.
Christ, like a slave, you washed the feet of your disciples; teach us deep humility.
Christ, have mercy.
Christ, like a Passover lamb, by your blood brought us to new life; lead our departed ones to that life you opened through your pierced side.
Lord, have mercy.

Invitation to the Lord's Prayer As we enter into the contemplation of those mighty acts by which God accomplished our redemption, let us draw closer to the Father.

Collect Almighty and everliving God, in your tender love for the human race you sent your Son our Savior Jesus Christ to take upon him our nature, and to suffer death upon the cross, giving us the example of his great humility: Mercifully grant that we may walk in the way of his suffering, and also share in his resurrection; through Jesus Christ our Lord, who lives and reigns with you and the Holy Spirit, one God, for ever and ever. Amen.

The Blessing
May we trust the word of Christ who said: You will weep and mourn, but the world will rejoice; you will have pain, but your pain will turn into joy. **Amen.**

Monday In Holy Week Morning Prayer

Invitatory The Lord is reigning from the tree: Come let us adore.

Hymn When I Survey The Wondrous Cross *Hymnal 474*

Antiphon 1 Here is my servant, whom I uphold, my chosen, in whom my soul delights.
Antiphon 2 I have given you as a covenant to the people, a light to the nations.
Antiphon 3 New things I now declare; before they spring forth, I tell you of them.

Responsory One (Mt. 16:24; Jn. 12:26)
If any want to become my followers
- **let them take up their cross and follow me.**

Where the Lord is there will his servant be
- **let them take up their cross and follow me.**

Glory to the Father and to the Son and to the Holy Spirit.
If any want to become my followers
- **let them take up their cross and follow me.**

Canticle – Canticle of the Servant Song IV *Quis credidit auditui*
(Isaiah 53: 1-11)

Antiphon He was despised and rejected by others; a man of suffering and acquainted with infirmity.

Who has believed what we have heard? *
    And to whom has the arm of the Lord been revealed?

For he grew up before him like a young plant, *
    and like a root out of dry ground.

He had no form or majesty that we should look at him, *
    nothing in his appearance that we should desire him.

He was despised and rejected by others; *
    a man of suffering and acquainted with infirmity.

He was as one from whom others hide their faces *
    he was despised, and we held him of no account.

Surely he has borne our infirmities and carried our diseases; *
    yet we accounted him stricken,
    struck down by God, and afflicted.

But he was wounded for our transgressions, *
    crushed for our iniquities.

Upon him was the punishment that made us whole, *
    and by his bruises we are healed.

Antiphon He was despised and rejected by others; a man of suffering and acquainted with infirmity.

Responsory Two (Ps. 88:18; Mk. 15:50)
My friend and my neighbor you have put away from me
    — darkness is my only companion.
All the disciples deserted Jesus and fled
    — darkness is my only companion.
Glory to the Father and to the Son and to the Holy Spirit.
My friend and my neighbor you have put away from me
    — darkness is my only companion.

Benedictus Antiphon Mary took a pound of costly perfume made of pure nard, anointed Jesus' feet, and wiped them with her hair. The house was filled with the fragrance of the perfume.

Litany
Strengthen us in our practice of almsgiving, prayer and fasting.
Lord, have mercy.
Purify us by our Lenten discipline to draw closer to you.
Christ, have mercy.
Return our hearts to a more faithful reception of your Sacraments and a consistent reading of your Word.
Lord, have mercy.

Invitation to the Lord's Prayer
We know that we are powerless to change our lives so we ask for the grace of repentance as we pray with you, O Christ.

Collect Almighty God, whose dear Son went not up to joy but first he suffered pain, and entered not into glory before he was crucified: Mercifully grant that we, walking in the way of the cross, may find it none other than the way of life and peace; through Jesus Christ your Son our Lord, who lives and reigns with you and the Holy Spirit, one God, for ever and ever. Amen.

The Blessing
May we rejoice insofar as we are sharing Christ's sufferings, so that we may also be glad and shout for joy when his glory is revealed. **Amen.**

Monday In Holy Week Noonday Prayer

Hymn To Mock Your Reign *Hymnal 170*

Antiphon My house shall be called a house of prayer for all the nations. But you have made it a den of robbers.

Reading Hebrews 2: 9-11
We do see Jesus, who for a little while was made lower than the angels, now crowned with glory and honor because of the suffering of death, so that by the grace of God he might taste death for everyone. It was fitting that God, for whom and through whom all things exist, in bringing many children to glory, should make the pioneer of their salvation perfect through sufferings. For the one who sanctifies and those who are sanctified all have one Father.

Verse and Response
If we suffer with Christ.
We will be glorified with Christ.

Collect *From Morning Prayer*

Monday In Holy Week Evening Prayer

Hymn Hail Thou Once Despised Jesus *Hymnal 495*

Antiphon 1 Christ entered once for all into the Holy Place, not with the blood of goats and calves, but with his own blood, thus obtaining eternal redemption.
Antiphon 2 How much more will the blood of Christ, who through the eternal Spirit offered himself without blemish to God, purify our conscience.
Antiphon 3 Christ is the mediator of a new covenant, so that those who are called may receive the promised eternal inheritance.

Responsory (Ps. 32:1; Mt. 5:8)
Blessed are they whose transgressions are forgiven
    – whose sin is put away.
Blessed are the pure of heart.
    – whose sin is put away.
Glory to the Father and to the Son and to the Holy Spirit.
Blessed **are they whose transgressions are forgiven**
    – whose sin is put away.

Magnificat Antiphon She bought this perfume so that she might keep it for the day of my burial. You always have the poor with you, but you do not always have me.

Litany
Kindle in our hearts an active love for our communities that with you we may build a world of justice and peace.
Lord, have mercy.
Visit the sick, comfort the sorrowful and strengthen the weak through the ministry of holy women and men.
Christ, have mercy.
You promised paradise to the repentant thief, bring all the dead to their heavenly mansion.
Lord, have mercy.

Invitation to the Lord's Prayer
Through Baptism we have become sharers of the divine nature, so we draw near with Christ and call out in the Spirit.

Collect *From Morning Prayer*

The Blessing
May we rejoice insofar as we are sharing Christ's sufferings, so that we may also be glad and shout for joy when his glory is revealed. **Amen.**

Tuesday In Holy Week Morning Prayer

Invitatory The Lord is reigning from the tree: Come let us adore.

Hymn Ah Holy Jesus *Hymnal 158*

Antiphon 1 The Lord God made me a polished arrow; in his quiver he hid me away.
Antiphon 2 I will give you as a light to the nations, that my salvation may reach to the end of the earth.
Antiphon 3 Kings shall see and stand up, because of the Holy One of Israel, who has chosen you.

Responsory One (Gal 6:4; Phil. 3:8)
May I never boast of anything
  − except the cross of our Lord Jesus Christ.
I consider all things as rubbish
  − except the cross of our Lord Jesus Christ.
Glory to the Father and to the Son and to the Holy Spirit.
May I never boast of anything
  − except the cross of our Lord Jesus Christ.

Canticle – Canticle of the Cross *Verbum enim crucis*
(1 Corinthians 1: 18-25)

Antiphon Christ Crucified is the power of God and the wisdom of God.

The message about the cross is foolishness *
   to those who are perishing.

But to us who are being saved *
   it is the power of God.

For it is written, 'I will destroy the wisdom of the wise, *
   and the discernment of the discerning I will thwart.'

Where is the one who is wise? *
   Where is the scribe?

Where is the debater of this age? *
   Has not God made foolish the wisdom of the world?

For since, in the wisdom of God, *
   the world did not know God through wisdom,

God decided, through the foolishness of our proclamation, *
   to save those who believe.

For Jews demand signs and Greeks desire wisdom, *
   but we proclaim Christ crucified.

Christ Crucified is a stumbling-block to Jews
and foolishness to Gentiles, *
   but to those who are the called, both Jews and Greeks,
   Christ is the power of God and the wisdom of God.

For God's foolishness is wiser than human wisdom, *
   and God's weakness is stronger than human strength.

Antiphon Christ Crucified is the power of God and the wisdom of God.

Responsory Two (2 Cor. 5:18; Eph. 4:32)
God reconciled us to himself through Christ
   – God has given us the ministry of reconciliation.
Forgive one another as God has forgiven you
   – God has given us the ministry of reconciliation.
Glory to the Father and to the Son and to the Holy Spirit.
God reconciled us to himself through Christ
   – God has given us the ministry of reconciliation.

Benedictus Antiphon Unless a grain of wheat falls into the earth and dies, it remains just a single grain; but if it dies, it bears much fruit.

Litany
Children are suffering from deprivation and want; feed their bodies, souls and spirits with your riches.
Lord, have mercy.
Parents lament their inability to adequately provide for their families; create new opportunities for all people to earn a just wage.
Christ, have mercy.
The poor endure poor living conditions in places of pollution and natural disasters; raise up businesses that build up the city of God among us.
Lord, have mercy.

Invitation to the Lord's Prayer You take the side of the poor and disadvantaged so we stand with our brothers and sisters in need as we pray.

Collect O God, by the passion of your blessed Son you made an instrument of shameful death to be for us the means of life: Grant us so to glory in the cross of Christ, that we may gladly suffer shame and loss for the sake of your Son our Savior Jesus Christ; who lives and reigns with you and the Holy Spirit, one God, for ever and ever. Amen.

The Blessing
May we rejoice in our sufferings, for in our flesh we are completing what is lacking in Christ's afflictions for the sake of his body, the church. **Amen.**

Tuesday In Holy Week Noonday Prayer
Hymn Cross of Jesus, cross of sorrow *Hymnal 160*

Antiphon By what authority are you doing these things? Who gave you this authority to do them?

Reading Zechariah 12: 10
I will pour out a spirit of compassion and supplication on the house of David and the inhabitants of Jerusalem, so that, when they look on the one whom they have pierced, they shall mourn for him, as one mourns for an only child, and weep bitterly over him, as one weeps over a firstborn.

Verse and Response
They have pierced my hands and my feet.
I can number all my bones.

Collect *From Morning Prayer*

Tuesday In Holy Week Evening Prayer

Hymn Glory Be To Jesus Who In Bitter Pain *Hymnal 479*

Antiphon 1 The message about the cross is foolishness to those who are perishing, but to us who are being saved it is the power of God.
Antiphon 2 We proclaim Christ crucified, the power of God and the wisdom of God.
Antiphon 3 God chose what is foolish in the world to shame the wise; God chose what is weak in the world to shame the strong.

Responsory (Eph. 2:15; Col. 1:20)
Christ created in himself one new humanity
    — **Christ has made peace.**
Through the blood of the cross
    — **Christ has made peace.**
Glory to the Father and to the Son and to the Holy Spirit.
Christ created in himself one new humanity
    — **Christ has made peace.**

Magnificat Antiphon The light is with you for a little longer. While you have the light, believe in the light, so that you may become children of light.

Litany
Turn our hearts to the needs of women and girls, men and boys who endure exploitation and bring an end to human trafficking.
Lord, have mercy.
Support police, firefighters, and emergency responders to come to the aid of people in dire conditions.
Christ, have mercy.
Lead the dying to behold the light of your glory and comfort them with faith in your presence.
Lord, have mercy.

Invitation to the Lord's Prayer We implore you to turn our hearts to you again, to renew our baptismal fervor and to draw us closer to you as we pray.

Collect *From Morning Prayer*

The Blessing
May we rejoice in our sufferings, for in our flesh we are completing what is lacking in Christ's afflictions for the sake of his body, the church. **Amen.**

Wednesday in Holy Week Morning Prayer

Invitatory The Lord is reigning from the tree: Come let us adore.

Hymn What Wondrous Love *Hymnal 439*

Antiphon 1 The Lord God has opened my ear, and I was not disobedient, I did not turn backward.
Antiphon 2 I gave my back to those who struck me, and my cheeks to those who pulled out the beard.
Antiphon 3 The Lord God helps me; therefore I have not been disgraced.

Responsory One (Eph. 1:7; Rom. 5:11)
In Christ we have redemption through his blood
– **the forgiveness of our trespasses.**
We have received reconciliation with God
– **the forgiveness of our trespasses.**
Glory to the Father and to the Son and to the Holy Spirit.
In Christ we have redemption through his blood
– **the forgiveness of our trespasses.**

Canticle of the Suffering Servant Song III *Dominus Deus aperuit*
(Isaiah 50: 5-9)

Antiphon I know that I shall not be put to shame; he who vindicates me is near.

The Lord God has given me the tongue of a teacher, *
  that I may know how to sustain the weary with a word.

Morning by morning he wakens *
  wakens my ear to listen as those who are taught.

The Lord God has opened my ear, *
  and I was not rebellious, I did not turn backward.

I gave my back to those who struck me, *
  and my cheeks to those who pulled out the beard;
  I did not hide my face from insult and spitting.

The Lord God helps me; *
  therefore I have not been disgraced.

I have set my face like flint, *
>> and I know that I shall not be put to shame;
>> he who vindicates me is near.

Who will contend with me? *
>> Let us stand up together.

Who are my adversaries? *
>> Let them confront me.

It is the Lord God who helps me; *
>> who will declare me guilty?

Antiphon I know that I shall not be put to shame; he who vindicates me is near.

Responsory Two (2 Cor. 5:19; 2 Cor. 13:11)
In Christ God was reconciling the world to himself
>> **− entrusting the message of reconciliation to us.**
Live in peace; and the God of love and peace will be with us
>> **− entrusting the message of reconciliation to us.**
Glory to the Father and to the Son and to the Holy Spirit.
In Christ God was reconciling the world to himself
>> **− entrusting the message of reconciliation to us.**

Benedictus Antiphon Jesus was troubled in spirit, and declared, "Very truly, I tell you, one of you will betray me."

Litany
Turn our hearts from seeking our own gain and attract our hearts to you in prayer.
Lord, have mercy.
Turn our minds from planning our own schemes and lead us to you through the study of your Word.
Christ, have mercy.
Turn our hands from selfish activity and sustain our service of our needy brothers and sisters.
Lord, have mercy.

Invitation to the Lord's Prayer
Draw near to us, O Christ, in our Lenten discipline and deepen the practice of our faith through prayer with you.

Collect Lord God, whose blessed Son our Savior gave his body to be whipped and his face to be spit upon: Give us grace to accept joyfully the sufferings of the present time, confident of the glory that shall be revealed; through Jesus Christ your Son our Lord, who lives and reigns with you and the Holy Spirit, one God, for ever and ever. Amen.

The Blessing
May we imitate and observe those who live according to the apostolic example and not live as enemies of the cross of Christ. **Amen.**

Wednesday in Holy Week Noonday Prayer
Hymn We Sing The Praise Of Him Who Died *Hymnal 471*

Antiphon The stone that the builders rejected has become the cornerstone; this was the Lord's doing.

Reading Hebrews 10: 12-14
When Christ had offered for all time a single sacrifice for sins, "he sat down at the right hand of God," and since then has been waiting "until his enemies would be made a footstool for his feet." For by a single offering he has perfected for all time those who are sanctified.

Verse and Response
You made on the cross by your one oblation of yourself.
A full, perfect and sufficient sacrifice for the sins of the whole world.

Collect *From Morning Prayer*

Wednesday in Holy Week Evening Prayer
Hymn The Royal Banners Forward Go *Hymnal 162*

Antiphon 1 Let us run with perseverance the race that is set before us, looking to Jesus the pioneer and perfecter of our faith.
Antiphon 2 For the sake of the joy that was set before him, Jesus endured the cross, disregarding its shame.
Antiphon 3 Consider Jesus who endured such hostility against himself from sinners, so that you may not grow weary or lose heart.

Responsory (Ps. 41:9; Lk. 22:48)
My best friend whom I trusted
  − he has turned against me.
Judas approached Jesus to kiss him
  − he has turned against me.
Glory to the Father and to the Son and to the Holy Spirit.
My best friend whom I trusted
  − he has turned against me.

Magnificat Antiphon Now the Son of Man has been glorified, and God has been glorified in him.

Litany
You endured betrayal and rejection; heal us of the times we have endured infidelity and were ourselves unfaithful.
Lord, have mercy.
You give us an example of humility in your passion; teach us obedience for the love of God.
Christ, have mercy.
You only are immortal, the creator and maker of us all; receive into the arms of your mercy all who have died.
Lord, have mercy.

Invitation to the Lord's Prayer
You took up the cross for our salvation, give us courage to take up our cross and strengthen us as we pray.

Collect *From Morning Prayer*

The Blessing
May we imitate and observe those who live according to the apostolic example and not live as enemies of the cross of Christ. **Amen.**

The Easter Triduum

Beginning with Maundy Thursday and throughout the Easter Triduum, Morning Prayer, Noonday Prayer and Evening Prayer have their own psalmody. The Responsories follow a distinct format.

Maundy Thursday Morning Prayer

Invitatory With great longing Christ has desired to eat this Passover with us: Come let us adore.

Hymn Sing my tongue the glorious battle *Hymnal 439*

Psalm 90 *Domine, refugium*

Antiphon Jesus knew that his hour had come to depart from this world and go to the Father.

1 Lord, you have been our refuge *
 from one generation to another.

2 Before the mountains were brought forth,
 or the land and the earth were born, *
 from age to age you are God.

3 You turn us back to the dust and say, *
 "Go back, O child of earth."

4 For a thousand years in your sight
 are like yesterday when it is past *
 and like a watch in the night.

5 You sweep us away like a dream; *
 we fade away suddenly like the grass.

6 In the morning it is green and flourishes; *
 in the evening it is dried up and withered.

7 For we consume away in your displeasure; *
 we are afraid because of your wrathful indignation.

8 Our iniquities you have set before you, *
 and our secret sins in the light of your countenance.

9 When you are angry, all our days are gone; *
 we bring our years to an end like a sigh.

10 The span of our life is seventy years,
   perhaps in strength even eighty; *
      yet the sum of them is but labor and sorrow,
      for they pass away quickly and we are gone.

11 Who regards the power of your wrath? *
      who rightly fears your indignation?

12 So teach us to number our days *
      that we may apply our hearts to wisdom.

13 Return, O LORD; how long will you tarry? *
      be gracious to your servants.

14 Satisfy us by your loving-kindness in the morning; *
      so shall we rejoice and be glad all the days of our life.

15 Make us glad by the measure of the days that you afflicted us *
      and the years in which we suffered adversity.

16 Show your servants your works *
      and your splendor to their children.

17 May the graciousness of the LORD our God be upon us; *
      prosper the work of our hands;
      prosper our handiwork.

Antiphon Jesus knew that his hour had come to depart from this world and go to the Father.

Psalm 36 *Dixit injustus*

Antiphon Having loved his own who were in the world, Jesus loved them to the end.

1 There is a voice of rebellion deep in the heart of the wicked; *
      there is no fear of God before his eyes.

2 He flatters himself in his own eyes *
      that his hateful sin will not be found out.

3 The words of his mouth are wicked and deceitful; *
      he has left off acting wisely and doing good.

4 He thinks up wickedness upon his bed
   and has set himself in no good way; *
      he does not abhor that which is evil.

5 Your love, O LORD, reaches to the heavens, *
      and your faithfulness to the clouds.

6 Your righteousness is like the strong mountains,
   your justice like the great deep; *
      you save both man and beast, O LORD.

7 How priceless is your love, O God! *
   your people take refuge
   under the shadow of your wings.

8 They feast upon the abundance of your house; *
   you give them drink from the river of your delights.

9 For with you is the well of life, *
   and in your light we see light.

10 Continue your loving-kindness to those who know you, *
   and your favor to those who are true of heart.

11 Let not the foot of the proud come near me, *
   nor the hand of the wicked push me aside.

12 See how they are fallen, those who work wickedness! *
   they are cast down and shall not be able to rise.

Antiphon Having loved his own who were in the world, Jesus loved them to the end.

Psalm 147 B *Lauda Hierusalem*

Antiphon Jesus took off his outer robe, poured water into a basin and began to wash the disciples' feet.

13 Worship the LORD, O Jerusalem; *
   praise your God, O Zion;

14 For he has strengthened the bars of your gates; *
   he has blessed your children within you.

15 He has established peace on your borders; *
   he satisfies you with the finest wheat.

16 He sends out his command to the earth, *
   and his word runs very swiftly.

17 He gives snow like wool; *
   he scatters hoarfrost like ashes.

18 He scatters his hail like bread crumbs; *
   who can stand against his cold?

19 He sends forth his word and melts them; *
   he blows with his wind, and the waters flow.

20 He declares his word to Jacob, *
 his statutes and his judgments to Israel.

21 He has not done so to any other nation; *
 to them he has not revealed his judgments.

Antiphon Jesus took off his outer robe, poured water into a basin and began to wash the disciples' feet.

Responsory One
On the Mount of Olives Jesus prayed to his Father,
"Father, if you are willing, remove this cup from me; yet, not my will but yours be done."
 —The spirit is willing but the flesh is weak.
Pray that you may not come into the time of trial.
 —The spirit is willing but the flesh is weak.

Canticle – Canticle of Confident Love *Non relinquam vos orfanos*
(John 15: 18-21, 23-24, 27-31)

Antiphon Those who love me will keep my word and my Father will love them. We will come to them and make our home with them.

I will not leave you orphaned; *
 I am coming to you.

In a little while the world will no longer see me,
but you will see me. *
 Because I live, you also will live.

On that day you will know that I am in my Father, *
 and you in me, and I in you.

They who have my commandments and keep them *
 are those who love me.

Those who love me will be loved by my Father, *
 and I will love them and reveal myself to them.

Those who love me will keep my word, *
 and my Father will love them.

We will come to them *
 and make our home with them.

Whoever does not love me does not keep my words; *
 and the word that you hear is not mine,
 but is from the Father who sent me.

Peace I leave with you; my peace I give to you. *
    I do not give to you as the world gives.

Do not let your hearts be troubled, *
    and do not let them be afraid.

You heard me say to you, *
    'I am going away, and I am coming to you.'

If you loved me, you would rejoice that I am going to the Father, *
    because the Father is greater than I.

And now I have told you this before it occurs, *
    so that when it does occur, you may believe.

I will no longer talk much with you, *
    for the ruler of this world is coming.

He has no power over me; *
    but I do as the Father has commanded me,
    so that the world may know that I love the Father.

Antiphon Those who love me will keep my word and my Father will love them. We will come to them and make our home with them.

Responsory after the Second Reading
Christ became obedient for us unto death.

Benedictus Antiphon Jesus, knowing that the Father had given all things into his hands, and that he had come from God and was going to God, began to wash the disciples' feet.

Litany
You were anointed by the Holy Spirit as prophet, priest and king; seal us with your Holy Spirit that we may share in your royal priesthood.
Lord, have mercy.
You walked the lonesome valley by yourself; awaken our hearts to know that you accompany all the abandoned and forsaken.
Christ, have mercy.
You prayed for the unity of your disciples; make our sad divisions to cease and draw us together in your sacrament of unity.
Lord, have mercy.

Invitation to the Lord's Prayer
We long for you, O Christ, to feed our hungry hearts so give us this day our daily bread.

Collect Almighty Father, whose dear Son, on the night before he suffered, instituted the Sacrament of his Body and Blood: Mercifully grant that we may receive it thankfully in remembrance of Jesus Christ our Lord, who in these holy mysteries gives us a pledge of eternal life; and who now lives and reigns with you and the Holy Spirit, one God, for ever and ever. Amen.

The Blessing
May we never boast of anything except the cross of our Lord Jesus Christ, by which the world has been crucified to us, and we to the world. **Amen.**

Maundy Thursday Noonday Prayer

Hymn When Jesus died to save us *Hymnal 322*

Psalm 2 *Quare fremuerunt gentes?*

Antiphon As often as you eat this bread and drink the cup, you proclaim the Lord's death until he comes.

1 Why are the nations in an uproar? *
    Why do the peoples mutter empty threats?

2 Why do the kings of the earth rise up in revolt,
    and the princes plot together, *
    against the LORD and against his Anointed?

3 "Let us break their yoke," they say; *
    "let us cast off their bonds from us."

4 He whose throne is in heaven is laughing; *
    the Lord has them in derision.

5 Then he speaks to them in his wrath, *
    and his rage fills them with terror.

6 "I myself have set my king *
    upon my holy hill of Zion."

7 Let me announce the decree of the LORD: *
    he said to me, "You are my Son;
    this day have I begotten you.

8 Ask of me, and I will give you
    the nations for your inheritance *
    and the ends of the earth for your possession.

9 You shall crush them with an iron rod *
    and shatter them like a piece of pottery."

10 And now, you kings, be wise; *
    be warned, you rulers of the earth.

11 Submit to the LORD with fear, *
    and with trembling bow before him;

12 Lest he be angry and you perish; *
    for his wrath is quickly kindled.

13 Blessed are they all *
    who take refuge in him!

Psalm 22 A *Deus, Deus meus*

1 My God, my God, why have you forsaken me? *
    and are so far from my cry
    and from the words of my distress?

2 O my God, I cry in the daytime, but you do not answer; *
    by night as well, but I find no rest.

3 Yet you are the Holy One, *
    enthroned upon the praises of Israel.

4 Our forefathers put their trust in you; *
    they trusted, and you delivered them.

5 They cried out to you and were delivered; *
    they trusted in you and were not put to shame.

6 But as for me, I am a worm and no man, *
    scorned by all and despised by the people.

7 All who see me laugh me to scorn; *
    they curl their lips and wag their heads, saying,

8 "He trusted in the LORD; let him deliver him; *
    let him rescue him, if he delights in him."

9 Yet you are he who took me out of the womb, *
    and kept me safe upon my mother's breast.

10 I have been entrusted to you ever since I was born; *
    you were my God
    when I was still in my mother's womb.

11 Be not far from me, for trouble is near, *
    and there is none to help.

12 Many young bulls encircle me; *
    strong bulls of Bashan surround me.

13 They open wide their jaws at me, *
    like a ravening and a roaring lion.

14 I am poured out like water;
    all my bones are out of joint; *
    my heart within my breast is melting wax.

15 My mouth is dried out like a pot-sherd;
    my tongue sticks to the roof of my mouth; *
    and you have laid me in the dust of the grave.

16 Packs of dogs close me in,
    and gangs of evildoers circle around me; *
    they pierce my hands and my feet;
    I can count all my bones.

17 They stare and gloat over me; *
    they divide my garments among them;
    they cast lots for my clothing.

18 Be not far away, O LORD; *
    you are my strength; hasten to help me.

19 Save me from the sword, *
    my life from the power of the dog.

20 Save me from the lion's mouth, *
    my wretched body from the horns of wild bulls.

Psalm 22 B *Narrabo nomen tuum*

21 I will declare your Name to my brethren; *
    in the midst of the congregation I will praise you.

22 Praise the LORD, you that fear him; *
    stand in awe of him, O offspring of Israel;
    all you of Jacob's line, give glory.

23 For he does not despise nor abhor the poor in their poverty;
    neither does he hide his face from them; *
    but when they cry to him he hears them.

24 My praise is of him in the great assembly; *
    I will perform my vows
    in the presence of those who worship him.

25 The poor shall eat and be satisfied,
    and those who seek the LORD shall praise him: *
    "May your heart live for ever!"

26 All the ends of the earth shall remember
    and turn to the LORD, *
        and all the families of the nations shall bow before him.

27 For kingship belongs to the LORD; *
    he rules over the nations.

28 To him alone all who sleep in the earth
    bow down in worship; *
        all who go down to the dust fall before him.

29 My soul shall live for him;
    my descendants shall serve him; *
        they shall be known as the LORD'S for ever.

30 They shall come and make known to a people yet unborn *
    the saving deeds that he has done.

Antiphon As often as you eat this bread and drink the cup, you proclaim the Lord's death until he comes.

Reading Hebrews 4: 14-15
Since, then, we have a great high priest who has passed through the heavens, Jesus, the Son of God, let us hold fast to our confession. For we do not have a high priest who is unable to sympathize with our weaknesses, but we have one who in every respect has been tested as we are, yet without sin.

Responsory after the Reading
Christ became obedient for us unto death.

Collect *From Morning Prayer*

Maundy Thursday Evening Prayer

Hymn Where true charity and love prevail *Hymnal 606*

Psalm 41 *Beatus qui intelligit*

Antiphon Jesus went with them to a place called Gethsemane; and he said to his disciples, "Sit here while I go over there and pray."

1 Blessed are they who consider the poor and needy! *
    the LORD will deliver them in the time of trouble.

2 The LORD preserves them and keeps them alive,
    so that they may be blessed in the land; *
        he does not hand them over to the will of their enemies.

3 The LORD sustains them on their sickbed *
    and ministers to them in their illness.

4 I said, "LORD, be merciful to me; *
    heal me, for I have sinned against you."

5 My enemies are saying wicked things about me: *
    "When will he die, and his name perish?"

6 Even if they come to see me, they speak empty words; *
    their heart collects false rumors;
    they go outside and spread them.

7 All my enemies whisper together about me *
    and devise evil against me.

8 "A deadly thing," they say, "has fastened on him; *
    he has taken to his bed and will never get up again."

9 Even my best friend, whom I trusted,
    who broke bread with me, *
    has lifted up his heel and turned against me.

10 But you, O LORD, be merciful to me and raise me up, *
    and I shall repay them.

11 By this I know you are pleased with me, *
    that my enemy does not triumph over me.

12 In my integrity you hold me fast, *
    and shall set me before your face for ever.

13 Blessed be the LORD God of Israel, *
    from age to age. Amen. Amen.

Antiphon Jesus went with them to a place called Gethsemane; and he said to his disciples, "Sit here while I go over there and pray."

Psalm 40 *Expectans, expectavi*

Antiphon My Father, if it is possible, let this cup pass from me; yet not what I want but what you want.

1 I waited patiently upon the LORD; *
    he stooped to me and heard my cry.

2 He lifted me out of the desolate pit, out of the mire and clay; *
    he set my feet upon a high cliff and made my footing sure.

3 He put a new song in my mouth,
    a song of praise to our God; *
        many shall see, and stand in awe,
        and put their trust in the LORD.

4 Blessed are they who trust in the LORD! *
    they do not resort to evil spirits or turn to false gods.

5 Great things are they that you have done, O LORD my God!
    how great your wonders and your plans for us! *
        there is none who can be compared with you.

6 Oh, that I could make them known and tell them! *
    but they are more than I can count.

7 In sacrifice and offering you take no pleasure *
    (you have given me ears to hear you);

8 Burnt-offering and sin-offering you have not required, *
    and so I said, "Behold, I come.

9 In the roll of the book it is written concerning me: *
    'I love to do your will, O my God;
    your law is deep in my heart.'"

10 I proclaimed righteousness in the great congregation; *
    behold, I did not restrain my lips;
    and that, O LORD, you know.

11 Your righteousness have I not hidden in my heart;
    I have spoken of your faithfulness and your deliverance; *
        I have not concealed your love and faithfulness
        from the great congregation.

12 You are the LORD;
    do not withhold your compassion from me; *
        let your love and your faithfulness keep me safe for ever,

13 For innumerable troubles have crowded upon me;
    my sins have overtaken me, and I cannot see; *
        they are more in number than the hairs of my head,
        and my heart fails me.

14 Be pleased, O LORD, to deliver me; *
    O LORD, make haste to help me.

15 Let them be ashamed and altogether dismayed
    who seek after my life to destroy it; *
        let them draw back and be disgraced
        who take pleasure in my misfortune.

16 Let those who say "Aha!" and gloat over me be confounded, *
        because they are ashamed.

17 Let all who seek you rejoice in you and be glad; *
        let those who love your salvation continually say,
        "Great is the LORD!"

18 Though I am poor and afflicted, *
        the Lord will have regard for me.

19 You are my helper and my deliverer; *
        do not tarry, O my God.

Antiphon My Father, if it is possible, let this cup pass from me; yet not what I want but what you want.

Psalm 108 *Paratum cor meum*

Antiphon Stay awake and pray that you may not come into the time of trial; the spirit indeed is willing, but the flesh is weak.

1 My heart is firmly fixed, O God, my heart is fixed; *
        I will sing and make melody.

2 Wake up, my spirit;
   awake, lute and harp; *
        I myself will waken the dawn.

3 I will confess you among the peoples, O LORD; *
        I will sing praises to you among the nations.

4 For your loving-kindness is greater than the heavens, *
        and your faithfulness reaches to the clouds.

5 Exalt yourself above the heavens, O God, *
        and your glory over all the earth.

6 So that those who are dear to you may be delivered, *
        save with your right hand and answer me.

7 God spoke from his holy place and said, *
        "I will exult and parcel out Shechem;
        I will divide the valley of Succoth.

8 Gilead is mine and Manasseh is mine; *
        Ephraim is my helmet and Judah my scepter.

9 Moab is my washbasin,
   on Edom I throw down my sandal to claim it, *
   and over Philistia will I shout in triumph."

10 Who will lead me into the strong city? *
   who will bring me into Edom?

11 Have you not cast us off, O God? *
   you no longer go out, O God, with our armies.

12 Grant us your help against the enemy, *
   for vain is the help of man.

13 With God we will do valiant deeds, *
   and he shall tread our enemies under foot.

Antiphon Stay awake and pray that you may not come into the time of trial; the spirit indeed is willing, but the flesh is weak.

Responsory after the Reading
Christ became obedient for us unto death.

Magnificat Antiphon I give you a new commandment, that you love one another. Just as I have loved you, you also should love one another.

Litany
Since we cherish you, O Christ, above all, lead us to follow you in the way of obedient humility.
Lord, have mercy.
As we renounce ourselves to follow you, O Christ, support us in the sacred fast that prepares us to celebrate your Resurrection.
Christ, have mercy.
Since we pray to never lose hope in you, O Christ, bring to your dwelling place all who have died in your faith and fear and all the departed.
Lord, have mercy.

Invitation to the Lord's Prayer
We hunger for you, O Christ, to feed our hungry hearts so give us this day the Bread of Life.

Collect *From Morning Prayer*

The Blessing
May we never boast of anything except the cross of our Lord Jesus Christ, by which the world has been crucified to us, and we to the world. **Amen.**

Compline for the Triduum

The Invitation
O God, make speed to save us.
**O Lord, make haste to help us.
Glory to the Father, and to the Son, and to the Holy Spirit:
as it was in the beginning, is now, and will be for ever. Amen.**

The Confession and Absolution
The Confession and Absolution follow. If a deacon is present, the deacon bids the congregation to the confession. If a bishop or priest are present they give the absolution. If there is no deacon, the bishop or priest bid the confession and give the absolution. If an ordained person is not present, the officiant bids the confession and gives the assurance of forgiveness.

Let us confess our sins to God.
A Period of Silence is observed.

Almighty God, our heavenly Father:
We have sinned against you,
through our own fault,
in thought, and word, and deed,
and in what we have left undone.
For the sake of your Son our Lord Jesus Christ,
forgive us all our offenses;
and grant that we may serve you
in newness of life, to the glory of your Name. Amen.

The Bishop, when present, or the Priest, stands and says
Almighty God have mercy on you, forgive you all your sins through our Lord Jesus Christ, strengthen you in all goodness, and by the power of the Holy Spirit keep you in eternal life. Amen.

Or in the absence of a bishop or priest:
Officiant May the Almighty God grant us forgiveness of all our sins, and the grace and comfort of the Holy Spirit. Amen.

Hymn To you before the close of day *Hymnal 44*

Psalm 4 *Cum invocarem*
1 Answer me when I call, O God, defender of my cause; *
    you set me free when I am hard-pressed;
    have mercy on me and hear my prayer.

2 "You mortals, how long will you dishonor my glory; *
    how long will you worship dumb idols
    and run after false gods?"

3 Know that the LORD does wonders for the faithful; *
    when I call upon the LORD, he will hear me.

4 Tremble, then, and do not sin; *
    speak to your heart in silence upon your bed.

5 Offer the appointed sacrifices *
    and put your trust in the LORD.

6 Many are saying, "Oh, that we might see better times!" *
    Lift up the light of your countenance upon us, O LORD.

7 You have put gladness in my heart, *
    more than when grain and wine and oil increase.

8 I lie down in peace; at once I fall asleep; *
    for only you, LORD, make me dwell in safety.

Psalm 91   *Qui habitat*

1 He who dwells in the shelter of the Most High, *
    abides under the shadow of the Almighty.

2 He shall say to the LORD,
  "You are my refuge and my stronghold, *
    my God in whom I put my trust."

3 He shall deliver you from the snare of the hunter *
    and from the deadly pestilence.

4 He shall cover you with his pinions,
  and you shall find refuge under his wings; *
    his faithfulness shall be a shield and buckler.

5 You shall not be afraid of any terror by night, *
    nor of the arrow that flies by day;

6 Of the plague that stalks in the darkness, *
    nor of the sickness that lays waste at mid-day.

7 A thousand shall fall at your side
  and ten thousand at your right hand, *
    but it shall not come near you.

8 Your eyes have only to behold *
    to see the reward of the wicked.

9 Because you have made the LORD your refuge, *
    and the Most High your habitation,

10 There shall no evil happen to you, *
   neither shall any plague come near your dwelling.

11 For he shall give his angels charge over you, *
   to keep you in all your ways.

12 They shall bear you in their hands, *
   lest you dash your foot against a stone.

13 You shall tread upon the lion and adder; *
   you shall trample the young lion
   and the serpent under your feet.

14 Because he is bound to me in love,
   therefore will I deliver him; *
   I will protect him, because he knows my Name.

15 He shall call upon me, and I will answer him; *
   I am with him in trouble;
   I will rescue him and bring him to honor.

16 With long life will I satisfy him, *
   and show him my salvation.

Psalm 134 *Ecce nunc*

1 Behold now, bless the LORD, all you servants of the LORD, *
   you that stand by night in the house of the LORD.

2 Lift up your hands in the holy place and bless the LORD; *
   the LORD who made heaven and earth
   bless you out of Zion.

Maundy Thursday
Reading 1 Peter 5:8-9
Discipline yourselves, keep alert. Like a roaring lion your adversary the devil prowls around, looking for someone to devour. Resist him, steadfast in your faith, for you know that your brothers and sisters in all the world are undergoing the same kinds of suffering.

Responsory after the Reading
Christ became obedient for us unto death.

Good Friday
Reading 1 Thessalonians 5:9-10
For God has destined us not for wrath but for obtaining salvation through our Lord Jesus Christ, who died for us, so that whether we are awake or asleep we may live with him. Christ became obedient for us unto death, death on the cross.

Responsory after the Reading
Christ became obedient for us unto death, even to death on the cross.

Holy Saturday
Reading Romans 5: 8-9
God proves his love for us in that while we still were sinners Christ died for us. Much more surely then, now that we have been justified by his blood, will we be saved through him from the wrath of God.

Responsory after the Reading
Christ became obedient for us unto death, even to death on the cross. Therefore God exalted him and gave him the Name which is above every name.

Canticle: Nunc Dimittis

Antiphon Christ himself bore our sins in his body on the cross that we might die to sin and live to righteousness.

The Song of Simeon *Nunc Dimittis*
Luke 2:29-32

Lord, you now have set your servant free *
    to go in peace as you have promised;

For these eyes of mine have seen the Savior, *
    whom you have prepared for all the world to see:

A Light to enlighten the nations, *
    and the glory of your people Israel.

Antiphon Christ himself bore our sins in his body on the cross that we might die to sin and live to righteousness.

The Lord's Prayer

Lord, have mercy.
Christ, have mercy.
Lord, have mercy.

Our Father in heaven,
>   hallowed be your Name,
>   your kingdom come,
>   your will be done, on earth as in heaven.
Give us today our daily bread.
Forgive us our sins
>   as we forgive those
>   who sin against us.
Save us from the time of trial,
>   and deliver us from evil.
For the kingdom, the power,
>   and the glory are yours,
>   now and for ever. Amen.

Collect Visit this place, O Lord, and drive far from it all snares of the enemy; let your holy angels dwell with us to preserve us in peace; and let your blessing be upon us always; through Jesus Christ our Lord. Amen.

Conclusion and Blessing
Let us bless the Lord.
Thanks be to God.

The Lord grant us a quiet night and a peaceful death.
Amen

Final Antiphon of the Blessed Virgin Mary

Ave Regina Caelorum
Hail, Queen of Heaven.
Hail, Queen of the Angels.
Hail, Root of Jesse and Gate of the morning,
From you the world's true light was born.
Rejoice, O Glorious Virgin,
Beautiful beyond all others.
O you who are fair beyond the fairest
Pray for us to Christ.

Good Friday Morning Prayer

Invitatory Christ, the Son of God, has redeemed us with his blood: Come let us adore.

Hymn Alone, Thou goest forth O Lord *Hymnal 164*

Psalm 88 *Domine, Deus*

Antiphon God did not withhold his own Son, but gave him up for all of us.

1 O LORD, my God, my Savior, *
    by day and night I cry to you.

2 Let my prayer enter into your presence; *
    incline your ear to my lamentation.

3 For I am full of trouble; *
    my life is at the brink of the grave.

4 I am counted among those who go down to the Pit; *
    I have become like one who has no strength;

5 Lost among the dead, *
    like the slain who lie in the grave,

6 Whom you remember no more, *
    for they are cut off from your hand.

7 You have laid me in the depths of the Pit, *
    in dark places, and in the abyss.

8 Your anger weighs upon me heavily, *
    and all your great waves overwhelm me.

9 You have put my friends far from me;
    you have made me to be abhorred by them; *
    I am in prison and cannot get free.

10 My sight has failed me because of trouble; *
    LORD, I have called upon you daily;
    I have stretched out my hands to you.

11 Do you work wonders for the dead? *
    will those who have died stand up and give you thanks?

12 Will your loving-kindness be declared in the grave? *
    your faithfulness in the land of destruction?

13 Will your wonders be known in the dark? *
    or your righteousness in the country
    where all is forgotten?

14 But as for me, O LORD, I cry to you for help; *
    in the morning my prayer comes before you.

15 LORD, why have you rejected me? *
    why have you hidden your face from me?

16 Ever since my youth, I have been wretched
    and at the point of death; *
    I have borne your terrors with a troubled mind.

17 Your blazing anger has swept over me; *
    your terrors have destroyed me;

18 They surround me all day long like a flood; *
    they encompass me on every side.

19 My friend and my neighbor you have put away from me, *
    and darkness is my only companion.

Antiphon God did not withhold his own Son, but gave him up for all of us.

Psalm 143 *Domine, exaudi*

Antiphon My spirit faints within me; my heart within me is desolate.

1 LORD, hear my prayer,
    and in your faithfulness heed my supplications; *
    answer me in your righteousness.

2 Enter not into judgment with your servant, *
    for in your sight shall no one living be justified.

3 For my enemy has sought my life;
    he has crushed me to the ground; *
    he has made me live in dark places
    like those who are long dead.

4 My spirit faints within me; *
    my heart within me is desolate.

5 I remember the time past;
    I muse upon all your deeds; *
    I consider the works of your hands.

6 I spread out my hands to you; *
    my soul gasps to you like a thirsty land.

7 O LORD, make haste to answer me; my spirit fails me; *
    do not hide your face from me
    or I shall be like those who go down to the Pit.

8 Let me hear of your loving-kindness in the morning,
    for I put my trust in you; *
    show me the road that I must walk,
    for I lift up my soul to you.

9 Deliver me from my enemies, O LORD, *
    for I flee to you for refuge.

10 Teach me to do what pleases you, for you are my God; *
    let your good Spirit lead me on level ground.

11 Revive me, O LORD, for your Name's sake; *
    for your righteousness' sake, bring me out of trouble.

Antiphon My spirit faints within me; my heart within me is desolate.

Psalm 147 *Lauda Hierusalem*

Antiphon Lord, remember me when you come into your kingdom.

13 Worship the LORD, O Jerusalem; *
    praise your God, O Zion;

14 For he has strengthened the bars of your gates; *
    he has blessed your children within you.

15 He has established peace on your borders; *
    he satisfies you with the finest wheat.

16 He sends out his command to the earth, *
    and his word runs very swiftly.

17 He gives snow like wool; *
    he scatters hoarfrost like ashes.

18 He scatters his hail like bread crumbs; *
    who can stand against his cold?

19 He sends forth his word and melts them; *
    he blows with his wind, and the waters flow.

20 He declares his word to Jacob, *
    his statutes and his judgments to Israel.

21 He has not done so to any other nation; *
    to them he has not revealed his judgments.

Antiphon Lord, remember me when you come into your kingdom.

Responsory One
The veil of the temple was torn in two. The earth shook and the rocks were split.
    —**The thief cried from the cross, "Jesus, remember me when you come into your reign."**
The women who had followed him from Galilee, stood at a distance, watching these things.
    —**The thief cried from the cross, "Jesus, remember me when you come into your reign."**

Canticle of the Suffering Servant V *Oblatus est*
(Isaiah 53: 7-12)

Antiphon He bore the sin of many, and made intercession for the transgressors.

He was oppressed, and he was afflicted, *
    yet he did not open his mouth.

Like a lamb that is led to the slaughter,
and like a sheep that before its shearers is silent, *
    so he did not open his mouth.

By a perversion of justice he was taken away. *
    Who could have imagined his future?

For he was cut off from the land of the living, *
    stricken for the transgression of my people.

They made his grave with the wicked *
    and his tomb with the rich.

He had done no violence, *
    and there was no deceit in his mouth
    yet it was the will of the Lord to crush him with pain.

When you make his life an offering for sin, *
    he shall see his offspring, and shall prolong his days;
    through him the will of the Lord shall prosper.

Out of his anguish he shall see light; *
    he shall find satisfaction through his knowledge.

The righteous one, my servant, shall make many righteous, *
  and he shall bear their iniquities.

Therefore I will allot him a portion with the great, *
  and he shall divide the spoil with the strong.

He poured out himself to death, *
  and was numbered with the transgressors.

Yet he bore the sin of many, *
  and made intercession for the transgressors.

Antiphon He bore the sin of many, and made intercession for the transgressors.

Responsory after the Second Reading
Christ became obedient for us unto death, even to death on the cross.

Benedictus Antiphon My kingdom is not from this world. For this I was born, and for this I came into the world, to testify to the truth. Everyone who belongs to the truth listens to my voice.

Litany
Christ, Crucified Lord, you willingly gave your life in obedience to the Father's will; teach us to obey our Father and find peace in God's will.
Lord, have mercy.
Christ, Suffering Servant, you offered yourself in loving freedom; let us prefer nothing whatever to you and bring us all together to everlasting life.
Christ, have mercy.
Christ, Forgiving Master, you pardoned those who crucified you; lead us to forgive our enemies.
Lord, have mercy.

Invitation to the Lord's Prayer
We surrender ourselves with Christ and entrust ourselves with Christ to the Father's love.

Collect Almighty God, we pray you graciously to behold this your family, for whom our Lord Jesus Christ was willing to be betrayed, and given into the hands of sinners, and to suffer death upon the cross; who now lives and reigns with you and the Holy Spirit, one God, for ever and ever. Amen.

The Blessing
May we set minds on things that are above, not on things that are on earth, for we have died, and our life is hidden with Christ in God.
Amen.

Good Friday Noonday Prayer

Hymn O sacred head sore wounded *Hymnal 168*

Psalm 69 A *Salvum me fac*

Antiphon Father, forgive them for they do not know what they are doing.

1 Save me, O God, *
 for the waters have risen up to my neck.

2 I am sinking in deep mire, *
 and there is no firm ground for my feet.

3 I have come into deep waters, *
 and the torrent washes over me.

4 I have grown weary with my crying;
 my throat is inflamed; *
 my eyes have failed from looking for my God.

5 Those who hate me without a cause
 are more than the hairs of my head;
 my lying foes who would destroy me are mighty. *
 Must I then give back what I never stole?

6 O God, you know my foolishness, *
 and my faults are not hidden from you.

7 Let not those who hope in you be put to shame through me,
 Lord God of hosts; *
 let not those who seek you be disgraced because of me,
 O God of Israel.

8 Surely, for your sake have I suffered reproach, *
 and shame has covered my face.

9 I have become a stranger to my own kindred, *
 an alien to my mother's children.

10 Zeal for your house has eaten me up; *
 the scorn of those who scorn you has fallen upon me.

11 I humbled myself with fasting, *
 but that was turned to my reproach.

12 I put on sack-cloth also, *
    and became a byword among them.

13 Those who sit at the gate murmur against me, *
    and the drunkards make songs about me.

Psalm 69 B *Ego vero*

14 But as for me, this is my prayer to you, *
    at the time you have set, O LORD:

15 "In your great mercy, O God, *
    answer me with your unfailing help.

16 Save me from the mire; do not let me sink; *
    let me be rescued from those who hate me
    and out of the deep waters.

17 Let not the torrent of waters wash over me,
   neither let the deep swallow me up; *
    do not let the Pit shut its mouth upon me.

18 Answer me, O LORD, for your love is kind; *
    in your great compassion, turn to me."

19 "Hide not your face from your servant; *
    be swift and answer me, for I am in distress.

20 Draw near to me and redeem me; *
    because of my enemies deliver me.

21 You know my reproach, my shame, and my dishonor; *
    my adversaries are all in your sight."

22 Reproach has broken my heart, and it cannot be healed; *
    I looked for sympathy, but there was none,
    for comforters, but I could find no one.

23 They gave me gall to eat, *
    and when I was thirsty, they gave me vinegar to drink.

24 Let the table before them be a trap *
    and their sacred feasts a snare.

25 Let their eyes be darkened, that they may not see, *
    and give them continual trembling in their loins.

26 Pour out your indignation upon them, *
    and let the fierceness of your anger overtake them.

27 Let their camp be desolate, *
    and let there be none to dwell in their tents.

28 For they persecute him whom you have stricken *
    and add to the pain of those whom you have pierced.

29 Lay to their charge guilt upon guilt, *
    and let them not receive your vindication.

30 Let them be wiped out of the book of the living *
    and not be written among the righteous.

Psalm 69 C *Ego sum pauper*

31 As for me, I am afflicted and in pain; *
    your help, O God, will lift me up on high.

32 I will praise the Name of God in song; *
    I will proclaim his greatness with thanksgiving.

33 This will please the LORD more than an offering of oxen, *
    more than bullocks with horns and hoofs.

34 The afflicted shall see and be glad; *
    you who seek God, your heart shall live.

35 For the LORD listens to the needy, *
    and his prisoners he does not despise.

36 Let the heavens and the earth praise him, *
    the seas and all that moves in them;

37 For God will save Zion and rebuild the cities of Judah; *
    they shall live there and have it in possession.

38 The children of his servants will inherit it, *
    and those who love his Name will dwell therein.

Antiphon Father, forgive them for they do not know what they are doing.

Reading Isaiah 53: 4-5
Surely he has borne our infirmities and carried our diseases; yet we accounted him stricken, struck down by God, and afflicted. But he was wounded for our transgressions, crushed for our iniquities; upon him was the punishment that made us whole, and by his bruises we are healed.

Responsory after the Reading
Christ became obedient for us unto death, even to death on the cross.

Kyrie

The Lord's Prayer

Collect Almighty God, we pray you graciously to behold this your family, for whom our Lord Jesus Christ was willing to be betrayed, and given into the hands of sinners, and to suffer death upon the cross; who now lives and reigns with you and the Holy Spirit, one God, for ever and ever. Amen.

Good Friday Evening Prayer

Hymn Sunset to sunrise changes now *Hymnal 163*

Psalm 116 *Dilexi, quoniam*

Antiphon Precious in the sight of the Lord is the death of his servants.

1 I love the LORD, because he has heard
 the voice of my supplication, *
   because he has inclined his ear to me
   whenever I called upon him.

2 The cords of death entangled me;
 the grip of the grave took hold of me; *
   I came to grief and sorrow.

3 Then I called upon the Name of the LORD: *
 "O LORD, I pray you, save my life."

4 Gracious is the LORD and righteous; *
 our God is full of compassion.

5 The LORD watches over the innocent; *
 I was brought very low, and he helped me.

6 Turn again to your rest, O my soul, *
 for the LORD has treated you well.

7 For you have rescued my life from death, *
 my eyes from tears, and my feet from stumbling.

8 I will walk in the presence of the LORD *
 in the land of the living.

9 I believed, even when I said,
 "I have been brought very low." *
   In my distress I said, "No one can be trusted."

10 How shall I repay the LORD *
 for all the good things he has done for me?

11 I will lift up the cup of salvation *
   and call upon the Name of the LORD.

12 I will fulfill my vows to the LORD *
   in the presence of all his people.

13 Precious in the sight of the LORD *
   is the death of his servants.

14 O LORD, I am your servant; *
   I am your servant and the child of your handmaid;
   you have freed me from my bonds.

15 I will offer you the sacrifice of thanksgiving *
   and call upon the Name of the LORD.

16 I will fulfill my vows to the LORD *
   in the presence of all his people,

17 In the courts of the LORD'S house, *
   in the midst of you, O Jerusalem.

Antiphon Precious in the sight of the Lord is the death of his servants.

Psalm 31 *In te, Domine, speravi*

Antiphon Into your hands I commend my spirit.

1 In you, O LORD, have I taken refuge;
   let me never be put to shame; *
      deliver me in your righteousness.

2 Incline your ear to me; *
      make haste to deliver me.

3 Be my strong rock, a castle to keep me safe,
   for you are my crag and my stronghold; *
      for the sake of your Name, lead me and guide me.

4 Take me out of the net that they have secretly set for me, *
      for you are my tower of strength.

5 Into your hands I commend my spirit, *
      for you have redeemed me,
      O LORD, O God of truth.

6 I hate those who cling to worthless idols, *
      and I put my trust in the LORD.

7 I will rejoice and be glad because of your mercy; *
　　for you have seen my affliction;
　　you know my distress.

8 You have not shut me up in the power of the enemy; *
　　you have set my feet in an open place.

9 Have mercy on me, O LORD, for I am in trouble; *
　　my eye is consumed with sorrow,
　　and also my throat and my belly.

10 For my life is wasted with grief,
　and my years with sighing; *
　　my strength fails me because of affliction,
　　and my bones are consumed.

11 I have become a reproach to all my enemies
　and even to my neighbors,
　　a dismay to those of my acquaintance; *
　　when they see me in the street they avoid me.

12 I am forgotten like a dead man, out of mind; *
　　I am as useless as a broken pot.

13 For I have heard the whispering of the crowd;
　fear is all around; *
　　they put their heads together against me;
　　they plot to take my life.

14 But as for me, I have trusted in you, O LORD. *
　　I have said, "You are my God.

15 My times are in your hand; *
　　rescue me from the hand of my enemies,
　　and from those who persecute me.

16 Make your face to shine upon your servant, *
　　and in your loving-kindness save me."

17 LORD, let me not be ashamed for having called upon you; *
　　rather, let the wicked be put to shame;
　　let them be silent in the grave.

18 Let the lying lips be silenced
　which speak against the righteous, *
　　haughtily, disdainfully, and with contempt.

19 How great is your goodness, O LORD!
    which you have laid up for those who fear you; *
        which you have done in the sight of all
        for those who put their trust in you.

20 You hide them in the covert of your presence
    from those who slander them; *
        you keep them in your shelter from the strife of tongues.

21 Blessed be the LORD! *
    for he has shown me the wonders of his love
    in a besieged city.

22 Yet I said in my alarm,
    "I have been cut off from the sight of your eyes." *
        Nevertheless, you heard the sound of my entreaty
        when I cried out to you.

23 Love the LORD, all you who worship him; *
    the LORD protects the faithful,
    but repays to the full those who act haughtily.

24 Be strong and let your heart take courage, *
    all you who wait for the LORD.

Antiphon Into your hands I commend my spirit.

Psalm 142 *Voce mea ad Dominum*

Antiphon Listen to my cry for help, for I have been brought very low.

1 I cry to the LORD with my voice; *
    to the LORD I make loud supplication.

2 I pour out my complaint before him *
    and tell him all my trouble.

3 When my spirit languishes within me, you know my path; *
    in the way wherein I walk they have hidden a trap for me.

4 I look to my right hand and find no one who knows me; *
    I have no place to flee to, and no one cares for me.

5 I cry out to you, O LORD; *
    I say, "You are my refuge,
    my portion in the land of the living."

6 Listen to my cry for help, for I have been brought very low; *
    save me from those who pursue me,
    for they are too strong for me.

7 Bring me out of prison, that I may give thanks to your Name; *
  when you have dealt bountifully with me,
  the righteous will gather around me.

Antiphon Listen to my cry for help, for I have been brought very low.

Responsory after the Reading
Christ became obedient for us unto death, even to death on the cross.

Magnificat Antiphon Jesus said, "It is finished." Then he bowed his head and gave up his spirit.

Litany
O Savior of the world, who by your cross and precious blood has redeemed us: save us and help us.
Lord, have mercy.
We adore you, O Christ, and we bless you, because by your holy cross you have redeemed the world.
Christ, have mercy.
We glory in your cross, O Lord, and praise and glorify your holy resurrection; for by virtue of your cross joy has come to the whole world.
Lord, have mercy.

Invitation to the Lord's Prayer
We surrender ourselves with Christ and entrust ourselves with Christ to the Father's love.

Collect Almighty God, we pray you graciously to behold this your family, for whom our Lord Jesus Christ was willing to be betrayed, and given into the hands of sinners, and to suffer death upon the cross; who now lives and reigns with you and the Holy Spirit, one God, for ever and ever. Amen.

The Blessing
May we set minds on things that are above, not on things that are on earth, for we have died, and our life is hidden with Christ in God.
Amen.

Compline as in Maundy Thursday (p. 96)

Holy Saturday Morning Prayer

Invitatory Christ suffered death on a cross and was buried for us: Come let us adore.

Hymn O sorrow deep *Hymnal 173*

Psalm 130 *De profundis*

Antiphon O death, I will be your death. O flames, I will be your destroyer.

1 Out of the depths have I called to you, O LORD;
  LORD, hear my voice; *
    let your ears consider well the voice of my supplication.

2 If you, LORD, were to note what is done amiss, *
    O LORD, who could stand?

3 For there is forgiveness with you; *
    therefore you shall be feared.

4 I wait for the LORD; my soul waits for him; *
    in his word is my hope.

5 My soul waits for the LORD,
  more than watchmen for the morning, *
    more than watchmen for the morning.

6 O Israel, wait for the LORD, *
    for with the LORD there is mercy;

7 With him there is plenteous redemption, *
    and he shall redeem Israel from all their sins.

Antiphon O death, I will be your death. O flames, I will be your destroyer.

Psalm 137 *Super flumina*

Antiphon Christ was put to death in the flesh, but made alive in the spirit, in which also he went and made a proclamation to the spirits in prison.

1 By the waters of Babylon we sat down and wept, *
    when we remembered you, O Zion.

2 As for our harps, we hung them up *
    on the trees in the midst of that land.

3 For those who led us away captive asked us for a song,
    and our oppressors called for mirth: *
        "Sing us one of the songs of Zion."

4 How shall we sing the LORD'S song *
    upon an alien soil?

5 If I forget you, O Jerusalem, *
    let my right hand forget its skill.

6 Let my tongue cleave to the roof of my mouth
    if I do not remember you, *
        if I do not set Jerusalem above my highest joy.

7 Remember the day of Jerusalem, O LORD,
    against the people of Edom, *
        who said, "Down with it! down with it!
        even to the ground!"

8 O Daughter of Babylon, doomed to destruction, *
    blessed the one who pays you back
    for what you have done to us!

9 Blessed shall he be who takes your little ones, *
    and dashes them against the rock!

Antiphon Christ was put to death in the flesh, but made alive in the spirit, in which also he went and made a proclamation to the spirits in prison.

Psalm 150 *Laudate Dominum*

Antiphon Is it nothing to you, all you who pass by? Look and see if there is any sorrow like my sorrow?

1 Praise God in his holy temple; *
    praise him in the firmament of his power.

2 Praise him for his mighty acts; *
    praise him for his excellent greatness.

3 Praise him with the blast of the ram's-horn; *
    praise him with lyre and harp.

4 Praise him with timbrel and dance; *
    praise him with strings and pipe.

5 Praise him with resounding cymbals; *
    praise him with loud-clanging cymbals.

6 Let everything that has breath *
      praise the Lord.

Antiphon Is it nothing to you, all you who pass by? Look and see if there is any sorrow like my sorrow?

Responsory One
Like a lamb that is led to the slaughter, he was afflicted, yet he did not open his mouth.
—**They made his grave with the wicked and his tomb with the rich.**
He poured out himself to death, and was numbered with the transgressors.
—**They made his grave with the wicked and his tomb with the rich.**

Canticle of Lamentation *O vos omnes*
(Lamentations 1:12,16; 3:19,22-24,26)

Antiphon I weep; my eyes flow with tears, for a comforter is far from me, one to revive my courage.

Is it nothing to you, all you who pass by? *
    Look and see if there is any sorrow like my sorrow,

Which was brought upon me, *
    inflicted by God's fierce anger.

For these things I weep; my eyes flow with tears, *
    for a comforter is far from me, one to revive my courage.

Remember my affliction and my bitterness, *
    wormwood and gall!

The steadfast love of God never ceases, *
    God's mercies never end.

They are new every morning; *
    great is your faithfulness.

"God is my portion," says my soul, *
    "therefore will I hope in God."

It is good that we should wait quietly *
    for the coming of God's salvation.

Antiphon I weep; my eyes flow with tears, for a comforter is far from me, one to revive my courage.

Responsory after the Second Reading
Christ became obedient for us unto death, even to death on the cross. Therefore God exalted him and gave him the Name which is above every name.

Benedictus Antiphon Joseph of Arimathea rolled a great stone to the door of the tomb and went away. Mary Magdalene and the other Mary were there, sitting opposite the tomb.

Litany
In the midst of life we are in death; from whom can we seek help? From you alone, O Lord, who by our sins are justly angered.
Lord, have mercy.
Lord, you know the secrets of our hearts; shut not your ears to our prayers, but spare us, O Lord.
Christ, have mercy.
O worthy and eternal Judge, do not let the pains of death turn us away from you at our last hour.
Lord, have mercy.

Invitation to the Lord's Prayer
In the mystery of Christ's burial we are hidden with Christ in God so we embrace our holy solitude as we pray with the solitary Christ.

Collect O God, Creator of heaven and earth: Grant that, as the crucified body of your dear Son was laid in the tomb and rested on this holy Sabbath, so we may await with him the coming of the third day, and rise with him to newness of life; who now lives and reigns with you and the Holy Spirit, one God, for ever and ever. Amen.

The Blessing
May we who have been buried with Christ by baptism into his death walk in newness of life. **Amen.**

Holy Saturday Noonday Prayer
Hymn From deepest woe I cry to thee *Hymnal 151*

Psalm 27 *Dominus illuminatio*
Antiphon I believe that I shall see the goodness of the Lord in the land of the living.

1 The LORD is my light and my salvation;
   whom then shall I fear? *
      the LORD is the strength of my life;
      of whom then shall I be afraid?

2 When evildoers came upon me to eat up my flesh, *
    it was they, my foes and my adversaries,
    who stumbled and fell.

3 Though an army should encamp against me, *
    yet my heart shall not be afraid;

4 And though war should rise up against me, *
    yet will I put my trust in him.

5 One thing have I asked of the LORD;
    one thing I seek; *
    that I may dwell in the house of the LORD
    all the days of my life;

6 To behold the fair beauty of the LORD *
    and to seek him in his temple.

7 For in the day of trouble
    he shall keep me safe in his shelter; *
    he shall hide me in the secrecy of his dwelling
    and set me high upon a rock.

8 Even now he lifts up my head *
    above my enemies round about me.

9 Therefore I will offer in his dwelling an oblation
    with sounds of great gladness; *
    I will sing and make music to the LORD.

10 Hearken to my voice, O LORD, when I call; *
    have mercy on me and answer me.

11 You speak in my heart and say, "Seek my face." *
    Your face, LORD, will I seek.

12 Hide not your face from me, *
    nor turn away your servant in displeasure.

13 You have been my helper;
    cast me not away; *
    do not forsake me, O God of my salvation.

14 Though my father and my mother forsake me, *
    the LORD will sustain me.

15 Show me your way, O LORD; *
    lead me on a level path, because of my enemies.

16 Deliver me not into the hand of my adversaries, *
      for false witnesses have risen up against me,
      and also those who speak malice.

17 What if I had not believed
      that I should see the goodness of the LORD *
      in the land of the living!

18 O tarry and await the LORD'S pleasure;
      be strong, and he shall comfort your heart; *
      wait patiently for the LORD.

Psalm 76 *Notus in Judæa*

1 In Judah is God known; *
      his Name is great in Israel.

2 At Salem is his tabernacle, *
      and his dwelling is in Zion.

3 There he broke the flashing arrows, *
      the shield, the sword, and the weapons of battle.

4 How glorious you are! *
      more splendid than the everlasting mountains!

5 The strong of heart have been despoiled;
      they sink into sleep; *
      none of the warriors can lift a hand.

6 At your rebuke, O God of Jacob, *
      both horse and rider lie stunned.

7 What terror you inspire! *
      who can stand before you when you are angry?

8 From heaven you pronounced judgment; *
      the earth was afraid and was still;

9 When God rose up to judgment *
      and to save all the oppressed of the earth.

10 Truly, wrathful Edom will give you thanks, *
      and the remnant of Hamath will keep your feasts.

11 Make a vow to the LORD your God and keep it; *
      let all around him bring gifts to him
      who is worthy to be feared.

12 He breaks the spirit of princes, *
      and strikes terror in the kings of the earth.

Holy Saturday Evening Prayer

Psalm 3 *Domine, quid multiplicati*

1 LORD, how many adversaries I have! *
 how many there are who rise up against me!

2 How many there are who say of me, *
 "There is no help for him in his God."

3 But you, O LORD, are a shield about me; *
 you are my glory, the one who lifts up my head.

4 I call aloud upon the LORD, *
 and he answers me from his holy hill;

5 I lie down and go to sleep; *
 I wake again, because the LORD sustains me.

6 I do not fear the multitudes of people *
 who set themselves against me all around.

7 Rise up, O LORD; set me free, O my God; *
 surely, you will strike all my enemies across the face,
 you will break the teeth of the wicked.

8 Deliverance belongs to the LORD. *
 Your blessing be upon your people!

Antiphon I believe that I shall see the goodness of the Lord in the land of the living.

Reading Hosea 6: 1-2
Come, let us return to the Lord; for it is he who has torn, and he will heal us; he has struck down, and he will bind us up. After two days he will revive us; on the third day he will raise us up, that we may live before him.

Responsory after the Reading
Christ became obedient for us unto death, even to death on the cross. Therefore God exalted him and gave him a name which is above all names.

Kyrie

The Lord's Prayer

Collect O God, Creator of heaven and earth: Grant that, as the crucified body of your dear Son was laid in the tomb and rested on this holy Sabbath, so we may await with him the coming of the third day, and rise with him to newness of life; who now lives and reigns with you and the Holy Spirit, one God, for ever and ever. Amen.

Holy Saturday Evening Prayer

Hymn There is a green hill far away *Hymnal 167*

Psalm 141 *Domine, clamavi*

Antiphon In you, Lord God, I take refuge; do not strip me of my life.

1 O Lord, I call to you; come to me quickly; *
    hear my voice when I cry to you.

2 Let my prayer be set forth in your sight as incense, *
    the lifting up of my hands as the evening sacrifice.

3 Set a watch before my mouth, O Lord,
    and guard the door of my lips; *
    let not my heart incline to any evil thing.

4 Let me not be occupied in wickedness with evildoers, *
    nor eat of their choice foods.

5 Let the righteous smite me in friendly rebuke;
    let not the oil of the unrighteous anoint my head; *
    for my prayer is continually against their wicked deeds.

6 Let their rulers be overthrown in stony places, *
    that they may know my words are true.

7 As when a plowman turns over the earth in furrows, *
    let their bones be scattered at the mouth of the grave.

8 But my eyes are turned to you, Lord God; *
    in you I take refuge;
    do not strip me of my life.

9 Protect me from the snare which they have laid for me *
    and from the traps of the evildoers.

10 Let the wicked fall into their own nets, *
    while I myself escape.

Antiphon In you, Lord God, I take refuge; do not strip me of my life.

Psalm 30 *Exaltabo te, Domine*

Antiphon You brought me up, O Lord, from the dead; you restored my life as I was going down to the grave.

1 I will exalt you, O Lord,
    because you have lifted me up *
    and have not let my enemies triumph over me.

2 O LORD my God, I cried out to you, *
　　and you restored me to health.

3 You brought me up, O LORD, from the dead; *
　　you restored my life as I was going down to the grave.

4 Sing to the LORD, you servants of his; *
　　give thanks for the remembrance of his holiness.

5 For his wrath endures but the twinkling of an eye, *
　　his favor for a lifetime.

6 Weeping may spend the night, *
　　but joy comes in the morning.

7 While I felt secure, I said,
　"I shall never be disturbed. *
　　　You, LORD, with your favor, made me
　　　as strong as the mountains."

8 Then you hid your face, *
　　and I was filled with fear.

9 I cried to you, O LORD; *
　　I pleaded with the Lord, saying,

10 "What profit is there in my blood, if I go down to the Pit? *
　　will the dust praise you or declare your faithfulness?

11 Hear, O LORD, and have mercy upon me; *
　　O LORD, be my helper."

12 You have turned my wailing into dancing; *
　　you have put off my sack-cloth and clothed me with joy.

13 Therefore my heart sings to you without ceasing; *
　　O LORD my God, I will give you thanks for ever.

Antiphon You brought me up, O Lord, from the dead; you restored my life as I was going down to the grave.

Psalm 86 *Inclina, Domine*

Antiphon Great is your love for me; you have delivered me from the nethermost Pit.

1 Bow down your ear, O LORD, and answer me, *
　　for I am poor and in misery.

2 Keep watch over my life, for I am faithful; *
　　save your servant who puts his trust in you.

3 Be merciful to me, O LORD, for you are my God; *
    I call upon you all the day long.

4 Gladden the soul of your servant, *
    for to you, O LORD, I lift up my soul.

5 For you, O LORD, are good and forgiving, *
    and great is your love toward all who call upon you.

6 Give ear, O LORD, to my prayer, *
    and attend to the voice of my supplications.

7 In the time of my trouble I will call upon you, *
    for you will answer me.

8 Among the gods there is none like you, O LORD, *
    nor anything like your works.

9 All nations you have made will come and
    worship you, O LORD, *
    and glorify your Name.

10 For you are great;
    you do wondrous things; *
    and you alone are God.

11 Teach me your way, O LORD,
    and I will walk in your truth; *
    knit my heart to you that I may fear your Name.

12 I will thank you, O LORD my God, with all my heart, *
    and glorify your Name for evermore.

13 For great is your love toward me; *
    you have delivered me from the nethermost Pit.

14 The arrogant rise up against me, O God,
    and a band of violent men seeks my life; *
    they have not set you before their eyes.

15 But you, O LORD, are gracious and full of compassion, *
    slow to anger, and full of kindness and truth.

16 Turn to me and have mercy upon me; *
    give your strength to your servant;
    and save the child of your handmaid.

17 Show me a sign of your favor,
    so that those who hate me may see it and be ashamed; *
    because you, O LORD, have helped me and comforted me.

Antiphon Great is your love for me; you have delivered me from the nethermost Pit.

Responsory after the Reading
Christ became obedient for us unto death, even to death on the cross. Therefore God exalted him and gave him the Name which is above every name.

Magnificat Antiphon Just as Jonah was three days and three nights in the belly of the sea monster, so for three days and three nights the Son of Man will be in the heart of the earth.

Litany
With the holy women, we sit in silence at your tomb; teach us to use our voices gently and seriously, modestly and briefly.
Lord, have mercy.
With those who mourn we stand in solidarity; teach us to hope in the face of despair.
Christ, have mercy.
With those preparing for Baptism we unite ourselves with you in your burial; lead all the dead into your Father's house.
Lord, have mercy.

Invitation to the Lord's Prayer
In the mystery of Christ's burial we are hidden with Christ in God so we embrace our holy solitude as we pray with the solitary Christ.

Collect O God, Creator of heaven and earth: Grant that, as the crucified body of your dear Son was laid in the tomb and rested on this holy Sabbath, so we may await with him the coming of the third day, and rise with him to newness of life; who now lives and reigns with you and the Holy Spirit, one God, for ever and ever. Amen.

The Blessing
May we who have been buried with Christ by baptism into his death walk in newness of life. **Amen.**

If Compline is prayed before the Great Vigil, the form is taken from that form used on Maundy Thursday, page 96. If Compline is prayer after the Great Vigil, the form is taken from the Ordinary with Easter antiphons.

The Easter Season

Introduction

The Easter Season begins with the Great Vigil of Easter. The Easter Offices are characterized by overflowing joy symbolized by the use of Alleluia. The Invitatory is found is the Ordinary of the Daily Office. Easter Day has its own proper office. Easter is celebrated with an Octave for eight days which concludes with Evening Prayer II of the Second Sunday of Easter. The Octave includes a proper Responsory at Morning Prayer and Evening Prayer. The traditional observance of the Octave includes using the Easter Day office with its proper antiphons and psalms on every day of the Octave. An alternative practice would use the proper antiphons with the weekday psalter and canticles. The proper Sunday Antiphons are found in the Proper of the Season. In the Proper and Common of the Saints, an Alleluia is added after the antiphons for the Psalms and Canticles. Compline has its seasonal character with a proper antiphon for the Nunc Dimittis. The offices for Easter Season conclude with a double alleluia. The Regina Caeli is the appropriate Marian Antiphon after Compline and is used in place of the Angelus as a devotional prayer.

Easter Day

Week 1

Principal Feast
Morning Prayer

Invitatory Alleluia. The Lord is risen indeed: Come let us adore him. Alleluia.

Hymn Hail thee festival day *Hymnal 175*

Antiphon 1 Alleluia. As the first day of the week was dawning, Mary Magdalene and the other Mary went to see the tomb. Alleluia. Alleluia.

Psalms from Sunday Week 1 Morning Prayer

Antiphon 2 Alleluia. Do not be afraid; I know that you are looking for Jesus who was crucified. He is not here; for he has been raised, as he said. Alleluia. Alleluia.

Antiphon 3 Alleluia. Go quickly and tell his disciples, "He has been raised from the dead, and indeed he is going ahead of you to Galilee; there you will see him." Alleluia. Alleluia.

Responsory One
This is the day the Lord has made. Let us rejoice and be glad in it. Alleluia.

Canticle You are God   *Te Deum laudamus, Page 667*

Alternate Easter Canticle
Based on the Pascha Troparion and the Easter Canon.

Antiphon Alleluia. Christ is risen from the dead, trampling down death by death, and giving life to those in the tomb. Alleluia. Alleluia.

It is the Day of Resurrection! Let us be radiant, O people of God!*
    Christ our God has delivered us from death to life,
        and from earth to heaven.

Christ, our Paschal Lamb, has sacrificed himself for us*
    The glorious Sun of Righteousness shines upon us from the tomb.

Let us arise with the dawn and sing a hymn to the Lord,*
    and we shall see Christ, the Sun of Righteousness,
        who brings life to shine on all.

Having beheld the Resurrection of Christ,*
    let us bow down before the Holy Lord Jesus,

We adore your Cross, O Christ, and we praise your Holy Resurrection*
    for you are our God, and we know no other God than you.

O come faithful people, come,
let us worship Christ's holy Resurrection.*
   Through the Cross joy has come to all the world.

Ever blessing the Lord, let us praise his Resurrection.*
   By suffering the Cross for us he destroyed death by death.

Antiphon Alleluia. Christ is risen from the dead, trampling down death by death, and giving life to those in the tomb. Alleluia. Alleluia.

Responsory Two
The stone rejected by the builders has become the cornerstone. Alleluia.

Benedictus Antiphon
Easter Day
Year A Alleluia. Jesus said to her, "Mary!" She turned and said to him, "Rabbouni!" Alleluia. Alleluia.
Year B Alleluia. Very early on the first day of the week, when the sun had risen Mary Magdalene, and Mary the mother of James, and Salome bought spices, so that they might go and anoint him. Alleluia. Alleluia.
Year C Alleluia. Why do you look for the living among the dead? He is not here, but has risen. Alleluia. Alleluia.

Litany
We praise you, Father, who raised Christ to glory; send us your Spirit that we may be raised to new life.
Lord, have mercy.
We praise you, Christ who commissioned Mary Magdalene as an Apostle; send us out as heralds of your resurrection.
Christ, have mercy.
We praise you, Spirit of holiness who raised Jesus from the dead; dwell in us that we may follow you in holiness of life.
Lord, have mercy.

Invitation to the Lord's Prayer
We glorify God who raised up Christ to new life in the resurrection and we celebrate God's victory as we pray.

Collect
Easter Day
Almighty God, who through your only-begotten Son Jesus Christ overcame death and opened to us the gate of everlasting life: Grant that we, who celebrate with joy the day of the Lord's resurrection, may be raised from the death of sin by your life-giving Spirit; through Jesus Christ

our Lord, who lives and reigns with you and the Holy Spirit, one God, now and for ever. Amen.

The Blessing
May we who have been raised with Christ, seek the things that are above, where Christ is, seated at the right hand of God. **Amen.**

Easter Day Noonday Prayer

Hymn The day of resurrection *Hymnal 210*

Antiphon You are looking for Jesus of Nazareth, who was crucified. He has been raised. Go, tell his disciples and Peter that he is going ahead of you to Galilee; there you will see him. Alleluia. Alleluia.
Psalms from Sunday Week 1 Noonday Prayer

Reading 1 Corinthians 15: 3b-6a
Christ died for our sins in accordance with the scriptures, he was buried, and he was raised on the third day in accordance with the scriptures, and he appeared to Cephas, then to the twelve. Then he appeared to more than five hundred brothers and sisters at one time

Verse and Response
This is the day the Lord has made. Alleluia.
Let us rejoice and be glad in it. Alleluia.

Collect *From Morning Prayer*

Easter Day Evening Prayer II

Hymn O sons and daughters *Hymnal 206*

Antiphon 1 Alleluia. While they were talking and discussing, Jesus himself came near and went with them, but their eyes were kept from recognizing him. Alleluia. Alleluia.
Psalms from Sunday Week 1 Evening Prayer II
Antiphon 2 Alleluia. "Stay with us, because it is almost evening and the day is now nearly over." So he went in to stay with them. Alleluia. Alleluia.
Antiphon 3 Alleluia. When Jesus was at the table with them, he took bread, blessed and broke it, and gave it to them. Then their eyes were opened, and they recognized him. Alleluia. Alleluia.

Responsory
This is the day the Lord has made. Let us rejoice and be glad in it. Alleluia.

Magnificat Antiphon
Easter Day
Year A Alleluia. I am ascending to my Father and your Father, to my God and your God. Alleluia. Alleluia.
Year B Alleluia. Do not be alarmed; you are looking for Jesus of Nazareth, who was crucified. He has been raised; he is not here. He is going ahead of you to Galilee; there you will see him. Alleluia. Alleluia.
Year C Alleluia. The Son of Man must be handed over to sinners, and be crucified, and on the third day rise again. They remembered his words, and returning from the tomb, they told all this to the eleven. Alleluia. Alleluia.

Litany
Your resurrection fills the world with hope; comfort those who are alone, homeless and unemployed.
Lord, have mercy.
Your resurrection fills the world with joy; sustain all who rejoice in your victory.
Christ, have mercy.
Your resurrection fills the world with expectation; bring all the departed to share in your victory over death.
Lord, have mercy.

Invitation to the Lord's Prayer We have walked with Christ from the cross to the empty tomb and we celebrate the Father's triumph in Christ the Son.

Collect
Easter Day O God, who for our redemption gave your only-begotten Son to the death of the cross, and by his glorious resurrection delivered us from the power of our enemy: Grant us so to die daily to sin, that we may evermore live with him in the joy of his resurrection; through Jesus Christ your Son our Lord, who lives and reigns with you and the Holy Spirit, one God, now and for ever. Amen.

The Blessing
May the God of peace, who brought back from the dead our Lord Jesus, the great shepherd of the sheep, by the blood of the eternal covenant, make us perfect in everything good so that we may do his will, working among us that which is pleasing in his sight. **Amen.**

Easter Season

The Easter Season Psalter Schedule
The First Sunday of Easter begins with Sunday Week 1 Morning Prayer.
The Second Sunday of Easter begins with Sunday Week 2 Evening Prayer I.
The Third Sunday of Easter begins with Sunday Week 3 Evening Prayer I.
The Fourth Sunday of Easter begins with Sunday Week 4 Evening Prayer I.
The Fifth Sunday of Easter begins with Sunday Week 1 Evening Prayer I.
The Sixth Sunday of Easter begins with Sunday Week 2 Evening Prayer I.
The Seventh Sunday of Easter begins with Sunday Week 3 Evening Prayer I.

Easter Season Sunday Evening Prayer I

The Offices for Easter Sunday and the Second Sunday of Easter are taken from Easter Day

Hymn Hail thee festival day *Hymnal 175*

Responsory for the Easter Octave.
This is the day the Lord has made. Let us rejoice and be glad in it. Alleluia.

Responsory (Lk. 24:34)
The Lord is truly risen.
 — **Alleluia, alleluia.**
The Lord appeared to Simon.
 — **Alleluia, alleluia.**
Glory to the Father and to the Son and to the Holy Spirit.
The Lord is truly risen.
 — **Alleluia, alleluia.**

Magnificat Antiphon
Second Sunday of Easter Alleluia. Unless I see the mark of the nails in his hands, and put my finger in the mark of the nails and my hand in his side, I will not believe. Alleluia. Alleluia.

Year A
Third Sunday of Easter Stay with us, because it is almost evening and the day is now nearly over. Alleluia.
Fourth Sunday of Easter The sheep hear the shepherd's voice. He calls his own sheep by name and leads them out. The sheep follow him because they know his voice. Alleluia.
Fifth Sunday of Easter Do not let your hearts be troubled. Believe in God, believe also in me. In my Father's house there are many dwelling places. Alleluia.

Sixth Sunday of Easter You know the Spirit of Truth, because he abides with you, and he will be in you. Alleluia.

Seventh Sunday of Easter Father, the hour has come; glorify your Son so that the Son may glorify you, since you have given him authority over all people. Alleluia.

Year B

Third Sunday of Easter Jesus himself stood among them and said to them, "Peace be with you." They were startled and terrified, and thought that they were seeing a ghost. Alleluia.

Fourth Sunday of Easter I am the good shepherd. The good shepherd lays down his life for the sheep. Alleluia.

Fifth Sunday of Easter I am the true vine, and my Father is the vinegrower. Every branch that bears fruit he prunes to make it bear more fruit. Abide in me as I abide in you. Alleluia.

Sixth Sunday of Easter As the Father has loved me, so I have loved you; abide in my love. If you keep my commandments, you will abide in my love. Alleluia.

Seventh Sunday of Easter Father, they know that everything you have given me is from you; for the words that you gave to me I have given to them, and they have received them and know in truth that I came from you. Alleluia.

Year C

Third Sunday of Easter Children, you have no fish, have you? Cast the net to the right side of the boat, and you will find some. Alleluia.

Fourth Sunday of Easter The works that I do in my Father's name testify to me; but you do not believe, because you do not belong to my sheep. Alleluia.

Fifth Sunday of Easter Now the Son of Man has been glorified, and God has been glorified in him. Alleluia.

Sixth Sunday of Easter Those who love me will keep my word, and my Father will love them, and we will come to them and make our home with them. Alleluia.

Seventh Sunday of Easter May they all be one as you, Father, are in me and I am in you, may they also be in us, so that the world may believe that you have sent me. Alleluia.

Litany

Since your first gift is peace, bring the peace of the resurrection to places torn by conflict and hearts broken by strife.
Lord, have mercy.

Since you transformed the fear of the women at the tomb, bring faith in your resurrection to replace our fear.
Christ, have mercy.
Since you opened the gates of heaven to all people, bring all the departed to the home you prepared for them.
Lord, have mercy.

Invitation to the Lord's Prayer Christ shines in our hearts by the light of the resurrection so illumined by Christ we pray in the Spirit.

Collect
Second Sunday of Easter
Almighty and everlasting God, who in the Paschal mystery established the new covenant of reconciliation: Grant that all who have been reborn into the fellowship of Christ's Body may show forth in their lives what they profess by their faith; through Jesus Christ our Lord, who lives and reigns with you and the Holy Spirit, one God, for ever and ever. Amen.
Third Sunday of Easter
O God, whose blessed Son made himself known to his disciples in the breaking of bread: Open the eyes of our faith, that we may behold him in all his redeeming work; who lives and reigns with you, in the unity of the Holy Spirit, one God, now and for ever. Amen.
Fourth Sunday of Easter
O God, whose Son Jesus is the good shepherd of your people; Grant that when we hear his voice we may know him who calls us each by name, and follow where he leads; who, with you and the Holy Spirit, lives and reigns, one God, for ever and ever. Amen.
Fifth Sunday of Easter
Almighty God, whom truly to know is everlasting life: Grant us so perfectly to know your Son Jesus Christ to be the way, the truth, and the life, that we may steadfastly follow his steps in the way that leads to eternal life; through Jesus Christ your Son our Lord, who lives and reigns with you, in the unity of the Holy Spirit, one God, for ever and ever. Amen.
Sixth Sunday of Easter
O God, you have prepared for those who love you such good things as surpass our understanding: Pour into our hearts such love towards you, that we, loving you in all things and above all things, may obtain your promises, which exceed all that we can desire; through Jesus Christ our Lord, who lives and reigns with you and the Holy Spirit, one God, for ever and ever. Amen.
Seventh Sunday of Easter
O God, the King of glory, you have exalted your only Son Jesus Christ with great triumph to your kingdom in heaven: Do not leave us

comfortless, but send us your Holy Spirit to strengthen us, and exalt us to that place where our Savior Christ has gone before; who lives and reigns with you and the Holy Spirit, one God, in glory everlasting. Amen.

The Blessing
May we know what is the hope to which God has called us, what are the riches of his glorious inheritance among the saints, and what is the immeasurable greatness of his power for us who believe. **Amen.**

Easter Season Sunday Morning Prayer

Invitatory Alleluia. The Lord is risen indeed: Come let us adore him. Alleluia.

Hymn Jesus Christ is risen today *Hymnal 207*

Responsory One for the Easter Octave.
This is the day the Lord has made. Let us rejoice and be glad in it. Alleluia.

Responsory One (Jn. 20:14; Song of Songs 3:3)
Mary Magdalene turned around and saw Jesus.
   – **Alleluia, alleluia.**
Have you seen him whom my soul loves?
   – **Alleluia, alleluia.**
Glory to the Father and to the Son and to the Holy Spirit.
Mary Magdalene turned around and saw Jesus.
   – **Alleluia, alleluia.**

Canticle You are God *Te Deum laudamus, Page 667*

Responsory Two for the Easter Octave.
The stone rejected by the builders has become the cornerstone. Alleluia.

Responsory Two (Lk. 24:5)
Why do you look for the living among the dead?
   – **Alleluia, alleluia.**
Christ is not here, but has risen.
   – **Alleluia, alleluia.**
Glory to the Father and to the Son and to the Holy Spirit.
Why do you look for the living among the dead?
   – **Alleluia, alleluia.**

Benedictus Antiphon
Second Sunday of Easter
Alleluia. Put your finger here and see my hands. Reach out your hand and put it in my side. Do not doubt but believe. Alleluia. Alleluia.

Year A
Third Sunday of Easter
Were not our hearts burning within us while he was talking to us on the road, while he was opening the scriptures to us? Alleluia.
Fourth Sunday of Easter
I am the gate. Whoever enters by me will be saved, and will come in and go out and find pasture. Alleluia.
Fifth Sunday of Easter
I am the way, and the truth, and the life. Alleluia.
Sixth Sunday of Easter
Because I live, you also will live. On that day you will know that I am in my Father, and you in me, and I in you. Alleluia.
Seventh Sunday of Easter
The words that you gave to me I have given to them, and they have received them and know in truth that I came from you. Alleluia.

Year B
Third Sunday of Easter
Look at my hands and my feet; see that it is I myself. Touch me and see; for a ghost does not have flesh and bones as you see that I have. Alleluia.
Fourth Sunday of Easter
I am the good shepherd. I know my own and my own know me, just as the Father knows me and I know the Father. And I lay down my life for the sheep. Alleluia.
Fifth Sunday of Easter
I am the vine, you are the branches. Those who abide in me and I in them bear much fruit, because apart from me you can do nothing. Alleluia.
Sixth Sunday of Easter
This is my commandment, that you love one another as I have loved you. No one has greater love than this, to lay down one's life for one's friends. Alleluia.
Seventh Sunday of Easter
Holy Father, protect them in your name that you have given me, so that they may be one, as we are one. Alleluia.

Year C
Third Sunday of Easter
Simon, son of John, do you love me more than these? Alleluia. Feed my lambs. Alleluia.
Fourth Sunday of Easter
My sheep hear my voice. I know them, and they follow me. I give them eternal life, and they will never perish. Alleluia.
Fifth Sunday of Easter
I give you a new commandment, that you love one another. Just as I have loved you, you also should love one another. Alleluia.
Sixth Sunday of Easter
The Advocate, the Holy Spirit, whom the Father will send in my name, will teach you everything, and remind you of all that I have said to you. Alleluia.
Seventh Sunday of Easter
Father, I desire that those also, whom you have given me, may be with me where I am, to see my glory, which you have given me because you loved me before the foundation of the world. Alleluia.

Litany
As we celebrate your Resurrection, open the eyes of our heart to experience you in the Breaking of the Bread.
Lord, have mercy.
Lead those in positions of public service to serve all people without discrimination or violence.
Christ, have mercy.
Strengthen families however they are organized to manifest you love, understanding and compassion.
Lord, have mercy.

Invitation to the Lord's Prayer Jesus opens our relationship with God as Father so we open our hearts in joy thanking God for the Resurrection.

Collect *From Evening Prayer I*

The Blessing
May we who have been raised with Christ, seek the things that are above, where Christ is, seated at the right hand of God. **Amen.**

Easter Season Sunday Noonday Prayer

Hymn The Day Of Resurrection *Hymnal 210*

Reading 1 Corinthians 15: 3b-6a
Christ died for our sins in accordance with the scriptures, he was buried, and he was raised on the third day in accordance with the scriptures, and he appeared to Cephas, then to the twelve. Then he appeared to more than five hundred brothers and sisters at one time.

Verse and Response
This is the day the Lord has made. Alleluia.
Let us rejoice and be glad in it. Alleluia.

Collect *From Morning Prayer*

Easter Season Sunday Evening Prayer II

Hymn O Sons And Daughters *Hymnal 206*

Responsory for the Easter Octave.
This is the day the Lord has made. Let us rejoice and be glad in it. Alleluia.

Responsory (Lk. 24:34)
The Lord is truly risen.
   − **Alleluia, alleluia.**
The Lord appeared to Simon.
   − **Alleluia, alleluia.**
Glory to the Father and to the Son and to the Holy Spirit.
The Lord is truly risen.
   − **Alleluia, alleluia.**

Magnificat Antiphon
Second Sunday of Easter
Alleluia. Have you believed because you have seen me? Blessed are those who have not seen and yet have come to believe. Alleluia. Alleluia.

Year A
Third Sunday of Easter
They told what had happened on the road, and how the Lord had been made known to them in the breaking of the bread. Alleluia.
Fourth Sunday of Easter
I came that they may have life, and have it abundantly. Alleluia.
Fifth Sunday of Easter
The Father who dwells in me does his works. Believe me that I am in the Father and the Father is in me. Alleluia.

Sixth Sunday of Easter
Those who love me will be loved by my Father, and I will love them and reveal myself to them. Alleluia.
Seventh Sunday of Easter
Holy Father, protect them in your name that you have given me, so that they may be one, as we are one. Alleluia.

Year B
Third Sunday of Easter
Everything written about me in the law of Moses, the prophets, and the psalms must be fulfilled. Then he opened their minds to understand the scriptures. Alleluia.
Fourth Sunday of Easter
I have other sheep that do not belong to this fold. I must bring them also, and they will listen to my voice. So there will be one flock, one shepherd. Alleluia.
Fifth Sunday of Easter
If you abide in me, and my words abide in you, ask for whatever you wish, and it will be done for you. My Father is glorified by this, that you bear much fruit and become my disciples. Alleluia.
Sixth Sunday of Easter
I have called you friends, because I have made known to you everything that I have heard from my Father. Alleluia.
Seventh Sunday of Easter
Sanctify them in the truth; your word is truth. As you have sent me into the world, so I have sent them into the world. Alleluia.

Year C
Third Sunday of Easter
When you grow old, you will stretch out your hands, and someone else will fasten a belt around you and take you where you do not wish to go. Alleluia.
Fourth Sunday of Easter
What my Father has given me is greater than all else, and no one can snatch it out of the Father's hand. The Father and I are one. Alleluia.
Fifth Sunday of Easter
By this everyone will know that you are my disciples, if you have love for one another. Alleluia.
Sixth Sunday of Easter
Peace I leave with you; my peace I give to you. I do not give to you as the world gives. Do not let your hearts be troubled, and do not let them be afraid. Alleluia.

Seventh Sunday of Easter
Righteous Father, I made your name known to them so that the love with which you have loved me may be in them, and I in them. Alleluia.

Litany
You walked with the disciples on the road to Emmaus, stay with us for the day is past.
Lord, have mercy.
You manifested yourself to the disciples during a meal; reveal your presence in our fellowship with each other.
Christ, have mercy.
You descended to the dead and proclaimed the Gospel of life to the departed; bring all the dead into the light of your risen life.
Lord, have mercy.

Invitation to the Lord's Prayer The Father raised Christ by the power of the Holy Spirit so in that Spirit we pray with Christ.

Collect *From Morning Prayer*

The Blessing
May the God of peace, who brought back from the dead our Lord Jesus, the great shepherd of the sheep, by the blood of the eternal covenant, make us perfect in everything good so that we may do his will, working among us that which is pleasing in his sight. **Amen.**

Easter Season Monday Morning Prayer

The Rogation Days are traditionally observed on Monday, Tuesday, and Wednesday before Ascension Day. On those days use the daily office of the day with proper parts taken from the Common of Rogation Days

Invitatory Alleluia. The Lord is risen indeed: Come let us adore him. Alleluia.

Hymn Welcome Happy Morning *Hymnal 179*

Responsory One for the Easter Octave
This is the day the Lord has made. Let us rejoice and be glad in it. Alleluia.

Responsory One (Jn. 14:27)
Peace I give you.
  – **Alleluia, alleluia.**
Not as the world gives do I give you peace.
  – **Alleluia, alleluia.**
Glory to the Father and to the Son and to the Holy Spirit.

Peace I give you.
   – **Alleluia, alleluia.**

Week 1 & 3 – Canticle of Unity *Pater venit hora*
(John 17: 1-10)

Antiphon Father, glorify me in your own presence, alleluia.

O Father, the hour has come; *
   glorify your Son so that the Son may glorify you.

You have given him authority over all people, *
   to give eternal life to all whom you have given him.

This is eternal life, that they may know you, the only true God, *
   and Jesus Christ whom you have sent.

I glorified you on earth *
   by finishing the work that you gave me to do.

So now, Father, glorify me in your own presence *
   with the glory that I had in your presence
   before the world existed.

I have made your name known *
   to those whom you gave me from the world.

They were yours, and you gave them to me, *
   and they have kept your word.

Now they know that everything you have given me is from you; *
   for the words that you gave to me I have given to them.

They have received them *
   and know in truth that I came from you;
   and they have believed that you sent me.

I am asking on their behalf;
I am not asking on behalf of the world, *
   but on behalf of those whom you gave me,
   because they are yours.

All mine are yours, and yours are mine; *
   and I have been glorified in them.

Antiphon Father, glorify me in your own presence, alleluia.

Weeks 2 & 4 – Canticle of Communion and Mission *Pater sanctifica eos*
(John 17: 17-26)

Antiphon As you, Father, are in me and I am in you, may they also be in us, alleluia.

Father, sanctify them in the truth; *
 your word is truth.

As you have sent me into the world, *
 so I have sent them into the world.

For their sakes I sanctify myself, *
 so that they also may be sanctified in truth.

I ask not only on behalf of these, *
 but also on behalf of those who will believe in me
 through their word.

May they all be one,
as you, Father, are in me and I am in you, *
 may they also be in us,
 so that the world may believe that you have sent me.

The glory that you have given me I have given them, *
 so that they may be one, as we are one,
 I in them and you in me.

May they become completely one, *
 so that the world may know that you have sent me
 and have loved them even as you have loved me.

Father, I desire that those also, whom you have given me, *
 may be with me where I am, to see my glory.

You have given me this glory *
 because you loved me before the foundation of the world.

Righteous Father, the world does not know you, *
 but I know you; and these know that you have sent me.

I made your name known to them, *
 and I will make it known.

So that the love with which you have loved me may be in them, *
 and I in them.

Antiphon As you, Father, are in me and I am in you, may they also be in us, alleluia.

Responsory Two for the Easter Octave
The stone rejected by the builders has become the cornerstone. Alleluia.

Responsory Two (Lk. 24: 1,4)
The women came to the tomb
   — Alleluia, alleluia.
Two men in dazzling clothes stood beside them.
   — Alleluia, alleluia.
Glory to the Father and to the Son and to the Holy Spirit.
The women came to the tomb
   — Alleluia, alleluia.

Benedictus Antiphon
Easter 1-6 God raised Jesus to life on the third day. Jesus then appeared not to the whole people but to witnesses whom God had chosen, alleluia.
Easter 7 If I do not go, the Advocate will not come; but if I go, I will send the Spirit to you, alleluia.

Litany
Enlighted the minds and hearts of all who foster education: librarians, teachers, researchers and scholars.
Lord, have mercy.
Accompany those who find themselves in difficult situations: the homeless, political refugees, the hungry and prisoners.
Christ, have mercy.
Bring healing to those who are ill: children with difficult diagnoses, those not accepting their approaching death and all with chronic disease.
Lord, have mercy.

Invitation to the Lord's Prayer By our Baptism, we are united with the Father in Christ by the Spirit, so let us pray to deepen our unity with God and one another.

Collect
Monday of Easter Week
Grant, we pray, Almighty God, that we who celebrate with awe the Paschal feast may be found worthy to attain to everlasting joys; through Jesus Christ our Lord, who lives and reigns with you and the Holy Spirit, one God, now and for ever. Amen.
Monday of the Second and Fifth Week of Easter
O God, you have united diverse peoples in the confession of your Name: Grant that all who have been born again in the font of Baptism may also be united in faith and love; through Jesus Christ our Lord, who lives and

reigns with you and the Holy Spirit, one God, for ever and ever. Amen.

Monday of the Third and Sixth Week of Easter
Let your people, O Lord, rejoice for ever that they have been renewed in spirit; and let the joy of our adoption as your sons and daughters strengthen the hope of our glorious resurrection in Jesus Christ our Lord; who lives and reigns with you and the Holy Spirit, one God, for ever and ever. Amen.

Monday of the Fourth Week of Easter
Grant, Almighty God, that the commemoration of our Lord's death and resurrection may continually transform our lives and be manifested in our deeds; through Jesus Christ our Lord, who lives and reigns with you and the Holy Spirit, one God, for ever and ever. Amen.

Monday of the Seventh Week of Easter
O God, by the resurrection of your Son you have given us a new birth into eternal life: Lift our hearts to our Savior, who is seated at your right hand, so that, when he comes again, we who have been reborn in Baptism may be clothed in a glorious immortality; through Jesus Christ our Lord, who lives and reigns with you and the Holy Spirit, one God, for ever and ever. Amen.

The Blessing
May the Lord direct our hearts to the love of God and to the steadfastness of Christ. **Amen.**

Easter Season Monday Noonday Prayer

Hymn Christ The Lord Is Risen Again *Hymnal 184*

Reading Colossians 3: 9, 10, 12
In Christ the whole fullness of deity dwells bodily, and you have come to fullness in him, who is the head of every ruler and authority. When you were buried with him in baptism, you were also raised with him through faith in the power of God, who raised him from the dead.

Verse and Response
May you know the love of Christ that surpasses knowledge. Alleluia.
That you may be filled with all the fullness of God. Alleluia.

Collect *From Morning Prayer*

Easter Season Monday Evening Prayer

Hymn At the Lamb's high feast we wing *Hymnal 174*

Responsory for the Easter Octave
This is the day the Lord has made. Let us rejoice and be glad in it. Alleluia.

Responsory (Jer. 31:3, 4)
I have loved you with an everlasting love.
  − Alleluia, alleluia.
You shall take your tambourines, and go forth in the dance.
  − Alleluia, alleluia.
Glory to the Father and to the Son and to the Holy Spirit.
I have loved you with an everlasting love.
  − Alleluia, alleluia.

Magnificat Antiphon
Easter 1-6 God, who raised Christ Jesus from the dead, will also give new life to your mortal bodies through the indwelling Spirit, alleluia
Easter 7 All who are moved by the Spirit of God are children of God and can cry, Abba! Alleluia.

Litany
Refresh us through the beauty of nature and friendships.
Lord, have mercy.
Nourish children with nutritious food and loving homes.
Christ, have mercy.
You trampled down death by your resurrection, bring all the departed to share the light of you face.
Lord, have mercy.

Invitation to the Lord's Prayer With the deep joy of the Resurrection of Christ, let us draw near to the Father. .

Collect *From Morning Prayer*

The Blessing
May we set our minds on things that are above, not on things that are on earth, for we have died, and our life is hidden with Christ in God. **Amen.**

Easter Season Tuesday Morning Prayer

Invitatory Alleluia. The glorious Sun of Righteousness shines upon us from the tomb. Come let us adore Christ. Alleluia.

Hymn Awake and Sing the Song Of Moses *Hymnal 181*

Responsory One for the Easter Octave
This is the day the Lord has made. Let us rejoice and be glad in it. Alleluia.

Responsory One (Rev. 21:23; Is. 49:6)
The glory of God is the city's light, and its lamp is the Lamb.
  − Alleluia, alleluia.

I will give you as a light to the nations.
> — **Alleluia, alleluia.**

Glory to the Father and to the Son and to the Holy Spirit.
The glory of God is the city's light, and its lamp is the Lamb.
> —Alleluia, alleluia.

Week 1 & 3 – Canticle of Generous Grace *Benedictus Deus*
(Ephesians 1: 3-10)

Antiphon The Father will gather up all things in heaven and things on earth in Christ, alleluia.

Blessed be the God and Father *
>   of our Lord Jesus Christ.

God has blessed us in Christ *
>   with every spiritual blessing in the heavens,

God chose us in Christ *
>   before the foundation of the world

To be holy and blameless *
>   before him in love.

He destined us for adoption *
>   as his children through Jesus Christ,

According to the good pleasure of his will, *
>   to the praise of his glorious grace
>   that he freely bestowed on us in the Beloved.

In Christ we have redemption through his blood, *
>   the forgiveness of our trespasses,

According to the riches of his grace *
>   that he lavished on us.

With all wisdom and insight *
>   he has made known to us the mystery of his will,

According to his good pleasure that he set forth in Christ, *
>   as a plan for the fullness of time,

To gather up all things in him, *
>   all things in heaven and things on earth.

Antiphon The Father will gather up all things in heaven and things on earth in Christ, alleluia.

Week 2 & 4 – Canticle of the Children of God *Quicumque enim Spiritu Dei*
(Romans 8: 14-17)

Antiphon The Spirit bears witness with our spirit that we are children of God, alleluia.

All who are led by the Spirit of God *
   are children of God.

You did not receive a spirit of slavery *
   to fall back into fear.

You have received a spirit of adoption *
   when we cry, "Abba! Father!"

It is that very Spirit bearing witness with our spirit *
   that we are children of God.

If we are children, then we are also heirs, *
   heirs of God and joint heirs with Christ.

We, however, must suffer with him *
   so that we may also be glorified with him.

Antiphon The Spirit bears witness with our spirit that we are children of God, alleluia.

Responsory Two for the Easter Octave
The stone rejected by the builders has become the cornerstone. Alleluia.

Responsory Two (1 Pt. 1:8; Jn. 20:29)
Though you do not see him now, you believe in him.
   – Alleluia, alleluia.
Blessed are those who have not seen and yet believe.
   – Alleluia, alleluia.
Glory to the Father and to the Son and to the Holy Spirit.
Though you do not see him now, you believe in him.
   – Alleluia, alleluia.

Benedictus Antiphon
Easter 1-6 Christ who died and was raised from the dead is at God's right hand and pleads our cause, alleluia.
Easter 7 After giving instructions through the Holy Spirit to the apostles, Jesus was taken up into heaven, alleluia.

Litany

You revealed yourself on the road to Emmaus; manifest yourself in the stranger.
Lord, have mercy.
You bring new members into your church in the waters of Baptism; deepen the commitment of all the newly baptized.
Christ, have mercy.
You manifested your presence to Thomas; strengthen our faltering faith.
Lord, have mercy.

Invitation to the Lord's Prayer Christ is the beginning of the Father's new creation so let us open our lips with words of praise.

Collect
Tuesday of Easter Week
O God, who by the glorious resurrection of your Son Jesus Christ destroyed death and brought life and immortality to light: Grant that we, who have been raised with him, may abide in his presence and rejoice in the hope of eternal glory; through Jesus Christ our Lord, to whom, with you and the Holy Spirit, be dominion and praise for ever and ever. Amen.

Tuesday of the Second and Fifth Week of Easter
O God, by the waters of Baptism you have renewed those who believe in you: Come to the help of those who have been reborn in Christ, that they may overcome the wiles of the devil, and continue faithful to the gifts of grace they have received from you; through Jesus Christ our Lord, who lives and reigns with you and the Holy Spirit, one God, for ever and ever. Amen.

Tuesday of the Third and Sixth Week of Easter
Almighty and everlasting God, you have given your Church the great joy of the resurrection of Jesus Christ: Give us also the greater joy of the kingdom of your elect, when the flock of your Son will share in the final victory of its Shepherd, Jesus Christ our Lord; who lives and reigns with you and the Holy Spirit, one God, now and for ever. Amen.

Tuesday of the Fourth Week of Easter
Hear our prayers, O Lord, and, as we confess that Christ, the Savior of the world, lives with you in glory, grant that, as he himself has promised, we may perceive him present among us also, to the end of the ages; who lives and reigns with you and the Holy Spirit, one God, for ever and ever. Amen.

Tuesday of the Seventh Week of Easter
O God, by the glorification of Jesus Christ and the coming of the Holy Spirit you have opened for us the gates of your kingdom: Grant that we, who have received such great gifts, may dedicate ourselves more diligently

to your service, and live more fully the riches of our faith; through Jesus Christ our Lord, who lives and reigns with you and the Holy Spirit, one God, for ever and ever. Amen.

The Blessing
May we who have died to the law through the body of Christ, so that we may belong to another, to Christ who has been raised from the dead, may we bear fruit for God. **Amen.**

Easter Season Tuesday Noonday Prayer
Hymn Through The Red Sea *Hymnal 187*

Reading 2 Timothy 2: 8, 11-13
Remember Jesus Christ, raised from the dead, a descendant of David. If we have died with him, we will also live with him; if we endure, we will also reign with him; if we deny him, he will also deny us; if we are faithless, he remains faithful— for he cannot deny himself.

Verse and Response
Christ was faithful over God's house as a son. Alleluia.
We are his house if we hold firm to hope. Alleluia.

Collect *From Morning Prayer*

Easter Season Tuesday Evening Prayer
Hymn Good Christians All Rejoice And Sing *Hymnal 205*

Responsory for the Easter Octave
This is the day the Lord has made. Let us rejoice and be glad in it. Alleluia.

Responsory (Acts 2:32; Acts 1:8)
God raised up Jesus, and of that all of us are witnesses.
　　− **Alleluia, alleluia.**
You will be my witnesses to the ends of the earth.
　　− **Alleluia, alleluia.**
Glory to the Father and to the Son and to the Holy Spirit.
God raised up Jesus, and of that all of us are witnesses.
　　− **Alleluia, alleluia.**

Magnificat Antiphon
Easter 1-6 God who raised Jesus to life will with Jesus raise us, too, and bring us in to God's holy presence, alleluia.
Easter 7 In Christ Jesus the life-giving law of the Spirit has set you free from the law of sin and death, alleluia.

Litany
You give us new life in the waters of Baptism; give us an inquiring and discerning heart.
Lord, have mercy.
You seal us with the Holy Spirit; may all anointed with the Holy Spirit share in the royal priesthood of Jesus Christ
Christ, have mercy.
You forgave our sins in Baptism; pardon the sins of all the departed and bring them into your presence.
Lord, have mercy.

Invitation to the Lord's Prayer Since we are sealed by the Holy Spirit in Baptism and marked as Christ's own for ever let us pray with Christ.

Collect *From Morning Prayer*

The Blessing
May we greatly rejoice in the Lord. May our whole being exult in our God who has clothed us with the garments of salvation, and has covered us with the robe of righteousness. **Amen.**

Easter Season Wednesday Morning Prayer

Invitatory Alleluia. The Lord is risen indeed: Come let us adore him. Alleluia.

Hymn On Earth Has Dawned This Day Of Days *Hymnal 201*

Responsory One for the Easter Octave
This is the day the Lord has made. Let us rejoice and be glad in it. Alleluia.

Responsory One (Jn. 20:20)
The disciples rejoiced
    – **Alleluia, alleluia.**
When they saw the Lord.
    – **Alleluia, alleluia.**
Glory to the Father and to the Son and to the Holy Spirit.
The disciples rejoiced. –
    Alleluia, alleluia.

Week 1 & 3 – Canticle of the Good Shepherd *Ego sum pastor bonus*
(John 10: 11-18)
Antiphon I am the good shepherd; I know my own and my own know me, alleluia.

I am the good shepherd. *
> The good shepherd lays down his life for the sheep.

The hired hand, who is not the shepherd *
> does not own the sheep.

The hired hand sees the wolf coming
and leaves the sheep and runs away *
> and the wolf snatches them and scatters them.

The hired hand runs away *
> because a hired hand does not care for the sheep.

I am the good shepherd. *
> I know my own and my own know me,

Just as the Father knows me *
> and I know the Father.

I lay down my life for the sheep. *
> I have other sheep
> that do not belong to this fold.

I must bring them also, *
> and they will listen to my voice.
> So there will be one flock, one shepherd.

For this reason the Father loves me, *
> because I lay down my life in order to take it up again.

No one takes it from me, *
> but I lay it down of my own accord.

I have power to lay it down, *
> and I have power to take it up again.
> I have received this command from my Father.

Antiphon I am the good shepherd; I know my own and my own know me, alleluia.

Week 2 & 4 – Canticle of Christ's Universal Vindication
Manifeste magnum est (1 Timothy 3: 16)

Antiphon Christ is proclaimed among the Gentiles, believed in throughout the world, alleluia.

The mystery of our religion is great: *
> Christ was revealed in flesh,

Christ was vindicated in spirit, *
    seen by angels,
Christ is proclaimed among the Gentiles, *
    believed in throughout the world,
    taken up in glory.

Antiphon Christ is proclaimed among the Gentiles, believed in throughout the world, alleluia.

Responsory Two for the Easter Octave
The stone rejected by the builders has become the cornerstone. Alleluia.

Responsory Two (Eph. 1:22)
God has made Christ the head over all things for the church.
    – Alleluia, alleluia.
The fullness of Christ fills all in all.
    – Alleluia, alleluia.
Glory to the Father and to the Son and to the Holy Spirit.
God has made Christ the head over all things for the church.
    – Alleluia, alleluia.

Benedictus Antiphon
Easter 1-6 It was Mary Magdalene, Joanna, Mary, the mother of James and the other women with them who told the apostles of Jesus' resurrection, alleluia.
Easter 7 You will receive power when the Holy Spirit comes upon you, and you will be my witnesses, alleluia.

Litany
You care for the earth and water it; sustain all who cultivate the earth and grow food for the people of the world.
Lord, have mercy.
Your wisdom created the universe; let us discover your plan for us in your world.
Christ, have mercy.
You make us caretakers of our planet; help us conserve the home you provide for us.
Lord, have mercy.

Invitation to the Lord's Prayer Christ is the Word through whom the universe is created so let us pray to know Christ in the Father's creation.

Collect

Wednesday of Easter Week

O God, whose blessed Son made himself known to his disciples in the breaking of bread: Open the eyes of our faith, that we may behold him in all his redeeming work; who lives and reigns with you, in the unity of the Holy Spirit, one God, now and for ever. Amen.

Wednesday of the Second and Fifth Week of Easter

Grant, O Lord, that we may so live in the Paschal mystery that the joy of these fifty days may continually strengthen us, and assure us of our salvation; through Jesus Christ your Son our Lord, who lives and reigns with you and the Holy Spirit, one God, for ever and ever. Amen.

Wednesday of the Third and Sixth Week of Easter

Almighty God, you show the light of your truth to those who are in error, to the intent that they may return to the way of righteousness: Grant to those who are admitted into the fellowship of Christ's religion that they may avoid those things that are contrary to their profession, and follow all such things as are agreeable to it; through Jesus Christ our Lord, who lives and reigns with you and the Holy Spirit, one God, for ever and ever. Amen.

Wednesday of the Fourth Week of Easter

O Lord, you have given us the grace to know the resurrection of your Son: Grant that the Holy Spirit, by his love, may raise us to newness of life; through Jesus Christ our Lord, who lives and reigns with you and the Holy Spirit, one God, for ever and ever. Amen.

Wednesday of the Seventh Week of Easter

O Lord, when your Son ascended into heaven he sent down upon the Apostles the Holy Spirit, as he had promised, that they might comprehend the mysteries of the kingdom: Distribute among us also, we pray, the gifts of the selfsame Spirit; through Jesus Christ our Lord, who lives and reigns with you and the Holy Spirit, one God, for ever and ever. Amen.

The Blessing

May the peace of Christ rule in our hearts to which indeed we were called in the one body. **Amen.**

Easter Season Wednesday Noonday Prayer

Hymn Love's Redeeming Work Is Done *Hymnal 188*

Reading Colossians 3: 1-3

If you have been raised with Christ, seek the things that are above, where Christ is, seated at the right hand of God. Set your minds on things that are above, not on things that are on earth, for you have died, and your life is hidden with Christ in God.

Verse and Response
Christ was raised from the dead by the glory of the Father. Alleluia.
That we too might walk in newness of life. Alleluia.
Collect *From Morning Prayer*

Easter Season Wednesday Evening Prayer

Hymn Christ Jesus Lay In Death's Strong Bands *Hymnal 185*

Responsory for the Easter Octave
This is the day the Lord has made. Let us rejoice and be glad in it. Alleluia.

Responsory (Rev. 1:18; Jn. 16:33)
I was dead, and see, I am alive forever and ever.
  – **Alleluia, alleluia.**
Take courage; I have conquered the world.
  – **Alleluia, alleluia.**
Glory to the Father and to the Son and to the Holy Spirit.
I was dead, and see, I am alive forever and ever.
  – **Alleluia, alleluia.**

Magnificat Antiphon
Easter 1-5 You have come to trust in God through Jesus who was raised from the dead and given glory, and so your faith and hope are fixed on God, alleluia.
Easter 7 Make fast with bonds of peace the unity the Spirit gives. There is one Body and one Spirit, alleluia.

Litany
You give us new life in the waters of Baptism; may we continue for ever in the risen life of Jesus Christ our Savior.
Lord, have mercy.
You seal us with the Holy Spirit; may all anointed with chrism share in the royal priesthood of Jesus Christ
Christ, have mercy.
You forgave our sins in Baptism and give us an inquiring and discerning heart, let all the dead continue to grow in knowledge and love of you.
Lord, have mercy.

Invitation to the Lord's Prayer Since we are sealed by the Holy Spirit in Baptism and marked as Christ's own for ever let us offer our sacrifice of praise and thanksgiving to the Father

Collect *From Morning Prayer*

The Blessing
May God make known how great among us are the riches of the glory of this mystery, which is Christ in us, our hope of glory. **Amen.**

Easter Season Thursday Morning Prayer

Invitatory Alleluia. Having beheld the Resurrection of Christ, let us bow down before the Holy Lord Jesus. Alleluia.

Hymn He is risen! *Hymnal 180*

Responsory One for the Easter Octave
This is the day the Lord has made. Let us rejoice and be glad in it. Alleluia.

Responsory One (Lk. 24:30)
Jesus took bread, blessed and broke it.
– Alleluia, alleluia.
They eyes were opened.
– Alleluia, alleluia.
Glory to the Father and to the Son and to the Holy Spirit.
Jesus took bread, blessed and broke it.
– Alleluia, alleluia.

Week 1 & 3 – Canticle of the Bread of Life *Ego sum panis vitae*
(John 6: 35-40, 50, 63)

Antiphon Those who eat my flesh and drink my blood abide in me, and I in them, alleluia.

I am the bread of life. *
   Whoever comes to me will never be hungry,
   and whoever believes in me will never be thirsty.

I am the bread of life. *
   Your ancestors ate the manna in the wilderness,
   and they died.

This is the bread that comes down from heaven, *
   so that one may eat of it and not die.

I am the living bread that came down from heaven. *
   Whoever eats of this bread will live forever;

The bread that I will give for the life of the world *
   is my flesh."

Unless you eat the flesh of the Son of Man and drink his blood, *
   you have no life in you.

Those who eat my flesh and drink my blood have eternal life, *
   and I will raise them up on the last day.

For my flesh is true food *
   and my blood is true drink.

Those who eat my flesh and drink my blood *
   abide in me, and I in them.

Just as the living Father sent me, and I live because of the Father, *
   so whoever eats me will live because of me.

Antiphon Those who eat my flesh and drink my blood abide in me, and I in them, alleluia.

Week 2 & 4 – Canticle of Christ the Vine *Ego sum vitis vera*
(John 15: 1-10)

Antiphon As the Father has loved me, so I have loved you; abide in my love, alleluia.

I am the true vine, *
   and my Father is the vine grower.

Abide in me *
   as I abide in you.

Just as the branch cannot bear fruit by itself *
   unless it abides in the vine,

Neither can you bear fruit *
   unless you abide in me.

I am the vine, *
   you are the branches.

Those who abide in me and I in them
bear much fruit, *
   because apart from me you can do nothing.

If you abide in me, and my words abide in you, *
   ask for whatever you wish, and it will be done for you.

My Father is glorified by this, *
   that you bear much fruit and become my disciples.

As the Father has loved me,
so I have loved you; *
   abide in my love.

If you keep my commandments, you will abide in my love, *
> just as I have kept my Father's commandments
> and abide in his love.

Antiphon As the Father has loved me, so I have loved you; abide in my love, alleluia.

Responsory Two for the Easter Octave
The stone rejected by the builders has become the cornerstone. Alleluia.

Responsory Two (Rev. 3:20; Lk. 24: 35)
I will come in to you and eat with you, and you with me.
> **− Alleluia, alleluia.**

He had been made known to them in the breaking of the bread.
> **− Alleluia, alleluia.**

Glory to the Father and to the Son and to the Holy Spirit.
I will come in to you and eat with you, and you with me.
> **− Alleluia, alleluia.**

Benedictus Antiphon
Easter 1-5 When he was at table with them, Jesus took bread, blessed and broke it and gave it to them. Then their eyes were opened, and they recognized him, alleluia.

Easter 7 When the Spurt of truth comes, he will guide you into all truth, alleluia.

Litany
Christ, Bread of Life, open our eyes to your abiding presence and deepen our love for you.
Lord, have mercy.
Christ, True Vine, purify us from all sin and strengthen us to bear fruit.
Christ, have mercy.
Christ, Risen Lord, manifest yourself in the least among us and draw us closer to you through humble service.
Lord, have mercy.

Invitation to the Lord's Prayer The Risen Christ illumines all who come to him so let us ask the Father to shine in our hearts.

Collect
Thursday of the First Week of Easter
Almighty and everlasting God, who in the Paschal mystery established the new covenant of reconciliation: Grant that all who have been reborn into the fellowship of Christ's Body may show forth in their lives what

they profess by their faith; through Jesus Christ our Lord, who lives and reigns with you and the Holy Spirit, one God, for ever and ever. Amen.

Thursday of the Second and Fifth Week of Easter
O Lord, you have saved us through the Paschal mystery of Christ: Continue to support your people with heavenly gifts, that we may attain true liberty, and enjoy the happiness of heaven which we have begun to taste on earth; through Jesus Christ our Lord, who lives and reigns with you and the Holy Spirit, one God, for ever and ever. Amen.

Thursday of the Third Week of Easter
God of infinite mercy, you renew the faith of your people by the yearly celebration of these fifty days: Stir up in us the gifts of your grace, that we may know more deeply that Baptism has cleansed us, the Spirit has quickened us, and the Blood of Christ has redeemed us; through Jesus Christ our Lord, who lives and reigns with you and the Holy Spirit, one God, for ever and ever. Amen.

Thursday of the Fourth Week of Easter
O Lord, you open the portals of your kingdom to those who have been reborn by water and the Spirit: Increase the grace you have given to your children, that those whom you have cleansed from sin may attain to all your promises; through Jesus Christ our Lord, who lives and reigns with you and the Holy Spirit, one God, for ever and ever. Amen..

Thursday of the Seventh Week of Easter
O loving Father, grant that your Church, being gathered by your Holy Spirit, may be dedicated more fully to your service, and live united in love, according to your will; through Jesus Christ our Lord, who lives and reigns with you and the Holy Spirit, one God, for ever and ever. Amen.

The Blessing
May we, for whom Christ, our Paschal Lamb, has been sacrificed, celebrate the feast, not with the old yeast, the yeast of malice and evil, but with the unleavened bread of sincerity and truth. **Amen.**

Easter Season Thursday Noonday Prayer

Hymn Over the Chaos *Hymnal 176*

Reading John 6: 54-57
Those who eat my flesh and drink my blood have eternal life, and I will raise them up on the last day; for my flesh is true food and my blood is true drink. Those who eat my flesh and drink my blood abide in me, and I in them. Just as the living Father sent me, and I live because of the Father, so whoever eats me will live because of me.

Verse and Response
I am the vine, you are the branches. Alleluia.
Those who abide in me and I in them bear much fruit. Alleluia.

Collect *From Morning Prayer*

Easter Season Thursday Evening Prayer

Hymn Alleluia, alleluia! Hearts and voices heavenward raise. *Hymnal 191*

Responsory for the Easter Octave
This is the day the Lord has made. Let us rejoice and be glad in it. Alleluia.

Responsory (Rev. 2:17; Lk. 24:30)
I will give you some of the hidden manna.
   — **Alleluia, alleluia.**
They recognized Jesus in the breaking of the bread.
   — **Alleluia, alleluia.**
Glory to the Father and to the Son and to the Holy Spirit.
I will give you some of the hidden manna.
   — **Alleluia, alleluia.**

Magnificat Antiphon
Easter 1-5 Your life is hidden with Christ in God. When Christ, your life, is revealed, then you also will be revealed with Christ in glory, alleluia.
Easter 7 Now the Lord is the Spirit, and where the Spirit of the Lord is, there is freedom, alleluia.

Litany
You are the light shining in the darkness; illumine judges and all involved with justice to be impartial in their decisions and actions.
Lord, have mercy.
You are the fire burning in the human heart; draw all spouses to a deeper love for one another.
Christ, have mercy.
You are the Evening Star illuminating the universe; bring all the dead to share in your life.
Lord, have mercy.

Invitation to the Lord's Prayer Deepen our faith and love, O Spirit, through our celebration of Christ's Paschal Mystery and draw us closer to the Father in prayer.

Collect *From Morning Prayer*

The Blessing
May we who eat the flesh and drink the blood of the Risen One, abide in Christ, and Christ in us. **Amen.**

Easter Season Friday Morning Prayer

Invitatory Alleluia. Come, let us worship the Risen Christ. For through the Cross joy has come into all the world. Alleluia.

Hymn Now the green blade riseth *Hymnal 204*

Responsory One for the Easter Octave
This is the day the Lord has made. Let us rejoice and be glad in it. Alleluia.

Responsory One (Rm. 6:9, 11)
Christ, being raised from the dead, will never die again.
  — **Alleluia, alleluia.**
You are dead to sin and alive to God in Christ.
  — **Alleluia, alleluia.**
Glory to the Father and to the Son and to the Holy Spirit.
Christ, being raised from the dead, will never die again.
  — **Alleluia, alleluia.**

Week 1 & 3 — Canticle of the Love of Christ *Si Deus pro nobis*
(Romans 8: 31-35. 37-39)

Antiphon In all these things we are more than conquerors through Christ who loved us, alleluia.

If God is for us, *
  who is against us?

God who did not withhold his own Son, *
  but gave him up for all of us.

Will he not with him *
  also give us everything else?

Who will bring any charge against God's elect? *
  It is God who justifies.

Who is to condemn? *
  It is Christ Jesus, who died.

Christ Jesus was raised and is at the right hand of God; *
  He intercedes for us.

Who will separate us from the love of Christ? *
    Will hardship, or distress, or persecution,
    or famine, or nakedness, or peril, or sword?

In all these things we are more than conquerors *
    through Christ who loved us.

For I am convinced that neither death, nor life, *
    nor angels, nor rulers,
    nor things present, nor things to come,

Nor powers, nor height, nor depth, *
    nor anything else in all creation,

Will be able to separate us from the love of God *
    in Christ Jesus our Lord.

Antiphon In all these things we are more than conquerors through Christ who loved us, alleluia.

Week 2 & 4 -- Canticle of Christ, the Image of God *Gratias agamus Deo*
(Colossians 1:12-20)

Antiphon Through Christ, God was pleased to reconcile to himself all things by making peace through the blood of his cross, alleluia.

Let us give thanks to the Father, who has made you worthy *
    to share in the inheritance of the saints in the light.

God has rescued us from the power of darkness *
    and transferred us into the kingdom of his beloved Son.

In Christ we have redemption, *
    the forgiveness of sins.

Christ is the image of the invisible God, *
    the firstborn of all creation.

In Christ all things in heaven and on earth were created, *
    things visible and invisible;

Thrones or dominions or rulers or powers *
    all things have been created through him and for him.

Christ is before all things, *
    and in him all things hold together.

Christ is the head of the body, the church; *
    he is the beginning, the firstborn from the dead.

In everything Christ has the first place. *
    In Christ all the fullness of God was pleased to dwell.

Through Christ God was pleased to reconcile to himself all things, *
    things on earth or in heaven,
    by making peace through the blood of his cross.

Antiphon Through Christ, God was pleased to reconcile to himself all things by making peace through the blood of his cross, alleluia.

Responsory Two for the Easter Octave
The stone rejected by the builders has become the cornerstone. Alleluia.

Responsory Two (Rev. 2:28; 2 Pt. 1:19)
To the one who conquers I will give the morning star.
    – **Alleluia, alleluia.**
The morning star rises in your hearts.
    – **Alleluia, alleluia.**
Glory to the Father and to the Son and to the Holy Spirit.
To the one who conquers I will give the morning star.
    – **Alleluia, alleluia.**

Benedictus Antiphon
Easter 1-5 Was it not necessary that the Messiah should suffer these things and then enter into his glory? Alleluia.
Easter 6-7 I will make your name known to them that the love with which you have loved me may be in them, and I in them, alleluia.

Litany
The cross has become the tree of life; bring endurance to all suffering chronic illness.
Lord, have mercy.
The cross has become the center of the world; gather all who seek God into its shade.
Christ, have mercy.
The cross has become our one reliance; bring us into new depths of hope when we are in crisis.
Lord, have mercy.

Invitation to the Lord's Christ has triumphed on the wood of the cross so we celebrate the Father's victory over death.

Collect
Friday of Easter Week
Almighty Father, who gave your only Son to die for our sins and to rise for our justification: Give us grace so to put away the leaven of malice and wickedness, that we may always serve you in pureness of living and truth; through Jesus Christ your Son our Lord, who lives and reigns with you and the Holy Spirit, one God, now and for ever. Amen.

Friday of the Second and Fourth Week of Easter
O Lord, the life of the faithful, the glory of the saints, and the delight of those who trust in you: Hear our supplications, and quench, we pray, the thirst of those who long for your promises; through Jesus Christ our Lord, who lives and reigns with you and the Holy Spirit, one God, for ever and ever. Amen..

Friday of the Third and Fifth Week of Easter
Lord God Almighty, for no merit on our part you have brought us out of death into life, out of sorrow into joy: Put no end to your gifts, fulfill your marvelous acts in us, and grant to us who have been justified by faith the strength to persevere in that faith; through Jesus Christ our Lord, who lives and reigns with you and the Holy Spirit, one God, for ever and ever. Amen.

Friday of the Sixth and Seventh Week of Easter
O God, by the resurrection of your Son you have given us a new birth into eternal life: Lift our hearts to our Savior, who is seated at your right hand, so that, when he comes again, we who have been reborn in Baptism may be clothed in a glorious immortality; through Jesus Christ our Lord, who lives and reigns with you and the Holy Spirit, one God, for ever and ever. Amen.

The Blessing
May the young women rejoice in the dance, and the young men and the old be merry. For God has turned our mourning into joy, has comforted us, and has given us gladness for sorrow. **Amen.**

Easter Season Friday Noonday Prayer
Hymn Christ Jesus lay in death's strong bands *Hymnal 186*

Reading Acts 4: 10-12
This man is standing before you in good health by the name of Jesus Christ of Nazareth, whom you crucified, whom God raised from the dead. This Jesus is "the stone that was rejected by you, the builders; it has become the cornerstone." There is salvation in no one else, for there is no other name under heaven given among mortals by which we must be saved.

Verse and Response
We build upon the foundation of the apostles and prophets. Alleluia.
Christ Jesus himself is the cornerstone. Alleluia.

Collect *From Morning Prayer*

Easter Season Friday Evening Prayer

Hymn Christ is alive! *Hymnal 182*

Responsory for the Easter Octave
This is the day the Lord has made. Let us rejoice and be glad in it. Alleluia.

Responsory (1 Cor. 5:7, 8)
Christ, our Paschal Lamb, has been sacrificed.
  – **Alleluia, alleluia.**
Let us celebrate with the unleavened bread of sincerity and truth.
  – **Alleluia, alleluia.**
Glory to the Father and to the Son and to the Holy Spirit.
Christ, our Paschal Lamb, has been sacrificed.
  – **Alleluia, alleluia.**

Magnificat Antiphon
Easter 1-5 Through Christ, God was please to reconcile to himself all things, whether on earth or in heaven, by making peace through the blood of his cross, alleluia.
Easter 6-7 Since the Spirit of God who raised Jesus from the dead dwells in you, God who raised Christ from the dead will give life to your mortal bodies also through his Spirit that dwells in you, alleluia.

Litany
You descended to the depths with your light; accompany those who battle addiction.
Lord, have mercy.
You overcame evil with good; transform us to see a new way in times of conflict.
Christ, have mercy.
You proclaimed the Gospel among the dead; bring all the departed into your new reign.
Lord, have mercy.

Invitation to the Lord's Prayer Confident of the power of the cross to overcome evil, let us join the Risen One in prayer.

Collect *From Morning Prayer*

The Blessing
May we who have not seen Christ yet love him and believe in him rejoice in Christ with an indescribable and glorious joy. **Amen.**

Easter Season Saturday Morning Prayer

Invitatory Alleluia. The glorious Sun of Righteousness shines upon us from the tomb. Come let us adore Christ. Alleluia.

Hymn Lift your voice rejoicing, Mary *Hymnal 190*

Responsory One for the Easter Octave
This is the day the Lord has made. Let us rejoice and be glad in it. Alleluia.

Responsory One (1 Pt. 1:3; Jn. 3:7)
God has given us a new birth into a living hope.
　− **Alleluia, alleluia.**
You must be born from above.
　− **Alleluia, alleluia.**
Glory to the Father and to the Son and to the Holy Spirit.
God has given us a new birth into a living hope.
　− **Alleluia, alleluia.**

Week 1 & 3 − Canticle of Wisdom *Reddidit Deus*
(Wisdom 10,17-21)

Antiphon Wisdom brought them over the Red Sea and led them through deep waters, alleluia.

Wisdom gave to holy people the reward of their labors; *
　she guided them along a marvelous way,

She became a shelter to them by day, *
　and a starry flame through the night.

She brought them over the Red Sea, *
　and led them through deep waters;

But she drowned their enemies, *
　and cast them up from the depth of the sea.

Therefore the righteous plundered the ungodly; *
　they sang hymns, O Lord, to your holy name,
　and praised with one accord your defending hand;

For wisdom opened the mouths of those who were mute, *
　and made the tongues of infants speak clearly.

Antiphon Wisdom brought them over the Red Sea and led them through deep waters, alleluia.

Week 2 & 4 – The Song of Moses *Cantemus Domino*
(Exodus 15:1-6, 11-13, 17-18)

Antiphon With your constant love you led the people you redeemed; with your might you brought them in safety to your holy dwelling, alleluia.

I will sing to the Lord, for he is lofty and uplifted; *
  the horse and its rider has he hurled into the sea.

The Lord is my strength and my refuge; *
  the Lord has become my Savior.

This is my God and I will praise him, *
  the God of my people and I will exalt him.

The Lord is a mighty warrior; *
  Yahweh is his Name.

The chariots of Pharaoh and his army has he hurled into the sea; *
  the finest of those who bear armor have been
  drowned in the Red Sea.

The fathomless deep has overwhelmed them; *
  they sank into the depths like a stone.

Your right hand, O Lord, is glorious in might; *
  your right hand, O Lord, has overthrown the enemy.

Who can be compared with you, O Lord, among the gods? *
  who is like you, glorious in holiness,
  awesome in renown, and worker of wonders?

You stretched forth your right hand; *
  the earth swallowed them up.

With your constant love you led the people you redeemed; *
  with your might you brought them in safety
  to your holy dwelling.

You will bring them in and plant them *
  on the mount of your possession,

The resting-place you have made for yourself, O Lord, *
  the sanctuary, O Lord, that your hand has established.

The Lord shall reign *
  for ever and for ever.

Antiphon With your constant love you led the people you redeemed; with your might you brought them in safety to your holy dwelling, alleluia.

Responsory Two for the Easter Octave
The stone rejected by the builders has become the cornerstone. Alleluia.

Responsory Two (Jn. 20:14; Jn. 20:18)
Mary Magdalene turned around and saw Jesus.
   — Alleluia, alleluia.
I have seen the Lord.
   — Alleluia, alleluia.
Glory to the Father and to the Son and to the Holy Spirit.
Mary Magdalene turned around and saw Jesus.
   — Alleluia, alleluia.

Benedictus Antiphon
Easter 1-5 Rejoice and be glad, O Virgin Mary, for the Lord is risen indeed, alleluia.
Easter 6-7 The disciples constantly devoted themselves to prayer, together with certain women, including Mary, the mother of Jesus, as well as his brothers, alleluia.

Litany
With the holy women who cared for your dead body, let us care for all who grieve and seek meaning in death's shadow.
Lord, have mercy.
With the holy women who beheld your empty tomb, let us remember your word and bear witness to your life.
Christ, have mercy.
With the holy women who proclaimed your Resurrection, let us show your presence among us in word and action.
Lord, have mercy.

Invitation to the Lord's Prayer You first appeared, O Christ, to the women at your empty tomb so with the faithful women of every generation we proclaim your Father's love.

Collect
Saturday of Easter Week
We thank you, heavenly Father, that you have delivered us from the dominion of sin and death and brought us into the kingdom of your Son; and we pray that, as by his death he has recalled us to life, so by his love

he may raise us to eternal joys; who lives and reigns with you, in the unity of the Holy Spirit, one God, now and forever. Amen.

Saturday of the Second and Fourth Week of Easter
O God, by the abundance of your grace you unfailingly increase the number of your children: Look with favor upon those whom you have chosen to be members of your Church, that, having been born again in Baptism, they may be granted a glorious resurrection; through Jesus Christ your Son our Lord, who lives and reigns with you and the Holy Spirit, one God, now and for ever. Amen.

Saturday of the Third and Fifth Week of Easter
O God, you continually increase your Church by the birth of new sons and daughters in Baptism: Grant that they may be obedient all the days of their life to the rule of faith which they received in that Sacrament; through Jesus Christ your Son our Lord, who lives and reigns with you and the Holy Spirit, one God, now and for ever. Amen.

Saturday of the Sixth and Seventh Week of Easter
O God, by the glorification of Jesus Christ and the coming of the Holy Spirit you have opened for us the gates of your kingdom: Grant that we, who have received such great gifts, may dedicate ourselves more diligently to your service, and live more fully the riches of our faith; through Jesus Christ our Lord, who lives and reigns with you and the Holy Spirit, one God, for ever and ever. Amen.

The Blessing
May God, who is rich in mercy, out of the great love with which he loved us even when we were dead through our trespasses, make us alive together with Christ. **Amen.**

Easter Season Saturday Noonday Prayer
Hymn That Easter day with joy was bright *Hymnal 193*

Reading Acts 1: 12-14
Then the apostles returned to Jerusalem from the mount called Olivet, which is near Jerusalem, a sabbath day's journey away. When they had entered the city, they went to the room upstairs where they were staying, Peter, and John, and James, and Andrew, Philip and Thomas, Bartholomew and Matthew, James son of Alphaeus, and Simon the Zealot, and Judas son of James. All these were constantly devoting themselves to prayer, together with certain women, including Mary the mother of Jesus, as well as his brothers.

Verse and Response
The Holy Spirit will come upon you. Alleluia.
The power of the Most High will overshadow you. Alleluia.

Collect *From Morning Prayer*

Ascension Day

Principal Feast
Evening Prayer I

Hymn See the conqueror mount in triumph *Hymnal 215*

Psalm 68 A *Exsurgat Deus*

Antiphon Men of Galilee, why do you stand looking up toward heaven? This Jesus, who has been taken up from you into heaven, will come in the same way as you saw him go into heaven. Alleluia.

1 Let God arise, and let his enemies be scattered; *
   let those who hate him flee before him.

2 Let them vanish like smoke when the wind drives it away; *
   as the wax melts at the fire, so let the wicked perish
   at the presence of God.

3 But let the righteous be glad and rejoice before God; *
   let them also be merry and joyful.

4 Sing to God, sing praises to his Name;
exalt him who rides upon the heavens; *
   YAHWEH is his Name, rejoice before him!

5 Father of orphans, defender of widows, *
   God in his holy habitation!

6 God gives the solitary a home
and brings forth prisoners into freedom; *
   but the rebels shall live in dry places.

7 O God, when you went forth before your people, *
   when you marched through the wilderness,

8 The earth shook, and the skies poured down rain,
at the presence of God, the God of Sinai, *
   at the presence of God, the God of Israel.

9 You sent a gracious rain, O God, upon your inheritance; *
   you refreshed the land when it was weary.

10 Your people found their home in it; *
   in your goodness, O God,
   you have made provision for the poor.

Antiphon Men of Galilee, why do you stand looking up toward heaven? This Jesus, who has been taken up from you into heaven, will come in the same way as you saw him go into heaven. Alleluia.

Psalm 68 B *Dominus dabit verbum*

Antiphon You will receive power when the Holy Spirit has come upon you; and you will be my witnesses in Jerusalem, in all Judea and Samaria, and to the ends of the earth. Alleluia.

11 The Lord gave the word; *
   great was the company of women who bore the tidings:

12 "Kings with their armies are fleeing away; *
   the women at home are dividing the spoils."

13 Though you lingered among the sheepfolds, *
   you shall be like a dove whose wings are covered with silver,
   whose feathers are like green gold.

14 When the Almighty scattered kings, *
   it was like snow falling in Zalmon.

15 O mighty mountain, O hill of Bashan! *
   O rugged mountain, O hill of Bashan!

16 Why do you look with envy, O rugged mountain,
   at the hill which God chose for his resting place? *
   truly, the LORD will dwell there for ever.

17 The chariots of God are twenty thousand,
   even thousands of thousands; *
   the Lord comes in holiness from Sinai.

18 You have gone up on high and led captivity captive;
   you have received gifts even from your enemies, *
   that the LORD God might dwell among them.

19 Blessed be the Lord day by day, *
   the God of our salvation, who bears our burdens.

20 He is our God, the God of our salvation; *
   God is the LORD, by whom we escape death.

21 God shall crush the heads of his enemies, *
   and the hairy scalp of those
   who go on still in their wickedness.

22 The Lord has said, "I will bring them back from Bashan; *
   I will bring them back from the depths of the sea;

23 That your foot may be dipped in blood, *
    the tongues of your dogs in the blood of your enemies."

Antiphon You will receive power when the Holy Spirit has come upon you; and you will be my witnesses in Jerusalem, in all Judea and Samaria, and to the ends of the earth. Alleluia.

Psalm 68 C *Viderunt ingressus tui Deus*

Antiphon As they were watching, he was lifted up, and a cloud took him out of their sight. Alleluia.

24 They see your procession, O God, *
    your procession into the sanctuary, my God and my King.

25 The singers go before, musicians follow after, *
    in the midst of maidens playing upon the hand-drums.

26 Bless God in the congregation; *
    bless the LORD, you that are of the fountain of Israel.

27 There is Benjamin, least of the tribes, at the head;
  the princes of Judah in a company; *
    and the princes of Zebulon and Naphtali.

28 Send forth your strength, O God; *
    establish, O God, what you have wrought for us.

29 Kings shall bring gifts to you, *
    for your temple's sake at Jerusalem.

30 Rebuke the wild beast of the reeds, *
    and the peoples, a herd of wild bulls with its calves.

31 Trample down those who lust after silver; *
    scatter the peoples that delight in war.

32 Let tribute be brought out of Egypt; *
    let Ethiopia stretch out her hands to God.

33 Sing to God, O kingdoms of the earth; *
    sing praises to the Lord.

34 He rides in the heavens, the ancient heavens; *
    he sends forth his voice, his mighty voice.

35 Ascribe power to God; *
    his majesty is over Israel;
    his strength is in the skies.

36 How wonderful is God in his holy places! *
   the God of Israel giving strength and power to his people!
   Blessed be God!

Antiphon As they were watching, he was lifted up, and a cloud took him out of their sight. Alleluia.

Responsory (Jn. 20:17)
I am ascending to my Father and your Father.
   – **Alleluia, alleluia.**
To my God and your God.
   – **Alleluia, alleluia.**
Glory to the Father and to the Son and to the Holy Spirit.
I am ascending to my Father and your Father.
   – **Alleluia, alleluia.**

Magnificat Antiphon Father, I have made your name known to those whom you gave me. I am praying for them because I am coming to you. Alleluia.

Litany
Christ, King of glory, as you have entered into the glory of the Father, draw us to you in heart and mind.
Lord, have mercy.
Christ, Center of the Cosmos, your fullness fills the universe, open our eyes to behold you in the natural world and in the people we meet.
Christ, have mercy.
Christ, Judge of the living and the dead, teach us to live upright lives that we may be worthy to join you in heaven.
Lord, have mercy.

Invitation to the Lord's Prayer The Father has opened the gates of heaven to receive his beloved Son so let our minds and hearts ascend with Christ to dwell with the Father.

Collect Almighty God, whose blessed Son our Savior Jesus Christ ascended far above all heavens that he might fill all things: Mercifully give us faith to perceive that, according to his promise, he abides with his Church on earth, even to the end of the ages; through Jesus Christ our Lord, who lives and reigns with you and the Holy Spirit, one God, in glory everlasting. Amen.

The Blessing
May we have the power to comprehend, with all the saints, what is the breadth and length and height and depth, and to know the love of Christ

that surpasses knowledge, so that we may be filled with all the fullness of God. **Amen.**

Ascension Day Morning Prayer

Invitatory Alleluia. Christ, the Lord is ascended into heaven: Come let us adore. Alleluia.

Hymn Hail thee festival day *Hymnal 216*

Antiphon 1 The eleven disciples went to Galilee, to the mountain to which Jesus had directed them. Alleluia.

Psalms from Sunday Week 2 Morning Prayer

Antiphon 2 All authority in heaven and on earth has been given to me. Go therefore and make disciples of all nations, and baptize them. Alleluia.

Antiphon 3 I am with you always, to the end of the age. Alleluia.

Responsory One (Eph. 4:8)
Christ ascended on high.
   – **Alleluia, alleluia.**
He made captivity itself a captive.
   – **Alleluia, alleluia.**
Glory to the Father and to the Son and to the Holy Spirit.
Christ ascended on high.
   – **Alleluia, alleluia.**

Canticle You are God   *Te Deum laudamus, Page 667*

Alternate Canticle Rejoice, all you people *Omnes gentes plaudite*
(Based on the Ascension Sequence Omnes Gentes Plaudite)

Antiphon The Savior returns to the home of heaven. O sound the trumpet! Alleluia.

O clap your hands, all you people.
Cry out to God, with a shout of gladness.
For Christ has triumphed
The Savior returns to the home of heaven.
O sound the trumpet!

Christ, the new Moses, enters into the tabernacle.
The people of God behold the wonder of this mystery.
Christ, the new Elijah, rides the fiery chariot into heaven.
Christ sends a double gift of the Spirit.
O sing your praise with lyre and harp!

Christ, the new Jacob, has crossed the Jordan
Carrying the staff of the wood of the cross
He has brought the grace of new life to God's people.
He has reconciled all who were estranged!
O praise with strings and pipe!

O King of Glory, strong and mighty,
You have shown yourself mighty in the battle with death.
The everlasting doors of life you open
To all who have clean hands and pure hearts.
O praise with resounding cymbals!

The Father draws you to your home in heaven
By the power of love, you have overcome death
The Spirit rejoices in your glorified body.
We praise you, Ascended Christ,
who has restored our human dignity.
O praise with every energy of the universe!

Antiphon The Savior returns to the home of heaven. O sound the trumpet! Alleluia.

Responsory Two (Ps. 47:5)
God has gone up with a shout.
   – Alleluia, alleluia.
The Lord with the sound of the ram's horn.
   – Alleluia, alleluia.
Glory to the Father and to the Son and to the Holy Spirit.
God has gone up with a shout.
   – Alleluia, alleluia.

Benedictus Antiphon I am ascending to my Father and to you Father, to my God and to your God. Alleluia.

Litany
Christ, Ascended Lord, shed your light into our hearts that we may be one with you and one with one another.
Lord, have mercy.
Christ, Victorious Lord, share your triumph with us that we may valiantly shun evil and seek holiness.
Christ, have mercy.
Christ, Exalted Lord, remember us in your reign that we may find our place with you in our heavenly homeland.
Lord, have mercy.

Invitation to the Lord's Prayer Christ promised to remain with us until the end of time so we raise our hearts to heaven and pray with Christ to the Father in heaven.

Collect Grant, we pray, Almighty God, that as we believe your only begotten Son our Lord Jesus Christ to have ascended into heaven, so we may also in heart and mind there ascend, and with him continually dwell; who lives and reigns with you and the Holy Spirit, one God, for ever and ever. Amen.

The Blessing
May we who have been raised with Christ, seek the things that are above, where Christ is, seated at the right hand of God. **Amen.**

Ascension Day Noonday Prayer

Hymn A hymn of glory let us sing *Hymnal 217*

Psalm 47 *Omnes gentes, plaudite*

Antiphon God has gone up with a shout. Alleluia.

1 Clap your hands, all you peoples; *
    shout to God with a cry of joy.

2 For the LORD Most High is to be feared; *
    he is the great King over all the earth.

3 He subdues the peoples under us, *
    and the nations under our feet.

4 He chooses our inheritance for us, *
    the pride of Jacob whom he loves.

5 God has gone up with a shout, *
    the LORD with the sound of the ram's-horn.

6 Sing praises to God, sing praises; *
    sing praises to our King, sing praises.

7 For God is King of all the earth; *
    sing praises with all your skill.

8 God reigns over the nations; *
    God sits upon his holy throne.

9 The nobles of the peoples have gathered together *
    with the people of the God of Abraham.

10 The rulers of the earth belong to God, *
    and he is highly exalted.

Psalm 48   *Magnus Dominus*

1 Great is the LORD, and highly to be praised; *
    in the city of our God is his holy hill.

2 Beautiful and lofty, the joy of all the earth,
  is the hill of Zion, *
    the very center of the world and the city of the great King.

3 God is in her citadels; *
    he is known to be her sure refuge.

4 Behold, the kings of the earth assembled *
    and marched forward together.

5 They looked and were astounded; *
    they retreated and fled in terror.

6 Trembling seized them there; *
    they writhed like a woman in childbirth,
    like ships of the sea when the east wind shatters them.

7 As we have heard, so have we seen,
  in the city of the LORD of hosts, in the city of our God; *
    God has established her for ever.

8 We have waited in silence on your loving-kindness, O God, *
    in the midst of your temple.

9 Your praise, like your Name, O God,
  reaches to the world's end; *
    your right hand is full of justice.

10 Let Mount Zion be glad
   and the cities of Judah rejoice, *
     because of your judgments.

11 Make the circuit of Zion;
   walk round about her; *
     count the number of her towers.

12 Consider well her bulwarks;
   examine her strongholds; *
     that you may tell those who come after.

13 This God is our God for ever and ever; *
     he shall be our guide for evermore.

Psalm 98 *Cantate Domino*

The throne of God and of the Lamb will be in it, and his servants will worship him; they will see his face. Rev. 22:3-4

1 Sing to the LORD a new song, *
 for he has done marvelous things.

2 With his right hand and his holy arm *
 has he won for himself the victory.

3 The LORD has made known his victory; *
 his righteousness has he openly shown
 in the sight of the nations.

4 He remembers his mercy and faithfulness
 to the house of Israel, *
 and all the ends of the earth have seen
 the victory of our God.

5 Shout with joy to the LORD, all you lands; *
 lift up your voice, rejoice, and sing.

6 Sing to the LORD with the harp, *
 with the harp and the voice of song.

7 With trumpets and the sound of the horn *
 shout with joy before the King, the LORD.

8 Let the sea make a noise and all that is in it, *
 the lands and those who dwell therein.

9 Let the rivers clap their hands, *
 and let the hills ring out with joy before the LORD,
 when he comes to judge the earth.

10 In righteousness shall he judge the world *
 and the peoples with equity.

Antiphon God has gone up with a shout. Alleluia.

Reading Hebrews 8: 1b-3a
We have such a high priest, one who is seated at the right hand of the throne of the Majesty in the heavens, a minister in the sanctuary and the true tent that the Lord, and not any mortal, has set up. For every high priest is appointed to offer gifts and sacrifices.

Verse and Response
Do not let your hearts be troubled. Alleluia.
I am going to the Father. Alleluia.

Collect Almighty God, whose blessed Son our Savior Jesus Christ ascended far above all heavens that he might fill all things: Mercifully give us faith to perceive that, according to his promise, he abides with his Church on earth, even to the end of the ages; through Jesus Christ our Lord, who lives and reigns with you and the Holy Spirit, one God, in glory everlasting. Amen.

Ascension Day Evening Prayer II

Hymn O Lord most high eternal King *Hymnal 220*

Antiphon 1 You have ascended in glory, O Christ, our God, giving joy to your disciples by the promise of the Holy Spirit. Alleluia.

Psalms from Sunday Week 2 Evening Prayer II

Antiphon 2 In your ascension into glory, O Christ, you united earth to heaven. Alleluia.

Antiphon 3 You are not separated from those who love you, O Christ, but you remain with them and assure them saying: I am with you and no one will be against you. Alleluia.

Responsory (Jn. 20:17)
I am ascending to my Father and your Father.
   – Alleluia, alleluia.
To my God and your God.
   – Alleluia, alleluia.
Glory to the Father and to the Son and to the Holy Spirit.
I am ascending to my Father and your Father.
   – Alleluia, alleluia.

Magnificat Antiphon Alleluia. O Christ, the King of glory, you opened the Kingdom of heaven to all believers. Do not abandon us but send us the Father's gift of the Spirit. Alleluia.

Litany
Giver of all good gifts, send us your Holy Spirit to cry out in our hearts: "Abba, Father."
Lord, have mercy.
Restorer of all brokenness, heal all that is broken in our hearts, bodies and souls.
Christ, have mercy.
Judge of all people, teach us holiness of life that we may join you with all the faithful departed.
Lord, have mercy.

Invitation to the Lord's Prayer The Father has opened the gates of heaven to receive his beloved Son so let our minds and hearts ascend with Christ to dwell with the Father.

Collect Grant, we pray, Almighty God, that as we believe your only begotten Son our Lord Jesus Christ to have ascended into heaven, so we may also in heart and mind there ascend, and with him continually dwell; who lives and reigns with you and the Holy Spirit, one God, for ever and ever. Amen.

The Blessing
May we have the power to comprehend, with all the saints, what is the breadth and length and height and depth, and to know the love of Christ that surpasses knowledge, so that we may be filled with all the fullness of God. **Amen.**

Pentecost

Principal Feast
Evening Prayer I

Hymn Hail this joyful day's return *Hymnal 223*

Antiphon 1 When the day of Pentecost had come, they were all together in one place. Alleluia.
Psalms from Sunday Week 1 Evening Prayer I
Antiphon 2 Divided tongues, as of fire, appeared among them, and a tongue rested on each of them. Alleluia.
Antiphon 3 All of them were filled with the Holy Spirit and began to speak in other languages, as the Spirit gave them ability. Alleluia.

Responsory (Jn. 14:16, 17)
The Father will send the Advocate.
    — Alleluia, alleluia.
You know the Advocate, because he abides with you.
    — Alleluia, alleluia.
Glory to the Father and to the Son and to the Holy Spirit.
The Father will send the Advocate.
    — Alleluia, alleluia.

Magnificat Antiphon Come, Holy Spirit, fill the hearts of your faithful people and kindle in them the fire of your love. While they speak diverse languages, you unite all people in the one faith. Alleluia. .

Litany
Your Spirit hovered over the creation and transformed chaos into order, resolve the conflicts in our world with your peaceful presence.
Lord, have mercy.
Your Spirit sanctified the waters at your baptism bringing a new holiness to our world; continue to make us holy by your sacraments.
Christ, have mercy.
Your Spirit raised up Christ from death to new life; so raise all the departed to enjoy you in heaven.
Lord, have mercy.

Invitation to the Lord's Prayer The Spirit cries out through us, Abba, Father, so with Christ, we pray in the Spirit.

Collect Almighty God, on this day you opened the way of eternal life to every race and nation by the promised gift of your Holy Spirit: Shed abroad this gift throughout the world by the preaching of the Gospel, that it may reach to the ends of the earth; through Jesus Christ our Lord, who lives and reigns with you, in the unity of the Holy Spirit, one God, for ever and ever. Amen.

The Blessing
May the grace of the Lord Jesus Christ, the love of God, and the communion of the Holy Spirit be with all of us. **Amen.**

Pentecost Morning Prayer

Invitatory Alleluia. The Spirit of the Lord renews the face of the earth: Come let us adore. Alleluia.

Hymn Come thou Holy Spirit *Hymnal 226*

Antiphon 1 The Spirit of the Lord has filled the world, and that which holds all things together knows what is said. Alleluia.
Psalms from Sunday Week 1 Morning Prayer
Antiphon 2 The wind blows where it chooses, and you hear the sound of it, but you do not know where it comes from or where it goes. So it is with everyone who is born of the Spirit. Alleluia.
Antiphon 3 Jesus breathed on them and said to them, "Receive the Holy Spirit." Alleluia.

Responsory One (Acts 2:4)
All of them were filled with the Holy Spirit.
    – Alleluia, alleluia.
They began to speak.
    – Alleluia, alleluia.

Glory to the Father and to the Son and to the Holy Spirit.
All of them were filled with the Holy Spirit.
– Alleluia, alleluia.

Canticle You are God   *Te Deum laudamus, Page 667*

Responsory Two (Wis. 1:7)
The Spirit of the Lord fills the earth.
– Alleluia, alleluia.
The Spirit embraces all things.
– Alleluia, alleluia.
Glory to the Father and to the Son and to the Holy Spirit.
The Spirit of the Lord fills the earth.
– Alleluia, alleluia.

Benedictus Antiphon The Advocate, the Holy Spirit, whom the Father will send in my name, will teach you everything, and remind you of all that I have said to you. Alleluia.

Litany
Holy Spirit, fire of God's love, burn in our hearts as the fire of the sun burns in the sky.
Lord, have mercy.
Holy Spirit, water of God's grace, satisfy our thirst as streams in the desert.
Christ, have mercy.
Holy Spirit, light of God's wisdom, expand our minds as the light of dawn fills the world.
Lord, have mercy.

Invitation to the Lord's Prayer Christ pours upon us the gift of the Spirit's love, let us return that love in the grace of the Spirit.

Collect O God, who on this day taught the hearts of your faithful people by sending to them the light of your Holy Spirit: Grant us by the same Spirit to have a right judgment in all things, and evermore to rejoice in his holy comfort; through Jesus Christ your Son our Lord, who lives and reigns with you, in the unity of the Holy Spirit, one God, for ever and ever. Amen.

The Blessing
May God grant that you may be strengthened in your inner being with power through his Spirit, and that Christ may dwell in your hearts through faith, as you are being rooted and grounded in love. **Amen.**

Pentecost Noonday Prayer

Hymn Holy Spirit ever living *Hymnal 511*

Antiphon God's love has been poured into our hearts through the Holy Spirit that has been given to us. Alleluia.
Psalms from Sunday Week 1 Noonday Prayer

Reading 2 Corinthians 3: 17-18
The Lord is the Spirit, and where the Spirit of the Lord is, there is freedom. And all of us, with unveiled faces, seeing the glory of the Lord as though reflected in a mirror, are being transformed into the same image from one degree of glory to another; for this comes from the Lord, the Spirit.

Verse and Response
The Spirit searches everything. Alleluia.
Even the depths of God. Alleluia.

Collect Almighty God, on this day you opened the way of eternal life to every race and nation by the promised gift of your Holy Spirit: Shed abroad this gift throughout the world by the preaching of the Gospel, that it may reach to the ends of the earth; through Jesus Christ our Lord, who lives and reigns with you, in the unity of the Holy Spirit, one God, for ever and ever. Amen.

Pentecost Evening Prayer II

Hymn Come Holy Ghost *Hymnal 502*

Antiphon 1 There is one body and one Spirit, just as you were called to the one hope of your calling, one Lord, one faith, one baptism. Alleluia.
Psalms from Sunday Week 1 Evening Prayer II
Antiphon 2 God has sent the Spirit of his Son into our hearts, crying, "Abba! Father!" Alleluia.
Antiphon 3 By this we know that we abide in God and God in us, because God has given us the Spirit. Alleluia.

Responsory (Acts 2:11)
The apostles spoke.
    – **Alleluia, alleluia.**
About God's deeds of power.
    – **Alleluia, alleluia.**
Glory to the Father and to the Son and to the Holy Spirit.
The apostles spoke.
    – **Alleluia, alleluia.**

Magnificat Antiphon Today we celebrate the fullness of the Paschal Feast. Alleluia. Today the Holy Spirit descended in fire on the assembled apostles. Alleluia. Today the Spirit sends us out into the world to preach the Gospel and baptize the nations. Alleluia. Alleluia.

Litany

Your Spirit hovered over the creation and transformed chaos into order, resolve the conflicts in our world with your peaceful presence.
Lord, have mercy.
Your Spirit sanctified the waters at your baptism bringing a new holiness to our world; continue to make us holy by your sacraments.
Christ, have mercy.
Your Spirit raised up Christ from death to new life; so raise all the departed to enjoy you in heaven.
Lord, have mercy.

Invitation to the Lord's Prayer The Spirit cries out through us, Abba, Father, so with Christ, we pray in the Spirit.

Collect O God, who on this day taught the hearts of your faithful people by sending to them the light of your Holy Spirit: Grant us by the same Spirit to have a right judgment in all things, and evermore to rejoice in his holy comfort; through Jesus Christ your Son our Lord, who lives and reigns with you, in the unity of the Holy Spirit, one God, for ever and ever. Amen.

The Blessing

May the grace of the Lord Jesus Christ, the love of God, and the communion of the Holy Spirit be with all of us. **Amen.**

The Easter Season concludes with Evening Prayer II of Pentecost.
The Ember Days, traditionally observed on the Wednesday, Friday, and Saturday
after the Day of Pentecost. On those days use the daily office of the day with proper
parts taken from the Common of Ember Days

The Ordinary Of The Daily Office

Morning Prayer

The Invitation
Officiant: Lord open our lips.
People: And our mouth shall proclaim your praise.
Officiant and People
Glory to the Father, and to the Son, and to the Holy Spirit:
as it was in the beginning, is now, and will be for ever. Amen.
Except in Lent, add **Alleluia.**

The Invitatory
The Daily Office begins with the Invitatory. While the Rule of St. Benedict provides for Psalm 95 this set of alternate Invitatory Psalms is taken from the Thesaurus Liturgiae Horarum Monasticae. The antiphon for the seasons or the proper or common of the saints are found in the assigned places. The antiphon is repeated after each section of the Invitatory Psalm.

Sunday Invitatory Psalm
Psalm 95 *Venite, exultemus*

(*Antiphon*)

1 Come, let us sing to the LORD; *
     let us shout for joy to the Rock of our salvation.
2 Let us come before his presence with thanksgiving *
     and raise a loud shout to him with psalms.

(*Antiphon*)

3 For the LORD is a great God, *
     and a great King above all gods.
4 In his hand are the caverns of the earth, *
     and the heights of the hills are his also.
5 The sea is his, for he made it, *
     and his hands have molded the dry land.

(*Antiphon*)

6 Come, let us bow down, and bend the knee, *
     and kneel before the LORD our Maker.
7 For he is our God,
     and we are the people of his pasture and the sheep of his hand. *
     Oh, that today you would hearken to his voice!

(*Antiphon*)

8 Harden not your hearts,
     as your forebears did in the wilderness,*
         at Meribah, and on that day at Massah,
         when they tempted me.
9 They put me to the test,*
     though they had seen my works.

(*Antiphon*)

10 Forty years long I detested that generation and said, *
     "This people are wayward in their hearts;
     they do not know my ways."
11 So I swore in my wrath, *
     "They shall not enter into my rest.

(*Antiphon*)

Monday Invitatory Psalm
Psalm 29 *Afferte Domino*

(*Antiphon*)
1 Ascribe to the LORD, you gods, *
    ascribe to the LORD glory and strength.
2 Ascribe to the LORD the glory due his Name; *
    worship the LORD in the beauty of holiness.
(*Antiphon*)

3 The voice of the LORD is upon the waters;
  the God of glory thunders; *
    the LORD is upon the mighty waters.
4 The voice of the LORD is a powerful voice; *
    the voice of the LORD is a voice of splendor.
(*Antiphon*)

5 The voice of the LORD breaks the cedar trees; *
    the LORD breaks the cedars of Lebanon;
6 He makes Lebanon skip like a calf, *
    and Mount Hermon like a young wild ox.
(*Antiphon*)

7 The voice of the LORD splits the flames of fire;
  the voice of the LORD shakes the wilderness; *
    the LORD shakes the wilderness of Kadesh.
8 The voice of the LORD makes the oak trees writhe *
    and strips the forests bare.
9 And in the temple of the LORD *
    all are crying, "Glory!"
(*Antiphon*)

10 The LORD sits enthroned above the flood; *
    the LORD sits enthroned as King for evermore.
11 The LORD shall give strength to his people; *
    the LORD shall give his people the blessing of peace.
(*Antiphon*)

Tuesday Invitatory Psalm
Psalm 8 *Domine, Dominus noster*

(*Antiphon*)

1 O Lᴏʀᴅ our Governor, *
    how exalted is your Name in all the world!
2 Out of the mouths of infants and children *
    your majesty is praised above the heavens.
3 You have set up a stronghold against your adversaries, *
    to quell the enemy and the avenger.

(*Antiphon*)

4 When I consider your heavens, the work of your fingers, *
    the moon and the stars you have set in their courses,
5 What is man that you should be mindful of him? *
    the son of man that you should seek him out?

(*Antiphon*)

6 You have made him but little lower than the angels; *
    you adorn him with glory and honor;
7 You give him mastery over the works of your hands; *
    you put all things under his feet:

(*Antiphon*)

8 All sheep and oxen, *
    even the wild beasts of the field,
9 The birds of the air, the fish of the sea, *
    and whatsoever walks in the paths of the sea.
10 O Lᴏʀᴅ our Governor, *
    how exalted is your Name in all the world!

(*Antiphon*)

Wednesday Invitatory Psalm
Psalm 95 *Venite, exultemus*

(Antiphon)

1 Come, let us sing to the LORD; *
    let us shout for joy to the Rock of our salvation.
2 Let us come before his presence with thanksgiving *
    and raise a loud shout to him with psalms.

(Antiphon)

3 For the LORD is a great God, *
    and a great King above all gods.
4 In his hand are the caverns of the earth, *
    and the heights of the hills are his also.
5 The sea is his, for he made it, *
    and his hands have molded the dry land.

(Antiphon)

6 Come, let us bow down, and bend the knee, *
    and kneel before the LORD our Maker.
7 For he is our God,
    and we are the people of his pasture and the sheep of his hand. *
    Oh, that today you would hearken to his voice!

(Antiphon)

8 Harden not your hearts,
    as your forebears did in the wilderness,*
        at Meribah, and on that day at Massah,
        when they tempted me.
9 They put me to the test,*
    though they had seen my works.

(Antiphon)

10 Forty years long I detested that generation and said, *
    "This people are wayward in their hearts;
    they do not know my ways."
11 So I swore in my wrath, *
    "They shall not enter into my rest.

(Antiphon)

Thursday Invitatory Psalm
Psalm 100 *Jubilate Deo*

(*Antiphon*)

1 Be joyful in the LORD, all you lands; *
    serve the LORD with gladness
    and come before his presence with a song.

(*Antiphon*)

2 Know this: The LORD himself is God; *
    he himself has made us, and we are his;
    we are his people and the sheep of his pasture.

(*Antiphon*)

3 Enter his gates with thanksgiving;
   go into his courts with praise; *
    give thanks to him and call upon his Name.

(*Antiphon*)

4 For the LORD is good;
   his mercy is everlasting; *
    and his faithfulness endures from age to age.

(*Antiphon*)

Friday Invitatory Psalm
Psalm 95 *Venite, exultemus*

(Antiphon)
1 Come, let us sing to the LORD; *
 let us shout for joy to the Rock of our salvation.
2 Let us come before his presence with thanksgiving *
 and raise a loud shout to him with psalms.

(Antiphon)

3 For the LORD is a great God, *
 and a great King above all gods.
4 In his hand are the caverns of the earth, *
 and the heights of the hills are his also.
5 The sea is his, for he made it, *
 and his hands have molded the dry land.

(Antiphon)

6 Come, let us bow down, and bend the knee, *
 and kneel before the LORD our Maker.
7 For he is our God,
 and we are the people of his pasture and the sheep of his hand. *
 Oh, that today you would hearken to his voice!

(Antiphon)

8 Harden not your hearts,
 as your forebears did in the wilderness,*
  at Meribah, and on that day at Massah,
  when they tempted me.
9 They put me to the test,*
 though they had seen my works.

(Antiphon)

10 Forty years long I detested that generation and said, *
 "This people are wayward in their hearts;
 they do not know my ways."
11 So I swore in my wrath, *
 "They shall not enter into my rest.

(Antiphon)

Saturday Invitatory Psalm
Psalm 122   *Lætatus sum*

(*Antiphon*)

1 I was glad when they said to me, *
    "Let us go to the house of the LORD."
2 Now our feet are standing *
    within your gates, O Jerusalem.

(*Antiphon*)

3 Jerusalem is built as a city *
    that is at unity with itself;
4 To which the tribes go up,
  the tribes of the LORD, *
    the assembly of Israel,
    to praise the Name of the LORD.
5 For there are the thrones of judgment, *
    the thrones of the house of David.

(*Antiphon*)

6 Pray for the peace of Jerusalem: *
    "May they prosper who love you.
7 Peace be within your walls *
    and quietness within your towers.

(*Antiphon*)

8 For my brethren and companions' sake, *
    I pray for your prosperity.
9 Because of the house of the LORD our God, *
    I will seek to do you good."

(*Antiphon*)

**In Easter Week, in place of an Invitatory Psalm,
the Pascha Nostra is said.
It may also be used daily until the Day of Pentecost.**

*The Antiphon for the Pascha Nostra is either of the season
or of the Feast of the day.*

Easter Alleluia. The Lord is risen indeed: Come let us adore. Alleluia.
Ascension Alleluia. Christ the Lord has ascended into heaven: Come let us adore him. Alleluia.
Pentecost Alleluia. The Spirit of the Lord renews the face of the earth: Come let us adore. Alleluia.

Christ our Passover *Pascha nostrum*
1 Corinthians 5:7-8; Romans 6:9-11; 1 Corinthians 15:20-22

(Antiphon)
Alleluia.
Christ our Passover has been sacrificed for us; *
    therefore let us keep the feast,
Not with old leaven, the leaven of malice and evil, *
    but with the unleavened bread of sincerity and truth. Alleluia.
(Antiphon)

Christ being raised from the dead will never die again; *
    death no longer has dominion over him.
The death that he died, he died to sin, once for all; *
    but the life he lives, he lives to God.
So also consider yourselves dead to sin, *
    and alive to God in Jesus Christ our Lord. Alleluia.
(Antiphon)

Christ has been raised from the dead, *
    the first fruits of those who have fallen asleep.
For since by a man came death, *
    by a man has come also the resurrection of the dead.
For as in Adam all die, *
    so in Christ shall all be made alive. Alleluia.
(Antiphon)

Hymn
The Hymn follows the Invitatory. The Hymn is found in the proper of either the season or of the saints.

Psalmody.
The Psalmody consists of three psalms with antiphons. The Psalms are found in the appropriate week of the Psalter. For major feasts and lesser feasts the antiphons are taken from the Proper of the day or from the Common of the Saints. The antiphons for the season are found in the Psalter.

Reading One
The office is structured so that there will be two readings at Morning Prayer. The readings are used in the order in which they appear in the Daily Office Lectionary. For Principal Feasts, Feasts of our Lord and Major Feasts, the readings are found in the lectionary for Holy Days.

Response to the Word of God
A period of silence appropriately follows the reading. The Responsory follows the period of silence.

The First Canticle
The First Canticle continues the prayer. An appropriate antiphon is included. The antiphons are found with the canticle. For Major and Lesser Feasts, the Canticle is taken from the proper of the saints. On Major Feasts, when a Proper Canticle is not assigned the *Te Deum laudamus* is used.

Canticle You are God *Te Deum laudamus*

You are God: we praise you;
You are the Lord: we acclaim you;
You are the eternal Father:
All creation worships you.
To you all angels, all the powers of heaven,
Cherubim and Seraphim, sing in endless praise:
   Holy, holy, holy Lord, God of power and might,
   heaven and earth are full of your glory.
The glorious company of apostles praise you.
The noble fellowship of prophets praise you.
The white-robed army of martyrs praise you.
Throughout the world the holy Church acclaims you;
   Father, of majesty unbounded,
   your true and only Son, worthy of all worship,
   and the Holy Spirit, advocate and guide.

You, Christ, are the king of glory,
the eternal Son of the Father.
When you became man to set us free
you did not shun the Virgin's womb.
You overcame the sting of death
and opened the kingdom of heaven to all believers.
You are seated at God's right hand in glory.
We believe that you will come and be our judge.
   Come then, Lord, and help your people,
   bought with the price of your own blood,
   and bring us with your saints
   to glory everlasting.

The Second Reading

Response to the Word of God
A period of silence appropriately follows the reading. The Responsory follows the period of silence.

The Gospel Canticle
The Gospel Canticle, the Song of Zechariah, continues the prayer. An appropriate antiphon is included. For the Seasons of the Church Year, the antiphon is found in the material for that day. For Major and Lesser Feasts, the antiphon is taken from the proper or common of the saints. The Sign of the Cross is made at the start of the Gospel Canticle.

The Song of Zechariah *Benedictus Dominus Deus*
Luke 1: 68-79

Blessed be the Lord, the God of Israel; *
   he has come to his people and set them free.
He has raised up for us a mighty savior, *
   born of the house of his servant David.
Through his holy prophets he promised of old,
   that he would save us from our enemies, *
   from the hands of all who hate us.
He promised to show mercy to our fathers *
   and to remember his holy covenant.
This was the oath he swore to our father Abraham, *
   to set us free from the hands of our enemies,
Free to worship him without fear, *
   holy and righteous in his sight
   all the days of our life.

You, my child, shall be called the prophet of the Most High, *
   for you will go before the Lord to prepare his way,
To give his people knowledge of salvation *
   by the forgiveness of their sins.
In the tender compassion of our God *
   the dawn from on high shall break upon us,
To shine on those who dwell in darkness and the
      shadow of death, *
   and to guide our feet into the way of peace.

The Litany
Intercessions are offered for the needs of the world, of the church and of the persons saying the office. Intercessions are found in the office of the day.

The Lord's Prayer
There is an Invitation to begin the Lord's Prayer.

Our Father in heaven,
   hallowed be your Name,
   your kingdom come,
   your will be done,
      on earth as in heaven.
Give us today our daily bread.
Forgive us our sins
   as we forgive those
      who sin against us.
Save us from the time of trial,
   and deliver us from evil.
For the kingdom, the power,
   and the glory are yours,
      now and for ever. Amen.

The Collect
After the Lord's Prayer, the concluding collect is said. It is said without an Invitation. The collect is taken from the Sunday, the season, or from the Major or Lesser Feast.

The Blessing
Let us bless the Lord. (Alleluia. Alleluia.)
Thanks be to God. (Alleluia. Alleluia.)

The Blessing is taken from the Season, the Sanctoral or the Ferial.

The Book of Common Prayer Conclusion of Morning Prayer

For those who prefer the structure of the office found in the Book of Common Prayer the following pattern would be followed after the second canticle. The Collect of the Day would be followed by a second collect and the collect for mission concludes the collects.

The Apostles' Creed

Officiant and People together, all standing

I believe in God, the Father almighty,
   creator of heaven and earth;
I believe in Jesus Christ, his only Son, our Lord.
   He was conceived by the power of the Holy Spirit
      and born of the Virgin Mary.
   He suffered under Pontius Pilate,
      was crucified, died, and was buried.
   He descended to the dead.
   On the third day he rose again.
   He ascended into heaven,
      and is seated at the right hand of the Father.
   He will come again to judge the living and the dead.
I believe in the Holy Spirit,
   the holy catholic Church,
   the communion of saints,
   the forgiveness of sins
   the resurrection of the body,
   and the life everlasting. Amen.

The Prayers

The People stand or kneel

Officiant   The Lord be with you.
People And also with you.
Officiant   Let us pray.

Our Father, who art in heaven,	Our Father in heaven,
hallowed be thy Name,	hallowed be your Name,
thy kingdom come,	your kingdom come,
thy will be done,	your will be done,
on earth as it is in heaven.	on earth as in heaven.
Give us this day our daily bread.	Give us today our daily bread.

And forgive us our trespasses,
    as we forgive those
        who trespass against us.
And lead us not into temptation,
    but deliver us from evil.
For thine is the kingdom,
    and the power, and the glory,
    for ever and ever. Amen.

Forgive us our sins
    as we forgive those
        who sin against us.
Save us from the time of trial,
    and deliver us from evil.
For the kingdom, the power,
    and the glory are yours,
    now and for ever. Amen.

Then follows one of these sets of Suffrages
Suffrages A
V. Show us your mercy, O Lord;
R. And grant us your salvation.
V. Clothe your ministers with righteousness;
R. Let your people sing with joy.
V. Give peace, O Lord, in all the world;
R. For only in you can we live in safety.
V. Lord, keep this nation under your care;
R. And guide us in the way of justice and truth.
V. Let your way be known upon earth;
R. Your saving health among all nations.
V. Let not the needy, O Lord, be forgotten;
R. Nor the hope of the poor be taken away.
V. Create in us clean hearts, O God;
R. And sustain us with your Holy Spirit.

Suffrages B
V. Save your people, Lord, and bless your inheritance;
R. Govern them and uphold them, now and always.
V. Day by day we bless you;
R. We praise your name for ever.
V. Lord, keep us from all sin today;
R. Have mercy upon us, Lord, have mercy.
V. Lord, show us your love and mercy;
R. For we put our trust in you.
V. In you, Lord, is our hope;
R. And we shall never hope in vain.

The Officiant then says one or more of the following Collects
The Collect of the Day

A Collect for Sundays
O God, you make us glad with the weekly remembrance of the glorious resurrection of your Son our Lord: Give us this day such blessing through our worship of you, that the week to come may be spent in your favor; through Jesus Christ our Lord. Amen.

A Collect for Fridays
Almighty God, whose most dear Son went not up to joy but first he suffered pain, and entered not into glory before he was crucified: Mercifully grant that we, walking in the way of the cross, may find it none other than the way of life and peace; through Jesus Christ our Lord. Amen.

A Collect for Saturdays
Almighty God, who after the creation of the world rested from all your works and sanctified a day of rest for all your creatures: Grant that we, putting away all earthly anxieties, may be duly prepared for the service of your sanctuary, and that our rest here upon earth may be a preparation for the eternal rest promised to your people in heaven; through Jesus Christ our Lord. Amen.

A Collect for the Renewal of Life
O God, the King eternal, whose light divides the day from the night and turns the shadow of death into the morning: Drive far from us all wrong desires, incline our hearts to keep your law, and guide our feet into the way of peace; that, having done your will with cheerfulness while it was day, we may, when night comes, rejoice to give you thanks; through Jesus Christ our Lord. Amen.

A Collect for Peace
O God, the author of peace and lover of concord, to know you is eternal life and to serve you is perfect freedom: Defend us, your humble servants, in all assaults of our enemies; that we, surely trusting in your defense, may not fear the power of any adversaries; through the might of Jesus Christ our Lord. Amen.

A Collect for Grace
Lord God, almighty and everlasting Father, you have brought us in safety to this new day: Preserve us with your mighty power, that we may not fall into sin, nor be overcome by adversity; and in all we do, direct us to the fulfilling of your purpose; through Jesus Christ our Lord. Amen.

A Collect for Guidance
Heavenly Father, in you we live and move and have our being: We humbly pray you so to guide and govern us by your Holy Spirit, that in all the cares and occupations of our life we may not forget you, but may remember that we are ever walking in your sight; through Jesus Christ our Lord. Amen.

Then, unless the Eucharist or a form of general intercession is to follow, one of these prayers for mission is added
Almighty and everlasting God, by whose Spirit the whole body of your faithful people is governed and sanctified: Receive our supplications and prayers which we offer before you for all members of your holy Church, that in their vocation and ministry they may truly and devoutly serve you; through our Lord and Savior Jesus Christ. Amen.
or this
O God, you have made of one blood all the peoples of the earth, and sent your blessed Son to preach peace to those who are far off and to those who are near: Grant that people everywhere may seek after you and find you; bring the nations into your fold; pour out your Spirit upon all flesh; and hasten the coming of your kingdom; through Jesus Christ our Lord. Amen.
or the following
Lord Jesus Christ, you stretched out your arms of love on the hard wood of the cross that everyone might come within the reach of your saving embrace: So clothe us in your Spirit that we, reaching forth our hands in love, may bring those who do not know you to the knowledge and love of you; for the honor of your Name. Amen.

Here may be sung a hymn or anthem.
Authorized intercessions and thanksgivings may follow.

Before the close of the Office one or both of the following may be used
The General Thanksgiving
Almighty God, Father of all mercies,
we your unworthy servants give you humble thanks
for all your goodness and loving-kindness
to us and to all whom you have made.
We bless you for our creation, preservation,
and all the blessings of this life;
but above all for your immeasurable love
in the redemption of the world by our Lord Jesus Christ;
for the means of grace, and for the hope of glory.
And, we pray, give us such an awareness of your mercies,

that with truly thankful hearts we may show forth your praise,
not only with our lips, but in our lives,
by giving up our selves to your service,
and by walking before you
in holiness and righteousness all our days;
through Jesus Christ our Lord,
to whom, with you and the Holy Spirit,
be honor and glory throughout all ages. Amen.

A Prayer of St. Chrysostom
Almighty God, you have given us grace at this time with one accord to make our common supplication to you; and you have promised through your well-beloved Son that when two or three are gathered together in his Name you will be in the midst of them: Fulfill now, O Lord, our desires and petitions as may be best for us; granting us in this world knowledge of your truth, and in the age to come life everlasting. Amen.

Then may be said

Let us bless the Lord.
Thanks be to God.

From Easter Day through the Day of Pentecost "Alleluia, alleluia" may be added to the preceding versicle and response.

The Officiant may then conclude with one of the following

The grace of our Lord Jesus Christ, and the love of God, and the fellowship of the Holy Spirit, be with us all evermore. **Amen.** *2 Corinthians 13:14*

May the God of hope fill us with all joy and peace in believing through the power of the Holy Spirit. **Amen.**
Romans 15:13

Glory to God whose power, working in us, can do infinitely more than we can ask or imagine: Glory to him from generation to generation in the Church, and in Christ Jesus for ever and ever. **Amen.**
Ephesians 3:20,21

Noonday Prayer

Officiant O God, make speed to save us.
People O Lord, make haste to help us.
Officiant and People
**Glory to the Father, and to the Son, and to the Holy Spirit:
as it was in the beginning, is now, and will be for ever. Amen.**
Except in Lent, add **Alleluia.**

Hymn

Psalmody

Reading

Verse and Response

The Short Litany
Officiant Let us pray for the needs of the world. *(Petitions are offered.)*
People Lord, have mercy.
Officiant Let us pray for the needs of the church. *(Petitions are offered.)*
People Christ, have mercy.
Officiant Let us pray for those who ask our prayer. *(Petitions are offered.)*
People Lord, have mercy.

Officiant Let us pray to the Father in the words of Christ, our Lord.
People Our Father in heaven,
   hallowed be your Name,
   your kingdom come,
   your will be done,
     on earth as in heaven.
Give us today our daily bread.
Forgive us our sins
   as we forgive those
     who sin against us.
Save us from the time of trial,
   and deliver us from evil.
For the kingdom, the power,
   and the glory are yours,
     now and for ever. Amen.

Concluding Prayer.
The concluding collect is taken from the proper of the season or the major or lesser feast.

The Conclusion
Officiant Let us bless the Lord. (Alleluia. Alleluia.)
People Thanks be to God. (Alleluia. Alleluia.)

The Book of Common Prayer Conclusion of Noonday Prayer
For those who prefer the structure of the office found in the Book of Common Prayer the following pattern would be followed after the Reading.

A meditation, silent or spoken, may follow.

The Officiant then begins the Prayers

Lord, have mercy.
Christ, have mercy.
Lord, have mercy.

Officiant and People

Our Father, who art in heaven,
  hallowed be thy Name,
    thy kingdom come,
    thy will be done,
      on earth as it is in heaven.
Give us this day our daily bread.
And forgive us our trespasses,
  as we forgive those
    who trespass against us.
And lead us not into temptation,
  but deliver us from evil.
For thine is the kingdom,
  and the power, and the glory,
    for ever and ever. Amen.
	Our Father in heaven,
	  hallowed be your Name,
	    your kingdom come,
	    your will be done,
	      on earth as in heaven.
	Give us today our daily bread.
	Forgive us our sins
	  as we forgive those
	    who sin against us.
	Save us from the time of trial,
	  and deliver us from evil.
	For the kingdom, the power,
	  and the glory are yours,
	    now and for ever. Amen.

Officiant Lord, hear our prayer.
People And let our cry come to you.
Officiant Let us prayer

The Officiant then says one of the following Collect. If desired, the Collect of the Day may be used.

Heavenly Father, send your Holy Spirit into our hearts, to direct and rule us according to your will, to comfort us in all our afflictions, to defend us from all error, and to lead us into all truth; through Jesus Christ our Lord. *Amen.*

Blessed Savior, at this hour you hung upon the cross, stretching out your loving arms: Grant that all the peoples of the earth may look to you and be saved; for your tender mercies' sake. *Amen.*

Almighty Savior, who at noonday called your servant Saint Paul to be an apostle to the Gentiles: We pray you to illumine the world with the radiance of your glory, that all nations may come and worship you; for you live and reign for ever and ever. *Amen.*

Lord Jesus Christ, you said to your apostles, "Peace I give to you; my peace I leave with you:" Regard not our sins, but the faith of your Church, and give to us the peace and unity of that heavenly city, where with the Father and the Holy Spirit you live and reign, now and for ever. *Amen.*

Free intercessions may be offered.

The service concludes as follows

Officiant Let us bless the Lord.
People   Thanks be to God.

Evening Prayer

The Invitation
Officiant O God, make speed to save us.
People O Lord, make haste to help us.
Officiant and People
**Glory to the Father, and to the Son, and to the Holy Spirit:
as it was in the beginning, is now, and will be for ever. Amen.**
Except in Lent, add **Alleluia.**

Hymn
The Hymn is found in the proper of either the season or of the saints.

Psalmody.
The Psalmody consists of three psalms with antiphons. For major feasts and lesser feasts the antiphons are taken from the Proper of the day or from the Common of the Saints. The antiphons for the seasons are found in the Psalter.

Reading
The readings is taken from the Daily Office Lectionary. At Evening Prayer, the reading is taken from the Gospel.

Response to the Word of God
A period of silence follows the reading. The Responsory follows the period of silence.

The Gospel Canticle
The Gospel Canticle, the Song of Mary, continues the prayer. An appropriate antiphon is included. The antiphons are found with the canticle. For Major and Lesser Feasts, the Canticle is taken from the proper of the saints. The Sign of the Cross is made at the start of the Gospel Canticle.

The Song of Mary *Magnificat*
Luke 1:46-55
My soul proclaims the greatness of the Lord,
    my spirit rejoices in God my Savior; *
        for he has looked with favor on his lowly servant.
From this day all generations will call me blessed: *
    the Almighty has done great things for me,
        and holy is his Name.
He has mercy on those who fear him *
    in every generation.

He has shown the strength of his arm, *
    he has scattered the proud in their conceit.
He has cast down the mighty from their thrones, *
    and has lifted up the lowly.
He has filled the hungry with good things, *
    and the rich he has sent away empty.
He has come to the help of his servant Israel, *
    for he has remembered his promise of mercy,
The promise he made to our fathers, *
    to Abraham and his children for ever.

Intercessions

The Rule of St. Benedict provides for intercessions after the Gospel Canticle. The intercessions are related to the season or the saint and ask God to look on the diverse needs of the world and the people of God.

The Lord's Prayer

There is an Invitation to begin the Lord's Prayer.

Our Father in heaven,
  hallowed be your Name,
  your kingdom come,
  your will be done,
    on earth as in heaven.
Give us today our daily bread.
Forgive us our sins
  as we forgive those
    who sin against us.
Save us from the time of trial,
  and deliver us from evil.
For the kingdom, the power,
  and the glory are yours,
    now and for ever. Amen.

The Collect

After the Lord's Prayer, the concluding collect is said. It is said without an Invitation. The collect is taken from the Sunday, the season, if available, or from the Major or Lesser Feast.

The Blessing

Let us bless the Lord. (Alleluia. Alleluia.)
Thanks be to God. (Alleluia. Alleluia.)

The Blessing is taken from the Season, the Sanctoral or the Ferial.

The Book of Common Prayer Conclusion of Evening Prayer

For those who prefer the structure of the office found in the Book of Common Prayer the following pattern would be followed after the canticle. The Collect of the Day would be followed by a second collect and the collect for mission concludes the collects.

The Apostles' Creed

Officiant and People together, all standing

I believe in God, the Father almighty,
   creator of heaven and earth;
I believe in Jesus Christ, his only Son, our Lord.
   He was conceived by the power of the Holy Spirit
      and born of the Virgin Mary.
   He suffered under Pontius Pilate,
      was crucified, died, and was buried.
   He descended to the dead.
   On the third day he rose again.
   He ascended into heaven,
      and is seated at the right hand of the Father.
   He will come again to judge the living and the dead.
I believe in the Holy Spirit,
   the holy catholic Church,
   the communion of saints,
   the forgiveness of sins
   the resurrection of the body,
   and the life everlasting. Amen.

The Prayers

The People stand or kneel

Officiant   The Lord be with you.
People And also with you.
Officiant   Let us pray.

Our Father, who art in heaven,
  hallowed be thy Name,
    thy kingdom come,
    thy will be done,
      on earth as it is in heaven.
Give us this day our daily bread.
	Our Father in heaven,
	  hallowed be your Name,
	    your kingdom come,
	    your will be done,
	      on earth as in heaven.
	Give us today our daily bread.

And forgive us our trespasses,
    as we forgive those
        who trespass against us.
And lead us not into temptation,
    but deliver us from evil.
For thine is the kingdom,
    and the power, and the glory,
        for ever and ever. Amen.
	Forgive us our sins
	    as we forgive those
	        who sin against us.
	Save us from the time of trial,
	    and deliver us from evil.
	For the kingdom, the power,
	    and the glory are yours,
	        now and for ever. Amen.

Then follows one of these sets of Suffrages

A

V. Show us your mercy, O Lord;
R. And grant us your salvation.
V. Clothe your ministers with righteousness;
R. Let your people sing with joy.
V. Give peace, O Lord, in all the world;
R. For only in you can we live in safety.

V. Lord, keep this nation under your care;
R. And guide us in the way of justice and truth.
V. Let your way be known upon earth;
R. Your saving health among all nations.
V. Let not the needy, O Lord, be forgotten;
R. Nor the hope of the poor be taken away.
V. Create in us clean hearts, O God;
R. And sustain us by your Holy Spirit.

B

That this evening may be holy, good, and peaceful,
We entreat you, O Lord.
That your holy angels may lead us in paths of peace and goodwill,
We entreat you, O Lord.
That we may be pardoned and forgiven for our sins and offenses,
We entreat you, O Lord.
That there may be peace to your Church and to the whole world,
We entreat you, O Lord.
That we may depart this life in your faith and fear, and not be condemned before the great judgment seat of Christ,
We entreat you, O Lord.

That we may be bound together by your Holy Spirit in the communion of [_____ and] all your saints, entrusting one another and all our life to Christ,
We entreat you, O Lord.

The Officiant then says one or more of the following Collects

The Collect of the Day

A Collect for Sundays
Lord God, whose Son our Savior Jesus Christ triumphed over the powers of death and prepared for us our place in the new Jerusalem: Grant that we, who have this day given thanks for his resurrection, may praise you in that City of which he is the light, and where he lives and reigns for ever and ever. Amen.

A Collect for Fridays
Lord Jesus Christ, by your death you took away the sting of death: Grant to us your servants so to follow in faith where you have led the way, that we may at length fall asleep peacefully in you and wake up in your likeness; for your tender mercies' sake. *Amen.*

A Collect for Saturdays
O God, the source of eternal light: Shed forth your unending day upon us who watch for you, that our lips may praise you, our lives may bless you, and our worship on the morrow give you glory; through Jesus Christ our Lord. *Amen.*

A Collect for Peace
Most holy God, the source of all good desires, all right judgements, and all just works: Give to us, your servants, that peace which the world cannot give, so that our minds may be fixed on the doing of your will, and that we, being delivered from the fear of all enemies, may live in peace and quietness; through the mercies of Christ Jesus our Savior. *Amen.*

A Collect for Aid against Perils
Be our light in the darkness, O Lord, and in your great mercy defend us from all perils and dangers of this night; for the love of your only Son, our Savior Jesus Christ. *Amen.*

A Collect for Protection
O God, the life of all who live, the light of the faithful, the strength of those who labor, and the repose of the dead: We thank you for the blessings of the day that is past, and humbly ask for your protection

through the coming night. Bring us in safety to the morning hours; through him who died and rose again for us, your Son our Savior Jesus Christ. *Amen.*

A Collect for the Presence of Christ
Lord Jesus, stay with us, for evening is at hand and the day is past; be our companion in the way, kindle our hearts, and awaken hope, that we may know you as you are revealed in Scripture and the breaking of bread. Grant this for the sake of your love. *Amen.*

Then, unless the Eucharist or a form of general intercession is to follow, one of these prayer for mission is added

O God and Father of all, whom the whole heavens adore: Let the whole earth also worship you, all nations obey you, all tongues confess and bless you, and men and women everywhere love you and serve you in peace; through Jesus Christ our Lord. *Amen.*

or this
Keep watch, dear Lord, with those who work, or watch, or weep this night, and give your angels charge over those who sleep. Tend the sick, Lord Christ; give rest to the weary, bless the dying, soothe the suffering, pity the afflicted, shield the joyous; and all for your love's sake. *Amen.*

or the following
O God, you manifest in your servants the signs of your presence: Send forth upon us the spirit of love, that in companionship with one another your abounding grace may increase among us; through Jesus Christ our Lord. Amen.

Here may be sung a hymn or anthem.

Authorized intercessions and thanksgivings may follow.

Before the close of the Office one or both of the following may be used

The General Thanksgiving
Almighty God, Father of all mercies,
we your unworthy servants give you humble thanks
for all your goodness and loving-kindness
to us and to all whom you have made.
We bless you for our creation, preservation,
and all the blessings of this life;
but above all for your immeasurable love
in the redemption of the world by our Lord Jesus Christ;

for the means of grace, and for the hope of glory.
And, we pray, give us such an awareness of your mercies,
that with truly thankful hearts we may show forth your praise,
not only with our lips, but in our lives,
by giving up our selves to your service,
and by walking before you
in holiness and righteousness all our days;
through Jesus Christ our Lord,
to whom, with you and the Holy Spirit,
be honor and glory throughout all ages. Amen.

A Prayer of St. Chrysostom
Almighty God, you have given us grace at this time with one accord to make our common supplication to you; and you have promised through your well-beloved Son that when two or three are gathered together in his Name you will be in the midst of them: Fulfill now, O Lord, our desires and petitions as may be best for us; granting us in this world knowledge of your truth, and in the age to come life everlasting. Amen.

Then may be said
Let us bless the Lord.
Thanks be to God.

From Easter Day through the Day of Pentecost "Alleluia, alleluia" may be added to the preceding versicle and response.

The Officiant may then conclude with one of the following

The grace of our Lord Jesus Christ, and the love of God, and the
fellowship of the Holy Spirit, be with us all evermore.
Amen.   *2 Corinthians 13:14*

May the God of hope fill us with all joy and peace in believing through
the power of the Holy Spirit. **Amen.**
Romans 15:13

Glory to God whose power, working in us, can do infinitely more than
we can ask or imagine: Glory to him from generation to generation in
the Church, and in Christ Jesus for ever and ever. **Amen.**
Ephesians 3:20,21

Compline

The Invitation
O God, make speed to save us.
O Lord, make haste to help us.
Glory to the Father, and to the Son, and to the Holy Spirit:
as it was in the beginning, is now, and will be for ever. Amen.
Except in Lent, add **Alleluia.**

The Confession and Absolution
The Confession and Absolution follow. If a deacon is present, the deacon bids the congregation to the confession. If a bishop or priest are present they give the absolution. If there is no deacon, the bishop or priest bid the confession and give the absolution. If an ordained person is not present, the officiant bids the confession and gives the assurance of forgiveness.

Let us confess our sins to God.
A Period of Silence is observed.

Almighty God, our heavenly Father:
We have sinned against you,
through our own fault,
in thought, and word, and deed,
and in what we have left undone.
For the sake of your Son our Lord Jesus Christ,
forgive us all our offenses;
and grant that we may serve you
in newness of life,
to the glory of your Name. Amen.

The Bishop, when present, or the Priest, stands and says
Almighty God have mercy on you, forgive you all your sins through our Lord Jesus Christ, strengthen you in all goodness, and by the power of the Holy Spirit keep you in eternal life. Amen.

Or in the absence of a bishop or priest:
Officiant May the Almighty God grant us forgiveness of all our sins, and the grace and comfort of the Holy Spirit. Amen.

Hymn
Week I & III
Before the ending of the day,
  Creator of the world, we pray,
  that with thy wonted favor thou
  wouldst be our guard and keeper now.

From all ill dreams defend our eyes,
 from nightly fears and fantasies;
 tread under foot our ghostly foe,
 that no pollution we may know.

O Father, that we ask be done,
 through Jesus Christ thine only Son,
 who, with the Holy Ghost and thee,
 doth live and reign eternally. Amen.
Author (attributed to): St. Ambrose; Translator: J. M. Neale (1852)

Week II & IV
All praise to You, my God, this night,
 For all the blessings of the light.
 Keep me, O keep me, King of kings,
 Beneath the shelter of Your wings.

Forgive me, Lord, for this I pray,
 The wrong that I have done this day.
 May peace with God and neighbor be,
 Before I sleep restored to me.

Lord, may I be at rest in You
 And sweetly sleep the whole night thro'.
 Refresh my strength, for Your own sake,
 So I may serve You when I wake.

Praise God, from whom all blessings flow;
 Praise Him all creatures here below;
 Praise Him above, ye heav'nly host;
 Praise Father, Son, and Holy Ghost.
Author: Thomas Ken

Psalm 4 *Cum invocarem*

1 Answer me when I call, O God, defender of my cause; *
 you set me free when I am hard-pressed;
 have mercy on me and hear my prayer.

2 "You mortals, how long will you dishonor my glory; *
 how long will you worship dumb idols
 and run after false gods?"

3 Know that the LORD does wonders for the faithful; *
 when I call upon the LORD, he will hear me.

4 Tremble, then, and do not sin; *
 speak to your heart in silence upon your bed.

5 Offer the appointed sacrifices *
 and put your trust in the LORD.

6 Many are saying, "Oh, that we might see better times!" *
 Lift up the light of your countenance upon us, O LORD.

7 You have put gladness in my heart, *
 more than when grain and wine and oil increase.

8 I lie down in peace; at once I fall asleep; *
 for only you, LORD, make me dwell in safety.

Psalm 91 *Qui habitat*

1 He who dwells in the shelter of the Most High, *
 abides under the shadow of the Almighty.

2 He shall say to the LORD,
 "You are my refuge and my stronghold, *
 my God in whom I put my trust."

3 He shall deliver you from the snare of the hunter *
 and from the deadly pestilence.

4 He shall cover you with his pinions,
 and you shall find refuge under his wings; *
 his faithfulness shall be a shield and buckler.

5 You shall not be afraid of any terror by night, *
 nor of the arrow that flies by day;

6 Of the plague that stalks in the darkness, *
 nor of the sickness that lays waste at mid-day.

7 A thousand shall fall at your side
 and ten thousand at your right hand, *
 but it shall not come near you.

8 Your eyes have only to behold *
 to see the reward of the wicked.

9 Because you have made the LORD your refuge, *
 and the Most High your habitation,

10 There shall no evil happen to you, *
 neither shall any plague come near your dwelling.

11 For he shall give his angels charge over you, *
   to keep you in all your ways.

12 They shall bear you in their hands, *
   lest you dash your foot against a stone.

13 You shall tread upon the lion and adder; *
   you shall trample the young lion
   and the serpent under your feet.

14 Because he is bound to me in love,
   therefore will I deliver him; *
   I will protect him, because he knows my Name.

15 He shall call upon me, and I will answer him; *
   I am with him in trouble;
   I will rescue him and bring him to honor.

16 With long life will I satisfy him, *
   and show him my salvation.

Psalm 134 *Ecce nunc*

1 Behold now, bless the LORD, all you servants of the LORD, *
   you that stand by night in the house of the LORD.

2 Lift up your hands in the holy place and bless the LORD; *
   the LORD who made heaven and earth
   bless you out of Zion.

Reading
Saturday
Jeremiah 14:9,22
Lord, you are in the midst of us, and we are called by your Name: Do not forsake us, O Lord our God.
People Thanks be to God.

Sunday
Hebrews 13:20-21
May the God of peace, who brought again from the dead our Lord Jesus, and great shepherd of the sheep, by the blood of the eternal covenant, equip you with everything good that you may do his will, working in you that which is pleasing in his sight; through Jesus Christ, to whom be glory for ever and ever.
People Thanks be to God.

Monday
Matthew 11:28-30
Come to me, all who labor and are heavy-laden, and I will give you rest. Take my yoke upon you, and learn from me; for I am gentle and lowly in heart, and you will find rest for your souls. For my yoke is easy, and my burden is light.
People   Thanks be to God.

Tuesday
1 Thessalonians 5: 9-10
God has destined us not for wrath but for obtaining salvation through our Lord Jesus Christ, who died for us, so that whether we are awake or asleep we may live with him.
People   Thanks be to God.

Wednesday
Ephesians 4: 26-67
Be angry but do not sin; do not let the sun go down on your anger, and do not make room for the devil.
People   Thanks be to God.

Thursday
1 Thessalonians 5: 223-24
May the God of peace himself sanctify you entirely; and may your spirit and soul and body be kept sound[f] and blameless at the coming of our Lord Jesus Christ. The one who calls you is faithful, and he will do this.
People   Thanks be to God.

Friday
1 Peter 5:8-9a
Be sober, be watchful. Your adversary the devil prowls around like a roaring lion, seeking someone to devour. Resist him, firm in your faith.
People   Thanks be to God.

Responsory
Into your hands, O Lord
    − I commend my spirit.
You have redeemed me, O Lord, O God of truth.
    − I commend my spirit.
Glory to the Father and to the Son and to the Holy Spirit.
Into your hands, O Lord
    − I commend my spirit.

Canticle: The Song of Simeon *Nunc Dimittis (Luke 2: 29-31*

The Canticle Nunc Dimittis is said with its proper antiphon.
Lent Antiphon Is not this the fast that I choose: to loose the bonds of injustice. to share your bread with the hungry? Then your light shall break forth like the dawn.
Easter Antiphon Alleluia. The Lord is risen as he said. Alleluia. Alleluia.
Pentecost Antiphon Alleluia. The Spirit, the Paraclete, will teach you all things. Alleluia. Alleluia.
Sanctoral Antiphon Shine in us, O God, with your light, and may you Spirt illumine the darkness of our hearts that we may abide in Christ, the light of the world.

The Song of Simeon *Nunc Dimittis*
Luke 2:29-32

Lord, you now have set your servant free *
   to go in peace as you have promised;
For these eyes of mine have seen the Savior, *
   whom you have prepared for all the world to see:
A Light to enlighten the nations, *
   and the glory of your people Israel.

Lent Antiphon Is not this the fast that I choose: to loose the bonds of injustice. to share your bread with the hungry? Then your light shall break forth like the dawn.
Easter Antiphon Alleluia. The Lord is risen as he said. Alleluia. Alleluia.
Pentecost Antiphon Alleluia. The Spirit, the Paraclete, will teach you all things. Alleluia. Alleluia.
Sanctoral Antiphon Shine in us, O God, with your light, and may you Spirt illumine the darkness of our hearts that we may abide in Christ, the light of the world.

The Lord's Prayer

Lord, have mercy.
Christ, have mercy.
Lord, have mercy.

Our Father in heaven,
   hallowed be your Name,
   your kingdom come,
   your will be done,

on earth as in heaven.
Give us today our daily bread.
Forgive us our sins
   as we forgive those
      who sin against us.
Save us from the time of trial,
   and deliver us from evil.
For the kingdom, the power,
   and the glory are yours,
      now and for ever. Amen.

Collect

Let us pray.

Saturday

We give you thanks, O God, for revealing your Son Jesus Christ to us by the light of his resurrection: Grant that as we sing your glory at the close of this day, our joy may abound in the morning as we celebrate the Paschal mystery; through Jesus Christ our Lord. Amen.

Sunday

Be our light in the darkness, O Lord, and in your great mercy defend us from all perils and dangers of this night; for the love of your only Son, our Savior Jesus Christ. Amen.

Monday

Be present, O merciful God, and protect us through the hours of this night, so that we who are wearied by the changes and chances of this life may rest in your eternal changelessness; through Jesus Christ our Lord. Amen.

Tuesday

Look down, O Lord, from your heavenly throne, and illumine this night with your celestial brightness; that by night as by day your people may glorify your holy Name; through Jesus Christ our Lord. Amen.

Wednesday

Visit this place, O Lord, and drive far from it all snares of the enemy; let your holy angels dwell with us to preserve us in peace; and let your blessing be upon us always; through Jesus Christ our Lord. Amen.

Thursday

Keep watch, dear Lord, with those who work, or watch, or weep this night, and give your angels charge over those who sleep. Tend the sick,

Lord Christ; give rest to the weary, bless the dying, soothe the suffering, pity the afflicted, shield the joyous; and all for your love's sake. Amen.

Friday
O God, your unfailing providence sustains the world we live in and the life we live: Watch over those, both night and day, who work while others sleep, and grant that we may never forget that our common life depends upon each other's toil; through Jesus Christ our Lord. Amen.

Conclusion and Blessing
Let us bless the Lord. (Alleluia. Alleluia.)
Thanks be to God. (Alleluia. Alleluia.)

The Lord grant us a quiet night and a peaceful death.
Amen

Final Antiphon of the Blessed Virgin Mary

February 2 through Good Friday
Ave Regina Caelorum
Hail, Queen of Heaven.
Hail, Queen of the Angels.
Hail, Root of Jesse and Gate of the morning,
From you the world's true light was born.
Rejoice, O Glorious Virgin,
Beautiful beyond all others.
O you who are fair beyond the fairest
Pray for us to Christ.

Easter
Regina Coeli
O Queen of heaven, rejoice, alleluia.
The Son whom you carried, alleluia,
Has risen according to his word, alleluia.
Pray for us to God, alleluia.

Rejoice and be glad, O Virgin Mary, alleluia!
— For the Lord is risen indeed, alleluia.

Alternate Traditional Marian Antiphons
Salve Regina
Hail, holy Queen, Mother of mercy;
our life, our sweetness and our hope.
To you do we cry, poor banished children of Eve.
To you do we raise our prayer,

grieving and lamenting in this desolate valley.
Turn then, most gracious intercessor,
your eyes of mercy toward us,
and after this exile
show us the blessed fruit of your womb, Jesus.
O clement, O loving, O sweet Virgin Mary.

Sub Tuum Praesidium
We turn to you for protection, O holy Mother of God.
Hear our prayers and help us in our needs.
Protect us from every danger, O glorious and blessed Virgin.

The Four Week Psalter

Week 1

Sunday Week 1 Evening Prayer I

Officiant: O God, make speed to save us.
People: **O Lord, make haste to help us.**
Officiant and People
**Glory to the Father, and to the Son, and to the Holy Spirit:
as it was in the beginning, is now, and will be for ever. Amen.**
Except in Lent, add **Alleluia.**

Hymn *From the Proper of the Season or of the Day*

Psalm 146 *Lauda, anima mea*
I will put my Spirit upon him, and he will proclaim justice to the Gentiles. Mt. 12:18

Lent When they breathe their last, they return to earth, and in that day their thoughts perish.
Easter The LORD shall reign for ever, your God, O Zion, throughout all generations. hallelujah!

1   Hallelujah!
    Praise the LORD, O my soul! *
        I will praise the LORD as long as I live;
        I will sing praises to my God while I have my being.

2   Put not your trust in rulers, nor in any child of earth, *
        for there is no help in them.

3   When they breathe their last, they return to earth, *
        and in that day their thoughts perish.

4   Blessed are they who have the God of Jacob for their help! *
        whose hope is in the LORD their God;

5   Who made heaven and earth, the seas, and all that is in them; *
        who keeps his promise for ever;

6   Who gives justice to those who are oppressed, *
        and food to those who hunger.

7   The LORD sets the prisoners free;
    the LORD opens the eyes of the blind; *
        the LORD lifts up those who are bowed down;

8   The LORD loves the righteous;
    the LORD cares for the stranger; *
        he sustains the orphan and widow,
        but frustrates the way of the wicked.

9 The LORD shall reign for ever, *
     your God, O Zion, throughout all generations.
     Hallelujah!

Glory to the Father, and to the Son, and to the Holy Spirit:
     as it was in the beginning, is now, and will be for ever. Amen.

Lent When they breathe their last, they return to earth, and in that day their thoughts perish.
Easter The LORD shall reign for ever, your God, O Zion, throughout all generations. hallelujah!

All Psalms and Canticles are concluded with the Gloria unless otherwise indicated.
The Antiphon is repeated after the Gloria.

Psalm 147 A *Laudate Dominum*
We give thanks to the Father, who has enabled us to share
in the inheritance of the saints in the light. Col. 1:12

Lent God heals the brokenhearted and binds up their wounds.
Easter The Lord rebuilds Jerusalem and heals the brokenhearted, hallelujah.

1 Hallelujah!
     How good it is to sing praises to our God! *
          how pleasant it is to honor him with praise!

2 The LORD rebuilds Jerusalem; *
     he gathers the exiles of Israel.

3 He heals the brokenhearted *
     and binds up their wounds.

4 He counts the number of the stars *
     and calls them all by their names.

5 Great is our LORD and mighty in power; *
     there is no limit to his wisdom.

6 The LORD lifts up the lowly, *
     but casts the wicked to the ground.

7 Sing to the LORD with thanksgiving; *
     make music to our God upon the harp.

8 He covers the heavens with clouds *
     and prepares rain for the earth;

9 He makes grass to grow upon the mountains *
     and green plants to serve mankind.

10 He provides food for flocks and herds *
     and for the young ravens when they cry.

11 He is not impressed by the might of a horse; *
     he has no pleasure in the strength of a man;

12 But the LORD has pleasure in those who fear him, *
     in those who await his gracious favor.

Lent God heals the brokenhearted and binds up their wounds.
Easter The Lord rebuilds Jerusalem and heals the brokenhearted, hallelujah.

Psalm 147 B *Lauda Hierusalem*
Let the peace of Christ rule in your hearts, to which indeed you were called in the one body. Col. 3:15
Lent God declares his word to Jacob, his statutes and his judgments to Israel.
Easter Come, I will show you the bride of the Lamb, hallelujah.

13 Worship the LORD, O Jerusalem; *
     praise your God, O Zion;

14 For he has strengthened the bars of your gates; *
     he has blessed your children within you.

15 He has established peace on your borders; *
     he satisfies you with the finest wheat.

16 He sends out his command to the earth, *
     and his word runs very swiftly.

17 He gives snow like wool; *
     he scatters hoarfrost like ashes.

18 He scatters his hail like bread crumbs; *
     who can stand against his cold?

19 He sends forth his word and melts them; *
     he blows with his wind, and the waters flow.

20 He declares his word to Jacob, *
     his statutes and his judgments to Israel.

21 He has not done so to any other nation; *
     to them he has not revealed his judgments.
     Hallelujah!

Lent God declares his word to Jacob, his statutes and his judgments to Israel.
Easter Come, I will show you the bride of the Lamb, hallelujah.

Reading
The Proper Reading is taken from the Lectionary.

Responsory, Magnificat Antiphon, Litany, Invitation to the Lord's Prayer, Collet and Dismissal are taken from the Proper of the Season .

Sunday Week 1 Morning Prayer
Officiant: Lord, open our lips.
People: **And our mouth shall proclaim your praise.**
Officiant and People **Glory to the Father ...**
Except in Lent, add **Alleluia.**

The Invitatory Psalm 95
From the Proper of the Season or of the Day

Hymn *From the Proper of the Season or of the Day*

Psalm 118 A *Confitemini Domino*
The God of our ancestors raised up Jesus…
God exalted him at his right hand as Leader and Savior. Acts 5: 30-31

Lent I was pressed so hard that I almost fell, but the LORD came to my help.
Easter The LORD is at my side to help me; I will triumph over those who hate me., hallelujah.

1 Give thanks to the LORD, for he is good; *
     his mercy endures for ever.

2 Let Israel now proclaim, *
     "His mercy endures for ever."

3 Let the house of Aaron now proclaim, *
     "His mercy endures for ever."

4 Let those who fear the LORD now proclaim, *
     "His mercy endures for ever."

5 I called to the LORD in my distress; *
     the LORD answered by setting me free.

6 The LORD is at my side, therefore I will not fear; *
     what can anyone do to me?

7 The LORD is at my side to help me; *
 I will triumph over those who hate me.

8 It is better to rely on the LORD *
 than to put any trust in flesh.

9 It is better to rely on the LORD *
 than to put any trust in rulers.

10 All the ungodly encompass me; *
 in the name of the LORD I will repel them.

11 They hem me in, they hem me in on every side; *
 in the name of the LORD I will repel them.

12 They swarm about me like bees;
 they blaze like a fire of thorns; *
 in the name of the LORD I will repel them.

13 I was pressed so hard that I almost fell, *
 but the LORD came to my help.

14 The LORD is my strength and my song, *
 and he has become my salvation.

Lent I was pressed so hard that I almost fell, but the LORD came to my help.
Easter The LORD is at my side to help me; I will triumph over those who hate me., hallelujah.

Psalm 118 B *Vox exsultationis*
*Christ entered into heaven itself,
now to appear in the presence of God on our behalf. Heb. 9: 24*

Lent The LORD has punished me sorely, but he did not hand me over to death.
Easter On this day the Lord has acted; we will rejoice and be glad in it, hallelujah.

15 There is a sound of exultation and victory *
 in the tents of the righteous:

16 "The right hand of the LORD has triumphed! *
 the right hand of the LORD is exalted!
 the right hand of the LORD has triumphed!"

17 I shall not die, but live, *
 and declare the works of the LORD.

18 The LORD has punished me sorely, *
    but he did not hand me over to death.

19 Open for me the gates of righteousness; *
    I will enter them;
    I will offer thanks to the LORD.

20 "This is the gate of the LORD; *
    he who is righteous may enter."

21 I will give thanks to you, for you answered me *
    and have become my salvation.

22 The same stone which the builders rejected *
    has become the chief cornerstone.

23 This is the LORD'S doing, *
    and it is marvelous in our eyes.

24 On this day the LORD has acted; *
    we will rejoice and be glad in it.

25 Hosannah, LORD, hosannah! *
    LORD, send us now success.

26 Blessed is he who comes in the name of the Lord; *
    we bless you from the house of the LORD.

27 God is the LORD; he has shined upon us; *
    form a procession with branches up to the horns of the altar.

28 "You are my God, and I will thank you; *
    you are my God, and I will exalt you."

29 Give thanks to the LORD, for he is good; *
    his mercy endures for ever.

Lent The LORD has punished me sorely, but he did not hand me over to death.
Easter On this day the Lord has acted; we will rejoice and be glad in it, hallelujah.

Psalm 100 *Jubilate Deo*
You are a chosen race, a royal priesthood, a holy nation, God's own people. 1 Pt. 2:9

Lent The LORD is good; his mercy is everlasting.
Easter Serve the Lord with gladness, hallelujah.

1 Be joyful in the LORD, all you lands; *
    serve the LORD with gladness
    and come before his presence with a song.

2 Know this: The LORD himself is God; *
     he himself has made us, and we are his;
     we are his people and the sheep of his pasture.

3 Enter his gates with thanksgiving;
  go into his courts with praise; *
     give thanks to him and call upon his Name.

4 For the LORD is good;
  his mercy is everlasting; *
     and his faithfulness endures from age to age.

Lent The LORD is good; his mercy is everlasting.
Easter Serve the Lord with gladness, hallelujah.

Readings

Responsories, Benedictus Antiphon, Litany, Invitation to the Lord's Prayer, Collet and Dismissal are taken from the Proper of the Season.

Sunday Week 1 Noonday Prayer

Officiant: O God, make speed to save us.
People: **O Lord, make haste to help us.**
Officiant and People **Glory to the Father...**
Except in Lent, add **Alleluia.**
Hymn *From the Proper of the Season or of the Day*

Psalm 1 *Beatus vir qui non abiit*
This is the person who comes to me, hears my words, and acts on them. Lk. 6:47

Lent The wicked are like chaff which the wind blows away.
Easter I know that the LORD gives victory to his anointed; he will answer him out of his holy heaven, hallelujah.

1 Blessed are they who have not walked
  in the counsel of the wicked, *
     nor lingered in the way of sinners,
     nor sat in the seats of the scornful!

2 Their delight is in the law of the LORD, *
     and they meditate on his law day and night.

3 They are like trees planted by streams of water,
  bearing fruit in due season, with leaves that do not wither; *
     everything they do shall prosper.

4 It is not so with the wicked; *
     they are like chaff which the wind blows away.

5 Therefore the wicked shall not stand upright
    when judgment comes, *
        nor the sinner in the council of the righteous.

6 For the LORD knows the way of the righteous, *
    but the way of the wicked is doomed.

Psalm 2 *Quare fremuerunt gentes?*
God put his power to work in Christ when he raised him from the dead and seated him at his right hand. Col. 1: 20

1 Why are the nations in an uproar? *
    Why do the peoples mutter empty threats?

2 Why do the kings of the earth rise up in revolt,
    and the princes plot together, *
        against the LORD and against his Anointed?

3 "Let us break their yoke," they say; *
    "let us cast off their bonds from us."

4 He whose throne is in heaven is laughing; *
    the Lord has them in derision.

5 Then he speaks to them in his wrath, *
    and his rage fills them with terror.

6 "I myself have set my king *
    upon my holy hill of Zion."

7 Let me announce the decree of the LORD: *
    he said to me, "You are my Son;
    this day have I begotten you.

8 Ask of me, and I will give you
    the nations for your inheritance *
        and the ends of the earth for your possession.

9 You shall crush them with an iron rod *
    and shatter them like a piece of pottery."

10 And now, you kings, be wise; *
    be warned, you rulers of the earth.

11 Submit to the LORD with fear, *
    and with trembling bow before him;

12 Lest he be angry and you perish; *
    for his wrath is quickly kindled.

13 Blessed are they all *
   who take refuge in him!

Psalm 20 *Exaudiat te Dominus*

Christ is the head of the body, the church; he is the beginning, the firstborn from the dead. Col. 1: 18

1 May the LORD answer you in the day of trouble, *
   the Name of the God of Jacob defend you;

2 Send you help from his holy place *
   and strengthen you out of Zion;

3 Remember all your offerings *
   and accept your burnt sacrifice;

4 Grant you your heart's desire *
   and prosper all your plans.

5 We will shout for joy at your victory
   and triumph in the Name of our God; *
   may the LORD grant all your requests.

6 Now I know that the LORD gives victory to his anointed; *
   he will answer him out of his holy heaven,
   with the victorious strength of his right hand.

7 Some put their trust in chariots and some in horses, *
   but we will call upon the Name of the LORD our God.

8 They collapse and fall down, *
   but we will arise and stand upright.

9 O LORD, give victory to the king *
   and answer us when we call.

Lent The wicked are like chaff which the wind blows away.
Easter I know that the LORD gives victory to his anointed; he will answer him out of his holy heaven, hallelujah.

Reading, Verse and Response, Collect and Conclusion as in the Proper of the Season or of the Day.

Sunday Week 1 Evening Prayer II

Officiant: O God, make speed to save us.
People: **O Lord, make haste to help us.**
Officiant and People **Glory to the Father ...**
Except in Lent, add **Alleluia.**

Hymn *From the Proper of the Season or of the Day*

Psalm 110 *Dixit Dominus*

Jesus has entered the inner sanctuary, having become a high priest forever according to the order of Melchizedek. Heb. 6:20

Lent He will drink from the brook beside the road; therefore he will lift high his head.
Easter The Lord has risen from the dead, and is seated at the right hand of God, hallelujah!

1 The LORD said to my Lord, "Sit at my right hand, *
    until I make your enemies your footstool."

2 The LORD will send the scepter of your power out of Zion, *
    saying, "Rule over your enemies round about you.

3 Princely state has been yours from the day of your birth; *
    in the beauty of holiness have I begotten you,
    like dew from the womb of the morning."

4 The LORD has sworn and he will not recant: *
    "You are a priest for ever after the order of Melchizedek."

5 The Lord who is at your right hand
    will smite kings in the day of his wrath; *
    he will rule over the nations.

6 He will heap high the corpses; *
    he will smash heads over the wide earth.

7 He will drink from the brook beside the road; *
    therefore he will lift high his head.

Lent He will drink from the brook beside the road; therefore he will lift high his head.
Easter The Lord has risen from the dead, and is seated at the right hand of God, hallelujah!

Psalm 111 *Confitebor tibi*

Christ entered once for all into the Holy Place, with his own blood, thus obtaining eternal redemption. Heb. 9:12

Lent We have been redeemed by the precious blood of Christ, the lamb without blemish.
Easter The Lord sent redemption to his people, hallelujah.

1 Hallelujah!
    I will give thanks to the LORD with my whole heart, *
        in the assembly of the upright, in the congregation.

Sunday Week 1 Evening Prayer II

2 Great are the deeds of the LORD! *
   they are studied by all who delight in them.

3 His work is full of majesty and splendor, *
   and his righteousness endures for ever.

4 He makes his marvelous works to be remembered; *
   the LORD is gracious and full of compassion.

5 He gives food to those who fear him; *
   he is ever mindful of his covenant.

6 He has shown his people the power of his works *
   in giving them the lands of the nations.

7 The works of his hands are faithfulness and justice; *
   all his commandments are sure.

8 They stand fast for ever and ever, *
   because they are done in truth and equity.

9 He sent redemption to his people;
   he commanded his covenant for ever; *
   holy and awesome is his Name.

10 The fear of the LORD is the beginning of wisdom; *
   those who act accordingly have a good understanding;
   his praise endures for ever.

Lent We have been redeemed by the precious blood of Christ, the lamb without blemish.
Easter The Lord sent redemption to his people, hallelujah.

Psalm 112 *Beatus vir*
The righteous will shine like the sun in the kingdom of their Father. Mt. 13: 43

Lent The righteous have given freely to the poor.
Easter God has shone in our hearts to give the light of the glory of God in the face of Jesus Christ., hallelujah.

1 Hallelujah!
   Blessed are they who fear the Lord *
   and have great delight in his commandments!
2 Their descendants will be mighty in the land; *
   the generation of the upright will be blessed.

3 Wealth and riches will be in their house, *
   and their righteousness will last for ever.

4 Light shines in the darkness for the upright; *
   the righteous are merciful and full of compassion.

5 It is good for them to be generous in lending *
   and to manage their affairs with justice.

6 For they will never be shaken; *
   the righteous will be kept in everlasting remembrance.

7 They will not be afraid of any evil rumors; *
   their heart is right;
   they put their trust in the Lord.

8 Their heart is established and will not shrink, *
   until they see their desire upon their enemies.

9 They have given freely to the poor, *
   and their righteousness stands fast for ever;
   they will hold up their head with honor.

10 The wicked will see it and be angry;
   they will gnash their teeth and pine away; *
   the desires of the wicked will perish.

Lent The righteous have given freely to the poor.
Easter God has shone in our hearts to give the light of the glory of God in the face of Jesus Christ., hallelujah.

Reading

Responsory, Magnificat Antiphon, Litany, Invitation to the Lord's Prayer, Collect and Dismissal are taken from the Proper of the Season.

Monday Week 1 Morning Prayer

Officiant: Lord, open our lips.
People: **And our mouth shall proclaim your praise.**
Officiant and People **Glory to the Father...**
Except in Lent, add **Alleluia.**

The Invitatory Psalm 29
From the Proper of the Season or of the Day

Hymn *From the Proper of the Season or of the Day*

Psalm 5 *Verba mea auribus*

*In the morning, while it was still very dark, he got up
and went out to a deserted place, and there he prayed. Mk. 1:35*

Lent Lead me, O LORD, in your righteousness, make your way straight before me.

Easter Those who love your Name will exult in you, hallelujah.

1 Give ear to my words, O LORD; *
    consider my meditation.

2 Hearken to my cry for help, my King and my God, *
    for I make my prayer to you.

3 In the morning, LORD, you hear my voice; *
    early in the morning I make my appeal and watch for you.

4 For you are not a God who takes pleasure in wickedness, *
    and evil cannot dwell with you.

5 Braggarts cannot stand in your sight; *
    you hate all those who work wickedness.

6 You destroy those who speak lies; *
    the bloodthirsty and deceitful, O LORD, you abhor.

7 But as for me, through the greatness of your mercy
    I will go into your house; *
    I will bow down toward your holy temple in awe of you.

8 Lead me, O LORD, in your righteousness,
    because of those who lie in wait for me; *
    make your way straight before me.

9 For there is no truth in their mouth; *
    there is destruction in their heart;

10 Their throat is an open grave; *
    they flatter with their tongue.

11 Declare them guilty, O God; *
    let them fall, because of their schemes.

12 Because of their many transgressions cast them out, *
    for they have rebelled against you.

13 But all who take refuge in you will be glad; *
    they will sing out their joy for ever.

14 You will shelter them, *
    so that those who love your Name may exult in you.

15 For you, O LORD, will bless the righteous; *
    you will defend them with your favor as with a shield.

Lent Lead me, O LORD, in your righteousness, make your way straight before me.
Easter Those who love your Name will exult in you, hallelujah.

Psalm 36 *Dixit injustus*
In him was life, and the life was the light of all people. Jn. 1:4

Lent Continue your loving-kindness to those who know you.
Easter With you, O Lord is the well of life, hallelujah.

1   There is a voice of rebellion deep in the heart of the wicked; *
    there is no fear of God before his eyes.

2   He flatters himself in his own eyes *
    that his hateful sin will not be found out.

3   The words of his mouth are wicked and deceitful; *
    he has left off acting wisely and doing good.

4   He thinks up wickedness upon his bed
    and has set himself in no good way; *
    he does not abhor that which is evil.

5   Your love, O LORD, reaches to the heavens, *
    and your faithfulness to the clouds.

6   Your righteousness is like the strong mountains,
    your justice like the great deep; *
    you save both man and beast, O LORD.

7   How priceless is your love, O God! *
    your people take refuge
    under the shadow of your wings.

8   They feast upon the abundance of your house; *
    you give them drink from the river of your delights.

9   For with you is the well of life, *
    and in your light we see light.

10 Continue your loving-kindness to those who know you, *
    and your favor to those who are true of heart.

11 Let not the foot of the proud come near me, *
    nor the hand of the wicked push me aside.

12 See how they are fallen, those who work wickedness! *
   they are cast down and shall not be able to rise.

Lent Continue your loving-kindness to those who know you.
Easter With you, O Lord is the well of life, hallelujah.

Psalm 148 *Laudate Dominum*

At Jesus' name every knee should bend, in heaven and on earth and under the earth. Phil 2:10
Lent Let all creatures praise the Name of the Lord; for he commanded, and they were created.
Easter The Name of the Lord is exalted above heaven and earth, hallelujah.

1 Hallelujah!
   Praise the LORD from the heavens; *
      praise him in the heights.

2 Praise him, all you angels of his; *
      praise him, all his host.

3 Praise him, sun and moon; *
      praise him, all you shining stars.

4 Praise him, heaven of heavens, *
      and you waters above the heavens.

5 Let them praise the Name of the LORD; *
      for he commanded, and they were created.

6 He made them stand fast for ever and ever; *
      he gave them a law which shall not pass away.

7 Praise the LORD from the earth, *
      you sea-monsters and all deeps;

8 Fire and hail, snow and fog, *
      tempestuous wind, doing his will;

9 Mountains and all hills, *
      fruit trees and all cedars;

10 Wild beasts and all cattle, *
      creeping things and wingèd birds;

11 Kings of the earth and all peoples, *
      princes and all rulers of the world;

12 Young men and maidens, *
      old and young together.

13 Let them praise the Name of the LORD, *
    for his Name only is exalted,
    his splendor is over earth and heaven.

14 He has raised up strength for his people
   and praise for all his loyal servants, *
       the children of Israel, a people who are near him.
       Hallelujah!

Lent Let all creatures praise the Name of the Lord; for he commanded, and they were created.
Easter The Name of the Lord is exalted above heaven and earth, hallelujah.

Readings

Responsories, Benedictus Antiphon, Litany, Invitation to the Lord's Prayer, Collet and Dismissal are taken from the Proper of the Season.

Monday Week 1 Noonday Prayer

Officiant: O God, make speed to save us.
People: **O Lord, make haste to help us.**
Officiant and People **Glory to the Father...**
Except in Lent, add **Alleluia.**

Hymn *From the Proper of the Season or of the Day*

Psalm 119 Aleph *Beati immaculate*
Blessed are those who hear the word of God and obey it. Lk. 11:28

Lent I love to do your will, O my God; your law is deep in my heart.
Easter The Lord has put a new song in my mouth; a song of praise to our God, hallelujah.

1 Blessed are they whose way is blameless, *
    who walk in the law of the LORD!

2 Blessed are they who observe his decrees *
    and seek him with all their hearts!

3 Who never do any wrong, *
    but always walk in his ways.

4 You laid down your commandments, *
    that we should fully keep them.

5 Oh, that my ways were made so direct *
    that I might keep your statutes!

6 Then I should not be put to shame, *
    when I regard all your commandments.

7 I will thank you with an unfeigned heart, *
    when I have learned your righteous judgments.

8 I will keep your statutes; *
    do not utterly forsake me.

Psalm 40 A *Expectans, expectavi*
I have come to call not the righteous but sinners. Mt. 9:13

1 I waited patiently upon the LORD; *
    he stooped to me and heard my cry.

2 He lifted me out of the desolate pit, out of the mire and clay; *
    he set my feet upon a high cliff and made my footing sure.

3 He put a new song in my mouth,
  a song of praise to our God; *
    many shall see, and stand in awe,
    and put their trust in the LORD.

4 Blessed are they who trust in the LORD! *
    they do not resort to evil spirits or turn to false gods.

5 Great things are they that you have done, O LORD my God!
  how great your wonders and your plans for us! *
    there is none who can be compared with you.

6 Oh, that I could make them known and tell them! *
    but they are more than I can count.

7 In sacrifice and offering you take no pleasure *
    (you have given me ears to hear you);

8 Burnt-offering and sin-offering you have not required, *
    and so I said, "Behold, I come.

9 In the roll of the book it is written concerning me: *
    'I love to do your will, O my God;
    your law is deep in my heart.'"

10 I proclaimed righteousness in the great congregation; *
    behold, I did not restrain my lips;
    and that, O LORD, you know.

11 Your righteousness have I not hidden in my heart;
I have spoken of your faithfulness and your deliverance; *
I have not concealed your love and faithfulness
from the great congregation.

12 You are the LORD;
do not withhold your compassion from me; *
let your love and your faithfulness keep me safe for ever,

13 For innumerable troubles have crowded upon me;
my sins have overtaken me, and I cannot see; *
they are more in number than the hairs of my head,
and my heart fails me.

Psalm 40 B *Complaceat tibi*
*Ask, and it will be given you; search, and you will find;
knock, and the door will be opened for you. Mt. 7:7*

14 Be pleased, O LORD, to deliver me; *
O LORD, make haste to help me.

15 Let them be ashamed and altogether dismayed
who seek after my life to destroy it; *
let them draw back and be disgraced
who take pleasure in my misfortune.

16 Let those who say "Aha!" and gloat over me be confounded, *
because they are ashamed.

17 Let all who seek you rejoice in you and be glad; *
let those who love your salvation continually say,
"Great is the LORD!"

18 Though I am poor and afflicted, *
the Lord will have regard for me.

19 You are my helper and my deliverer; *
do not tarry, O my God.

Lent I love to do your will, O my God; your law is deep in my heart.
Easter The Lord has put a new song in my mouth; a song of praise to our God, hallelujah.

Reading, Verse and Response, Collect and Conclusion as in the Proper of the Season or of the Day.

Monday Week 1 Evening Prayer

Officiant: O God, make speed to save us.
People: **O Lord, make haste to help us.**
Officiant and People **Glory to the Father...**
Except in Lent, add **Alleluia.**

Hymn *From the Proper of the Season or of the Day*

Psalm 139 A *Domine, probasti*
The peace of God, which surpasses all understanding,
will guard your hearts and your minds in Christ Jesus. Phil 4:7

Lent Where can I go then from your Spirit? Where can I flee from your presence?

Easter You know my sitting down and my rising up, you discern my thoughts from afar, hallelujah.

1 LORD, you have searched me out and known me; *
    you know my sitting down and my rising up;
    you discern my thoughts from afar.

2 You trace my journeys and my resting-places *
    and are acquainted with all my ways.

3 Indeed, there is not a word on my lips, *
    but you, O LORD, know it altogether.

4 You press upon me behind and before *
    and lay your hand upon me.

5 Such knowledge is too wonderful for me; *
    it is so high that I cannot attain to it.

6 Where can I go then from your Spirit? *
    where can I flee from your presence?

7 If I climb up to heaven, you are there; *
    if I make the grave my bed, you are there also.

8 If I take the wings of the morning *
    and dwell in the uttermost parts of the sea,

9 Even there your hand will lead me *
    and your right hand hold me fast.

10 If I say, "Surely the darkness will cover me, *
    and the light around me turn to night,"

11 Darkness is not dark to you;
   the night is as bright as the day; *
      darkness and light to you are both alike.

Lent Where can I go then from your Spirit? Where can I flee from your presence?
Easter You know my sitting down and my rising up, you discern my thoughts from afar, hallelujah.

Psalm 139 B *Quia tu*

If anyone is in Christ, there is a new creation: everything old has passed away;
see, everything has become new. 2 Cor. 5:17

Lent I, the Lord, search the mind and test the heart, to give to each one as their deeds deserve.
Easter O the depth of the riches and wisdom and knowledge of God! How unsearchable are his judgments and how inscrutable his ways! Hallelujah.

12 For you yourself created my inmost parts; *
    you knit me together in my mother's womb.

13 I will thank you because I am marvelously made; *
    your works are wonderful, and I know it well.

14 My body was not hidden from you, *
    while I was being made in secret
    and woven in the depths of the earth.

15 Your eyes beheld my limbs, yet unfinished in the womb;
   all of them were written in your book; *
      they were fashioned day by day,
      when as yet there was none of them.

16 How deep I find your thoughts, O God! *
    how great is the sum of them!

17 If I were to count them,
   they would be more in number than the sand; *
      to count them all, my life span
      would need to be like yours.

18 Oh, that you would slay the wicked, O God! *
    You that thirst for blood, depart from me.

19 They speak despitefully against you; *
    your enemies take your Name in vain.

20 Do I not hate those, O LORD, who hate you? *
   and do I not loathe those who rise up against you?

21 I hate them with a perfect hatred; *
   they have become my own enemies.

22 Search me out, O God, and know my heart; *
   try me and know my restless thoughts.

23 Look well whether there be any wickedness in me *
   and lead me in the way that is everlasting.

Lent I, the Lord, search the mind and test the heart, to give to each one as their deeds deserve.
Easter O the depth of the riches and wisdom and knowledge of God! How unsearchable are his judgments and how inscrutable his ways! Hallelujah.

Psalm 11 *In Domino confido*
Strive first for the kingdom of God and his righteousness, and all these things will be given to you as well. Mt. 6: 33

Lent The LORD weighs the righteous as well as the wicked, but those who delight in violence he abhors.
Easter I will write on you the name of my God, and the name of the city of my God, the new Jerusalem, and my own new name, hallelujah.

1 In the LORD have I taken refuge; *
   how then can you say to me,
      "Fly away like a bird to the hilltop;

2 For see how the wicked bend the bow
   and fit their arrows to the string, *
      to shoot from ambush at the true of heart.

3 When the foundations are being destroyed, *
   what can the righteous do?"

4 The LORD is in his holy temple; *
   the LORD'S throne is in heaven.

5 His eyes behold the inhabited world; *
   his piercing eye weighs our worth.

6 The LORD weighs the righteous as well as the wicked, *
   but those who delight in violence he abhors.

7 Upon the wicked he shall rain
   coals of fire and burning sulphur; *
      a scorching wind shall be their lot.

8 For the LORD is righteous;
   he delights in righteous deeds; *
      and the just shall see his face.

Lent The LORD weighs the righteous as well as the wicked, but those who delight in violence he abhors.
Easter I will write on you the name of my God, and the name of the city of my God, the new Jerusalem, and my own new name, hallelujah.

Reading

Responsory, Magnificat Antiphon, Litany, Invitation to the Lord's Prayer, Collect and Dismissal are taken from the Proper of the Season.

Tuesday Week 1 Morning Prayer

Officiant: Lord, open our lips.
People: **And our mouth shall proclaim your praise.**
Officiant and People **Glory to the Father…**
Except in Lent, add **Alleluia.**

The Invitatory Psalm 8
From the Proper of the Season or of the Day

Hymn *From the Proper of the Season or of the Day*

Psalm 57 *Miserere mei, Deus*
Do not fear those who kill the body but cannot kill the soul. Mt. 10:28

Lent My heart is firmly fixed, O God, my heart is fixed.
Easter Exalt yourself above the heavens, O God, hallelujah.

1 Be merciful to me, O God, be merciful,
   for I have taken refuge in you; *
      in the shadow of your wings will I take refuge
      until this time of trouble has gone by.

2 I will call upon the Most High God, *
      the God who maintains my cause.

3 He will send from heaven and save me;
   he will confound those who trample upon me; *
      God will send forth his love and his faithfulness.

4 I lie in the midst of lions that devour the people; *
      their teeth are spears and arrows,
      their tongue a sharp sword.

5 They have laid a net for my feet,
  and I am bowed low; *
    they have dug a pit before me,
    but have fallen into it themselves.

6 Exalt yourself above the heavens, O God, *
    and your glory over all the earth.

7 My heart is firmly fixed, O God, my heart is fixed; *
    I will sing and make melody.

8 Wake up, my spirit;
  awake, lute and harp; *
    I myself will waken the dawn.

9 I will confess you among the peoples, O LORD; *
    I will sing praise to you among the nations.

10 For your loving-kindness is greater than the heavens, *
    and your faithfulness reaches to the clouds.

11 Exalt yourself above the heavens, O God, *
    and your glory over all the earth.

Lent My heart is firmly fixed, O God, my heart is fixed.
Easter Exalt yourself above the heavens, O God, hallelujah.

Psalm 3 *Domine, quid multiplicati*
*You will be betrayed even by parents and brothers, by relatives and friends;
and they will put some of you to death. Lk. 21:16*

Lent I do not fear the multitudes of people who set themselves against me all around.
Easter I lie down and go to sleep; I wake again, because the LORD sustains me, hallelujah.

1 LORD, how many adversaries I have! *
    how many there are who rise up against me!

2 How many there are who say of me, *
    "There is no help for him in his God."

3 But you, O LORD, are a shield about me; *
    you are my glory, the one who lifts up my head.

4 I call aloud upon the LORD, *
    and he answers me from his holy hill;

5 I lie down and go to sleep; *
    I wake again, because the LORD sustains me.

6 I do not fear the multitudes of people *
    who set themselves against me all around.

7 Rise up, O LORD; set me free, O my God; *
    surely, you will strike all my enemies across the face,
    you will break the teeth of the wicked.

8 Deliverance belongs to the LORD. *
    Your blessing be upon your people!

Lent I do not fear the multitudes of people who set themselves against me all around.

Easter I lie down and go to sleep; I wake again, because the LORD sustains me, hallelujah.

Psalm 98 *Cantate Domino*
The throne of God and of the Lamb will be in it, and his servants will worship him; they will see his face. Rev. 22:3-4

Lent The Lord remembers his mercy and faithfulness to the house of Israel.

Easter All the ends of the earth have seen the victory of our God, hallelujah.

1 Sing to the LORD a new song, *
    for he has done marvelous things.

2 With his right hand and his holy arm *
    has he won for himself the victory.

3 The LORD has made known his victory; *
    his righteousness has he openly shown
    in the sight of the nations.

4 He remembers his mercy and faithfulness
    to the house of Israel, *
    and all the ends of the earth have seen
    the victory of our God.

5 Shout with joy to the LORD, all you lands; *
    lift up your voice, rejoice, and sing.

6 Sing to the LORD with the harp, *
    with the harp and the voice of song.

7 With trumpets and the sound of the horn *
    shout with joy before the King, the LORD.

8 Let the sea make a noise and all that is in it, *
    the lands and those who dwell therein.

9 Let the rivers clap their hands, *
   and let the hills ring out with joy before the LORD,
   when he comes to judge the earth.

10 In righteousness shall he judge the world *
   and the peoples with equity.

Lent The Lord remembers his mercy and faithfulness to the house of Israel.
Easter All the ends of the earth have seen the victory of our God, hallelujah.

Readings

Responsories, Benedictus Antiphon, Litany, Invitation to the Lord's Prayer, Collet and Dismissal are taken from the Proper of the Season.

Tuesday Week 1 Noonday Prayer

Officiant: O God, make speed to save us.
People: **O Lord, make haste to help us.**
Officiant and People **Glory to the Father…**
Except in Lent, add **Alleluia.**

Hymn *From the Proper of the Season or of the Day*

Psalm 119 Beth *In quo corrigit?*

If you wish to be perfect, go, sell your possessions, and give the money to the poor, and you will have treasure in heaven; then come, follow me. Mt. 19:21

Lent Then they cried to the LORD in their trouble, and he delivered them from their distress.
Easter The Lord shatters the doors of bronze and breaks in two the iron bars, hallelujah.

9 How shall a young man cleanse his way? *
   By keeping to your words.

10 With my whole heart I seek you; *
   let me not stray from your commandments.

11 I treasure your promise in my heart, *
   that I may not sin against you.

12 Blessed are you, O LORD; *
   instruct me in your statutes.

13 With my lips will I recite *
   all the judgments of your mouth.

14 I have taken greater delight in the way of your decrees *
    than in all manner of riches.

15 I will meditate on your commandments *
    and give attention to your ways.

16 My delight is in your statutes; *
    I will not forget your word.

Psalm 107 A *Confitemini Domino*

*Many will come from east and west and will eat with Abraham and Isaac and Jacob
in the kingdom of heaven. Mt. 8:11*

1 Give thanks to the LORD, for he is good, *
    and his mercy endures for ever.

2 Let all those whom the LORD has redeemed proclaim *
    that he redeemed them from the hand of the foe.

3 He gathered them out of the lands; *
    from the east and from the west,
    from the north and from the south.

4 Some wandered in desert wastes; *
    they found no way to a city where they might dwell.

5 They were hungry and thirsty; *
    their spirits languished within them.

6 Then they cried to the LORD in their trouble, *
    and he delivered them from their distress.

7 He put their feet on a straight path *
    to go to a city where they might dwell.

8 Let them give thanks to the LORD for his mercy *
    and the wonders he does for his children.

9 For he satisfies the thirsty *
    and fills the hungry with good things.

Psalm 107 B *Sedentes in tenebris*

*The dead man came out, his hands and feet bound with strips of cloth, and his face
wrapped in a cloth. Jesus said to them, "Unbind him, and let him go." Jn. 11:44*

10 Some sat in darkness and deep gloom, *
    bound fast in misery and iron;

11 Because they rebelled against the words of God *
    and despised the counsel of the Most High.

12 So he humbled their spirits with hard labor; *
   they stumbled, and there was none to help.

13 Then they cried to the LORD in their trouble, *
   and he delivered them from their distress.

14 He led them out of darkness and deep gloom *
   and broke their bonds asunder.

15 Let them give thanks to the LORD for his mercy *
   and the wonders he does for his children.

16 For he shatters the doors of bronze *
   and breaks in two the iron bars.

17 Some were fools and took to rebellious ways; *
   they were afflicted because of their sins.

18 They abhorred all manner of food *
   and drew near to death's door.

19 Then they cried to the LORD in their trouble, *
   and he delivered them from their distress.

20 He sent forth his word and healed them *
   and saved them from the grave.

21 Let them give thanks to the LORD for his mercy *
   and the wonders he does for his children.

22 Let them offer a sacrifice of thanksgiving *
   and tell of his acts with shouts of joy.

Lent Then they cried to the LORD in their trouble, and he delivered them from their distress.
Easter The Lord shatters the doors of bronze and breaks in two the iron bars, hallelujah.

Reading, Verse and Response, Collect and Conclusion as in the Proper of the Season or of the Day.

Tuesday Week 1 Evening Prayer

Officiant: O God, make speed to save us.
People: **O Lord, make haste to help us.**
Officiant and People **Glory to the Father...**
Except in Lent, add **Alleluia.**

Hymn *From the Proper of the Season or of the Day*

Psalm 131 *Domine, non est*

Whoever does not receive the kingdom of God as a little child will never enter it. Lk. 18:19

Lent The ladder is our life in the world, which the Lord raises up to heaven if our heart is humbled.
Easter Learn from me for I am gentle and humble of heart, hallelujah.

1 O LORD, I am not proud; *
 I have no haughty looks.

2 I do not occupy myself with great matters, *
 or with things that are too hard for me.

3 But I still my soul and make it quiet,
 like a child upon its mother's breast; *
 my soul is quieted within me.

4 O Israel, wait upon the LORD, *
 from this time forth for evermore.

Lent The ladder is our life in the world, which the Lord raises up to heaven if our heart is humbled.
Easter Learn from me for I am gentle and humble of heart, hallelujah.

Psalm 132 *Memento, Domine*

He will be called the Son of the Most High, and the Lord God will give to him the throne of his ancestor David. Lk. 1:32

Lent Let us fall upon our knees before God's footstool.
Easter Arise, O LORD, into your resting-place, hallelujah.

1 LORD, remember David, *
 and all the hardships he endured;

2 How he swore an oath to the LORD *
 and vowed a vow to the Mighty One of Jacob:

3 "I will not come under the roof of my house, *
 nor climb up into my bed;

4 I will not allow my eyes to sleep, *
 nor let my eyelids slumber;

5 Until I find a place for the LORD, *
 a dwelling for the Mighty One of Jacob."

6 "The ark! We heard it was in Ephratah; *
 we found it in the fields of Jearim.

7 Let us go to God's dwelling place; *
 let us fall upon our knees before his footstool."

8 Arise, O LORD, into your resting-place, *
    you and the ark of your strength.

9 Let your priests be clothed with righteousness; *
    let your faithful people sing with joy.

10 For your servant David's sake, *
    do not turn away the face of your Anointed.

11 The LORD has sworn an oath to David; *
    in truth, he will not break it:

12 "A son, the fruit of your body *
    will I set upon your throne.

13 If your children keep my covenant
    and my testimonies that I shall teach them, *
    their children will sit upon your throne for evermore."

14 For the LORD has chosen Zion; *
    he has desired her for his habitation:

15 "This shall be my resting-place for ever; *
    here will I dwell, for I delight in her.

16 I will surely bless her provisions, *
    and satisfy her poor with bread.

17 I will clothe her priests with salvation, *
    and her faithful people will rejoice and sing.

18 There will I make the horn of David flourish; *
    I have prepared a lamp for my Anointed.

19 As for his enemies, I will clothe them with shame; *
    but as for him, his crown will shine."

Lent Let us fall upon our knees before God's footstool.
Easter Arise, O LORD, into your resting-place, hallelujah.

Psalm 133 *Ecce, quam bonum!*
*Lead a life worthy of the calling to which you have been called,
with all humility and gentleness. Eph. 4: 1-2*

Lent Be of the same mind, having the same love, being in full accord and of one mind.
Easter They devoted themselves to the apostles' teaching and fellowship, to the breaking of bread and the prayers, hallelujah.

1 Oh, how good and pleasant it is, *
    when brethren live together in unity!

2 It is like fine oil upon the head *
   that runs down upon the beard,

3 Upon the beard of Aaron, *
   and runs down upon the collar of his robe.

4 It is like the dew of Hermon *
   that falls upon the hills of Zion.

5 For there the LORD has ordained the blessing: *
   life for evermore.

Lent Be of the same mind, having the same love, being in full accord and of one mind.
Easter They devoted themselves to the apostles' teaching and fellowship, to the breaking of bread and the prayers, hallelujah.

Reading

Responsory, Magnificat Antiphon, Litany, Invitation to the Lord's Prayer, Collet and Dismissal are taken from the Proper of the Season.

Wednesday Week 1 Morning Prayer

Officiant: Lord, open our lips.
People: **And our mouth shall proclaim your praise.**
Officiant and People **Glory to the Father ...**
Except in Lent, add **Alleluia.**

The Invitatory Psalm 95
From the Proper of the Season or of the Day

Hymn *From the Proper of the Season or of the Day*

Psalm 64 *Exaudi, Deus*
Jesus knew all people and needed no one to bear witness of people;
for he himself knew what was in people. Jn. 2:25

Lent Hide me from the conspiracy of the wicked, from the mob of evildoers.
Easter Everyone will stand in awe and declare God's deeds; they will recognize his works, hallelujah.

1 Hear my voice, O God, when I complain; *
   protect my life from fear of the enemy.

2 Hide me from the conspiracy of the wicked, *
   from the mob of evildoers.

3 They sharpen their tongue like a sword, *
    and aim their bitter words like arrows,

4 That they may shoot down the blameless from ambush;
    they shoot without warning and are not afraid.

5 They hold fast to their evil course; *
    they plan how they may hide their snares.

6 They say, "Who will see us?
  who will find out our crimes? *
    we have thought out a perfect plot."

7 The human mind and heart are a mystery; *
    but God will loose an arrow at them,
    and suddenly they will be wounded.

8 He will make them trip over their tongues, *
    and all who see them will shake their heads.

9 Everyone will stand in awe and declare God's deeds; *
    they will recognize his works.

10 The righteous will rejoice in the LORD and put their trust in him, *
    and all who are true of heart will glory.

Lent Hide me from the conspiracy of the wicked, from the mob of evildoers.
Easter Everyone will stand in awe and declare God's deeds; they will recognize his works, hallelujah.

Psalm 99 *Dominus regnavit*
I saw no temple in the city, for its temple is the Lord God the Almighty and the Lamb. Rev. 21:22

Lent You were a God who forgave them, yet punished them for their evil deeds.
Easter The Lord is great in Zion; he is high above all peoples, hallelujah!

1 The LORD is King;
  let the people tremble; *
    he is enthroned upon the cherubim;
    let the earth shake.

2 The LORD is great in Zion; *
    he is high above all peoples.

3 Let them confess his Name, which is great and awesome; *
    he is the Holy One.

4 "O mighty King, lover of justice,
   you have established equity; *
      you have executed justice and righteousness in Jacob."

5 Proclaim the greatness of the LORD our God
   and fall down before his footstool; *
      he is the Holy One.

6 Moses and Aaron among his priests,
      and Samuel among those who call upon his Name, *
      they called upon the LORD, and he answered them.

7 He spoke to them out of the pillar of cloud; *
      they kept his testimonies and the decree that he gave them.

8 "O LORD our God, you answered them indeed; *
      you were a God who forgave them,
      yet punished them for their evil deeds."

9 Proclaim the greatness of the LORD our God
   and worship him upon his holy hill; *
      for the LORD our God is the Holy One.

Lent You were a God who forgave them, yet punished them for their evil deeds.
Easter The Lord is great in Zion; he is high above all peoples, hallelujah!

Psalm 67 *Deus misereatur*

I thank my God through Jesus Christ for all of you, because your faith is proclaimed throughout the world. Rm 1:8

Lent Let your ways be known upon earth, your saving health among all nations.
Easter Let the peoples praise you, O God; let all the peoples praise you, hallelujah.

1 May God be merciful to us and bless us, *
      show us the light of his countenance and come to us.

2 Let your ways be known upon earth, *
      your saving health among all nations.

3 Let the peoples praise you, O God; *
      let all the peoples praise you.

4 Let the nations be glad and sing for joy, *
      for you judge the peoples with equity
      and guide all the nations upon earth.

5 Let the peoples praise you, O God; *
   let all the peoples praise you.

6 The earth has brought forth her increase; *
   may God, our own God, give us his blessing.

7 May God give us his blessing, *
   and may all the ends of the earth stand in awe of him.

Lent Let your ways be known upon earth, your saving health among all nations.
Easter Let the peoples praise you, O God; let all the peoples praise you, hallelujah.

Readings

Responsories, Benedictus Antiphon, Litany, Invitation to the Lord's Prayer, Collect and Dismissal are taken from the Proper of the Season.

Wednesday Week 1 Noonday Prayer

Officiant: O God, make speed to save us.
People: **O Lord, make haste to help us.**
Officiant and People **Glory to the Father...**
Except in Lent, add **Alleluia.**

Hymn *From the Proper of the Season or of the Day*

Psalm 119 Gimel *Retribue servo tuo*

Jesus said to the blind man, "Go; your faith has made you well."
Immediately he regained his sight and followed Jesus on the way. Mk. 10:52

Lent They cried to the LORD in their trouble, and he delivered them from their distress.
Easter What sort of man is this that even the winds and the sea obey him, hallelujah.

17 Deal bountifully with your servant, *
   that I may live and keep your word.

18 Open my eyes, that I may see *
   the wonders of your law.

19 I am a stranger here on earth; *
   do not hide your commandments from me.

20 My soul is consumed at all times *
   with longing for your judgments.

21 You have rebuked the insolent; *
    cursed are they who stray from your commandments!

22 Turn from me shame and rebuke, *
    for I have kept your decrees.

23 Even though rulers sit and plot against me, *
    I will meditate on your statutes.

24 For your decrees are my delight, *
    and they are my counselors.

Psalm 107 C *Qui descendunt mare*
He woke up and rebuked the wind, and said to the sea, "Peace! Be still!" Mk. 4:39

23 Some went down to the sea in ships *
    and plied their trade in deep waters;

24 They beheld the works of the LORD *
    and his wonders in the deep.

25 Then he spoke, and a stormy wind arose, *
    which tossed high the waves of the sea.

26 They mounted up to the heavens and fell back to the depths; *
    their hearts melted because of their peril.

27 They reeled and staggered like drunkards *
    and were at their wits' end.

28 Then they cried to the LORD in their trouble, *
    and he delivered them from their distress.

29 He stilled the storm to a whisper *
    and quieted the waves of the sea.

30 Then were they glad because of the calm, *
    and he brought them to the harbor they were bound for.

31 Let them give thanks to the LORD for his mercy *
    and the wonders he does for his children.

32 Let them exalt him in the congregation of the people *
    and praise him in the council of the elders.

Psalm 107 D *Posuit flumina*
God has brought down the powerful from their thrones, and lifted up the lowly. Lk. 1:52

33 The LORD changed rivers into deserts, *
    and water-springs into thirsty ground,

34 A fruitful land into salt flats, *
 because of the wickedness of those who dwell there.

35 He changed deserts into pools of water *
 and dry land into water-springs.

36 He settled the hungry there, *
 and they founded a city to dwell in.

37 They sowed fields, and planted vineyards, *
 and brought in a fruitful harvest.

38 He blessed them, so that they increased greatly; *
 he did not let their herds decrease.

39 Yet when they were diminished and brought low, *
 through stress of adversity and sorrow,

40 (He pours contempt on princes *
 and makes them wander in trackless wastes)

41 He lifted up the poor out of misery *
 and multiplied their families like flocks of sheep.

42 The upright will see this and rejoice, *
 but all wickedness will shut its mouth.

43 Whoever is wise will ponder these things, *
 and consider well the mercies of the LORD.

Lent They cried to the LORD in their trouble, and he delivered them from their distress.
Easter What sort of man is this that even the winds and the sea obey him, hallelujah.

Reading, Verse and Response, Collect and Conclusion as in the Proper of the Season or of the Day.

Wednesday Week 1 Evening Prayer

Officiant: O God, make speed to save us.
People: **O Lord, make haste to help us.**
Officiant and People **Glory to the Father...**
Except in Lent, add **Alleluia.**

Hymn *From the Proper of the Season or of the Day*

Psalm 135 A *Laudate nomen*

Jesus Christ purified for himself a people of his own who are zealous for good deeds. Titus 2:15

Lent It was not because you were more numerous than any other people that the Lord set his heart on you and chose you.
Easter In Christ all the fullness of God was pleased to dwell, hallelujah.

1 Hallelujah!
 Praise the Name of the LORD; *
  give praise, you servants of the LORD,

2 You who stand in the house of the LORD, *
  in the courts of the house of our God.

3 Praise the LORD, for the LORD is good; *
  sing praises to his Name, for it is lovely.

4 For the LORD has chosen Jacob for himself *
  and Israel for his own possession.

5 For I know that the LORD is great, *
  and that our Lord is above all gods.

6 The LORD does whatever pleases him, in heaven and on earth, *
  in the seas and all the deeps.

7 He brings up rain clouds from the ends of the earth; *
  he sends out lightning with the rain,
  and brings the winds out of his storehouse.

8 It was he who struck down the firstborn of Egypt, *
  the firstborn both of man and beast.

9 He sent signs and wonders into the midst of you, O Egypt, *
  against Pharaoh and all his servants.

10 He overthrew many nations *
  and put mighty kings to death:

11 Sihon, king of the Amorites,
  and Og, the king of Bashan, *
  and all the kingdoms of Canaan.

12 He gave their land to be an inheritance, *
  an inheritance for Israel his people.

Lent It was not because you were more numerous than any other people that the Lord set his heart on you and chose you.
Easter In Christ all the fullness of God was pleased to dwell, hallelujah.

Psalm 135 B *Domine nomen tuum*
Will not God grant justice to his chosen ones who cry to him day and night? Lk. 18:7

Lent The Lord loved you and kept the oath that he swore to your ancestors that he brought you out of Egypt.
Easter Through Christ God was pleased to reconcile to himself all things by making peace through the blood of his cross, hallelujah.

13 O Lord, your Name is everlasting; *
 your renown, O Lord, endures from age to age.

14 For the Lord gives his people justice *
 and shows compassion to his servants.

15 The idols of the heathen are silver and gold, *
 the work of human hands.

16 They have mouths, but they cannot speak; *
 eyes have they, but they cannot see.

17 They have ears, but they cannot hear; *
 neither is there any breath in their mouth.

18 Those who make them are like them, *
 and so are all who put their trust in them.

19 Bless the Lord, O house of Israel; *
 O house of Aaron, bless the Lord.

20 Bless the Lord, O house of Levi; *
 you who fear the Lord, bless the Lord.

21 Blessed be the Lord out of Zion, *
 who dwells in Jerusalem.
 Hallelujah!

Lent The Lord loved you and kept the oath that he swore to your ancestors that he brought you out of Egypt.
Easter Through Christ God was pleased to reconcile to himself all things by making peace through the blood of his cross, hallelujah.

Psalm 138 *Confitebor tibi*
The Lord is faithful; he will strengthen you and guard you from the evil one. 2 Thes. 3:3

Lent O Lord, your love endures for ever; do not abandon the works of your hands.
Easter Though I walk in the midst of trouble, you keep me safe, hallelujah.

1   I will give thanks to you, O LORD, with my whole heart; *
      before the gods I will sing your praise.

2   I will bow down toward your holy temple
      and praise your Name, *
      because of your love and faithfulness;

3   For you have glorified your Name *
      and your word above all things.

4   When I called, you answered me; *
      you increased my strength within me.

5   All the kings of the earth will praise you, O LORD, *
      when they have heard the words of your mouth.

6   They will sing of the ways of the LORD, *
      that great is the glory of the LORD.

7   Though the LORD be high, he cares for the lowly; *
      he perceives the haughty from afar.

8   Though I walk in the midst of trouble, you keep me safe; *
      you stretch forth your hand against the fury of my enemies;
      your right hand shall save me.

9   The LORD will make good his purpose for me; *
      O LORD, your love endures for ever;
      do not abandon the works of your hands.

Lent O Lord, your love endures for ever; do not abandon the works of your hands.
Easter Though I walk in the midst of trouble, you keep me safe, hallelujah.

Reading

Responsory, Magnificat Antiphon, Litany, Invitation to the Lord's Prayer, Collet and Dismissal are taken from the Proper of the Season.

Thursday Week 1 Morning Prayer

Officiant: Lord, open our lips.
People: **And our mouth shall proclaim your praise.**
Officiant and People **Glory to the Father…**
Except in Lent, add **Alleluia.**

The Invitatory Psalm 100
From the Proper of the Season or of the Day

Hymn *From the Proper of the Season or of the Day*

Psalm 16 *Conserva me, Domine*
This Jesus God raised up, and of that all of us are witnesses. Acts 2:32

Lent You will not abandon me to the grave, nor let your holy one see the Pit.
Easter You will show me the path of life, hallelujah.

1 Protect me, O God, for I take refuge in you; *
 I have said to the LORD, "You are my Lord,
 my good above all other."

2 All my delight is upon the godly that are in the land, *
 upon those who are noble among the people.

3 But those who run after other gods *
 shall have their troubles multiplied.

4 Their libations of blood I will not offer, *
 nor take the names of their gods upon my lips.

5 O LORD, you are my portion and my cup; *
 it is you who uphold my lot.

6 My boundaries enclose a pleasant land; *
 indeed, I have a goodly heritage.

7 I will bless the LORD who gives me counsel; *
 my heart teaches me, night after night.

8 I have set the LORD always before me; *
 because he is at my right hand I shall not fall.

9 My heart, therefore, is glad, and my spirit rejoices; *
 my body also shall rest in hope.

10 For you will not abandon me to the grave, *
 nor let your holy one see the Pit.

11 You will show me the path of life; *
 in your presence there is fullness of joy,
 and in your right hand are pleasures for evermore.

Lent You will not abandon me to the grave, nor let your holy one see the Pit.
Easter You will show me the path of life, hallelujah.

Psalm 42 *Quemadmodum*

The water that I will give will become in them a spring of water gushing up to eternal life. Jn. 4:14

Lent Why are you so full of heaviness, O my soul?
Easter The water that I will give will become in them a spring of water gushing up to eternal life, hallelujah.

1 As the deer longs for the water-brooks, *
     so longs my soul for you, O God.

2 My soul is athirst for God, athirst for the living God; *
     when shall I come to appear before the presence of God?

3 My tears have been my food day and night, *
     while all day long they say to me,
     "Where now is your God?"

4 I pour out my soul when I think on these things: *
     how I went with the multitude
     and led them into the house of God,

5 With the voice of praise and thanksgiving, *
     among those who keep holy-day.

6 Why are you so full of heaviness, O my soul? *
     and why are you so disquieted within me?

7 Put your trust in God; *
     for I will yet give thanks to him,
     who is the help of my countenance, and my God.

8 My soul is heavy within me; *
     therefore I will remember you from the land of Jordan,
     and from the peak of Mizar among the heights of Hermon.

9 One deep calls to another in the noise of your cataracts; *
     all your rapids and floods have gone over me.

10 The LORD grants his loving-kindness in the daytime; *
     in the night season his song is with me,
     a prayer to the God of my life.

11 I will say to the God of my strength,
     "Why have you forgotten me? *
     and why do I go so heavily
     while the enemy oppresses me?"

12 While my bones are being broken, *
     my enemies mock me to my face;

13 All day long they mock me *
and say to me, "Where now is your God?"

14 Why are you so full of heaviness, O my soul? *
and why are you so disquieted within me?

15 Put your trust in God; *
for I will yet give thanks to him,
who is the help of my countenance, and my God.

Lent Why are you so full of heaviness, O my soul?
Easter The water that I will give will become in them a spring of water gushing up to eternal life, hallelujah.

Psalm 149 *Cantate Domino*
All who see them shall acknowledge that they are a people whom the Lord has blessed. Is. 61: 9
Lent There is joy in the presence of the angels of God over one sinner who repents.
Easter Let the faithful rejoice in triumph, hallelujah.

1 Hallelujah!
Sing to the LORD a new song; *
sing his praise in the congregation of the faithful.

2 Let Israel rejoice in his Maker; *
let the children of Zion be joyful in their King.

3 Let them praise his Name in the dance; *
let them sing praise to him with timbrel and harp.

4 For the LORD takes pleasure in his people *
and adorns the poor with victory.

5 Let the faithful rejoice in triumph; *
let them be joyful on their beds.

6 Let the praises of God be in their throat *
and a two-edged sword in their hand;

7 To wreak vengeance on the nations *
and punishment on the peoples;

8 To bind their kings in chains *
and their nobles with links of iron;

9 To inflict on them the judgment decreed; *
this is glory for all his faithful people.
Hallelujah!

Lent There is joy in the presence of the angels of God over one sinner who repents.
Easter Let the faithful rejoice in triumph, hallelujah.

Readings

Responsories, Benedictus Antiphon, Litany, Invitation to the Lord's Prayer, Collect and Dismissal are taken from the Proper of the Season.

Thursday Week 1 Noonday Prayer

Officiant: O God, make speed to save us.
People: **O Lord, make haste to help us.**
Officiant and People **Glory to the Father...**
Except in Lent, add **Alleluia.**

Hymn *From the Proper of the Season or of the Day*

Psalm 119 Daleth *Adhæsit pavimento*

We shall run on the path of God's commandments, our hearts overflowing with the inexpressible delights of love. RB Prol 49

Lent My eyes are fixed on you, O my Strength; for you, O God, are my stronghold.
Easter To you, O my Strength, will I sing; for you, O God, are my stronghold and my merciful God, hallelujah.

25 My soul cleaves to the dust; *
    give me life according to your word.

26 I have confessed my ways, and you answered me; *
    instruct me in your statutes.

27 Make me understand the way of your commandments, *
    that I may meditate on your marvelous works.

28 My soul melts away for sorrow; *
    strengthen me according to your word.

29 Take from me the way of lying; *
    let me find grace through your law.

30 I have chosen the way of faithfulness; *
    I have set your judgments before me.

31 I hold fast to your decrees; *
    O LORD, let me not be put to shame.

32 I will run the way of your commandments, *
    for you have set my heart at liberty.

Psalm 59 A *Eripe me de inimicis*
The assembly rose as a body and brought Jesus before Pilate. Lk. 23:1

1 Rescue me from my enemies, O God; *
    protect me from those who rise up against me.

2 Rescue me from evildoers *
    and save me from those who thirst for my blood.

3 See how they lie in wait for my life,
  how the mighty gather together against me; *
    not for any offense or fault of mine, O LORD.

4 Not because of any guilt of mine *
    they run and prepare themselves for battle.

5 Rouse yourself, come to my side, and see; *
    for you, LORD God of hosts, are Israel's God.

6 Awake, and punish all the ungodly; *
    show no mercy to those who are faithless and evil.

7 They go to and fro in the evening; *
    they snarl like dogs and run about the city.

8 Behold, they boast with their mouths,
  and taunts are on their lips; *
    "For who," they say, "will hear us?"

9 But you, O LORD, you laugh at them; *
    you laugh all the ungodly to scorn.

10 My eyes are fixed on you, O my Strength; *
    for you, O God, are my stronghold.

11 My merciful God comes to meet me; *
    God will let me look in triumph on my enemies.

Psalm 59 B *Et tu, Domine*
This is your hour, and the power of darkness. Lk. 22:53

12 Slay them, O God, lest my people forget; *
    send them reeling by your might
    and put them down, O Lord our shield.

13 For the sins of their mouths, for the words of their lips,
   for the cursing and lies that they utter, *
    let them be caught in their pride.

14 Make an end of them in your wrath; *
    make an end of them, and they shall be no more.

15 Let everyone know that God rules in Jacob; *
    and to the ends of the earth.

16 They go to and fro in the evening; *
    they snarl like dogs and run about the city.

17 They forage for food, *
    and if they are not filled, they howl.

18 For my part, I will sing of your strength; *
    I will celebrate your love in the morning;

19 For you have become my stronghold, *
    a refuge in the day of my trouble.

20 To you, O my Strength, will I sing; *
    for you, O God, are my stronghold and my merciful God.

Lent My eyes are fixed on you, O my Strength; for you, O God, are my stronghold.
Easter To you, O my Strength, will I sing; for you, O God, are my stronghold and my merciful God, hallelujah.

Reading, Verse and Response, Collect and Conclusion as in the Proper of the Season or of the Day.

Thursday Week 1 Evening Prayer

Officiant: O God, make speed to save us.
People: **O Lord, make haste to help us.**
Officiant and People **Glory to the Father ...**
Except in Lent, add **Alleluia.**

Hymn *From the Proper of the Season or of the Day*

Psalm 78 Part I A *Attendite, popule*
You faithless generation, how much longer must I be among you? Mk. 9:19

Lent They did not keep the covenant of God, and refused to walk in his law.
Easter The Lord split open the sea and let them pass through; he made the waters stand up like walls, hallelujah.

1 Hear my teaching, O my people; *
    incline your ears to the words of my mouth.

2 I will open my mouth in a parable; *
    I will declare the mysteries of ancient times.

3 That which we have heard and known,
    and what our forefathers have told us, *
        we will not hide from their children.

4 We will recount to generations to come
    the praiseworthy deeds and the power of the LORD, *
        and the wonderful works he has done.

5 He gave his decrees to Jacob
    and established a law for Israel, *
        which he commanded them to teach their children;

6 That the generations to come might know,
    and the children yet unborn; *
        that they in their turn might tell it to their children;

7 So that they might put their trust in God, *
        and not forget the deeds of God,
        but keep his commandments;

8 And not be like their forefathers,
    a stubborn and rebellious generation, *
        a generation whose heart was not steadfast,
        and whose spirit was not faithful to God.

9 The people of Ephraim, armed with the bow, *
        turned back in the day of battle;

10 They did not keep the covenant of God, *
        and refused to walk in his law;

11 They forgot what he had done, *
        and the wonders he had shown them.

12 He worked marvels in the sight of their forefathers, *
        in the land of Egypt, in the field of Zoan.

13 He split open the sea and let them pass through; *
        he made the waters stand up like walls.

14 He led them with a cloud by day, *
        and all the night through with a glow of fire.

15 He split the hard rocks in the wilderness *
        and gave them drink as from the great deep.

16 He brought streams out of the cliff, *
        and the waters gushed out like rivers.

17 But they went on sinning against him, *
    rebelling in the desert against the Most High.

Lent They did not keep the covenant of God, and refused to walk in his law.
Easter The Lord split open the sea and let them pass through; he made the waters stand up like walls, hallelujah.

Psalm 78 Part I B *Et appposuerunt*
When the Son of Man comes, will he find faith on earth? Lk. 18:8

Lent They had no faith in God, nor did they put their trust in his saving power.
Easter My flesh is true food and my blood is true drink. Those who eat my flesh and drink my blood abide in my and I in them, hallelujah.

18 They tested God in their hearts, *
    demanding food for their craving.

19 They railed against God and said, *
    "Can God set a table in the wilderness?

20 True, he struck the rock, the waters gushed out,
    and the gullies overflowed; *
    but is he able to give bread
    or to provide meat for his people?"

21 When the LORD heard this, he was full of wrath; *
    a fire was kindled against Jacob,
    and his anger mounted against Israel;

22 For they had no faith in God, *
    nor did they put their trust in his saving power.

23 So he commanded the clouds above *
    and opened the doors of heaven.

24 He rained down manna upon them to eat *
    and gave them grain from heaven.

25 So mortals ate the bread of angels; *
    he provided for them food enough.

26 He caused the east wind to blow in the heavens *
    and led out the south wind by his might.

27 He rained down flesh upon them like dust *
    and wingèd birds like the sand of the sea.

28 He let it fall in the midst of their camp *
    and round about their dwellings.

29 So they ate and were well filled, *
    for he gave them what they craved.

Lent They had no faith in God, nor did they put their trust in his saving power.
Easter My flesh is true food and my blood is true drink. Those who eat my flesh and drink my blood abide in my and I in them, hallelujah.

Psalm 78 Part I C *Non sunt fraudati*
Be steadfast, immovable, always excelling in the work of the Lord, because you know that in the Lord your labor is not in vain. 1 Cor. 15:58

Lent You were so merciful that you forgave their sins and did not destroy them.
Easter Just as the living Father sent me, and I live because of the Father, so whoever eats me will live because of me, hallelujah.

30 But they did not stop their craving, *
    though the food was still in their mouths.

31 So God's anger mounted against them; *
    he slew their strongest men
    and laid low the youth of Israel.

32 In spite of all this, they went on sinning *
    and had no faith in his wonderful works.

33 So he brought their days to an end like a breath *
    and their years in sudden terror.

34 Whenever he slew them, they would seek him, *
    and repent, and diligently search for God.

35 They would remember that God was their rock, *
    and the Most High God their redeemer.

36 But they flattered him with their mouths *
    and lied to him with their tongues.

37 Their heart was not steadfast toward him, *
    and they were not faithful to his covenant.

38 But he was so merciful that he forgave their sins
    and did not destroy them; *
    many times he held back his anger
    and did not permit his wrath to be roused.

39 For he remembered that they were but flesh, *
   a breath that goes forth and does not return.

Lent You were so merciful that you forgave their sins and did not destroy them.
Easter Just as the living Father sent me, and I live because of the Father, so whoever eats me will live because of me, hallelujah.

Reading

Responsory, Magnificat Antiphon, Litany, Invitation to the Lord's Prayer, Collect and Dismissal are taken from the Proper of the Season.

Friday Week 1 Morning Prayer

Officiant: Lord, open our lips.
People: **And our mouth shall proclaim your praise.**
Officiant and People **Glory to the Father…**
Except in Lent, add **Alleluia.**

The Invitatory Psalm 95
From the Proper of the Season or of the Day

Hymn *From the Proper of the Season or of the Day*

Psalm 51 *Miserere mei, Deus*
How much more will the blood of Christ, who through the eternal Spirit offered himself without blemish to God, purify our conscience from dead works to worship the living God! Heb. 9: 15

Lent Purge me from my sin, and I shall be pure; wash me, and I shall be clean indeed.
Easter Make me hear of joy and gladness, that the body you have broken may rejoice, hallelujah.

1 Have mercy on me, O God,
   according to your loving-kindness; *
   in your great compassion blot out my offenses.

2 Wash me through and through from my wickedness *
   and cleanse me from my sin.

3 For I know my transgressions, *
   and my sin is ever before me.

4 Against you only have I sinned *
   and done what is evil in your sight.

5 And so you are justified when you speak *
   and upright in your judgment.

6 Indeed, I have been wicked from my birth, *
   a sinner from my mother's womb.

7 For behold, you look for truth deep within me, *
   and will make me understand wisdom secretly.

8 Purge me from my sin, and I shall be pure; *
   wash me, and I shall be clean indeed.

9 Make me hear of joy and gladness, *
   that the body you have broken may rejoice.

10 Hide your face from my sins *
   and blot out all my iniquities.

11 Create in me a clean heart, O God, *
   and renew a right spirit within me.

12 Cast me not away from your presence *
   and take not your holy Spirit from me.

13 Give me the joy of your saving help again *
   and sustain me with your bountiful Spirit.

14 I shall teach your ways to the wicked, *
   and sinners shall return to you.

15 Deliver me from death, O God, *
   and my tongue shall sing of your righteousness,
   O God of my salvation.

16 Open my lips, O Lord, *
   and my mouth shall proclaim your praise.

17 Had you desired it, I would have offered sacrifice, *
   but you take no delight in burnt-offerings.

18 The sacrifice of God is a troubled spirit; *
   a broken and contrite heart, O God, you will not despise.

19 Be favorable and gracious to Zion, *
   and rebuild the walls of Jerusalem.

20 Then you will be pleased with the appointed sacrifices,
  with burnt-offerings and oblations; *
   then shall they offer young bullocks upon your altar.

Lent Purge me from my sin, and I shall be pure; wash me, and I shall be clean indeed.

Easter Make me hear of joy and gladness, that the body you have broken may rejoice, hallelujah.

Psalm 88 A *Domine, Deus*
Joseph of Arimathea, who was a disciple of Jesus,
asked Pilate to let him take away the body of Jesus. Jn. 19:38

Lent The Lord, the Redeemer of Israel, says to one deeply despised, abhorred by the nations, the slave of rulers, "Kings shall see and stand up."
Easter Let us give thanks to the Father, who has called you to share in the inheritance of the saints in the light, hallelujah.

1 O LORD, my God, my Savior, *
   by day and night I cry to you.

2 Let my prayer enter into your presence; *
   incline your ear to my lamentation.

3 For I am full of trouble; *
   my life is at the brink of the grave.

4 I am counted among those who go down to the Pit; *
   I have become like one who has no strength;

5 Lost among the dead, *
   like the slain who lie in the grave,

6 Whom you remember no more, *
   for they are cut off from your hand.

7 You have laid me in the depths of the Pit, *
   in dark places, and in the abyss.

8 Your anger weighs upon me heavily, *
   and all your great waves overwhelm me.

9 You have put my friends far from me;
   you have made me to be abhorred by them; *
   I am in prison and cannot get free.

10 My sight has failed me because of trouble; *
   LORD, I have called upon you daily;
   I have stretched out my hands to you.

Lent The Lord, the Redeemer of Israel, says to one deeply despised, abhorred by the nations, the slave of rulers, "Kings shall see and stand up."
Easter Let us give thanks to the Father, who has called you to share in the inheritance of the saints in the light, hallelujah.

Psalm 88 B *Numquid mortuis*

In the garden there was a new tomb in which no one had ever been laid. Because the tomb was nearby, they laid Jesus there. Jn. 19:41-42

Lent My friend and my neighbor you have put away from me, and darkness is my only companion.
Easter God has rescued us from the power of darkness and transferred us into the kingdom of his Beloved Son, hallelujah.

11 Do you work wonders for the dead? *
 will those who have died stand up and give you thanks?

12 Will your loving-kindness be declared in the grave? *
 your faithfulness in the land of destruction?

13 Will your wonders be known in the dark? *
 or your righteousness in the country
 where all is forgotten?

14 But as for me, O LORD, I cry to you for help; *
 in the morning my prayer comes before you.

15 LORD, why have you rejected me? *
 why have you hidden your face from me?

16 Ever since my youth, I have been wretched
 and at the point of death; *
 I have borne your terrors with a troubled mind.

17 Your blazing anger has swept over me; *
 your terrors have destroyed me;

18 They surround me all day long like a flood; *
 they encompass me on every side.

19 My friend and my neighbor you have put away from me, *
 and darkness is my only companion.

Lent My friend and my neighbor you have put away from me, and darkness is my only companion.
Easter God has rescued us from the power of darkness and transferred us into the kingdom of his Beloved Son, hallelujah.

Readings

Responsories, Benedictus Antiphon, Litany, Invitation to the Lord's Prayer, Collet and Dismissal are taken from the Proper of the Season.

Friday Week 1 Noonday Prayer

Officiant: O God, make speed to save us.
People: **O Lord, make haste to help us.**
Officiant and People **Glory to the Father...**
Except in Lent, add **Alleluia.**

Hymn *From the Proper of the Season or of the Day*

Psalm 119 He *Legem pone*
*They hear the word, hold it fast in an honest and good heart,
and bear fruit with patient endurance. Lk. 8:15*

Lent Be merciful, just as your Father is merciful.
Easter I will give great thanks to the LORD with my mouth; in the midst of the multitude will I praise him, hallelujah.

33 Teach me, O LORD, the way of your statutes, *
 and I shall keep it to the end.

34 Give me understanding, and I shall keep your law; *
 I shall keep it with all my heart.

35 Make me go in the path of your commandments, *
 for that is my desire.

36 Incline my heart to your decrees *
 and not to unjust gain.

37 Turn my eyes from watching what is worthless; *
 give me life in your ways.

38 Fulfill your promise to your servant, *
 which you make to those who fear you.

39 Turn away the reproach which I dread, *
 because your judgments are good.

40 Behold, I long for your commandments; *
 in your righteousness preserve my life.

Psalm 109 A *Deus, laudem*
*The soldiers began saluting Jesus, "Hail, King of the Jews!" They struck his head with a reed,
spat upon him, and knelt down in homage to him. Mk. 16:18-19*

1 Hold not your tongue, O God of my praise; *
 for the mouth of the wicked,
 the mouth of the deceitful, is opened against me.

2 They speak to me with a lying tongue; *
 they encompass me with hateful words
 and fight against me without a cause.

3 Despite my love, they accuse me; *
    but as for me, I pray for them.

4 They repay evil for good, *
    and hatred for my love.

5 Set a wicked man against him, *
    and let an accuser stand at his right hand.

6 When he is judged, let him be found guilty, *
    and let his appeal be in vain.

7 Let his days be few, *
    and let another take his office.

8 Let his children be fatherless, *
    and his wife become a widow.

9 Let his children be waifs and beggars; *
    let them be driven from the ruins of their homes.

10 Let the creditor seize everything he has; *
    let strangers plunder his gains.

11 Let there be no one to show him kindness, *
    and none to pity his fatherless children.

12 Let his descendants be destroyed, *
    and his name be blotted out in the next generation.

13 Let the wickedness of his fathers
  be remembered before the LORD, *
    and his mother's sin not be blotted out;

14 Let their sin be always before the LORD; *
    but let him root out their names from the earth;

15 Because he did not remember to show mercy, *
    but persecuted the poor and needy
    and sought to kill the brokenhearted.

16 He loved cursing,
  let it come upon him; *
    he took no delight in blessing,
    let it depart from him.

17 He put on cursing like a garment, *
    let it soak into his body like water
    and into his bones like oil;

18 Let it be to him like the cloak
   which he wraps around himself, *
      and like the belt that he wears continually.

19 Let this be the recompense from the LORD to my accusers, *
      and to those who speak evil against me.

Psalm 109 B *Et tu, Domine*

*They compelled a passer-by, who was coming in from the country, to carry his cross;
it was Simon of Cyrene. Mk 15:21*

20 But you, O Lord my God,
   oh, deal with me according to your Name; *
      for your tender mercy's sake, deliver me.

21 For I am poor and needy, *
      and my heart is wounded within me.

22 I have faded away like a shadow when it lengthens; *
      I am shaken off like a locust.

23 My knees are weak through fasting, *
      and my flesh is wasted and gaunt.

24 I have become a reproach to them; *
      they see and shake their heads.

25 Help me, O LORD my God; *
      save me for your mercy's sake.

26 Let them know that this is your hand, *
      that you, O LORD, have done it.

27 They may curse, but you will bless; *
      let those who rise up against me be put to shame,
      and your servant will rejoice.

28 Let my accusers be clothed with disgrace *
      and wrap themselves in their shame as in a cloak.

29 I will give great thanks to the LORD with my mouth; *
      in the midst of the multitude will I praise him;

30 Because he stands at the right hand of the needy, *
      to save his life from those who would condemn him.

Lent Be merciful, just as your Father is merciful.
Easter I will give great thanks to the LORD with my mouth; in the midst of the multitude will I praise him, hallelujah.

Reading, Verse and Response, Collect and Conclusion as in the Proper of the Season or of the Day.

Friday Week 1 Evening Prayer

Officiant: O God, make speed to save us.
People: **O Lord, make haste to help us.**
Officiant and People **Glory to the Father…**
Except in Lent, add **Alleluia.**

Hymn *From the Proper of the Season or of the Day*

Psalm 130 *De profundis*

*Jesus offered up prayers and supplications, with loud cries and tears,
to the one who was able to save him from death. Heb 5:7*

Lent With the Lord there is plenteous redemption, and God shall redeem Israel from all their sins
Easter I will be joyful in the LORD; I will glory in God's victory, hallelujah.

1. Out of the depths have I called to you, O LORD;
   LORD, hear my voice; *
   let your ears consider well the voice of my supplication.

2. If you, LORD, were to note what is done amiss, *
   O LORD, who could stand?

3. For there is forgiveness with you; *
   therefore you shall be feared.

4. I wait for the LORD; my soul waits for him; *
   in his word is my hope.

5. My soul waits for the LORD,
   more than watchmen for the morning, *
   more than watchmen for the morning.

6. O Israel, wait for the LORD, *
   for with the LORD there is mercy;

7. With him there is plenteous redemption, *
   and he shall redeem Israel from all their sins.

Lent With the Lord there is plenteous redemption, and God shall redeem Israel from all their sins
Easter I will be joyful in the LORD; I will glory in God's victory, hallelujah.

Psalm 35 *Judica, Domine*

The people stood by, watching; but the leaders scoffed at him, saying,
"He saved others; let him save himself if he is the Messiah of God. Lk. 23:35

Lent They came together and laid plans to capture Jesus by treachery and put him to death.
Easter I will give you thanks in the great congregation; I will praise you in the mighty throng, hallelujah.

1 Fight those who fight me, O LORD; *
    attack those who are attacking me.

2 Take up shield and armor *
    and rise up to help me.

3 Draw the sword and bar the way
    against those who pursue me; *
    say to my soul, "I am your salvation."

4 Let those who seek after my life be shamed and humbled; *
    let those who plot my ruin fall back and be dismayed.

5 Let them be like chaff before the wind, *
    and let the angel of the LORD drive them away.

6 Let their way be dark and slippery, *
    and let the angel of the LORD pursue them.

7 For they have secretly spread a net for me without a cause; *
    without a cause they have dug a pit to take me alive.

8 Let ruin come upon them unawares; *
    let them be caught in the net they hid;
    let them fall into the pit they dug.

9 Then I will be joyful in the LORD; *
    I will glory in his victory.

10 My very bones will say, "LORD, who is like you? *
    You deliver the poor from those who are too strong for them,
    the poor and needy from those who rob them."

11 Malicious witnesses rise up against me; *
    they charge me with matters I know nothing about.

12 They pay me evil in exchange for good; *
    my soul is full of despair.

13 But when they were sick I dressed in sack-cloth *
    and humbled myself by fasting;

14 I prayed with my whole heart,
   as one would for a friend or a brother; *
      I behaved like one who mourns for his mother,
      bowed down and grieving.

15 But when I stumbled, they were glad and gathered together;
   they gathered against me; *
      strangers whom I did not know tore me to pieces
      and would not stop.

16 They put me to the test and mocked me; *
      they gnashed at me with their teeth.

17 O Lord, how long will you look on? *
      rescue me from the roaring beasts,
      and my life from the young lions.

18 I will give you thanks in the great congregation; *
      I will praise you in the mighty throng.

19 Do not let my treacherous foes rejoice over me, *
      nor let those who hate me without a cause
      wink at each other.

20 For they do not plan for peace, *
      but invent deceitful schemes
      against the quiet in the land.

21 They opened their mouths at me and said, *
      "Aha! we saw it with our own eyes."

22 You saw it, O Lord; do not be silent; *
      O Lord, be not far from me.

23 Awake, arise, to my cause! *
      to my defense, my God and my Lord!

24 Give me justice, O Lord my God,
   according to your righteousness; *
      do not let them triumph over me.

25 Do not let them say in their hearts,
   "Aha! just what we want!" *
      Do not let them say, "We have swallowed him up."

26 Let all who rejoice at my ruin be ashamed and disgraced; *
      let those who boast against me
      be clothed with dismay and shame.

27 Let those who favor my cause sing out with joy and be glad; *
   let them say always, "Great is the LORD,
   who desires the prosperity of his servant."

28 And my tongue shall be talking of your righteousness *
   and of your praise all the day long.

Lent They came together and laid plans to capture Jesus by treachery and put him to death.
Easter I will give you thanks in the great congregation; I will praise you in the mighty throng, hallelujah.

Psalm 142 *Voce mea ad Dominum*
Jesus gave a loud cry and breathed his last. Mk. 15:37

Lent In the days of his flesh, Jesus offered up prayers and supplications, with loud cries and tears and he was heard because of his reverence.
Easter When you have dealt bountifully with me, the righteous will gather around me, hallelujah.

1 I cry to the LORD with my voice; *
   to the LORD I make loud supplication.

2 I pour out my complaint before him *
   and tell him all my trouble.

3 When my spirit languishes within me, you know my path; *
   in the way wherein I walk they have hidden a trap for me.

4 I look to my right hand and find no one who knows me; *
   I have no place to flee to, and no one cares for me.

5 I cry out to you, O LORD; *
   I say, "You are my refuge,
   my portion in the land of the living."

6 Listen to my cry for help, for I have been brought very low; *
   save me from those who pursue me,
   for they are too strong for me.

7 Bring me out of prison, that I may give thanks to your Name; *
   when you have dealt bountifully with me,
   the righteous will gather around me.

Lent In the days of his flesh, Jesus offered up prayers and supplications, with loud cries and tears and he was heard because of his reverence.
Easter When you have dealt bountifully with me, the righteous will gather around me, hallelujah.

Reading

Responsory, Magnificat Antiphon, Litany, Invitation to the Lord's Prayer, Collect and Dismissal are taken from the Proper of the Season.

Saturday Week 1 Morning Prayer

Officiant: Lord, open our lips.
People: **And our mouth shall proclaim your praise.**
Officiant and People **Glory to the Father...**
Except in Lent, add **Alleluia.**

The Invitatory Psalm 122
From the Proper of the Season or of the Day

Hymn *From the Proper of the Season or of the Day*

Psalm 9 *Confitebor tibi*
I was dead, and see, I am alive forever and ever; and I have the keys of Death and of Hades. Rev. 1:18

Lent Have pity on me, O LORD, you who lift me up from the gate of death

Easter I will tell of all your praises in the gates of the city of Zion, hallelujah.

1 I will give thanks to you, O LORD, with my whole heart; *
 I will tell of all your marvelous works.

2 I will be glad and rejoice in you; *
 I will sing to your Name, O Most High.

3 When my enemies are driven back, *
 they will stumble and perish at your presence.

4 For you have maintained my right and my cause; *
 you sit upon your throne judging right.

5 You have rebuked the ungodly and destroyed the wicked; *
 you have blotted out their name for ever and ever.

6 As for the enemy, they are finished, in perpetual ruin, *
 their cities ploughed under, the memory of them perished;

7 But the LORD is enthroned for ever; *
 he has set up his throne for judgment.

8 It is he who rules the world with righteousness; *
 he judges the peoples with equity.

9 The LORD will be a refuge for the oppressed, *
   a refuge in time of trouble.

10 Those who know your Name will put their trust in you, *
   for you never forsake those who seek you, O LORD.

11 Sing praise to the LORD who dwells in Zion; *
   proclaim to the peoples the things he has done.

12 The Avenger of blood will remember them; *
   he will not forget the cry of the afflicted.

13 Have pity on me, O LORD; *
   see the misery I suffer from those who hate me,
   O you who lift me up from the gate of death;

14 So that I may tell of all your praises
   and rejoice in your salvation *
   in the gates of the city of Zion.

15 The ungodly have fallen into the pit they dug, *
   and in the snare they set is their own foot caught.

16 The LORD is known by his acts of justice; *
   the wicked are trapped in the works of their own hands.

17 The wicked shall be given over to the grave, *
   and also all the peoples that forget God.

18 For the needy shall not always be forgotten, *
   and the hope of the poor shall not perish for ever.

19 Rise up, O LORD, let not the ungodly have the upper hand; *
   let them be judged before you.

20 Put fear upon them, O LORD; *
   let the ungodly know they are but mortal.

Lent Have pity on me, O LORD, you who lift me up from the gate of death
Easter I will tell of all your praises in the gates of the city of Zion, hallelujah.

Psalm 101 *Misericordiam et judicium*
Everyone who does what is right is righteous, just as he is righteous. 1 Jn. 3:7

Lent A crooked heart shall be far from me; I will not know evil.
Easter Those who do the will of my Father will enter into the kingdom of heaven, hallelujah.

1 I will sing of mercy and justice; *
    to you, O LORD, will I sing praises.

2 I will strive to follow a blameless course;
    oh, when will you come to me? *
    I will walk with sincerity of heart within my house.

3 I will set no worthless thing before my eyes; *
    I hate the doers of evil deeds;
    they shall not remain with me.

4 A crooked heart shall be far from me; *
    I will not know evil.

5 Those who in secret slander their neighbors I will destroy; *
    those who have a haughty look and a proud heart
    I cannot abide.

6 My eyes are upon the faithful in the land,
    that they may dwell with me, *
    and only those who lead a blameless life
    shall be my servants.

7 Those who act deceitfully shall not dwell in my house, *
    and those who tell lies shall not continue in my sight.

8 I will soon destroy all the wicked in the land, *
    that I may root out all evildoers from the city of the LORD.

Lent A crooked heart shall be far from me; I will not know evil.
Easter Those who do the will of my Father will enter into the kingdom of heaven, hallelujah.

Psalm 150 *Laudate Dominum*
The whole multitude of the disciples began to praise God joyfully with a loud voice. Lk. 19: 37

Lent Praise the Lord in the firmament of his power.
Easter Worship God who is seated upon the throne, saying, Amen, hallelujah.

1 Hallelujah!
   Praise God in his holy temple; *
    praise him in the firmament of his power.

2 Praise him for his mighty acts; *
    praise him for his excellent greatness.

3 Praise him with the blast of the ram's-horn; *
    praise him with lyre and harp.

4 Praise him with timbrel and dance; *
    praise him with strings and pipe.

5 Praise him with resounding cymbals; *
    praise him with loud-clanging cymbals.

6 Let everything that has breath *
    praise the Lord.
    Hallelujah!

Lent Praise the Lord in the firmament of his power.
Easter Worship God who is seated upon the throne, saying, Amen, hallelujah.

Readings

Responsories, Benedictus Antiphon, Litany, Invitation to the Lord's Prayer, Collet and Dismissal are taken from the Proper of the Season.

Saturday Week 1 Noonday Prayer

Officiant: O God, make speed to save us.
People: **O Lord, make haste to help us.**
Officiant and People **Glory to the Father ...**
Except in Lent, add **Alleluia.**

Hymn *From the Proper of the Season or of the Day*

Psalm 119 Waw *Et veniat super me*
You will know the truth, and the truth will make you free. Jn. 8:32

Lent If we wish to dwell in the tent of that kingdom, we must run to it by good deeds.
Easter You have rescued my soul from death that I may walk before God in the light of the living, hallelujah.

41 Let your loving-kindness come to me, O LORD, *
    and your salvation, according to your promise.

42 Then shall I have a word for those who taunt me, *
    because I trust in your words.

43 Do not take the word of truth out of my mouth, *
    for my hope is in your judgments.

44 I shall continue to keep your law; *
    I shall keep it for ever and ever.

45 I will walk at liberty, *
    because I study your commandments.

46 I will tell of your decrees before kings *
   and will not be ashamed.

47 I delight in your commandments, *
   which I have always loved.

48 I will lift up my hands to your commandments, *
   and I will meditate on your statutes.

Psalm 30 *Exaltabo te, Domine*

Jesus Christ, our Lord, was declared to be Son of God with power according to the spirit of holiness by resurrection from the dead. Rm. 1:4

1 I will exalt you, O LORD,
  because you have lifted me up *
    and have not let my enemies triumph over me.

2 O LORD my God, I cried out to you, *
   and you restored me to health.

3 You brought me up, O LORD, from the dead; *
   you restored my life as I was going down to the grave.

4 Sing to the LORD, you servants of his; *
   give thanks for the remembrance of his holiness.

5 For his wrath endures but the twinkling of an eye, *
   his favor for a lifetime.

6 Weeping may spend the night, *
   but joy comes in the morning.

7 While I felt secure, I said,
  "I shall never be disturbed. *
    You, LORD, with your favor,
    made me as strong as the mountains."

8 Then you hid your face, *
   and I was filled with fear.

9 I cried to you, O LORD; *
   I pleaded with the Lord, saying,

10 "What profit is there in my blood, if I go down to the Pit? *
    will the dust praise you or declare your faithfulness?

11 Hear, O LORD, and have mercy upon me; *
    O LORD, be my helper."

12 You have turned my wailing into dancing; *
    you have put off my sack-cloth and clothed me with joy.

13 Therefore my heart sings to you without ceasing; *
    O LORD my God, I will give you thanks for ever.

Psalm 56 *Miserere mei, Deus*
Do not let your hearts be troubled, and do not let them be afraid. Jn. 14:27

1 Have mercy on me, O God,
   for my enemies are hounding me; *
    all day long they assault and oppress me.

2 They hound me all the day long; *
    truly there are many who fight against me, O Most High.

3 Whenever I am afraid, *
    I will put my trust in you.

4 In God, whose word I praise,
   In God I trust and will not be afraid, *
    for what can flesh do to me?

5 All day long they damage my cause; *
    their only thought is to do me evil.

6 They band together; they lie in wait; *
    they spy upon my footsteps;
    because they seek my life.

7 Shall they escape despite their wickedness? *
    O God, in your anger, cast down the peoples.

8 You have noted my lamentation;
   put my tears into your bottle; *
    are they not recorded in your book?

9 Whenever I call upon you, my enemies will be put to flight; *
    this I know, for God is on my side.

10 In God the LORD, whose word I praise,
    in God I trust and will not be afraid, *
     for what can mortals do to me?

11 I am bound by the vow I made to you, O God; *
    I will present to you thank-offerings;

12 For you have rescued my soul from death
   and my feet from stumbling, *
    that I may walk before God in the light of the living.

Lent If we wish to dwell in the tent of that kingdom, we must run to it by good deeds.

Easter You have rescued my soul from death that I may walk before God in the light of the living, hallelujah.

Reading, Verse and Response, Collect and Conclusion as in the Proper of the Season or of the Day.

Week 2

Sunday Week 2 Evening Prayer I

Officiant: O God, make speed to save us.
People: **O Lord, make haste to help us.**
Officiant and People **Glory to the Father...**
Except in Lent, add **Alleluia.**

Hymn *From the Proper of the Season or of the Day*

Psalm 146 *Lauda, anima mea*
I will put my Spirit upon him, and he will proclaim justice to the Gentiles. Mt. 12:18

Lent When they breathe their last, they return to earth, and in that day their thoughts perish.
Easter The LORD shall reign for ever, your God, O Zion, throughout all generations. hallelujah!

1 Hallelujah!
   Praise the LORD, O my soul! *
      I will praise the LORD as long as I live;
      I will sing praises to my God while I have my being.

2 Put not your trust in rulers, nor in any child of earth, *
      for there is no help in them.

3 When they breathe their last, they return to earth, *
      and in that day their thoughts perish.

4 Blessed are they who have the God of Jacob for their help! *
      whose hope is in the LORD their God;

5 Who made heaven and earth, the seas, and all that is in them; *
      who keeps his promise for ever;

6 Who gives justice to those who are oppressed, *
      and food to those who hunger.

7 The LORD sets the prisoners free;
   the LORD opens the eyes of the blind; *
      the LORD lifts up those who are bowed down;

8 The LORD loves the righteous;
   the LORD cares for the stranger; *
      he sustains the orphan and widow,
      but frustrates the way of the wicked.

9 The LORD shall reign for ever, *
      your God, O Zion, throughout all generations.
      Hallelujah!

Lent When they breathe their last, they return to earth, and in that day their thoughts perish.
Easter The LORD shall reign for ever, your God, O Zion, throughout all generations. hallelujah!

Psalm 147 A *Laudate Dominum*
We give thanks to the Father, who has enabled us to share
in the inheritance of the saints in the light. Col. 1:12

Lent God heals the brokenhearted and binds up their wounds.
Easter The Lord rebuilds Jerusalem and heals the brokenhearted, hallelujah.

1 Hallelujah!
   How good it is to sing praises to our God! *
      how pleasant it is to honor him with praise!

2 The LORD rebuilds Jerusalem; *
      he gathers the exiles of Israel.

3 He heals the brokenhearted *
      and binds up their wounds.

4 He counts the number of the stars *
      and calls them all by their names.

5 Great is our LORD and mighty in power; *
      there is no limit to his wisdom.

6 The LORD lifts up the lowly, *
      but casts the wicked to the ground.

7 Sing to the LORD with thanksgiving; *
      make music to our God upon the harp.

8 He covers the heavens with clouds *
      and prepares rain for the earth;

9 He makes grass to grow upon the mountains *
      and green plants to serve mankind.

10 He provides food for flocks and herds *
      and for the young ravens when they cry.

11 He is not impressed by the might of a horse; *
      he has no pleasure in the strength of a man;

12 But the LORD has pleasure in those who fear him, *
      in those who await his gracious favor.

Lent God heals the brokenhearted and binds up their wounds.
Easter The Lord rebuilds Jerusalem and heals the brokenhearted, hallelujah.

Psalm 147 B *Lauda Hierusalem*

Let the peace of Christ rule in your hearts, to which indeed you were called in the one body. Col. 3:15

Lent God declares his word to Jacob, his statutes and his judgments to Israel.
Easter Come, I will show you the bride of the Lamb, hallelujah.

13 Worship the LORD, O Jerusalem; *
    praise your God, O Zion;

14 For he has strengthened the bars of your gates; *
    he has blessed your children within you.

15 He has established peace on your borders; *
    he satisfies you with the finest wheat.

16 He sends out his command to the earth, *
    and his word runs very swiftly.

17 He gives snow like wool; *
    he scatters hoarfrost like ashes.

18 He scatters his hail like bread crumbs; *
    who can stand against his cold?

19 He sends forth his word and melts them; *
    he blows with his wind, and the waters flow.

20 He declares his word to Jacob, *
    his statutes and his judgments to Israel.

21 He has not done so to any other nation; *
    to them he has not revealed his judgments.
    Hallelujah!

Lent God declares his word to Jacob, his statutes and his judgments to Israel.
Easter Come, I will show you the bride of the Lamb, hallelujah.

Reading

Responsory, Magnficat Antiphon, Litany, Invitation to the Lord's Prayer, Collet and Dismissal are taken from the Proper of the Season.

Sunday Week 2 Morning Prayer

Officiant: Lord, open our lips.
People: **And our mouth shall proclaim your praise.**
Officiant and People **Glory to the Father…**
Except in Lent, add **Alleluia.**

The Invitatory Psalm 95
From the Proper of the Season or of the Day

Hymn *From the Proper of the Season or of the Day*

Psalm 93 *Dominus regnavit*
Jesus Christ is the faithful witness, the firstborn of the dead, and the ruler of the kings of the earth. Rev. 1:5

Lent Your testimonies are very sure, O Lord, and mightier than the sound of many waters.
Easter The Lord has put on splendid apparel, hallelujah.

1 The LORD is King;
    he has put on splendid apparel; *
        the LORD has put on his apparel
        and girded himself with strength.

2 He has made the whole world so sure *
        that it cannot be moved;

3 Ever since the world began, your throne has been established; *
        you are from everlasting.

4 The waters have lifted up, O LORD,
    the waters have lifted up their voice; *
        the waters have lifted up their pounding waves.

5 Mightier than the sound of many waters,
    mightier than the breakers of the sea, *
        mightier is the LORD who dwells on high.

6 Your testimonies are very sure, *
        and holiness adorns your house, O LORD,
        for ever and for evermore.

Lent Your testimonies are very sure, O Lord, and mightier than the sound of many waters.
Easter The Lord has put on splendid apparel, hallelujah.

Psalm 63 *Deus, Deus meus*
Let anyone who is thirsty come to me, and let the one who believes in me drink. Jn. 7: 37-38

Lent You have been my helper, O my God.
Easter Let whoever thirsts take the water of life without price, hallelujah.

1 O God, you are my God; eagerly I seek you; *
   my soul thirsts for you, my flesh faints for you,
   as in a barren and dry land where there is no water.

2 Therefore I have gazed upon you in your holy place, *
   that I might behold your power and your glory.

3 For your loving-kindness is better than life itself; *
   my lips shall give you praise.

4 So will I bless you as long as I live *
   and lift up my hands in your Name.

5 My soul is content, as with marrow and fatness, *
   and my mouth praises you with joyful lips,

6 When I remember you upon my bed, *
   and meditate on you in the night watches.

7 For you have been my helper, *
   and under the shadow of your wings I will rejoice.

8 My soul clings to you; *
   your right hand holds me fast.

9 May those who seek my life to destroy it *
   go down into the depths of the earth;

10 Let them fall upon the edge of the sword, *
   and let them be food for jackals.

11 But the king will rejoice in God;
   all those who swear by him will be glad; *
   for the mouth of those who speak lies shall be stopped.

Lent You have been my helper, O my God.
Easter Let whoever thirsts take the water of life without price, hallelujah.

Psalm 47 *Omnes gentes, plaudite*

God has made him the head over all things for the church, which is his body, the fullness of him who fills all in all. Eph. 1:22-23

Lent The LORD Most High is to be feared; he is the great King over all the earth.

Easter God has gone up with a shout, the LORD with the sound of the ram's-horn, hallelujah.

1 Clap your hands, all you peoples; *
    shout to God with a cry of joy.

2 For the LORD Most High is to be feared; *
    he is the great King over all the earth.

3 He subdues the peoples under us, *
    and the nations under our feet.

4 He chooses our inheritance for us, *
    the pride of Jacob whom he loves.

5 God has gone up with a shout, *
    the LORD with the sound of the ram's-horn.

6 Sing praises to God, sing praises; *
    sing praises to our King, sing praises.

7 For God is King of all the earth; *
    sing praises with all your skill.

8 God reigns over the nations; *
    God sits upon his holy throne.

9 The nobles of the peoples have gathered together *
    with the people of the God of Abraham.

10 The rulers of the earth belong to God, *
    and he is highly exalted.

Lent The LORD Most High is to be feared; he is the great King over all the earth.

Easter God has gone up with a shout, the LORD with the sound of the ram's-horn, hallelujah.

Readings

Responsories, Benedictus Antiphon, Litany, Invitation to the Lord's Prayer, Collet and Dismissal are taken from the Proper of the Season.

Sunday Week 2 Noonday Prayer

Officiant: O God, make speed to save us.
People: **O Lord, make haste to help us.**
Officiant and People **Glory to the Father …**
Except in Lent, add **Alleluia.**

Hymn *From the Proper of the Season or of the Day*

Psalm 72 A *Deus, judicium*
On entering the house, they saw the child with Mary his mother;
and they knelt down and paid him homage. Mt. 2:11

Lent The LORD is good; God's mercy is everlasting.
Easter May his Name remain for ever and be established as long as the sun endures; may all the nations bless themselves in him and call him blessed., hallelujah.

1 Give the King your justice, O God, *
 and your righteousness to the King's Son;

2 That he may rule your people righteously *
 and the poor with justice;

3 That the mountains may bring prosperity to the people, *
 and the little hills bring righteousness.

4 He shall defend the needy among the people; *
 he shall rescue the poor and crush the oppressor.

5 He shall live as long as the sun and moon endure, *
 from one generation to another.

6 He shall come down like rain upon the mown field, *
 like showers that water the earth.

7 In his time shall the righteous flourish; *
 there shall be abundance of peace
 till the moon shall be no more.

8 He shall rule from sea to sea, *
 and from the River to the ends of the earth.

9 His foes shall bow down before him, *
 and his enemies lick the dust.

10 The kings of Tarshish and of the isles shall pay tribute, *
 and the kings of Arabia and Saba offer gifts.

11 All kings shall bow down before him, *
 and all the nations do him service.

Psalm 72 B *Quia liberabit*

Jesus saw a great crowd; and he had compassion for them and cured their sick. Mt. 14:14

12 For he shall deliver the poor who cries out in distress, *
    and the oppressed who has no helper.

13 He shall have pity on the lowly and poor; *
    he shall preserve the lives of the needy.

14 He shall redeem their lives from oppression and violence, *
    and dear shall their blood be in his sight.

15 Long may he live!
   and may there be given to him gold from Arabia; *
      may prayer be made for him always,
      and may they bless him all the day long.

16 May there be abundance of grain on the earth,
   growing thick even on the hilltops; *
      may its fruit flourish like Lebanon,
      and its grain like grass upon the earth.

17 May his Name remain for ever
   and be established as long as the sun endures; *
      may all the nations bless themselves in him
      and call him blessed.

18 Blessed be the LORD God, the God of Israel, *
    who alone does wondrous deeds!

19 And blessed be his glorious Name for ever! *
    and may all the earth be filled with his glory.
    Amen. Amen.

Psalm 117 *Laudate Dominum*

Once you were not a people, but now you are God's people. 1 Pt. 2:10

1 Praise the LORD, all you nations; *
    laud him, all you peoples.

2 For his loving-kindness toward us is great, *
    and the faithfulness of the LORD endures for ever.
    Hallelujah!

Lent The LORD is good; God's mercy is everlasting.
Easter May his Name remain for ever and be established as long as the sun endures; may all the nations bless themselves in him and call him blessed., hallelujah.

Reading, Verse and Response, Collect and Conclusion as in the Proper of the Season or of the Day.

Sunday Week 2 Evening Prayer II

Officiant: O God, make speed to save us.
People: **O Lord, make haste to help us.**
Officiant and People **Glory to the Father ...**
Except in Lent, add **Alleluia.**

Hymn *From the Proper of the Season or of the Day*

Psalm 113 *Laudate, pueri*
Salvation belongs to our God who is seated on the throne, and to the Lamb! Rev. 7:10

Lent The Lord takes up the weak out of the dust and lifts up the poor from the ashes.
Easter The Lord, who is high above all nations, has raised us up with Christ Jesus, hallelujah.

1 Hallelujah!
  Give praise, you servants of the LORD; *
    praise the Name of the LORD.

2 Let the Name of the LORD be blessed, *
    from this time forth for evermore.

3 From the rising of the sun to its going down *
    let the Name of the LORD be praised.

4 The LORD is high above all nations, *
    and his glory above the heavens.

5 Who is like the LORD our God, who sits enthroned on high, *
    but stoops to behold the heavens and the earth?

6 He takes up the weak out of the dust *
    and lifts up the poor from the ashes.

7 He sets them with the princes, *
    with the princes of his people.

8 He makes the woman of a childless house *
    to be a joyful mother of children.

Lent The Lord takes up the weak out of the dust and lifts up the poor from the ashes.
Easter The Lord, who is high above all nations, has raised us up with Christ Jesus, hallelujah.

Psalm 114 *In exitu Israel*

Now have come the salvation and the power and the kingdom of our God and the authority of his Messiah. Rev. 12:10

Lent I will never forget any of their injustices. Shall not the land tremble on this account?
Easter He has delivered us from the dominion of darkness, and brought us into the kingdom of his Son, hallelujah.

1 Hallelujah!
   When Israel came out of Egypt, *
      the house of Jacob from a people of strange speech,

2 Judah became God's sanctuary *
      and Israel his dominion.

3 The sea beheld it and fled; *
      Jordan turned and went back.

4 The mountains skipped like rams, *
      and the little hills like young sheep.

5 What ailed you, O sea, that you fled? *
      O Jordan, that you turned back?

6 You mountains, that you skipped like rams? *
      you little hills like young sheep?

7 Tremble, O earth, at the presence of the Lord, *
      at the presence of the God of Jacob,

8 Who turned the hard rock into a pool of water *
      and flint-stone into a flowing spring.

Lent I will never forget any of their injustices. Shall not the land tremble on this account?
Easter He has delivered us from the dominion of darkness, and brought us into the kingdom of his Son, hallelujah.

Psalm 115 *Non nobis, Domine*

Jesus Christ loves us and freed us from our sins by his blood, and made us to be a kingdom, priests serving his God and Father. Rev. 1:5-6

Lent What wrong did your ancestors find in me that they went far from me, and went after worthless things, and became worthless themselves?
Easter We have been turned from the worship of idols to serve the living God, hallelujah.

1 Not to us, O LORD, not to us,
    but to your Name give glory; *
        because of your love and because of your faithfulness.

2 Why should the heathen say, *
    "Where then is their God?"

3 Our God is in heaven; *
    whatever he wills to do he does.

4 Their idols are silver and gold, *
    the work of human hands.

5 They have mouths, but they cannot speak; *
    eyes have they, but they cannot see;

6 They have ears, but they cannot hear; *
    noses, but they cannot smell;

7 They have hands, but they cannot feel;
    feet, but they cannot walk; *
        they make no sound with their throat.

8 Those who make them are like them, *
    and so are all who put their trust in them.

9 O Israel, trust in the LORD; *
    he is their help and their shield.

10 O house of Aaron, trust in the LORD; *
    he is their help and their shield.

11 You who fear the LORD, trust in the LORD; *
    he is their help and their shield.

12 The LORD has been mindful of us, and he will bless us; *
    he will bless the house of Israel;
    he will bless the house of Aaron;

13 He will bless those who fear the LORD, *
    both small and great together.

14 May the LORD increase you more and more, *
    you and your children after you.

15 May you be blessed by the LORD, *
    the maker of heaven and earth.

16 The heaven of heavens is the LORD'S, *
    but he entrusted the earth to its peoples.

17 The dead do not praise the LORD, *
    nor all those who go down into silence;

18 But we will bless the LORD, *
    from this time forth for evermore.
    Hallelujah!

Lent What wrong did your ancestors find in me that they went far from me, and went after worthless things, and became worthless themselves?
Easter We have been turned from the worship of idols to serve the living God, hallelujah.

Reading

Responsory, Magnificat Antiphon, Litany, Invitation to the Lord's Prayer, Collect and Dismissal are taken from the Proper of the Season.

Monday Week 2 Morning Prayer

Officiant: Lord, open our lips.
People: **And our mouth shall proclaim your praise.**
Officiant and People **Glory to the Father...**
Except in Lent, add **Alleluia.**

The Invitatory Psalm 29
From the Proper of the Season or of the Day

Hymn *From the Proper of the Season or of the Day*

Psalm 19 *Cæli enarrant*
For you who revere my name the sun of righteousness shall rise, with healing in its wings. Mal 4:2

Lent Keep your servant from presumptuous sins; let them not get dominion over me.
Easter The glory of God is the light of the city, and its lamp is the Lamb, hallelujah.

1   The heavens declare the glory of God, *
    and the firmament shows his handiwork.

2   One day tells its tale to another, *
    and one night imparts knowledge to another.

3   Although they have no words or language, *
    and their voices are not heard,

4   Their sound has gone out into all lands, *
    and their message to the ends of the world.

5 In the deep has he set a pavilion for the sun; *
   it comes forth like a bridegroom out of his chamber;
   it rejoices like a champion to run its course.

6 It goes forth from the uttermost edge of the heavens
   and runs about to the end of it again; *
   nothing is hidden from its burning heat.

7 The law of the LORD is perfect
   and revives the soul; *
   the testimony of the LORD is sure
   and gives wisdom to the innocent.

8 The statutes of the LORD are just
   and rejoice the heart; *
   the commandment of the LORD is clear
   and gives light to the eyes.

9 The fear of the LORD is clean
   and endures for ever; *
   the judgments of the LORD are true
   and righteous altogether.

10 More to be desired are they than gold,
   more than much fine gold, *
   sweeter far than honey,
   than honey in the comb.

11 By them also is your servant enlightened, *
   and in keeping them there is great reward.

12 Who can tell how often he offends? *
   cleanse me from my secret faults.

13 Above all, keep your servant from presumptuous sins;
   let them not get dominion over me; *
   then shall I be whole and sound,
   and innocent of a great offense.

14 Let the words of my mouth and the meditation of my heart
   be acceptable in your sight, *
   O LORD, my strength and my redeemer.

Lent Keep your servant from presumptuous sins; let them not get dominion over me.
Easter The glory of God is the light of the city, and its lamp is the Lamb, hallelujah.

Psalm 65 *Te decet hymnus*

Jesus got up and rebuked the winds and the sea; and there was a dead calm. Mt. 8:26

Lent Our sins are stronger than we are, but you will blot them out.
Easter You visit the earth and water it abundantly, hallelujah.

1 You are to be praised, O God, in Zion; *
    to you shall vows be performed in Jerusalem.

2 To you that hear prayer shall all flesh come, *
    because of their transgressions.

3 Our sins are stronger than we are, *
    but you will blot them out.

4 Blessed are they whom you choose
    and draw to your courts to dwell there! *
        they will be satisfied by the beauty of your house,
        by the holiness of your temple.

5 Awesome things will you show us in your righteousness,
    O God of our salvation, *
        O Hope of all the ends of the earth
        and of the seas that are far away.

6 You make fast the mountains by your power; *
    they are girded about with might.

7 You still the roaring of the seas, *
    the roaring of their waves,
    and the clamor of the peoples.

8 Those who dwell at the ends of the earth
    will tremble at your marvelous signs; *
        you make the dawn and the dusk to sing for joy.

9 You visit the earth and water it abundantly;
    you make it very plenteous; *
        the river of God is full of water.

10 You prepare the grain, *
    for so you provide for the earth.

11 You drench the furrows and smooth out the ridges; *
    with heavy rain you soften the ground and bless its increase.

12 You crown the year with your goodness, *
    and your paths overflow with plenty.

13 May the fields of the wilderness be rich for grazing, *
      and the hills be clothed with joy.

14 May the meadows cover themselves with flocks,
    and the valleys cloak themselves with grain; *
      let them shout for joy and sing.

Lent Our sins are stronger than we are, but you will blot them out.
Easter You visit the earth and water it abundantly, hallelujah.

Psalm 148 *Laudate Dominum*

At Jesus' name every knee should bend, in heaven and on earth and under the earth. Phil 2:10
Lent Let all creatures praise the Name of the Lord; for he commanded, and they were created.
Easter The Name of the Lord is exalted above heaven and earth, hallelujah.

1 Hallelujah!
    Praise the LORD from the heavens; *
      praise him in the heights.

2 Praise him, all you angels of his; *
      praise him, all his host.

3 Praise him, sun and moon; *
      praise him, all you shining stars.

4 Praise him, heaven of heavens, *
      and you waters above the heavens.

5 Let them praise the Name of the LORD; *
      for he commanded, and they were created.

6 He made them stand fast for ever and ever; *
      he gave them a law which shall not pass away.

7 Praise the LORD from the earth, *
      you sea-monsters and all deeps;

8 Fire and hail, snow and fog, *
      tempestuous wind, doing his will;

9 Mountains and all hills, *
      fruit trees and all cedars;

10 Wild beasts and all cattle, *
      creeping things and wingèd birds;

11 Kings of the earth and all peoples, *
     princes and all rulers of the world;

12 Young men and maidens, *
     old and young together.

13 Let them praise the Name of the LORD, *
     for his Name only is exalted,
     his splendor is over earth and heaven.

14 He has raised up strength for his people
   and praise for all his loyal servants, *
     the children of Israel, a people who are near him.
     Hallelujah!

Lent Let all creatures praise the Name of the Lord; for he commanded, and they were created.
Easter The Name of the Lord is exalted above heaven and earth, hallelujah.

Readings

Responsories, Benedictus Antiphon, Litany, Invitation to the Lord's Prayer, Collect and Dismissal are taken from the Proper of the Season.

Monday Week 2 Noonday Prayer

Officiant: O God, make speed to save us.
People: **O Lord, make haste to help us.**
Officiant and People **Glory to the Father ...**
Except in Lent, add **Alleluia.**

Hymn *From the Proper of the Season or of the Day*

Psalm 119 Zayin *Memor esto verbi tui*

Suffering produces endurance, and endurance produces character, and character produces hope, and hope does not disappoint us. Rm. 5: 3-5

Lent The breakers of death rolled over me, and the torrents of oblivion made me afraid.
Easter They went out and fled from the tomb, for terror and amazement has seized them, hallelujah.

49 Remember your word to your servant, *
     because you have given me hope.

50 This is my comfort in my trouble, *
     that your promise gives me life.

51 The proud have derided me cruelly, *
    but I have not turned from your law.

52 When I remember your judgments of old, *
    O LORD, I take great comfort.

53 I am filled with a burning rage , *
    because of the wicked who forsake your law.

54 Your statutes have been like songs to me *
    wherever I have lived as a stranger.

55 I remember your Name in the night, O LORD, *
    and dwell upon your law.

56 This is how it has been with me, *
    because I have kept your commandments.

Psalm 18 Part I A *Diligam te, Domine*
Jesus began to be distressed and agitated. "I am deeply grieved, even to death." Mk. 14:33-35

1 I love you, O LORD my strength, *
    O LORD my stronghold, my crag, and my haven.

2 My God, my rock in whom I put my trust, *
    my shield, the horn of my salvation, and my refuge;
    you are worthy of praise.

3 I will call upon the LORD, *
    and so shall I be saved from my enemies.

4 The breakers of death rolled over me, *
    and the torrents of oblivion made me afraid.

5 The cords of hell entangled me, *
    and the snares of death were set for me.

6 I called upon the LORD in my distress *
    and cried out to my God for help.

7 He heard my voice from his heavenly dwelling; *
    my cry of anguish came to his ears.

Psalm 18 Part I B *Commota est*
Jesus gave a loud cry and breathed his last.
And the curtain of the temple was torn in two, from top to bottom. Mk. 15:37-38

8 The earth reeled and rocked; *
    the roots of the mountains shook;
    they reeled because of his anger.

9 Smoke rose from his nostrils
and a consuming fire out of his mouth; *
hot burning coals blazed forth from him.

10 He parted the heavens and came down *
with a storm cloud under his feet.

11 He mounted on cherubim and flew; *
he swooped on the wings of the wind.

12 He wrapped darkness about him; *
he made dark waters and thick clouds his pavilion.

13 From the brightness of his presence, through the clouds, *
burst hailstones and coals of fire.

14 The LORD thundered out of heaven; *
the Most High uttered his voice.

15 He loosed his arrows and scattered them; *
he hurled thunderbolts and routed them.

16 The beds of the seas were uncovered,
and the foundations of the world laid bare, *
at your battle cry, O LORD,
at the blast of the breath of your nostrils.

17 He reached down from on high and grasped me; *
he drew me out of great waters.

18 He delivered me from my strong enemies
and from those who hated me; *
for they were too mighty for me.

19 They confronted me in the day of my disaster; *
but the LORD was my support.

20 He brought me out into an open place; *
he rescued me because he delighted in me.

Lent The breakers of death rolled over me, and the torrents of oblivion made me afraid.
Easter They went out and fled from the tomb, for terror and amazement has seized them, hallelujah.

Reading, Verse and Response, Collect and Conclusion as in the Proper of the Season or of the Day.

Monday Week 2 Evening Prayer

Officiant: O God, make speed to save us.
People: **O Lord, make haste to help us.**
Officiant and People **Glory to the Father ...**
Except in Lent, add **Alleluia.**

Hymn *From the Proper of the Season or of the Day*

Psalm 33 A *Exultate, justi*
All things came into being through the Word, and without him not one thing came into being. Jn. 1:3
Lent Let all the earth fear the LORD; let all who dwell in the world stand in awe of him.
Easter The loving-kindness of the Lord fills the whole earth, hallelujah.

1 Rejoice in the LORD, you righteous; *
 it is good for the just to sing praises.

2 Praise the LORD with the harp; *
 play to him upon the psaltery and lyre.

3 Sing for him a new song; *
 sound a fanfare with all your skill upon the trumpet.

4 For the word of the LORD is right, *
 and all his works are sure.

5 He loves righteousness and justice; *
 the loving-kindness of the LORD fills the whole earth.

6 By the word of the LORD were the heavens made, *
 by the breath of his mouth all the heavenly hosts.

7 He gathers up the waters of the ocean as in a water-skin *
 and stores up the depths of the sea.

8 Let all the earth fear the LORD; *
 let all who dwell in the world stand in awe of him.

9 For he spoke, and it came to pass; *
 he commanded, and it stood fast.

10 The LORD brings the will of the nations to naught; *
 he thwarts the designs of the peoples.

11 But the LORD'S will stands fast for ever, *
 and the designs of his heart from age to age.

12 Blessed is the nation whose God is the LORD! *
 blessed the people he has chosen to be his own!

Lent Let all the earth fear the LORD; let all who dwell in the world stand in awe of him.
Easter The loving-kindness of the Lord fills the whole earth, hallelujah.

Psalm 33 B *De caelo respexit*
We are what he has made us, created in Christ Jesus for good works, which God prepared beforehand to be our way of life. Eph. 2:10

Lent Our soul waits for the LORD who is our help and our shield.
Easter To the King of the ages, immortal, invisible, the only God, be honor and glory, hallelujah.

13 The LORD looks down from heaven, *
    and beholds all the people in the world.

14 From where he sits enthroned he turns his gaze *
    on all who dwell on the earth.

15 He fashions all the hearts of them *
    and understands all their works.

16 There is no king that can be saved by a mighty army; *
    a strong man is not delivered by his great strength.

17 The horse is a vain hope for deliverance; *
    for all its strength it cannot save.

18 Behold, the eye of the LORD is upon those who fear him, *
    on those who wait upon his love,

19 To pluck their lives from death, *
    and to feed them in time of famine.

20 Our soul waits for the LORD; *
    he is our help and our shield.

21 Indeed, our heart rejoices in him, *
    for in his holy Name we put our trust.

22 Let your loving-kindness, O LORD, be upon us, *
    as we have put our trust in you.

Lent Our soul waits for the LORD who is our help and our shield.
Easter To the King of the ages, immortal, invisible, the only God, be honor and glory, hallelujah.

Psalm 94 *Deus ultionum*

I thank you, Father, Lord of heaven and earth, because you have hidden these things from the wise and the intelligent and have revealed them to infants. Lk. 10:21

Lent The LORD knows our human thoughts; how like a puff of wind they are.

Easter The LORD has become my stronghold, and my God the rock of my trust, hallelujah.

1 O LORD God of vengeance, *
   O God of vengeance, show yourself.

2 Rise up, O Judge of the world; *
   give the arrogant their just deserts.

3 How long shall the wicked, O LORD, *
   how long shall the wicked triumph?

4 They bluster in their insolence; *
   all evildoers are full of boasting.

5 They crush your people, O LORD, *
   and afflict your chosen nation.

6 They murder the widow and the stranger *
   and put the orphans to death.

7 Yet they say, "The LORD does not see, *
   the God of Jacob takes no notice."

8 Consider well, you dullards among the people; *
   when will you fools understand?

9 He that planted the ear, does he not hear? *
   he that formed the eye, does he not see?

10 He who admonishes the nations, will he not punish? *
   he who teaches all the world, has he no knowledge?

11 The LORD knows our human thoughts; *
   how like a puff of wind they are.

12 Blessed are they whom you instruct, O Lord! *
   whom you teach out of your law;

13 To give them rest in evil days, *
   until a pit is dug for the wicked.

14 For the LORD will not abandon his people, *
   nor will he forsake his own.

15 For judgment will again be just, *
    and all the true of heart will follow it.

16 Who rose up for me against the wicked? *
    who took my part against the evildoers?

17 If the LORD had not come to my help, *
    I should soon have dwelt in the land of silence.

18 As often as I said, "My foot has slipped," *
    your love, O LORD, upheld me.

19 When many cares fill my mind, *
    your consolations cheer my soul.

20 Can a corrupt tribunal have any part with you, *
    one which frames evil into law?

21 They conspire against the life of the just *
    and condemn the innocent to death.

22 But the LORD has become my stronghold, *
    and my God the rock of my trust.

23 He will turn their wickedness back upon them
    and destroy them in their own malice; *
    the LORD our God will destroy them.

Lent The LORD knows our human thoughts; how like a puff of wind they are.
Easter The LORD has become my stronghold, and my God the rock of my trust, hallelujah.

Reading

Responsory, Magnificat Antiphon, Litany, Invitation to the Lord's Prayer, Collet and Dismissal are taken from the Proper of the Season.

Tuesday Week 2 Morning Prayer

Officiant: Lord, open our lips.
People: **And our mouth shall proclaim your praise.**
Officiant and People **Glory to the Father...**
Except in Lent, add **Alleluia.**

The Invitatory Psalm 8
From the Proper of the Season or of the Day

Hymn *From the Proper of the Season or of the Day*

Psalm 27 *Dominus illuminatio*

If you keep my commandments, you will abide in my love, just as I have kept my Father's commandments and abide in his love. Jn. 15:10

Lent Though an army should encamp against me, yet my heart shall not be afraid.

Easter I believe that I shall see the goodness of the Lord in the land of the living, hallelujah.

1 The LORD is my light and my salvation;
 whom then shall I fear? *
   the LORD is the strength of my life;
   of whom then shall I be afraid?

2 When evildoers came upon me to eat up my flesh, *
   it was they, my foes and my adversaries,
   who stumbled and fell.

3 Though an army should encamp against me, *
   yet my heart shall not be afraid;

4 And though war should rise up against me, *
   yet will I put my trust in him.

5 One thing have I asked of the LORD;
 one thing I seek; *
   that I may dwell in the house of the LORD all the days of my life;

6 To behold the fair beauty of the LORD *
   and to seek him in his temple.

7 For in the day of trouble
 he shall keep me safe in his shelter; *
   he shall hide me in the secrecy of his dwelling
   and set me high upon a rock.

8 Even now he lifts up my head *
   above my enemies round about me.

9 Therefore I will offer in his dwelling an oblation
 with sounds of great gladness; *
   I will sing and make music to the LORD.

10 Hearken to my voice, O LORD, when I call; *
   have mercy on me and answer me.

11 You speak in my heart and say, "Seek my face." *
   Your face, LORD, will I seek.

12 Hide not your face from me, *
    nor turn away your servant in displeasure.

13 You have been my helper;
   cast me not away; *
    do not forsake me, O God of my salvation.

14 Though my father and my mother forsake me, *
    the LORD will sustain me.

15 Show me your way, O LORD; *
    lead me on a level path, because of my enemies.

16 Deliver me not into the hand of my adversaries, *
    for false witnesses have risen up against me,
    and also those who speak malice.

17 What if I had not believed
   that I should see the goodness of the LORD *
    in the land of the living!

18 O tarry and await the LORD'S pleasure;
   be strong, and he shall comfort your heart; *
    wait patiently for the LORD.

Lent Though an army should encamp against me, yet my heart shall not be afraid.
Easter I believe that I shall see the goodness of the Lord in the land of the living, hallelujah.

Psalm 76 *Notus in Judæa*

In the world you face persecution. But take courage; I have conquered the world. Jn. 16:33

Lent What terror you inspire! Who can stand before you when you are angry?
Easter The name of the Lord is great in Israel, hallelujah.

1 In Judah is God known; *
    his Name is great in Israel.

2 At Salem is his tabernacle, *
    and his dwelling is in Zion.

3 There he broke the flashing arrows, *
    the shield, the sword, and the weapons of battle.

4 How glorious you are! *
    more splendid than the everlasting mountains!

5 The strong of heart have been despoiled;
  they sink into sleep; *
    none of the warriors can lift a hand.

6 At your rebuke, O God of Jacob, *
    both horse and rider lie stunned.

7 What terror you inspire! *
    who can stand before you when you are angry?

8 From heaven you pronounced judgment; *
    the earth was afraid and was still;

9 When God rose up to judgment *
    and to save all the oppressed of the earth.

10 Truly, wrathful Edom will give you thanks, *
    and the remnant of Hamath will keep your feasts.

11 Make a vow to the LORD your God and keep it; *
    let all around him bring gifts to him
    who is worthy to be feared.

12 He breaks the spirit of princes, *
    and strikes terror in the kings of the earth.

Lent What terror you inspire! Who can stand before you when you are angry?
Easter The name of the Lord is great in Israel, hallelujah.

Psalm 98 *Cantate Domino*

The throne of God and of the Lamb will be in it, and his servants will worship him; they will see his face. Rev. 22:3-4

Lent The Lord remembers his mercy and faithfulness to the house of Israel.
Easter All the ends of the earth have seen the victory of our God, hallelujah.

1 Sing to the LORD a new song, *
    for he has done marvelous things.

2 With his right hand and his holy arm *
    has he won for himself the victory.

3 The LORD has made known his victory; *
    his righteousness has he openly shown
    in the sight of the nations.

4 He remembers his mercy and faithfulness
   to the house of Israel, *
      and all the ends of the earth have seen
      the victory of our God.

5 Shout with joy to the LORD, all you lands; *
      lift up your voice, rejoice, and sing.

6 Sing to the LORD with the harp, *
      with the harp and the voice of song.

7 With trumpets and the sound of the horn *
      shout with joy before the King, the LORD.

8 Let the sea make a noise and all that is in it, *
      the lands and those who dwell therein.

9 Let the rivers clap their hands, *
      and let the hills ring out with joy before the LORD,
      when he comes to judge the earth.

10 In righteousness shall he judge the world *
      and the peoples with equity.

Lent The Lord remembers his mercy and faithfulness to the house of Israel.
Easter All the ends of the earth have seen the victory of our God, hallelujah.

Readings

Responsories, Benedictus Antiphon, Litany, Invitation to the Lord's Prayer, Collet and Dismissal are taken from the Proper of the Season.

Tuesday Week 2 Noonday Prayer

Officiant: O God, make speed to save us.
People: **O Lord, make haste to help us.**
Officiant and People **Glory to the Father …**
Except in Lent, add **Alleluia.**

Hymn *From the Proper of the Season or of the Day*

Psalm 119 Heth *Portio mea, Domine*
Be renewed in the spirit of your minds, and put on the new nature, created after the likeness of God. Eph. 4:33-34

Lent You will save a lowly people, but you will humble the haughty eyes.
Easter The Lord lives! Exalted is the God of my salvation, hallelujah.

57 You only are my portion, O LORD; *
   I have promised to keep your words.

58 I entreat you with all my heart, *
   be merciful to me according to your promise.

59 I have considered my ways *
   and turned my feet toward your decrees.

60 I hasten and do not tarry *
   to keep your commandments.

61 Though the cords of the wicked entangle me, *
   I do not forget your law.

62 At midnight I will rise to give you thanks, *
   because of your righteous judgments.

63 I am a companion of all who fear you *
   and of those who keep your commandments.

64 The earth, O LORD, is full of your love; *
   instruct me in your statutes.

Psalm 18: Part II A *Et retribuet mihi*
The light shines in the darkness, and the darkness has not overcome it. Jn. 1:5

21 The LORD rewarded me because of my righteous dealing; *
   because my hands were clean he rewarded me;

22 For I have kept the ways of the LORD *
   and have not offended against my God;

23 For all his judgments are before my eyes, *
   and his decrees I have not put away from me;

24 For I have been blameless with him *
   and have kept myself from iniquity;

25 Therefore the LORD rewarded me
   according to my righteous dealing, *
   because of the cleanness of my hands in his sight.

26 With the faithful you show yourself faithful, O God; *
   with the forthright you show yourself forthright.

27 With the pure you show yourself pure, *
   but with the crooked you are wily.

28 You will save a lowly people, *
   but you will humble the haughty eyes.

29 You, O LORD, are my lamp; *
    my God, you make my darkness bright.

30 With you I will break down an enclosure; *
    with the help of my God I will scale any wall.

31 As for God, his ways are perfect;
   the words of the LORD are tried in the fire; *
    he is a shield to all who trust in him.

Psalm 18: Part II B *Quoniam quis*

Take the whole armor of God, that you may be able to withstand in the evil day, and having done all, to stand. Eph. 6:13

32 For who is God, but the LORD? *
    who is the Rock, except our God?

33 It is God who girds me about with strength *
    and makes my way secure.

34 He makes me sure-footed like a deer *
    and lets me stand firm on the heights.

35 He trains my hands for battle *
    and my arms for bending even a bow of bronze.

36 You have given me your shield of victory; *
    your right hand also sustains me;
    your loving care makes me great.

37 You lengthen my stride beneath me, *
    and my ankles do not give way.

38 I pursue my enemies and overtake them; *
    I will not turn back till I have destroyed them.

39 I strike them down, and they cannot rise; *
    they fall defeated at my feet.

40 You have girded me with strength for the battle; *
    you have cast down my adversaries beneath me;
    you have put my enemies to flight.

41 I destroy those who hate me;
   they cry out, but there is none to help them; *
    they cry to the LORD, but he does not answer.

42 I beat them small like dust before the wind; *
    I trample them like mud in the streets.

43 You deliver me from the strife of the peoples; *
    you put me at the head of the nations.

44 A people I have not known shall serve me;
  no sooner shall they hear than they shall obey me; *
    strangers will cringe before me.

45 The foreign peoples will lose heart; *
    they shall come trembling out of their strongholds.

46 The LORD lives! Blessed is my Rock! *
    Exalted is the God of my salvation!

47 He is the God who gave me victory *
    and cast down the peoples beneath me.

48 You rescued me from the fury of my enemies;
  you exalted me above those who rose against me; *
    you saved me from my deadly foe.

49 Therefore will I extol you among the nations, O LORD, *
    and sing praises to your Name.

50 He multiplies the victories of his king; *
    he shows loving-kindness to his anointed,
    to David and his descendants for ever.

Lent You will save a lowly people, but you will humble the haughty eyes.
Easter The Lord lives! Exalted is the God of my salvation, hallelujah.

Reading, Verse and Response, Collect and Conclusion as in the Proper of the Season or of the Day.

Tuesday Week 2 Evening Prayer

Officiant: O God, make speed to save us.
People: **O Lord, make haste to help us.**
Officiant and People **Glory to the Father...**
Except in Lent, add **Alleluia.**

Hymn *From the Proper of the Season or of the Day*

Psalm 45 A *Eructavit cor meum*
Here is the bridegroom! Come out to meet him. Mt. 25:6

Lent I will take you for my wife in righteousness and in justice, in steadfast love, and in mercy.
Easter Blessed are those who are called to the wedding feast of the Lamb, hallelujah.

1 My heart is stirring with a noble song;
    let me recite what I have fashioned for the king; *
        my tongue shall be the pen of a skilled writer.

2 You are the fairest of men; *
    grace flows from your lips,
    because God has blessed you for ever.

3 Strap your sword upon your thigh, O mighty warrior, *
    in your pride and in your majesty.

4 Ride out and conquer in the cause of truth *
    and for the sake of justice.

5 Your right hand will show you marvelous things; *
    your arrows are very sharp, O mighty warrior.

6 The peoples are falling at your feet, *
    and the king's enemies are losing heart.

7 Your throne, O God, endures for ever and ever, *
    a scepter of righteousness is the scepter of your kingdom;
    you love righteousness and hate iniquity.

8 Therefore God, your God, has anointed you *
    with the oil of gladness above your fellows.

9 All your garments are fragrant with myrrh, aloes, and cassia, *
    and the music of strings from ivory palaces makes you glad.

10 Kings' daughters stand among the ladies of the court; *
    on your right hand is the queen,
    adorned with the gold of Ophir.

Lent I will take you for my wife in righteousness and in justice, in steadfast love, and in mercy.
Easter Blessed are those who are called to the wedding feast of the Lamb, hallelujah.

Psalm 45 B *Audi filia et vide*
Come, I will show you the bride, the wife of the Lamb. Rev. 21:9

Lent I will go and return to my husband.
Easter The Bride of the Lamb has made herself ready; she has been clothed with fine linen, bright and pure, hallelujah.

11 "Hear, O daughter; consider and listen closely; *
    forget your people and your father's house.

12 The king will have pleasure in your beauty; *
  he is your master; therefore do him honor.

13 The people of Tyre are here with a gift; *
  the rich among the people seek your favor."

14 All glorious is the princess as she enters; *
  her gown is cloth-of-gold.

15 In embroidered apparel she is brought to the king; *
  after her the bridesmaids follow in procession.

16 With joy and gladness they are brought, *
  and enter into the palace of the king.

17 "In place of fathers, O king, you shall have sons; *
  you shall make them princes over all the earth.

18 I will make your name to be remembered
  from one generation to another; *
  therefore nations will praise you for ever and ever."

Lent I will go and return to my husband.
Easter The Bride of the Lamb has made herself ready; she has been clothed with fine linen, bright and pure, hallelujah.

Psalm 46 *Deus noster refugium*
I am with you always, to the close of the age. Mt. 28:20

Lent The nations make much ado, and the kingdoms are shaken; God has spoken, and the earth shall melt away.
Easter There is a river whose streams make glad the city of God, hallelujah.

1 God is our refuge and strength, *
  a very present help in trouble.

2 Therefore we will not fear, though the earth be moved, *
  and though the mountains be toppled
  into the depths of the sea;

3 Though its waters rage and foam, *
  and though the mountains tremble at its tumult.

4 The LORD of hosts is with us; *
  the God of Jacob is our stronghold.

5 There is a river whose streams make glad the city of God, *
  the holy habitation of the Most High.

6 God is in the midst of her;
   she shall not be overthrown; *
      God shall help her at the break of day.

7 The nations make much ado, and the kingdoms are shaken; *
      God has spoken, and the earth shall melt away.

8 The LORD of hosts is with us; *
      the God of Jacob is our stronghold.

9 Come now and look upon the works of the LORD, *
      what awesome things he has done on earth.

10 It is he who makes war to cease in all the world; *
      he breaks the bow, and shatters the spear,
      and burns the shields with fire.

11 "Be still, then, and know that I am God; *
      I will be exalted among the nations;
      I will be exalted in the earth."

12 The LORD of hosts is with us; *
      the God of Jacob is our stronghold.

Lent The nations make much ado, and the kingdoms are shaken; God has spoken, and the earth shall melt away.
Easter There is a river whose streams make glad the city of God, hallelujah.

Reading

Responsory, Magnificat Antiphon, Litany, Invitation to the Lord's Prayer, Collet and Dismissal are taken from the Proper of the Season.

Wednesday Week 2 Morning Prayer

Officiant: Lord, open our lips.
People: **And our mouth shall proclaim your praise.**
Officiant and People **Glory to the Father...**
Except in Lent, add **Alleluia.**

The Invitatory Psalm 95
From the Proper of the Season or of the Day

Hymn *From the Proper of the Season or of the Day*

Psalm 28 *Ad te, Domine*

When he has found the lost sheep, he lays it on his shoulders, rejoicing. Lk. 15:5

Lent They have no understanding of the Lord's doings, nor of the works of his hands.
Easter The Lord is a safe refuge for his anointed, hallelujah.

1 O Lord, I call to you;
  my Rock, do not be deaf to my cry; *
    lest, if you do not hear me,
    I become like those who go down to the Pit.

2 Hear the voice of my prayer when I cry out to you, *
    when I lift up my hands to your holy of holies.

3 Do not snatch me away with the wicked
  or with the evildoers, *
    who speak peaceably with their neighbors,
    while strife is in their hearts.

4 Repay them according to their deeds, *
    and according to the wickedness of their actions.

5 According to the work of their hands repay them, *
    and give them their just deserts.

6 They have no understanding of the Lord's doings,
  nor of the works of his hands; *
    therefore he will break them down
    and not build them up.

7 Blessed is the Lord! *
    for he has heard the voice of my prayer.

8 The Lord is my strength and my shield; *
    my heart trusts in him, and I have been helped;

9 Therefore my heart dances for joy, *
    and in my song will I praise him.

10 The Lord is the strength of his people, *
    a safe refuge for his anointed.

11 Save your people and bless your inheritance; *
    shepherd them and carry them for ever.

Lent They have no understanding of the Lord's doings, nor of the works of his hands.
Easter The Lord is a safe refuge for his anointed, hallelujah.

Psalm 96 *Cantate Domino*

For us there is one God, the Father, from whom are all things and for whom we exist, and one Lord, Jesus Christ, through whom are all things and through whom we exist. 1 Cor. 8:6

Lent The Lord will judge the world with righteousness.
Easter Tell it out among the nations: The Lord is King, hallelujah.

1 Sing to the LORD a new song; *
    sing to the LORD, all the whole earth.

2 Sing to the LORD and bless his Name; *
    proclaim the good news of his salvation from day to day.

3 Declare his glory among the nations *
    and his wonders among all peoples.

4 For great is the LORD and greatly to be praised; *
    he is more to be feared than all gods.

5 As for all the gods of the nations, they are but idols; *
    but it is the LORD who made the heavens.

6 Oh, the majesty and magnificence of his presence! *
    Oh, the power and the splendor of his sanctuary!

7 Ascribe to the LORD, you families of the peoples; *
    ascribe to the LORD honor and power.

8 Ascribe to the LORD the honor due his Name; *
    bring offerings and come into his courts.

9 Worship the LORD in the beauty of holiness; *
    let the whole earth tremble before him.

10 Tell it out among the nations: "The LORD is King! *
    he has made the world so firm that it cannot be moved;
    he will judge the peoples with equity."

11 Let the heavens rejoice, and let the earth be glad;
    let the sea thunder and all that is in it; *
    let the field be joyful and all that is therein.

12 Then shall all the trees of the wood shout for joy
  before the LORD when he comes, *
    when he comes to judge the earth.

13 He will judge the world with righteousness *
    and the peoples with his truth.

Lent The Lord will judge the world with righteousness.

Easter Tell it out among the nations: The Lord is King, hallelujah.

Psalm 67 *Deus misereatur*

I thank my God through Jesus Christ for all of you, because your faith is proclaimed throughout the world. Rm 1:8

Lent Let your ways be known upon earth, your saving health among all nations.

Easter Let the peoples praise you, O God; let all the peoples praise you, hallelujah.

1 May God be merciful to us and bless us, *
    show us the light of his countenance and come to us.

2 Let your ways be known upon earth, *
    your saving health among all nations.

3 Let the peoples praise you, O God; *
    let all the peoples praise you.

4 Let the nations be glad and sing for joy, *
    for you judge the peoples with equity
    and guide all the nations upon earth.

5 Let the peoples praise you, O God; *
    let all the peoples praise you.

6 The earth has brought forth her increase; *
    may God, our own God, give us his blessing.

7 May God give us his blessing, *
    and may all the ends of the earth stand in awe of him.

Lent Let your ways be known upon earth, your saving health among all nations.

Easter Let the peoples praise you, O God; let all the peoples praise you, hallelujah.

Readings

Responsories, Benedictus Antiphon, Litany, Invitation to the Lord's Prayer, Collect and Dismissal are taken from the Proper of the Season.

Wednesday Week 2 Noonday Prayer

Officiant: O God, make speed to save us.
People: **O Lord, make haste to help us.**
Officiant and People **Glory to the Father...**
Except in Lent, add **Alleluia.**

Hymn *From the Proper of the Season or of the Day*

Psalm 119 Teth *Bonitatem fecisti*
If you continue in my word, you are truly my disciples. Jn. 8: 31

Lent Have mercy upon us, O LORD, have mercy.
Easter We have escaped like a bird from the snare of the fowler. hallelujah.

65 O LORD, you have dealt graciously with your servant, *
 according to your word.

66 Teach me discernment and knowledge, *
 for I have believed in your commandments.

67 Before I was afflicted I went astray, *
 but now I keep your word.

68 You are good and you bring forth good; *
 instruct me in your statutes.

69 The proud have smeared me with lies, *
 but I will keep your commandments with my whole heart.

70 Their heart is gross and fat, *
 but my delight is in your law.

71 It is good for me that I have been afflicted, *
 that I might learn your statutes.

72 The law of your mouth is dearer to me *
 than thousands in gold and silver.

Psalm 123 *Ad te levavi oculos meos*
With the eyes of your heart enlightened, you may know what is the hope to which he has called you. Eph. 1: 18

1 To you I lift up my eyes, *
 to you enthroned in the heavens.

2 As the eyes of servants look to the hand of their masters, *
 and the eyes of a maid to the hand of her mistress,

3 So our eyes look to the LORD our God, *
 until he show us his mercy.

4 Have mercy upon us, O LORD, have mercy, *
 for we have had more than enough of contempt,

5 Too much of the scorn of the indolent rich, *
 and of the derision of the proud.

Wednesday Week 2 Evening Prayer

Psalm 124 *Nisi quia Dominus*
Do not fear those who kill the body but cannot kill the soul. Mt. 10: 28

1 If the LORD had not been on our side, *
    let Israel now say;

2 If the LORD had not been on our side, *
    when enemies rose up against us;

3 Then would they have swallowed us up alive *
    in their fierce anger toward us;

4 Then would the waters have overwhelmed us *
    and the torrent gone over us;

5 Then would the raging waters *
    have gone right over us.

6 Blessed be the LORD! *
    he has not given us over to be a prey for their teeth.

7 We have escaped like a bird from the snare of the fowler; *
    the snare is broken, and we have escaped.

8 Our help is in the Name of the LORD, *
    the maker of heaven and earth.

Lent Have mercy upon us, O LORD, have mercy.
Easter We have escaped like a bird from the snare of the fowler. hallelujah.

Reading, Verse and Response, Collect and Conclusion as in the Proper of the Season or of the Day.

Wednesday Week 2 Evening Prayer

Officiant: O God, make speed to save us.
People: **O Lord, make haste to help us.**
Officiant and People **Glory to the Father ...**
Except in Lent, add **Alleluia.**

Hymn *From the Proper of the Season or of the Day*

Psalm 105 A *Confitemini Domino*
God had provided something better so that our ancestors would not, apart from us, be made perfect. Heb 11: 40

Lent He is the LORD our God; his judgments prevail in all the world.
Easter The Lord has been mindful of his covenant, the promise he made for a thousand generations, hallelujah.

1 Give thanks to the LORD and call upon his Name; *
    make known his deeds among the peoples.

2 Sing to him, sing praises to him, *
    and speak of all his marvelous works.

3 Glory in his holy Name; *
    let the hearts of those who seek the LORD rejoice.

4 Search for the LORD and his strength; *
    continually seek his face.

5 Remember the marvels he has done, *
    his wonders and the judgments of his mouth,

6 O offspring of Abraham his servant, *
    O children of Jacob his chosen.

7 He is the LORD our God; *
    his judgments prevail in all the world.

8 He has always been mindful of his covenant, *
    the promise he made for a thousand generations:

9 The covenant he made with Abraham, *
    the oath that he swore to Isaac,

10 Which he established as a statute for Jacob, *
    an everlasting covenant for Israel,

11 Saying, "To you will I give the land of Canaan *
    to be your allotted inheritance."

12 When they were few in number, *
    of little account, and sojourners in the land,

13 Wandering from nation to nation *
    and from one kingdom to another,

14 He let no one oppress them *
    and rebuked kings for their sake,

15 Saying, "Do not touch my anointed *
    and do my prophets no harm."

16 Then the LORD called for a famine in the land *
    and destroyed the supply of bread.

17 He sent a man before them, *
    Joseph, who was sold as a slave.

18 They bruised his feet in fetters; *
   his neck they put in an iron collar.

19 Until his prediction came to pass, *
   the word of the LORD tested him.

20 The king sent and released him; *
   the ruler of the peoples set him free.

21 He set him as a master over his household, *
   as a ruler over all his possessions,

22 To instruct his princes according to his will *
   and to teach his elders wisdom.

Lent He is the LORD our God; his judgments prevail in all the world.
Easter The Lord has been mindful of his covenant, the promise he made for a thousand generations, hallelujah.

Psalm 105 B *Et intravit Israel*

By faith Moses left Egypt, unafraid of the king's anger; for he persevered as though he saw him who is invisible. Heb. 11: 27

Lent Moses considered abuse suffered for the Christ to be greater than the treasures of Egypt for he was looking ahead to the reward.
Easter By faith Moses left Egypt, unafraid of the king's anger, for he persevered as though he saw him who is invisible, hallelujah.

23 Israel came into Egypt, *
   and Jacob became a sojourner in the land of Ham.

24 The LORD made his people exceedingly fruitful; *
   he made them stronger than their enemies;

25 Whose heart he turned, so that they hated his people, *
   and dealt unjustly with his servants.

26 He sent Moses his servant, *
   and Aaron whom he had chosen.

27 They worked his signs among them, *
   and portents in the land of Ham.

28 He sent darkness, and it grew dark; *
   but the Egyptians rebelled against his words.

29 He turned their waters into blood *
   and caused their fish to die.

30 Their land was overrun by frogs, *
    in the very chambers of their kings.

31 He spoke, and there came swarms of insects *
    and gnats within all their borders.

32 He gave them hailstones instead of rain, *
    and flames of fire throughout their land.

33 He blasted their vines and their fig trees *
    and shattered every tree in their country.

34 He spoke, and the locust came, *
    and young locusts without number,

35 Which ate up all the green plants in their land *
    and devoured the fruit of their soil.

36 He struck down the firstborn of their land, *
    the firstfruits of all their strength.

Lent Moses considered abuse suffered for the Christ to be greater than the treasures of Egypt for he was looking ahead to the reward.
Easter By faith Moses left Egypt, unafraid of the king's anger, for he persevered as though he saw him who is invisible, hallelujah.

Psalm 105 C *Et eduxit eos*

By faith the people passed through the Red Sea as if it were dry land. Heb. 11: 29

Lent By faith Moses kept the Passover and the sprinkling of blood. By faith the people passed through the Red Sea as if it were dry land.
Easter God led forth his people with gladness and his chosen with shouts of joy, hallelujah.

37 The LORD led out his people with silver and gold; *
    in all their tribes there was not one that stumbled.

38 Egypt was glad of their going, *
    because they were afraid of them.

39 He spread out a cloud for a covering *
    and a fire to give light in the night season.

40 They asked, and quails appeared, *
    and he satisfied them with bread from heaven.

41 He opened the rock, and water flowed, *
    so the river ran in the dry places.

42 For God remembered his holy word *
    and Abraham his servant.

43 So he led forth his people with gladness, *
    his chosen with shouts of joy.

44 He gave his people the lands of the nations, *
    and they took the fruit of others' toil,

45 That they might keep his statutes *
    and observe his laws.
    Hallelujah!

Lent By faith Moses kept the Passover and the sprinkling of blood. By faith the people passed through the Red Sea as if it were dry land. **Easter** God led forth his people with gladness and his chosen with shouts of joy, hallelujah.

Reading

Responsory, Magnificat Antiphon, Litany, Invitation to the Lord's Prayer, Collect and Dismissal are taken from the Proper of the Season.

Thursday Week 2 Morning Prayer

Officiant: Lord, open our lips.
People: **And our mouth shall proclaim your praise.**
Officiant and People **Glory to the Father...**
Except in Lent, add **Alleluia.**

The Invitatory Psalm 100
From the Proper of the Season or of the Day

Hymn *From the Proper of the Season or of the Day*

Psalm 34 *Benedicam Dominum*
*All of us, with unveiled faces, seeing the glory of the Lord,
are being transformed into the same image. 2 Cor. 3:18*

Lent Turn from evil and do good; seek peace and pursue it.
Easter Taste and see that the Lord is good, hallelujah.

1 I will bless the LORD at all times; *
    his praise shall ever be in my mouth.

2 I will glory in the LORD; *
    let the humble hear and rejoice.

3 Proclaim with me the greatness of the LORD; *
    let us exalt his Name together.

4 I sought the LORD, and he answered me *
   and delivered me out of all my terror.

5 Look upon him and be radiant, *
   and let not your faces be ashamed.

6 I called in my affliction and the LORD heard me *
   and saved me from all my troubles.

7 The angel of the LORD encompasses those who fear him, *
   and he will deliver them.

8 Taste and see that the LORD is good; *
   blessed are they who trust in him!

9 Fear the LORD, you that are his saints, *
   for those who fear him lack nothing.

10 The young lions lack and suffer hunger, *
   but those who seek the LORD lack nothing that is good.

11 Come, children, and listen to me; *
   I will teach you the fear of the LORD.

12 Who among you loves life *
   and desires long life to enjoy prosperity?

13 Keep your tongue from evil-speaking *
   and your lips from lying words.

14 Turn from evil and do good; *
   seek peace and pursue it.

15 The eyes of the LORD are upon the righteous, *
   and his ears are open to their cry.

16 The face of the LORD is against those who do evil, *
   to root out the remembrance of them from the earth.

17 The righteous cry, and the LORD hears them *
   and delivers them from all their troubles.

18 The LORD is near to the brokenhearted *
   and will save those whose spirits are crushed.

19 Many are the troubles of the righteous, *
   but the LORD will deliver him out of them all.

20 He will keep safe all his bones; *
   not one of them shall be broken.

21 Evil shall slay the wicked, *
    and those who hate the righteous will be punished.

22 The LORD ransoms the life of his servants, *
    and none will be punished who trust in him.

Lent Turn from evil and do good; seek peace and pursue it.
Easter Taste and see that the Lord is good, hallelujah.

Psalm 122   *Lætatus sum*

I saw the holy city, the new Jerusalem, coming down out of heaven from God, prepared as a bride adorned for her husband. Rev. 21: 2

Lent See, we are going up to Jerusalem, and everything that is written about the Son of Man will be accomplished.
Easter May the peace of Christ fill your hearts with joy, hallelujah.

1 I was glad when they said to me, *
    "Let us go to the house of the LORD."

2 Now our feet are standing *
    within your gates, O Jerusalem.

3 Jerusalem is built as a city *
    that is at unity with itself;

4 To which the tribes go up,
    the tribes of the LORD, *
        the assembly of Israel,
        to praise the Name of the LORD.

5 For there are the thrones of judgment, *
    the thrones of the house of David.

6 Pray for the peace of Jerusalem: *
    "May they prosper who love you.

7 Peace be within your walls *
    and quietness within your towers.

8 For my brethren and companions' sake, *
    I pray for your prosperity.

9 Because of the house of the LORD our God, *
    I will seek to do you good."

Lent See, we are going up to Jerusalem, and everything that is written about the Son of Man will be accomplished.
Easter May the peace of Christ fill your hearts with joy, hallelujah.

Psalm 149 *Cantate Domino*

All who see them shall acknowledge that they are a people whom the Lord has blessed. Is. 61: 9

Lent There is joy in the presence of the angels of God over one sinner who repents.
Easter Let the faithful rejoice in triumph, hallelujah.

1 Hallelujah!
 Sing to the LORD a new song; *
  sing his praise in the congregation of the faithful.

2 Let Israel rejoice in his Maker; *
  let the children of Zion be joyful in their King.

3 Let them praise his Name in the dance; *
  let them sing praise to him with timbrel and harp.

4 For the LORD takes pleasure in his people *
  and adorns the poor with victory.

5 Let the faithful rejoice in triumph; *
  let them be joyful on their beds.

6 Let the praises of God be in their throat *
  and a two-edged sword in their hand;

7 To wreak vengeance on the nations *
  and punishment on the peoples;

8 To bind their kings in chains *
  and their nobles with links of iron;

9 To inflict on them the judgment decreed; *
  this is glory for all his faithful people.
  Hallelujah!

Lent There is joy in the presence of the angels of God over one sinner who repents.
Easter Let the faithful rejoice in triumph, hallelujah.

Readings

Responsories, Benedictus Antiphon, Litany, Invitation to the Lord's Prayer, Collect and Dismissal are taken from the Proper of the Season.

Thursday Week 2 Noonday Prayer

Officiant: O God, make speed to save us.
People: **O Lord, make haste to help us.**
Officiant and People **Glory to the Father...**
Except in Lent, add **Alleluia.**

Hymn *From the Proper of the Season or of the Day*

Psalm 119 Yodh *Manus tuæ fecerunt me*
I tell you, anyone who hears my word and believes him who sent me has eternal life. Jn. 5: 24
Lent For this reason the Father loves me, because I lay down my life in order to take it up again.
Easter When you have brought out all your own, you go ahead of them and the sheep follow you because they know your voice, hallelujah.

73 Your hands have made me and fashioned me; *
    give me understanding,
    that I may learn your commandments.

74 Those who fear you will be glad when they see me, *
    because I trust in your word.

75 I know, O LORD, that your judgments are right *
    and that in faithfulness you have afflicted me.

76 Let your loving-kindness be my comfort, *
    as you have promised to your servant.

77 Let your compassion come to me, that I may live, *
    for your law is my delight.

78 Let the arrogant be put to shame,
  for they wrong me with lies; *
    but I will meditate on your commandments.

79 Let those who fear you turn to me, *
    and also those who know your decrees.

80 Let my heart be sound in your statutes, *
    that I may not be put to shame.

Psalm 78 C *Quotiens exacerbaverunt*
You faithless generation, how much longer must I be among you? Mk. 9: 19

40 How often the people disobeyed God in the wilderness *
    and offended him in the desert!

41 Again and again they tempted God *
    and provoked the Holy One of Israel.

42 They did not remember his power *
    in the day when he ransomed them from the enemy;

43 How he wrought his signs in Egypt *
    and his omens in the field of Zoan.

44 He turned their rivers into blood, *
    so that they could not drink of their streams.

45 He sent swarms of flies among them, which ate them up, *
    and frogs, which destroyed them.

46 He gave their crops to the caterpillar, *
    the fruit of their toil to the locust.

47 He killed their vines with hail *
    and their sycamores with frost.

48 He delivered their cattle to hailstones *
    and their livestock to hot thunderbolts.

49 He poured out upon them his blazing anger: *
    fury, indignation, and distress,
    a troop of destroying angels.

50 He gave full rein to his anger;
    did not spare their souls from death; *
    but delivered their lives to the plague.

51 He struck down all the firstborn of Egypt, *
    the flower of manhood in the dwellings of Ham.

52 He led out his people like sheep *
    and guided them in the wilderness like a flock.

53 He led them to safety, and they were not afraid; *
    but the sea overwhelmed their enemies.

54 He brought them to his holy land, *
    the mountain his right hand had won.

55 He drove out the Canaanites before them
    apportioned an inheritance to them by lot; *
    he made the tribes of Israel to dwell in their tents.

Psalm 78 D *Et tentaverunt*
I am the good shepherd. I know my own and my own know me. Jn. 10:14

56 But they tested the Most High God, and defied him, *
    and did not keep his commandments.

57 They turned away and were disloyal like their fathers; *
    they were undependable like a warped bow.

58 They grieved him with their hill-altars *
    and provoked his displeasure with their idols.

59 When God heard this, he was angry *
    and utterly rejected Israel.

60 He forsook the shrine at Shiloh, *
    the tabernacle where he had lived among his people.

61 He delivered the ark into captivity, *
    his glory into the adversary's hand.

62 He gave his people to the sword *
    and was angered against his inheritance.

63 The fire consumed their young men; *
    there were no wedding songs for their maidens.

64 Their priests fell by the sword, *
    and their widows made no lamentation.

65 Then the LORD woke as though from sleep, *
    like a warrior refreshed with wine.

66 He struck his enemies on the backside *
    and put them to perpetual shame.

67 He rejected the tent of Joseph *
    and did not choose the tribe of Ephraim;

68 He chose instead the tribe of Judah *
    and Mount Zion, which he loved.

69 He built his sanctuary like the heights of heaven, *
    like the earth which he founded for ever.

70 He chose David his servant, *
    and took him away from the sheepfolds.

71 He brought him from following the ewes, *
    to be a shepherd over Jacob his people
    and over Israel his inheritance.

72 So he shepherded them with a faithful and true heart *
    and guided them with the skillfulness of his hands.

Lent For this reason the Father loves me, because I lay down my life in order to take it up again.

Easter When you have brought out all your own, you go ahead of them and the sheep follow you because they know your voice, hallelujah.

Reading, Verse and Response, Collect and Conclusion as in the Proper of the Season or of the Day.

Thursday Week 2 Evening Prayer

Officiant: O God, make speed to save us.
People: **O Lord, make haste to help us.**
Officiant and People **Glory to the Father**
Except in Lent, add **Alleluia.**

Hymn *From the Proper of the Season or of the Day*

Psalm 116 *Dilexi, quoniam*
This cup that is poured out for you is the new covenant in my blood. Lk. 22: 20

Lent I will fulfill my vows to the LORD in the presence of all his people.
Easter You have freed me from my bonds, O Lord: I will offer you the sacrifice of thanksgiving, hallelujah.

1 I love the LORD, because he has heard
 the voice of my supplication, *
  because he has inclined his ear to me whenever I called upon him.

2 The cords of death entangled me;
 the grip of the grave took hold of me; *
  I came to grief and sorrow.

3 Then I called upon the Name of the LORD: *
  "O LORD, I pray you, save my life."

4 Gracious is the LORD and righteous; *
  our God is full of compassion.

5 The LORD watches over the innocent; *
  I was brought very low, and he helped me.

6 Turn again to your rest, O my soul, *
  for the LORD has treated you well.

7 For you have rescued my life from death, *
  my eyes from tears, and my feet from stumbling.

8 I will walk in the presence of the LORD *
  in the land of the living.

9 I believed, even when I said,
   "I have been brought very low." *
      In my distress I said, "No one can be trusted."

10 How shall I repay the LORD *
   for all the good things he has done for me?

11 I will lift up the cup of salvation *
   and call upon the Name of the LORD.

12 I will fulfill my vows to the LORD *
   in the presence of all his people.

13 Precious in the sight of the LORD *
   is the death of his servants.

14 O LORD, I am your servant; *
   I am your servant and the child of your handmaid;
   you have freed me from my bonds.

15 I will offer you the sacrifice of thanksgiving *
   and call upon the Name of the LORD.

16 I will fulfill my vows to the LORD *
   in the presence of all his people,

17 In the courts of the LORD'S house, *
   in the midst of you, O Jerusalem.

Lent I will fulfill my vows to the LORD in the presence of all his people.
Easter You have freed me from my bonds, O Lord: I will offer you the sacrifice of thanksgiving, hallelujah.

Psalm 144 *Benedictus Dominus*

*Do not worry about your life, what you will eat or what you will drink,
or about your body, what you will wear. Mt. 6: 25*

Lent We are like a puff of wind; our days are like a passing shadow.
Easter You have stretched out your hand from on high; you rescued me and delivered me, hallelujah.

1 Blessed be the LORD my rock! *
   who trains my hands to fight and my fingers to battle;

2 My help and my fortress, my stronghold and my deliverer, *
   my shield in whom I trust,
   who subdues the peoples under me.

3 O LORD, what are we that you should care for us? *
   mere mortals that you should think of us?

4 We are like a puff of wind; *
    our days are like a passing shadow.

5 Bow your heavens, O LORD, and come down; *
    touch the mountains, and they shall smoke.

6 Hurl the lightning and scatter them; *
    shoot out your arrows and rout them.

7 Stretch out your hand from on high; *
    rescue me and deliver me from the great waters,
    from the hand of foreign peoples,

8 Whose mouths speak deceitfully *
    and whose right hand is raised in falsehood.

9 O God, I will sing to you a new song; *
    I will play to you on a ten-stringed lyre.

10 You give victory to kings *
    and have rescued David your servant.

11 Rescue me from the hurtful sword *
    and deliver me from the hand of foreign peoples,

12 Whose mouths speak deceitfully *
    and whose right hand is raised in falsehood.

13 May our sons be like plants well nurtured from their youth, *
    and our daughters like sculptured corners of a palace.

14 May our barns be filled to overflowing
    with all manner of crops; *
        may the flocks in our pastures increase
        by thousands and tens of thousands;
        may our cattle be fat and sleek.

15 May there be no breaching of the walls, no going into exile, *
    no wailing in the public squares.

16 Blessed are the people of whom this is so! *
    blessed are the people whose God is the LORD!

Lent We are like a puff of wind; our days are like a passing shadow.
Easter You have stretched out your hand from on high; you rescued me and delivered me, hallelujah.

Psalm 84 *Quam dilecta!*

*Though you do not see him now, you believe in him
and rejoice with an indescribable and glorious joy. 1 Pt. 1: 8*

Lent Behold our defender, O God, and look upon the face of your Anointed.

Easter My heart and my flesh rejoice in the living God, hallelujah.

1 How dear to me is your dwelling, O LORD of hosts! *
　My soul has a desire and longing
　　for the courts of the LORD;
　　my heart and my flesh rejoice in the living God.

2 The sparrow has found her a house
　and the swallow a nest where she may lay her young; *
　　by the side of your altars, O LORD of hosts,
　　my King and my God.

3 Blessed are they who dwell in your house! *
　they will always be praising you.

4 Blessed are the people whose strength is in you! *
　whose hearts are set on the pilgrims' way.

5 Those who go through the desolate valley
　will find it a place of springs, *
　　for the early rains have covered it with pools of water.

6 They will climb from height to height, *
　and the God of gods will reveal himself in Zion.

7 LORD God of hosts, hear my prayer; *
　hearken, O God of Jacob.

8 Behold our defender, O God; *
　and look upon the face of your Anointed.

9 For one day in your courts is better
　than a thousand in my own room, *
　　and to stand at the threshold of the house of my God
　　than to dwell in the tents of the wicked.

10 For the LORD God is both sun and shield; *
　he will give grace and glory;

11 No good thing will the LORD withhold *
　from those who walk with integrity.

12 O LORD of hosts, *
　　blessed are they who put their trust in you!

Lent Behold our defender, O God, and look upon the face of your Anointed.
Easter My heart and my flesh rejoice in the living God, hallelujah.

Reading

Responsory, Magnificat Antiphon, Litany, Invitation to the Lord's Prayer, Collet and Dismissal are taken from the Proper of the Season.

Friday Week 2 Morning Prayer

Officiant: Lord, open our lips.
People: **And our mouth shall proclaim your praise.**
Officiant and People **Glory to the Father...**
Except in Lent, add **Alleluia.**

The Invitatory Psalm 95
From the Proper of the Season or of the Day

Hymn *From the Proper of the Season or of the Day*

Psalm 38 *Domine, ne in furore*
*Many women were also there, looking on from a distance;
they had followed Jesus from Galilee and had provided for him. Mt. 27: 55*

Lent My friends and companions draw back from my affliction.
Easter I press on toward the goal for the prize of the heavenly call of God in Christ Jesus, hallelujah.

1　O LORD, do not rebuke me in your anger; *
　　do not punish me in your wrath.

2　For your arrows have already pierced me, *
　　and your hand presses hard upon me.

3　There is no health in my flesh,
　　because of your indignation; *
　　　there is no soundness in my body, because of my sin.

4　For my iniquities overwhelm me; *
　　like a heavy burden they are too much for me to bear.

5　My wounds stink and fester *
　　by reason of my foolishness.

6　I am utterly bowed down and prostrate; *
　　I go about in mourning all the day long.

7 My loins are filled with searing pain; *
   there is no health in my body.

8 I am utterly numb and crushed; *
   I wail, because of the groaning of my heart.

9 O Lord, you know all my desires, *
   and my sighing is not hidden from you.

10 My heart is pounding, my strength has failed me, *
   and the brightness of my eyes is gone from me.

11 My friends and companions draw back from my affliction; *
   my neighbors stand afar off.

12 Those who seek after my life lay snares for me; *
   those who strive to hurt me speak of my ruin
   and plot treachery all the day long.

13 But I am like the deaf who do not hear, *
   like those who are mute and do not open their mouth.

14 I have become like one who does not hear *
   and from whose mouth comes no defense.

15 For in you, O LORD, have I fixed my hope; *
   you will answer me, O Lord my God.

16 For I said, "Do not let them rejoice at my expense, *
   those who gloat over me when my foot slips."

17 Truly, I am on the verge of falling, *
   and my pain is always with me.

18 I will confess my iniquity *
   and be sorry for my sin.

19 Those who are my enemies without cause are mighty, *
   and many in number are those who wrongfully hate me.

20 Those who repay evil for good slander me, *
   because I follow the course that is right.

21 O LORD, do not forsake me; *
   be not far from me, O my God.

22 Make haste to help me, *
   O Lord of my salvation.

Lent My friends and companions draw back from my affliction.

Easter I press on toward the goal for the prize of the heavenly call of God in Christ Jesus, hallelujah.

Psalm 140 *Eripe me, Domine*
The Pharisees went and plotted to entrap him in what he said. Mt. 22: 15

Lent The Son of Man will be handed over to wicked men.
Easter The Lord God is the strength of my salvation, hallelujah.

1 Deliver me, O LORD, from evildoers; *
    protect me from the violent,

2 Who devise evil in their hearts *
    and stir up strife all day long.

3 They have sharpened their tongues like a serpent; *
    adder's poison is under their lips.

4 Keep me, O LORD, from the hands of the wicked; *
    protect me from the violent,
    who are determined to trip me up.

5 The proud have hidden a snare for me
    and stretched out a net of cords; *
    they have set traps for me along the path.

6 I have said to the LORD, "You are my God; *
    listen, O LORD, to my supplication.

7 O LORD God, the strength of my salvation, *
    you have covered my head in the day of battle.

8 Do not grant the desires of the wicked, O LORD, *
    nor let their evil plans prosper.

9 Let not those who surround me lift up their heads; *
    let the evil of their lips overwhelm them.

10 Let hot burning coals fall upon them; *
    let them be cast into the mire, never to rise up again."

11 A slanderer shall not be established on the earth, *
    and evil shall hunt down the lawless.

12 I know that the LORD will maintain the cause of the poor *
    and render justice to the needy.

13 Surely, the righteous will give thanks to your Name, *
    and the upright shall continue in your sight.

Lent The Son of Man will be handed over to wicked men.
Easter The Lord God is the strength of my salvation, hallelujah.

Psalm 41 *Beatus qui intelligit*
Blessed are those slaves whom the master finds alert when he comes; truly I tell you, he will fasten his belt and have them sit down to eat, and he will come and serve them. Lk. 12:37

Lent My best friend, whom I trusted, who broke bread with me, has lifted up his heel and turned against me.

Easter In my integrity you hold me fast, and shall set me before your face for ever, hallelujah.

1 Blessed are they who consider the poor and needy! *
   the LORD will deliver them in the time of trouble.

2 The LORD preserves them and keeps them alive,
   so that they may be blessed in the land; *
   he does not hand them over to the will of their enemies.

3 The LORD sustains them on their sickbed *
   and ministers to them in their illness.

4 I said, "LORD, be merciful to me; *
   heal me, for I have sinned against you."

5 My enemies are saying wicked things about me: *
   "When will he die, and his name perish?"

6 Even if they come to see me, they speak empty words; *
   their heart collects false rumors;
   they go outside and spread them.

7 All my enemies whisper together about me *
   and devise evil against me.

8 "A deadly thing," they say, "has fastened on him; *
   he has taken to his bed and will never get up again."

9 Even my best friend, whom I trusted,
   who broke bread with me, *
   has lifted up his heel and turned against me.

10 But you, O LORD, be merciful to me and raise me up, *
    and I shall repay them.

11 By this I know you are pleased with me, *
    that my enemy does not triumph over me.

12 In my integrity you hold me fast, *
    and shall set me before your face for ever.

13 Blessed be the LORD God of Israel, *
>   from age to age. Amen. Amen.

Lent My best friend, whom I trusted, who broke bread with me, has lifted up his heel and turned against me.
Easter In my integrity you hold me fast, and shall set me before your face for ever, hallelujah.

Readings

Responsories, Benedictus Antiphon, Litany, Invitation to the Lord's Prayer, Collet and Dismissal are taken from the Proper of the Season.

Friday Week 2 Noonday Prayer

Officiant: O God, make speed to save us.
People: **O Lord, make haste to help us.**
Officiant and People **Glory to the Father…**
Except in Lent, add **Alleluia.**

Hymn *From the Proper of the Season or of the Day*

Psalm 119 Kaph *Defecit in salutare*

Joseph bought a linen cloth, and taking down the body, wrapped it in the linen cloth, and laid it in a tomb that had been hewn out of the rock. Mk. 15:46

Lent 'Destroy this temple, and in three days I will raise it up.' He was speaking of the temple of his body.
Easter I saw water flowing from the right side of the temple, hallelujah, and all to whom this water came were saved and shall say: hallelujah.

81 My soul has longed for your salvation; *
>   I have put my hope in your word.

82 My eyes have failed from watching for your promise, *
>   and I say, "When will you comfort me?"

83 I have become like a leather flask in the smoke, *
>   but I have not forgotten your statutes.

84 How much longer must I wait? *
>   when will you give judgment
>   against those who persecute me?

85 The proud have dug pits for me; *
>   they do not keep your law.

86 All your commandments are true; *
>   help me, for they persecute me with lies.

87 They had almost made an end of me on earth, *
    but I have not forsaken your commandments.

88 In your loving-kindness, revive me, *
    that I may keep the decrees of your mouth.

Psalm 129 *Sæpe expugnaverunt*
After they have flogged him, they will kill him, and on the third day he will rise again. Lk. 18: 33

1 "Greatly have they oppressed me since my youth," *
    let Israel now say;

2 "Greatly have they oppressed me since my youth, *
    but they have not prevailed against me."

3 The plowmen plowed upon my back *
    and made their furrows long.

4 The LORD, the Righteous One, *
    has cut the cords of the wicked.

5 Let them be put to shame and thrown back, *
    all those who are enemies of Zion.

6 Let them be like grass upon the housetops, *
    which withers before it can be plucked;

7 Which does not fill the hand of the reaper, *
    nor the bosom of him who binds the sheaves;

8 So that those who go by say not so much as,
    "The LORD prosper you. *
    We wish you well in the Name of the LORD."

Psalm 74 *Ut quid, Deus?*
Destroy this temple, and in three days I will raise it up. Jn. 2: 19

1 O God, why have you utterly cast us off? *
    why is your wrath so hot against the sheep of your pasture?

2 Remember your congregation that you purchased long ago, *
    the tribe you redeemed to be your inheritance,
    and Mount Zion where you dwell.

3 Turn your steps toward the endless ruins; *
    the enemy has laid waste everything in your sanctuary.

4 Your adversaries roared in your holy place; *
    they set up their banners as tokens of victory.

5 They were like men coming up with axes to a grove of trees; *
    they broke down all your carved work
    with hatchets and hammers.

6 They set fire to your holy place; *
    they defiled the dwelling-place of your Name
    and razed it to the ground.

7 They said to themselves, "Let us destroy them altogether." *
    They burned down
    all the meeting-places of God in the land.

8 There are no signs for us to see;
    there is no prophet left; *
    there is not one among us who knows how long.

9 How long, O God, will the adversary scoff? *
    will the enemy blaspheme your Name for ever?

10 Why do you draw back your hand? *
    why is your right hand hidden in your bosom?

11 Yet God is my King from ancient times, *
    victorious in the midst of the earth.

12 You divided the sea by your might *
    and shattered the heads of the dragons upon the waters;

13 You crushed the heads of Leviathan *
    and gave him to the people of the desert for food.

14 You split open spring and torrent; *
    you dried up ever-flowing rivers.

15 Yours is the day, yours also the night; *
    you established the moon and the sun.

16 You fixed all the boundaries of the earth; *
    you made both summer and winter.

17 Remember, O Lord, how the enemy scoffed, *
    how a foolish people despised your Name.

18 Do not hand over the life of your dove to wild beasts; *
    never forget the lives of your poor.

19 Look upon your covenant; *
    the dark places of the earth are haunts of violence.

20 Let not the oppressed turn away ashamed; *
    let the poor and needy praise your Name.

21 Arise, O God, maintain your cause; *
    remember how fools revile you all day long.

22 Forget not the clamor of your adversaries, *
    the unending tumult of those who rise up against you.

Lent 'Destroy this temple, and in three days I will raise it up.' He was speaking of the temple of his body.
Easter I saw water flowing from the right side of the temple, hallelujah, and all to whom this water came were saved and shall say: hallelujah.

Reading, Verse and Response, Collect and Conclusion as in the Proper of the Season or of the Day.

Friday Week 2 Evening Prayer

Officiant: O God, make speed to save us.
People: **O Lord, make haste to help us.**
Officiant and People **Glory to the Father...**
Except in Lent, add **Alleluia.**

Hymn *From the Proper of the Season or of the Day*

Psalm 79 *Deus, venerunt*

This fellow said, "I am able to destroy the temple of God and to build it in three days." Mt. 26: 51

Lent Remember not our past sins; let your compassion be swift to meet us
Easter Destroy this temple and in three days I will raise it up, hallelujah.

1 O God, the heathen have come into your inheritance;
   they have profaned your holy temple; *
      they have made Jerusalem a heap of rubble.

2 They have given the bodies of your servants
   as food for the birds of the air, *
      and the flesh of your faithful ones
      to the beasts of the field.

3 They have shed their blood like water
   on every side of Jerusalem, *
      and there was no one to bury them.

4 We have become a reproach to our neighbors, *
      an object of scorn and derision to those around us.

5 How long will you be angry, O LORD? *
    will your fury blaze like fire for ever?

6 Pour out your wrath upon the heathen
    who have not known you *
        and upon the kingdoms
        that have not called upon your Name.

7 For they have devoured Jacob *
    and made his dwelling a ruin.

8 Remember not our past sins;
    let your compassion be swift to meet us; *
        for we have been brought very low.

9 Help us, O God our Savior, for the glory of your Name; *
    deliver us and forgive us our sins, for your Name's sake.

10 Why should the heathen say, "Where is their God?" *
    Let it be known among the heathen and in our sight
    that you avenge the shedding of your servants' blood.

11 Let the sorrowful sighing of the prisoners come before you, *
    and by your great might
    spare those who are condemned to die.

12 May the revilings with which they reviled you, O Lord, *
    return seven-fold into their bosoms.

13 For we are your people and the sheep of your pasture; *
    we will give you thanks for ever
    and show forth your praise from age to age.

Lent Remember not our past sins; let your compassion be swift to meet us
Easter Destroy this temple and in three days I will raise it up, hallelujah.

Psalm 6 *Domine, ne in furore*
I am deeply grieved, even to death; remain here, and stay awake with me. Mt. 26: 38

Lent If we wish to dwell in the tent of that kingdom, we must run to it by good deeds.
Easter The Lord has heard my supplication; the Lord accepts my prayer, hallelujah.

1 LORD, do not rebuke me in your anger; *
    do not punish me in your wrath.

2 Have pity on me, LORD, for I am weak; *
  heal me, LORD, for my bones are racked.

3 My spirit shakes with terror; *
  how long, O LORD, how long?

4 Turn, O LORD, and deliver me; *
  save me for your mercy's sake.

5 For in death no one remembers you; *
  and who will give you thanks in the grave?

6 I grow weary because of my groaning; *
  every night I drench my bed
  and flood my couch with tears.

7 My eyes are wasted with grief *
  and worn away because of all my enemies.

8 Depart from me, all evildoers, *
  for the LORD has heard the sound of my weeping.

9 The LORD has heard my supplication; *
  the LORD accepts my prayer.

10 All my enemies shall be confounded and quake with fear; *
  they shall turn back and suddenly be put to shame.

Lent If we wish to dwell in the tent of that kingdom, we must run to it by good deeds.
Easter The Lord has heard my supplication; the Lord accepts my prayer, hallelujah.

Psalm 77 *Voce mea ad Dominum*
My Father, if this cannot pass unless I drink it, your will be done. Mt. 26: 42

Lent In the day of my trouble I sought the Lord; my hands were stretched out by night and did not tire.
Easter Was it not necessary that the Messiah should suffer these things and then enter into his glory, hallelujah.

1 I will cry aloud to God; *
  I will cry aloud, and he will hear me.

2 In the day of my trouble I sought the Lord; *
  my hands were stretched out by night and did not tire;
  I refused to be comforted.

3 I think of God, I am restless, *
  I ponder, and my spirit faints.

4 You will not let my eyelids close; *
    I am troubled and I cannot speak.

5 I consider the days of old; *
    I remember the years long past;

6 I commune with my heart in the night; *
    I ponder and search my mind.

7 Will the Lord cast me off for ever? *
    will he no more show his favor?

8 Has his loving-kindness come to an end for ever? *
    has his promise failed for evermore?

9 Has God forgotten to be gracious? *
    has he, in his anger, withheld his compassion?

10 And I said, "My grief is this: *
    the right hand of the Most High has lost its power."

11 I will remember the works of the LORD, *
    and call to mind your wonders of old time.

12 I will meditate on all your acts *
    and ponder your mighty deeds.

13 Your way, O God, is holy; *
    who is so great a god as our God?

14 You are the God who works wonders *
    and have declared your power among the peoples.

15 By your strength you have redeemed your people, *
    the children of Jacob and Joseph.

16 The waters saw you, O God;
    the waters saw you and trembled; *
        the very depths were shaken.

17 The clouds poured out water;
    the skies thundered; *
        your arrows flashed to and fro;

18 The sound of your thunder was in the whirlwind;
    your lightnings lit up the world; *
        the earth trembled and shook.

19 Your way was in the sea,
   and your paths in the great waters, *
      yet your footsteps were not seen.

20 You led your people like a flock *
      by the hand of Moses and Aaron.

Lent In the day of my trouble I sought the Lord; my hands were stretched out by night and did not tire.
Easter Was it not necessary that the Messiah should suffer these things and then enter into his glory, hallelujah.

Reading

Responsory, Magnificat Antiphon, Litany, Invitation to the Lord's Prayer, Collect and Dismissal are taken from the Proper of the Season.

Saturday Week 2 Morning Prayer

Officiant: Lord, open our lips.
People: **And our mouth shall proclaim your praise.**
Officiant and People **Glory to the Father...**
Except in Lent, add **Alleluia.**

The Invitatory Psalm 122
From the Proper of the Season or of the Day

Hymn *From the Proper of the Season or of the Day*

Psalm 49 A *Audite hæc, omnes*
Those who want to save their life will lose it, and those who lose their life for my sake will find it. Mt. 16:25

Lent Whoever wants to be my disciple must deny themselves and take up their cross daily and follow me.
Easter May you have the knowledge of God's mystery, that is Christ himself, in whom are hidden all the treasures of wisdom and knowledge, hallelujah.

1 Hear this, all you peoples;
   hearken, all you who dwell in the world, *
      you of high degree and low, rich and poor together.

2 My mouth shall speak of wisdom, *
      and my heart shall meditate on understanding.

3 I will incline my ear to a proverb *
      and set forth my riddle upon the harp.

4 Why should I be afraid in evil days, *
    when the wickedness of those at my heels surrounds me,

5 The wickedness of those who put their trust in their goods, *
    and boast of their great riches?

6 We can never ransom ourselves, *
    or deliver to God the price of our life;

7 For the ransom of our life is so great, *
    that we should never have enough to pay it,

8 In order to live for ever and ever, *
    and never see the grave.

Lent Whoever wants to be my disciple must deny themselves and take up their cross daily and follow me.
Easter May you have the knowledge of God's mystery, that is Christ himself, in whom are hidden all the treasures of wisdom and knowledge, hallelujah.

Psalm 49 B *Cum viderit*

For what will it profit them if they gain the whole world but forfeit their life? Mt. 16:26

Lent The message of the cross is foolishness to those who are perishing, but to us who are being saved it is the power of God.
Easter From the grasp of death, God has ransomed my life, hallelujah.

9 For we see that the wise die also;
    like the dull and stupid they perish *
        and leave their wealth to those who come after them.

10 Their graves shall be their homes for ever,
    their dwelling places from generation to generation, *
        though they call the lands after their own names.

11 Even though honored, they cannot live for ever; *
    they are like the beasts that perish.

12 Such is the way of those who foolishly trust in themselves, *
    and the end of those who delight in their own words.

13 Like a flock of sheep they are destined to die;
    Death is their shepherd; *
        they go down straightway to the grave.

14 Their form shall waste away, *
    and the land of the dead shall be their home.

15 But God will ransom my life; *
    he will snatch me from the grasp of death.

16 Do not be envious when some become rich, *
    or when the grandeur of their house increases;

17 For they will carry nothing away at their death, *
    nor will their grandeur follow them.

18 Though they thought highly of themselves while they lived, *
    and were praised for their success,

19 They shall join the company of their forebears, *
    who will never see the light again.

20 Those who are honored, but have no understanding, *
    are like the beasts that perish.

Lent The message of the cross is foolishness to those who are perishing, but to us who are being saved it is the power of God.
Easter From the grasp of death, God has ransomed my life, hallelujah.

Psalm 150 *Laudate Dominum*
The whole multitude of the disciples began to praise God joyfully with a loud voice. Lk. 19: 37
Lent Praise the Lord in the firmament of his power.
Easter Worship God who is seated upon the throne, saying, Amen, hallelujah.

1 Hallelujah!
   Praise God in his holy temple; *
       praise him in the firmament of his power.

2 Praise him for his mighty acts; *
       praise him for his excellent greatness.

3 Praise him with the blast of the ram's-horn; *
       praise him with lyre and harp.

4 Praise him with timbrel and dance; *
       praise him with strings and pipe.

5 Praise him with resounding cymbals; *
       praise him with loud-clanging cymbals.

6 Let everything that has breath *
       praise the Lord.
       Hallelujah!

Lent Praise the Lord in the firmament of his power.
Easter Worship God who is seated upon the throne, saying, Amen, hallelujah.

Readings

Responsories, Benedictus Antiphon, Litany, Invitation to the Lord's Prayer, Collet and Dismissal are taken from the Proper of the Season.

Saturday Week 2 Noonday Prayer

Officiant: O God, make speed to save us.
People: **O Lord, make haste to help us.**
Officiant and People **Glory to the Father...**
Except in Lent, add **Alleluia.**

Hymn *From the Proper of the Season or of the Day*

Psalm 119 Lamedh *In æternum, Domine*
The words that I have spoken to you are spirit and life. Jn. 6: 63

Lent Be merciful to me, O LORD, for you are my God.
Easter Great is your love toward me; you have delivered me from the nethermost Pit, hallelujah.

89 O LORD, your word is everlasting; *
   it stands firm in the heavens.

90 Your faithfulness remains from one generation to another; *
   you established the earth, and it abides.

91 By your decree these continue to this day, *
   for all things are your servants.

92 If my delight had not been in your law, *
   I should have perished in my affliction.

93 I will never forget your commandments, *
   because by them you give me life.

94 I am yours; oh, that you would save me! *
   for I study your commandments.

95 Though the wicked lie in wait for me to destroy me, *
   I will apply my mind to your decrees.

96 I see that all things come to an end, *
   but your commandment has no bounds.

Psalm 86 A *Inclina, Domine*

Jesus told them a parable about their need to pray always and not to lose heart. Lk. 18:1

1 Bow down your ear, O LORD, and answer me, *
   for I am poor and in misery.

2 Keep watch over my life, for I am faithful; *
   save your servant who puts his trust in you.

3 Be merciful to me, O LORD, for you are my God; *
   I call upon you all the day long.

4 Gladden the soul of your servant, *
   for to you, O LORD, I lift up my soul.

5 For you, O LORD, are good and forgiving, *
   and great is your love toward all who call upon you.

6 Give ear, O LORD, to my prayer, *
   and attend to the voice of my supplications.

7 In the time of my trouble I will call upon you, *
   for you will answer me.

8 Among the gods there is none like you, O LORD, *
   nor anything like your works.

Psalm 86 B *Omnes gentes*

All nations will come and worship before you, for your judgments have been revealed. Rev. 15:4

9 All nations you have made will come
   and worship you, O LORD, *
   and glorify your Name.

10 For you are great;
   you do wondrous things; *
   and you alone are God.

11 Teach me your way, O LORD,
   and I will walk in your truth; *
   knit my heart to you that I may fear your Name.

12 I will thank you, O LORD my God, with all my heart, *
   and glorify your Name for evermore.

13 For great is your love toward me; *
   you have delivered me from the nethermost Pit.

14 The arrogant rise up against me, O God,
   and a band of violent men seeks my life; *
   they have not set you before their eyes.

15 But you, O LORD, are gracious and full of compassion, *
    slow to anger, and full of kindness and truth.

16 Turn to me and have mercy upon me; *
    give your strength to your servant;
    and save the child of your handmaid.

17 Show me a sign of your favor,
    so that those who hate me may see it and be ashamed; *
    because you, O LORD, have helped me and comforted me.

Lent Be merciful to me, O LORD, for you are my God.
Easter Great is your love toward me; you have delivered me from the nethermost Pit, hallelujah.

Reading, Verse and Response, Collect and Conclusion as in the Proper of the Season or of the Day.

Week 3

Sunday Week 3 Evening Prayer I

Officiant: O God, make speed to save us.
People: **O Lord, make haste to help us.**
Officiant and People **Glory to the Father...**
Except in Lent, add **Alleluia.**

Hymn *From the Proper of the Season or of the Day*

Psalm 21 *Domine, in virtute tua*
*God has put all things under Christ's feet and has made him
the head over all things for the church. Eph. 1: 28*

Lent Though they intend evil against you they shall not prevail.
Easter You meet him with blessings of prosperity, and set a crown of fine gold upon his head, hallelujah.

1 The king rejoices in your strength, O LORD; *
   how greatly he exults in your victory!

2 You have given him his heart's desire; *
   you have not denied him the request of his lips.

3 For you meet him with blessings of prosperity, *
   and set a crown of fine gold upon his head.

4 He asked you for life, and you gave it to him: *
   length of days, for ever and ever.

5 His honor is great, because of your victory; *
   splendor and majesty have you bestowed upon him.

6 For you will give him everlasting felicity *
   and will make him glad with the joy of your presence.

7 For the king puts his trust in the LORD; *
   because of the loving-kindness of the Most High,
   he will not fall.

8 Your hand will lay hold upon all your enemies; *
   your right hand will seize all those who hate you.

9 You will make them like a fiery furnace *
   at the time of your appearing, O LORD;

10 You will swallow them up in your wrath, *
   and fire shall consume them.

11 You will destroy their offspring from the land *
   and their descendants from among the peoples of the earth.

12 Though they intend evil against you
 and devise wicked schemes, *
  yet they shall not prevail.

13 For you will put them to flight *
  and aim your arrows at them.

14 Be exalted, O LORD, in your might; *
  we will sing and praise your power.

Lent Though they intend evil against you they shall not prevail.
Easter You meet him with blessings of prosperity, and set a crown of fine gold upon his head, hallelujah.

Psalm 136 A *Confitemini*
God has confirmed the promises given to the patriarchs, in order that the Gentiles might glorify God for his mercy. Rm. 15: 8-9

Lent Give thanks to the Lord who does great wonders; for his mercy endures for ever.
Easter In Christ are hidden all the treasures of wisdom and knowledge, hallelujah.

1 Give thanks to the LORD, for he is good, *
   for his mercy endures for ever.

2 Give thanks to the God of gods, *
   for his mercy endures for ever.

3 Give thanks to the Lord of lords, *
   for his mercy endures for ever.

4 Who only does great wonders, *
   for his mercy endures for ever;

5 Who by wisdom made the heavens, *
   for his mercy endures for ever;

6 Who spread out the earth upon the waters, *
   for his mercy endures for ever;

7 Who created great lights, *
   for his mercy endures for ever;

8 The sun to rule the day, *
   for his mercy endures for ever;

9 The moon and the stars to govern the night, *
   for his mercy endures for ever.

Lent Give thanks to the Lord who does great wonders; for his mercy endures for ever.
Easter In Christ are hidden all the treasures of wisdom and knowledge, hallelujah.

Psalm 136 B *Qui percussit*
God, who is rich in mercy, out of the great love with which he loved us, made us alive together with Christ Eph. 2:4-5

Lent The Lord remembered us, and delivered us from our enemies.
Easter With a mighty hand and a stretched out arm, he brought Israel out of Egypt, hallelujah.

10 Who struck down the firstborn of Egypt, *
    for his mercy endures for ever;

11 And brought out Israel from among them, *
    for his mercy endures for ever;

12 With a mighty hand and a stretched-out arm, *
    for his mercy endures for ever;

13 Who divided the Red Sea in two, *
    for his mercy endures for ever;

14 And made Israel to pass through the midst of it, *
    for his mercy endures for ever;

15 But swept Pharaoh and his army into the Red Sea, *
    for his mercy endures for ever;

16 Who led his people through the wilderness, *
    for his mercy endures for ever.

17 Who struck down great kings, *
    for his mercy endures for ever;

18 And slew mighty kings, *
    for his mercy endures for ever;

19 Sihon, king of the Amorites, *
    for his mercy endures for ever;

20 And Og, the king of Bashan, *
    for his mercy endures for ever;

21 And gave away their lands for an inheritance, *
    for his mercy endures for ever;

22 An inheritance for Israel his servant, *
　　for his mercy endures for ever.

23 Who remembered us in our low estate, *
　　for his mercy endures for ever;

24 And delivered us from our enemies, *
　　for his mercy endures for ever;

25 Who gives food to all creatures, *
　　for his mercy endures for ever.

26 Give thanks to the God of heaven, *
　　for his mercy endures for ever.

Lent The Lord remembered us, and delivered us from our enemies.
Easter With a mighty hand and a stretched out arm, he brought Israel out of Egypt, hallelujah.

Reading

Responsory, Magnificat Antiphon, Litany, Invitation to the Lord's Prayer, Collet and Dismissal are taken from the Proper of the Season.

Sunday Week 3 Morning Prayer

Officiant: Lord, open our lips.
People: **And our mouth shall proclaim your praise.**
Officiant and People **Glory to the Father...**
Except in Lent, add **Alleluia.**

The Invitatory Psalm 95
From the Proper of the Season or of the Day

Hymn *From the Proper of the Season or of the Day 7*

Psalm 118 A *Confitemini Domino*
The God of our ancestors raised up Jesus...
God exalted him at his right hand as Leader and Savior. Acts 5: 30-31

Lent I was pressed so hard that I almost fell, but the LORD came to my help.
Easter The LORD is at my side to help me; I will triumph over those who hate me, hallelujah.

1　Give thanks to the LORD, for he is good; *
　　his mercy endures for ever.

2　Let Israel now proclaim, *
　　"His mercy endures for ever."

3   Let the house of Aaron now proclaim, *
       "His mercy endures for ever."

4   Let those who fear the LORD now proclaim, *
       "His mercy endures for ever."

5   I called to the LORD in my distress; *
       the LORD answered by setting me free.

6   The LORD is at my side, therefore I will not fear; *
       what can anyone do to me?

7   The LORD is at my side to help me; *
       I will triumph over those who hate me.

8   It is better to rely on the LORD *
       than to put any trust in flesh.

9   It is better to rely on the LORD *
       than to put any trust in rulers.

10 All the ungodly encompass me; *
       in the name of the LORD I will repel them.

11 They hem me in, they hem me in on every side; *
       in the name of the LORD I will repel them.

12 They swarm about me like bees;
    they blaze like a fire of thorns; *
       in the name of the LORD I will repel them.

13 I was pressed so hard that I almost fell, *
       but the LORD came to my help.

14 The LORD is my strength and my song, *
       and he has become my salvation.

Lent I was pressed so hard that I almost fell, but the LORD came to my help.
Easter The LORD is at my side to help me; I will triumph over those who hate me, hallelujah.

Psalm 118 B *Vox exsultationis*
*Christ entered into heaven itself,
now to appear in the presence of God on our behalf. Heb. 9: 24*

Lent The LORD has punished me sorely, but he did not hand me over to death.
Easter On this day the Lord has acted; we will rejoice and be glad in it, hallelujah.

15 There is a sound of exultation and victory *
    in the tents of the righteous:

16 "The right hand of the LORD has triumphed! *
    the right hand of the LORD is exalted!
    the right hand of the LORD has triumphed!"

17 I shall not die, but live, *
    and declare the works of the LORD.

18 The LORD has punished me sorely, *
    but he did not hand me over to death.

19 Open for me the gates of righteousness; *
    I will enter them;
    I will offer thanks to the LORD.

20 "This is the gate of the LORD; *
    he who is righteous may enter."

21 I will give thanks to you, for you answered me *
    and have become my salvation.

22 The same stone which the builders rejected *
    has become the chief cornerstone.

23 This is the LORD'S doing, *
    and it is marvelous in our eyes.

24 On this day the LORD has acted; *
    we will rejoice and be glad in it.

25 Hosannah, LORD, hosannah! *
    LORD, send us now success.

26 Blessed is he who comes in the name of the Lord; *
    we bless you from the house of the LORD.

27 God is the LORD; he has shined upon us; *
    form a procession with branches up to the horns of the altar.

28 "You are my God, and I will thank you; *
    you are my God, and I will exalt you."

29 Give thanks to the LORD, for he is good; *
    his mercy endures for ever.

Lent The LORD has punished me sorely, but he did not hand me over to death.

Easter On this day the Lord has acted; we will rejoice and be glad in it, hallelujah.

Psalm 100 *Jubilate Deo*
You are a chosen race, a royal priesthood, a holy nation, God's own people. 1 Pt. 2:9

Lent The LORD is good; his mercy is everlasting.
Easter Serve the Lord with gladness, hallelujah.

1 Be joyful in the LORD, all you lands; *
    serve the LORD with gladness
    and come before his presence with a song.

2 Know this: The LORD himself is God; *
    he himself has made us, and we are his;
    we are his people and the sheep of his pasture.

3 Enter his gates with thanksgiving;
    go into his courts with praise; *
    give thanks to him and call upon his Name.

4 For the LORD is good;
    his mercy is everlasting; *
    and his faithfulness endures from age to age.

Lent The LORD is good; his mercy is everlasting.
Easter Serve the Lord with gladness, hallelujah.

Readings

Responsories, Benedictus Antiphon, Litany, Invitation to the Lord's Prayer, Collet and Dismissal are taken from the Proper of the Season.

Sunday Week 3 Noonday Prayer

Officiant: O God, make speed to save us.
People: **O Lord, make haste to help us.**
Officiant and People **Glory to the Father…**
Except in Lent, add **Alleluia.**

Hymn *From the Proper of the Season or of the Day*

Psalm 1 *Beatus vir qui non abiit*
This is the person who comes to me, hears my words, and acts on them. Lk. 6:47

Lent The wicked are like chaff which the wind blows away.
Easter I know that the LORD gives victory to his anointed; he will answer him out of his holy heaven, hallelujah.

1 Blessed are they who have not walked
    in the counsel of the wicked, *
        nor lingered in the way of sinners,
        nor sat in the seats of the scornful!

2 Their delight is in the law of the LORD, *
    and they meditate on his law day and night.

3 They are like trees planted by streams of water,
    bearing fruit in due season, with leaves that do not wither; *
        everything they do shall prosper.

4 It is not so with the wicked; *
    they are like chaff which the wind blows away.

5 Therefore the wicked shall not stand upright
    when judgment comes, *
        nor the sinner in the council of the righteous.

6 For the LORD knows the way of the righteous, *
    but the way of the wicked is doomed.

Psalm 2 *Quare fremuerunt gentes?*
God put his power to work in Christ when he raised him from the dead and seated him at his right hand. Col. 1: 20

1 Why are the nations in an uproar? *
    Why do the peoples mutter empty threats?

2 Why do the kings of the earth rise up in revolt,
    and the princes plot together, *
        against the LORD and against his Anointed?

3 "Let us break their yoke," they say; *
    "let us cast off their bonds from us."

4 He whose throne is in heaven is laughing; *
    the Lord has them in derision.

5 Then he speaks to them in his wrath, *
    and his rage fills them with terror.

6 "I myself have set my king *
    upon my holy hill of Zion."

7 Let me announce the decree of the LORD: *
    he said to me, "You are my Son;
    this day have I begotten you.

8 Ask of me, and I will give you
 the nations for your inheritance *
  and the ends of the earth for your possession.

9 You shall crush them with an iron rod *
  and shatter them like a piece of pottery."

10 And now, you kings, be wise; *
  be warned, you rulers of the earth.

11 Submit to the LORD with fear, *
  and with trembling bow before him;

12 Lest he be angry and you perish; *
  for his wrath is quickly kindled.

13 Blessed are they all *
  who take refuge in him!

Psalm 20 *Exaudiat te Dominus*

Christ is the head of the body, the church; he is the beginning, the firstborn from the dead. Col. 1: 18

1 May the LORD answer you in the day of trouble, *
  the Name of the God of Jacob defend you;

2 Send you help from his holy place *
  and strengthen you out of Zion;

3 Remember all your offerings *
  and accept your burnt sacrifice;

4 Grant you your heart's desire *
  and prosper all your plans.

5 We will shout for joy at your victory
 and triumph in the Name of our God; *
  may the LORD grant all your requests.

6 Now I know that the LORD gives victory to his anointed; *
  he will answer him out of his holy heaven,
  with the victorious strength of his right hand.

7 Some put their trust in chariots and some in horses, *
  but we will call upon the Name of the LORD our God.

8 They collapse and fall down, *
  but we will arise and stand upright.

9 O LORD, give victory to the king *
  and answer us when we call.

Lent The wicked are like chaff which the wind blows away.
Easter I know that the LORD gives victory to his anointed; he will answer him out of his holy heaven, hallelujah.

Reading, Verse and Response, Collect and Conclusion as in the Proper of the Season or of the Day.

Sunday Week 3 Evening Prayer II

Officiant: O God, make speed to save us.
People: **O Lord, make haste to help us.**
Officiant and People **Glory to the Father…**
Except in Lent, add **Alleluia.**

Hymn *From the Proper of the Season or of the Day*

Psalm 110 *Dixit Dominus*
Jesus has entered the inner sanctuary, having become a high priest forever according to the order of Melchizedek. Heb. 6:20

Lent He will drink from the brook beside the road; therefore he will lift high his head.
Easter The Lord has risen from the dead, and is seated at the right hand of God, hallelujah!

1 The LORD said to my Lord, "Sit at my right hand, *
 until I make your enemies your footstool."

2 The LORD will send the scepter of your power out of Zion, *
 saying, "Rule over your enemies round about you.

3 Princely state has been yours from the day of your birth; *
 in the beauty of holiness have I begotten you,
 like dew from the womb of the morning."

4 The LORD has sworn and he will not recant: *
 "You are a priest for ever after the order of Melchizedek."

5 The Lord who is at your right hand
 will smite kings in the day of his wrath; *
 he will rule over the nations.

6 He will heap high the corpses; *
 he will smash heads over the wide earth.

7 He will drink from the brook beside the road; *
 therefore he will lift high his head.

Lent He will drink from the brook beside the road; therefore he will lift high his head.

Easter The Lord has risen from the dead, and is seated at the right hand of God, hallelujah!

Psalm 111 *Confitebor tibi*
Christ entered once for all into the Holy Place, with his own blood,
thus obtaining eternal redemption. Heb. 9:12

Lent We have been redeemed by the precious blood of Christ, the lamb without blemish.
Easter The Lord sent redemption to his people, hallelujah.

1 Hallelujah!
   I will give thanks to the LORD with my whole heart, *
      in the assembly of the upright, in the congregation.

2 Great are the deeds of the LORD! *
      they are studied by all who delight in them.

3 His work is full of majesty and splendor, *
      and his righteousness endures for ever.

4 He makes his marvelous works to be remembered; *
      the LORD is gracious and full of compassion.

5 He gives food to those who fear him; *
      he is ever mindful of his covenant.

6 He has shown his people the power of his works *
      in giving them the lands of the nations.

7 The works of his hands are faithfulness and justice; *
      all his commandments are sure.

8 They stand fast for ever and ever, *
      because they are done in truth and equity.

9 He sent redemption to his people;
   he commanded his covenant for ever; *
      holy and awesome is his Name.

10 The fear of the LORD is the beginning of wisdom; *
       those who act accordingly have a good understanding;
       his praise endures for ever.

Lent We have been redeemed by the precious blood of Christ, the lamb without blemish.
Easter The Lord sent redemption to his people, hallelujah.

Psalm 112 *Beatus vir*

The righteous will shine like the sun in the kingdom of their Father. Mt. 13: 43

Lent The righteous have given freely to the poor.
Easter God has shone in our hearts to give the light of the glory of God in the face of Jesus Christ, hallelujah.

1 Hallelujah!
 Blessed are they who fear the Lord *
  and have great delight in his commandments!

2 Their descendants will be mighty in the land; *
  the generation of the upright will be blessed.

3 Wealth and riches will be in their house, *
  and their righteousness will last for ever.

4 Light shines in the darkness for the upright; *
  the righteous are merciful and full of compassion.

5 It is good for them to be generous in lending *
  and to manage their affairs with justice.

6 For they will never be shaken; *
  the righteous will be kept in everlasting remembrance.

7 They will not be afraid of any evil rumors; *
  their heart is right;
  they put their trust in the Lord.

8 Their heart is established and will not shrink, *
  until they see their desire upon their enemies.

9 They have given freely to the poor, *
  and their righteousness stands fast for ever;
  they will hold up their head with honor.

10 The wicked will see it and be angry;
  they will gnash their teeth and pine away; *
  the desires of the wicked will perish.

Lent The righteous have given freely to the poor.
Easter God has shone in our hearts to give the light of the glory of God in the face of Jesus Christ, hallelujah.

Reading

Responsory, Magnificat Antiphon, Litany, Invitation to the Lord's Prayer, Collect and Dismissal are taken from the Proper of the Season.

Monday Week 3 Morning Prayer

Officiant: Lord, open our lips.
People: **And our mouth shall proclaim your praise.**
Officiant and People **Glory to the Father ...**
Except in Lent, add **Alleluia.**

The Invitatory Psalm 29
From the Proper of the Season or of the Day

Hymn *From the Proper of the Season or of the Day*

Psalm 17 *Exaudi, Domine*
Seeing the glory of the Lord, we are being transformed into the same image from one degree of glory to another. 2 Cor. 3:18

Lent Weigh my heart, summon me by night, melt me down; you will find no impurity in me.

Easter When I awake, I shall be satisfied, beholding your likeness, hallelujah.

1 Hear my plea of innocence, O LORD;
  give heed to my cry; *
    listen to my prayer, which does not come from lying lips.

2 Let my vindication come forth from your presence; *
    let your eyes be fixed on justice.

3 Weigh my heart, summon me by night, *
    melt me down; you will find no impurity in me.

4 I give no offense with my mouth as others do; *
    I have heeded the words of your lips.

5 My footsteps hold fast to the ways of your law; *
    in your paths my feet shall not stumble.

6 I call upon you, O God, for you will answer me; *
    incline your ear to me and hear my words.

7 Show me your marvelous loving-kindness, *
    O Savior of those who take refuge at your right hand
    from those who rise up against them.

8 Keep me as the apple of your eye; *
    hide me under the shadow of your wings,

9 From the wicked who assault me, *
    from my deadly enemies who surround me.

10 They have closed their heart to pity, *
    and their mouth speaks proud things.

11 They press me hard,
    now they surround me, *
    watching how they may cast me to the ground,

12 Like a lion, greedy for its prey, *
    and like a young lion lurking in secret places.

13 Arise, O LORD; confront them and bring them down; *
    deliver me from the wicked by your sword.

14 Deliver me, O LORD, by your hand *
    from those whose portion in life is this world;

15 Whose bellies you fill with your treasure, *
    who are well supplied with children
    and leave their wealth to their little ones.

16 But at my vindication I shall see your face; *
    when I awake, I shall be satisfied,
    beholding your likeness.

Lent Weigh my heart, summon me by night, melt me down; you will find no impurity in me.
Easter When I awake, I shall be satisfied, beholding your likeness, hallelujah.

Psalm 108 *Paratum cor meum*
*The nations will walk by its light,
and the kings of the earth will bring their glory into it. Rev. 21: 24*

Lent My heart is ready, O God, my heart is ready.
Easter Exalt yourself above the heavens, O God, hallelujah.

1 My heart is firmly fixed, O God, my heart is fixed; *
    I will sing and make melody.

2 Wake up, my spirit;
    awake, lute and harp; *
    I myself will waken the dawn.

3 I will confess you among the peoples, O LORD; *
    I will sing praises to you among the nations.

4 For your loving-kindness is greater than the heavens, *
    and your faithfulness reaches to the clouds.

5 Exalt yourself above the heavens, O God, *
    and your glory over all the earth.

6 So that those who are dear to you may be delivered, *
    save with your right hand and answer me.

7 God spoke from his holy place and said, *
    "I will exult and parcel out Shechem;
    I will divide the valley of Succoth.

8 Gilead is mine and Manasseh is mine; *
    Ephraim is my helmet and Judah my scepter.

9 Moab is my washbasin,
    on Edom I throw down my sandal to claim it, *
    and over Philistia will I shout in triumph."

10 Who will lead me into the strong city? *
    who will bring me into Edom?

11 Have you not cast us off, O God? *
    you no longer go out, O God, with our armies.

12 Grant us your help against the enemy, *
    for vain is the help of man.

13 With God we will do valiant deeds, *
    and he shall tread our enemies under foot.

Lent My heart is ready, O God, my heart is ready.
Easter Exalt yourself above the heavens, O God, hallelujah.

Psalm 148 *Laudate Dominum*
*At Jesus' name every knee should bend, in heaven and on earth
and under the earth. Phil 2:10*

Lent Let all creatures praise the Name of the Lord; for he commanded, and they were created.
Easter The Name of the Lord is exalted above heaven and earth, hallelujah.

1 Hallelujah!
    Praise the LORD from the heavens; *
        praise him in the heights.

2 Praise him, all you angels of his; *
    praise him, all his host.

3 Praise him, sun and moon; *
    praise him, all you shining stars.

4 Praise him, heaven of heavens, *
    and you waters above the heavens.

5 Let them praise the Name of the LORD; *
    for he commanded, and they were created.

6 He made them stand fast for ever and ever; *
    he gave them a law which shall not pass away.

7 Praise the LORD from the earth, *
    you sea-monsters and all deeps;

8 Fire and hail, snow and fog, *
    tempestuous wind, doing his will;

9 Mountains and all hills, *
    fruit trees and all cedars;

10 Wild beasts and all cattle, *
    creeping things and wingèd birds;

11 Kings of the earth and all peoples, *
    princes and all rulers of the world;

12 Young men and maidens, *
    old and young together.

13 Let them praise the Name of the LORD, *
    for his Name only is exalted,
    his splendor is over earth and heaven.

14 He has raised up strength for his people
    and praise for all his loyal servants, *
        the children of Israel, a people who are near him.
        Hallelujah!

Lent Let all creatures praise the Name of the Lord; for he commanded, and they were created.
Easter The Name of the Lord is exalted above heaven and earth, hallelujah.

Readings

Responsories, Benedictus Antiphon, Litany, Invitation to the Lord's Prayer, Collet and Dismissal are taken from the Proper of the Season.

Monday Week 3 Noonday Prayer

Officiant: O God, make speed to save us.
People: **O Lord, make haste to help us.**
Officiant and People **Glory to the Father...**
Except in Lent, add **Alleluia.**

Hymn *From the Proper of the Season or of the Day*

Psalm 119   Mem   *Quomodo dilexi!*
*They found him in the temple, sitting among the teachers,
listening to them and asking them questions. Lk. 2:46*

Lent I have come not to bring peace but a sword.
Easter Peace I give you, my peace I give to you, hallelujah.

97 Oh, how I love your law! *
    all the day long it is in my mind.

98 Your commandment has made me wiser than my enemies, *
    and it is always with me.

99 I have more understanding than all my teachers, *
    for your decrees are my study.

100 I am wiser than the elders, *
    because I observe your commandments.

101 I restrain my feet from every evil way, *
    that I may keep your word.

102 I do not shrink from your judgments, *
    because you yourself have taught me.

103 How sweet are your words to my taste! *
    they are sweeter than honey to my mouth.

104 Through your commandments I gain understanding; *
    therefore I hate every lying way.

Psalm 120   *Ad Dominum*
If you, even you, had only recognized on this day the things that make for peace! Lk: 19:42

1 When I was in trouble, I called to the LORD; *
    I called to the LORD, and he answered me.

2 Deliver me, O LORD, from lying lips *
    and from the deceitful tongue.

3 What shall be done to you, and what more besides, *
    O you deceitful tongue?

4 The sharpened arrows of a warrior, *
   along with hot glowing coals.

5 How hateful it is that I must lodge in Meshech *
   and dwell among the tents of Kedar!

6 Too long have I had to live *
   among the enemies of peace.

7 I am on the side of peace, *
   but when I speak of it, they are for war.

Psalm 121 *Levavi oculos*

*Holy Father, protect them in your name that you have given me,
so that they may be one, as we are one. Jn. 17:11*

1 I lift up my eyes to the hills; *
   from where is my help to come?

2 My help comes from the LORD, *
   the maker of heaven and earth.

3 He will not let your foot be moved *
   and he who watches over you will not fall asleep.

4 Behold, he who keeps watch over Israel *
   shall neither slumber nor sleep;

5 The LORD himself watches over you; *
   the LORD is your shade at your right hand,

6 So that the sun shall not strike you by day, *
   nor the moon by night.

7 The LORD shall preserve you from all evil; *
   it is he who shall keep you safe.

8 The LORD shall watch over your going out
   and your coming in, *
   from this time forth for evermore.

Lent I have come not to bring peace but a sword.
Easter Peace I give you, my peace I give to you, hallelujah.

Reading, Verse and Response, Collect and Conclusion as in the Proper of the Season or of the Day.

Monday Week 3 Evening Prayer

Officiant: O God, make speed to save us.
People: **O Lord, make haste to help us.**
Officiant and People **Glory to the Father...**
Except in Lent, add **Alleluia.**

Hymn *From the Proper of the Season or of the Day*

Psalm 8 *Domine, Dominus noster*

We do see Jesus, who for a little while was made lower than the angels, now crowned with glory and honor. Heb. 2:9

Lent God has put all things under his feet, and made him the head of the Church, which is his body.

Easter We see Jesus, who for a little while was made lower than the angels, crowned with glory and honor, hallelujah!

1 O LORD our Governor, *
    how exalted is your Name in all the world!

2 Out of the mouths of infants and children *
    your majesty is praised above the heavens.

3 You have set up a stronghold against your adversaries, *
    to quell the enemy and the avenger.

4 When I consider your heavens, the work of your fingers, *
    the moon and the stars you have set in their courses,

5 What is man that you should be mindful of him? *
    the son of man that you should seek him out?

6 You have made him but little lower than the angels; *
    you adorn him with glory and honor;

7 You give him mastery over the works of your hands; *
    you put all things under his feet:

8 All sheep and oxen, *
    even the wild beasts of the field,

9 The birds of the air, the fish of the sea, *
    and whatsoever walks in the paths of the sea.

10 O LORD our Governor, *
    how exalted is your Name in all the world!

Lent God has put all things under his feet, and made him the head of the Church, which is his body.

Easter We see Jesus, who for a little while was made lower than the angels, crowned with glory and honor, hallelujah!

Psalm 52 *Quid gloriaris?*
I know the one in whom I have put my trust. 1 Tim. 1:12

Lent For all of us make many mistakes in speaking. Anyone who makes no mistakes is perfect.

Easter On either side of the river is the tree of life; and the leaves of the tree are for the healing of the nations, hallelujah!

1 You tyrant, why do you boast of wickedness *
  against the godly all day long?

2 You plot ruin;
  your tongue is like a sharpened razor, *
  O worker of deception.

3 You love evil more than good *
  and lying more than speaking the truth.

4 You love all words that hurt, *
  O you deceitful tongue.

5 Oh, that God would demolish you utterly, *
  topple you, and snatch you from your dwelling,
  and root you out of the land of the living!

6 The righteous shall see and tremble, *
  and they shall laugh at him, saying,

7 "This is the one who did not take God for a refuge, *
  but trusted in great wealth
  and relied upon wickedness."

8 But I am like a green olive tree in the house of God; *
  I trust in the mercy of God for ever and ever.

9 I will give you thanks for what you have done *
  and declare the goodness of your Name
  in the presence of the godly.

Lent For all of us make many mistakes in speaking. Anyone who makes no mistakes is perfect.

Easter On either side of the river is the tree of life; and the leaves of the tree are for the healing of the nations, hallelujah!

Psalm 128 *Beati omnes*
Living in the fear of the Lord and in the comfort of the Holy Spirit, the church increased in numbers. Acts 9:31

Lent The one who fears the LORD shall thus indeed be blessed.
Easter May you live to see your children's children; may peace be upon Israel, hallelujah.

1 Blessed are they all who fear the LORD, *
    and who follow in his ways!

2 You shall eat the fruit of your labor; *
    happiness and prosperity shall be yours.

3 Your wife shall be like a fruitful vine within your house, *
    your children like olive shoots round about your table.

4 The man who fears the LORD *
    shall thus indeed be blessed.

5 The LORD bless you from Zion, *
    and may you see the prosperity of Jerusalem
    all the days of your life.

6 May you live to see your children's children; *
    may peace be upon Israel.

Lent The one who fears the LORD shall thus indeed be blessed.
Easter May you live to see your children's children; may peace be upon Israel, hallelujah.

Reading

Responsory, Magnficat Antiphon, Litany, Invitation to the Lord's Prayer, Collet and Dismissal are taken from the Proper of the Season.

Tuesday Week 3 Morning Prayer
Officiant: Lord, open our lips.
People: **And our mouth shall proclaim your praise.**
Officiant and People **Glory to the Father...**
Except in Lent, add **Alleluia.**

The Invitatory Psalm 8
From the Proper of the Season or of the Day

Hymn *From the Proper of the Season or of the Day*

Psalm 87 *Fundamenta ejus*

Sarah corresponds to the Jerusalem above; she is free, and she is our mother. Gal. 4:26

Lent Jerusalem, Jerusalem the city that kills the prophets and stones those who are sent to it!
Easter The singers and the dancers will say: All my fresh springs are in you, O city of God, hallelujah.

1 On the holy mountain stands the city he has founded; *
    the LORD loves the gates of Zion
    more than all the dwellings of Jacob.

2 Glorious things are spoken of you, *
    O city of our God.

3 I count Egypt and Babylon among those who know me; *
    behold Philistia, Tyre, and Ethiopia:
    in Zion were they born.

4 Of Zion it shall be said, "Everyone was born in her, *
    and the Most High himself shall sustain her."

5 The LORD will record as he enrolls the peoples, *
    "These also were born there."

6 The singers and the dancers will say, *
    "All my fresh springs are in you."

Lent Jerusalem, Jerusalem the city that kills the prophets and stones those who are sent to it!
Easter The singers and the dancers will say: All my fresh springs are in you, O city of God, hallelujah.

Psalm 48 *Magnus Dominus*

I saw the holy city, the new Jerusalem, coming down out of heaven from God, prepared as a bride adorned for her husband. Rev. 21:2

Lent Your right hand is full of justice.
Easter This God shall be our guide for evermore, hallelujah.

1 Great is the LORD, and highly to be praised; *
    in the city of our God is his holy hill.

2 Beautiful and lofty, the joy of all the earth,
is the hill of Zion, *
    the very center of the world and the city of the great King.

3 God is in her citadels; *
    he is known to be her sure refuge.

4 Behold, the kings of the earth assembled *
    and marched forward together.

5 They looked and were astounded; *
    they retreated and fled in terror.

6 Trembling seized them there; *
    they writhed like a woman in childbirth,
    like ships of the sea when the east wind shatters them.

7 As we have heard, so have we seen,
  in the city of the LORD of hosts, in the city of our God; *
    God has established her for ever.

8 We have waited in silence on your loving-kindness, O God, *
    in the midst of your temple.

9 Your praise, like your Name, O God,
  reaches to the world's end; *
    your right hand is full of justice.

10 Let Mount Zion be glad
   and the cities of Judah rejoice, *
     because of your judgments.

11 Make the circuit of Zion;
   walk round about her; *
     count the number of her towers.

12 Consider well her bulwarks;
   examine her strongholds; *
     that you may tell those who come after.

13 This God is our God for ever and ever; *
     he shall be our guide for evermore.

Lent Your right hand is full of justice.
Easter This God shall be our guide for evermore, hallelujah.

Psalm 98 *Cantate Domino*

The throne of God and of the Lamb will be in it, and his servants will worship him; they will see his face. Rev. 22:3-4

Lent The Lord remembers his mercy and faithfulness to the house of Israel.
Easter All the ends of the earth have seen the victory of our God, hallelujah.

1 Sing to the L ORD a new song, *
   for he has done marvelous things.

2 With his right hand and his holy arm *
   has he won for himself the victory.

3 The L ORD has made known his victory; *
   his righteousness has he openly shown
   in the sight of the nations.

4 He remembers his mercy and faithfulness
   to the house of Israel, *
   and all the ends of the earth have seen
   the victory of our God.

5 Shout with joy to the L ORD, all you lands; *
   lift up your voice, rejoice, and sing.

6 Sing to the L ORD with the harp, *
   with the harp and the voice of song.

7 With trumpets and the sound of the horn *
   shout with joy before the King, the L ORD.

8 Let the sea make a noise and all that is in it, *
   the lands and those who dwell therein.

9 Let the rivers clap their hands, *
   and let the hills ring out with joy before the L ORD,
   when he comes to judge the earth.

10 In righteousness shall he judge the world *
   and the peoples with equity.

Lent The Lord remembers his mercy and faithfulness to the house of Israel.

Easter All the ends of the earth have seen the victory of our God, hallelujah.

Readings

Responsories, Benedictus Antiphon, Litany, Invitation to the Lord's Prayer, Collect and Dismissal are taken from the Proper of the Season.

Tuesday Week 3 Noonday Prayer

Officiant: O God, make speed to save us.
People: **O Lord, make haste to help us.**
Officiant and People **Glory to the Father...**
Except in Lent, add **Alleluia.**

Hymn *From the Proper of the Season or of the Day*

Psalm 119 Nun *Lucerna pedibus meis*

I have no greater joy than this, to hear that my children are walking in the truth. 3 Jn. 1:4

Lent As far as the east is from the west, so far has he removed our sins from us.
Easter The LORD has set his throne in heaven, and his kingship has dominion over all, hallelujah.

105 Your word is a lantern to my feet *
    and a light upon my path.

106 I have sworn and am determined *
    to keep your righteous judgments.

107 I am deeply troubled; *
    preserve my life, O LORD, according to your word.

108 Accept, O LORD, the willing tribute of my lips, *
    and teach me your judgments.

109 My life is always in my hand, *
    yet I do not forget your law.

110 The wicked have set a trap for me, *
    but I have not strayed from your commandments.

111 Your decrees are my inheritance for ever; *
    truly, they are the joy of my heart.

112 I have applied my heart to fulfill your statutes *
    for ever and to the end.

Psalm 103 A *Benedic, anima mea*

Together may you with one voice glorify the God and Father of our Lord Jesus Christ. Rm 15:6

1 Bless the LORD, O my soul, *
    and all that is within me, bless his holy Name.

2 Bless the LORD, O my soul, *
    and forget not all his benefits.

3 He forgives all your sins *
    and heals all your infirmities;

4 He redeems your life from the grave *
    and crowns you with mercy and loving-kindness;

5 He satisfies you with good things, *
    and your youth is renewed like an eagle's.

6 The LORD executes righteousness *
    and judgment for all who are oppressed.

7 He made his ways known to Moses *
    and his works to the children of Israel.

8 The LORD is full of compassion and mercy, *
    slow to anger and of great kindness.

9 He will not always accuse us, *
    nor will he keep his anger for ever.

10 He has not dealt with us according to our sins, *
    nor rewarded us according to our wickedness.

11 For as the heavens are high above the earth, *
    so is his mercy great upon those who fear him.

12 As far as the east is from the west, *
    so far has he removed our sins from us.

13 As a father cares for his children, *
    so does the LORD care for those who fear him.

14 For he himself knows whereof we are made; *
    he remembers that we are but dust.

Psalm 103 B *Homo, sicut*

You have been born anew, not of perishable but of imperishable seed, through the living and enduring word of God. 1 Pt. 1:23

15 Our days are like the grass; *
    we flourish like a flower of the field;

16 When the wind goes over it, it is gone, *
    and its place shall know it no more.

17 But the merciful goodness of the LORD endures for ever
   on those who fear him, *
    and his righteousness on children's children;

18 On those who keep his covenant *
    and remember his commandments and do them.

19 The LORD has set his throne in heaven, *
    and his kingship has dominion over all.

20 Bless the LORD, you angels of his,
  you mighty ones who do his bidding, *
    and hearken to the voice of his word.

21 Bless the LORD, all you his hosts, *
    you ministers of his who do his will.

22 Bless the LORD, all you works of his,
  in all places of his dominion; *
    bless the LORD, O my soul.

Lent As far as the east is from the west, so far has he removed our sins from us.
Easter The LORD has set his throne in heaven, and his kingship has dominion over all, hallelujah.

Reading, Verse and Response, Collect and Conclusion as in the Proper of the Season or of the Day.

Tuesday Week 3 Evening Prayer

Officiant: O God, make speed to save us.
People: **O Lord, make haste to help us.**
Officiant and People **Glory to the Father**
Except in Lent, add **Alleluia.**

Hymn *From the Proper of the Season or of the Day*

Psalm 85 *Benedixisti, Domine*

Glory to God in the highest heaven, and on earth peace among those whom he favors! Lk. 2:14

Lent You have forgiven the iniquity of your people and blotted out all their sins.
Easter Jesus came and stood among them and said, "Peace be with you." Hallelujah.

1 You have been gracious to your land, O LORD, *
    you have restored the good fortune of Jacob.

2 You have forgiven the iniquity of your people *
    and blotted out all their sins.

3 You have withdrawn all your fury *
    and turned yourself from your wrathful indignation.

4 Restore us then, O God our Savior; *
    let your anger depart from us.

5 Will you be displeased with us for ever? *
    will you prolong your anger from age to age?

6 Will you not give us life again, *
    that your people may rejoice in you?

7 Show us your mercy, O LORD, *
    and grant us your salvation.

8 I will listen to what the LORD God is saying, *
    for he is speaking peace to his faithful people
    and to those who turn their hearts to him.

9 Truly, his salvation is very near to those who fear him, *
    that his glory may dwell in our land.

10 Mercy and truth have met together; *
    righteousness and peace have kissed each other.

11 Truth shall spring up from the earth, *
    and righteousness shall look down from heaven.

12 The LORD will indeed grant prosperity, *
    and our land will yield its increase.

13 Righteousness shall go before him, *
    and peace shall be a pathway for his feet.

Lent You have forgiven the iniquity of your people and blotted out all their sins.
Easter Jesus came and stood among them and said, "Peace be with you." Hallelujah.

Psalm 62 *Nonne Deo?*
*To one who without works trusts him who justifies the ungodly,
such faith is reckoned as righteousness. Rm. 4:5*

Lent Put your trust in God always, O people, pour out your hearts before God, for God is our refuge.
Easter Let not your hearts be troubled; believe in me, hallelujah.

1 For God alone my soul in silence waits; *
    from him comes my salvation.

2 He alone is my rock and my salvation, *
    my stronghold, so that I shall not be greatly shaken.

3 How long will you assail me to crush me,
    all of you together, *
    as if you were a leaning fence, a toppling wall?

4 They seek only to bring me down from my place of honor; *
    lies are their chief delight.

5 They bless with their lips, *
    but in their hearts they curse.

6 For God alone my soul in silence waits; *
    truly, my hope is in him.

7 He alone is my rock and my salvation, *
    my stronghold, so that I shall not be shaken.

8 In God is my safety and my honor; *
    God is my strong rock and my refuge.

9 Put your trust in him always, O people, *
    pour out your hearts before him, for God is our refuge.

10 Those of high degree are but a fleeting breath, *
    even those of low estate cannot be trusted.

11 On the scales they are lighter than a breath, *
    all of them together.

12 Put no trust in extortion;
    in robbery take no empty pride; *
    though wealth increase, set not your heart upon it.

13 God has spoken once, twice have I heard it, *
    that power belongs to God.

14 Steadfast love is yours, O Lord, *
    for you repay everyone according to his deeds.

Lent Put your trust in God always, O people, pour out your hearts before God, for God is our refuge.
Easter Let not your hearts be troubled; believe in me, hallelujah.

Psalm 125 *Qui confidunt*

For those who will follow this rule—peace be upon them, and mercy, and upon the Israel of God. Gal. 6:16

Lent When the days drew near for him to be taken up, Jesus set his face to go to Jerusalem.

Easter You have come to Jesus, the mediator of a new covenant, and to the sprinkled blood that speaks more eloquently than the blood of Abel, hallelujah.

1 Those who trust in the LORD are like Mount Zion, *
    which cannot be moved, but stands fast for ever.

2 The hills stand about Jerusalem; *
    so does the LORD stand round about his people,
    from this time forth for evermore.

3 The scepter of the wicked shall not hold sway
    over the land allotted to the just, *
    so that the just shall not put their hands to evil.

4 Show your goodness, O LORD, to those who are good *
    and to those who are true of heart.

5 As for those who turn aside to crooked ways,
    the LORD will lead them away with the evildoers; *
    but peace be upon Israel.

Lent When the days drew near for him to be taken up, Jesus set his face to go to Jerusalem.

Easter You have come to Jesus, the mediator of a new covenant, and to the sprinkled blood that speaks more eloquently than the blood of Abel, hallelujah.

Reading

Responsory, Magnificat Antiphon, Litany, Invitation to the Lord's Prayer, Collet and Dismissal are taken from the Proper of the Season.

Wednesday Week 3 Morning Prayer

Officiant: Lord, open our lips.
People: **And our mouth shall proclaim your praise.**
Officiant and People **Glory to the Father...**
Except in Lent, add **Alleluia.**

The Invitatory Psalm 95

From the Proper of the Season or of the Day

Hymn *From the Proper of the Season or of the Day*

Psalm 90 *Domine, refugium*
With the Lord one day is like a thousand years, and a thousand years are like one day. 2 Pt. 3:8

Lent Our iniquities you have set before you, and our secret sins in the light of your countenance.

Easter Christ has risen from the dead and will never die again, hallelujah.

1 Lord, you have been our refuge *
    from one generation to another.

2 Before the mountains were brought forth,
   or the land and the earth were born, *
    from age to age you are God.

3 You turn us back to the dust and say, *
    "Go back, O child of earth."

4 For a thousand years in your sight
   are like yesterday when it is past *
    and like a watch in the night.

5 You sweep us away like a dream; *
    we fade away suddenly like the grass.

6 In the morning it is green and flourishes; *
    in the evening it is dried up and withered.

7 For we consume away in your displeasure; *
    we are afraid because of your wrathful indignation.

8 Our iniquities you have set before you, *
    and our secret sins in the light of your countenance.

9 When you are angry, all our days are gone; *
    we bring our years to an end like a sigh.

10 The span of our life is seventy years,
   perhaps in strength even eighty; *
    yet the sum of them is but labor and sorrow,
    for they pass away quickly and we are gone.

11 Who regards the power of your wrath? *
    who rightly fears your indignation?

12 So teach us to number our days *
    that we may apply our hearts to wisdom.

13 Return, O LORD; how long will you tarry? *
    be gracious to your servants.

14 Satisfy us by your loving-kindness in the morning; *
    so shall we rejoice and be glad all the days of our life.

15 Make us glad by the measure of the days that you afflicted us *
    and the years in which we suffered adversity.

16 Show your servants your works *
    and your splendor to their children.

17 May the graciousness of the LORD our God be upon us; *
    prosper the work of our hands;
    prosper our handiwork.

Lent Our iniquities you have set before you, and our secret sins in the light of your countenance.
Easter Christ has risen from the dead and will never die again, hallelujah.

Psalm 75 *Confitebimur tibi*
God, through Jesus Christ, will judge the secret thoughts of all. Rm. 2:16

Lent I will say to the boasters, "Boast no more."
Easter I will rejoice for ever; I will sing praises to the God of Jacob, hallelujah.

1 We give you thanks, O God, we give you thanks, *
    calling upon your Name
    and declaring all your wonderful deeds.

2 "I will appoint a time," says God; *
    "I will judge with equity.

3 Though the earth and all its inhabitants are quaking, *
    I will make its pillars fast.

4 I will say to the boasters, 'Boast no more,' *
    and to the wicked, 'Do not toss your horns;

5 Do not toss your horns so high, *
    nor speak with a proud neck.'"

6 For judgment is neither from the east nor from the west, *
    nor yet from the wilderness or the mountains.

7 It is God who judges; *
    he puts down one and lifts up another.

8 For in the LORD'S hand there is a cup,
  full of spiced and foaming wine, which he pours out, *
    and all the wicked of the earth
    shall drink and drain the dregs.

9 But I will rejoice for ever; *
    I will sing praises to the God of Jacob.

10 He shall break off all the horns of the wicked; *
    but the horns of the righteous shall be exalted.

Lent I will say to the boasters, "Boast no more."
Easter I will rejoice for ever; I will sing praises to the God of Jacob, hallelujah.

Psalm 67 *Deus misereatur*

*I thank my God through Jesus Christ for all of you,
because your faith is proclaimed throughout the world. Rm 1:8*

Lent Let your ways be known upon earth, your saving health among all nations.

Easter : Let the peoples praise you, O God; let all the peoples praise you, hallelujah.

1 May God be merciful to us and bless us, *
    show us the light of his countenance and come to us.

2 Let your ways be known upon earth, *
    your saving health among all nations.

3 Let the peoples praise you, O God; *
    let all the peoples praise you.

4 Let the nations be glad and sing for joy, *
    for you judge the peoples with equity
    and guide all the nations upon earth.

5 Let the peoples praise you, O God; *
    let all the peoples praise you.

6 The earth has brought forth her increase; *
    may God, our own God, give us his blessing.

7 May God give us his blessing, *
    and may all the ends of the earth stand in awe of him.

Readings

Responsories, Benedictus Antiphon, Litany, Invitation to the Lord's Prayer, Collet and Dismissal are taken from the Proper of the Season.

Wednesday Week 3 Noonday Prayer

Officiant: O God, make speed to save us.
People: **O Lord, make haste to help us.**
Officiant and People **Glory to the Father…**
Except in Lent, add **Alleluia.**

Hymn *From the Proper of the Season or of the Day*

Psalm 119 Samekh *Iniquos odio habui*
The monastic who is to be received comes before the community in the oratory and promises stability, fidelity to monastic life and obedience. RB 58:17

Lent Jesus was filled with fear and distress.
Easter At Jesus' Name every knee should bend in heaven and on earth, hallelujah.

113 I hate those who have a divided heart, *
   but your law do I love.

114 You are my refuge and shield; *
   my hope is in your word.

115 Away from me, you wicked! *
   I will keep the commandments of my God.

116 Sustain me according to your promise, that I may live, *
   and let me not be disappointed in my hope.

117 Hold me up, and I shall be safe, *
   and my delight shall be ever in your statutes.

118 You spurn all who stray from your statutes; *
   their deceitfulness is in vain.

119 In your sight all the wicked of the earth are but dross; *
   therefore I love your decrees.

120 My flesh trembles with dread of you; *
   I am afraid of your judgments.

Psalm 12 *Salvum me fac*
All of them deserted Jesus and fled. Mk. 14:50

1 Help me, LORD, for there is no godly one left; *
   the faithful have vanished from among us.

2 Everyone speaks falsely with his neighbor; *
   with a smooth tongue they speak from a double heart.

3 Oh, that the LORD would cut off all smooth tongues, *
    and close the lips that utter proud boasts!

4 Those who say, "With our tongue will we prevail; *
    our lips are our own; who is lord over us?"

5 "Because the needy are oppressed,
  and the poor cry out in misery, *
    I will rise up," says the LORD,
    "and give them the help they long for."

6 The words of the LORD are pure words, *
    like silver refined from ore
    and purified seven times in the fire.

7 O LORD, watch over us *
    and save us from this generation for ever.

8 The wicked prowl on every side, *
    and that which is worthless is highly prized by everyone.

Psalm 83 *Deus, quis similis?*
You will be hated by all because of my name.
But the one who endures to the end will be saved. Mk. 13:13

1 O God, do not be silent; *
    do not keep still nor hold your peace, O God;

2 For your enemies are in tumult, *
    and those who hate you have lifted up their heads.

3 They take secret counsel against your people *
    and plot against those whom you protect.

4 They have said, "Come, let us wipe them out
  from among the nations; *
    let the name of Israel be remembered no more."

5 They have conspired together; *
    they have made an alliance against you:

6 The tents of Edom and the Ishmaelites; *
    the Moabites and the Hagarenes;

7 Gebal, and Ammon, and Amalek; *
    the Philistines and those who dwell in Tyre.

8 The Assyrians also have joined them, *
    and have come to help the people of Lot.

9 Do to them as you did to Midian, *
     to Sisera, and to Jabin at the river of Kishon:

10 They were destroyed at Endor; *
     they became like dung upon the ground.

11 Make their leaders like Oreb and Zeëb, *
     and all their commanders like Zebah and Zalmunna,

12 Who said, "Let us take for ourselves *
     the fields of God as our possession."

13 O my God, make them like whirling dust *
     and like chaff before the wind;

14 Like fire that burns down a forest, *
     like the flame that sets mountains ablaze.

15 Drive them with your tempest *
     and terrify them with your storm;

16 Cover their faces with shame, O LORD, *
     that they may seek your Name.

17 Let them be disgraced and terrified for ever; *
     let them be put to confusion and perish.

18 Let them know that you, whose Name is YAHWEH, *
     you alone are the Most High over all the earth.

Lent Jesus was filled with fear and distress.
Easter At Jesus' Name every knee should bend in heaven and on earth, hallelujah.

Reading, Verse and Response, Collect and Conclusion as in the Proper of the Season or of the Day.

Wednesday Week 3 Evening Prayer

Officiant: O God, make speed to save us.
People: **O Lord, make haste to help us.**
Officiant and People **Glory to the Father...**
Except in Lent, add **Alleluia.**

Hymn *From the Proper of the Season or of the Day*

Psalm 106 A *Confitemini Domino*

*Our ancestors were unwilling to obey Moses; instead, they pushed him aside,
and in their hearts they turned back to Egypt. Acts 7:39*

Lent We have sinned as our forebears did; we have done wrong and dealt wickedly.

Easter Was it not necessary that the Messiah should suffer these things and then enter into his glory, hallelujah.

1 Hallelujah!
  Give thanks to the LORD, for he is good, *
    for his mercy endures for ever.

2 Who can declare the mighty acts of the LORD *
    or show forth all his praise?

3 Blessed are those who act with justice *
    and always do what is right!

4 Remember me, O LORD,
  with the favor you have for your people, *
    and visit me with your saving help;

5 That I may see the prosperity of your elect
  and be glad with the gladness of your people, *
    that I may glory with your inheritance.

6 We have sinned as our forebears did; *
    we have done wrong and dealt wickedly.

7 In Egypt they did not consider your marvelous works,
  nor remember the abundance of your love; *
    they defied the Most High at the Red Sea.

8 But he saved them for his Name's sake, *
    to make his power known.

9 He rebuked the Red Sea, and it dried up, *
    and he led them through the deep as through a desert.

10 He saved them from the hand of those who hated them *
    and redeemed them from the hand of the enemy.

11 The waters covered their oppressors; *
    not one of them was left.

12 Then they believed his words *
    and sang him songs of praise.

13 But they soon forgot his deeds *
    and did not wait for his counsel.

14 A craving seized them in the wilderness, *
    and they put God to the test in the desert.

15 He gave them what they asked, *
    but sent leanness into their soul.

16 They envied Moses in the camp, *
    and Aaron, the holy one of the LORD.

17 The earth opened and swallowed Dathan *
    and covered the company of Abiram.

18 Fire blazed up against their company, *
    and flames devoured the wicked.

Lent We have sinned as our forebears did; we have done wrong and dealt wickedly.
Easter Was it not necessary that the Messiah should suffer these things and then enter into his glory, hallelujah.

Psalm 106 B *Et fecerunt*
God turned away from them and handed them over to worship the host of heaven. Acts 7:42
Lent They forgot God their Savior, who had done great things in Egypt.
Easter Beginning with Moses and all the prophets Jesus interpreted to them the things about himself in all the scripture, hallelujah.

19 Israel made a bull-calf at Horeb *
    and worshiped a molten image;

20 And so they exchanged their Glory *
    for the image of an ox that feeds on grass.

21 They forgot God their Savior, *
    who had done great things in Egypt,

22 Wonderful deeds in the land of Ham, *
    and fearful things at the Red Sea.

23 So he would have destroyed them,
    had not Moses his chosen stood before him in the breach, *
    to turn away his wrath from consuming them.

24 They refused the pleasant land *
    and would not believe his promise.

25 They grumbled in their tents *
>   and would not listen to the voice of the LORD.

26 So God lifted his hand against them, *
>   to overthrow them in the wilderness,

27 To cast out their seed among the nations, *
>   and to scatter them throughout the lands.

28 They joined themselves to Baal-Peor *
>   and ate sacrifices offered to the dead.

29 They provoked him to anger with their actions, *
>   and a plague broke out among them.

30 Then Phinehas stood up and interceded, *
>   and the plague came to an end.

31 This was reckoned to him as righteousness *
>   throughout all generations for ever.

32 Again they provoked his anger at the waters of Meribah, *
>   so that he punished Moses because of them;

33 For they so embittered his spirit *
>   that he spoke rash words with his lips.

Lent They forgot God their Savior, who had done great things in Egypt.
Easter Beginning with Moses and all the prophets Jesus interpreted to them the things about himself in all the scripture, hallelujah.

Psalm 106 C *Non disperdiderunt*

You stiff-necked people, uncircumcised in heart and ears, you are forever opposing the Holy Spirit, just as your ancestors used to do. Acts 7:51

Lent God is faithful and will not let you be tested beyond your strength.
Easter I want to know Christ and the power of his resurrection and the sharing of his sufferings by becoming like him in his death, if somehow I may attain the resurrection from the dead, hallelujah.

34 They did not destroy the peoples *
>   as the LORD had commanded them.

35 They intermingled with the heathen *
>   and learned their pagan ways,

36 So that they worshiped their idols, *
>   which became a snare to them.

37 They sacrificed their sons *
    and their daughters to evil spirits.

38 They shed innocent blood,
  the blood of their sons and daughters, *
    which they offered to the idols of Canaan,
    and the land was defiled with blood.

39 Thus they were polluted by their actions *
    and went whoring in their evil deeds.

40 Therefore the wrath of the LORD was kindled against his people *
    and he abhorred his inheritance.

41 He gave them over to the hand of the heathen, *
    and those who hated them ruled over them.

42 Their enemies oppressed them, *
    and they were humbled under their hand.

43 Many a time did he deliver them,
  but they rebelled through their own devices, *
    and were brought down in their iniquity.

44 Nevertheless, God saw their distress, *
    when he heard their lamentation.

45 He remembered his covenant with them *
    and relented in accordance with his great mercy.

46 He caused them to be pitied *
    by those who held them captive.

47 Save us, O LORD our God,
  and gather us from among the nations, *
    that we may give thanks to your holy Name
    and glory in your praise.

48 Blessed be the LORD, the God of Israel,
  from everlasting and to everlasting; *
    and let all the people say, "Amen!"
    Hallelujah!

Lent God is faithful and will not let you be tested beyond your strength.
Easter I want to know Christ and the power of his resurrection and the sharing of his sufferings by becoming like him in his death, if somehow I may attain the resurrection from the dead, hallelujah.

Reading

Responsory, Magnificat Antiphon, Litany, Invitation to the Lord's Prayer, Collet and Dismissal are taken from the Proper of the Season.

Thursday Week 3 Morning Prayer

Officiant: Lord, open our lips.
People: **And our mouth shall proclaim your praise.**
Officiant and People **Glory to the Father...**
Except in Lent, add **Alleluia.**

The Invitatory Psalm 100
From the Proper of the Season or of the Day

Hymn *From the Proper of the Season or of the Day*

Psalm 23 *Dominus regit me*
The good shepherd lays down his life for the sheep. Jn. 10:11

Lent Though I walk through the valley of the shadow of death, I shall fear no evil; for you are with me.
Easter I am the Good Shepherd. I know my own and my own know me, just as the Father knows me and I know the Father, hallelujah.

1 The LORD is my shepherd; *
 I shall not be in want.

2 He makes me lie down in green pastures *
 and leads me beside still waters.

3 He revives my soul *
 and guides me along right pathways for his Name's sake.

4 Though I walk through the valley of the shadow of death,
 I shall fear no evil; *
 for you are with me;
 your rod and your staff, they comfort me.

5 You spread a table before me
 in the presence of those who trouble me; *
 you have anointed my head with oil,
 and my cup is running over.

6 Surely your goodness and mercy shall follow me
 all the days of my life, *
 and I will dwell in the house of the LORD for ever.

Lent Though I walk through the valley of the shadow of death, I shall fear no evil; for you are with me.

Easter I am the Good Shepherd. I know my own and my own know me, just as the Father knows me and I know the Father, hallelujah.

Psalm 81 *Exultate Deo*
Those who eat my flesh and drink my blood abide in me, and I in them. Jn. 6:56

Lent My people did not hear my voice, and Israel would not obey me.
Easter I am the bread of life. Those who eat my flesh and drink my blood abide in me and I in them, hallelujah.

1 Sing with joy to God our strength *
    and raise a loud shout to the God of Jacob.

2 Raise a song and sound the timbrel, *
    the merry harp, and the lyre.

3 Blow the ram's-horn at the new moon, *
    and at the full moon, the day of our feast.

4 For this is a statute for Israel, *
    a law of the God of Jacob.

5 He laid it as a solemn charge upon Joseph, *
    when he came out of the land of Egypt.

6 I heard an unfamiliar voice saying, *
    "I eased his shoulder from the burden;
    his hands were set free from bearing the load."

7 You called on me in trouble, and I saved you; *
    I answered you from the secret place of thunder
    and tested you at the waters of Meribah.

8 Hear, O my people, and I will admonish you: *
    O Israel, if you would but listen to me!

9 There shall be no strange god among you; *
    you shall not worship a foreign god.

10 I am the LORD your God,
    who brought you out of the land of Egypt and said, *
    "Open your mouth wide, and I will fill it."

11 And yet my people did not hear my voice, *
    and Israel would not obey me.

12 So I gave them over to the stubbornness of their hearts, *
    to follow their own devices.

13 Oh, that my people would listen to me! *
  that Israel would walk in my ways!

14 I should soon subdue their enemies *
  and turn my hand against their foes.

15 Those who hate the LORD would cringe before him, *
  and their punishment would last for ever.

16 But Israel would I feed with the finest wheat *
  and satisfy him with honey from the rock.

Lent My people did not hear my voice, and Israel would not obey me.
Easter I am the bread of life. Those who eat my flesh and drink my blood abide in me and I in them, hallelujah.

Psalm 149 *Cantate Domino*

All who see them shall acknowledge that they are a people whom the Lord has blessed. Is. 61: 9

Lent There is joy in the presence of the angels of God over one sinner who repents.
Easter Let the faithful rejoice in triumph; let them be joyful on their beds, hallelujah.

1 Hallelujah!
  Sing to the LORD a new song; *
  sing his praise in the congregation of the faithful.

2 Let Israel rejoice in his Maker; *
  let the children of Zion be joyful in their King.

3 Let them praise his Name in the dance; *
  let them sing praise to him with timbrel and harp.

4 For the LORD takes pleasure in his people *
  and adorns the poor with victory.

5 Let the faithful rejoice in triumph; *
  let them be joyful on their beds.

6 Let the praises of God be in their throat *
  and a two-edged sword in their hand;

7 To wreak vengeance on the nations *
  and punishment on the peoples;

8 To bind their kings in chains *
  and their nobles with links of iron;

9 To inflict on them the judgment decreed; *
    this is glory for all his faithful people.
    Hallelujah!

Lent There is joy in the presence of the angels of God over one sinner who repents.
Easter Let the faithful rejoice in triumph; let them be joyful on their beds, hallelujah.

Readings

Responsories, Benedictus Antiphon, Litany, Invitation to the Lord's Prayer, Collet and Dismissal are taken from the Proper of the Season.

Thursday Week 3 Noonday Prayer

Officiant: O God, make speed to save us.
People: **O Lord, make haste to help us.**
Officiant and People **Glory to the Father…**
Except in Lent, add **Alleluia.**

Hymn *From the Proper of the Season or of the Day*

Psalm 119 Ayin *Feci judicium*
Blessed is that slave whom his master will find at work when he arrives. Lk. 12:43
Lent Let us fall upon our knees before God's footstool.
Easter Arise, O LORD, into your resting-place, hallelujah.

121 I have done what is just and right; *
    do not deliver me to my oppressors.

122 Be surety for your servant's good; *
    let not the proud oppress me.

123 My eyes have failed from watching for your salvation *
    and for your righteous promise.

124 Deal with your servant according to your loving-kindness *
    and teach me your statutes.

125 I am your servant; grant me understanding, *
    that I may know your decrees.

126 It is time for you to act, O LORD, *
    for they have broken your law.

127 Truly, I love your commandments *
    more than gold and precious stones.

128 I hold all your commandments to be right for me; *
   all paths of falsehood I abhor.

Psalm 127 *Nisi Dominus*

Everyone then who hears these words of mine and acts on them will be like a wise man who built his house on rock. Mt. 7: 24

1 Unless the LORD builds the house, *
   their labor is in vain who build it.

2 Unless the LORD watches over the city, *
   in vain the watchman keeps his vigil.

3 It is in vain that you rise so early and go to bed so late; *
   vain, too, to eat the bread of toil,
   for he gives to his beloved sleep.

4 Children are a heritage from the LORD, *
   and the fruit of the womb is a gift.

5 Like arrows in the hand of a warrior *
   are the children of one's youth.

6 Blessed is the man who has his quiver full of them! *
   he shall not be put to shame
   when he contends with his enemies in the gate.

Psalm 128 *Beati omnes*

Living in the fear of the Lord and in the comfort of the Holy Spirit, the church increased in numbers. Acts 9:31

1 Happy are they all who fear the LORD, *
   and who follow in his ways!

2 You shall eat the fruit of your labor; *
   happiness and prosperity shall be yours.

3 Your wife shall be like a fruitful vine within your house, *
   your children like olive shoots round about your table.

4 The man who fears the LORD *
   shall thus indeed be blessed.

5 The LORD bless you from Zion, *
   and may you see the prosperity of Jerusalem
   all the days of your life.

6 May you live to see your children's children; *
   may peace be upon Israel.

Lent Let us fall upon our knees before God's footstool.

Easter Arise, O LORD, into your resting-place, hallelujah.

Reading, Verse and Response, Collect and Conclusion as in the Proper of the Season or of the Day.

Thursday Week 3 Evening Prayer

Officiant: O God, make speed to save us.
People: **O Lord, make haste to help us.**
Officiant and People **Glory to the Father...**
Except in Lent, add **Alleluia.**

Hymn *From the Proper of the Season or of the Day*

Psalm 104 A *Benedic, anima mea*
Consider the lilies, how they grow: they neither toil nor spin; yet I tell you, even Solomon in all his glory was not clothed like one of these. Lk. 12:27

Lent I form light and create darkness, I make weal and create woe; I the Lord do all these things.
Easter Through Christ and in Christ were all things created; he is the image of the invisible God, and the first-born of all creation, hallelujah.

1 Bless the LORD, O my soul; *
 O LORD my God, how excellent is your greatness!
 you are clothed with majesty and splendor.

2 You wrap yourself with light as with a cloak *
 and spread out the heavens like a curtain.

3 You lay the beams of your chambers in the waters above; *
 you make the clouds your chariot;
 you ride on the wings of the wind.

4 You make the winds your messengers *
 and flames of fire your servants.

5 You have set the earth upon its foundations, *
 so that it never shall move at any time.

6 You covered it with the Deep as with a mantle; *
 the waters stood higher than the mountains.

7 At your rebuke they fled; *
 at the voice of your thunder they hastened away.

8 They went up into the hills and down to the valleys beneath, *
 to the places you had appointed for them.

9 You set the limits that they should not pass; *
    they shall not again cover the earth.

10 You send the springs into the valleys; *
    they flow between the mountains.

11 All the beasts of the field drink their fill from them, *
    and the wild asses quench their thirst.

12 Beside them the birds of the air make their nests *
    and sing among the branches.

13 You water the mountains from your dwelling on high; *
    the earth is fully satisfied by the fruit of your works.

14 You make grass grow for flocks and herds *
    and plants to serve mankind;

15 That they may bring forth food from the earth, *
    and wine to gladden our hearts,

16 Oil to make a cheerful countenance, *
    and bread to strengthen the heart.

17 The trees of the LORD are full of sap, *
    the cedars of Lebanon which he planted,

18 In which the birds build their nests, *
    and in whose tops the stork makes his dwelling.

19 The high hills are a refuge for the mountain goats, *
    and the stony cliffs for the rock badgers.

20 You appointed the moon to mark the seasons, *
    and the sun knows the time of its setting.

21 You make darkness that it may be night, *
    in which all the beasts of the forest prowl.

22 The lions roar after their prey *
    and seek their food from God.

23 The sun rises, and they slip away *
    and lay themselves down in their dens.

24 Man goes forth to his work *
    and to his labor until the evening.

Lent I form light and create darkness, I make weal and create woe; I the Lord do all these things.

Easter Through Christ and in Christ were all things created; he is the image of the invisible God, and the first-born of all creation, hallelujah.

Psalm 104 B *Quam magnificata sunt*
The heavenly Father will give the Holy Spirit to those who ask him. Lk. 11:13

Lent You hide your face, and they are terrified; you take away their breath, and they die and return to their dust.
Easter You send forth your Spirit, and they are created, hallelujah.

25 O LORD, how manifold are your works! *
    in wisdom you have made them all;
    the earth is full of your creatures.

26 Yonder is the great and wide sea
    with its living things too many to number, *
    creatures both small and great.

27 There move the ships,
  and there is that Leviathan, *
    which you have made for the sport of it.

28 All of them look to you *
    to give them their food in due season.

29 You give it to them; they gather it; *
    you open your hand, and they are filled with good things.

30 You hide your face, and they are terrified; *
    you take away their breath,
    and they die and return to their dust.

31 You send forth your Spirit, and they are created; *
    and so you renew the face of the earth.

Lent You hide your face, and they are terrified; you take away their breath, and they die and return to their dust.
Easter You send forth your Spirit, and they are created, hallelujah.

Psalm 104 C *Sit gloria Domini*
*People will faint from fear and foreboding of what is coming upon the world,
for the powers of the heavens will be shaken. Lk. 21:26*

Lent Let sinners be consumed out of the earth, and the wicked be no more.
Easter I will sing to the LORD as long as I live, hallelujah.

32 May the glory of the LORD endure for ever; *
    may the LORD rejoice in all his works.

33 He looks at the earth and it trembles; *
    he touches the mountains and they smoke.

34 I will sing to the LORD as long as I live; *
    I will praise my God while I have my being.

35 May these words of mine please him; *
    I will rejoice in the LORD.

36 Let sinners be consumed out of the earth, *
    and the wicked be no more.

37 Bless the LORD,
    O my soul. *
        Hallelujah!

Lent Let sinners be consumed out of the earth, and the wicked be no more.
Easter I will sing to the LORD as long as I live, hallelujah.

Reading

Responsory, Magnificat Antiphon, Litany, Invitation to the Lord's Prayer, Collect and Dismissal are taken from the Proper of the Season.

Friday Week 3 Morning Prayer

Officiant: Lord, open our lips.
People: **And our mouth shall proclaim your praise.**
Officiant and People **Glory to the Father...**
Except in Lent, add **Alleluia.**

The Invitatory Psalm 95
From the Proper of the Season or of the Day

Hymn *From the Proper of the Season or of the Day*

Psalm 143 *Domine, exaudi*
*The Son of Man must undergo great suffering, and be killed,
and on the third day be raised. Lk. 9:22*

Lent I spread out my hands to you; my soul gasps to you like a thirsty land.
Easter Revive me, O LORD, for your Name's sake; for your righteousness' sake, bring me out of trouble, hallelujah.

1 LORD, hear my prayer,
    and in your faithfulness heed my supplications; *
        answer me in your righteousness.

2 Enter not into judgment with your servant, *
    for in your sight shall no one living be justified.

3 For my enemy has sought my life;
  he has crushed me to the ground; *
    he has made me live in dark places
    like those who are long dead.

4 My spirit faints within me; *
    my heart within me is desolate.

5 I remember the time past;
  I muse upon all your deeds; *
    I consider the works of your hands.

6 I spread out my hands to you; *
    my soul gasps to you like a thirsty land.

7 O LORD, make haste to answer me; my spirit fails me; *
    do not hide your face from me
    or I shall be like those who go down to the Pit.

8 Let me hear of your loving-kindness in the morning,
  for I put my trust in you; *
    show me the road that I must walk,
    for I lift up my soul to you.

9 Deliver me from my enemies, O LORD, *
    for I flee to you for refuge.

10 Teach me to do what pleases you, for you are my God; *
    let your good Spirit lead me on level ground.

11 Revive me, O LORD, for your Name's sake; *
    for your righteousness' sake, bring me out of trouble.

Lent I spread out my hands to you; my soul gasps to you like a thirsty land.
Easter Revive me, O LORD, for your Name's sake; for your righteousness' sake, bring me out of trouble, hallelujah.

Psalm 39 *Dixi, custodiam*
Jesus gave Pilate no answer. Jn. 19:9

Lent LORD, let me know my end and the number of my days.
Easter Jesus offered up prayers and supplications, with loud cries and tears, to God who saved him from death because of his reverent submission, hallelujah.

1 I said, "I will keep watch upon my ways, *
    so that I do not offend with my tongue.

2 I will put a muzzle on my mouth *
    while the wicked are in my presence."

3 So I held my tongue and said nothing; *
    I refrained from rash words;
    but my pain became unbearable.

4 My heart was hot within me;
    while I pondered, the fire burst into flame; *
    I spoke out with my tongue:

5 LORD, let me know my end and the number of my days, *
    so that I may know how short my life is.

6 You have given me a mere handful of days,
    and my lifetime is as nothing in your sight; *
    truly, even those who stand erect are but a puff of wind.

7 We walk about like a shadow,
    and in vain we are in turmoil; *
    we heap up riches and cannot tell who will gather them.

8 And now, what is my hope? *
    O Lord, my hope is in you.

9 Deliver me from all my transgressions *
    and do not make me the taunt of the fool.

10 I fell silent and did not open my mouth, *
    for surely it was you that did it.

11 Take your affliction from me; *
    I am worn down by the blows of your hand.

12 With rebukes for sin you punish us;
    like a moth you eat away all that is dear to us; *
    truly, everyone is but a puff of wind.

13 Hear my prayer, O LORD,
    and give ear to my cry; *
    hold not your peace at my tears.

14 For I am but a sojourner with you, *
    a wayfarer, as all my forebears were.

15 Turn your gaze from me, that I may be glad again, *
    before I go my way and am no more.

Lent LORD, let me know my end and the number of my days.
Easter Jesus offered up prayers and supplications, with loud cries and tears, to God who saved him from death because of his reverent submission, hallelujah.

Psalm 32 *Beati quorum*
*There will be more joy in heaven over one sinner who repents
than over ninety-nine righteous persons who need no repentance. Lk. 15:7*

Lent I said, "I will confess my transgressions to the LORD." Then you forgave me the guilt of my sin.
Easter We have been reconciled to God through the death of his Son. hallelujah.

1 Blessed are they whose transgressions are forgiven, *
    and whose sin is put away!

2 Blessed are they to whom the LORD imputes no guilt, *
    and in whose spirit there is no guile!

3 While I held my tongue, my bones withered away, *
    because of my groaning all day long.

4 For your hand was heavy upon me day and night; *
    my moisture was dried up as in the heat of summer.

5 Then I acknowledged my sin to you, *
    and did not conceal my guilt.

6 I said, "I will confess my transgressions to the LORD." *
    Then you forgave me the guilt of my sin.

7 Therefore all the faithful will make their prayers to you
    in time of trouble; *
    when the great waters overflow, they shall not reach them.

8 You are my hiding-place;
    you preserve me from trouble; *
    you surround me with shouts of deliverance.

9 "I will instruct you and teach you
    in the way that you should go; *
    I will guide you with my eye.

10 Do not be like horse or mule, which have no understanding; *
    who must be fitted with bit and bridle,
    or else they will not stay near you."

11 Great are the tribulations of the wicked; *
    but mercy embraces those who trust in the LORD.

12 Be glad, you righteous, and rejoice in the LORD; *
    shout for joy, all who are true of heart.

Lent I said, "I will confess my transgressions to the LORD." Then you forgave me the guilt of my sin.
Easter We have been reconciled to God through the death of his Son. hallelujah.

Readings

Responsories, Benedictus Antiphon, Litany, Invitation to the Lord's Prayer, Collect and Dismissal are taken from the Proper of the Season.

Friday Week 3 Noonday Prayer

Officiant: O God, make speed to save us.
People: **O Lord, make haste to help us.**
Officiant and People **Glory to the Father…**
Except in Lent, add **Alleluia.**

Hymn *From the Proper of the Season or of the Day*

Psalm 119 Pe *Mirabilia*

While you have the light, believe in the light, so that you may become children of light. Jn. 12:36

Lent They gave me gall to eat, and when I was thirsty, they gave me vinegar to drink.
Easter After he was raised from the dead, his disciples remembered that he has said these words, and they believed the scripture and the word that Jesus had spoken, hallelujah.

129 Your decrees are wonderful; *
    therefore I obey them with all my heart.

130 When your word goes forth it gives light; *
    it gives understanding to the simple.

131 I open my mouth and pant; *
    I long for your commandments.

132 Turn to me in mercy, *
    as you always do to those who love your Name.

133 Steady my footsteps in your word; *
   let no iniquity have dominion over me.

134 Rescue me from those who oppress me, *
   and I will keep your commandments.

135 Let your countenance shine upon your servant *
   and teach me your statutes.

136 My eyes shed streams of tears, *
   because people do not keep your law.

Psalm 69 A *Salvum me fac*

When Jesus knew that all was now finished, he said (in order to fulfill the scripture), "I am thirsty." Jn. 19:29

1 Save me, O God, *
   for the waters have risen up to my neck.

2 I am sinking in deep mire, *
   and there is no firm ground for my feet.

3 I have come into deep waters, *
   and the torrent washes over me.

4 I have grown weary with my crying;
   my throat is inflamed; *
   my eyes have failed from looking for my God.

5 Those who hate me without a cause
   are more than the hairs of my head;
   my lying foes who would destroy me are mighty. *
       Must I then give back what I never stole?

6 O God, you know my foolishness, *
   and my faults are not hidden from you.

7 Let not those who hope in you be put to shame through me,
   Lord God of hosts; *
   let not those who seek you be disgraced because of me,
       O God of Israel.

8 Surely, for your sake have I suffered reproach, *
   and shame has covered my face.

9 I have become a stranger to my own kindred, *
   an alien to my mother's children.

10 Zeal for your house has eaten me up; *
   the scorn of those who scorn you has fallen upon me.

11 I humbled myself with fasting, *
    but that was turned to my reproach.

12 I put on sack-cloth also, *
    and became a byword among them.

13 Those who sit at the gate murmur against me, *
    and the drunkards make songs about me.

Psalm 69 B *Ego vero*

They offered Jesus wine to drink, mixed with gall; but when he tasted it,
he would not drink it. Mt. 27:34

14 But as for me, this is my prayer to you, *
    at the time you have set, O LORD:

15 "In your great mercy, O God, *
    answer me with your unfailing help.

16 Save me from the mire; do not let me sink; *
    let me be rescued from those who hate me
    and out of the deep waters.

17 Let not the torrent of waters wash over me,
    neither let the deep swallow me up; *
    do not let the Pit shut its mouth upon me.

18 Answer me, O LORD, for your love is kind; *
    in your great compassion, turn to me."

19 "Hide not your face from your servant; *
    be swift and answer me, for I am in distress.

20 Draw near to me and redeem me; *
    because of my enemies deliver me.

21 You know my reproach, my shame, and my dishonor; *
    my adversaries are all in your sight."

22 Reproach has broken my heart, and it cannot be healed; *
    I looked for sympathy, but there was none,
    for comforters, but I could find no one.

23 They gave me gall to eat, *
    and when I was thirsty, they gave me vinegar to drink.

24 Let the table before them be a trap *
    and their sacred feasts a snare.

25 Let their eyes be darkened, that they may not see, *
    and give them continual trembling in their loins.

26 Pour out your indignation upon them, *
    and let the fierceness of your anger overtake them.

27 Let their camp be desolate, *
    and let there be none to dwell in their tents.

28 For they persecute him whom you have stricken *
    and add to the pain of those whom you have pierced.

29 Lay to their charge guilt upon guilt, *
    and let them not receive your vindication.

30 Let them be wiped out of the book of the living *
    and not be written among the righteous.

31 As for me, I am afflicted and in pain; *
    your help, O God, will lift me up on high.

32 I will praise the Name of God in song; *
    I will proclaim his greatness with thanksgiving.

33 This will please the LORD more than an offering of oxen, *
    more than bullocks with horns and hoofs.

34 The afflicted shall see and be glad; *
    you who seek God, your heart shall live.

35 For the LORD listens to the needy, *
    and his prisoners he does not despise.

36 Let the heavens and the earth praise him, *
    the seas and all that moves in them;

37 For God will save Zion and rebuild the cities of Judah; *
    they shall live there and have it in possession.

38 The children of his servants will inherit it, *
    and those who love his Name will dwell therein.

Lent They gave me gall to eat, and when I was thirsty, they gave me vinegar to drink.
Easter After he was raised from the dead, his disciples remembered that he has said these words, and they believed the scripture and the word that Jesus had spoken, hallelujah.

Reading, Verse and Response, Collect and Conclusion as in the Proper of the Season or of the Day.

Friday Week 3 Evening Prayer

Officiant: O God, make speed to save us.
People: **O Lord, make haste to help us.**
Officiant and People **Glory to the Father...**
Except in Lent, add **Alleluia.**

Hymn *From the Proper of the Season or of the Day*

Psalm 31 *In te, Domine, speravi*
Jesus gave a loud cry and breathed his last. Mk. 15:37

Lent Into your hands I commend my spirit, for you have redeemed me.
Easter Love the LORD, all you who worship him; the LORD protects the faithful, hallelujah.

1 In you, O LORD, have I taken refuge;
 let me never be put to shame; *
  deliver me in your righteousness.

2 Incline your ear to me; *
  make haste to deliver me.

3 Be my strong rock, a castle to keep me safe,
 for you are my crag and my stronghold; *
  for the sake of your Name, lead me and guide me.

4 Take me out of the net that they have secretly set for me, *
  for you are my tower of strength.

5 Into your hands I commend my spirit, *
  for you have redeemed me,
  O LORD, O God of truth.

6 I hate those who cling to worthless idols, *
  and I put my trust in the LORD.

7 I will rejoice and be glad because of your mercy; *
  for you have seen my affliction;
  you know my distress.

8 You have not shut me up in the power of the enemy; *
  you have set my feet in an open place.

9 Have mercy on me, O LORD, for I am in trouble; *
  my eye is consumed with sorrow,
  and also my throat and my belly.

10 For my life is wasted with grief,
    and my years with sighing; *
        my strength fails me because of affliction,
        and my bones are consumed.

11 I have become a reproach to all my enemies
    and even to my neighbors,
    a dismay to those of my acquaintance; *
        when they see me in the street they avoid me.

12 I am forgotten like a dead man, out of mind; *
    I am as useless as a broken pot.

13 For I have heard the whispering of the crowd;
    fear is all around; *
        they put their heads together against me;
        they plot to take my life.

14 But as for me, I have trusted in you, O LORD. *
    I have said, "You are my God.

15 My times are in your hand; *
    rescue me from the hand of my enemies,
    and from those who persecute me.

16 Make your face to shine upon your servant, *
    and in your loving-kindness save me."

17 LORD, let me not be ashamed for having called upon you; *
    rather, let the wicked be put to shame;
    let them be silent in the grave.

18 Let the lying lips be silenced
    which speak against the righteous, *
        haughtily, disdainfully, and with contempt.

19 How great is your goodness, O LORD!
    which you have laid up for those who fear you; *
        which you have done in the sight of all
        for those who put their trust in you.

20 You hide them in the covert of your presence
    from those who slander them; *
        you keep them in your shelter from the strife of tongues.

21 Blessed be the LORD! *
    for he has shown me the wonders of his love
    in a besieged city.

22 Yet I said in my alarm,
   "I have been cut off from the sight of your eyes." *
      Nevertheless, you heard the sound of my entreaty
      when I cried out to you.

23 Love the LORD, all you who worship him; *
      the LORD protects the faithful,
      but repays to the full those who act haughtily.

24 Be strong and let your heart take courage, *
      all you who wait for the LORD.

Lent Into your hands I commend my spirit, for you have redeemed me.
Easter Love the LORD, all you who worship him; the LORD protects the faithful, hallelujah.

Psalm 13 *Usquequo, Domine?*

"Now my soul is troubled. And what should I say— 'Father, save me from this hour'?
Father, glorify your name." Jn. 12:27-28

Lent How long will you hide your face from me? How long shall I have perplexity in my mind?
Easter I will sing to the LORD, for he has dealt with me richly; I will praise the Name of the Lord Most High, hallelujah.

1 How long, O LORD?
   will you forget me for ever? *
      how long will you hide your face from me?

2 How long shall I have perplexity in my mind,
   and grief in my heart, day after day? *
      how long shall my enemy triumph over me?

3 Look upon me and answer me, O LORD my God; *
      give light to my eyes, lest I sleep in death;

4 Lest my enemy say, "I have prevailed over him," *
      and my foes rejoice that I have fallen.

5 But I put my trust in your mercy; *
      my heart is joyful because of your saving help.

6 I will sing to the LORD, for he has dealt with me richly; *
      I will praise the Name of the Lord Most High.

Lent How long will you hide your face from me? How long shall I have perplexity in my mind?

Easter I will sing to the LORD, for he has dealt with me richly; I will praise the Name of the Lord Most High, hallelujah.

Psalm 71 *In te, Domine, speravi*
Those who passed by derided Jesus, shaking their heads. Mk. 15:29

Lent I have become a portent to many; but you are my refuge and my strength.

Easter Be my strong rock, a castle to keep me safe; you are my crag and my stronghold, hallelujah.

1 In you, O LORD, have I taken refuge; *
　　let me never be ashamed.

2 In your righteousness, deliver me and set me free; *
　　incline your ear to me and save me.

3 Be my strong rock, a castle to keep me safe; *
　　you are my crag and my stronghold.

4 Deliver me, my God, from the hand of the wicked, *
　　from the clutches of the evildoer and the oppressor.

5 For you are my hope, O LORD God, *
　　my confidence since I was young.

6 I have been sustained by you ever since I was born;
　　from my mother's womb you have been my strength; *
　　my praise shall be always of you.

7 I have become a portent to many; *
　　but you are my refuge and my strength.

8 Let my mouth be full of your praise *
　　and your glory all the day long.

9 Do not cast me off in my old age; *
　　forsake me not when my strength fails.

10 For my enemies are talking against me, *
　　and those who lie in wait for my life take counsel together.

11 They say, "God has forsaken him;
　go after him and seize him; *
　　because there is none who will save."

12 O God, be not far from me; *
　　come quickly to help me, O my God.

13 Let those who set themselves against me
    be put to shame and be disgraced; *
        let those who seek to do me evil
        be covered with scorn and reproach.

14 But I shall always wait in patience, *
    and shall praise you more and more.

15 My mouth shall recount your mighty acts
    and saving deeds all day long; *
        though I cannot know the number of them.

16 I will begin with the mighty works of the Lord God; *
    I will recall your righteousness, yours alone.

17 O God, you have taught me since I was young, *
    and to this day I tell of your wonderful works.

18 And now that I am old and gray-headed,
    O God, do not forsake me, *
        till I make known your strength to this generation
        and your power to all who are to come.

19 Your righteousness, O God, reaches to the heavens; *
    you have done great things;
    who is like you, O God?

20 You have showed me great troubles and adversities, *
    but you will restore my life
    and bring me up again from the deep places of the earth.

21 You strengthen me more and more; *
    you enfold and comfort me,

22 Therefore I will praise you upon the lyre
    for your faithfulness, O my God; *
        I will sing to you with the harp, O Holy One of Israel.

23 My lips will sing with joy when I play to you, *
    and so will my soul, which you have redeemed.

24 My tongue will proclaim your righteousness all day long, *
    for they are ashamed and disgraced
    who sought to do me harm.

Lent I have become a portent to many; but you are my refuge and my strength.

Easter Be my strong rock, a castle to keep me safe; you are my crag and my stronghold, hallelujah.

Reading

Responsory, Magnificat Antiphon, Litany, Invitation to the Lord's Prayer, Collect and Dismissal are taken from the Proper of the Season.

Saturday Week 3 Morning Prayer

Officiant: Lord, open our lips.
People: **And our mouth shall proclaim your praise.**
Officiant and People **Glory to the Father...**
Except in Lent, add **Alleluia.**

The Invitatory Psalm 122
From the Proper of the Season or of the Day

Hymn *From the Proper of the Season or of the Day*

Psalm 73 *Quam bonus Israel!*
So it is with those who store up treasures for themselves but are not rich toward God. Lk. 12:21

Lent I have been afflicted all day long, and punished every morning.
Easter The people shall come in awe to the Lord and to God's goodness, hallelujah.

1 Truly, God is good to Israel, *
   to those who are pure in heart.

2 But as for me, my feet had nearly slipped; *
   I had almost tripped and fallen;

3 Because I envied the proud *
   and saw the prosperity of the wicked:

4 For they suffer no pain, *
   and their bodies are sleek and sound;

5 In the misfortunes of others they have no share; *
   they are not afflicted as others are;

6 Therefore they wear their pride like a necklace *
   and wrap their violence about them like a cloak.

7 Their iniquity comes from gross minds, *
   and their hearts overflow with wicked thoughts.

8 They scoff and speak maliciously; *
   out of their haughtiness they plan oppression.

9 They set their mouths against the heavens, *
   and their evil speech runs through the world.

10 And so the people turn to them *
   and find in them no fault.

11 They say, "How should God know? *
   is there knowledge in the Most High?"
12 So then, these are the wicked; *
   always at ease, they increase their wealth.

13 In vain have I kept my heart clean, *
   and washed my hands in innocence.

14 I have been afflicted all day long, *
   and punished every morning.

Lent I have been afflicted all day long, and punished every morning.
Easter The people shall come in awe to the Lord and to God's goodness, hallelujah.

Psalm 73 B *Si dicebam*
If then you have not been faithful with the dishonest wealth,
who will entrust to you the true riches? Lk. 16:11

Lent Though my flesh and my heart should waste away, God is the strength of my heart and my portion for ever.
Easter I will speak of all your works in the gates of the city of Zion, hallelujah.

15 Had I gone on speaking this way, *
   I should have betrayed the generation of your children.

16 When I tried to understand these things, *
   it was too hard for me;

17 Until I entered the sanctuary of God *
   and discerned the end of the wicked.

18 Surely, you set them in slippery places; *
   you cast them down in ruin.

19 Oh, how suddenly do they come to destruction, *
   come to an end, and perish from terror!

20 Like a dream when one awakens, O Lord, *
   when you arise you will make their image vanish.

21 When my mind became embittered, *
   I was sorely wounded in my heart.

22 I was stupid and had no understanding; *
    I was like a brute beast in your presence.

23 Yet I am always with you; *
    you hold me by my right hand.

24 You will guide me by your counsel, *
    and afterwards receive me with glory.

25 Whom have I in heaven but you? *
    and having you I desire nothing upon earth.

26 Though my flesh and my heart should waste away, *
    God is the strength of my heart and my portion for ever.

27 Truly, those who forsake you will perish; *
    you destroy all who are unfaithful.

28 But it is good for me to be near God; *
    I have made the LORD God my refuge.

29 I will speak of all your works *
    in the gates of the city of Zion.

Lent Though my flesh and my heart should waste away, God is the strength of my heart and my portion for ever.
Easter I will speak of all your works in the gates of the city of Zion, hallelujah.

Psalm 150 *Laudate Dominum*

The whole multitude of the disciples began to praise God joyfully with a loud voice. Lk. 19: 37

Lent Praise the Lord in the firmament of his power.
Easter Worship God who is seated upon the throne, saying, Amen, hallelujah.

1 Hallelujah!
    Praise God in his holy temple; *
        praise him in the firmament of his power.

2 Praise him for his mighty acts; *
        praise him for his excellent greatness.

3 Praise him with the blast of the ram's-horn; *
        praise him with lyre and harp.

4 Praise him with timbrel and dance; *
        praise him with strings and pipe.

5 Praise him with resounding cymbals; *
    praise him with loud-clanging cymbals.

6 Let everything that has breath *
    praise the Lord. Hallelujah!

Lent Praise the Lord in the firmament of his power.
Easter Worship God who is seated upon the throne, saying, Amen, hallelujah.

Readings

Responsories, Benedictus Antiphon, Litany, Invitation to the Lord's Prayer, Collet and Dismissal are taken from the Proper of the Season.

Saturday Week 3 Noonday Prayer

Officiant: O God, make speed to save us.
People: **O Lord, make haste to help us.**
Officiant and People **Glory to the Father…**
Except in Lent, add **Alleluia.**

Hymn *From the Proper of the Season or of the Day*

Psalm 119 Sadhe *Justus es, Domine*
Let the word of Christ dwell in you richly. Col. 3:16

Lent I will confess my transgressions to the LORD.
Easter At Jesus' Name every knee should bend in heaven and on earth, hallelujah.

137 You are righteous, O LORD, *
    and upright are your judgments.

138 You have issued your decrees *
    with justice and in perfect faithfulness.

139 My indignation has consumed me, *
    because my enemies forget your words.

140 Your word has been tested to the uttermost, *
    and your servant holds it dear.

141 I am small and of little account, *
    yet I do not forget your commandments.

142 Your justice is an everlasting justice *
    and your law is the truth.

143 Trouble and distress have come upon me, *
  yet your commandments are my delight.

144 The righteousness of your decrees is everlasting; *
  grant me understanding, that I may live.

Psalm 82 *Deus stetit*

*All the nations will be gathered before the Son of Man,
and he will separate people one from another. Mt. 25: 32*

1 God takes his stand in the council of heaven; *
  he gives judgment in the midst of the gods:

2 "How long will you judge unjustly, *
  and show favor to the wicked?

3 Save the weak and the orphan; *
  defend the humble and needy;

4 Rescue the weak and the poor; *
  deliver them from the power of the wicked.

5 They do not know, neither do they understand;
  they go about in darkness; *
  all the foundations of the earth are shaken.

6 Now I say to you, 'You are gods, *
  and all of you children of the Most High;

7 Nevertheless, you shall die like mortals, *
  and fall like any prince.'"

8 Arise, O God, and rule the earth, *
  for you shall take all nations for your own.

Psalm 7 *Domine, Deus meus*

You also must be ready, for the Son of Man is coming at an unexpected hour. Mt. 24:44

1 O LORD my God, I take refuge in you; *
  save and deliver me from all who pursue me;

2 Lest like a lion they tear me in pieces *
  and snatch me away with none to deliver me.

3 O LORD my God, if I have done these things: *
  if there is any wickedness in my hands,

4 If I have repaid my friend with evil, *
  or plundered him who without cause is my enemy;

5 Then let my enemy pursue and overtake me, *
    trample my life into the ground,
    and lay my honor in the dust.

6 Stand up, O LORD, in your wrath; *
    rise up against the fury of my enemies.

7 Awake, O my God, decree justice; *
    let the assembly of the peoples gather round you.

8 Be seated on your lofty throne, O Most High; *
    O LORD, judge the nations.

9 Give judgment for me
  according to my righteousness, O LORD, *
    and according to my innocence, O Most High.

10 Let the malice of the wicked come to an end,
   but establish the righteous; *
     for you test the mind and heart, O righteous God.

11 God is my shield and defense; *
     he is the savior of the true in heart.

12 God is a righteous judge; *
     God sits in judgment every day.

13 If they will not repent, God will whet his sword; *
     he will bend his bow and make it ready.

14 He has prepared his weapons of death; *
     he makes his arrows shafts of fire.

15 Look at those who are in labor with wickedness, *
     who conceive evil, and give birth to a lie.

16 They dig a pit and make it deep *
     and fall into the hole that they have made.

17 Their malice turns back upon their own head; *
     their violence falls on their own scalp.
18 I will bear witness that the LORD is righteous; *
     I will praise the Name of the LORD Most High.

Lent I will confess my transgressions to the LORD.
Easter At Jesus' Name every knee should bend in heaven and on earth, hallelujah.

Reading, Verse and Response, Collect and Conclusion as in the Proper of the Season or of the Day.

Week 4

Sunday Week 4 Evening Prayer I

Officiant: O God, make speed to save us.
People: **O Lord, make haste to help us.**
Officiant and People **Glory to the Father ...**
Except in Lent, add **Alleluia.**

Hymn *From the Proper of the Season or of the Day*

Psalm 141 *Domine, clamavi*
*The smoke of the incense, with the prayers of the saints,
rose before God from the hand of the angel. Rev. 8:4*

Lent Set a watch before my mouth, O LORD, and guard the door of my lips.

Easter Were not our hearts burning within us while he was talking to us on the road, while he was opening the scripture to us, hallelujah.

1 O LORD, I call to you; come to me quickly; *
    hear my voice when I cry to you.

2 Let my prayer be set forth in your sight as incense, *
    the lifting up of my hands as the evening sacrifice.

3 Set a watch before my mouth, O LORD,
    and guard the door of my lips; *
    let not my heart incline to any evil thing.

4 Let me not be occupied in wickedness with evildoers, *
    nor eat of their choice foods.

5 Let the righteous smite me in friendly rebuke;
    let not the oil of the unrighteous anoint my head; *
    for my prayer is continually against their wicked deeds.

6 Let their rulers be overthrown in stony places, *
    that they may know my words are true.

7 As when a plowman turns over the earth in furrows, *
    let their bones be scattered at the mouth of the grave.

8 But my eyes are turned to you, Lord God; *
    in you I take refuge;
    do not strip me of my life.

9 Protect me from the snare which they have laid for me *
    and from the traps of the evildoers.

10 Let the wicked fall into their own nets, *
    while I myself escape.

Lent Set a watch before my mouth, O LORD, and guard the door of my lips.

Easter Were not our hearts burning within us while he was talking to us on the road, while he was opening the scripture to us, hallelujah.

Psalm 145 A *Exaltabo te, Deus*

Many will come from east and west and will eat with Abraham and Isaac and Jacob in the kingdom of heaven. Mt. 8:11

Lent The LORD is gracious and full of compassion, slow to anger and of great kindness.

Easter Every day will I bless you and praise your Name for ever and ever, hallelujah.

1 I will exalt you, O God my King, *
    and bless your Name for ever and ever.

2 Every day will I bless you *
    and praise your Name for ever and ever.

3 Great is the LORD and greatly to be praised; *
    there is no end to his greatness.

4 One generation shall praise your works to another *
    and shall declare your power.

5 I will ponder the glorious splendor of your majesty *
    and all your marvelous works.

6 They shall speak of the might of your wondrous acts, *
    and I will tell of your greatness.

7 They shall publish the remembrance of your great goodness; *
    they shall sing of your righteous deeds.

8 The LORD is gracious and full of compassion, *
    slow to anger and of great kindness.

9 The LORD is loving to everyone *
    and his compassion is over all his works.

Lent The LORD is gracious and full of compassion, slow to anger and of great kindness.

Easter Every day will I bless you and praise your Name for ever and ever, hallelujah.

Psalm 145 B *Confiteantur tibi*

The kingdom of God has come near to you. Lk. 10:9

Lent The Lord fulfills the desire of those who fear him; he hears their cry and helps them.

Easter Let all flesh bless God's holy Name for ever and ever, hallelujah.

10 All your works praise you, O LORD, *
   and your faithful servants bless you.

11 They make known the glory of your kingdom *
   and speak of your power;

12 That the peoples may know of your power *
   and the glorious splendor of your kingdom.

13 Your kingdom is an everlasting kingdom; *
   your dominion endures throughout all ages.

14 The LORD is faithful in all his words *
   and merciful in all his deeds.

15 The LORD upholds all those who fall; *
   he lifts up those who are bowed down.

16 The eyes of all wait upon you, O LORD, *
   and you give them their food in due season.

17 You open wide your hand *
   and satisfy the needs of every living creature.

18 The LORD is righteous in all his ways *
   and loving in all his works.

19 The LORD is near to those who call upon him, *
   to all who call upon him faithfully.

20 He fulfills the desire of those who fear him; *
   he hears their cry and helps them.

21 The LORD preserves all those who love him, *
   but he destroys all the wicked.

22 My mouth shall speak the praise of the LORD; *
   let all flesh bless his holy Name for ever and ever.

Lent The Lord fulfills the desire of those who fear him; he hears their cry and helps them.
Easter Let all flesh bless God's holy Name for ever and ever, hallelujah.

Reading

Responsory, Magnificat Antiphon, Litany, Invitation to the Lord's Prayer, Collect and Dismissal are taken from the Proper of the Season.

Sunday Week 4 Morning Prayer

Officiant: Lord, open our lips.
People: **And our mouth shall proclaim your praise.**
Officiant and People **Glory to the Father...**
Except in Lent, add **Alleluia.**

The Invitatory Psalm 95
From the Proper of the Season or of the Day

Hymn *From the Proper of the Season or of the Day*

Psalm 93 *Dominus regnavit*
*Jesus Christ is the faithful witness, the firstborn of the dead,
and the ruler of the kings of the earth. Rev. 1:5*

Lent Your testimonies are very sure, O Lord, and mightier than the sound of many waters.
Easter The Lord has put on splendid apparel, hallelujah.

1 The LORD is King;
   he has put on splendid apparel; *
     the LORD has put on his apparel
     and girded himself with strength.

2 He has made the whole world so sure *
     that it cannot be moved;

3 Ever since the world began, your throne has been established; *
     you are from everlasting.

4 The waters have lifted up, O LORD,
   the waters have lifted up their voice; *
     the waters have lifted up their pounding waves.

5 Mightier than the sound of many waters,
   mightier than the breakers of the sea, *
     mightier is the LORD who dwells on high.

6 Your testimonies are very sure, *
     and holiness adorns your house, O LORD,
     for ever and for evermore.

Lent Your testimonies are very sure, O Lord, and mightier than the sound of many waters.
Easter The Lord has put on splendid apparel, hallelujah.

Psalm 29 *Afferte Domino*

God chose to make known how great among the Gentiles are the riches of the glory of this mystery, which is Christ in you, the hope of glory. Col. 1: 27

Lent Blessed is the king who comes in the name of the Lord! Peace in heaven, and glory in the highest heaven!
Easter Father, glorify me in your own presence with the glory that I had in your presence before the world existed, hallelujah.

1 Ascribe to the LORD, you gods, *
    ascribe to the LORD glory and strength.

2 Ascribe to the LORD the glory due his Name; *
    worship the LORD in the beauty of holiness.

3 The voice of the LORD is upon the waters;
  the God of glory thunders; *
    the LORD is upon the mighty waters.

4 The voice of the LORD is a powerful voice; *
    the voice of the LORD is a voice of splendor.

5 The voice of the LORD breaks the cedar trees; *
    the LORD breaks the cedars of Lebanon;

6 He makes Lebanon skip like a calf, *
    and Mount Hermon like a young wild ox.

7 The voice of the LORD splits the flames of fire;
  the voice of the LORD shakes the wilderness; *
    the LORD shakes the wilderness of Kadesh.

8 The voice of the LORD makes the oak trees writhe *
    and strips the forests bare.

9 And in the temple of the LORD *
    all are crying, "Glory!"

10 The LORD sits enthroned above the flood; *
    the LORD sits enthroned as King for evermore.

11 The LORD shall give strength to his people; *
    the LORD shall give his people the blessing of peace.

Lent Blessed is the king who comes in the name of the Lord! Peace in heaven, and glory in the highest heaven!
Easter Father, glorify me in your own presence with the glory that I had in your presence before the world existed, hallelujah.

Psalm 47 *Omnes gentes, plaudite*

God has made him the head over all things for the church, which is his body,
the fullness of him who fills all in all. Eph. 1:22-23

Lent The LORD Most High is to be feared; he is the great King over all the earth.

Easter God has gone up with a shout, the LORD with the sound of the ram's-horn, hallelujah.

1 Clap your hands, all you peoples; *
    shout to God with a cry of joy.

2 For the LORD Most High is to be feared; *
    he is the great King over all the earth.

3 He subdues the peoples under us, *
    and the nations under our feet.

4 He chooses our inheritance for us, *
    the pride of Jacob whom he loves.

5 God has gone up with a shout, *
    the LORD with the sound of the ram's-horn.

6 Sing praises to God, sing praises; *
    sing praises to our King, sing praises.

7 For God is King of all the earth; *
    sing praises with all your skill.

8 God reigns over the nations; *
    God sits upon his holy throne.

9 The nobles of the peoples have gathered together *
    with the people of the God of Abraham.

10 The rulers of the earth belong to God, *
    and he is highly exalted.

Lent The LORD Most High is to be feared; he is the great King over all the earth.

Easter God has gone up with a shout, the LORD with the sound of the ram's-horn, hallelujah.

Readings

Responsories, Benedictus Antiphon, Litany, Invitation to the Lord's Prayer, Collet and Dismissal are taken from the Proper of the Season.

Sunday Week 4 Noonday Prayer

Officiant: O God, make speed to save us.
People: **O Lord, make haste to help us.**
Officiant and People **Glory to the Father…**
Except in Lent, add **Alleluia.**

Hymn *From the Proper of the Season or of the Day*

Psalm 72 A *Deus, judicium*

*On entering the house, they saw the child with Mary his mother;
and they knelt down and paid him homage. Mt. 2:11*

Lent The LORD is good; God's mercy is everlasting.
Easter May his Name remain for ever and be established as long as the sun endures; may all the nations bless themselves in him and call him blessed, hallelujah.

1 Give the King your justice, O God, *
     and your righteousness to the King's Son;

2 That he may rule your people righteously *
     and the poor with justice;

3 That the mountains may bring prosperity to the people, *
     and the little hills bring righteousness.

4 He shall defend the needy among the people; *
     he shall rescue the poor and crush the oppressor.

5 He shall live as long as the sun and moon endure, *
     from one generation to another.

6 He shall come down like rain upon the mown field, *
     like showers that water the earth.

7 In his time shall the righteous flourish; *
     there shall be abundance of peace
     till the moon shall be no more.

8 He shall rule from sea to sea, *
     and from the River to the ends of the earth.

9 His foes shall bow down before him, *
     and his enemies lick the dust.

10 The kings of Tarshish and of the isles shall pay tribute, *
     and the kings of Arabia and Saba offer gifts.

11 All kings shall bow down before him, *
     and all the nations do him service.

Psalm 72 B *Quia liberabit*
Jesus saw a great crowd; and he had compassion for them and cured their sick. Mt. 14:14

12 For he shall deliver the poor who cries out in distress, *
 and the oppressed who has no helper.

13 He shall have pity on the lowly and poor; *
 he shall preserve the lives of the needy.

14 He shall redeem their lives from oppression and violence, *
 and dear shall their blood be in his sight.

15 Long may he live!
 and may there be given to him gold from Arabia; *
 may prayer be made for him always,
 and may they bless him all the day long.

16 May there be abundance of grain on the earth,
 growing thick even on the hilltops; *
 may its fruit flourish like Lebanon,
 and its grain like grass upon the earth.

17 May his Name remain for ever
 and be established as long as the sun endures; *
 may all the nations bless themselves in him
 and call him blessed.

18 Blessed be the LORD God, the God of Israel, *
 who alone does wondrous deeds!

19 And blessed be his glorious Name for ever! *
 and may all the earth be filled with his glory.
 Amen. Amen.

Psalm 117 *Laudate Dominum*
Once you were not a people, but now you are God's people. 1 Pt. 2:10

1 Praise the LORD, all you nations; *
 laud him, all you peoples.

2 For his loving-kindness toward us is great, *
 and the faithfulness of the LORD endures for ever.
 Hallelujah!

Lent The LORD is good; God's mercy is everlasting.
Easter May his Name remain for ever and be established as long as the sun endures; may all the nations bless themselves in him and call him blessed, hallelujah.

Reading, Verse and Response, Collect and Conclusion as in the Proper of the Season or of the Day.

Sunday Week 4 Evening Prayer II

Officiant: O God, make speed to save us.
People: **O Lord, make haste to help us.**
Officiant and People **Glory to the Father...**
Except in Lent, add **Alleluia.**

Hymn *From the Proper of the Season or of the Day*

Psalm 113 *Laudate, pueri*
Salvation belongs to our God who is seated on the throne, and to the Lamb! Rev. 7:10

Lent The Lord takes up the weak out of the dust and lifts up the poor from the ashes.
Easter The Lord, who is high above all nations, has raised us up with Christ Jesus, hallelujah.

1 Hallelujah!
   Give praise, you servants of the LORD; *
     praise the Name of the LORD.

2 Let the Name of the LORD be blessed, *
     from this time forth for evermore.

3 From the rising of the sun to its going down *
     let the Name of the LORD be praised.

4 The LORD is high above all nations, *
     and his glory above the heavens.

5 Who is like the LORD our God, who sits enthroned on high, *
     but stoops to behold the heavens and the earth?

6 He takes up the weak out of the dust *
     and lifts up the poor from the ashes.

7 He sets them with the princes, *
     with the princes of his people.

8 He makes the woman of a childless house *
     to be a joyful mother of children.

Lent The Lord takes up the weak out of the dust and lifts up the poor from the ashes.
Easter The Lord, who is high above all nations, has raised us up with Christ Jesus, hallelujah.

Psalm 114 *In exitu Israel*

Now have come the salvation and the power and the kingdom of our God and the authority of his Messiah. Rev. 12:10

Lent I will never forget any of their injustices. Shall not the land tremble on this account?
Easter He has delivered us from the dominion of darkness, and brought us into the kingdom of his Son, hallelujah.

1 Hallelujah!
  When Israel came out of Egypt, *
    the house of Jacob from a people of strange speech,

2 Judah became God's sanctuary *
    and Israel his dominion.

3 The sea beheld it and fled; *
    Jordan turned and went back.

4 The mountains skipped like rams, *
    and the little hills like young sheep.

5 What ailed you, O sea, that you fled? *
    O Jordan, that you turned back?

6 You mountains, that you skipped like rams? *
    you little hills like young sheep?

7 Tremble, O earth, at the presence of the Lord, *
    at the presence of the God of Jacob,

8 Who turned the hard rock into a pool of water *
    and flint-stone into a flowing spring.

Lent I will never forget any of their injustices. Shall not the land tremble on this account?
Easter He has delivered us from the dominion of darkness, and brought us into the kingdom of his Son, hallelujah.

Psalm 115 *Non nobis, Domine*

Jesus Christ loves us and freed us from our sins by his blood, and made us to be a kingdom, priests serving his God and Father. Rev. 1:5-6

Lent What wrong did your ancestors find in me that they went far from me, and went after worthless things, and became worthless themselves?
Easter We have been turned from the worship of idols to serve the living God, hallelujah.

1 Not to us, O Lord, not to us,
    but to your Name give glory; *
        because of your love and because of your faithfulness.

2 Why should the heathen say, *
    "Where then is their God?"

3 Our God is in heaven; *
    whatever he wills to do he does.

4 Their idols are silver and gold, *
    the work of human hands.

5 They have mouths, but they cannot speak; *
    eyes have they, but they cannot see;

6 They have ears, but they cannot hear; *
    noses, but they cannot smell;

7 They have hands, but they cannot feel;
    feet, but they cannot walk; *
        they make no sound with their throat.

8 Those who make them are like them, *
    and so are all who put their trust in them.

9 O Israel, trust in the Lord; *
    he is their help and their shield.

10 O house of Aaron, trust in the Lord; *
    he is their help and their shield.

11 You who fear the Lord, trust in the Lord; *
    he is their help and their shield.

12 The Lord has been mindful of us, and he will bless us; *
    he will bless the house of Israel;
    he will bless the house of Aaron;

13 He will bless those who fear the Lord, *
    both small and great together.

14 May the Lord increase you more and more, *
    you and your children after you.

15 May you be blessed by the Lord, *
    the maker of heaven and earth.

16 The heaven of heavens is the Lord's, *
    but he entrusted the earth to its peoples.

Monday Week 4 Morning Prayer

17 The dead do not praise the LORD, *
nor all those who go down into silence;

18 But we will bless the LORD, *
from this time forth for evermore.
Hallelujah!

Lent What wrong did your ancestors find in me that they went far from me, and went after worthless things, and became worthless themselves?
Easter We have been turned from the worship of idols to serve the living God, hallelujah.

Reading

Responsory, Magnificat Antiphon, Litany, Invitation to the Lord's Prayer, Collect and Dismissal are taken from the Proper of the Season.

Monday Week 4 Morning Prayer

Officiant: Lord, open our lips.
People: **And our mouth shall proclaim your praise.**
Officiant and People **Glory to the Father...**
Except in Lent, add **Alleluia.**

The Invitatory Psalm 29
From the Proper of the Season or of the Day

Hymn *From the Proper of the Season or of the Day*

Psalm 97 *Dominus regnavit*
*You will see the Son of Man seated at the right hand of Power
and coming on the clouds of heaven. Mt. 26:64*

Lent The LORD loves those who hate evil; and delivers them from the hand of the wicked.
Easter Light has sprung up for the righteous, and joyful gladness for those who are truehearted, hallelujah.

1 The LORD is King;
let the earth rejoice; *
let the multitude of the isles be glad.

2 Clouds and darkness are round about him, *
righteousness and justice are the foundations of his throne.

3 A fire goes before him *
and burns up his enemies on every side.

4 His lightnings light up the world; *
the earth sees it and is afraid.

5 The mountains melt like wax at the presence of the LORD, *
   at the presence of the Lord of the whole earth.

6 The heavens declare his righteousness, *
   and all the peoples see his glory.

7 Confounded be all who worship carved images
   and delight in false gods! *
   Bow down before him, all you gods.

8 Zion hears and is glad, and the cities of Judah rejoice, *
   because of your judgments, O LORD.

9 For you are the LORD,
   most high over all the earth; *
   you are exalted far above all gods.

10 The LORD loves those who hate evil; *
   he preserves the lives of his saints
   and delivers them from the hand of the wicked.

11 Light has sprung up for the righteous, *
   and joyful gladness for those who are truehearted.

12 Rejoice in the LORD, you righteous, *
   and give thanks to his holy Name.

Lent The LORD loves those who hate evil; and delivers them from the hand of the wicked.
Easter Light has sprung up for the righteous, and joyful gladness for those who are truehearted, hallelujah.

Psalm 24 *Domini est terra*
The aim of instruction is love that comes from a pure heart, a good conscience, and sincere faith. 1 Tim. 1:5

Lent Who can ascent the hill of the Lord? Those who have clean hands and a pure heart.
Easter He who came down from heaven has ascended far above all heavens. He is the King of glory, hallelujah.

1 The earth is the LORD'S and all that is in it, *
   the world and all who dwell therein.

2 For it is he who founded it upon the seas *
   and made it firm upon the rivers of the deep.

3 "Who can ascend the hill of the LORD? *
   and who can stand in his holy place?"

4 "Those who have clean hands and a pure heart, *
    who have not pledged themselves to falsehood,
    nor sworn by what is a fraud.

5 They shall receive a blessing from the Lord *
    and a just reward from the God of their salvation."

6 Such is the generation of those who seek him, *
    of those who seek your face, O God of Jacob.

7 Lift up your heads, O gates;
  lift them high, O everlasting doors; *
    and the King of glory shall come in.

8 "Who is this King of glory?" *
    "The LORD, strong and mighty,
    the LORD, mighty in battle."

9 Lift up your heads, O gates;
  lift them high, O everlasting doors; *
    and the King of glory shall come in.

10 "Who is he, this King of glory?" *
    "The LORD of hosts,
    he is the King of glory."

Lent Who can ascent the hill of the Lord? Those who have clean hands and a pure heart.
Easter He who came down from heaven has ascended far above all heavens. He is the King of glory, hallelujah.

Psalm 148 *Laudate Dominum*
At Jesus' name every knee should bend, in heaven and on earth and under the earth. Phil 2:10

Lent Let all creatures praise the Name of the Lord; for he commanded, and they were created.
Easter The Name of the Lord is exalted above heaven and earth, hallelujah.

1 Hallelujah!
  Praise the LORD from the heavens; *
    praise him in the heights.

2 Praise him, all you angels of his; *
    praise him, all his host.

3 Praise him, sun and moon; *
    praise him, all you shining stars.

4 Praise him, heaven of heavens, *
    and you waters above the heavens.

5 Let them praise the Name of the LORD; *
    for he commanded, and they were created.

6 He made them stand fast for ever and ever; *
    he gave them a law which shall not pass away.

7 Praise the LORD from the earth, *
    you sea-monsters and all deeps;

8 Fire and hail, snow and fog, *
    tempestuous wind, doing his will;

9 Mountains and all hills, *
    fruit trees and all cedars;

10 Wild beasts and all cattle, *
    creeping things and wingèd birds;

11 Kings of the earth and all peoples, *
    princes and all rulers of the world;

12 Young men and maidens, *
    old and young together.

13 Let them praise the Name of the LORD, *
    for his Name only is exalted,
    his splendor is over earth and heaven.

14 He has raised up strength for his people
    and praise for all his loyal servants, *
        the children of Israel, a people who are near him.
        Hallelujah!

Lent Let all creatures praise the Name of the Lord; for he commanded, and they were created.
Easter The Name of the Lord is exalted above heaven and earth, hallelujah.

Readings

Responsories, Benedictus Antiphon, Litany, Invitation to the Lord's Prayer, Collet and Dismissal are taken from the Proper of the Season.

Monday Week 4 Noonday Prayer

Officiant: O God, make speed to save us.
People: **O Lord, make haste to help us.**
Officiant and People **Glory to the Father...**
Except in Lent, add **Alleluia.**

Hymn *From the Proper of the Season or of the Day*

Psalm 119 Qoph *Clamavi in toto corde meo*
Have pity on us and help us. Mk. 9:22

Lent If we wish to dwell in the tent of that kingdom, we must run to it by good deeds.
Easter The Lord is the refuge of the wise one who has sought the Lord, hallelujah.

145 I call with my whole heart; *
    answer me, O LORD, that I may keep your statutes.

146 I call to you;
    oh, that you would save me! *
    I will keep your decrees.

147 Early in the morning I cry out to you, *
    for in your word is my trust.

148 My eyes are open in the night watches, *
    that I may meditate upon your promise.

149 Hear my voice, O LORD, according to your loving-kindness; *
    according to your judgments, give me life.

150 They draw near who in malice persecute me; *
    they are very far from your law.

151 You, O LORD, are near at hand, *
    and all your commandments are true.

152 Long have I known from your decrees *
    that you have established them for ever.

Psalm 14 *Dixit insipiens*
God is righteous and justifies the one who has faith in Jesus. Rm. 3:26

1 The fool has said in his heart, "There is no God." *
    All are corrupt and commit abominable acts;
    there is none who does any good.

2 The LORD looks down from heaven upon us all, *
    to see if there is any who is wise,
    if there is one who seeks after God.

3   Every one has proved faithless;
    all alike have turned bad; *
        there is none who does good; no, not one.

4   Have they no knowledge, all those evildoers *
        who eat up my people like bread
        and do not call upon the LORD?

5   See how they tremble with fear, *
        because God is in the company of the righteous.

6   Their aim is to confound the plans of the afflicted, *
        but the LORD is their refuge.

7   Oh, that Israel's deliverance would come out of Zion! *
        when the LORD restores the fortunes of his people,
        Jacob will rejoice and Israel be glad.

Psalm 15 *Domine, quis habitabit?*
Blessed are the pure in heart, for they will see God. Mt. 5:8

1   LORD, who may dwell in your tabernacle? *
        who may abide upon your holy hill?

2   Whoever leads a blameless life and does what is right, *
        who speaks the truth from his heart.

3   There is no guile upon his tongue;
    he does no evil to his friend; *
        he does not heap contempt upon his neighbor.

4   In his sight the wicked is rejected, *
        but he honors those who fear the LORD.

5   He has sworn to do no wrong *
        and does not take back his word.

6   He does not give his money in hope of gain, *
        nor does he take a bribe against the innocent.

7   Whoever does these things *
        shall never be overthrown.

Lent If we wish to dwell in the tent of that kingdom, we must run to it by good deeds.
Easter The Lord is the refuge of the wise one who has sought the Lord, hallelujah.

Reading, Verse and Response, Collect and Conclusion as in the Proper of the Season or of the Day.

Monday Week 4 Evening Prayer

Officiant: O God, make speed to save us.
People: **O Lord, make haste to help us.**
Officiant and People **Glory to the Father…**
Except in Lent, add **Alleluia.**

Hymn *From the Proper of the Season or of the Day*

Psalm 68 A *Exsurgat Deus*
Blessed are you who are poor, for yours is the kingdom of God. Lk. 6:20

Lent O God, you went forth before your people, you marched with them through the wilderness.
Easter Sing to God, sing praises to his Name; exalt him who rides upon the heavens, hallelujah.

1 Let God arise, and let his enemies be scattered; *
    let those who hate him flee before him.

2 Let them vanish like smoke when the wind drives it away; *
    as the wax melts at the fire, so let the wicked perish
    at the presence of God.

3 But let the righteous be glad and rejoice before God; *
    let them also be merry and joyful.

4 Sing to God, sing praises to his Name;
   exalt him who rides upon the heavens; *
    YAHWEH is his Name, rejoice before him!

5 Father of orphans, defender of widows, *
    God in his holy habitation!

6 God gives the solitary a home
   and brings forth prisoners into freedom; *
    but the rebels shall live in dry places.

7 O God, when you went forth before your people, *
    when you marched through the wilderness,

8 The earth shook, and the skies poured down rain,
   at the presence of God, the God of Sinai, *
    at the presence of God, the God of Israel.

9 You sent a gracious rain, O God, upon your inheritance; *
    you refreshed the land when it was weary.

10 Your people found their home in it; *
    in your goodness, O God,
    you have made provision for the poor.

Lent O God, you went forth before your people, you marched with them through the wilderness.

Easter Sing to God, sing praises to his Name; exalt him who rides upon the heavens, hallelujah.

Psalm 68 B *Dominus dabit*
Our Savior Christ Jesus, abolished death and brought life and immortality to light through the gospel. 2 Tim. 1:10

Lent God is the LORD, by whom we escape death.

Easter You have gone up on high and led captivity captive; that you might dwell among them, hallelujah.

11 The Lord gave the word; *
 great was the company of women who bore the tidings:

12 "Kings with their armies are fleeing away; *
 the women at home are dividing the spoils."

13 Though you lingered among the sheepfolds, *
 you shall be like a dove whose wings are covered with silver,
 whose feathers are like green gold.

14 When the Almighty scattered kings, *
 it was like snow falling in Zalmon.

15 O mighty mountain, O hill of Bashan! *
 O rugged mountain, O hill of Bashan!

16 Why do you look with envy, O rugged mountain,
 at the hill which God chose for his resting place? *
 truly, the LORD will dwell there for ever.

17 The chariots of God are twenty thousand,
 even thousands of thousands; *
 the Lord comes in holiness from Sinai.

18 You have gone up on high and led captivity captive;
 you have received gifts even from your enemies, *
 that the LORD God might dwell among them.

19 Blessed be the Lord day by day, *
 the God of our salvation, who bears our burdens.

20 He is our God, the God of our salvation; *
 God is the LORD, by whom we escape death.

21 God shall crush the heads of his enemies, *
 and the hairy scalp of those
 who go on still in their wickedness.

22 The Lord has said, "I will bring them back from Bashan; *
    I will bring them back from the depths of the sea;

23 That your foot may be dipped in blood, *
    the tongues of your dogs in the blood of your enemies."

Lent God is the LORD, by whom we escape death.
Easter You have gone up on high and led captivity captive; that you might dwell among them, hallelujah.

Psalm 68 C *Viderunt ingressus tui*
*Look! He is coming with the clouds; every eye will see him,
even those who pierced him. Rev. 1:7*

Lent Trample down those who lust after silver; scatter the peoples that delight in war.
Easter The Lord is the God of our salvation, the Lord by whom we escape death, hallelujah.

24 They see your procession, O God, *
    your procession into the sanctuary, my God and my King.

25 The singers go before, musicians follow after, *
    in the midst of maidens playing upon the hand-drums.

26 Bless God in the congregation; *
    bless the LORD, you that are of the fountain of Israel.

27 There is Benjamin, least of the tribes, at the head;
    the princes of Judah in a company; *
    and the princes of Zebulon and Naphtali.

28 Send forth your strength, O God; *
    establish, O God, what you have wrought for us.

29 Kings shall bring gifts to you, *
    for your temple's sake at Jerusalem.

30 Rebuke the wild beast of the reeds, *
    and the peoples, a herd of wild bulls with its calves.

31 Trample down those who lust after silver; *
    scatter the peoples that delight in war.

32 Let tribute be brought out of Egypt; *
    let Ethiopia stretch out her hands to God.

33 Sing to God, O kingdoms of the earth; *
    sing praises to the Lord.

34 He rides in the heavens, the ancient heavens; *
    he sends forth his voice, his mighty voice.

35 Ascribe power to God; *
    his majesty is over Israel;
    his strength is in the skies.

36 How wonderful is God in his holy places! *
    the God of Israel giving strength and power to his people!
    Blessed be God!

Lent Trample down those who lust after silver; scatter the peoples that delight in war.
Easter The Lord is the God of our salvation, the Lord by whom we escape death, hallelujah.

Reading

Responsory, Magnificat Antiphon, Litany, Invitation to the Lord's Prayer, Collect and Dismissal are taken from the Proper of the Season .

Tuesday Week 4 Morning Prayer

Officiant: Lord, open our lips.
People: **And our mouth shall proclaim your praise.**
Officiant and People **Glory to the Father...**
Except in Lent, add **Alleluia.**

The Invitatory Psalm 8
From the Proper of the Season or of the Day

Hymn *From the Proper of the Season or of the Day*

Psalm 89 Part I A *Misericordias Domini*
Jacob was the father of Joseph the husband of Mary, of whom Jesus was born, who is called the Messiah. Mt. 1:16

Lent Have mercy on us, Lord, Son of David.
Easter The Lion of the tribe of Judah, the Root of David, has conquered, hallelujah.

1 Your love, O LORD, for ever will I sing; *
    from age to age my mouth will proclaim your faithfulness.

2 For I am persuaded that your love is established for ever; *
    you have set your faithfulness firmly in the heavens.

3 "I have made a covenant with my chosen one; *
    I have sworn an oath to David my servant:

4 'I will establish your line for ever, *
 and preserve your throne for all generations.'"

Lent Have mercy on us, Lord, Son of David.
Easter The Lion of the tribe of Judah, the Root of David, has conquered, hallelujah.

Psalm 89 Part I B *Confitebuntur caeli*

Jesus woke up and rebuked the wind and the raging waves; they ceased, and there was a calm. Lk. 8:24

Lent Who in the skies can be compared to the LORD? Who is like the LORD among the gods?
Easter You are the glory of their strength, and by your favor our might is exalted, hallelujah.

5 The heavens bear witness to your wonders, O LORD, *
 and to your faithfulness in the assembly of the holy ones;

6 For who in the skies can be compared to the LORD? *
 who is like the LORD among the gods?

7 God is much to be feared in the council of the holy ones, *
 great and terrible to all those round about him.

8 Who is like you, LORD God of hosts? *
 O mighty LORD, your faithfulness is all around you.

9 You rule the raging of the sea *
 and still the surging of its waves.

10 You have crushed Rahab of the deep with a deadly wound; *
 you have scattered your enemies with your mighty arm.

11 Yours are the heavens; the earth also is yours; *
 you laid the foundations of the world and all that is in it.

12 You have made the north and the south; *
 Tabor and Hermon rejoice in your Name.

13 You have a mighty arm; *
 strong is your hand and high is your right hand.

14 Righteousness and justice are the foundations of your throne; *
 love and truth go before your face.

15 Blessed are the people who know the festal shout! *
 they walk, O LORD, in the light of your presence.

16 They rejoice daily in your Name; *
 they are jubilant in your righteousness.

17 For you are the glory of their strength, *
　　and by your favor our might is exalted.

18 Truly, the LORD is our ruler; *
　　the Holy One of Israel is our King.

Lent Who in the skies can be compared to the LORD? Who is like the LORD among the gods?
Easter You are the glory of their strength, and by your favor our might is exalted, hallelujah.

Psalm 98 *Cantate Domino*

The throne of God and of the Lamb will be in it, and his servants will worship him; they will see his face. Rev. 22:3-4

Lent The Lord remembers his mercy and faithfulness to the house of Israel.
Easter All the ends of the earth have seen the victory of our God, hallelujah.

1 Sing to the LORD a new song, *
　　for he has done marvelous things.

2 With his right hand and his holy arm *
　　has he won for himself the victory.

3 The LORD has made known his victory; *
　　his righteousness has he openly shown
　　in the sight of the nations.

4 He remembers his mercy and faithfulness
　　to the house of Israel, *
　　and all the ends of the earth have seen
　　the victory of our God.

5 Shout with joy to the LORD, all you lands; *
　　lift up your voice, rejoice, and sing.

6 Sing to the LORD with the harp, *
　　with the harp and the voice of song.

7 With trumpets and the sound of the horn *
　　shout with joy before the King, the LORD.

8 Let the sea make a noise and all that is in it, *
　　the lands and those who dwell therein.

9 Let the rivers clap their hands, *
　　and let the hills ring out with joy before the LORD,
　　when he comes to judge the earth.

10 In righteousness shall he judge the world *
    and the peoples with equity.

Lent The Lord remembers his mercy and faithfulness to the house of Israel.
Easter All the ends of the earth have seen the victory of our God, hallelujah.

Readings

Responsories, Benedictus Antiphon, Litany, Invitation to the Lord's Prayer, Collet and Dismissal are taken from the Proper of the Season.

Tuesday Week 4 Noonday Prayer

Officiant: O God, make speed to save us.
People: **O Lord, make haste to help us.**
Officiant and People **Glory to the Father…**
Except in Lent, add **Alleluia.**

Hymn *From the Proper of the Season or of the Day*

Psalm 119 Resh *Vide humilitatem*
Sanctify them in the truth; your word is truth. Jn. 17:17

Lent I will offer you a freewill sacrifice and praise your Name, O LORD, for it is good.
Easter God is my helper; it is the Lord who sustains my life, hallelujah.

153 Behold my affliction and deliver me, *
    for I do not forget your law.

154 Plead my cause and redeem me; *
    according to your promise, give me life.

155 Deliverance is far from the wicked, *
    for they do not study your statutes.

156 Great is your compassion, O LORD; *
    preserve my life, according to your judgments.

157 There are many who persecute and oppress me, *
    yet I have not swerved from your decrees.

158 I look with loathing at the faithless, *
    for they have not kept your word.

159 See how I love your commandments! *
    O LORD, in your mercy, preserve me.

160 The heart of your word is truth; *
    all your righteous judgments endure for evermore.

Psalm 54 *Deus, in nomine*

Do not be afraid, little flock, for it is your Father's good pleasure to give you the kingdom. Lk. 12:32

1 Save me, O God, by your Name; *
    in your might, defend my cause.

2 Hear my prayer, O God; *
    give ear to the words of my mouth.

3 For the arrogant have risen up against me,
and the ruthless have sought my life, *
    those who have no regard for God.

4 Behold, God is my helper; *
    it is the Lord who sustains my life.

5 Render evil to those who spy on me; *
    in your faithfulness, destroy them.

6 I will offer you a freewill sacrifice *
    and praise your Name, O LORD, for it is good.

7 For you have rescued me from every trouble, *
    and my eye has seen the ruin of my foes.

Psalm 70 *Deus, in adjutorium*

Will not God grant justice to his chosen ones who cry to him day and night? Lk. 18:7

1 Be pleased, O God, to deliver me; *
    O LORD, make haste to help me.

2 Let those who seek my life be ashamed
and altogether dismayed; *
    let those who take pleasure in my misfortune
    draw back and be disgraced.

3 Let those who say to me "Aha!" and gloat over me turn back, *
    because they are ashamed.

4 Let all who seek you rejoice and be glad in you; *
    let those who love your salvation say for ever,
    "Great is the LORD!"

5 But as for me, I am poor and needy; *
    come to me speedily, O God.

6 You are my helper and my deliverer; *
    O LORD, do not tarry.

Lent I will offer you a freewill sacrifice and praise your Name, O LORD, for it is good.
Easter God is my helper; it is the Lord who sustains my life, hallelujah.

Reading, Verse and Response, Collect and Conclusion as in the Proper of the Season or of the Day.

Tuesday Week 4 Evening Prayer

Officiant: O God, make speed to save us.
People: **O Lord, make haste to help us.**
Officiant and People **Glory to the Father…**
Except in Lent, add **Alleluia.**

Hymn *From the Proper of the Season or of the Day*

Psalm 89 Part II A *Tunc locutus es*

The Holy Spirit descended upon him in bodily form like a dove. Lk. 3:22

Lent My hand will hold him fast and my arm will make him strong.
Easter I will make him my firstborn and higher than the kings of the earth, hallelujah.

19 You spoke once in a vision and said to your faithful people: *
　　"I have set the crown upon a warrior
　　and have exalted one chosen out of the people.

20 I have found David my servant; *
　　with my holy oil have I anointed him.

21 My hand will hold him fast *
　　and my arm will make him strong.

22 No enemy shall deceive him, *
　　nor any wicked man bring him down.

23 I will crush his foes before him *
　　and strike down those who hate him.

24 My faithfulness and love shall be with him, *
　　and he shall be victorious through my Name.

25 I shall make his dominion extend *
　　from the Great Sea to the River.

26 He will say to me, 'You are my Father, *
　　my God, and the rock of my salvation.'

27 I will make him my firstborn *
　　and higher than the kings of the earth.

28 I will keep my love for him for ever, *
    and my covenant will stand firm for him.

29 I will establish his line for ever *
    and his throne as the days of heaven."

Lent My hand will hold him fast and my arm will make him strong.
Easter I will make him my firstborn and higher than the kings of the earth, hallelujah.

Psalm 89 Part II B *Si autem*

*They will not leave within you one stone upon another;
because you did not recognize the time of your visitation from God. Lk. 19:44*

Lent You have cast off and rejected your anointed; you have become enraged at him.
Easter I will place on his shoulder the key of the house of David, hallelujah.

30 "If his children forsake my law *
    and do not walk according to my judgments;

31 If they break my statutes *
    and do not keep my commandments;

32 I will punish their transgressions with a rod *
    and their iniquities with the lash;

33 But I will not take my love from him, *
    nor let my faithfulness prove false.

34 I will not break my covenant, *
    nor change what has gone out of my lips.

35 Once for all I have sworn by my holiness: *
    'I will not lie to David.

36 His line shall endure for ever *
    and his throne as the sun before me;

37 It shall stand fast for evermore like the moon, *
    the abiding witness in the sky.'"

38 But you have cast off and rejected your anointed; *
    you have become enraged at him.

39 You have broken your covenant with your servant, *
    defiled his crown, and hurled it to the ground.

40 You have breached all his walls *
    and laid his strongholds in ruins.

41 All who pass by despoil him; *
   he has become the scorn of his neighbors.

42 You have exalted the right hand of his foes *
   and made all his enemies rejoice.

43 You have turned back the edge of his sword *
   and have not sustained him in battle.

44 You have put an end to his splendor *
   and cast his throne to the ground.

45 You have cut short the days of his youth *
   and have covered him with shame.

Lent You have cast off and rejected your anointed; you have become enraged at him.
Easter I will place on his shoulder the key of the house of David, hallelujah.

Psalm 89 Part II C *Usquequo, Domine*
The Son of Man will be handed over to the Gentiles;
and he will be mocked and insulted and spat upon. Lk. 18:32

Lent Remember, LORD, how short life is, how frail you have made all flesh.
Easter Remember Jesus Christ, raised from the dead, a descendant of David, hallelujah.

46 How long will you hide yourself, O LORD?
   will you hide yourself for ever? *
      how long will your anger burn like fire?

47 Remember, LORD, how short life is, *
   how frail you have made all flesh.

48 Who can live and not see death? *
   who can save himself from the power of the grave?

49 Where, Lord, are your loving-kindnesses of old, *
   which you promised David in your faithfulness?

50 Remember, Lord, how your servant is mocked, *
   how I carry in my bosom the taunts of many peoples,

51 The taunts your enemies have hurled, O LORD, *
   which they hurled at the heels of your anointed.

52 Blessed be the LORD for evermore! *
   Amen, I say, Amen.

Lent Remember, LORD, how short life is, how frail you have made all flesh.
Easter Remember Jesus Christ, raised from the dead, a descendant of David, hallelujah.

Reading

Responsory, Magnificat Antiphon, Litany, Invitation to the Lord's Prayer, Collect and Dismissal are taken from the Proper of the Season.

Wednesday Week 4 Morning Prayer

Officiant: Lord, open our lips.
People: **And our mouth shall proclaim your praise.**
Officiant and People **Glory to the Father...**
Except in Lent, add **Alleluia.**

The Invitatory Psalm 95
From the Proper of the Season or of the Day

Hymn *From the Proper of the Season or of the Day*

Psalm 66 *Jubilate Deo*
You have given him authority over all people,
to give eternal life to all whom you have given him. Jn. 17:2

Lent Come and listen, all you who fear God, and I will tell you what he has done for me.
Easter Bless our God, who holds our souls in life, hallelujah.

1 Be joyful in God, all you lands; *
    sing the glory of his Name;
    sing the glory of his praise.

2 Say to God, "How awesome are your deeds! *
    because of your great strength
    your enemies cringe before you.

3 All the earth bows down before you, *
    sings to you, sings out your Name."

4 Come now and see the works of God, *
    how wonderful he is in his doing toward all people.

5 He turned the sea into dry land,
    so that they went through the water on foot, *
    and there we rejoiced in him.

6 In his might he rules for ever;
    his eyes keep watch over the nations; *
    let no rebel rise up against him.

7 Bless our God, you peoples; *
    make the voice of his praise to be heard;

8 Who holds our souls in life, *
    and will not allow our feet to slip.

9 For you, O God, have proved us; *
    you have tried us just as silver is tried.

10 You brought us into the snare; *
    you laid heavy burdens upon our backs.

11 You let enemies ride over our heads;
   we went through fire and water; *
       but you brought us out into a place of refreshment.

12 I will enter your house with burnt-offerings
   and will pay you my vows, *
       which I promised with my lips
       and spoke with my mouth when I was in trouble.

13 I will offer you sacrifices of fat beasts
   with the smoke of rams; *
       I will give you oxen and goats.

14 Come and listen, all you who fear God, *
    and I will tell you what he has done for me.

15 I called out to him with my mouth, *
    and his praise was on my tongue.

16 If I had found evil in my heart, *
    the Lord would not have heard me;

17 But in truth God has heard me; *
    he has attended to the voice of my prayer.

18 Blessed be God, who has not rejected my prayer, *
    nor withheld his love from me.

Lent Come and listen, all you who fear God, and I will tell you what he has done for me.
Easter Bless our God, who holds our souls in life, hallelujah.

Psalm 50 *Deus deorum*

You, then, that teach others, will you not teach yourself? Rm. 2:21

Lent Call upon me in the day of trouble; I will deliver you, and you shall honor me.

Easter Offer to God a sacrifice of thanksgiving, and make good your vows to the Most High, hallelujah.

1 The LORD, the God of gods, has spoken; *
   he has called the earth
   from the rising of the sun to its setting.

2 Out of Zion, perfect in its beauty, *
   God reveals himself in glory.

3 Our God will come and will not keep silence; *
   before him there is a consuming flame,
   and round about him a raging storm.

4 He calls the heavens and the earth from above *
   to witness the judgment of his people.

5 "Gather before me my loyal followers, *
   those who have made a covenant with me
   and sealed it with sacrifice."

6 Let the heavens declare the rightness of his cause; *
   for God himself is judge.

7 Hear, O my people, and I will speak:
   "O Israel, I will bear witness against you; *
   for I am God, your God.

8 I do not accuse you because of your sacrifices; *
   your offerings are always before me.

9 I will take no bull-calf from your stalls, *
   nor he-goats out of your pens;

10 For all the beasts of the forest are mine, *
   the herds in their thousands upon the hills.

11 I know every bird in the sky, *
   and the creatures of the fields are in my sight.

12 If I were hungry, I would not tell you, *
   for the whole world is mine and all that is in it.

13 Do you think I eat the flesh of bulls, *
   or drink the blood of goats?

14 Offer to God a sacrifice of thanksgiving *
   and make good your vows to the Most High.

15 Call upon me in the day of trouble; *
    I will deliver you, and you shall honor me."

16 But to the wicked God says: *
    "Why do you recite my statutes,
    and take my covenant upon your lips;

17 Since you refuse discipline, *
    and toss my words behind your back?

18 When you see a thief, you make him your friend, *
    and you cast in your lot with adulterers.

19 You have loosed your lips for evil, *
    and harnessed your tongue to a lie.

20 You are always speaking evil of your brother *
    and slandering your own mother's son.

21 These things you have done, and I kept still, *
    and you thought that I am like you."

22 I have made my accusation; *
    I have put my case in order before your eyes.

23 Consider this well, you who forget God, *
    lest I rend you and there be none to deliver you.

24 Whoever offers me the sacrifice of thanksgiving honors me; *
    but to those who keep in my way
    will I show the salvation of God."

Lent Call upon me in the day of trouble; I will deliver you, and you shall honor me.
Easter Offer to God a sacrifice of thanksgiving, and make good your vows to the Most High, hallelujah.

Psalm 67 *Deus misereatur*
*I thank my God through Jesus Christ for all of you,
because your faith is proclaimed throughout the world. Rm 1:8*

Lent Let your ways be known upon earth, your saving health among all nations.
Easter Let the peoples praise you, O God; let all the peoples praise you, hallelujah.

1 May God be merciful to us and bless us, *
    show us the light of his countenance and come to us.

2 Let your ways be known upon earth, *
    your saving health among all nations.

3 Let the peoples praise you, O God; *
    let all the peoples praise you.

4 Let the nations be glad and sing for joy, *
    for you judge the peoples with equity
    and guide all the nations upon earth.

5 Let the peoples praise you, O God; *
    let all the peoples praise you.

6 The earth has brought forth her increase; *
    may God, our own God, give us his blessing.

7 May God give us his blessing, *
    and may all the ends of the earth stand in awe of him.

Lent Let your ways be known upon earth, your saving health among all nations.
Easter Let the peoples praise you, O God; let all the peoples praise you, hallelujah.

Readings

Responsories, Benedictus Antiphon, Litany, Invitation to the Lord's Prayer, Collet and Dismissal are taken from the Proper of the Season.

Wednesday Week 4 Noonday Prayer

Officiant: O God, make speed to save us.
People: **O Lord, make haste to help us.**
Officiant and People **Glory to the Father...**
Except in Lent, add **Alleluia.**

Hymn *From the Proper of the Season or of the Day*

Psalm 119 Shin *Principes persecuti sunt*
I have said this to you, so that in me you may have peace. Jn. 16:33

Lent You, O God, have heard my vows; you have granted me the heritage of those who fear your Name.
Easter Let the King sit enthroned before God for ever, hallelujah.

161 Rulers have persecuted me without a cause, *
    but my heart stands in awe of your word.

162 I am as glad because of your promise *
    as one who finds great spoils.

163 As for lies, I hate and abhor them, *
    but your law is my love.

164 Seven times a day do I praise you, *
    because of your righteous judgments.

165 Great peace have they who love your law; *
    for them there is no stumbling block.

166 I have hoped for your salvation, O LORD, *
    and have fulfilled your commandments.

167 I have kept your decrees *
    and I have loved them deeply.

168 I have kept your commandments and decrees, *
    for all my ways are before you.

Psalm 61 *Exaudi, Deus*
*How often have I desired to gather your children together
as a hen gathers her brood under her wings. Lk. 13:34*

1 Hear my cry, O God, *
    and listen to my prayer.

2 I call upon you from the ends of the earth
with heaviness in my heart; *
    set me upon the rock that is higher than I.

3 For you have been my refuge, *
    a strong tower against the enemy.

4 I will dwell in your house for ever; *
    I will take refuge under the cover of your wings.

5 For you, O God, have heard my vows; *
    you have granted me the heritage
    of those who fear your Name.

6 Add length of days to the king's life; *
    let his years extend over many generations.

7 Let him sit enthroned before God for ever; *
    bid love and faithfulness watch over him.

8 So will I always sing the praise of your Name, *
    and day by day I will fulfill my vows.

Psalm 53 *Dixit insipiens*

Since all have sinned and fall short of the glory of God;
they are now justified by his grace as a gift. Rm. 3:23

1 The fool has said in his heart, "There is no God." *
    All are corrupt and commit abominable acts;
    there is none who does any good.

2 God looks down from heaven upon us all, *
    to see if there is any who is wise,
    if there is one who seeks after God.

3 Every one has proved faithless;
  all alike have turned bad; *
    there is none who does good; no, not one.

4 Have they no knowledge, those evildoers *
    who eat up my people like bread
    and do not call upon God?

5 See how greatly they tremble,
  such trembling as never was; *
    for God has scattered the bones of the enemy;
    they are put to shame, because God has rejected them.

6 Oh, that Israel's deliverance would come out of Zion! *
    when God restores the fortunes of his people
    Jacob will rejoice and Israel be glad.

Lent You, O God, have heard my vows; you have granted me the heritage of those who fear your Name.
Easter Let the King sit enthroned before God for ever, hallelujah.

Reading, Verse and Response, Collect and Conclusion as in the Proper of the Season or of the Day.

Wednesday Week 4 Evening Prayer

Officiant: O God, make speed to save us.
People: **O Lord, make haste to help us.**
Officiant and People **Glory to the Father...**
Except in Lent, add **Alleluia.**

Hymn *From the Proper of the Season or of the Day*

Psalm 25 A *Ad te, Domine, levavi*

All who exalt themselves will be humbled, and all who humble themselves will be exalted. Mt. 23:12

Lent Remember not the sins of my youth and my transgressions; remember me according to your love.

Easter Christ is the head of the body, the church; he is the beginning, the firstborn from the dead, hallelujah.

1 To you, O LORD, I lift up my soul;
    my God, I put my trust in you; *
        let me not be humiliated,
        nor let my enemies triumph over me.

2 Let none who look to you be put to shame; *
        let the treacherous be disappointed in their schemes.

3 Show me your ways, O LORD, *
        and teach me your paths.

4 Lead me in your truth and teach me, *
        for you are the God of my salvation;
        in you have I trusted all the day long.

5 Remember, O LORD, your compassion and love, *
        for they are from everlasting.

6 Remember not the sins of my youth and my transgressions; *
        remember me according to your love
        and for the sake of your goodness, O LORD.

7 Gracious and upright is the LORD; *
        therefore he teaches sinners in his way.

8 He guides the humble in doing right *
        and teaches his way to the lowly.

Lent Remember not the sins of my youth and my transgressions; remember me according to your love.
Easter Christ is the head of the body, the church; he is the beginning, the firstborn from the dead, hallelujah.

Psalm 25 B *Universae viae Domini*
Blessed are the meek, for they will inherit the earth. Mt. 5:5

Lent For your Name's sake, O LORD, forgive my sin, for it is great.
Easter In Christ all the fullness of God was pleased to dwell, and through him God was pleased to reconcile to himself all things, hallelujah.

9 All the paths of the LORD are love and faithfulness *
        to those who keep his covenant and his testimonies.

10 For your Name's sake, O LORD, *
        forgive my sin, for it is great.

11 Who are they who fear the LORD? *
    he will teach them the way that they should choose.

12 They shall dwell in prosperity, *
    and their offspring shall inherit the land.

13 The LORD is a friend to those who fear him *
    and will show them his covenant.

14 My eyes are ever looking to the LORD, *
    for he shall pluck my feet out of the net.

15 Turn to me and have pity on me, *
    for I am left alone and in misery.

16 The sorrows of my heart have increased; *
    bring me out of my troubles.

17 Look upon my adversity and misery *
    and forgive me all my sin.

18 Look upon my enemies, for they are many, *
    and they bear a violent hatred against me.

19 Protect my life and deliver me; *
    let me not be put to shame, for I have trusted in you.

20 Let integrity and uprightness preserve me, *
    for my hope has been in you.

21 Deliver Israel, O God, *
    out of all his troubles.

Lent For your Name's sake, O LORD, forgive my sin, for it is great.
Easter In Christ all the fullness of God was pleased to dwell, and through him God was pleased to reconcile to himself all things, hallelujah.

Psalm 27 *Dominus illuminatio*
Do not be afraid, for I have overcome the world Jn. 16:33

Lent Though an army should encamp against me, yet my heart shall not be afraid.
Easter I believe that I shall see the goodness of the Lord in the land of the living, hallelujah.

1 The LORD is my light and my salvation;
   whom then shall I fear? *
      the LORD is the strength of my life;
      of whom then shall I be afraid?

2 When evildoers came upon me to eat up my flesh, *
   it was they, my foes and my adversaries,
   who stumbled and fell.

3 Though an army should encamp against me, *
   yet my heart shall not be afraid;

4 And though war should rise up against me, *
   yet will I put my trust in him.

5 One thing have I asked of the LORD;
  one thing I seek; *
   that I may dwell in the house of the LORD
   all the days of my life;

6 To behold the fair beauty of the LORD *
   and to seek him in his temple.

7 For in the day of trouble he shall keep me safe
  in his shelter; *
   he shall hide me in the secrecy of his dwelling
   and set me high upon a rock.

8 Even now he lifts up my head *
   above my enemies round about me.

9 Therefore I will offer in his dwelling an oblation
  with sounds of great gladness; *
   I will sing and make music to the LORD.

10 Hearken to my voice, O LORD, when I call; *
   have mercy on me and answer me.

11 You speak in my heart and say, "Seek my face." *
   Your face, LORD, will I seek.

12 Hide not your face from me, *
   nor turn away your servant in displeasure.

13 You have been my helper;
  cast me not away; *
   do not forsake me, O God of my salvation.

14 Though my father and my mother forsake me, *
   the LORD will sustain me.

15 Show me your way, O LORD; *
   lead me on a level path, because of my enemies.

16 Deliver me not into the hand of my adversaries, *
    for false witnesses have risen up against me,
    and also those who speak malice.

17 What if I had not believed
    that I should see the goodness of the LORD *
    in the land of the living!

18 O tarry and await the LORD'S pleasure;
    be strong, and he shall comfort your heart; *
    wait patiently for the LORD.

Lent Though an army should encamp against me, yet my heart shall not be afraid.
Easter I believe that I shall see the goodness of the Lord in the land of the living, hallelujah.

Reading

Responsory, Magnificat Antiphon, Litany, Invitation to the Lord's Prayer, Collet and Dismissal are taken from the Proper of the Season.

Thursday Week 4 Morning Prayer

Officiant: Lord, open our lips.
People: **And our mouth shall proclaim your praise.**
Officiant and People **Glory to the Father...**
Except in Lent, add **Alleluia.**

The Invitatory Psalm 100
From the Proper of the Season or of the Day

Hymn *From the Proper of the Season or of the Day*

Psalm 43 *Judica me, Deus*
*We are going up to Jerusalem, and everything that is written
about the Son of Man by the prophets will be accomplished. Lk. 18:31*

Lent Defend my cause against an ungodly people, O God; deliver me from the deceitful and the wicked.
Easter I will go to the altar of God, to the God of my joy and gladness, hallelujah.

1 Give judgment for me, O God,
    and defend my cause against an ungodly people; *
    deliver me from the deceitful and the wicked.

2 For you are the God of my strength;
why have you put me from you? *
  and why do I go so heavily
  while the enemy oppresses me?

3 Send out your light and your truth, that they may lead me, *
  and bring me to your holy hill
  and to your dwelling;

4 That I may go to the altar of God,
to the God of my joy and gladness; *
  and on the harp I will give thanks to you, O God my God.

5 Why are you so full of heaviness, O my soul? *
  and why are you so disquieted within me?

6 Put your trust in God; *
  for I will yet give thanks to him,
  who is the help of my countenance, and my God.

Lent Defend my cause against an ungodly people, O God; deliver me from the deceitful and the wicked.
Easter I will go to the altar of God, to the God of my joy and gladness, hallelujah.

Psalm 26 *Judica me, Domine*

The blood of Christ will purify our conscience from dead works to worship the living God. Heb. 9:14

Lent Test me, O LORD, and try me; examine my heart and my mind.
Easter Lord, I love the house in which you dwell, and the place where your glory abides, hallelujah.

1 Give judgment for me, O LORD,
for I have lived with integrity; *
  I have trusted in the Lord and have not faltered.

2 Test me, O LORD, and try me; *
  examine my heart and my mind.

3 For your love is before my eyes; *
  I have walked faithfully with you.

4 I have not sat with the worthless, *
  nor do I consort with the deceitful.

5 I have hated the company of evildoers; *
  I will not sit down with the wicked.

6 I will wash my hands in innocence, O LORD, *
  that I may go in procession round your altar,

7 Singing aloud a song of thanksgiving *
    and recounting all your wonderful deeds.

8 LORD, I love the house in which you dwell *
    and the place where your glory abides.

9 Do not sweep me away with sinners, *
    nor my life with those who thirst for blood,

10 Whose hands are full of evil plots, *
    and their right hand full of bribes.

11 As for me, I will live with integrity; *
    redeem me, O LORD, and have pity on me.

12 My foot stands on level ground; *
    in the full assembly I will bless the LORD.

Lent Test me, O LORD, and try me; examine my heart and my mind.
Easter Lord, I love the house in which you dwell, and the place where your glory abides, hallelujah.

Psalm 149 *Cantate Domino*
All who see them shall acknowledge that they are a people whom the Lord has blessed. Is. 61: 9

Lent There is joy in the presence of the angels of God over one sinner who repents.
Easter Let the faithful rejoice in triumph, hallelujah.

1 Hallelujah!
   Sing to the LORD a new song; *
     sing his praise in the congregation of the faithful.

2 Let Israel rejoice in his Maker; *
    let the children of Zion be joyful in their King.

3 Let them praise his Name in the dance; *
    let them sing praise to him with timbrel and harp.

4 For the LORD takes pleasure in his people *
    and adorns the poor with victory.

5 Let the faithful rejoice in triumph; *
    let them be joyful on their beds.

6 Let the praises of God be in their throat *
    and a two-edged sword in their hand;

7 To wreak vengeance on the nations *
    and punishment on the peoples;

8 To bind their kings in chains *
   and their nobles with links of iron;

9 To inflict on them the judgment decreed; *
   this is glory for all his faithful people.
   Hallelujah!

Lent There is joy in the presence of the angels of God over one sinner who repents.
Easter Let the faithful rejoice in triumph, hallelujah.

Readings

Responsories, Benedictus Antiphon, Litany, Invitation to the Lord's Prayer, Collect and Dismissal are taken from the Proper of the Season.

Thursday Week 4 Noonday Prayer

Officiant: O God, make speed to save us.
People: **O Lord, make haste to help us.**
Officiant and People **Glory to the Father…**
Except in Lent, add **Alleluia.**

Hymn *From the Proper of the Season or of the Day*

Psalm 119 Taw *Appropinquet deprecatio*
Rejoice with me, for I have found my sheep that was lost. Lk. 15:6

Lent I have gone astray like a sheep that is lost; search for your servant
Easter Blessed are the meek for they shall inherit the earth, hallelujah.

169 Let my cry come before you, O LORD; *
   give me understanding, according to your word.

170 Let my supplication come before you; *
   deliver me, according to your promise.

171 My lips shall pour forth your praise, *
   when you teach me your statutes.

172 My tongue shall sing of your promise, *
   for all your commandments are righteous.

173 Let your hand be ready to help me, *
   for I have chosen your commandments.

174 I long for your salvation, O LORD, *
   and your law is my delight.

175 Let me live, and I will praise you, *
   and let your judgments help me.

176 I have gone astray like a sheep that is lost; *
 search for your servant,
  for I do not forget your commandments.

Psalm 10 A *Ut quid, Domine?*

When they hand you over, do not worry about how you are to speak or what you are to say;
for what you are to say will be given to you at that time. Mt. 10:19

1 Why do you stand so far off, O LORD, *
 and hide yourself in time of trouble?

2 The wicked arrogantly persecute the poor, *
 but they are trapped in the schemes they have devised.

3 The wicked boast of their heart's desire; *
 the covetous curse and revile the LORD.

4 The wicked are so proud that they care not for God; *
 their only thought is, "God does not matter."

5 Their ways are devious at all times;
 your judgments are far above out of their sight; *
  they defy all their enemies.

6 They say in their heart, "I shall not be shaken; *
 no harm shall happen to me ever."

7 Their mouth is full of cursing, deceit, and oppression; *
 under their tongue are mischief and wrong.

8 They lurk in ambush in public squares
 and in secret places they murder the innocent; *
  they spy out the helpless.

9 They lie in wait, like a lion in a covert;
 they lie in wait to seize upon the lowly; *
  they seize the lowly and drag them away in their net.

10 The innocent are broken and humbled before them; *
 the helpless fall before their power.

11 They say in their heart, "God has forgotten; *
 he hides his face; he will never notice."

Psalm 10 B *Exsurge Domine Deus*

You will be hated by all because of my name.
But the one who endures to the end will be saved. Mt. 10:22

12 Rise up, O LORD;
 lift up your hand, O God; *
  do not forget the afflicted.

13 Why should the wicked revile God? *
    why should they say in their heart, "You do not care"?

14 Surely, you behold trouble and misery; *
    you see it and take it into your own hand.

15 The helpless commit themselves to you, *
    for you are the helper of orphans.

16 Break the power of the wicked and evil; *
    search out their wickedness until you find none.

17 The LORD is King for ever and ever; *
    the ungodly shall perish from his land.

18 The LORD will hear the desire of the humble; *
    you will strengthen their heart and your ears shall hear;

19 To give justice to the orphan and oppressed, *
    so that mere mortals may strike terror no more.

Lent I have gone astray like a sheep that is lost; search for your servant
Easter Blessed are the meek for they shall inherit the earth, hallelujah.

Reading, Verse and Response, Collect and Conclusion as in the Proper of the Season or of the Day.

Thursday Week 4 Evening Prayer

Officiant: O God, make speed to save us.
People: **O Lord, make haste to help us.**
Officiant and People **Glory to the Father...**
Except in Lent, add **Alleluia.**

Hymn *From the Proper of the Season or of the Day*

Psalm 80 A *Qui regis Israel*
*Just as the branch cannot bear fruit by itself unless it abides in the vine,
neither can you unless you abide in me. Jn. 15:4*

Lent You have fed them with the bread of tears; you have given them bowls of tears to drink.
Easter I am the vine and you are the branches, hallelujah.

1 Hear, O Shepherd of Israel, leading Joseph like a flock; *
    shine forth, you that are enthroned upon the cherubim.

2 In the presence of Ephraim, Benjamin, and Manasseh, *
    stir up your strength and come to help us.

3 Restore us, O God of hosts; *
   show the light of your countenance, and we shall be saved.

4 O L<small>ORD</small> God of hosts, *
   how long will you be angered
   despite the prayers of your people?

5 You have fed them with the bread of tears; *
   you have given them bowls of tears to drink.

6 You have made us the derision of our neighbors, *
   and our enemies laugh us to scorn.

7 Restore us, O God of hosts; *
   show the light of your countenance, and we shall be saved.

Lent You have fed them with the bread of tears; you have given them bowls of tears to drink.
Easter I am the vine and you are the branches, hallelujah.

Psalm 80 B *Vineam de Aegypto*
Those who abide in me and I in them bear much fruit,
because apart from me you can do nothing. Jn. 15:5

Lent Restore us, O God of hosts, show the light of your countenance and we shall be saved.
Easter Those who abide in my and I in them bear much fruit, because apart from me you can do nothing, hallelujah.

8 You have brought a vine out of Egypt; *
   you cast out the nations and planted it.

9 You prepared the ground for it; *
   it took root and filled the land.

10 The mountains were covered by its shadow *
   and the towering cedar trees by its boughs.

11 You stretched out its tendrils to the Sea *
   and its branches to the River.

12 Why have you broken down its wall, *
   so that all who pass by pluck off its grapes?

13 The wild boar of the forest has ravaged it, *
   and the beasts of the field have grazed upon it.

14 Turn now, O God of hosts, look down from heaven;
   behold and tend this vine; *
   preserve what your right hand has planted.

15 They burn it with fire like rubbish; *
    at the rebuke of your countenance let them perish.

16 Let your hand be upon the man of your right hand, *
    the son of man you have made so strong for yourself.

17 And so will we never turn away from you; *
    give us life, that we may call upon your Name.

18 Restore us, O LORD God of hosts; *
    show the light of your countenance, and we shall be saved.

Lent Restore us, O God of hosts, show the light of your countenance and we shall be saved.
Easter Those who abide in my and I in them bear much fruit, because apart from me you can do nothing, hallelujah.

Psalm 126 *In convertendo*
I consider that the sufferings of this present time are not worth comparing with the glory about to be revealed to us. Rm. 8:18

Lent They go out weeping, carrying the seed.
Easter The LORD has done great things for us, and we are glad indeed, hallelujah.

1 When the LORD restored the fortunes of Zion, *
    then were we like those who dream.

2 Then was our mouth filled with laughter, *
    and our tongue with shouts of joy.

3 Then they said among the nations, *
    "The LORD has done great things for them."

4 The LORD has done great things for us, *
    and we are glad indeed.

5 Restore our fortunes, O LORD, *
    like the watercourses of the Negev.

6 Those who sowed with tears *
    will reap with songs of joy.

7 Those who go out weeping, carrying the seed, *
    will come again with joy, shouldering their sheaves.

Lent They go out weeping, carrying the seed.
Easter The LORD has done great things for us, and we are glad indeed, hallelujah.

Reading

Responsory, Magnificat Antiphon, Litany, Invitation to the Lord's Prayer, Collect and Dismissal are taken from the Proper of the Season.

Friday Week 4 Morning Prayer

Officiant: Lord, open our lips.
People: **And our mouth shall proclaim your praise.**
Officiant and People **Glory to the Father...**
Except in Lent, add **Alleluia.**

The Invitatory Psalm 95
From the Proper of the Season or of the Day

Hymn *From the Proper of the Season or of the Day*

Psalm 44 A *Deus, auribus*
*He humbled himself and became obedient to the point of death—
even death on a cross. Phil 2:8*

Lent Here is the Lamb of God who takes away the sin of the world.
Easter You have favored your people; you are my King and my God, hallelujah.

1 We have heard with our ears, O God,
   our forefathers have told us, *
      the deeds you did in their days,
      in the days of old.

2 How with your hand you drove the peoples out
   and planted our forefathers in the land; *
      how you destroyed nations and made your people flourish.

3 For they did not take the land by their sword,
   nor did their arm win the victory for them; *
      but your right hand, your arm,
      and the light of your countenance,
      because you favored them.

4 You are my King and my God; *
      you command victories for Jacob.

5 Through you we pushed back our adversaries; *
      through your Name we trampled
      on those who rose up against us.

6 For I do not rely on my bow, *
      and my sword does not give me the victory.

7 Surely, you gave us victory over our adversaries *
 and put those who hate us to shame.

8 Every day we gloried in God, *
 and we will praise your Name for ever.

9 Nevertheless, you have rejected and humbled us *
 and do not go forth with our armies.

10 You have made us fall back before our adversary, *
 and our enemies have plundered us.

11 You have made us like sheep to be eaten *
 and have scattered us among the nations.

12 You are selling your people for a trifle *
 and are making no profit on the sale of them.

13 You have made us the scorn of our neighbors, *
 a mockery and derision to those around us.

14 You have made us a byword among the nations, *
 a laughing-stock among the peoples.

15 My humiliation is daily before me, *
 and shame has covered my face;

16 Because of the taunts of the mockers and blasphemers, *
 because of the enemy and avenger.

Lent Here is the Lamb of God who takes away the sin of the world.
Easter You have favored your people; you are my King and my God, hallelujah.

Psalm 44 B *Haec omnia venerunt*

*Jesus threw himself on the ground and prayed that,
if it were possible, the hour might pass from him. Mk. 14:35*

Lent You thrust us down into a place of misery, and covered us over with deep darkness.
Easter Rise up, and help us, and save us, for the sake of your steadfast love, hallelujah.

17 All this has come upon us; *
 yet we have not forgotten you,
 nor have we betrayed your covenant.

18 Our heart never turned back, *
 nor did our footsteps stray from your path;

19 Though you thrust us down into a place of misery, *
    and covered us over with deep darkness.

20 If we have forgotten the Name of our God, *
    or stretched out our hands to some strange god,

21 Will not God find it out? *
    for he knows the secrets of the heart.

22 Indeed, for your sake we are killed all the day long; *
    we are accounted as sheep for the slaughter.

23 Awake, O Lord! why are you sleeping? *
    Arise! do not reject us for ever.

24 Why have you hidden your face *
    and forgotten our affliction and oppression?

25 We sink down into the dust; *
    our body cleaves to the ground.

26 Rise up, and help us, *
    and save us, for the sake of your steadfast love.

Lent You thrust us down into a place of misery, and covered us over with deep darkness.
Easter Rise up, and help us, and save us, for the sake of your steadfast love, hallelujah.

Psalm 137 *Super flumina*
The women who had come with Jesus from Galilee followed, and they saw the tomb and how his body was laid. Lk. 23:5

Lent Lay hold of your thoughts while they are still young and dash them against Christ.
Easter Stay in Jerusalem until you have been clothed with power from on high, hallelujah.

1 By the waters of Babylon we sat down and wept, *
    when we remembered you, O Zion.

2 As for our harps, we hung them up *
    on the trees in the midst of that land.

3 For those who led us away captive asked us for a song,
    and our oppressors called for mirth: *
        "Sing us one of the songs of Zion."

4 How shall we sing the LORD'S song *
    upon an alien soil?

5 If I forget you, O Jerusalem, *
    let my right hand forget its skill.

6 Let my tongue cleave to the roof of my mouth
    if I do not remember you, *
    if I do not set Jerusalem above my highest joy.

7 Remember the day of Jerusalem, O LORD,
    against the people of Edom, *
    who said, "Down with it! down with it!
    even to the ground!"

8 O Daughter of Babylon, doomed to destruction, *
    blessed the one who pays you back
    for what you have done to us!

9 Blessed shall he be who takes your little ones, *
    and dashes them against the rock!

Lent Lay hold of your thoughts while they are still young and dash them against Christ.
Easter Stay in Jerusalem until you have been clothed with power from on high, hallelujah.

Readings

Responsories, Benedictus Antiphon, Litany, Invitation to the Lord's Prayer, Collect and Dismissal are taken from the Proper of the Season.

Friday Week 4 Noonday Prayer

Officiant: O God, make speed to save us.
People: **O Lord, make haste to help us.**
Officiant and People **Glory to the Father...**
Except in Lent, add **Alleluia.**

Hymn *From the Proper of the Season or of the Day*

Psalm 60 *Deus, repulisti nos*
At that moment the curtain of the temple was torn in two, from top to bottom.
The earth shook, and the rocks were split. Mt. 26;51

Lent My companion stretched forth his hand against his comrade; he has broken his covenant.
Easter With God we will do valiant deeds, and he shall tread our enemies under foot, hallelujah.

1 O God, you have cast us off and broken us; *
    you have been angry;
    oh, take us back to you again.

2 You have shaken the earth and split it open; *
    repair the cracks in it, for it totters.

3 You have made your people know hardship; *
    you have given us wine that makes us stagger.

4 You have set up a banner for those who fear you, *
    to be a refuge from the power of the bow.

5 Save us by your right hand and answer us, *
    that those who are dear to you may be delivered.

6 God spoke from his holy place and said: *
    "I will exult and parcel out Shechem;
    I will divide the valley of Succoth.

7 Gilead is mine and Manasseh is mine; *
    Ephraim is my helmet and Judah my scepter.

8 Moab is my wash-basin,
    on Edom I throw down my sandal to claim it, *
    and over Philistia will I shout in triumph."

9 Who will lead me into the strong city? *
    who will bring me into Edom?

10 Have you not cast us off, O God? *
    you no longer go out, O God, with our armies.

11 Grant us your help against the enemy, *
    for vain is the help of man.

12 With God we will do valiant deeds, *
    and he shall tread our enemies under foot.

Psalm 55 A *Exaudi, Deus*

In his anguish Jesus prayed more earnestly, and his sweat became like great drops of blood falling down on the ground. Lk. 22:44

1 Hear my prayer, O God; *
    do not hide yourself from my petition.

2 Listen to me and answer me; *
    I have no peace, because of my cares.

3 I am shaken by the noise of the enemy *
    and by the pressure of the wicked;

4 For they have cast an evil spell upon me *
    and are set against me in fury.

5 My heart quakes within me, *
    and the terrors of death have fallen upon me.

6 Fear and trembling have come over me, *
    and horror overwhelms me.

7 And I said, "Oh, that I had wings like a dove! *
    I would fly away and be at rest.

8 I would flee to a far-off place *
    and make my lodging in the wilderness.

9 I would hasten to escape *
    from the stormy wind and tempest."

10 Swallow them up, O Lord;
    confound their speech; *
    for I have seen violence and strife in the city.

11 Day and night the watchmen
    make their rounds upon her walls, *
    but trouble and misery are in the midst of her.

Psalm 55 B *Insidiae in vitalibus*

They asked Peter, "You are not also one of his disciples, are you?"
He denied it and said, "I am not." Jn. 18: 25

12 There is corruption at her heart; *
    her streets are never free of oppression and deceit.

13 For had it been an adversary who taunted me,
    then I could have borne it; *
    or had it been an enemy who vaunted himself against me,
    then I could have hidden from him.

14 But it was you, a man after my own heart, *
    my companion, my own familiar friend.

15 We took sweet counsel together, *
    and walked with the throng in the house of God.

16 Let death come upon them suddenly;
    let them go down alive into the grave; *
    for wickedness is in their dwellings, in their very midst.

17 But I will call upon God, *
    and the LORD will deliver me.

18 In the evening, in the morning, and at noonday,
    I will complain and lament, *
    and he will hear my voice.

19 He will bring me safely back
   from the battle waged against me; *
      for there are many who fight me.

20 God, who is enthroned of old, will hear me
   and bring them down; *
      they never change; they do not fear God.

21 My companion stretched forth his hand against his comrade; *
      he has broken his covenant.

22 His speech is softer than butter, *
      but war is in his heart.

23 His words are smoother than oil, *
      but they are drawn swords.

24 Cast your burden upon the LORD,
   and he will sustain you; *
      he will never let the righteous stumble.

25 For you will bring the bloodthirsty and deceitful *
      down to the pit of destruction, O God.

26 They shall not live out half their days, *
      but I will put my trust in you.

Lent My companion stretched forth his hand against his comrade; he has broken his covenant.
Easter With God we will do valiant deeds, and he shall tread our enemies under foot, hallelujah.

Reading, Verse and Response, Collect and Conclusion as in the Proper of the Season or of the Day.

Friday Week 4 Evening Prayer

Officiant: O God, make speed to save us.
People: **O Lord, make haste to help us.**
Officiant and People **Glory to the Father...**
Except in Lent, add **Alleluia.**

Hymn *From the Proper of the Season or of the Day*

Psalm 22 A *Deus, Deus meus*
At three o'clock Jesus cried out with a loud voice,
"My God, my God, why have you forsaken me?" Mk 15:34

Lent They pierce my hands and my feet; I can count all my bones.
Easter Although he was a Son, Jesus learned obedience through what he suffered, hallelujah.

1 My God, my God, why have you forsaken me? *
    and are so far from my cry
    and from the words of my distress?

2 O my God, I cry in the daytime, but you do not answer; *
    by night as well, but I find no rest.

3 Yet you are the Holy One, *
    enthroned upon the praises of Israel.

4 Our forefathers put their trust in you; *
    they trusted, and you delivered them.

5 They cried out to you and were delivered; *
    they trusted in you and were not put to shame.

6 But as for me, I am a worm and no man, *
    scorned by all and despised by the people.

7 All who see me laugh me to scorn; *
    they curl their lips and wag their heads, saying,

8 "He trusted in the LORD; let him deliver him; *
    let him rescue him, if he delights in him."

9 Yet you are he who took me out of the womb, *
    and kept me safe upon my mother's breast.

10 I have been entrusted to you ever since I was born; *
    You were my God
    when I was still in my mother's womb.

11 Be not far from me, for trouble is near, *
    and there is none to help.

12 Many young bulls encircle me; *
    strong bulls of Bashan surround me.

13 They open wide their jaws at me, *
    like a ravening and a roaring lion.

14 I am poured out like water;
    all my bones are out of joint; *
    my heart within my breast is melting wax.

15 My mouth is dried out like a pot-sherd;
    my tongue sticks to the roof of my mouth; *
    and you have laid me in the dust of the grave.

16 Packs of dogs close me in,
   and gangs of evildoers circle around me; *
      they pierce my hands and my feet;
      I can count all my bones.

17 They stare and gloat over me; *
      they divide my garments among them;
      they cast lots for my clothing.

18 Be not far away, O LORD; *
      you are my strength; hasten to help me.

19 Save me from the sword, *
      my life from the power of the dog.

20 Save me from the lion's mouth, *
      my wretched body from the horns of wild bulls.

Lent They pierce my hands and my feet; I can count all my bones.
Easter Although he was a Son, Jesus learned obedience through what he suffered, hallelujah.

Psalm 22 B *Narrabo nomen tuum*

Jesus said to the women, "Do not be afraid; go and tell my brothers to go to Galilee; there they will see me." Mt. 28:10

Lent God does not despise nor abhor the poor in their poverty; neither does he hide his face from them.
Easter My soul shall live for him; my descendants shall serve him; they shall be known as the LORD'S for ever, hallelujah

21 I will declare your Name to my brethren; *
      in the midst of the congregation I will praise you.

22 Praise the LORD, you that fear him; *
      stand in awe of him, O offspring of Israel;
      all you of Jacob's line, give glory.

23 For he does not despise nor abhor the poor in their poverty;
   neither does he hide his face from them; *
      but when they cry to him he hears them.

24 My praise is of him in the great assembly; *
      I will perform my vows
      in the presence of those who worship him.

25 The poor shall eat and be satisfied,
   and those who seek the LORD shall praise him: *
      "May your heart live for ever!"

26 All the ends of the earth shall remember
 and turn to the LORD, *
  and all the families of the nations shall bow before him.

27 For kingship belongs to the LORD; *
  he rules over the nations.

28 To him alone all who sleep in the earth
 bow down in worship; *
  all who go down to the dust fall before him.

29 My soul shall live for him;
 my descendants shall serve him; *
  they shall be known as the LORD'S for ever.

30 They shall come and make known to a people yet unborn *
  the saving deeds that he has done.

Lent God does not despise nor abhor the poor in their poverty; neither does he hide his face from them.
Easter My soul shall live for him; my descendants shall serve him; they shall be known as the LORD'S for ever, hallelujah

Psalm 102 *Domine, exaudi*
Just as the sufferings of Christ are abundant for us,
so also our consolation is abundant through Christ. 2 Cor. 1:5

Lent My days pass away like a shadow, and I wither like the grass.
Easter You will arise and have compassion on Zion, for it is time to have mercy upon her, hallelujah.

1 LORD, hear my prayer, and let my cry come before you; *
  hide not your face from me in the day of my trouble.

2 Incline your ear to me; *
  when I call, make haste to answer me,

3 For my days drift away like smoke, *
  and my bones are hot as burning coals.

4 My heart is smitten like grass and withered, *
  so that I forget to eat my bread.

5 Because of the voice of my groaning *
  I am but skin and bones.

6 I have become like a vulture in the wilderness, *
  like an owl among the ruins.

7 I lie awake and groan; *
    I am like a sparrow, lonely on a house-top.

8 My enemies revile me all day long, *
    and those who scoff at me have taken an oath against me.

9 For I have eaten ashes for bread *
    and mingled my drink with weeping.

10 Because of your indignation and wrath *
    you have lifted me up and thrown me away.

11 My days pass away like a shadow, *
    and I wither like the grass.

12 But you, O LORD, endure for ever, *
    and your Name from age to age.

13 You will arise and have compassion on Zion,
    for it is time to have mercy upon her; *
    indeed, the appointed time has come.

14 For your servants love her very rubble, *
    and are moved to pity even for her dust.

15 The nations shall fear your Name, O LORD, *
    and all the kings of the earth your glory.

16 For the LORD will build up Zion, *
    and his glory will appear.

17 He will look with favor on the prayer of the homeless; *
    he will not despise their plea.

18 Let this be written for a future generation, *
    so that a people yet unborn may praise the LORD.

19 For the LORD looked down from his holy place on high; *
    from the heavens he beheld the earth;

20 That he might hear the groan of the captive *
    and set free those condemned to die;

21 That they may declare in Zion the Name of the LORD, *
    and his praise in Jerusalem;

22 When the peoples are gathered together, *
    and the kingdoms also, to serve the LORD.

23 He has brought down my strength before my time; *
    he has shortened the number of my days;

24 And I said, "O my God,
do not take me away in the midst of my days; *
your years endure throughout all generations.

25 In the beginning, O LORD,
you laid the foundations of the earth, *
and the heavens are the work of your hands;

26 They shall perish, but you will endure;
they all shall wear out like a garment; *
as clothing you will change them,
and they shall be changed;

27 But you are always the same, *
and your years will never end.

28 The children of your servants shall continue, *
and their offspring shall stand fast in your sight."

Lent My days pass away like a shadow, and I wither like the grass.
Easter You will arise and have compassion on Zion, for it is time to have mercy upon her, hallelujah.

Reading

Responsory, Magnificat Antiphon, Litany, Invitation to the Lord's Prayer, Collet and Dismissal are taken from the Proper of the Season.

Saturday Week 4 Morning Prayer

Officiant: Lord, open our lips.
People: **And our mouth shall proclaim your praise.**
Officiant and People **Glory to the Father...**
Except in Lent, add **Alleluia.**

The Invitatory Psalm 122
From the Proper of the Season or of the Day

Hymn *From the Proper of the Season or of the Day*

Psalm 30 *Exaltabo te, Domine*
Jesus was put to death in the flesh, but made alive in the spirit,
in which also he went and made a proclamation to the spirits in prison. 1 Pt. 3:18-19

Lent Weeping may spend the night, but joy comes in the morning.
Easter You brought me up, O LORD, from the dead; you restored my life, hallelujah.

1 I will exalt you, O LORD,
    because you have lifted me up *
        and have not let my enemies triumph over me.

2 O LORD my God, I cried out to you, *
    and you restored me to health.

3 You brought me up, O LORD, from the dead; *
    you restored my life as I was going down to the grave.

4 Sing to the LORD, you servants of his; *
    give thanks for the remembrance of his holiness.

5 For his wrath endures but the twinkling of an eye, *
    his favor for a lifetime.

6 Weeping may spend the night, *
    but joy comes in the morning.

7 While I felt secure, I said,
    "I shall never be disturbed. *
    You, LORD, with your favor,
    made me as strong as the mountains."

8 Then you hid your face, *
    and I was filled with fear.

9 I cried to you, O LORD; *
    I pleaded with the Lord, saying,

10 "What profit is there in my blood, if I go down to the Pit? *
    will the dust praise you or declare your faithfulness?

11 Hear, O LORD, and have mercy upon me; *
    O LORD, be my helper."

12 You have turned my wailing into dancing; *
    you have put off my sack-cloth and clothed me with joy.

13 Therefore my heart sings to you without ceasing; *
    O LORD my God, I will give you thanks for ever.

Lent Weeping may spend the night, but joy comes in the morning.
Easter You brought me up, O LORD, from the dead; you restored my life, hallelujah.

Psalm 92 *Bonum est confiteri*
With gratitude in your hearts sing psalms, hymns, and spiritual songs to God. Eph. 3:16

Lent The wicked flourish only to be destroyed for ever; but you, O LORD, are exalted for evermore.

Easter You have made me glad, O Lord, and I shout for joy because of the works of your hands, hallelujah.

1 It is a good thing to give thanks to the LORD, *
    and to sing praises to your Name, O Most High;

2 To tell of your loving-kindness early in the morning *
    and of your faithfulness in the night season;

3 On the psaltery, and on the lyre, *
    and to the melody of the harp.

4 For you have made me glad by your acts, O LORD; *
    and I shout for joy because of the works of your hands.

5 LORD, how great are your works! *
    your thoughts are very deep.

6 The dullard does not know,
  nor does the fool understand, *
    that though the wicked grow like weeds,
    and all the workers of iniquity flourish,

7 They flourish only to be destroyed for ever; *
    but you, O LORD, are exalted for evermore.

8 For lo, your enemies, O LORD,
  lo, your enemies shall perish, *
    and all the workers of iniquity shall be scattered.

9 But my horn you have exalted like the horns of wild bulls; *
    I am anointed with fresh oil.

10 My eyes also gloat over my enemies, *
    and my ears rejoice to hear the doom of the wicked
    who rise up against me.

11 The righteous shall flourish like a palm tree, *
    and shall spread abroad like a cedar of Lebanon.

12 Those who are planted in the house of the LORD *
    shall flourish in the courts of our God;

13 They shall still bear fruit in old age; *
    they shall be green and succulent;

14 That they may show how upright the LORD is, *
    my Rock, in whom there is no fault.

Lent The wicked flourish only to be destroyed for ever; but you, O LORD, are exalted for evermore.
Easter You have made me glad, O Lord, and I shout for joy because of the works of your hands, hallelujah.

Psalm 143 *Domine, exaudi*
*The Son of Man must undergo great suffering, and be killed,
and on the third day be raised. Lk. 9:22*

Lent I spread out my hands to you; my soul gasps to you like a thirsty land.
Easter Revive me, O LORD, for your Name's sake; for your righteousness' sake, bring me out of trouble., hallelujah.

1 LORD, hear my prayer,
 and in your faithfulness heed my supplications; *
  answer me in your righteousness.

2 Enter not into judgment with your servant, *
  for in your sight shall no one living be justified.

3 For my enemy has sought my life;
 he has crushed me to the ground; *
  he has made me live in dark places
  like those who are long dead.

4 My spirit faints within me; *
  my heart within me is desolate.

5 I remember the time past;
 I muse upon all your deeds; *
  I consider the works of your hands.

6 I spread out my hands to you; *
  my soul gasps to you like a thirsty land.

7 O LORD, make haste to answer me; my spirit fails me; *
  do not hide your face from me
  or I shall be like those who go down to the Pit.

8 Let me hear of your loving-kindness in the morning,
 for I put my trust in you; *
  show me the road that I must walk,
  for I lift up my soul to you.

9 Deliver me from my enemies, O LORD, *
  for I flee to you for refuge.

10 Teach me to do what pleases you, for you are my God; *
    let your good Spirit lead me on level ground.

11 Revive me, O LORD, for your Name's sake; *
    for your righteousness' sake, bring me out of trouble.

Lent I spread out my hands to you; my soul gasps to you like a thirsty land.
Easter Revive me, O LORD, for your Name's sake; for your righteousness' sake, bring me out of trouble., hallelujah.

Readings

Responsories, Benedictus Antiphon, Litany, Invitation to the Lord's Prayer, Collet and Dismissal are taken from the Proper of the Season.

Saturday Week 4 Noonday Prayer

Officiant: O God, make speed to save us.
People: **O Lord, make haste to help us.**
Officiant and People **Glory to the Father...**
Except in Lent, add **Alleluia.**

Hymn *From the Proper of the Season or of the Day*

Psalm 37 A *Noli æmulari*
Blessed are the meek, for they will inherit the earth. Mt. 5:5

Lent Turn from evil, and do good, and dwell in the land for ever.
Easter Take delight in the LORD, and he shall give you your heart's desire, hallelujah.

1 Do not fret yourself because of evildoers; *
    do not be jealous of those who do wrong.

2 For they shall soon wither like the grass, *
    and like the green grass fade away.

3 Put your trust in the LORD and do good; *
    dwell in the land and feed on its riches.

4 Take delight in the LORD, *
    and he shall give you your heart's desire.

5 Commit your way to the LORD and put your trust in him, *
    and he will bring it to pass.

6 He will make your righteousness as clear as the light *
    and your just dealing as the noonday.

7 Be still before the LORD *
    and wait patiently for him.

8 Do not fret yourself over the one who prospers, *
    the one who succeeds in evil schemes.

9 Refrain from anger, leave rage alone; *
    do not fret yourself; it leads only to evil.

10 For evildoers shall be cut off, *
    but those who wait upon the LORD shall possess the land.

11 In a little while the wicked shall be no more; *
    you shall search out their place, but they will not be there.

12 But the lowly shall possess the land; *
    they will delight in abundance of peace.

13 The wicked plot against the righteous *
    and gnash at them with their teeth.

14 The Lord laughs at the wicked, *
    because he sees that their day will come.

15 The wicked draw their sword and bend their bow
  to strike down the poor and needy, *
    to slaughter those who are upright in their ways.

16 Their sword shall go through their own heart, *
    and their bow shall be broken.

17 The little that the righteous has *
    is better than great riches of the wicked.

18 For the power of the wicked shall be broken, *
    but the LORD upholds the righteous.

Psalm 37 B *Novit Dominus*
May you be filled with the knowledge of God's will
in all spiritual wisdom and understanding. Col. 1:9

19 The LORD cares for the lives of the godly, *
    and their inheritance shall last for ever.

20 They shall not be ashamed in bad times, *
    and in days of famine they shall have enough.

21 As for the wicked, they shall perish, *
   and the enemies of the LORD,
   like the glory of the meadows, shall vanish;
   they shall vanish like smoke.

22 The wicked borrow and do not repay, *
   but the righteous are generous in giving.

23 Those who are blessed by God shall possess the land, *
   but those who are cursed by him shall be destroyed.

24 Our steps are directed by the LORD; *
   he strengthens those in whose way he delights.

25 If they stumble, they shall not fall headlong, *
   for the LORD holds them by the hand.

26 I have been young and now I am old, *
   but never have I seen the righteous forsaken,
   or their children begging bread.

27 The righteous are always generous in their lending, *
   and their children shall be a blessing.

28 Turn from evil, and do good, *
   and dwell in the land for ever.

29 For the LORD loves justice; *
   he does not forsake his faithful ones.

30 They shall be kept safe for ever, *
   but the offspring of the wicked shall be destroyed.

31 The righteous shall possess the land *
   and dwell in it for ever.

32 The mouth of the righteous utters wisdom, *
   and their tongue speaks what is right.

33 The law of their God is in their heart, *
   and their footsteps shall not falter.

Psalm 37 C *Considerat peccator*

Show how by your good life that your works are done with gentleness born of wisdom. Jm. 3:13

34 The wicked spy on the righteous *
   and seek occasion to kill them.

35 The LORD will not abandon them to their hand, *
   nor let them be found guilty when brought to trial.

36 Wait upon the LORD and keep his way; *
    he will raise you up to possess the land,
    and when the wicked are cut off, you will see it.

37 I have seen the wicked in their arrogance, *
    flourishing like a tree in full leaf.

38 I went by, and behold, they were not there; *
    I searched for them, but they could not be found.

39 Mark those who are honest;
   observe the upright; *
    for there is a future for the peaceable.

40 Transgressors shall be destroyed, one and all; *
    the future of the wicked is cut off.

41 But the deliverance of the righteous comes from the LORD; *
    he is their stronghold in time of trouble.

42 The LORD will help them and rescue them; *
    he will rescue them from the wicked and deliver them,
    because they seek refuge in him.

Lent Turn from evil, and do good, and dwell in the land for ever.
Easter Take delight in the LORD, and he shall give you your heart's desire, hallelujah.

Reading, Verse and Response, Collect and Conclusion as in the Proper of the Season or of the Day.

The Proper of the Saints

February

February 4
Cornelius the Centurion
Lesser Feast

From the Common of Holy Persons Page 628 with the following proper antiphons

Benedictus Antiphon In Caesarea there was a man named Cornelius, a centurion. He was a devout man who feared God with all his household; he gave alms generously to the people and prayed constantly to God.

Magnificat Antiphon Peter said, "Can anyone withhold the water for baptizing these people who have received the Holy Spirit just as we have?" So he ordered them to be baptized in the name of Jesus Christ.

Collect O God, by your Spirit you called Cornelius the Centurion to be the first Christian among the Gentiles: Grant to your Church such a ready will to go where you send and to do what you command, that under your guidance it may welcome all who turn to you in love and faith, and proclaim the Gospel to all nations; through Jesus Christ our Lord, who lives and reigns with you and the Holy Spirit, one God, for ever and ever. Amen.

February 5
Agatha of Sicily
Martyr c. 251
Lesser Feast

From the Common of Martyrs Page 597 with the following proper antiphons

Benedictus Antiphon As a bride going to her wedding chamber, Agatha went rejoicing to prison and offered herself as an oblation to God.

Magnificat Antiphon Lord Jesus Christ, my Good Master, I thank you for you have sustained me in my torments. Draw me, my Lord, into your glory which never fades.

Collect Almighty and everlasting God, who strengthened your martyr Agatha with constancy and courage: Grant us for the love of you to make no peace with oppression, to fear no adversity, and to have no tolerance for those who would use their power to abuse or exploit; Through Jesus Christ our Lord, to whom with you and the Holy Spirit be all honor and glory, now and for ever. Amen.

February 6
The Martyrs of Japan
1597
Lesser Feast
From the Common of Martyrs Page 597 with the following proper antiphons
Benedictus Antiphon When you walk through fire you shall not be burned, and the flame shall not consume you.

Magnificat Antiphon May I never boast of anything except the cross of our Lord Jesus Christ, by which the world has been crucified to me, and I to the world.

Collect O God our Father, source of strength to all your saints, you brought the holy martyrs of Japan through the suffering of the cross to the joys of eternal life: Grant that we, encouraged by their example, may hold fast the faith we profess, even to death itself; through Jesus Christ our Lord, who lives and reigns with you and the Holy Spirit, one God, now and for ever. Amen.

February 9
Anne Ayers
Professed Religious and Founder of the Sisterhood of the Holy Communion, 1896
Lesser Feast
From the Common of Professed Religious Page 624
Collect O God, whose blessed Son became poor that we through his poverty might be rich: Deliver us from an inordinate love of this world, that we, inspired by the devotion of your servant Anne Ayers, may serve you with singleness of heart, and attain to the riches of the age to come; through Jesus Christ our Lord, who lives and reigns with you, in the unity of the Holy Spirit, one God, now and for ever.
Amen.

February 10
Scholastica
Nun and Foundress
Principal Feast
From the Common of Monastics Page 620 with the following proper parts
Evening Prayer I
Hymn Blessed City Heavenly Salem *Hymnal 519*

Antiphon 1 The holy Nun Scholastica entreated her brother Benedict to stay with her all night that they might speak of the joys of heaven.
Psalms from Sunday Week 1 Evening Prayer I

February 10

Antiphon 2 In answer to her prayer, such a storm arose that Benedict could not put his head out of doors.

Antiphon 3 Scholastica said to her brother, "I desired you to stay, and you would not hear me; I have desired it of our good Lord, and he has granted my petition."

Reading I John 4: 7-16

Responsory (Jn. 15:7,4)
If you abide in me, and my words abide in you
  —ask for whatever you wish, and it will be done for you.
Abide in me as I abide in you
  —ask for whatever you wish, and it will be done for you.
Glory to the Father and to the Son and to the Holy Spirit.
If you abide in me, and my words abide in you
  —ask for whatever you wish, and it will be done for you.

Magnificat Antiphon Now this wise virgin has gone to Christ. Among the choirs of virgins, she is radiant as the sun in the heavens. Come, spouse of Christ, receive the crown the Lord has prepared for you.

Collect Almighty and ever-living God, who in your only-begotten Son opened for us a door of hope in this valley of tears, grant that we, like the virgin Saint Scholastica, may sing to you as in the days of our youth with purity of heart recovered and holy innocence restored, so that, having preferred nothing to the love of the Bridegroom Christ, it may be given us to sing your praise forever at the wedding feast of the Lamb through the same Christ our Lord. Amen.

The Blessing
May we run in the path of God's commandments, our hearts overflowing with the inexpressible delight of love. **Amen.**

Scholastica Morning Prayer

Invitatory Let us all rejoice in the Lord, celebrating the feast in honor of St. Scholastica, in whose blessed solemnity the angels rejoice and praise the Son of God.

Hymn Come Down O Love Divine *Hymnal 516*

Antiphon 1 I desired you to stay, and you would not hear me; I have desired it of our good Lord, and he has granted my petition.
Psalms from Sunday Week 1 Morning Prayer
Antiphon 2 Brother, if you can now depart, in God's name return to your monastery, and leave me here alone.

Antiphon 3 She who loved more, did more.

Reading One Song of Songs 8:1-7

Responsory One (Song 6:9)
The maidens saw her
  —**they called her blessed.**
My dove, my perfect one, is the only one.
  —**they called her blessed.**
Glory to the Father and to the Son and to the Holy Spirit.
The maidens saw her
  —**they called her blessed.**

    Canticle You are God *Te Deum laudamus, Page 667*

Canticle During Lent
Canticle of Jerusalem Betrothed *Propter Sion non tacebo*
(Isaiah 62:1-5)

Antiphon You shall be a crown of beauty in the hand of the Lord, and a royal diadem in the hand of your God.

For Zion's sake I will not keep silent, *
  and for Jerusalem's sake I will not rest,

Until her vindication shines out like the dawn, *
  and her salvation like a burning torch.

The nations shall see your vindication, *
  and all the kings your glory.

You shall be called by a new name *
  spoken by the mouth of the Lord.

You shall be a crown of beauty in the hand of the Lord, *
  and a royal diadem in the hand of your God.

You shall no more be termed "Forsaken," *
  and your land shall no more be termed "Desolate;"

You shall be called "My Delight," *
  and your land "Espoused."

For the Lord delights in you, *
  and your land shall be married.

For as a young man marries a young woman, *
  so shall your builder marry you,

And as the bridegroom rejoices over the bride, *
　so shall your God rejoice over you.

Antiphon You shall be a crown of beauty in the hand of the Lord, and a royal diadem in the hand of your God.

Reading Two Luke 10: 38-42

Responsory (Ps. 133:1,5)
Oh, how good and pleasant it is
　—when brethren live together in unity.
There the Lord has ordained the blessing
　—when brethren live together in unity.
Glory to the Father and to the Son and to the Holy Spirit.
Oh, how good and pleasant it is
　—when brethren live together in unity.

Benedictus Antiphon Arise my love, my fair one, my dove, who dwell in the cleft of the rock. Come and receive the crown which Christ has prepared for you.

Collect O Lord, who made Saint Scholastica resplendent with the brightness of an incomparable purity, grant that we may please you by the transparency of our daily lives and, by faithfulness in the school of your service, be found worthy of praising you in heaven with all the angels and saints. We make our prayer through our Lord Jesus Christ, your Son, who lives and reigns with you in the unity of the Holy Spirit, God forever and ever. Amen.

The Blessing
May we prefer nothing whatever to Christ, and may he bring us all together to everlasting life. **Amen.**

Scholastica Noonday Prayer
Hymn Like The Murmur Of The Dove's Song *Hymnal 513*

Antiphon At midnight there was a shout, "Look! Here is the bridegroom! Come out to meet him."
Psalms from Sunday Week 1 Noonday Prayer

Reading
2 Cor. 11: 2b
I promised you in marriage to one husband, to present you as a chaste virgin to Christ.

Verse and Response
You speak in my heart.
Your face, Lord, will I seek.

Collect O Lord, who made Saint Scholastica resplendent with the brightness of an incomparable purity, grant that we may please you by the transparency of our daily lives and, by faithfulness in the school of your service, be found worthy of praising you in heaven with all the angels and saints. We make our prayer through our Lord Jesus Christ, your Son, who lives and reigns with you in the unity of the Holy Spirit, God forever and ever. Amen.

Scholastica Evening Prayer II

Hymn Jerusalem The Golden *Hymnal 624*

Antiphon 1 You are beautiful, my love; you are beautiful; your eyes are doves.
Psalms from Sunday Week 1 Evening Prayer II
Antiphon 2 I slept, but my heart was awake. Listen! my beloved is knocking. "Open to me, my sister, my love, my dove, my perfect one."
Antiphon 3 Oh, that I had wings like a dove. I would fly away and be at rest.

Reading I John 3: 1-3, 21-23

Responsory (Lk 10:41)
She received more than her brother did from the Lord of her heart
   —because she loved him so much.
She has chosen the better part
   —because she loved him so much.
Glory to the Father and to the Son and to the Holy Spirit.
She received more than her brother did from the Lord of her heart
   —because she loved him so much.

Magnificat Antiphon Standing in his cell, and lifting up his eyes to heaven, Benedict beheld the soul of his sister Scholastica ascend into heaven in the likeness of a dove.

Collect God of love, to show us the beauty of holiness, you caused the soul of St. Scholastica to go up into heaven in the form of a dove. Grant that by her example, we may live in such peace and purity of heart as to enjoy everlasting happiness with her. Grant this through our Lord Jesus Christ, your Son, who lives and reigns with you in the unity of the Holy Spirit, God, for ever and ever. Amen.

The Blessing
May we run in the path of God's commandments, our hearts overflowing with the inexpressible delight of love. **Amen.**

February 13

Absalom Jones
Priest, 1818
Lesser Feast

From the Common of Pastors Page 601 with the following proper antiphons

Benedictus Antiphon We desire to walk in the liberty wherewith Christ has made us free that following peace with all, we may have our fruit unto holiness, and in the end, everlasting life.

Magnificat Antiphon We have gone forward to erect a house for the glory of God, and our mutual advantage to meet in for clarification and social religious worship and more particularly to keep an open door for those of our race.

Collect Set us free, heavenly Father, from every bond of prejudice and fear; that, honoring the steadfast courage of your servant Absalom Jones, we may show forth in our lives the reconciling love and true freedom of the children of God, which you have given us in your Son our Savior Jesus Christ; who lives and reigns with you and the Holy Spirit, one God, now and for ever. Amen.

February 14

Cyril, Monk, and Methodius, Bishop
Missionaries to the Slavs, 869, 885
Lesser Feast

From the Common of Missionaries Page 612

Collect Almighty and everlasting God, by the power of the Holy Spirit you moved your servant Cyril and his brother Methodius to bring the light of the Gospel to a hostile and divided people: Overcome all bitterness and strife among us by the love of Christ, and make us one united family under the banner of the Prince of Peace; who lives and reigns with you and the Holy Spirit, one God, now and for ever. Amen.

February 15

Thomas Bray
Priest and Missionary, 1730
Lesser Feast

From the Common of Missionaries Page 612

Collect O God of compassion, you opened the eyes of your servant Thomas Bray to see the needs of the Church in the New World, and led him to found societies to meet those needs: Make the Church in this land diligent at all times to propagate the Gospel among those who have not received it, and to promote the spread of Christian knowledge; through Jesus Christ our Lord, who lives and reigns with you and the Holy Spirit, one God, for ever and ever. Amen.

February 17
Janani Luwum
Archbishop of Uganda, and Martyr, 1977
Lesser Feast

From the Common of Martyrs Page 597

Collect O God, whose Son the Good Shepherd laid down his life for the sheep: We give you thanks for your faithful shepherd Janani Luwum, who after his Savior's example, gave up his life for the people of Uganda. Grant us to be so inspired by his witness that we make no peace with oppression, but live as those who are sealed with the cross of Christ, who died and rose again, and now lives and reigns with you and the Holy Spirit, one God, for ever and ever. Amen.

February 18
Martin Luther
Reformer, 1546
Lesser Feast

From the Common of Theologians and Teachers Page 605

Collect O God, our refuge and our strength: You raised up your servant Martin Luther to reform and renew your Church in the light of your word. Defend and purify the Church in our own day and grant that, through faith, we may boldly proclaim the riches of your grace which you have made known in Jesus Christ our Savior, who with you and the Holy Spirit, lives and reigns, one God, now and for ever. Amen.

February 22
Margaret of Cortona
Franciscan Tertiary, 1297
Lesser Feast

From the Common of Holy Persons Page 628

Collect O God, as your servant Margaret of Cortona found a home where her repentance led to a life of prayer, service, and leadership, Grant that we may always seek to dwell where estrangement yields to reconciliation, through Jesus Christ, who is himself the goal of all our seeking and the answer to our desires, unto whom, with you and the Holy Spirit, be honor and glory, now and forever. Amen.

February 23

Polycarp
Bishop and Martyr of Smyrna, 156
Lesser Feast

From the Common of Martyrs Page 597 with the following proper antiphons

Benedictus Antiphon Eighty six years have I have served him and he has done me no wrong. How can I blaspheme my King and my Savior?"

Magnificat Antiphon O Lord God Almighty I give you thanks that you count me worthy to be numbered among your martyrs, sharing the cup of Christ and the resurrection to eternal life, both of soul and body, through the immortality of the Holy Spirit.

Collect O God, the maker of heaven and earth, you gave your venerable servant, the holy and gentle Polycarp, boldness to confess Jesus Christ as King and Savior, and steadfastness to die for his faith: Give us grace, following his example, to share the cup of Christ and rise to eternal life; through Jesus Christ our Lord, who lives and reigns with you and the Holy Spirit, one God, now and for ever. Amen.

February 24

Saint Matthias the Apostle
Major Feast

From the Common of Apostles Page 579 with the following proper antiphons

Benedictus Antiphon So one of the men who have accompanied us during all the time that the Lord Jesus went in and out among us, one of these must become a witness with us to his resurrection.

Magnificat Antiphon Lord, you know everyone's heart. They cast lots for them, and the lot fell on Matthias; and he was added to the eleven apostles.

Collect Almighty God, who in the place of Judas chose your faithful servant Matthias to be numbered among the Twelve: Grant that your Church, being delivered from false apostles, may always be guided and governed by faithful and true pastors; through Jesus Christ our Lord, who lives and reigns with you, in the unity of the Holy Spirit, one God, now and for ever. Amen.

February 25
Walburga
Benedictine Abbess of Double Monastery of Heidenheim and Missionary, c 777
Lesser Feast

From the Common of Monastics Page 620 with the following proper antiphons

Benedictus Antiphon Walburga, a model of monastic life, gathered together nuns consecrated to Christ and fulfilled the Lord's command with all zeal and eagerness.

Magnificat Antiphon You, Lord, to whom I have been dedicated from my earliest youth, have made me worthy, I who am unworthy, to receive of your divine light to lead me home.

Collect Almighty and merciful God, by your grace blessed Walburga left all things to follow the poor and humble Christ. Perfect the work of conversion which you have begun in us; through Jesus Christ our Lord, who lives and reigns with you and the Holy Spirit, one God, for ever and ever. Amen.

February 26
Photini, The Samaritan Woman
Equal to the Apostles
Lesser Feast
Morning Prayer

From the Common of the Apostles Page 580 with the following proper parts.

Invitatory Christ is the Living Water; come let us drink from the well of salvation.

Hymn The eternal gifts of Christ the King *Hymnal 233*

Antiphon 1 Jesus came to a Samaritan city called Sychar. Jacob's well was there, and Jesus, tired out by his journey, was sitting by the well.
Psalms from the current day of the week.
Antiphon 2 A Samaritan woman came to draw water, and Jesus said to her, "Give me a drink." The Samaritan woman said to him, "How is it that you, a Jew, ask a drink of me, a woman of Samaria?"
Antiphon 3 If you knew the gift of God, and who it is that is saying to you, 'Give me a drink,' you would have asked him, and he would have given you living water.

Reading One 2 Kings 17:28-41

Responsory One (Jn. 4;23; Jn. 9:31)
The true worshipers will worship the Father
— in spirit and truth.
God listens to one who worships him and obeys his will
— in spirit and truth.
Glory to the Father and to the Son and to the Holy Spirit.
The true worshipers will worship the Father
— **in spirit and truth.**

Canticle – Song of the Mystery of Christ *In mysterio Christi*
(Ephesians 3: 5-10)

Antiphon I will give water as a gift from the spring of the water of life.

The mystery of Christ was not made known to humankind *
in former generations.

It has now been revealed *
to his holy apostles and prophets by the Spirit.

The Gentiles have become fellow-heirs,
members of the same body, *
and sharers in the promise in Christ Jesus through the gospel.

Of this gospel I have become a servant *
according to the gift of God's grace.

The Gospel was given to me *
by the working of God's power.

Although I am the very least of all the saints, *
this grace was given to me:

To bring to the Gentiles
the news of the boundless riches of Christ, *
and to make everyone see what is the plan of the mystery.

That mystery of Christ lay hidden for ages in God *
who created all things;

So that through the church *
the wisdom of God in its rich variety

Might now be made known *
to the rulers and authorities in the heavenly places.

Antiphon I will give water as a gift from the spring of the water of life.

Reading Two John 4:1–26

February 26

Responsory Two (Song 4:15: Gen. 24: 13)
You are a garden fountain, a well of living water
  – and flowing streams from Lebanon.
I am standing here by the spring of water
  – and flowing streams from Lebanon.
Glory to the Father and to the Son and to the Holy Spirit.
You are a garden fountain, a well of living water
  – and flowing streams from Lebanon.

Benedictus Antiphon The hour is coming, and is now here, when the true worshipers will worship the Father in spirit and truth, for the Father seeks such as these to worship him. God is spirit, and those who worship him must worship in spirit and truth."

Collect O Almighty God, whose most blessed Son revealed to the Samaritan woman that He is indeed the Christ, the Savior of the World; grant us to drink of the well that springs up to everlasting life that we may worship you in spirit and in truth through your Son, Jesus Christ our Lord. Amen.

Photini, The Samaritan Woman Noonday Prayer

Antiphon Illuminated by the Holy Spirit, Photini, equal to the apostles, drank the water of salvation from Christ the Savior. With an open hand she gave it to those who thirst.
Psalms from the current day of the week.

Reading Isaiah 55: 1-3
Ho, everyone who thirsts, come to the waters; and you that have no money, come, buy and eat! Come, buy wine and milk without money and without price. Why do you spend your money for that which is not bread, and your labor for that which does not satisfy? Listen carefully to me, and eat what is good, and delight yourselves in rich food. Incline your ear, and come to me; listen, so that you may live.

Verse and Response
My food is to do the will of him who sent me.
And to complete my Father's work.

Collect *From Morning Prayer*

Photini, The Samaritan Woman Evening Prayer
From the Common of the Apostles Page 583 with the following proper parts

Hymn Jesus Lover of my soul *Hymnal 699*

Antiphon 1 Those who drink of the water that I will give them will never be thirsty. The water that I will give will become in them a spring of water gushing up to eternal life.
Psalms from the current day of the week.
Antiphon 2 The hour is coming when you will worship the Father neither on this mountain nor in Jerusalem. The true worshipers will worship the Father in spirit and truth
Antiphon 3 The woman left her water jar and went back to the city. She said to the people, "Come and see a man who told me everything I have ever done! He cannot be the Messiah, can he?"

Reading Isaiah 55: 1-5

Responsory (Jn. 7:37-38; Is. 12:4)
Let anyone who is thirsty come to me
    – let the one who believes in me drink.
With joy you will draw water from the wells of salvation
    – let the one who believes in me drink.
Glory to the Father and to the Son and to the Holy Spirit.
Let anyone who is thirsty come to me
    – **let the one who believes in me drink.**

Magnificat Antiphon The woman said to him, "I know that Messiah is coming. When he comes, he will proclaim all things to us." Jesus said to her, "I am he, the one who is speaking to you."

Collect *From Morning Prayer*

February 27
George Herbert
Priest, 1633
Lesser Feast
From the Common of Theologians and Teachers Page 605 with the following antiphons
Benedictus Antiphon Come, my Light, my Feast, my Strength : such a Light, as shows a feast; such a Feast, as mends in length : such a Strength, as makes his guest.

Magnificat Antiphon My God, thou art all love. And in this love, more than in bed, I rest.

Collect Our God and King, you called your servant George Herbert from the pursuit of worldly honors to be a pastor of souls, a poet, and a priest in your temple: Give us grace, we pray, joyfully to perform the tasks you give us to do, knowing that nothing is menial or common that is done for your sake; through Jesus Christ our Lord, who lives and reigns with you and the Holy Spirit, one God, for ever and ever. Amen.

February 28

Anna Julia Haywood Cooper
Educator, 1964
Lesser Feast

From the Common of Holy Persons Page 628

Collect Almighty God, you inspired your servant Anna Julia Haywood Cooper with the love of learning and the skill of teaching: Enlighten us more and more through the discipline of learning, and deepen our commitment to the education of all your children; through Jesus Christ our Lord, who lives and reigns with you and the Holy Spirit, one God, for ever and ever. Amen.

March

March 1

David
Bishop of Menevia, Wales, c. 544
Lesser Feast

From the Common of Pastors Page 601

Collect Almighty God, you called your servant David to be a faithful and wise steward of your mysteries for the people of Wales: Mercifully grant that, following his purity of life and zeal for the Gospel of Christ, we may with him receive our heavenly reward; through Jesus Christ our Lord, who lives and reigns with you and the Holy Spirit, one God, for ever and ever. Amen.

March 2

Chad
Bishop of Lichfield, 672
Lesser Feast

From the Common of Pastors Page 601

Collect Almighty God, for the peace of the Church your servant Chad relinquished cheerfully the honors that had been thrust upon him, only to be rewarded with equal responsibility: Keep us, we pray, from thinking of ourselves more highly than we ought to think, and ready at all times to step aside for others, that the cause of Christ may be advanced; through him who lives and reigns with you and the Holy Spirit, one God, now and for ever. Amen.

March 3
John and Charles Wesley
Priests, 1791, 1788
Lesser Feast

From the Common of Pastors Page 601
Collect Lord God, you inspired your servants John and Charles Wesley with burning zeal for the sanctification of souls, and endowed them with eloquence in speech and song: Kindle in your Church, we entreat you, such fervor, that those whose faith has cooled may be warmed, and those who have not known Christ may turn to him and be saved; who lives and reigns with you and the Holy Spirit, one God, now and for ever. Amen.

March 7
Perpetua, Felicitas and their Companions
Martyrs at Carthage, 202
Lesser Feast

From the Common of Martyrs Page 597 with the following proper antiphons
Benedictus Antiphon The day of the martyrs' victory dawned. They marched from their cells into the amphitheater, as if into heaven. If they trembled it was for joy and not for fear.

Magnificat Antiphon I began to walk in triumph towards the Gate of Life. I knew that I would win the victory.

Collect O God the King of saints, you strengthened your servants Perpetua and Felicitas and their companions to make a good confession, staunchly resisting, for the cause of Christ, the claims of human affection, and encouraging one another in their time of trial: Grant that we who cherish their blessed memory may share their pure and steadfast faith, and win with them the palm of victory; through Jesus Christ our Lord, who lives and reigns with you and the Holy Spirit, one God, for ever and ever. Amen.

March 9
Gregory
Bishop of Nyssa, c. 394
Lesser Feast

From the Common of Theologians and Teachers Page 605
Collect Almighty God, you have revealed to your Church your eternal Being of glorious majesty and perfect love as one God in Trinity of

Persons: Give us grace that, like your bishop Gregory of Nyssa, we may continue steadfast in the confession of this faith, and constant in our worship of you, Father, Son, and Holy Spirit; for you live and reign for ever and ever. Amen.

March 9
Frances of Rome
Married Woman, Religious Founder, Benedictine Oblate, 1440
Lesser Feast

From the Common of Monastics Page 620

Collect Father of mercy, you called Frances of Rome to serve you in marriage and as a Benedictine oblate. Give us grace to balance our life commitments and focus our hearts on you; through Jesus Christ our Lord, who lives and reigns with you and the Holy Spirit, one God, for ever and ever. Amen.

March 12
Gregory the Great
Monk, Bishop of Rome and Teacher of the Faith, 604
Lesser Feast

From the Common of Teacher of the Faith Page 608 with the following antiphons

Benedictus Antiphon In the midst of the Church, he spoke with great persuasion. The Lord filled him with the Spirit of wisdom and understanding.

Magnificat Antiphon O Blessed Gregory, wise and learned teacher of the church, servant of the servants of God, lover of the monastic life, we join you in prayer to God.

Collect Almighty and merciful God, you raised up Gregory of Rome to be a servant of the servants of God, and inspired him to send missionaries to preach the Gospel to the English people: Preserve in your Church the catholic and apostolic faith they taught, that your people, being fruitful in every good work, may receive the crown of glory that never fades away; through Jesus Christ our Lord, who lives and reigns with you and the Holy Spirit, one God, for ever and ever. Amen.

March 13
James Theodore Holly
Bishop of Haiti, and of the Dominican Republic, 1911
Lesser Feast

From the Common of Pastors Page 601

Collect Most gracious God, by the calling of your servant James Theodore Holly you gave us our first bishop of African American heritage. In his quest for life and freedom, he led your people from bondage into a new land and established the Church in Haiti. Grant that, inspired by his testimony, we may overcome our prejudice and honor those whom you call from every family, language, people, and nation; through Jesus Christ our Lord, who lives and reigns with you and the Holy Spirit, one God, now and for ever. Amen.

March 17

Patrick
Bishop and Missionary of Ireland, 461
Lesser Feast

From the Common of Missionaries Page 612

Collect Almighty God, in your providence you chose your servant Patrick to be the apostle of the Irish people, to bring those who were wandering in darkness and error to the true light and knowledge of you: Grant us so to walk in that light that we may come at last to the light of everlasting life; through Jesus Christ our Lord, who lives and reigns with you and the Holy Spirit, one God, for ever and ever. Amen.

March 18

Cyril
Bishop of Jerusalem and Teacher of the Faith, 386
Lesser Feast

From the Common of Teacher of the Faith Page 608

Collect Strengthen, O Lord, the bishops of your Church in their special calling to be teachers and ministers of the Sacraments, so that they, like your servant Cyril of Jerusalem, may effectively instruct your people in Christian faith and practice; and that we, taught by them, may enter more fully into the celebration of the Paschal mystery; through Jesus Christ our Lord, who lives and reigns with you and the Holy Spirit, one God, now and for ever. Amen.

March 19

Saint Joseph
Major Feast
Evening Prayer I

Hymn Come now, and praise the humble saint *Hymnal 260*

Antiphon 1 Jacob was the father of Joseph the husband of Mary, of whom Jesus was born, who is called the Messiah. (Alleluia)
Psalms from Sunday Week 1 Evening Prayer I

Antiphon 2 Now the birth of Jesus the Messiah took place in this way. When his mother Mary had been engaged to Joseph, but before they lived together, she was found to be with child from the Holy Spirit. (Alleluia)

Antiphon 3 Joseph, son of David, do not be afraid to take Mary as your wife, for the child conceived in her is from the Holy Spirit. She will bear a son, and you are to name him Jesus. (Alleluia)

Reading 2 Chronicles 6: 12-17

Responsory (1 Kg. 8:23; Mt. 1:21)
O Lord, God of Israel, there is no God like you,
     −you keep your steadfast love with your servants.
You are to name him Jesus, for he will save his people from their sins
     −you keep your steadfast love with your servants.
Glory to the Father, and to the Son and to the Holy Spirit.
O Lord, God of Israel, there is no God like you,
     −you keep your steadfast love with your servants.

Magnificat Antiphon When Joseph awoke from sleep, he did as the angel of the Lord commanded him; he took Mary as his wife. (Alleluia)

Litany
Joseph was the spouse of Mary and head of the holy family of Nazareth, may you strengthen us in our different families.
Lord, have mercy.
Joseph endured the uncertainty of life as a refugee, may you uphold all who are in exile and all who are displaced.
Christ, have mercy.
Joseph entered into the promised life of the blessed in heaven, may you rescue all the dead from the power of darkness and draw them into the light of life.
Lord, have mercy.

Invitation to the Lord's Prayer
As we bow before the Father, from whom every family in heaven and on earth is named, let us pray that according to the riches of God's glory we may be strengthened with might through the Spirit.

Collect O God, who from the family of your servant David raised up Joseph to be the guardian of your incarnate Son and the spouse of his virgin mother: Give us grace to imitate his uprightness of life and his obedience to your commands; through Jesus Christ our Lord, who lives and reigns with you and the Holy Spirit, one God, for ever and ever. Amen.

The Blessing
May we rejoice and sing for the Lord, our God, is in our midst: the God who will rejoice over us with gladness, who will renew us in his love; who will exult over us with loud singing. **Amen.**

Saint Joseph Morning Prayer

Invitatory Let us celebrate the feast of St. Joseph: Come let us worship Christ, the Incarnate Word. (Alleluia)

Hymn By the Creator, Joseph was appointed *Hymnal 261*

Antiphon 1 The angel Gabriel was sent by God to a town in Galilee called Nazareth, to a virgin engaged to a man whose name was Joseph, of the house of David. The virgin's name was Mary. (Alleluia)

Psalms from Sunday Week 1 Morning Prayer

Antiphon 2 Joseph went from the town of Nazareth in Galilee to Judea, to the city of David called Bethlehem, because he was descended from the house and family of David. (Alleluia)

Antiphon 3 While they were there, the time came for her to deliver her child. And she gave birth to her firstborn son and wrapped him in bands of cloth, and laid him in a manger, because there was no place for them in the inn. (Alleluia)

Reading One Isaiah 63: 1-13

Responsory (Is. 63:9; Is. 63:7)
It was no messenger or angel but his presence that saved them
 — **he lifted them up and carried them all the days of old.**
God has shown them great favor according to his mercy.
 — **he lifted them up and carried them all the days of old.**
Glory to the Father, and to the Son and to the Holy Spirit.
It was no messenger or angel but his presence that saved them
 — **he lifted them up and carried them all the days of old.**

Canticle of the Incarnate Word *In principio*
(John 1: 1-5, 9-12, 14, 16, 18)

Antiphon For his faithfulness and meekness God consecrated him, choosing him out of all humankind. (Alleluia)

In the beginning was the Word, *
 and the Word was with God,

The Word was God. *
    He was in the beginning with God;
All things were made through him, *
    and without him was not anything made that was made.

In him was life, *
    and the life was the light of all.

The light shines in the darkness, *
    and the darkness has not overcome it.

The true light that enlightens everyone *
    was coming into the world.

He was in the world, *
    and the world was made through him,
    yet the world knew him not.

He came to his own home, *
    and his own people received him not.

But to all who received him, who believed in his name, *
    he gave power to become children of God;

And the Word became flesh *
    and dwelt among us,
    full of grace and truth;

We have beheld his glory, *
    glory as of the only Son from the Father.

And from his fullness have we all received, *
    grace upon grace.

No one has ever seen God; *
    the only Son, who is in the bosom of the Father,
    he has made him known.

Antiphon For his faithfulness and meekness God consecrated him, choosing him out of all humankind. (Alleluia)

Reading Two Matthew 1: 18-25

Responsory (Mt. 1:21, 22)
Joseph, son of David, do not be afraid to take Mary as your wife
    – the child conceived in her is from the Holy Spirit.
The child to be born will be holy; he will be called Son of God.
    – the child conceived in her is from the Holy Spirit.

Glory to the Father, and to the Son and to the Holy Spirit.
Joseph, son of David, do not be afraid to take Mary as your wife
  —the child conceived in her is from the Holy Spirit.

Benedictus Antiphon The shepherds went with haste and found Mary and Joseph, and the child lying in the manger. They made known what had been told them about this child. (Alleluia)

Litany
Joseph showed his righteousness and shielded Mary from disgrace; may you raise up champions to answer the victims of human trafficking and abuse.
Lord, have mercy.
Joseph raised Jesus to grow in wisdom and grace; may your Spirit accompany all children to develop wisdom through your Spirit.
Christ, have mercy.
Joseph came from the ancient line of Abraham; may you help us understand our connection in faith with Jews and Muslims who share the faith of Abraham
Lord, have mercy.

Invitation to the Lord's Prayer
As we celebrate Joseph and his obedience to your word, open our hearts to hear your Spirit speaking in us as we pray.

Collect *From Evening Prayer I*

The Blessing
May we rejoice and sing for the Lord, our God, is in our midst: the God who will rejoice over us with gladness, who will renew us in his love; who will exult over us with loud singing. **Amen.**

Saint Joseph Noonday Prayer
Hymn By all thy saints still striving *Hymnal 231*

Antiphon An angel of the Lord appeared to Joseph in a dream and said, 'Get up, take the child and his mother, and flee to Egypt, and remain there until I tell you; for Herod is seeking the child, to destroy him.' (Alleluia)
Psalms from Sunday Week 1 Noonday Prayer

Reading Hebrews 11: 13-16
All of these died in faith without having received the promises, but from a distance they saw and greeted them. They confessed that they were strangers and foreigners on the earth, for people who speak in this way

make it clear that they are seeking a homeland. If they had been thinking of the land that they had left behind, they would have had opportunity to return. But as it is, they desire a better country, that is, a heavenly one. Therefore God is not ashamed to be called their God; indeed, he has prepared a city for them.

Verse and Response
The just man was strengthened in his faith. (Alleluia)
Therefore through faith he was counted as justified. (Alleluia)

Collect *From Evening Prayer I*

Saint Joseph Evening Prayer II

Hymn Come now, and praise the humble saint *Hymnal 260*

Antiphon 1 Philip found Nathanael and said to him, 'We have found him about whom Moses in the law and also the prophets wrote, Jesus son of Joseph from Nazareth.' (Alleluia)

Psalms from Sunday Week 1 Evening Prayer II

Antiphon 2 All spoke well of him and were amazed at the gracious words that came from his mouth. They said, 'Is not this Joseph's son?' (Alleluia)

Antiphon 3 'Is not this Jesus, the son of Joseph, whose father and mother we know? How can he now say, "I have come down from heaven?"' (Alleluia)

Reading Ephesians 3: 14-21

Responsory (Eph. 3:17, 19)
May Christ dwell in your hearts through faith,
  –as you are being rooted and grounded in love.
May you be filled with all the fullness of God.
  –as you are being rooted and grounded in love.
Glory to the Father, and to the Son and to the Holy Spirit.
May Christ dwell in your hearts through faith,
  –as you are being rooted and grounded in love.

Magnificat Antiphon He will be great, and will be called the Son of the Most High, and the Lord God will give to him the throne of his ancestor David. He will reign over the house of Jacob for ever, and of his kingdom there will be no end. (Alleluia)

Litany

Joseph was the spouse of Mary and head of the holy family of Nazareth, may you strengthen us in our different families.
Lord, have mercy.
Joseph endured the uncertainty of life as a refugee, may you uphold all who are in exile and all who are displaced.
Christ, have mercy.
Joseph entered into the promised life of the blessed in heaven, may you rescue all the dead from the power of darkness and draw them into the light of life.
Lord, have mercy.

Invitation to the Lord's Prayer

As we bow before the Father, from whom every family in heaven and on earth is named, let us pray that according to the riches of God's glory we may be strengthened with might through his Spirit.

Collect *From Evening Prayer I*

The Blessing

May we rejoice and sing for the Lord, our God, is in our midst: the God who will rejoice over us with gladness, who will renew us in his love; who will exult over us with loud singing. **Amen.**

March 20

Cuthbert
Monk and Bishop of Lindisfarne, 687
Lesser Feast

From the Common of Pastors, Page 601

Collect Almighty God, you called Cuthbert from following the flock to be a shepherd of your people: Mercifully grant that, as he sought in dangerous and remote places those who had erred and strayed from your ways, so we may seek the indifferent and the lost, and lead them back to you; through Jesus Christ our Lord, who lives and reigns with you and the Holy Spirit, one God, for ever and ever. Amen.

March 21

Transitus of St. Benedict
Principal Feast
Evening Prayer I

Hymn Jerusalem My Happy Home *Hymnal 620*

Antiphon 1 Benedict never lost hope in God's mercy. He received the reward the Lord promised. (Alleluia)

Psalms from Sunday Week 1 Evening Prayer I

Antiphon 2 He cherished Christ above all and entered the glory of everlasting life. (Alleluia)

Antiphon 3 Blessed Benedict preferred nothing to Christ who has brought him with the saints to everlasting life. (Alleluia)

Reading Romans 12: 1-14

Responsory
Holy Father Benedict
    —pray for us.
That we may be worthy of the promises of Christ
    —pray for us.
Glory to the Father, and to the Son and to the Holy Spirit.
Holy Father Benedict
    —pray for us.

Magnificat Antiphon Today Holy Benedict, in the presence of his disciples, ascended to heaven. Today with hand uplifted, he died between the words of his prayer. Today he was received into glory by the Holy Angels. (Alleluia)

Litany
You opened our ears and we have answered your call, teach us the hidden way of obedience.
Lord, have mercy.
You sent us your Spirit and we heard your voice inviting us, deepen our conversion that we may discern your love showing us the way of life.
Christ, have mercy.
You summoned our holy Father Benedict, your beloved, to walk a glorious road to heaven, so take all departed Benedictines and all the dead to follow him on that same path.
Lord, have mercy.

Invitation to the Lord's Prayer
Together with St. Benedict, St. Scholastica and holy monks, nuns and oblates of all times and places, let us raise our voices in prayer to the Father.

Collect Lord, our God, you filled the blessed abbot Benedict with the spirit of your Son and made him a master in the way of perfection. As we celebrate his entrance into glory, may we attain that love, which surpasses all understanding. Through Jesus Christ, our Lord, who lives and reigns with you in the unity of the Holy Spirit, one God forever and ever. Amen.

The Blessing
May the word of Christ dwell in us richly as we teach and admonish one another in all wisdom. **Amen.**

Transitus of St. Benedict Morning Prayer

Invitatory Let us all rejoice in the Lord, who bestowed a robe of glory on our Father Benedict. (Alleluia)

Hymn Blessed City Heavenly Salem *Hymnal 519*

Antiphon 1 There was a man of holy life, Benedict, blessed by grace and name; from his youth, he manifested the mind of a mature man. (Alleluia)

Psalms from Sunday Week 1 Morning Prayer

Antiphon 2 The confessor of the Lord, lead the angelic life on earth. He rejoices with Christ forever in heaven. (Alleluia)

Antiphon 3 Benedict was adorned with angelic ways; although dwelling on earth, he lived as among the saints in heaven. (Alleluia)

Reading One Sirach 45: 1-5

Responsory One (Sir 45: 1,9)
The Lord loved him
—and clothed him with a robe of glory.
The Lord made an everlasting covenant with him
—and clothed him with a robe of glory.
Glory to the Father, and to the Son and to the Holy Spirit.
The Lord loved him
—and clothed him with a robe of glory.

Canticle You are God *Te Deum laudamus, Page 667*

Canticle During Lent
Canticle of the Learned *Beatus qui in sapientia*
(Sirach 14:22; 15:3.4.6b)

Antiphon Blessed Benedict, beloved of the Lord, was anointed with the Spirit of the Lord and was filled with the spirit of all the righteous.

Blessed are they who meditate on wisdom *
    and reason intelligently,

Who reflect in their hearts on her ways *
    and ponder her secrets,

She will feed them with the bread of learning, *
    and give them the water of wisdom to drink.

They will lean on her and not fall, *
> and they will rely on her and not be put to shame.

She will exalt them above their neighbors, *
> and will open their mouths in the midst of the assembly.

They will find gladness and a crown of rejoicing, *
> and will inherit an everlasting name.

Antiphon Blessed Benedict, beloved of the Lord, was anointed with the Spirit of the Lord and was filled with the spirit of all the righteous.

Reading Two Hebrews 11: 8-16

Responsory Two (Sir 45:1,3)
He was beloved by God and people,
> **—his memory is blessed.**

For his faithfulness and meekness the Lord consecrated him
> **—his memory is blessed.**

Glory to the Father, and to the Son and to the Holy Spirit.
He was beloved by God and people,
> **—his memory is blessed.**

Benedictus Antiphon Benedict, father and guide of monks, nuns and oblates, most holy Confessor of the Lord, intercede for us and for our salvation. (Alleluia)

Litany
With Benedictine monks, nuns and oblates, we join with all monastics, of the West and the East, and pray that you lead us deeper into your mystery.
Lord, have mercy.
As we have risen from sleep, open our eyes to your deifying light that we may live this day as your beloved daughters and sons.
Christ, have mercy.
Since God has given us the light of life, let us run this day and do what will profit us forever.
Lord, have mercy.

Invitation to the Lord's Prayer
Together with St. Benedict, St. Scholastica and holy monks, nuns and oblates of all times and places, let us raise our voices in prayer to the Father.

Collect *From Evening Prayer I*

The Blessing
May we prefer nothing whatever to Christ, and may he bring us all together to everlasting life. **Amen.**

Transitus of St. Benedict Noonday Prayer

Hymn Blest Are The Pure Of Heart *Hymnal 656*

Antiphon He persevered as though he saw him who is invisible. (Alleluia)
Psalms from Sunday Week 1 Noonday Prayer

Reading Exodus 17: 10-12
Joshua did as Moses told him, and fought with Amalek, while Moses, Aaron, and Hur went up to the top of the hill. Whenever Moses held up his hand, Israel prevailed; and whenever he lowered his hand, Amalek prevailed. But Moses' hands grew weary; so they took a stone and put it under him, and he sat on it. Aaron and Hur held up his hands, one on one side, and the other on the other side; so his hands were steady until the sun set.

Verse and Response
On the arms of his brethren, he stood with his hands raised to heaven. (Alleluia)
As he prayed, he breathed his last. (Alleluia)

Collect *From Evening Prayer I*

Transitus of St. Benedict Evening Prayer II

Hymn Jerusalem The Golden *Hymnal 624*

Antiphon 1 Benedict's disciples carried him to the Oratory where Benedict did arm himself for his death by receiving the Body and Blood of our Lord. (Alleluia)
Psalms from Sunday Week 1 Evening Prayer II
Antiphon 2 His disciples supported his weak limbs. Benedict stood up, his hands lifted toward heaven and with prayer he breathed forth his soul. (Alleluia)
Antiphon 3 The monks beheld a way stretching from his cell to heaven spread with garments and shining with numerous lamps. This is the way by which Benedict, beloved of the Lord, ascended to God. (Alleluia)

Reading Luke 14:26-33

Responsory (Sir 45: 1,9)
The Lord loved him
  —and clothed him with a robe of glory.
The Lord made an everlasting covenant with him
  —and clothed him with a robe of glory.
Glory to the Father, and to the Son and to the Holy Spirit.
The Lord loved him
  —and clothed him with a robe of glory.

Magnificat Antiphon Today Holy Benedict, in the presence of his disciples, ascended to heaven. Today with hand uplifted, he died between the words of his prayer. Today he was received into glory by the Holy Angels. (Alleluia)

Litany
You opened our ears and we have answered your call, teach us the hidden way of obedience.
Lord, have mercy.
You sent us your Spirit and we heard your voice inviting us, deepen our conversion that we may discern your love showing us the way of life.
Christ, have mercy.
You summoned our holy Father Benedict, your beloved, to walk a glorious road to heaven, so take all departed Benedictines and all the dead to follow him on that same path.
Lord, have mercy.

Invitation to the Lord's Prayer
Together with St. Benedict, St. Scholastica and holy monks, nuns and oblates of all times and places, let us raise our voices in prayer to the Father.

Collect *From Evening Prayer I*

The Blessing
May the word of Christ dwell in us richly as we teach and admonish one another in all wisdom. **Amen.**

March 22

James De Koven
Priest, 1879
Lesser Feast

From the Common of Pastors Page 601
Collect Almighty and everlasting God, the source and perfection of all virtues, you inspired your servant James De Koven to do what is right

and to preach what is true: Grant that all ministers and stewards of your mysteries may impart to your faithful people, by word and example, the knowledge of your grace; through Jesus Christ our Lord, who lives and reigns with you and the Holy Spirit, one God, for ever and ever. Amen.

March 23
Gregory the Illuminator
Bishop and Missionary of Armenia, c. 332
Lesser Feast

From the Common of Missionaries Page 612

Collect Almighty God, whose will it is to be glorified in your saints, and who raised up your servant Gregory the Illuminator to be a light in the world, and to preach the Gospel to the people of Armenia: Shine, we pray, in our hearts, that we also in our generation may show forth your praise, who called us out of darkness into your marvelous light; through Jesus Christ our Lord, who lives and reigns with you and the Holy Spirit, one God, now and for ever. Amen.

March 24
Óscar Romero
Archbishop of San Salvador and Martyr, 1980
Maura Clarke and Ita Ford, Maryknoll Sisters; Dorothy Kazel, Ursuline Sister, and Jean Donovan, Lay Missionary
Martyrs, 1980
Ignacio Ellacuría, Ignacio Martín-Baró, Segundo Montes, Juan Ramón Moreno, Joaquín López y López, Amando López,
Jesuits and Martyrs, 1989
Elba Ramos and Celina Ramos
Martyrs, 1989
Lesser Feast

From the Common of Martyrs Page 597 with the following proper antiphons

Canticle Antiphon One who is committed to the poor must risk the same fate as the poor.

Benedictus Antiphon I hope that you come to find that which gives life a deep meaning for you. Something worth living for – maybe even worth dying for.

Collect Almighty God, you called your servant Oscar Romero and the Martyrs of San Salvador to be a voice for the voiceless poor, and to give their lives as seeds of freedom and signs of hope: Grant that, inspired by their sacrifice, we may without fear or favor witness to your Word who abides, your Word who is Life, even Jesus Christ our Lord, to whom, with you and the Holy Spirit, be praise and glory now and for ever. Amen.

March 25
The Annunciation of Our Lord Jesus Christ
to the Blessed Virgin Mary
Feast of our Lord
Evening Prayer I

Hymn The angel Gabriel from heaven came *Hymnal 265*

Antiphon 1 The Lord said to me, you are my Son; this day have I begotten you. (Alleluia)
Psalms from Sunday Week 1 Evening Prayer I
Antiphon 2 The Lord God has given him the throne of his father David, and he will reign for ever and ever. (Alleluia)
Antiphon 3 When the Son came into the world he said: I have come to do your will, O God. (Alleluia)

Reading Genesis 3:1-15 or Romans 5:12-21 or Galatians 4:1-7

Responsory (Gal. 4:4; Jn. 8:42)
When the fullness of time had come
　　—**God sent his Son, born of a woman.**
I came from God and now I am here
　　—**God sent his Son, born of a woman.**
Glory to the Father, and to the Son and to the Holy Spirit.
When the fullness of time had come
　　—**God sent his Son, born of a woman.**

Magnificat Antiphon The Holy Spirit will come upon you, O Mary, and the power of the Most High will overshadow you. (Alleluia)

Litany
You called Mary to be the Mother of your Incarnate Word; give insight and strength to all families who are raising children.
Lord, have mercy.
You taught Mary to see Jesus not only as her son but also as her Lord; deepen our discipleship of Christ, our Teacher.
Christ, have mercy.
You deepened Mary's faith by revealing to the Church the risen Christ; bring all the dead to share in Christ's risen life.
Lord, have mercy.

March 25

Invitation to the Lord's Prayer
As you called Mary to serve you as the Mother of Christ, may we answer your invitation to a more faithful following of Christ as we pray.

Collect Pour your grace into our hearts, O Lord, that we who have known the incarnation of your Son Jesus Christ, announced by an angel to the Virgin Mary, may by his cross and passion be brought to the glory of his resurrection; who lives and reigns with you, in the unity of the Holy Spirit, one God, now and for ever. Amen.

The Blessing
May we rejoice and sing for the Lord, our God, is in our midst: the God who will rejoice over us with gladness, who will renew us in his love; who will exult over us with loud singing. **Amen.**

The Annunciation of Our Lord Jesus Christ to the Blessed Virgin Mary
Morning Prayer

Invitatory (Alleluia) The Word was made flesh and dwelt among us: Come let us adore. (Alleluia)

Hymn The Word whom earth and sea and sky *Hymnal 263*

Antiphon 1 The Angel Gabriel was sent by God to a virgin engaged to a man whose name was Joseph of the house of David. The Virgin's name was Mary. (Alleluia)

Psalms from Sunday Week 1 Morning Prayer

Antiphon 2 Do not be afraid, Mary, for you have found favor with God. You will conceive in your womb and bear a son, and you will name him Jesus. (Alleluia)

Antiphon 3 Here am I, the servant of the Lord; let it be with me according to your word. (Alleluia)

Reading One Isaiah 52:7-12

Responsory One (Zech. 2:10; Is. 12:6)
Sing and rejoice, O daughter Zion!
  — **I will come and dwell in your midst.**
Great in your midst is the Holy One of Israel
  — **I will come and dwell in your midst.**
Glory to the Father and to the Son and to the Holy Spirit.
Sing and rejoice, O daughter Zion!
  — **I will come and dwell in your midst.**

March 25

Canticle of the Annunciation *Ave gratia plena*
(Luke 1: 28, 30-33, 35, 38, 42, 45)

Antiphon Blessed is she who believed that there would be a fulfilment of what was spoken to her by the Lord. (Alleluia)

Greetings, favored one! *
   The Lord is with you.'
   for you have found favor with God.

You will conceive in your womb and bear a son, *
   and you will name him Jesus.

He will be great, and will be called the Son of the Most High, *
   and the Lord God will give to him
   the throne of his ancestor David.

The Holy Spirit will come upon you, *
   and the power of the Most High will overshadow you;

Therefore the child to be born will be holy; *
   he will be called Son of God.

Here am I, the servant of the Lord; *
   let it be with me according to your word.

Blessed are you among women, *
   and blessed is the fruit of your womb.

Blessed is she who believed *
   that there would be a fulfilment
   of what was spoken to her by the Lord.

Antiphon Blessed is she who believed that there would be a fulfilment of what was spoken to her by the Lord. (Alleluia)

Reading Two Hebrews 2:5-10

Responsory Two (Lk. 11:27; Lk. 1:45)
Blessed is the womb that bore you
    —Blessed are those who hear the word of God and obey it.
Blessed is she who believed
    —Blessed are those who hear the word of God and obey it.
Glory to the Father and to the Son and to the Holy Spirit.
Blessed is the womb that bore you
    —Blessed are those who hear the word of God and obey it.

Benedictus Antiphon When the fullness of time had come, God sent his Son, born of a woman, born under the law, so that we might receive adoption as children. (Alleluia)

Litany
Mary endured the estrangement of her unconventional motherhood; comfort all who are victims of sexual violence.
Lord, have mercy.
Mary followed your Son even in his agony; support all who endure the inequalities of our justice system.
Christ, have mercy.
Mary joined the disciples in prayer for the Spirit; deepen the prayer of all committed to contemplation.
Lord, have mercy.

Invitation to the Lord's Prayer
As your Word took flesh from Blessed Mary, may you send us your Spirit that we may discern the Mystical Body of your Son as we pray to you.

Collect *From Evening Prayer I*

The Blessing
May we rejoice and sing for the Lord, our God, is in our midst: the God who will rejoice over us with gladness, who will renew us in his love; who will exult over us with loud singing. **Amen.**

The Annunciation of Our Lord Jesus Christ to the Blessed Virgin Mary
Noonday Prayer

Hymn Virgin Born, we bow before thee *Hymnal 258*

Antiphon The virgin shall conceive and bear a son, and they shall name him Emmanuel. (Alleluia)
Psalms from Sunday Week 1 Noonday Prayer

Reading Isaiah 11: 1-2
A shoot shall come out from the stump of Jesse, and a branch shall grow out of his roots. The spirit of the Lord shall rest on him, the spirit of wisdom and understanding, the spirit of counsel and might, the spirit of knowledge and the fear of the Lord.

Verse and Response
The Word was made flesh. (Alleluia)
And pitched his tent among us. (Alleluia)

March 25

Collect *From Evening Prayer I*

The Annunciation of Our Lord Jesus Christ to the Blessed Virgin Mary
Evening Prayer II

Hymn God himself is with us *Hymnal 475*

Antiphon 1 The Lord said to me, you are my Son; this day have I begotten you. (Alleluia)
Psalms from Sunday Week 1 Evening Prayer II
Antiphon 2 The Lord God has given him the throne of his father David, and he will reign for ever and ever. (Alleluia)
Antiphon 3 When the Son came into the world he said: A body you have prepared for me. I have come to do your will, O God. (Alleluia)

Reading Wisdom 9:1-12 or John 1:9-14

Responsory (Lk. 1:42; Lk. 11:28)
Blessed are you among women
   —blessed is the fruit of your womb.
Blessed are they who hear the word of God and keep it.
   —blessed is the fruit of your womb.
Glory to the Father, and to the Son and to the Holy Spirit.
Blessed are you among women
   —blessed is the fruit of your womb

Magnificat Antiphon God's love was revealed among us in this way: God sent his only Son into the world so that we might live through him. (Alleluia)

Litany
The Father has chosen Mary to be the mother of his Son; let us rejoice with Christ in being called beloved children of God.
Lord have mercy.
Mary proclaimed that God would feed the hungry and lift the downtrodden; may we open our hands and our hearts to serve Christ in the hungry and oppressed.
Christ have mercy.
Mary has entered into the dwelling place prepared for her by Christ; may all the dead enter their heavenly home.
Lord have mercy.

Invitation to the Lord's Prayer
Rejoicing in God's love made manifest in the Incarnation, as members of Christ's body let us pray with our Risen Lord.

Collect *From Evening Prayer I*

The Blessing
May we rejoice and sing for the Lord, our God, is in our midst: the God who will rejoice over us with gladness, who will renew us in his love; who will exult over us with loud singing. **Amen.**

March 26
Harriet Monsell
Professed Religious, Founder of the Community of St. John Baptist, 1883
Lesser Feast
From the Common of Professed Religious Page 624
Collect Gracious God, who led your servant Harriet Monsell through grief to a new vocation; grant that we, inspired by her example, may grow in the life of prayer and the work of service so that in sorrow or joy, your presence may increase among us and our lives reveal the mind of Jesus Christ, to whom, with you and the Holy Spirit be honor and glory, now and forever. Amen.

March 27
Charles Henry Brent
Bishop of the Philippines, and of Western New York, 1929
Lesser Feast
From the Common of Missionaries Page 612
Collect Heavenly Father, whose Son prayed that we all might be one: Deliver us from arrogance and prejudice, and give us wisdom and forbearance, that, following your servant Charles Henry Brent, we may be united in one family with all who confess the Name of your Son Jesus Christ; who lives and reigns with you and the Holy Spirit, one God, now and for ever. Amen.

March 29
John Keble
Priest, 1866
Lesser Feast
From the Common of Theologians and Teachers Page 605
Collect Grant, O God, that in all time of our testing we may know your presence and obey your will; that, following the example of your servant John Keble, we may accomplish with integrity and courage what you give us to do, and endure what you give us to bear; through Jesus Christ our

Lord, who lives and reigns with you and the Holy Spirit, one God, for ever and ever. Amen.

March 31

John Donne
Priest, 1631
Lesser Feast

From the Common of Theologians and Teachers Page 605 with the following proper antiphons

Benedictus Antiphon As to others' souls I preach'd thy word, be this my text, my sermon to mine own: "Therefore that he may raise, the Lord throws down." (Alleluia)

Magnificat Antiphon I turne my backe to thee, but to receive corrections. Restore thine Image, so much, by thy grace, that thou may'st know me, and I'll turne my face. (Alleluia)

Collect Almighty God, the root and fountain of all being: Open our eyes to see, with your servant John Donne, that whatever has any being is a mirror in which we may behold you; through Jesus Christ our Lord, who lives and reigns with you and the Holy Spirit, one God, for ever and ever. Amen.

April

April 1

Frederick Denison Maurice
Priest, 1872
Lesser Feast

From the Common of Theologian and Teacher Page 605

Collect Almighty God, you restored our human nature to heavenly glory through the perfect obedience of our Savior Jesus Christ: Keep alive in your Church, we pray, a passion for justice and truth; that, like your servant Frederick Denison Maurice, we may work and pray for the triumph of the kingdom of your Christ; who lives and reigns with you and the Holy Spirit, one God, now and for ever. Amen.

April 2

James Lloyd Breck
Priest, 1876
Lesser Feast

From the Common of Missionaries Page 612

Collect Teach your Church, O Lord, we pray, to value and support pioneering and courageous missionaries, whom you call, as you called your servant James Lloyd Breck, to preach, and teach, and plant your

Church on new frontiers; through Jesus Christ our Lord, who lives and reigns with you and the Holy Spirit, one God, for ever and ever. Amen.

April 3

Richard
Bishop of Chichester, 1253
Lesser Feast

From the Common of Pastors Page 601
Collect We thank you, Lord God, for all the benefits you have given us in your Son Jesus Christ, our most merciful Redeemer, Friend, and Brother, and for all the pains and insults he has borne for us; and we pray that, following the example of your saintly bishop Richard of Chichester, we may see Christ more clearly, love him more dearly, and follow him more nearly; who lives and reigns with you and the Holy Spirit, one God, now and for ever. Amen.

April 3

Mary of Egypt
Monastic, c. 421
Lesser Feast

From the Common of Monastics Page 620
Collect Merciful Lord, who raises up sinners by your boundless compassion and mercy: Cause the desert sun to burn away our coarseness and to melt our hardness of heart, that, like your servant Mary of Egypt, we may not depart from this life until we understand the ways of repentance and the benefits of prayer; through Jesus Christ our Lord, who lives and reigns with you and the Holy Spirit, one God, now and forever. Amen.

April 4

Martin Luther King, Jr.
Baptist Pastor, Civil Rights Leader, Martyr 1968
Lesser Feast

From the Common of Martyrs Page 597 with the following proper antiphons
Benedictus Antiphon I have a dream today that we will be able to speed up that day when all of God's children will be able to join hands and sing in the words of the old Negro spiritual: Free at last! Free at last! Thank God Almighty, we are free at last! (Alleluia)

Magnificat Antiphon I just want to do God's will. And I've seen the Promised Land. I may not get there with you. I'm not fearing any man. Mine eyes have seen the glory of the coming of the Lord. (Alleluia)

Collect Almighty God, by the hand of Moses your servant you led your people out of slavery, and made them free at last: Grant that your Church, following the example of your prophet Martin Luther King, may resist oppression in the name of your love, and may secure for all your children the blessed liberty of the Gospel of Jesus Christ; who lives and reigns with you and the Holy Spirit, one God, now and for ever. Amen.

April 5
Harriet Starr Cannon
Professed Religious, and Founder of the Community of St. Mary, 1896
Lesser Feast
From the Common of Professed Religious Page 624

Collect Gracious God, who called Harriet Starr Cannon and her companions to revive the monastic vocation in the Episcopal Church and to dedicate their lives to you: Grant that we, after their example, may ever surrender ourselves to the revelation of your holy will; through our Lord and Savior Jesus Christ, who lives and reigns with you and the Holy Spirit, one God, for ever and ever. Amen.

April 7
Tikhon
Patriarch of Russia, Confessor and Ecumenist, 1925
Lesser Feast
From the Common of Pastors Page 601

Collect Holy God, holy and mighty, you call us together into one communion and fellowship: Open our eyes, we pray, as you opened the eyes of your servant Tikhon, that we may see the faithfulness of others as we strive to be steadfast in the faith delivered to us, that the world may see and know you; through Jesus Christ our Lord, to whom, with you and the Holy Spirit, be glory and praise unto ages of ages. Amen.

April 8
William Augustus Muhlenberg
Priest, 1877
Lesser Feast
From the Common of Pastors Page 601

Collect Do not let your Church close its eyes, O Lord, to the plight of the poor and neglected, the homeless and destitute, the old and the sick, the lonely and those who have none to care for them. Give us the vision and compassion with which you so richly endowed your servant William Augustus Muhlenberg, that we may labor tirelessly to heal those who are broken in body or spirit, and to turn their sorrow into joy; through Jesus

Christ our Lord, who lives and reigns with you and the Holy Spirit, one God, for ever and ever. Amen.

April 9

Dietrich Bonhoeffer

Lutheran Pastor, Theologian and Martyr, 1945
Lesser Feast

From the Common of Martyrs Page 597 with the following proper antiphons

Benedictus Antiphon Costly grace is the gospel which must be sought again and again, the gift which must be asked for, the door at which a person must knock. (Alleluia)

Magnificat Antiphon When Christ calls us, he bids us come and die. It is that dying of the old person which is the result of our encounter with Christ. (Alleluia)

Collect Gracious God, the Beyond in the midst of our life, you gave grace to your servant Dietrich Bonhoeffer to know and to teach the truth as it is in Jesus Christ, and to bear the cost of following him: Grant that we, strengthened by his teaching and example, may receive your word and embrace its call with an undivided heart; through Jesus Christ our Savior, who lives and reigns with you and the Holy Spirit, one God, for ever and ever. Amen.

April 10

William Law

Priest, 1761
Lesser Feast

From the Common of Theologians and Teachers Page 605

Collect God, by whose grace your servant William Law, kindled with the flame of your love, became a burning and shining light in your Church: Grant that we also may be aflame with the spirit of love and discipline, and walk before you as children of light; through Jesus Christ our Lord, who lives and reigns with you, in the unity of the Holy Spirit, one God, now and for ever. Amen.

April 11

George Augustus Selwyn

Bishop of New Zealand, and of Lichfield, 1878
Lesser Feast

From the Common of Missionaries Page 612

Collect Almighty and everlasting God, we thank you for your servant George Augustus Selwyn, whom you called to preach the Gospel to the people of New Zealand and Melanesia, and to lay a firm foundation for the growth of your Church in many nations. Raise up in this and every land evangelists and heralds of your kingdom, that your Church may proclaim the unsearchable riches of our Savior Jesus Christ; who lives and reigns with you and the Holy Spirit, one God, now and for ever. Amen.

April 19

Alphege

Archbishop of Canterbury, and Martyr, 1012
Lesser Feast

From the Common of Martyrs Page 597

Collect O loving God, your martyr bishop Alphege of Canterbury suffered violent death when he refused to permit a ransom to be extorted from his people: Grant that all pastors of your flock may pattern themselves on the Good Shepherd, who laid down his life for the sheep; and who with you and the Holy Spirit lives and reigns, one God, for ever and ever. Amen.

April 21

Anselm

Monk, Archbishop of Canterbury and Teacher of the Faith, 1109
Lesser Feast

From the Common of Teacher of the Faith Page 608 with the following proper antiphons

Benedictus Antiphon I desire in some measure to understand your truth, which my heart believes and loves. For I do not seek to understand in order that I may believe, but I believe in order to understand. (Alleluia)

Magnificat Antiphon Indeed, except for you alone, whatever else exists can be thought not to exist. Therefore, you alone exist most truly of all and thus most greatly of all. (Alleluia)

Collect Almighty God, you raised up your servant Anselm to teach the Church of his day to understand its faith in your eternal Being, perfect justice, and saving mercy: Provide your Church in every age with devout and learned scholars and teachers, that we may be able to give a reason for the hope that is in us; through Jesus Christ our Lord, who lives and reigns with you and the Holy Spirit, one God, for ever and ever. Amen.

April 22

Hadewijch of Brabant

Beguine, Poet and Mystic, 13th century
Lesser Feast

From the Common of Theologian and Teacher Page 605 with the following proper antiphons

Benedictus Antiphon God, who ever was and evermore shall be the foundation of veritable Love and perfect faith, is for us the perfect pledge of the most perfect Love. (Alleluia)

Magnificat Antiphon O Love, were I but love, and would I but love you, Love, with love! O Love, for love's sake, grant that I, having become love, may know Love wholly as Love! (Alleluia)

Collect Triune God of Love, overwhelming and all-encompassing, visit us in our solitude and in our companionship, and draw us ever more deeply into union with you, who are ever present and ever mysterious, that we like your servant Hadewijch might know you ever more fully, even as we have been fully known. through Jesus Christ our Lord, who lives and reigns with you and the Holy Spirit, one God, for ever and ever. Amen.

April 25
Saint Mark the Evangelist
Major Feast

From the Common of Evangelists Page 587 with the following proper antiphons
Benedictus Antiphon Jesus came to Galilee, proclaiming the good news of God, and saying, "The time is fulfilled, and the kingdom of God has come near; repent, and believe in the good news." Alleluia.

Magnificat Antiphon *(For Evening Prayer I and Evening Prayer II)* For those who want to save their life will lose it, and those who lose their life for my sake, and for the sake of the gospel, will save it. Alleluia.

Collect Almighty God, by the hand of Mark the evangelist you have given to your Church the Gospel of Jesus Christ the Son of God: We thank you for this witness, and pray that we may be firmly grounded in its truth; through Jesus Christ our Lord, who lives and reigns with you and the Holy Spirit, one God, for ever and ever. Amen.

April 29
Catherine of Siena
Third Order Dominican, Mystic and Teacher of the Faith, 1380
Lesser Feast

From the Common of Teacher of the Faith Page 608 with the following proper antiphons
Benedictus Antiphon Eternal Trinity, Godhead, mystery deep as the sea, you could give me no greater gift than the gift of yourself. For you

are a fire ever burning and never consumed, which itself consumes all the selfish love that fills my being. Alleluia.

Magnificat Antiphon Always and everywhere Catherine desired and discovered God. Through the power of her love, she entered into communion with the Lord. Alleluia.

Collect Everlasting God, you so kindled the flame of holy love in the heart of blessed Catherine of Siena, as she meditated on the passion of your Son our Savior, that she devoted her life to the poor and the sick, and to the peace and unity of the Church: Grant that we also may share in the mystery of Christ's death, and rejoice in the revelation of his glory; who lives and reigns with you and the Holy Spirit, one God, now and for ever. Amen.

May

May 1

Saint Philip and Saint James
Apostles
Major Feast

From the Common of Apostles Page 579 with the following proper antiphons

Benedictus Antiphon Do not let your hearts be troubled. Believe in God, believe also in me. In my Father's house there are many dwelling-places. Alleluia.

Magnificat Antiphon Have I been with you all this time, Philip, and you still do not know me? Whoever has seen me has seen the Father. Alleluia.

Collect Almighty God, who gave to your apostles Philip and James grace and strength to bear witness to the truth: Grant that we, being mindful of their victory of faith, may glorify in life and death the Name of our Lord Jesus Christ; who lives and reigns with you and the Holy Spirit, one God, now and for ever. Amen.

May 2

Athanasius
Bishop of Alexandria and Teacher of the Faith, 373
Lesser Feast

From the Common of Teacher of the Faith Page 608

Collect Uphold your Church, O God of truth, as you upheld your servant Athanasius, to maintain and proclaim boldly the catholic faith against all opposition, trusting solely in the grace of your eternal Word, who took upon himself our humanity that we might share his divinity; who lives and reigns with you and the Holy Spirit, one God, now and for ever. Amen.

May 4

Monnica
Mother of Augustine of Hippo, 387
Lesser Feast

From the Common of Holy Persons Page 628

Collect O Lord, through spiritual discipline you strengthened your servant Monnica to persevere in offering her love and prayers and tears for the conversion of her husband and of Augustine their son: Deepen our devotion, we pray, and use us in accordance with your will to bring others, even our own kindred, to acknowledge Jesus Christ as Savior and Lord; who with you and the Holy Spirit lives and reigns, one God, for ever and ever. Amen

May 8

Dame Julian of Norwich
Mystic, c. 1417
Lesser Feast

From the Common of Theologian and Teacher Page 605 with the following proper antiphons

Benedictus Antiphon Love was his meaning. Who showed it to you? Love. What did he show you? Love. Why did he show it? For love. Keep yourself therein and you shall know and understand more in the same.

Magnificat Antiphon Our Father created us and keeps us within Him. The deep Wisdom of the Trinity is our Mother in whom we are all enclosed. The exalted Goodness of the Trinity is our Lord and in Him we are enclosed and He in us.

Collect Lord God, in your compassion you granted to the Lady Julian many revelations of your nurturing and sustaining love: Move our hearts, like hers, to seek you above all things, for in giving us yourself you give us all; through Jesus Christ our Lord, who lives and reigns with you and the Holy Spirit, one God, for ever and ever. Amen.

May 9

Gregory of Nazianzus
Bishop of Constantinople and Teacher of the Faith, 389
Lesser Feast

From the Common of Teacher of the Faith Page 608

Collect Almighty God, you have revealed to your Church your eternal Being of glorious majesty and perfect love as one God in Trinity of Persons: Give us grace that, like your bishop Gregory of Nazianzus, we may continue steadfast in the confession of this faith, and constant in our worship of you, Father, Son, and Holy Spirit; for you live and reign for ever and ever. Amen.

May 11

The Holy Abbots of Cluny:
Odo, Mayeul, Odilo, Hugh and Peter the Venerable
Lesser Feast

From the Common of Monastics Page 620 with the following proper antiphons
Benedictus Antiphon Blessed are you, O Saints of God, who have been found worthy to share in the delight of heaven and to rejoice in the honor of great renown. Alleluia

Magnificat Antiphon You have left everything to follow me. You shall have it all returned a hundredfold and inherit eternal life. Alleluia.

Collect Lord our God, you are the shield and glorious reward of those who walk blamelessly before you. Keep us steadfast in your holy service so that by the example and intercession of the blessed abbots of Cluny, we may with open hearts run the path of perfect charity. We ask this through our Lord Jesus Christ, your Son, who lives and reigns with you and the Holy Spirit, one God, for ever and ever. Amen.

May 13

Bede Griffiths
Benedictine Monk, Yogi, Priest 1993

From the Common of Theologians and Teachers Page 605
Collect Holy Wisdom, dwelling in all creation, you manifested yourself to Bede through the mystery of your presence in the sacred writings of Hinduism; continue to shine in the wonder of your diverse manifestations but chiefly through Jesus Christ our Savior, who with you and the Holy Spirit, lives and reigns, one God, now and for ever. Amen.

May 15

Pachomius
Abbot, 348
Lesser Feast

From the Common of Monastics Page 620
Collect Lord our God, you raised the blessed abbot Pachomius to the heights of virtue and doctrine. Through his example may we seek before all else the bread of your word which enlightens our minds and brings peace to our hearts. We ask this through our Lord Jesus Christ, your Son, who lives and reigns with you and the Holy Spirit, one God, for ever and ever. Amen.

May 15

Junia and Andronicus
Coworkers of the Apostle Paul
Lesser Feast

From the Common of the Apostles Page 580 with the following proper antiphons

Benedictus Antiphon Greet Andronicus and Junia, my relatives who were in prison with me; they are prominent among the apostles, and they were in Christ before I was.

Magnificat Antiphon Peace be with you. As the Father has sent me, so I send you.

Collect Almighty God, whose Son, the risen Christ, sent forth your apostles Junia and Andronicus to proclaim the gospel and extend your reign: send us forth in your Holy Spirit, that women and men may minister as one in faithful witness to the gospel of Jesus Christ; who lives and reigns with you and the Holy Spirit in perfect unity, one God, now and for ever. Amen.

May 16

The Martyrs of the Sudan
1983-2011
Lesser Feast

From the Common of Martyrs Page 597

Collect O God, steadfast in the midst of persecution, by your providence the blood of the martyrs is the seed of the Church: As the martyrs of the Sudan refused to abandon Christ even in the face of torture and death, and so by their sacrifice brought forth a plentiful harvest, may we, too, be steadfast in our faith in Jesus Christ; who with you and the Holy Spirit lives and reigns, one God, for ever and ever. Amen.

May 19

Dunstan
Monk, Abbot, Restorer of the Monastic Life and Archbishop of Canterbury, 988
Lesser Feast

From the Common of Pastors Page 601

Collect O God of truth and beauty, you richly endowed your bishop Dunstan with skill in music and the working of metals, and with gifts of administration and reforming zeal: Teach us, we pray, to see in you the source of all our talents, and move us to offer them for the adornment of worship and the advancement of true religion; through Jesus Christ our Lord, who lives and reigns with you and the Holy Spirit, one God, now and for ever. Amen.

May 20

Alcuin
Deacon and Abbot of Tours, 804
Lesser Feast

From the Common of Monastics Page 620

Collect Almighty God, in a rude and barbarous age you raised up your deacon Alcuin to rekindle the light of learning: Illumine our minds, we pray, that amid the uncertainties and confusions of our own time we may show forth your eternal truth; through Jesus Christ our Lord, who lives and reigns with you and the Holy Spirit, one God, for ever and ever. Amen.

May 22

Lydia of Thyatira,
Coworker of the Apostle Paul
Lesser Feast

From the Common of the Apostles Page 580 with the following proper antiphons

Benedictus Antiphon Lydia was a worshiper of God and a dealer in purple cloth. The Lord opened her heart to listen eagerly to what was said by Paul.

Magnificat Antiphon When Lydia and her household were baptized, she urged Paul, Silas and Timothy, saying, "If you have judged me to be faithful to the Lord, come and stay at my home."

Collect Eternal God, who gives good gifts to all people, and who teaches us to have the same spirit of generosity: Give us, we pray you, hearts that are always open to hear your word, that following the example of your servant Lydia, we may show hospitality to all who are in any need or trouble, through Jesus Christ our Lord who lives and reigns with you and the Holy Spirit, one God, now and for ever. Amen.

May 24

Jackson Kemper
First Missionary Bishop in the United States, 1870
Lesser Feast

From the Common of Missionaries Page 612

Collect Lord God, in your providence Jackson Kemper was chosen first missionary bishop in this land, and by his arduous labor and travel congregations were established in scattered settlements of the West: Grant that the Church may always be faithful to its mission, and have the vision, courage, and perseverance to make known to all people the Good News of Jesus Christ; who with you and the Holy Spirit lives and reigns, one God, for ever and ever. Amen.

May 25

Bede, the Venerable

Monk of Jarrow, Priest and Teacher of the Faith, 735
Lesser Feast

From the Common of Teacher of the Faith Page 608 with the following proper antiphons

Benedictus Antiphon Christ is the Morning Star who, when the night of this world is past, brings to his saints the promise of the light of life and opens everlasting day.

Magnificat Antiphon I pray you, loving Jesus, that as you have graciously given me to drink in with delight the words of your knowledge, so you would mercifully grant me to attain one day to you, the fountain of all wisdom, and to appear forever before your face.

Collect Heavenly Father, you called your servant Bede, while still a child, to devote his life to your service in the disciplines of religion and scholarship: Grant that as he labored in the Spirit to bring the riches of your truth to his generation, so we, in our various vocations, may strive to make you known in all the world; through Jesus Christ our Lord, who lives and reigns with you and the Holy Spirit, one God, for ever and ever. Amen.

May 26

Augustine

Monk, First Archbishop of Canterbury, 605
Lesser Feast

From the Common of Pastors Page 601

Collect O Lord our God, by your Son Jesus Christ you called your apostles and sent them forth to preach the Gospel to the nations: We bless your holy Name for your servant Augustine, first Archbishop of Canterbury, whose labors in propagating your Church among the English people we commemorate today; and we pray that all whom you call and send may do your will, and bide your time, and see your glory; through Jesus Christ our Lord, who lives and reigns with you and the Holy Spirit, one God, for ever and ever. Amen.

May 28

Mechthild of Magdeburg,

Mystic, Beguine, Benedictine Nun c.1282
Lesser Feast

From the Common of Monastics Page 620

Collect Draw near to the souls of your people, O God, that like your servant Mechthild we may yearn to know you ever more, just as we are known intimately by you, who knows each one of us better than we can know ourselves. All this we ask through Jesus Christ our Lord, who lives and reigns with you and the Holy Spirit, one God now and for ever. Amen.

May 31
The Visitation of the Blessed Virgin Mary
Feast of our Lord
Evening Prayer I

From the Common of the Blessed Virgin Mary Page 569 with the following proper parts

Hymn Ye who claim the faith of Jesus *Hymnal 268*

Antiphon 1 Mary set out and went in haste to a Judean town in the hill country, where she entered the house of Zechariah and greeted Elizabeth. Alleluia.

Psalms from the Common of the Blessed Virgin Mary Evening Prayer I Page 546

Antiphon 2 When Elizabeth heard Mary's greeting, the child leaped in her womb and Elizabeth was filled with the Holy Spirit. Alleluia.

Antiphon 3 Blessed are you among women and blessed is the fruit of your womb. Alleluia.

Reading Isaiah 11:1-10 or Hebrews 2:11-18

Responsory (Is. 11:1, 10)
A shoot shall come out from the stock of Jesse,
  – and a branch shall grow out of his roots.
His dwelling shall be glorious
  – and a branch shall grow out of his roots.
Glory to the Father and to the Son and to the Holy Spirit.
A shoot shall come out from the stock of Jesse,
  – and a branch shall grow out of his roots.

Magnificat Antiphon Blessed are you, O Mary, for you believed that there would be a fulfillment of what was spoken to you by the Lord. Alleluia.

Litany
You called Mary to be the Mother of your Incarnate Word; give insight and strength to all families who are raising children.
Lord, have mercy.
You taught Mary to see Jesus not only as her son but also as her Lord; deepen our discipleship of Christ, our Teacher.
Christ, have mercy.
You deepened Mary's faith by revealing to the Church the risen Christ; bring all the dead to share in Christ's risen life.
Lord, have mercy.

Invitation to the Lord's Prayer
As you called Mary to serve you as the Mother of Christ, may we answer your invitation to a more faithful following of Christ as we pray.

Collect Father in heaven, by your grace the virgin mother of your incarnate Son was blessed in bearing him, but still more blessed in keeping your word: Grant us who honor the exaltation of her lowliness to follow the example of her devotion to your will; through Jesus Christ our Lord, who lives and reigns with you and the Holy Spirit, one God, for ever and ever. Amen.

The Blessing
May we be glad and rejoice forever in what God is creating; for God is creating Jerusalem as a joy, and its people as a delight. **Amen.**

The Visitation of the Blessed Virgin Mary
Morning Prayer

Invitatory Let us celebrate the Visitation of St. Mary. Come let us worship Christ, the Incarnate Word. Alleluia.

Hymn Praise we the Lord this day *Hymnal 267*

Antiphon 1 Elizabeth exclaimed, "Why has this happened that the mother of my Lord comes to me?" Alleluia.
Psalms from Sunday Week 1 Morning Prayer
Antiphon 2 As soon as I heard the sound of your greeting, the child in my womb leaped for joy. Alleluia.
Antiphon 3 Mary remained with her about three months and then returned to her home. Alleluia.

Reading One 1 Samuel 1: 1-20

Responsory One (Zech. 2:10; Is. 12:6)
Sing and rejoice, O daughter Zion!
    — I will come and dwell in your midst.
Sing and rejoice, O daughter Zion!
    — I will come and dwell in your midst.
Great in your midst is the Holy One of Israel
    — I will come and dwell in your midst.
Glory to the Father and to the Son and to the Holy Spirit.
Sing and rejoice, O daughter Zion!
    — I will come and dwell in your midst.

Canticle of the Annunciation *Ave gratia plena*
(Luke 1: 28, 30-33, 35, 38, 42, 45)

Antiphon Blessed is she who believed that there would be a fulfilment of what was spoken to her by the Lord. Alleluia.

Greetings, favored one! *
    The Lord is with you.'
    for you have found favor with God.

You will conceive in your womb and bear a son, *
    and you will name him Jesus.

He will be great, and will be called the Son of the Most High, *
    and the Lord God will give to him
    the throne of his ancestor David.

The Holy Spirit will come upon you, *
    and the power of the Most High will overshadow you;

Therefore the child to be born will be holy; *
    he will be called Son of God.

Here am I, the servant of the Lord; *
    let it be with me according to your word.

Blessed are you among women, *
    and blessed is the fruit of your womb.

Blessed is she who believed *
    that there would be a fulfilment
    of what was spoken to her by the Lord.

Antiphon Blessed is she who believed that there would be a fulfilment of what was spoken to her by the Lord. Alleluia.

Reading Two Hebrews 3: 1-6

Responsory Two (Lk. 11:27; Lk. 1:45)
Blessed is the womb that bore you
  —**Blessed are those who hear the word of God and obey it.**
Blessed is she who believed
  —**Blessed are those who hear the word of God and obey it.**
Glory to the Father and to the Son and to the Holy Spirit.
Blessed is the womb that bore you
  —**Blessed are those who hear the word of God and obey it.**

Benedictus Antiphon When Elizabeth heard the sound of Mary's greeting, the child leaped in her womb for joy. Blessed is she who believed that there would be a fulfillment of what was spoken to her by the Lord. Alleluia.

Litany
Mary endured the estrangement of her unconventional motherhood; comfort all who are victims of sexual violence.
Lord, have mercy.
Mary followed your Son even in his agony; support all who endure the inequalities of our justice system.
Christ, have mercy.
Mary joined the disciples in prayer for the Spirit; deepen the prayer of all committed to contemplation.
Lord, have mercy.

Invitation to the Lord's Prayer
As your Word took flesh from Blessed Mary, may you send us your Spirit to us that we may discern the Mystical Body of your Son as we pray.

Collect *From Evening Prayer I*

The Blessing
May we sing aloud, rejoice and exult with all our hearts for the king of Israel, the Lord, is in our midst. **Amen.**

The Visitation of the Blessed Virgin Mary
Noonday Prayer

Hymn Virgin-born, we bow before thee *Hymnal 258*

Antiphon Hark! My lover – here he comes springing over the mountains, leaping over the hills. Alleluia.
Psalms from Sunday Week 1 Noonday Prayer

May 31

Reading Sirach 24: 8-12
Then the Creator of all things gave me a command, and my Creator chose the place for my tent. He said, 'Make your dwelling in Jacob, and in Israel receive your inheritance.' Before the ages, in the beginning, he created me, and for all the ages I shall not cease to be. In the holy tent I ministered before him, and so I was established in Zion. Thus in the beloved city he gave me a resting place, and in Jerusalem was my domain. I took root in an honored people, in the portion of the Lord, his heritage.

Verse and Response
Blessed are you among women. Alleluia
And blessed is the fruit of your womb. Alleluia

Collect *From Evening Prayer I*

The Visitation of the Blessed Virgin Mary
Evening Prayer II

Hymn Ye who claim the faith of Jesus *Hymnal 269*

Antiphon 1 Mary set out and went in haste to a Judean town in the hill country, where she entered the house of Zechariah and greeted Elizabeth. Alleluia.
Psalms from Evening Prayer II of the Common of the Blessed Virgin Mary, Page 575
Antiphon 2 When Elizabeth heard Mary's greeting, the child leaped in her womb and Elizabeth was filled with the Holy Spirit. Alleluia.
Antiphon 3 Blessed are you among women and blessed is the fruit of your womb. Alleluia.

Reading Zechariah 2:10-13 or John 3:25-30

Responsory (Luke 1: 42; Luke 11: 28)
Blessed are you among women;
    —blessed is the fruit of your womb.
Blessed are they who hear the word of God and keep it.
    —blessed is the fruit of your womb.
Glory to the Father, and to the Son and to the Holy Spirit.
Blessed are you among women;
    —blessed is the fruit of your womb

Magnificat Antiphon All generations shall call me blessed for the Mighty One has done great things for me and holy is his name. Alleluia.

Litany
You called Mary to be the Mother of your Incarnate Word; give insight and strength to all families who are raising children.
Lord, have mercy.
You taught Mary to see Jesus not only as her son but also as her Lord; deepen our discipleship of Christ, our Teacher.
Christ, have mercy.
You deepened Mary's faith by revealing to the Church the risen Christ; bring all the dead to share in Christ's risen life.
Lord, have mercy.

Collect *From Evening Prayer I*

The Blessing
May we be glad and rejoice forever in what God is creating; for God is creating Jerusalem as a joy, and its people as a delight. **Amen.**

June

June 1

Justin
Martyr at Rome, c. 167
Lesser Feast

From the Common of Martyrs Page 597

Collect Almighty and everlasting God, you found your martyr Justin wandering from teacher to teacher, seeking the true God, and you revealed to him the sublime wisdom of your eternal Word: Grant that all who seek you, or a deeper knowledge of you, may find and be found by you; through Jesus Christ our Lord, who lives and reigns with you and the Holy Spirit, one God, for ever and ever. Amen.

June 2

Blandina and her Companions
Martyrs of Lyons, 177
Lesser Feast

From the Common of Martyrs Page 597

Collect Grant, O Lord, that we who keep the feast of the holy martyrs Blandina and her companions may be rooted and grounded in love of you, and may endure the sufferings of this life for the glory that shall be revealed in us; through Jesus Christ our Lord, who lives and reigns with you and the Holy Spirit, one God, now and for ever. Amen.

June 3

The Martyrs of Uganda
1886
Lesser Feast

From the Common of Martyrs Page 597

Collect O God, by your providence the blood of the martyrs is the seed of the Church: Grant that we who remember before you the blessed martyrs of Uganda, may, like them, be steadfast in our faith in Jesus Christ, to whom they gave obedience, even to death, and by their sacrifice brought forth a plentiful harvest; through Jesus Christ our Lord, who lives and reigns with you and the Holy Spirit, one God, for ever and ever. Amen.

June 5

Boniface
Monk, Archbishop of Mainz, Missionary to Germany, and Martyr, 754
Lesser Feast

From the Common of Martyrs Page 597

Collect Almighty God, you called your faithful servant Boniface to be a witness and martyr in Germany, and by his labor and suffering you raised up a people for your own possession: Pour out your Holy Spirit upon your Church in every land, that by the service and sacrifice of many your holy Name may be glorified and your kingdom enlarged; through Jesus Christ our Lord, who lives and reigns with you and the Holy Spirit, one God, for ever and ever. Amen.

June 6

Ini Kopuria
Founder of the Melanesian Brotherhood, 1945
Lesser Feast

From the Common of Professed Religious Page 624

Collect Loving God, we bless your Name for the witness of Ini Kopuria, police officer and founder of the Melanesian Brotherhood, whose members saved many American pilots in a time of war, and who continue to minister courageously to the islanders of Melanesia. Open our eyes that we, with these Anglican brothers, may establish peace and hope in service to others, for the sake of Jesus Christ; who with you and the Holy Spirit lives and reigns, one God, for ever and ever. Amen.

June 8
Melania the Elder
Monastic, 410
Lesser Feast

From the Common of Monastics Page 620

Collect Most High and Merciful God, who called your servant Melania to forsake earthly comforts in order to devote herself to studying the scriptures and to welcoming the poor; instruct us in the ways of poverty and the grace of hospitality, that we might comfort those who have no place to rest and teach the way of your love; through Jesus Christ our Lord. Amen.

June 9
Columba
Abbot of Iona, 597
Lesser Feast

From the Common of Monastics Page 620 with the following proper antiphons

Benedictus Antiphon By some divine intuition, and through a wonderful expansion of his inner soul, he beheld the whole universe drawn together and laid open to his sight, as in one ray of the sun.

Magnificat Antiphon If you thus follow the example of the holy fathers, God, the Comforter of the good, will be your Helper and I, abiding with Him, will intercede for you.

Collect O God, by the preaching of your blessed servant Columba you caused the light of the Gospel to shine in Scotland: Grant, we pray, that, having his life and labors in remembrance, we may show our thankfulness to you by following the example of his zeal and patience; through Jesus Christ our Lord, who lives and reigns with you and the Holy Spirit, one God, for ever and ever. Amen.

June 10
Ephrem of Edessa
Deacon and Teacher of the Faith, 373
Lesser Feast

From the Common of Teacher of the Faith Page 608

Collect Pour out on us, O Lord, that same Spirit by which your deacon Ephrem rejoiced to proclaim in sacred song the mysteries of faith; and so gladden our hearts that we, like him, may be devoted to you alone; through Jesus Christ our Lord, who lives and reigns with you and the Holy Spirit, one God, now and for ever. Amen.

June 11
Saint Barnabas the Apostle
Major Feast

From the Common of Apostles Page 580 with the following proper antiphons

Benedictus Antiphon There was a Levite, Joseph, to whom the apostles gave the name Barnabas (which means "son of encouragement"). He sold his field and brought the money to the apostles.

Magnificat Antiphon The whole assembly kept silence, and listened to Barnabas and Paul as they told of all the signs and wonders that God had done through them among the Gentiles.

Collect Grant, O God, that we may follow the example of your faithful servant Barnabas, who, seeking not his own renown but the wellbeing of your Church, gave generously of his life and substance for the relief of the poor and the spread of the Gospel; through Jesus Christ our Lord, who lives and reigns with you and the Holy Spirit, one God, for ever and ever. Amen.

June 12
Enmegahbowh
Priest and Missionary, 1902
Lesser Feast

From the Common of Missionaries Page 612

Collect Almighty God, you led your pilgrim people of old with fire and cloud: Grant that the ministers of your Church, following the example of blessed Enmegahbowh, may stand before your holy people, leading them with fiery zeal and gentle humility. This we ask through Jesus, the Christ, who lives and reigns with you in the unity of the Holy Spirit, one God now and for ever. Amen.

June 14
Basil the Great
Monk, Author of a Monastic Rule, Bishop of Caesarea, Teacher of the Faith, 379
Lesser Feast

From the Common of Teacher of the Faith Page 608

Collect Almighty God, you have revealed to your Church your eternal Being of glorious majesty and perfect love as one God in Trinity of Persons: Give us grace that, like your bishop Basil of Caesarea, we may continue steadfast in the confession of this faith, and constant in our worship of you, Father, Son, and Holy Spirit; for you live and reign for ever and ever. Amen.

Common of the Saints

Common of the Dedication of a Church
Evening Prayer I

Hymn Blessed city, heavenly Salem *Hymnal 519*

Psalm 147 A *Laudate Dominum*

Antiphon I will go to the altar of God and adore in your holy temple. (Alleluia)

1. Hallelujah!
   How good it is to sing praises to our God! *
      how pleasant it is to honor him with praise!

2 The LORD rebuilds Jerusalem; *
      he gathers the exiles of Israel.

3 He heals the brokenhearted *
      and binds up their wounds.

4 He counts the number of the stars *
      and calls them all by their names.

5 Great is our LORD and mighty in power; *
      there is no limit to his wisdom.

6 The LORD lifts up the lowly, *
      but casts the wicked to the ground.

7 Sing to the LORD with thanksgiving; *
      make music to our God upon the harp.

8 He covers the heavens with clouds *
      and prepares rain for the earth;

9 He makes grass to grow upon the mountains *
      and green plants to serve mankind.

10 He provides food for flocks and herds *
      and for the young ravens when they cry.

11 He is not impressed by the might of a horse; *
      he has no pleasure in the strength of a man;

12 But the LORD has pleasure in those who fear him, *
      in those who await his gracious favor.

Antiphon I will go to the altar of God and adore in your holy temple. (Alleluia)

Psalm 147 B *Lauda Hierusalem*

Antiphon The Lord is in his holy temple, the Lord, whose throne is in heaven. (Alleluia)

13 Worship the LORD, O Jerusalem; *
    praise your God, O Zion;

14 For he has strengthened the bars of your gates; *
    he has blessed your children within you.

15 He has established peace on your borders; *
    he satisfies you with the finest wheat.

16 He sends out his command to the earth, *
    and his word runs very swiftly.

17 He gives snow like wool; *
    he scatters hoarfrost like ashes.

18 He scatters his hail like bread crumbs; *
    who can stand against his cold?

19 He sends forth his word and melts them; *
    he blows with his wind, and the waters flow.

20 He declares his word to Jacob, *
    his statutes and his judgments to Israel.

21 He has not done so to any other nation; *
    to them he has not revealed his judgments.
    Hallelujah!

Antiphon The Lord is in his holy temple, the Lord, whose throne is in heaven. (Alleluia)

Psalm 65 *Te decet hymnus*

Antiphon Open wide the doors and gates for Christ the Lord. (Alleluia)

1 You are to be praised, O God, in Zion; *
    to you shall vows be performed in Jerusalem.

2 To you that hear prayer shall all flesh come, *
    because of their transgressions.

3 Our sins are stronger than we are, *
    but you will blot them out.

4 Blessed are they whom you choose
and draw to your courts to dwell there! *
    they will be satisfied by the beauty of your house,
    by the holiness of your temple.

5 Awesome things will you show us in your righteousness,
O God of our salvation, *
    O Hope of all the ends of the earth
    and of the seas that are far away.

6 You make fast the mountains by your power; *
    they are girded about with might.

7 You still the roaring of the seas, *
    the roaring of their waves,
    and the clamor of the peoples.

8 Those who dwell at the ends of the earth
will tremble at your marvelous signs; *
    you make the dawn and the dusk to sing for joy.

9 You visit the earth and water it abundantly;
you make it very plenteous; *
    the river of God is full of water.

10 You prepare the grain, *
    for so you provide for the earth.

11 You drench the furrows and smooth out the ridges; *
    with heavy rain you soften the ground and bless its increase.

12 You crown the year with your goodness, *
    and your paths overflow with plenty.

13 May the fields of the wilderness be rich for grazing, *
    and the hills be clothed with joy.

14 May the meadows cover themselves with flocks,
and the valleys cloak themselves with grain; *
    let them shout for joy and sing.

Antiphon Open wide the doors and gates for Christ the Lord. (Alleluia)

Reading Haggai 2:1-9 or 1 Corinthians 3:9-17

Responsory (Ps. 5:7,8)
I will go into your house
    — **I will bow down toward your holy temple.**
Lead me, O Lord, in your righteousness
    — **I will bow down toward your holy temple.**
Glory to the Father and to the Son and to the Holy Spirit.
I will go into your house
    — **I will bow down toward your holy temple.**

Magnificat Antiphon Rejoice with Jerusalem, and be glad for her, all you who love her; rejoice with her in joy. (Alleluia)

Litany
For the Church universal, of which these visible buildings are the symbol, we thank you, Lord.
Lord, have mercy.
For your presence whenever two or three have gathered together in your Name, we thank you, Lord.
Christ, have mercy.
For the faith of those who have gone before us and for our encouragement by their perseverance, we thank you, Lord.
Lord, have mercy.

Invitation to the Lord's Prayer
As living stones built into Christ's temple, let us offer our sacrifice of praise to the Father.

Collect Almighty God, to whose glory we celebrate the dedication of this house of prayer: We give you thanks for the fellowship of those who have worshiped in this place, and we pray that all who seek you here may find you, and be filled with your joy and peace; through Jesus Christ our Lord, who lives and reigns with you, in the unity of the Holy Spirit, one God, now and for ever. Amen.

The Blessing
May we, who celebrate the mystery of the Church, the Bride of Christ, know ourselves to be loved and sanctified by Christ, our Bridegroom.
Amen.

Common of the Dedication of a Church
Morning Prayer

Invitatory Christ loves the church: Come let us worship. (Alleluia)

Hymn Glorious things of thee are spoken *Hymnal 522*

Antiphon 1 My house shall be called a house of prayer for all peoples.(Alleluia)

Psalms from Sunday Week 1 Morning Prayer

Antiphon 2 This is none other than the house of God, and this is the gate of heaven. (Alleluia)

Antiphon 3 Like living stones, let yourselves be built into a spiritual house, to be a holy priesthood, to offer spiritual sacrifices (Alleluia)

Reading One 1 Kings 8:1-13

Responsory (Ps. 48:1; Ps. 61:4)
Great is the Lord, and highly to be praised
  – in the city of our God is his holy hill.
I will dwell in your house for ever
  – in the city of our God is his holy hill.
Glory to the Father and to the Son and to the Holy Spirit.
Great is the Lord, and highly to be praised
  – in the city of our God is his holy hill.

Canticle of Zion *Erit in novissimis*
(Isaiah 2: 2-5)

Antiphon Come, let us go up to the mountain of the Lord, to the house of the God of Jacob. (Alleluia)

In days to come the mountain of the Lord's house *
  shall be established as the highest of the mountains.

It shall be raised above the hills; *
  all the nations shall stream to it.

Many peoples shall come and say, *
  "Come, let us go up to the mountain of the Lord,
  to the house of the God of Jacob.

The Lord will teach us his ways *
  that we may walk in his paths."

For out of Zion shall go forth instruction, *
  and the word of the Lord from Jerusalem.

He shall judge between the nations, *
  and shall arbitrate for many peoples.

They shall beat their swords into plowshares, *
  and their spears into pruning hooks.

Nation shall not lift up sword against nation, *
    neither shall they learn war any more.

Antiphon Come, let us go up to the mountain of the Lord, to the house of the God of Jacob. (Alleluia)

Reading Two John 10:22-30

Responsory Two (Ps 65:4; Ps. 48:10)
Your people will be satisfied by the beauty of your house
    − by the holiness of your temple.
Let Mount Zion be glad
    − by the holiness of your temple.
Glory to the Father and to the Son and to the Holy Spirit.
Your people will be satisfied by the beauty of your house
    − by the holiness of your temple.

Benedictus Antiphon Zacchaeus, hurry and come down; for I must stay at your house today. So he hurried down and joyfully welcome Christ for salvation came to his house that day. (Alleluia)

Litany
Father, we thank you that through the waters of Baptism we die to sin and are made new in Christ. Grant through your Spirit that those baptized at the Font may enjoy the liberty of the children of God.
Lord, have mercy.
Eternal Word, you speak to us through the words of Holy Scripture. Give us ears to hear and
hearts to obey.
Christ, have mercy.
Lord God, you sanctified the Holy Table dedicated to you. Accept here the continual recalling of the sacrifice of your Son.
Lord, have mercy.

Invitation to the Lord's Prayer
Christ illumines the Church with the Holy Spirit and draws us into the light of the Father. Let us rejoice in the Father's light.

Collect *From Evening Prayer I*

The Blessing
May all who eat and drink at Table of Christ be fed and refreshed by his flesh and blood, be forgiven for their sins, united with one another, and strengthened for holy service. **Amen.**

Common of the Dedication of a Church
Noonday Prayer

Hymn Singing songs of expectation *Hymnal 527*

Antiphon You are God's temple and God's Spirit dwells in you. (Alleluia)

Psalms from Sunday Week 1 Noonday Prayer

Reading 2 Cor. 6: 16
We are the temple of the living God; as God said, "I will live in them and walk among them, and I will be their God, and they shall be my people.

Verse and Response
Blessed are they whom you choose. (Alleluia)
And draw to your courts to dwell there! (Alleluia)

Collect *From Evening Prayer I*

Common of the Dedication of a Church
Evening Prayer II

Hymn Christ is made the sure foundation *Hymnal 518*

Psalm 46   *Deus noster refugium*

Antiphon I will dwell in your house for ever; I will take refuge under the cover of your wings. (Alleluia)

1 God is our refuge and strength, *
   a very present help in trouble.

2 Therefore we will not fear, though the earth be moved, *
   and though the mountains be toppled
   into the depths of the sea;

3 Though its waters rage and foam, *
   and though the mountains tremble at its tumult.

4 The LORD of hosts is with us; *
   the God of Jacob is our stronghold.

5 There is a river whose streams make glad the city of God, *
   the holy habitation of the Most High.

6 God is in the midst of her;
   she shall not be overthrown; *
   God shall help her at the break of day.

7 The nations make much ado, and the kingdoms are shaken; *
    God has spoken, and the earth shall melt away.

8 The LORD of hosts is with us; *
    the God of Jacob is our stronghold.

9 Come now and look upon the works of the LORD, *
    what awesome things he has done on earth.

10 It is he who makes war to cease in all the world; *
    he breaks the bow, and shatters the spear,
    and burns the shields with fire.

11 "Be still, then, and know that I am God; *
    I will be exalted among the nations;
    I will be exalted in the earth."

12 The LORD of hosts is with us; *
    the God of Jacob is our stronghold.

Antiphon I will dwell in your house for ever; I will take refuge under the cover of your wings. (Alleluia)

Psalm 122 *Lætatus sum*

Antiphon Destroy this temple, and in three days I will raise it up. He was speaking of the temple of his body. (Alleluia)

1 I was glad when they said to me, *
    "Let us go to the house of the LORD."

2 Now our feet are standing *
    within your gates, O Jerusalem.

3 Jerusalem is built as a city *
    that is at unity with itself;

4 To which the tribes go up,
    the tribes of the LORD, *
      the assembly of Israel,
      to praise the Name of the LORD.

5 For there are the thrones of judgment, *
    the thrones of the house of David.

6 Pray for the peace of Jerusalem: *
    "May they prosper who love you.

7 Peace be within your walls *
    and quietness within your towers.

8 For my brethren and companions' sake, *
    I pray for your prosperity.

9 Because of the house of the LORD our God, *
    I will seek to do you good."

Antiphon Destroy this temple, and in three days I will raise it up. He was speaking of the temple of his body. (Alleluia)

Psalm 27 A *Dominus illuminatio*

Antiphon In Christ the whole structure is joined together and grows into a holy temple in the Lord. (Alleluia)

1 The LORD is my light and my salvation;
   whom then shall I fear? *
    the LORD is the strength of my life;
    of whom then shall I be afraid?

2 When evildoers came upon me to eat up my flesh, *
    it was they, my foes and my adversaries,
    who stumbled and fell.

3 Though an army should encamp against me, *
    yet my heart shall not be afraid;

4 And though war should rise up against me, *
    yet will I put my trust in him.

5 One thing have I asked of the LORD;
   one thing I seek; *
    that I may dwell in the house of the LORD
    all the days of my life;

6 To behold the fair beauty of the LORD *
    and to seek him in his temple.

7 For in the day of trouble
   he shall keep me safe in his shelter; *
    he shall hide me in the secrecy of his dwelling
    and set me high upon a rock.

8 Even now he lifts up my head *
    above my enemies round about me.

Antiphon In Christ the whole structure is joined together and grows into a holy temple in the Lord. (Alleluia)

Reading 1 Kings 8:54-62 or Hebrews 10:19-25

Responsory (Rev. 21:2)
I saw the holy city, the new Jerusalem
    – **coming down out of heaven from God.**
She was prepared as a bride adorned for her husband
    – **coming down out of heaven from God.**
Glory to the Father and to the Son and to the Holy Spirit.
I saw the holy city, the new Jerusalem
    – **coming down out of heaven from God.**

Magnificat Antiphon They are before the throne of God, and worship him day and night within his temple, and the one who is seated on the throne will shelter them. (Alleluia)

Litany
Christ Jesus, Living Temple, you provide a place for all people in your house of prayer; open your church to embrace all whom you welcome.
Lord, have mercy.
Christ Jesus, Foundation of the Church, you support all who are established on you; build us up into a living temple in you.
Christ, have mercy.
Christ Jesus, Keystone of the Universe, all creation finds its order in you; lead the dead to find themselves recreated in your image.
Lord, have mercy.

Invitation to the Lord's Prayer
As living stones built into Christ's temple, let us offer our sacrifice of praise to the Father.

Collect *From Evening Prayer I*

The Blessing
May we, who celebrate the mystery of the Church, the Bride of Christ, know ourselves to be loved and sanctified by Christ, our Bridegroom.
Amen.

Common of the Founding of the Community Evening Prayer I

Hymn Rejoice, ye pure in heart! *Hymnal 556*

Antiphon 1 All who believed were together and had all things in common; they would sell their possessions and goods and distribute the proceeds to all, as any had need. (Alleluia)
Psalms from Sunday Week One Evening Prayer I

Antiphon 2 Day by day, as they spent much time together in the temple, they broke bread at home and ate their food with glad and generous hearts. (Alleluia)

Antiphon 3 They praised God and enjoyed the goodwill of all the people. Day by day the Lord added to their number those who were being saved. (Alleluia)

Reading Luke 10: 38-42

Responsory (John 13: 34-35)
Just as I have loved you
    — **you also should love one another.**
I give you a new commandment
    — **you also should love one another.**
Glory to the Father and to the Son and to the Holy Spirit.
Just as I have loved you
    — **you also should love one another.**

Magnificat Antiphon If you have any encouragement from being united with Christ, then make my joy complete by being like-minded, having the same love, being one in spirit and of one mind. (Alleluia)

Litany
You raised up this community in the power of the Holy Spirit; call new women and men to follow you in the consecrated life.
Lord, have mercy.
You form your disciples in the pattern of contemplation and work; send your Spirit to sanctify monastics who live in the world.
Christ, have mercy.
You promise eternal life to all who faithfully follow you in the consecrated life; bring our departed brothers and sisters to your banquet in heaven.
Lord, have mercy.

Invitation to the Lord's Prayer
Faithful to the pledge we make of mutual forgiveness, let us ask God to cleanse our hearts as we pray with Christ.

Collect Gracious God, you raised up N. to be a religious community in the church. Help us to remain faithful to our charism until we dwell with you, O Father, and the Incarnate Word and the Holy Spirit in inexpressible joy, forever and ever. Amen.

The Blessing
May the word of Christ dwell in us richly as we teach and admonish one another in all wisdom. **Amen.**

Common of the Founding of the Community
Morning Prayer

Invitatory Christ calls to follow him in the common life: Come let us adore. (Alleluia)

Hymn Over the chaos of the empty waters *Hymnal 176*

Antiphon 1 As God's chosen ones, holy and beloved, clothe yourselves with compassion, kindness, humility, meekness, and patience. (Alleluia)
Psalms from Sunday Week 1 Morning Prayer
Antiphon 2 I have taught you the way of wisdom; I have led you in the paths of uprightness. (Alleluia)
Antiphon 3 Who is wise and understanding among you? Let them show it by their good life, by deeds done in the humility that comes from wisdom. (Alleluia)

Reading One Hosea 2: 14-23

Responsory One (Ps. 62:1, 6)
For God alone
    — **my soul in silence waits.**
My hope is in God
    — **my soul in silence waits.**
Glory to the Father and to the Son and to the Holy Spirit.
For God alone
    — **my soul in silence waits.**

      Canticle You are God   *Te Deum laudamus, Page 667*

Reading Two Acts 2: 37-47

Responsory Two (Ps. 133:1; Phil. 4:5)
How good and pleasant it is
    — **when brethren live together in unity.**
Let your gentleness be known to everyone
    — **when brethren live together in unity.**
Glory to the Father and to the Son and to the Holy Spirit.
How good and pleasant it is
    — **when brethren live together in unity.**

Benedictus Antiphon Those who love me will keep my word, and my Father will love them, and we will come to them and make our home with them. (Alleluia)

Litany
Christ Jesus was obedient even to death on the cross; teach us obedience in our following the Gospel and the Rule.
Lord, have mercy.
Christ Jesus took on our human flesh and dwelled among us; support us in our stability to our sisters and brothers.
Christ, have mercy.
Christ Jesus preached a change of mind and heart; deepen our commitment to live the common life.
Lord, have mercy.

Invitation to the Lord's Prayer
In fellowship with consecrated women and men from centuries past and yet to come, let us approach the throne of grace and pray with Christ.

Collect *From Evening Prayer I*

The Blessing
May we prefer nothing whatever to Christ, and may he bring us all together to everlasting life. **Amen.**

Common of the Founding of the Community
Noonday Prayer
Hymn God of the prophets *Hymnal 359*

Antiphon One thing I asked of the Lord: to live in the house of the Lord all the days of my life, to behold the beauty of the Lord. (Alleluia)
Psalms from Sunday Week 1 Noonday Prayer

Reading John 17: 14-19
I have given them your word, and the world has hated them because they do not belong to the world, just as I do not belong to the world. I am not asking you to take them out of the world, but I ask you to protect them from the evil one. They do not belong to the world, just as I do not belong to the world. Sanctify them in the truth; your word is truth. As you have sent me into the world, so I have sent them into the world. And for their sakes I sanctify myself, so that they also may be sanctified in truth.

Verse and Response
I made your name known to them, and I will make it known. (Alleluia)
So that the love with which you have loved me may be in them, and I in them. (Alleluia)

Collect *From Evening Prayer I*

Common of the Founding of the Community
Evening Prayer II

Hymn God is Love, let heaven adore him *Hymnal 379*

Antiphon 1 All who believed were together and had all things in common; they would sell their possessions and goods and distribute the proceeds to all, as any had need. (Alleluia)
Psalms from Sunday Evening Prayer II Week One
Antiphon 2 Day by day, as they spent much time together in the temple, they broke bread at home and ate their food with glad and generous hearts, praising God and having the goodwill of all the people. (Alleluia)
Antiphon 3 For those who will follow this rule—peace be upon them, and mercy, and upon the Israel of God. (Alleluia)

Reading John 17: 21b – 26

Responsory (John 13: 34-35)
Just as I have loved you
  – you also should love one another.
I give you a new commandment
  – you also should love one another.
Glory to the Father and to the Son and to the Holy Spirit.
Just as I have loved you
  – you also should love one another.

Magnificat Antiphon Peace be to the whole community, and love with faith, from God the Father and the Lord Jesus Christ. Grace be with all who have an undying love for our Lord Jesus Christ. (Alleluia)

Litany
You raised up this community in the power of the Holy Spirit; call new women and men to follow you.
Lord, have mercy.
You form your disciples in the pattern of contemplation and work; send your Spirit to sanctify your people.
Christ, have mercy.

You promise eternal life to all who faithfully follow you in the monastic life; bring our departed sisters and brothers to your banquet in heaven.
Lord, have mercy.

Invitation to the Lord's Prayer
Faithful to the pledge we make of mutual forgiveness, let us ask God to cleanse our hearts as we pray with Christ.

Collect *From Evening Prayer I*

The Blessing
May the word of Christ dwell in us richly as we teach and admonish one another in all wisdom. **Amen.**

Common of the Blessed Virgin Mary
Evening Prayer I

Hymn The angel Gabriel from heaven came *Hymnal 265*

Psalm 113 *Laudate, pueri*

Antiphon Blessed are you among women, and blessed is the fruit of your womb. (Alleluia)

1 Hallelujah!
   Give praise, you servants of the LORD; *
      praise the Name of the LORD.

2 Let the Name of the LORD be blessed, *
      from this time forth for evermore.

3 From the rising of the sun to its going down *
      let the Name of the LORD be praised.

4 The LORD is high above all nations, *
      and his glory above the heavens.

5 Who is like the LORD our God, who sits enthroned on high, *
      but stoops to behold the heavens and the earth?

6 He takes up the weak out of the dust *
      and lifts up the poor from the ashes.

7 He sets them with the princes, *
      with the princes of his people.

8 He makes the woman of a childless house *
      to be a joyful mother of children.

Antiphon Blessed are you among women, and blessed is the fruit of your womb. (Alleluia)

Psalm 45 B *Audi filia et vide*

Antiphon All glorious is the princess as she enters; her gown is cloth-of-gold. (Alleluia)

11 "Hear, O daughter; consider and listen closely; *
      forget your people and your father's house.

12 The king will have pleasure in your beauty; *
      he is your master; therefore do him honor.

13 The people of Tyre are here with a gift; *
      the rich among the people seek your favor."

14 All glorious is the princess as she enters; *
    her gown is cloth of gold.

15 In embroidered apparel she is brought to the king; *
    after her the bridesmaids follow in procession.

16 With joy and gladness they are brought, *
    and enter into the palace of the king.

17 "In place of fathers, O king, you shall have sons; *
    you shall make them princes over all the earth.

18 I will make your name to be remembered
    from one generation to another; *
    therefore nations will praise you for ever and ever."

Antiphon All glorious is the princess as she enters; her gown is cloth-of-gold. (Alleluia)

Psalm 145 *Exaltabo te, Deus*

Antiphon You are the glory of Jerusalem, the joy of Israel. You are the honor of our people. (Alleluia)

1 I will exalt you, O God my King, *
    and bless your Name for ever and ever.

2 Every day will I bless you *
    and praise your Name for ever and ever.

3 Great is the LORD and greatly to be praised; *
    there is no end to his greatness.

4 One generation shall praise your works to another *
    and shall declare your power.

5 I will ponder the glorious splendor of your majesty *
    and all your marvelous works.

6 They shall speak of the might of your wondrous acts, *
    and I will tell of your greatness.

7 They shall publish the remembrance of your great goodness; *
    they shall sing of your righteous deeds.

8 The LORD is gracious and full of compassion, *
    slow to anger and of great kindness.

9 The LORD is loving to everyone *
    and his compassion is over all his works.

10 All your works praise you, O LORD, *
    and your faithful servants bless you.

11 They make known the glory of your kingdom *
    and speak of your power;

12 That the peoples may know of your power *
    and the glorious splendor of your kingdom.

13 Your kingdom is an everlasting kingdom; *
    your dominion endures throughout all ages.

14 The LORD is faithful in all his words *
    and merciful in all his deeds.

15 The LORD upholds all those who fall; *
    he lifts up those who are bowed down.

16 The eyes of all wait upon you, O LORD, *
    and you give them their food in due season.

17 You open wide your hand *
    and satisfy the needs of every living creature.

18 The LORD is righteous in all his ways *
    and loving in all his works.

19 The LORD is near to those who call upon him, *
    to all who call upon him faithfully.

20 He fulfills the desire of those who fear him; *
    he hears their cry and helps them.

21 The LORD preserves all those who love him, *
    but he destroys all the wicked.

22 My mouth shall speak the praise of the LORD; *
    let all flesh bless his holy Name for ever and ever.

Antiphon You are the glory of Jerusalem, the joy of Israel. You are the honor of our people. (Alleluia)

Reading *From the Proper of the Day*

Responsory (Gal. 4:4; Jn. 8:42)
When the fullness of time had come
    – God sent his Son, born of a woman.
I came from God and now I am here
    – God sent his Son, born of a woman.

Glory to the Father, and to the Son and to the Holy Spirit.
When the fullness of time had come
— **God sent his Son, born of a woman.**

Magnificat Antiphon *From the Proper of the Day*

Litany
You called Mary to be the Mother of your Incarnate Word; give insight and strength to all families who are raising children.
Lord, have mercy.
You taught Mary to see Jesus not only as her son but also as her Lord; deepen our discipleship of Christ, our Teacher.
Christ, have mercy.
You deepened Mary's faith by revealing to the Church the risen Christ; bring all the dead to share in Christ's risen life.
Lord, have mercy.

Invitation to the Lord's Prayer
As you called Mary to serve you as the Mother of Christ, may we answer your invitation to a more faithful following of Christ as we pray.

Collect *From the Proper of the Day*

The Blessing
May we who celebrate Mary whose womb bore Christ and whose breasts nursed Christ be more blessed in hearing the word of God and obeying it. **Amen.**

Common of the Blessed Virgin Mary Morning Prayer

Invitatory The Word was made flesh: Come let us worship. (Alleluia)

Hymn Praise we the Lord this day *Hymnal 267*

Antiphon 1 The Angel Gabriel was sent by God to a virgin engaged to a man whose name was Joseph of the house of David. The Virgin's name was Mary. (Alleluia)
Psalms from Sunday of Week 1 Morning Prayer
Antiphon 2 Do not be afraid, Mary, for you have found favor with God. You will conceive in your womb and bear a son, and you will name him Jesus. (Alleluia)
Antiphon 3 Here am I, the servant of the Lord; let it be with me according to your word. (Alleluia)

Reading One *From the Proper of the Day*

Responsory (Zech. 2:10; Is. 12:6)
Sing and rejoice, O daughter Zion!
> – **I will come and dwell in your midst.**

Great in your midst is the Holy One of Israel
> – **I will come and dwell in your midst.**

Glory to the Father and to the Son and to the Holy Spirit.
Sing and rejoice, O daughter Zion!
> – **I will come and dwell in your midst.**

Canticle – Song of the Annunciation *Ave gratia plena*
(Luke 1: 28, 30-33, 35, 38, 42, 45)

Antiphon Blessed is she who believed that there would be a fulfilment of what was spoken to her by the Lord. (Alleluia)

Greetings, favored one! *
> The Lord is with you.'
> for you have found favor with God.

You will conceive in your womb and bear a son, *
> and you will name him Jesus.

He will be great, and will be called the Son of the Most High, *
> and the Lord God will give to him
> the throne of his ancestor David.

The Holy Spirit will come upon you, *
> and the power of the Most High will overshadow you;

Therefore the child to be born will be holy; *
> he will be called Son of God.

Here am I, the servant of the Lord; *
> let it be with me according to your word.

Blessed are you among women, *
> and blessed is the fruit of your womb.

Blessed is she who believed *
> that there would be a fulfilment
> of what was spoken to her by the Lord.

Antiphon Blessed is she who believed that there would be a fulfilment of what was spoken to her by the Lord. (Alleluia)

Reading Two *From the Proper of the Day*

Responsory Two (Lk. 11:27; Lk. 1:45)
Blessed is the womb that bore you
— Blessed are those who hear the word of God and obey it.
Blessed is she who believed
— Blessed are those who hear the word of God and obey it.
Glory to the Father and to the Son and to the Holy Spirit.
Blessed is the womb that bore you
— Blessed are those who hear the word of God and obey it.

Benedictus Antiphon *From the Proper of the Day*

Litany
Mary endured the estrangement of her unconventional motherhood; comfort all who are victims of sexual violence.
Lord, have mercy.
Mary followed your Son even in his agony; support all who endure the inequalities of our justice system.
Christ, have mercy.
Mary joined the disciples in prayer for the Spirit; deepen the prayer of all committed to contemplation.
Lord, have mercy.

Invitation to the Lord's Prayer As your Word took flesh from Blessed Mary, may you send us your Spirit that we may discern the Mystical Body of your Son as we pray to you.

Collect *From the Proper of the Day*

The Blessing
May we who believe that God sent his Son, born of a woman, born under the law, be blessed in our redemption and our adoption as children of God. **Amen.**

Common of the Blessed Virgin Mary
Noonday Prayer

Hymn Virgin Born, we bow before thee *Hymnal 258*

Antiphon Mary treasured all these words and pondered them in her heart. (Alleluia)
Psalms from Sunday of Week One Noonday Prayer

Reading Zechariah 9:9
Rejoice greatly, O daughter Zion! Shout aloud, O daughter Jerusalem! Lo, your king comes to you.

Verse and Response
Blessed is the womb that bore you and the breasts that nursed you. (Alleluia)
Blessed rather are those who hear the word of God and obey it. (Alleluia)

Collect *From the Proper of the Day or one of the following*

Common of the Blessed Virgin Mary Evening Prayer II

Hymn Sing we of the Blessed Mother Hymnal 278

Psalm 113 *Laudate, pueri*

Antiphon Blessed are you among women, and blessed is the fruit of your womb. (Alleluia)

1 Hallelujah!
 Give praise, you servants of the LORD; *
  praise the Name of the LORD.

2 Let the Name of the LORD be blessed, *
  from this time forth for evermore.

3 From the rising of the sun to its going down *
  let the Name of the LORD be praised.

4 The LORD is high above all nations, *
  and his glory above the heavens.

5 Who is like the LORD our God, who sits enthroned on high, *
  but stoops to behold the heavens and the earth?

6 He takes up the weak out of the dust *
  and lifts up the poor from the ashes.

7 He sets them with the princes, *
  with the princes of his people.

8 He makes the woman of a childless house *
  to be a joyful mother of children.

Antiphon Blessed are you among women, and blessed is the fruit of your womb. (Alleluia)

Psalm 122 *Lætatus sum*

Antiphon All glorious is the princess as she enters; her gown is cloth-of-gold. (Alleluia)

1 I was glad when they said to me, *
    "Let us go to the house of the LORD."

2 Now our feet are standing *
    within your gates, O Jerusalem.

3 Jerusalem is built as a city *
    that is at unity with itself;

4 To which the tribes go up,
    the tribes of the LORD, *
    the assembly of Israel,
    to praise the Name of the LORD.

5 For there are the thrones of judgment, *
    the thrones of the house of David.

6 Pray for the peace of Jerusalem: *
    "May they prosper who love you.

7 Peace be within your walls *
    and quietness within your towers.

8 For my brethren and companions' sake, *
    I pray for your prosperity.

9 Because of the house of the LORD our God, *
    I will seek to do you good."

Antiphon All glorious is the princess as she enters; her gown is cloth-of-gold. (Alleluia)

Psalm 127 *Nisi Dominus*

Antiphon You are the glory of Jerusalem, the joy of Israel. You are the honor of our people. (Alleluia)

1 Unless the LORD builds the house, *
    their labor is in vain who build it.

2 Unless the LORD watches over the city, *
    in vain the watchman keeps his vigil.

3 It is in vain that you rise so early and go to bed so late; *
    vain, too, to eat the bread of toil,
    for he gives to his beloved sleep.

4 Children are a heritage from the LORD, *
   and the fruit of the womb is a gift.

5 Like arrows in the hand of a warrior *
   are the children of one's youth.

6 Blessed is the man who has his quiver full of them! *
   he shall not be put to shame
   when he contends with his enemies in the gate.

Antiphon You are the glory of Jerusalem, the joy of Israel. You are the honor of our people. (Alleluia)

Reading *From the Proper of the Day*

Responsory (Luke 1: 42; Luke 11: 28)
Blessed are you among women
   — blessed is the fruit of your womb.
Blessed are they who hear the word of God and keep it
   — blessed is the fruit of your womb.
Glory to the Father, and to the Son and to the Holy Spirit.
Blessed are you among women
   — blessed is the fruit of your womb.

Magnificat Antiphon *From the Proper of the Day*

Litany
The Father has chosen Mary to be the mother of his Son; let us rejoice with Christ in being called beloved children of God.
Lord have mercy.
Mary proclaimed that God would feed the hungry and lift the downtrodden; may we open our hands and our hearts to serve Christ in the hungry and oppressed.
Christ have mercy.
Mary has entered into the dwelling place prepared for her by Christ; may all the dead enter their heavenly home.
Lord have mercy.

Invitation to the Lord's Prayer
Rejoicing in our hope of sharing the glory of God, let us long for the kingdom of God in the words of Christ.

Collect *From the Proper of the Day*

Blessing
May we who celebrate Mary whose womb bore Christ and whose breasts nursed Christ be more blessed in hearing the word of God and obeying it. **Amen.**

Common of the Blessed Virgin Mary on Saturday Morning Prayer

Hymn Praise we the Lord this day *Hymnal 267*

Psalms from Saturday of the Current Week.

Benedictus Antiphon
Lent 1-4 A sword will pierce your own soul.
Lent 5 Woman here is your son. Here is your mother.
Easter 1-5 Rejoice and be glad, O Virgin Mary, for the Lord is risen indeed, hallelujah.
Easter 6-7 They constantly devoted themselves to prayer, together with certain women, including Mary, the mother of Jesus, as well as his brothers, hallelujah.

Litany
Mary endured the estrangement of her unconventional motherhood; comfort all who are victims of sexual violence.
Lord, have mercy.
Mary followed your Son even in his agony; support all who endure the inequalities of our justice system.
Christ, have mercy.
Mary joined the disciples in prayer for the Spirit; deepen the prayer of all committed to contemplation.
Lord, have mercy.

Invitation to the Lord's Prayer As your Word took flesh from Blessed Mary, may you send us your Spirit that we may discern the Mystical Body of your Son as we pray to you.

Collect
Pour your grace into our hearts, O Lord, that we who have known the incarnation of your Son Jesus Christ, announced by an angel to the Virgin Mary, may by his cross and passion be brought to the glory of his resurrection; who lives and reigns with you, in the unity of the Holy Spirit, one God, now and for ever. Amen.

The Blessing
May we who celebrate Mary whose womb bore Christ and whose breasts nursed Christ be more blessed in hearing the word of God and obeying it. **Amen.**

or

May we who believe that God sent his Son, born of a woman, born under the law, be blessed in our redemption and our adoption as children of God. **Amen.**

Common of the Blessed Virgin Mary on Saturday
Noonday Prayer

Hymn Virgin Born, we bow before thee Hymnal 258

Antiphon You are the glory of Jerusalem, the joy of Israel, the highest honor of our people. (Alleluia)

Reading Zechariah 9:9
Rejoice greatly, O daughter Zion! Shout aloud, O daughter Jerusalem! Lo, your king comes to you.

Verse and Response
Blessed is the womb that bore you and the breasts that nursed you. (Alleluia)
Blessed are those who hear the word of God and obey it. (Alleluia)

Collect Father in heaven, by your grace the virgin mother of your incarnate Son was blessed in bearing him, but still more blessed in keeping your word: Grant us who honor the exaltation of her lowliness to follow the example of her devotion to your will; through Jesus Christ our Lord, who lives and reigns with you and the Holy Spirit, one God, for ever and ever. Amen.

Common of the Apostles
Evening Prayer I

Hymn The eternal gifts of Christ the King *Hymnal 233*

Antiphon 1 I give you a new commandment, that you love one another. (Alleluia)
Psalms from Sunday Week 1 Evening Prayer I
or Sunday Evening Prayer I of the Current Week.
Antiphon 2 No one has greater love than this, to lay down one's life for one's friends. (Alleluia)

Antiphon 3 You are my friends if you do what I command you. (Alleluia)

Reading *From the Proper of the Day*

Responsory (Jn. 13:35)
By this everyone will know
　　− you are my disciples.
If you have love for one another
　　− you are my disciples.
Glory to the Father, and to the Son and to the Holy Spirit.
By this everyone will know
　　− you are my disciples.

Magnificat Antiphon You did not choose me but I chose you. And I appointed you to go and bear fruit, fruit that will endure. (Alleluia)

Litany
The apostles endured depravation and hardship; come to the aid of the hungry, the homeless and those in prison.
Lord, have mercy.
The apostles preached a gospel of peace; restore peace to those places torn by conflict.
Christ, have mercy.
The apostles proclaimed the Jesus was risen from the dead; bring all the departed into the light of your glory.
Lord, have mercy.

Invitation to the Lord's Prayer
Impelled by the Spirit to carry out Christ's mission to all people, let us pray that Christ restore all people to unity with God and one another in God's heavenly kingdom.

Collect *From the Proper of the Day*

The Blessing
Let us pray for one another that the word of the Lord may spread rapidly and be glorified everywhere, just as it is among us. **Amen.**

Common of the Apostles
Morning Prayer

Invitatory Christ is the Lord of the Apostles: Come let us adore. (Alleluia)

Hymn A mighty sound from heaven *Hymnal 230*

Antiphon 1 Go and make disciples of all nations, baptizing them and teaching them to obey everything that I have commanded you. (Alleluia)
Psalms from Sunday Week 1 Morning Prayer
or Sunday Morning Prayer of the Current Week.
Antiphon 2 I am among you as one who serves. (Alleluia)
Antiphon 3 You are those who have stood by me in my trials. (Alleluia)

Reading One *From the Proper of the Day*

Responsory (1 Jn. 1:3)
We declare to you what we have seen and heard
　　— **that you may have fellowship with us.**
Our fellowship is with the Father and with his Son
　　— **that you may have fellowship with us.**
Glory to the Father, and to the Son and to the Holy Spirit
We declare to you what we have seen and heard
　　— **that you may have fellowship with us.**

Canticle – Song of the Apostles　　*Vos sacerdotes Domini*
(Isaiah 61: 6-9)
Antiphon In former generations this mystery was not made known to humankind, as it has now been revealed to his holy apostles and prophets by the Spirit. (Alleluia.)

You shall be called priests of the Lord, *
　　you shall be named ministers of our God;

You shall enjoy the wealth of the nations, *
　　and in their riches you shall glory.

Because their shame was double, *
　　and dishonor was proclaimed as their lot,

Therefore they shall possess a double portion; *
　　everlasting joy shall be theirs.

For I the Lord love justice, *
　　I hate robbery and wrongdoing;

I will faithfully give them their recompense, *
　　and I will make an everlasting covenant with them.

Their descendants shall be known among the nations, *
　　and their offspring among the peoples;

All who see them shall acknowledge *
　　that they are a people whom the Lord has blessed.

Antiphon In former generations this mystery was not made known to humankind, as it has now been revealed to his holy apostles and prophets by the Spirit. (Alleluia.)

Reading Two *From the Proper of the Day*

Responsory (Jn. 13:34)
I give you a new commandment
    – love one another.
Just as I have loved you
    – love one another.
Glory to the Father and **to** the Son and to the Holy Spirit.
I give you a new commandment
    – love one another.

Benedictus Antiphon I do not call you servants; but I have called you friends, because I have made known to you everything that I have heard from my Father. (Alleluia)

Litany
Strengthen us in the faith we have received that we may continue in the apostles' teaching and fellowship, in the breaking of bread and in the prayers.
Lord, have mercy.
Empower us in the faith we have received that we may proclaim by word and example the Good News of God in Christ.
Christ, have mercy.
Confirm us in the faith we have received that we may strive for justice and peace among all people and respect the dignity of every human being.
Lord, have mercy.

Invitation to the Lord's Prayer
Baptized into the faith we received from the apostles, let us open our hearts in prayer to our Father.

Collect *From the Proper of the Day*

The Blessing
May we rejoice that we are no longer strangers and aliens, but that we are citizens with the saints and members of the household of God, built upon the foundation of the apostles and prophets, with Christ Jesus himself as the cornerstone. **Amen.**

Common of the Apostles
Noonday Prayer

Hymn They cast their nets in Galilee *Hymnal 661*

Antiphon We preach Christ crucified, the power of God and the wisdom of God. (Alleluia)
Psalms from Sunday Week 1 Noonday Prayer
Reading Acts 5:41-42
As they left the council, the apostles rejoiced that they were considered worthy to suffer dishonor for the sake of the name. And every day in the temple and at home they did not cease to teach and proclaim Jesus as the Messiah.

Verse and Response
Rejoice and be glad. (Alleluia)
That your names are written in heaven. (Alleluia)

Collect *From the Proper of the Day*

Common of the Apostles
Evening Prayer II

Hymn By all your saints still striving *Hymnal 231-232 (using the appropriate second verse)*

Psalm 112 *Beatus vir*

Antiphon 1 No one has greater love than this, to lay down one's life for one's friends. (Alleluia)

1 Hallelujah!
   Blessed are they who fear the Lord *
      and have great delight in his commandments!

2 Their descendants will be mighty in the land; *
      the generation of the upright will be blessed.

3 Wealth and riches will be in their house, *
      and their righteousness will last for ever.

4 Light shines in the darkness for the upright; *
      the righteous are merciful and full of compassion.

5 It is good for them to be generous in lending *
      and to manage their affairs with justice.

6 For they will never be shaken; *
      the righteous will be kept in everlasting remembrance.

7 They will not be afraid of any evil rumors; *
    their heart is right;
    they put their trust in the Lord.

8 Their heart is established and will not shrink, *
    until they see their desire upon their enemies.

9 They have given freely to the poor, *
    and their righteousness stands fast for ever;
    they will hold up their head with honor.

10 The wicked will see it and be angry;
    they will gnash their teeth and pine away; *
    the desires of the wicked will perish.

Antiphon 1 No one has greater love than this, to lay down one's life for one's friends. (Alleluia)

Psalm 115 *Non nobis, Domine*

Antiphon I have chosen you out of the world—therefore the world hates you. (Alleluia)

1 Not to us, O Lord, not to us,
    but to your Name give glory; *
    because of your love and because of your faithfulness.

2 Why should the heathen say, *
    "Where then is their God?"

3 Our God is in heaven; *
    whatever he wills to do he does.

4 Their idols are silver and gold, *
    the work of human hands.

5 They have mouths, but they cannot speak; *
    eyes have they, but they cannot see;

6 They have ears, but they cannot hear; *
    noses, but they cannot smell;

7 They have hands, but they cannot feel;
    feet, but they cannot walk; *
    they make no sound with their throat.

8 Those who make them are like them, *
    and so are all who put their trust in them.

9 O Israel, trust in the LORD; *
    he is their help and their shield.

10 O house of Aaron, trust in the LORD; *
    he is their help and their shield.

11 You who fear the LORD, trust in the LORD; *
    he is their help and their shield.

12 The LORD has been mindful of us, and he will bless us; *
    he will bless the house of Israel;
    he will bless the house of Aaron;

13 He will bless those who fear the LORD, *
    both small and great together.

14 May the LORD increase you more and more, *
    you and your children after you.

15 May you be blessed by the LORD, *
    the maker of heaven and earth.

16 The heaven of heavens is the LORD'S, *
    but he entrusted the earth to its peoples.

17 The dead do not praise the LORD, *
    nor all those who go down into silence;

18 But we will bless the LORD, *
    from this time forth for evermore.
    Hallelujah!

Antiphon I have chosen you out of the world—therefore the world hates you. (Alleluia)

Psalm 138 *Confitebor tibi*

Antiphon Servants are not greater than their master. If they persecuted me, they will persecute you. (Alleluia)

1   I will give thanks to you, O LORD, with my whole heart; *
    before the gods I will sing your praise.

2   I will bow down toward your holy temple
    and praise your Name, *
    because of your love and faithfulness;

3   For you have glorified your Name *
    and your word above all things.

4 When I called, you answered me; *
    you increased my strength within me.

5 All the kings of the earth will praise you, O LORD, *
    when they have heard the words of your mouth.

6 They will sing of the ways of the LORD, *
    that great is the glory of the LORD.

7 Though the LORD be high, he cares for the lowly; *
    he perceives the haughty from afar.

8 Though I walk in the midst of trouble, you keep me safe; *
    you stretch forth your hand against the fury of my enemies;
    your right hand shall save me.

9 The LORD will make good his purpose for me; *
    O LORD, your love endures for ever;
    do not abandon the works of your hands.

Antiphon Servants are not greater than their master. If they persecuted me, they will persecute you. (Alleluia)

Reading *From the Proper of the Day*

Responsory (Ps. 96:3; Mk. 16:15)
Declare God's glory among the nations
    – **the Lord's marvelous works among all the peoples.**
Proclaim the good news to the whole creation
    – **the Lord's marvelous works among all the peoples.**
Glory to the Father and to the Son and to the Holy Spirit.
Declare God's glory among the nations
    – **the Lord's marvelous works among all the peoples.**

Magnificat Antiphon Servants are not greater than their master, nor are messengers greater than the one who sent them. If you know these things, you are blessed if you do them. (Alleluia)

Litany
The apostles endured depravation and hardship; come to the aid of the hungry, the homeless and those in prison.
Lord, have mercy.
The apostles preached a gospel of peace; restore peace to those places torn by conflict.
Christ, have mercy.

The apostles proclaimed that Jesus was raised from the dead; bring all the departed into the light of your glory.
Lord, have mercy.

Invitation to the Lord's Prayer
Since we share the apostles' mission as ambassadors of reconciliation, let us ask the Father to hasten the coming of the kingdom.

Collect *From the Proper of the Day*

The Blessing
Let us pray for one another that the word of the Lord may spread rapidly and be glorified everywhere, just as it is among us. **Amen.**

Common of Evangelists Evening Prayer I

Hymn Thanks be to God whose Word was spoken *Hymnal 630*

Psalm 110 *Dixit Dominus*
Antiphon The Gentiles have become fellow-heirs, members of the same body, through the gospel. (Alleluia)

1 The LORD said to my Lord, "Sit at my right hand, *
    until I make your enemies your footstool."

2 The LORD will send the scepter of your power out of Zion, *
    saying, "Rule over your enemies round about you.

3 Princely state has been yours from the day of your birth; *
    in the beauty of holiness have I begotten you,
    like dew from the womb of the morning."

4 The LORD has sworn and he will not recant: *
    "You are a priest for ever after the order of Melchizedek."

5 The Lord who is at your right hand
    will smite kings in the day of his wrath; *
    he will rule over the nations.

6 He will heap high the corpses; *
    he will smash heads over the wide earth.

7 He will drink from the brook beside the road; *
    therefore he will lift high his head.

Antiphon The Gentiles have become fellow-heirs, members of the same body, through the gospel. (Alleluia)

Psalm 96 *Cantate Domino*

Antiphon I do it all for the sake of the gospel, so that I may share in its blessings. (Alleluia)

1 Sing to the LORD a new song; *
 sing to the LORD, all the whole earth.

2 Sing to the LORD and bless his Name; *
 proclaim the good news of his salvation from day to day.

3 Declare his glory among the nations *
 and his wonders among all peoples.

4 For great is the LORD and greatly to be praised; *
 he is more to be feared than all gods.

5 As for all the gods of the nations, they are but idols; *
 but it is the LORD who made the heavens.

6 Oh, the majesty and magnificence of his presence! *
 Oh, the power and the splendor of his sanctuary!

7 Ascribe to the LORD, you families of the peoples; *
 ascribe to the LORD honor and power.

8 Ascribe to the LORD the honor due his Name; *
 bring offerings and come into his courts.

9 Worship the LORD in the beauty of holiness; *
 let the whole earth tremble before him.

10 Tell it out among the nations: "The LORD is King! *
 he has made the world so firm that it cannot be moved;
 he will judge the peoples with equity."

11 Let the heavens rejoice, and let the earth be glad;
 let the sea thunder and all that is in it; *
 let the field be joyful and all that is therein.

12 Then shall all the trees of the wood shout for joy
 before the LORD when he comes, *
 when he comes to judge the earth.

13 He will judge the world with righteousness *
 and the peoples with his truth.

Antiphon I do it all for the sake of the gospel, so that I may share in its blessings. (Alleluia)

Psalm 145 *Exaltabo te, Deus*

Antiphon We have heard of your faith in Christ Jesus because of the hope laid up for you in heaven. You have heard of this hope in the word of the truth, the gospel. (Alleluia)

1 I will exalt you, O God my King, *
    and bless your Name for ever and ever.

2 Every day will I bless you *
    and praise your Name for ever and ever.

3 Great is the LORD and greatly to be praised; *
    there is no end to his greatness.

4 One generation shall praise your works to another *
    and shall declare your power.

5 I will ponder the glorious splendor of your majesty *
    and all your marvelous works.

6 They shall speak of the might of your wondrous acts, *
    and I will tell of your greatness.

7 They shall publish the remembrance of your great goodness; *
    they shall sing of your righteous deeds.

8 The LORD is gracious and full of compassion, *
    slow to anger and of great kindness.

9 The LORD is loving to everyone *
    and his compassion is over all his works.

10 All your works praise you, O LORD, *
    and your faithful servants bless you.

11 They make known the glory of your kingdom *
    and speak of your power;

12 That the peoples may know of your power *
    and the glorious splendor of your kingdom.

13 Your kingdom is an everlasting kingdom; *
    your dominion endures throughout all ages.

14 The LORD is faithful in all his words *
    and merciful in all his deeds.

15 The LORD upholds all those who fall; *
    he lifts up those who are bowed down.

16 The eyes of all wait upon you, O LORD, *
    and you give them their food in due season.

17 You open wide your hand *
    and satisfy the needs of every living creature.

18 The LORD is righteous in all his ways *
    and loving in all his works.

19 The LORD is near to those who call upon him, *
    to all who call upon him faithfully.

20 He fulfills the desire of those who fear him; *
    he hears their cry and helps them.

21 The LORD preserves all those who love him, *
    but he destroys all the wicked.

22 My mouth shall speak the praise of the LORD; *
    let all flesh bless his holy Name for ever and ever.

Antiphon We have heard of your faith in Christ Jesus because of the hope laid up for you in heaven. You have heard of this hope in the word of the truth, the gospel. (Alleluia)

Reading *From the Proper of the Day*

Responsory (Is. 61:1; Lk. 4:18)
The Spirit of the Lord is upon me
    – to bring good news to the poor.
He has sent me to proclaim release to the captives
    – to bring good news to the poor.
Glory to the Father, and to the Son and to the Holy Spirit.
The Spirit of the Lord is upon me
    – to bring good news to the poor.

Magnificat Antiphon *From the Proper of the Day*

Litany
Father you revealed the mystery to bring all people together in Christ's body; manifest that mystery among those who are estranged.
Lord, have mercy.
You brought healing to a world broken by conflict and intolerance; restore those yearning for your word of grace and compassion. .
Christ, have mercy.

You gather into one the dispersed children of God; bring the dead to enjoy the light of your love.
Lord, have mercy.

Invitation to the Lord's Prayer We have received the word of truth in the Gospel so form us by the Spirit in the likeness of Christ as we pray.

Collect *From the Proper of the Day*

The Blessing
May we clothe ourselves with faith and the performance of good works and set out on the way, with the Gospel as our guide, that we may deserve to see him who has called us to his kingdom. **Amen.**

Common of Evangelists Morning Prayer

Invitatory Christ is the Lord and Teacher of the Evangelists: Come let us adore. (Alleluia)

Hymn Lamp of our feet, whereby we trace *Hymnal 627*

Antiphon 1 God's grace has now been revealed through the appearing of our Savior Christ Jesus, who brought life and immortality to light through the gospel. (Alleluia)
Psalms from Sunday Week 1 Morning Prayer
Antiphon 2 God is able to strengthen you according to my gospel and the proclamation of Jesus Christ. (Alleluia)
Antiphon 3 I am not ashamed of the gospel; it is the power of God for salvation to everyone who has faith. (Alleluia)

Reading One *From the Proper of the Day*

Responsory (1 Cor. 9:23; Rom. 1:9)
I do it all for the sake of the gospel
— so that I may share in its blessings.
I serve God by announcing the gospel of his Son
— so that I may share in its blessings.
Glory to the Father and to the Son and to the Holy Spirit.
I do it all for the sake of the gospel
— so that I may share in its blessings.

Canticle – Song of the Mystery of Christ *In mysterio Christi*
(Ephesians 3: 5-10)
Antiphon I have become a servant of the Gospel according to the gift of God's grace. (Alleluia)

The mystery of Christ was not made known to humankind *
  in former generations.

It has now been revealed *
  to his holy apostles and prophets by the Spirit.

The Gentiles have become fellow-heirs,
members of the same body, *
  and sharers in the promise in Christ Jesus through the gospel.

Of this gospel I have become a servant *
  according to the gift of God's grace.

The Gospel was given to me *
  by the working of God's power.

Although I am the very least of all the saints, *
  this grace was given to me:

To bring to the Gentiles the news
of the boundless riches of Christ, *
  and to make everyone see what is the plan of the mystery.

That mystery of Christ lay hidden for ages in God *
  who created all things;

So that through the church the wisdom of God in its rich variety *
  might now be made known
  to the rulers and authorities in the heavenly places.

Antiphon I have become a servant of the Gospel according to the gift of God's grace. (Alleluia)

Reading Two *From the Proper of the Day*

Responsory Two (Eph. 3:5, 6)
In former times this mystery was not made known to humankind
  — as it has now been revealed by the Spirit.
Through the Gospel, the Gentiles become members of the same body.
  — as it has now been revealed by the Spirit.
Glory to the Father, and to the Son and to the Holy Spirit.
In former times this mystery was not made known to humankind
  — as it has now been revealed by the Spirit.

Benedictus Antiphon *From the Proper of the Day*

Litany
You called your holy evangelists to proclaim the good news of Jesus, your Son; continue to call faithful ministers of your word.
Lord, have mercy.
You manifested your healing to a broken world through the ministry of your beloved Son; continue your healing work through contemplative prayer.
Christ, have mercy.
You summoned the Gentiles to be joint heirs of the promises you gave to Abraham and Sarah; continue to call all people to share the table of your Holy Word.
Lord, have mercy.

Invitation to the Lord's Prayer We have received in the Gospel the full mystery of the Incarnate Word so we pray with Christ to the Father.

Collect *From the Proper of the Day*

The Blessing
May we do everything for the sake of the gospel, so that we may share in its blessings. **Amen.**

Common of Evangelists Noonday Prayer

Hymn Come sing, ye choirs exultant *Hymnal 235*

Antiphon Live your life in a manner worthy of the gospel of Christ. (Alleluia)
Psalms from Sunday Week 1 Noonday Prayer

Reading Ephesians 4: 11-13
The gifts he gave were that some would be apostles, some prophets, some evangelists, some pastors and teachers, to equip the saints for the work of ministry, for building up the body of Christ, until all of us come to the unity of the faith and of the knowledge of the Son of God, to maturity, to the measure of the full stature of Christ.

Verse and Response
Our message of the gospel came to you not in word only. (Alleluia)
But in power and in the Holy Spirit. (Alleluia)

Collect *From the Proper of the Day*

Common of Evangelists Evening Prayer II

Hymn Spread, O spread, thou mighty word *Hymnal 530*

Psalm 116 *Dilexi, quoniam*

Antiphon The Gentiles have become fellow-heirs, members of the same body, through the gospel. (Alleluia)

1 I love the LORD, because he has heard
 the voice of my supplication, *
  because he has inclined his ear to me
  whenever I called upon him.

2 The cords of death entangled me;
 the grip of the grave took hold of me; *
  I came to grief and sorrow.

3 Then I called upon the Name of the LORD: *
  "O LORD, I pray you, save my life."

4 Gracious is the LORD and righteous; *
  our God is full of compassion.

5 The LORD watches over the innocent; *
  I was brought very low, and he helped me.

6 Turn again to your rest, O my soul, *
  for the LORD has treated you well.

7 For you have rescued my life from death, *
  my eyes from tears, and my feet from stumbling.

8 I will walk in the presence of the LORD *
  in the land of the living.

9 I believed, even when I said,
 "I have been brought very low." *
  In my distress I said, "No one can be trusted."

10 How shall I repay the LORD *
  for all the good things he has done for me?

11 I will lift up the cup of salvation *
  and call upon the Name of the LORD.

12 I will fulfill my vows to the LORD *
  in the presence of all his people.

13 Precious in the sight of the LORD *
   is the death of his servants.

14 O LORD, I am your servant; *
   I am your servant and the child of your handmaid;
   you have freed me from my bonds.

15 I will offer you the sacrifice of thanksgiving *
   and call upon the Name of the LORD.

16 I will fulfill my vows to the LORD *
   in the presence of all his people,

17 In the courts of the LORD'S house, *
   in the midst of you, O Jerusalem.
   Hallelujah!

Antiphon The Gentiles have become fellow-heirs, members of the same body, through the gospel. (Alleluia)

Psalm 126 *In convertendo*

Antiphon I do it all for the sake of the gospel, so that I may share in its blessings. (Alleluia)

1 When the LORD restored the fortunes of Zion, *
   then were we like those who dream.

2 Then was our mouth filled with laughter, *
   and our tongue with shouts of joy.

3 Then they said among the nations, *
   "The LORD has done great things for them."

4 The LORD has done great things for us, *
   and we are glad indeed.

5 Restore our fortunes, O LORD, *
   like the watercourses of the Negev.

6 Those who sowed with tears *
   will reap with songs of joy.

7 Those who go out weeping, carrying the seed, *
   will come again with joy, shouldering their sheaves.

Antiphon I do it all for the sake of the gospel, so that I may share in its blessings. (Alleluia)

Psalm 138 *Confitebor tibi*

Antiphon We have heard of your faith in Christ Jesus and of the love that you have for all the saints, because of the hope laid up for you in heaven. You have heard of this hope in the gospel. (Alleluia)

1 I will give thanks to you, O LORD, with my whole heart; *
    before the gods I will sing your praise.

2 I will bow down toward your holy temple
    and praise your Name, *
    because of your love and faithfulness;

3 For you have glorified your Name *
    and your word above all things.

4 When I called, you answered me; *
    you increased my strength within me.

5 All the kings of the earth will praise you, O LORD, *
    when they have heard the words of your mouth.

6 They will sing of the ways of the LORD, *
    that great is the glory of the LORD.

7 Though the LORD be high, he cares for the lowly; *
    he perceives the haughty from afar.

8 Though I walk in the midst of trouble, you keep me safe; *
    you stretch forth your hand against the fury of my enemies;
    your right hand shall save me.

9 The LORD will make good his purpose for me; *
    O LORD, your love endures for ever;
    do not abandon the works of your hands.

Antiphon We have heard of your faith in Christ Jesus and of the love that you have for all the saints, because of the hope laid up for you in heaven. You have heard of this hope in the gospel. (Alleluia)

Reading *From the Proper of the Day*

Responsory (Is. 61:1; Lk. 4:18)
The Spirit of the Lord is upon me
    − to bring good news to the poor.
He has sent me to proclaim release to the captives
    − to bring good news to the poor.
Glory to the Father, and to the Son and to the Holy Spirit.

The Spirit of the Lord is upon me
  — **to bring good news to the poor.**

Magnificat Antiphon *From the Proper of the Day*

Litany
Father you revealed the mystery to bring all people together in Christ's body; manifest that mystery among those who are estranged.
Lord, have mercy.
You brought healing to a world broken by conflict and intolerance; restore those yearning for your word of grace and compassion. .
Christ, have mercy.
You gather into one the dispersed children of God; bring the dead to enjoy the light of your love.
Lord, have mercy.

Invitation to the Lord's Prayer In the Gospel, the Father reveals himself to us in Christ by the Spirit. In that Spirit, we pray with Christ to the Father.

Collect *From the Proper of the Day*

The Blessing
May we clothe ourselves with faith and the performance of good works and set out on the way, with the Gospel as our guide, that we may deserve to see God who has called us to his kingdom. **Amen.**

Common of Martyrs Morning Prayer

Invitatory Christ calls us to carry the cross: Come let us worship the King of Martyrs. (Alleluia)

Hymn Let us now our voices raise *Hymnal 237*

Antiphon 1 Whoever acknowledges me before others, the Son of Man also will acknowledge before the angels of God. (Alleluia)
Antiphon 2 We share abundantly in Christ's sufferings, so through Christ we share abundantly in his consolation. (Alleluia)
Antiphon 3 If you would serve me, you must follow me; and where I am, there also shall my servant be. (Alleluia)

Reading One *From the Proper of the Day*

Responsory One (Jn. 12:24; 1 Cor. 15:36)
If the grain of wheat dies
    — **it bears much fruit.**
What is sown is perishable, what is raised is imperishable
    — **it bears much fruit.**
Glory to the Father and to the Son and to the Holy Spirit.
If the grain of wheat dies
    — **it bears much fruit.**

Canticle — Song of the Martyrs *Iustoium animae*
(Wisdom 3: 1-6)

Antiphon If any want to become my followers, let them deny themselves and take up their cross and follow me. (Alleluia)

The souls of the righteous are in the hand of God, *
    and no torment will ever touch them.

In the eyes of the foolish they seemed to have died, *
    and their departure was thought to be a disaster.

Their going from us was considered to be their destruction; *
    but they are at peace.

For though in the sight of others they were punished, *
    their hope is full of immortality.

Having been disciplined a little, they will receive great good, *
    because God tested them and found them worthy of himself.

Like gold in the furnace he tried them, *
    and like a sacrificial burnt offering he accepted them.

Antiphon If any want to become my followers, let them deny themselves and take up their cross and follow me. (Alleluia)

Reading Two *From the Proper of the Day*

Responsory Two (Ps. 59:10, 11)
My eyes are fixed on you, O my Strength
    — **for you, O God, are my stronghold.**
My merciful God comes to meet me
    — **for you, O God, are my stronghold.**
Glory to the Father and to the Son and to the Holy Spirit.
My eyes are fixed on you, O my Strength
    — **for you, O God, are my stronghold.**

Benedictus Antiphon Those who hate their life in this world will keep it for eternal life. (Alleluia)

Litany
The martyrs show your strength made perfect in their weakness; support us in our frailty.
Lord, have mercy.
The martyrs bore witness to you name by their death; let us proclaim you in word and action.
Christ, have mercy.
The martyrs discovered your power coming to their aid in their suffering; lift up all who experience pain and abandonment.
Lord, have mercy.

Invitation to the Lord's Prayer
As the martyrs gave their lives as an offering of love, forgiving those who killed them, let us seek the image of God in those who offend us by asking God to forgive us as we forgive others.

Collect *From the Proper of the Day*

The Blessing
May we always carry in our bodies the death of Jesus so that the life of Jesus may also be made visible in our bodies. **Amen.**

Common of Martyrs Noonday Prayer
Hymn King of the martyrs noble band *Hymnal 236*

Antiphon They have washed their robes and made them white in the blood of the Lamb. (Alleluia)

Reading James 1: 12
Blessed is anyone who endures temptation. Such a one has stood the test and will receive the crown of life that the Lord has promised to those who love him.

Verse and Response
Be faithful until death. (Alleluia)
And I will give you the crown of life. (Alleluia)

Collect *From the Proper of the Day or one of the following*
Almighty God, who gave your servant N. boldness to confess the Name of our Savior Jesus Christ before the rulers of this world, and courage to die for this faith: Grant that we may always be ready to give a reason for the hope that is in us, and to suffer gladly for the sake of our Lord Jesus

Christ; who lives and reigns with you and the Holy Spirit, one God, for ever and ever. Amen.

or this
Almighty God, by whose grace and power your holy martyr N. triumphed over suffering and was faithful even to death: Grant us, who now remember him in thanksgiving, to be so faithful in our witness to you in this world, that we may receive with him the crown of life; through Jesus Christ our Lord, who lives and reigns with you and the Holy Spirit, one God, for ever and ever. Amen.

or this (for a Virgin Martyr)
Almighty and everlasting God, who kindled the flame of your love in the heart of your holy martyr N.: Grant to us, your humble servants, a like faith and power of love, that we who rejoice in her triumph may profit by her example; through Jesus Christ our Lord, who lives and reigns with you and the Holy Spirit, one God, for ever and ever. Amen.

Common of Martyrs Evening Prayer

Hymn Blessed feasts of blessed martyrs *Hymnal 239*

Antiphon 1 You will be hated by all because of my name but the one who endures to the end will be saved. (Alleluia)
Antiphon 2 I consider that the sufferings of this present time are not worth comparing with the glory about to be revealed to us. (Alleluia)
Antiphon 3 Whoever follows me will never walk in darkness but will have the light of life. (Alleluia)

Reading *From the Proper of the Day*

Responsory (Ps. 66:9,11)
You, O God, have proved us
    – you have tried us just as silver is tried.
You brought us out into a place of refreshment
    – you have tried us just as silver is tried.
Glory to the Father and to the Son and to the Holy Spirit.
You, O God, have proved us
    – you have tried us just as silver is tried.

Magnificat Antiphon The holy friends of Christ rejoice in heaven. They followed in his footsteps to the end. They have shed their blood for love of him and will reign with him forever. (Alleluia)

Litany

By shedding their blood, the martyrs gave their greatest witness to Christ. Strengthen our faith by the example of the martyrs.
Lord, have mercy.
By shedding their blood, the martyrs surrendered all for love of you. Deepen our attachment to you and our detachment from passing things.
Christ, have mercy.
By shedding their blood, the martyrs were united with Christ in his self-offering. May the martyrs come to welcome all the dead and lead them to the holy city, the new and eternal Jerusalem.
Lord, have mercy.

Invitation to the Lord's Prayer

Christ joined the martyrs to himself in union with the Father. Let us pray to become one with the Father through prayer and holiness of life.

Collect *From the Proper of the Day*

The Blessing

May we rejoice in our sufferings for the church, for in our flesh we are completing what is lacking in Christ's afflictions for the sake of his body, that is, the church. **Amen.**

Common of Pastors Morning Prayer

Invitatory Christ is the Shepherd of the flock: Come let us adore. (Alleluia)

Hymn Shepherd of souls, refresh and bless *Hymnal 343*

Antiphon 1 You are the light of the world. A city built on a hill cannot be hid. (Alleluia)
Antiphon 2 Let your light shine before others, so that they may see your good works and give glory to your Father in heaven. (Alleluia)
Antiphon 3 Whoever wishes to be great among you must be your servant. (Alleluia)

Reading One *From the Proper of the Day*

Responsory (Ez. 34:15; Jn. 10:14)
I myself will be the shepherd of my sheep
   – and I will make them lie down.
I know my sheep and my sheep know me
   – and I will make them lie down
Glory to the Father and to the Son and to the Holy Spirit.

I myself will be the shepherd of my sheep
  – and I will make them lie down.

Canticle – Song of the Learned   *Beatus qui in sapientia*
(Sirach 14:22; 15:3.4.6b)

Antiphon Tend the flock of God that is in your charge, exercising the oversight, as God would have you do. Be examples to the flock. (Alleluia)

Blessed are they who meditate on wisdom *
  and reason intelligently,

Who reflect in their hearts on her ways *
  and ponder her secrets,

She will feed them with the bread of learning, *
  and give them the water of wisdom to drink.

They will lean on her and not fall, *
  and they will rely on her and not be put to shame.

She will exalt them above their neighbors, *
  and will open their mouths in the midst of the assembly.

They will find gladness and a crown of rejoicing, *
  and will inherit an everlasting name.

Antiphon Tend the flock of God that is in your charge, exercising the oversight, as God would have you do. Be examples to the flock. (Alleluia)

Reading Two *From the Proper of the Day*

Responsory Two (Ez. 3:17)
I have made you a watchman for the house of Israel
  – you shall give them warning from me.
Whenever you hear a word from my mouth
  – you shall give them warning from me.
Glory to the Father and to the Son and to the Holy Spirit.
I have made you a watchman for the house of Israel
  – you shall give them warning from me.

Benedictus Antiphon The Lord God will feed his flock like a shepherd, he will gather the lambs in his arms; he will carry them in his bosom, and gently lead those that are with young. (Alleluia)

Litany
We thank you for raising up faithful pastors from among your people; give wisdom to our leaders that they may lead us in ways both new and old.
Lord, have mercy.
Your leaders championed the cause of the poor and alienated; open the ears of our leaders to hear your voice in the marginalized and outcast.
Christ, have mercy.
Your leaders spoke a word inspired by tradition in a language understood by the people of their day; open the minds and lips of our leaders to speak a faithful yet innovative word.
Lord, have mercy.

Invitation to the Lord's Prayer
You continue to call shepherds to pastor your flock so with our shepherds and all your faithful people we pray.

Collect *From the Proper of the Day*

The Blessing
May we remember our leaders, those who spoke the word of God to us; consider the outcome of their way of life, and imitate their faith. **Amen.**

Common of Pastors Noonday Prayer

Hymn Savior, like a shepherd lead us *Hymnal 708*

Antiphon As the Father has sent me, so I send you. (Alleluia)

Reading 1 Tim. 1: 12
I am grateful to Christ Jesus our Lord, who has strengthened me, because he judged me faithful and appointed me to his service.

Verse and Response
Unless the Lord builds the house. (Alleluia)
Their labor is in vain who build it. (Alleluia)

Collect *From the Proper of the Day or the following*
Heavenly Father, Shepherd of your people, we thank you for your servant N., who was faithful in the care and nurture of your flock; and we pray that, following his example and the teaching of his holy life, we may by your grace grow into the stature of the fullness of our Lord and Savior Jesus Christ; who lives and reigns with you and the Holy Spirit, one God, for ever and ever. Amen.

Common of Pastors Evening Prayer

Hymn My Shepherd will supply my need *Hymnal 664*

Antiphon 1 Well done, good and trustworthy slave; enter into the joy of your master. (Alleluia)
Antiphon 2 I am sending you out like sheep into the midst of wolves; so be wise as serpents and innocent as doves. (Alleluia)
Antiphon 3 You received without paying, give without pay. (Alleluia)

Reading *From the Proper of the Day*

Responsory (1 Pt. 4:5; Rev. 2:10)
When the chief shepherd appears
  – you will win the crown of glory.
Be faithful until death, and I will give you the crown of life
  – you will win the crown of glory.
Glory to the Father and to the Son and to the Holy Spirit.
When the chief shepherd appears
  – you will win the crown of glory.

Magnificat Antiphon How beautiful upon the mountains are the feet of the messenger who announces peace, who says to Zion, "Your God reigns." (Alleluia)

Litany
Your pastors reconciled people in conflict; bring your harmony where there is discord.
Lord, have mercy.
Your pastors continued your ministry of healing; restore human frailty with your gentleness.
Christ, have mercy.
Your pastors comforted the dying and buried the dead; console those who mourn and lead the dead into your glory.
Lord, have mercy.

Invitation to the Lord's Prayer
Your pastors lead your people in fervent prayer so let us pray with Christ, the Shepherd of our souls.

Collect *From the Proper of the Day*

The Blessing
May we not quench the Spirit, not despise the words of prophets, but test everything, hold fast to what is good and abstain from every form of evil.
Amen.

Common of Theologians and Teachers Morning Prayer

Invitatory Christ alone is our Teacher: Come let us sit at his feet and worship. (Alleluia)

Hymn We limit not the truth of God *Hymnal 629*

Antiphon 1 They are well instructed; their God teaches them. (Alleluia)
Antiphon 2 Your ears shall hear a word behind you, saying, "This is the way; walk in it." (Alleluia)
Antiphon 3 The beginning of wisdom is the most sincere desire for instruction, and concern for instruction is love of her. (Alleluia)

Reading One *From the Proper of the Day*

Responsory One (Ps. 25:4; Ps. 43:3)
Lead me in your truth and teach me
　　− **for you are the God of my salvation.**
Send out your light and your truth
　　− **for you are the God of my salvation.**
Glory to the Father and to the Son and to the Holy Spirit.
Lead me in your truth and teach me
　　− **for you are the God of my salvation.**

Canticle – Song of the Lord, our Rock　*Audite caeli*
(Deuteronomy 32: 1-6)

Antiphon Let the earth hear the words of my mouth. (Alleluia)

Give ear, O heavens, and I will speak; *
　let the earth hear the words of my mouth.

May my teaching drop like the rain, *
　my speech condense like the dew;

Like gentle rain on grass, *
　like showers on new growth.

For I will proclaim the name of the LORD; *
　ascribe greatness to our God!

The Rock, his work is perfect, *
　and all his ways are just.

A faithful God, without deceit, *
　just and upright is he.

Antiphon Let the earth hear the words of my mouth. (Alleluia)

Reading Two *From the Proper of the Day*

Responsory Two (Eph. 4:11, 12; 1 Cor. 12:4)
The gifts he gave were that some would be pastors and teachers
    — to equip the saints for the work of ministry.
There are varieties of gifts
    — to equip the saints for the work of ministry.
Glory to the Father and to the Son and to the Holy Spirit.
The gifts he gave were that some would be pastors and teachers
    — to equip the saints for the work of ministry.

Benedictus Antiphon A disciple is not above the teacher, nor a slave above the master. (Alleluia)

Litany
At the dawn of day, illumine our minds and hearts to understand your Word and follow your commands.
Lord, have mercy.
As you kindle your light among us, so shine in our minds that we may understand your teaching and put it into practice.
Christ, have mercy.
With your never-failing wisdom, send your Spirit to all who teach, all who study and all who seek you.
Lord, have mercy.

Invitation to the Lord's Prayer
Since the Holy Spirit gives to some the word of wisdom, to others the word of knowledge, and to others the word of faith we praise God's Name for the gifts of grace in the church.

Collect *From the Proper of the Day*

The Blessing
May the God of our Lord Jesus Christ, the Father of glory, give us a spirit of wisdom and revelation that we may come to know God more deeply. **Amen.**

Common of Theologians and Teachers
Noonday Prayer

Hymn Lord be thy word my rule *Hymnal 626*

Antiphon The mouth of the righteous utters wisdom; the law of their God is in their heart. (Alleluia)

Reading Isaiah 50: 4
The Lord God has given me the tongue of a teacher, that I may know how to sustain the weary with a word. Morning by morning he wakens—wakens my ear to listen as those who are taught.

Verse and Response
Out of Zion shall go forth instruction. (Alleluia)
And the word of the Lord from Jerusalem. (Alleluia)

Collect *From the Proper of the Day or one of the following*
O God, by your Holy Spirit you give to some the word of wisdom, to others the word of knowledge, and to others the word of faith: We praise your Name for the gifts of grace manifested in your servant N., and we pray that your Church may never be destitute of such gifts; through Jesus Christ our Lord, who with you and the Holy Spirit lives and reigns, one God, for ever and ever. Amen.

Almighty God, you gave to your servant N. special gifts of grace to understand and teach the truth as it is in Christ Jesus: Grant that by this teaching we may know you, the one true God, and Jesus Christ whom you have sent; who lives and reigns with you and the Holy Spirit, one God, for ever and ever. Amen.

Common of Theologians and Teachers Evening Prayer

Hymn Word of God come down on earth *Hymnal 633*

Antiphon 1 Teach them the statutes and instructions and make known to them the way they are to go. (Alleluia)
Antiphon 2 As the Lord my God has charged me, I now teach you statutes and ordinances for you to observe. (Alleluia)
Antiphon 3 Hear, my child, your father's instruction, and do not reject your mother's teaching. (Alleluia)

Reading *From the Proper of the Day*

Responsory (Pro. 9:9; Pro. 6:23)
Give instruction to the wise, and they will become wiser still
 – teach the righteous and they will gain in learning.
The commandment is a lamp and the teaching a light
 – teach the righteous and they will gain in learning.
Glory to the Father and to the Son and to the Holy Spirit.
Give instruction to the wise, and they will become wiser still
 – teach the righteous and they will gain in learning.

Magnificat Antiphon You shall put these words of mine in your heart and soul, and you shall bind them as a sign on your hand, and fix them as an emblem on your forehead. (Alleluia)

Litany
As the light moves into darkness, continue to shine in those places torn by misunderstanding.
Lord, have mercy.
With the approaching evening, give rest to our bodies and refreshment to our minds.
Christ, have mercy.
You alone are the rest of the dead, lead all the departed into your undying light.
Lord, have mercy.

Invitation to the Lord's Prayer
The Spirit bestows special gifts of grace to understand and teach the truth as it is in Christ Jesus: Grant that by this teaching we may know you, the one true God.

Collect *From the Proper of the Day*

The Blessing
May God become manifest in us, God who is the source of our life in Christ Jesus, who became for us wisdom from God, and righteousness and sanctification and redemption. **Amen.**

Common of Teacher of the Faith Morning Prayer

Invitatory The Lord is the fountain of wisdom: Come let us worship. (Alleluia)

Hymn Praise To The Holiest In the Height *Hymnal 446*

Antiphon 1 The fear of the Lord is the beginning of wisdom. (Alleluia)
Antiphon 2 Wisdom will come into your heart, and knowledge will be pleasant to your soul. (Alleluia)
Antiphon 3 I love those who love me, and those who seek me diligently find me. (Alleluia)

Reading One *From the Proper of the Day*

Responsory One (Prov. 9:10; Jas. 1:5)
The fear of the Lord is the beginning of wisdom
  – **knowledge of the Holy One is insight.**

If any of you lacks wisdom, let him ask God
- **knowledge of the Holy One is insight.**
Glory to the Father and **to** the Son and to the Holy Spirit.
The fear of the Lord is the beginning of wisdom
- **knowledge of the Holy One is insight.**

Canticle – Song of Wisdom's Feast *Sapientia aedificavit*
(Proverbs 8: 1-6, 10-11)

Antiphon Give instruction to the wise, and they will become wiser still. (Alleluia)

Wisdom has built her house, *
  she has hewn her seven pillars.

She has slaughtered her animals, she has mixed her wine, *
  she has also set her table.

She has sent out her servant-girls, she calls
from the highest places in the town. *
  "You that are simple, turn in here!"

To those without sense she says, *
  "Come, eat of my bread*
  and drink of the wine I have mixed.

"Lay aside immaturity, and live, *
  and walk in the way of insight."

Give instruction to the wise, and they will become wiser still; *
  teach the righteous and they will gain in learning.

The fear of the Lord is the beginning of wisdom, *
  and the knowledge of the Holy One is insight.

For by me your days will be multiplied, *
  and years will be added to your life.

Antiphon Give instruction to the wise, and they will become wiser still. (Alleluia)

Reading Two *From the Proper of the Day*

Responsory Two (Ps. 37:30; Ps. 51:6)
The mouths of the righteous utter wisdom
  — and their tongues speak justice.
You made them understand wisdom secretly
  — and their tongues speak justice.
Glory to the Father, and to the Son and to the Holy Spirit

The mouths of the righteous utter wisdom
- and their tongues speak justice.

Benedictus Antiphon for a Female Teacher of the Faith In the midst of the church she spoke with great persuasion. The Lord filled her with the Spirit of wisdom and understanding. (Alleluia)

Benedictus Antiphon for a Male Teacher of the Faith In the midst of the church he spoke with great persuasion. The Lord filled him with the Spirit of wisdom and understanding. (Alleluia)

Litany
You illumine the minds and hearts of your holy teachers; let your Spirit kindle your truth in schools, colleges and universities.
Lord, have mercy.
You trained your holy teachers to speak your truth in their generation; let writers lead people to ever greater wisdom through fidelity to your Word.
Christ, have mercy.
You opened the mouth of your holy teachers to speak the truth in love; let us learn civility and graciousness in our dealings with one another.
Lord, have mercy.

Invitation to the Lord's Prayer
As the morning star illumines the earth, let us ask Christ, the Light of the world, to shine in our minds and hearts and lead us to the Father.

Collect *From the Proper of the Day*

The Blessing
May Christ, the Living Word and Wisdom of God, shine in us and through us. **Amen.**

Common of Teacher of the Faith Noonday Prayer
Hymn Can We By Searching Find Out God *Hymnal 476*

Antiphon Wisdom will come into your heart, and knowledge will be pleasant to your soul. (Alleluia)

Reading Wisdom 7: 13-14
I learned without guile and I impart without grudging; I do not hide her wealth, for wisdom is an unfailing treasure for mortals; those who get it obtain friendship with God, commended for the gifts that come from instruction.

Verse and Response
They will pour forth their words of wisdom. (Alleluia)
In prayer they will give thanks to the Lord. (Alleluia)

Collect *From the Proper of the Day or the following*
Almighty God, you gave to your servant N. special gifts of grace to understand and teach the truth as it is in Christ Jesus: Grant that by this teaching we may know you, the one true God, and Jesus Christ whom you have sent; who lives and reigns with you and the Holy Spirit, one God, for ever and ever. Amen.

Common of Teacher of the Faith Evening Prayer

Hymn Immortal, Invisible, God Only Wise *Hymnal 423*

Antiphon 1 Wisdom from above is first pure, then peaceable, gentle, willing to yield, full of mercy and good fruits (Alleluia)
Antiphon 2 The mouth of the just tells of wisdom. The law of God is in their hearts. (Alleluia)
Antiphon 3 In Christ are hidden all the treasures of wisdom and knowledge. (Alleluia)

Reading *From the Proper of the Day*

Responsory (Sir. 15:5)
In the midst of the Church
   − **they spoke with understanding.**
The Lord filled them with a spirit of wisdom and insight
   − **they spoke with understanding.**
Glory to the Father and to the Son and to the Holy Spirit.
In the midst of the Church
   − **they spoke with understanding.**

Magnificat Antiphon O holy N. foremost teacher, light of the church, lover of the Gospel, pray for us to the Word of God. (Alleluia)
- January 13 Hilary
- January 27 John Chrysostom
- January 28 Thomas Aquinas
- March 12 Gregory the Great
- March 18 Cyril of Jerusalem
- April 21 Anselm
- April 29, Catherine of Siena
- May 2 Athanasius
- May 9 Gregory of Nazianzus

- May 29 Bede, the Venerable
- June 10 Ephrem of Edessa
- June 14 Basil the Great
- August 20 Bernard
- August 28 Augustine
- September 17 Hildegard
- September 30 Jerome
- October 15 Teresa of Jesus
- November 10 Leo
- December 4 John of Damascus
- December 5 Clement of Alexandria
- December 7 Ambrose
- December 14 John of the Cross

Litany
Your wisdom led our teachers by the prompting of the Spirit; continue to guide scholars in their study and teaching.
Lord, have mercy.
Your wisdom embraced diverse forms of human understanding; make yourself known to us in ways that make sense in our generation.
Christ, have mercy.
Your wisdom is revealed in the mystery of Christ; lead all the dead who sought you to discover you in the heaven.
Lord, have mercy.

Invitation to the Lord's Prayer
Let us pray to God, the source of all wisdom, in the words given to us by Christ, the Word of God.

Collect *From the Proper of the Day*

The Blessing
May the God of our Lord Jesus Christ, the Father of glory, give us a spirit of wisdom and revelation that we may come to know God more deeply. **Amen.**

Common of Missionaries Morning Prayer

Invitatory Christ sends disciples to the ends of the earth: Come, all nations, and worship God. (Alleluia)

Hymn Christ for the world we sing *Hymnal 537*

Antiphon 1 I will give you as a light to the nations (Alleluia)
Antiphon 2 Nations shall come to your light, and kings to the brightness of your dawn. (Alleluia)
Antiphon 3 Let your light shine before others so that they may see your good works and give glory to your Father in heaven. (Alleluia)

Reading One *From the Proper of the Day*

Responsory One (Ps. 67:5; Mk. 16:15)
Let the peoples praise you, O God
    — let the nations be glad and sing for joy.
Go out to all the world and proclaim the gospel
    — let the nations be glad and sing for joy.
Glory to the Father and to the Son and to the Holy Spirit.
Let the peoples praise you, O God
    — let the nations be glad and sing for joy.

Canticle – Song of the Evangelist *Quam pulchri super montes*
(Isaiah 52: 7–10)
Antiphon The herald of the Gospel brings good news and announces salvation. (Alleluia.)

How beautiful upon the mountains *
    are the feet of the messenger who announces peace.

The herald brings good news, *
    announces salvation,
    and says to Zion, "Your God reigns."

Listen! Your sentinels lift up their voices, *
    together they sing for joy.

In plain sight they see *
    the return of the LORD to Zion.

Break forth together into singing, *
    you ruins of Jerusalem.

The LORD has comforted his people, *
    he has redeemed Jerusalem.

The LORD has bared his holy arm *
    before the eyes of all the nations.

All the ends of the earth shall see *
    the salvation of our God.

Antiphon The herald of the Gospel brings good news and announces salvation. (Alleluia.)

Reading Two *From the Proper of the Day*

Responsory Two (Ps. 98:3; Rev. 7:9)
All the ends of the earth
 — **have seen the victory of our God.**
People from every tribe and tongue
 — **have seen the victory of our God.**
Glory to the Father and to the Son and to the Holy Spirit.
All the ends of the earth
 — **have seen the victory of our God.**

Benedictus Antiphon God will teach us his ways that we may walk in his paths. (Alleluia)

Litany
You sent your disciples to the ends of the earth; send us out as heralds of the Gospel in our communities.
Lord, have mercy.
You stirred up missionaries in every age to discover your presence in different cultures; continue to reveal yourself in the patterns you inspire.
Christ, have mercy.
You draw all the world to yourself through the proclamation of your word; gather the scattered children of God into the fellowship of your church.
Lord, have mercy.

Invitation to the Lord's Prayer
Since the missionary impulse flows from the very nature of God who sends forth the Son and the Spirit, let us join in the prayer of Christ for the coming of God's reign.

Collect *From the Proper of the Day*

The Blessing
May God make known how great among us are the riches of the glory of this mystery, which is Christ in us, the hope of glory. **Amen.**

Common of Missionaries Noonday Prayer

Hymn When Jesus left his Father's throne *Hymnal 480*

Antiphon We must work the works of God who sent me while it is day. (Alleluia)

Reading Matthew 26: 18-20
Jesus came and said to them, "All authority in heaven and on earth has been given to me. Go therefore and make disciples of all nations, baptizing them in the name of the Father and of the Son and of the Holy Spirit, and teaching them to obey everything that I have commanded you. And remember, I am with you always, to the end of the age."

Verse and Response
We declare to you what we have that you may have fellowship with us. (Alleluia)
Our fellowship is with the Father and with his Son Jesus Christ. (Alleluia)

Collect *From the Proper of the Day or the following*
Almighty God, whose will it is to be glorified in your saints, and who raised up your servant N. to be a light in the world: Shine, we pray, in our hearts, that we also in our generation may show forth your praise, who called us out of darkness into your marvelous light; through Jesus Christ our Lord, who lives and reigns with you and the Holy Spirit, one God, now and for ever. Amen.

Common of Missionaries Evening Prayer

Hymn Spread, O spread, thy mighty Word *Hymnal 530*

Antiphon 1 You will be my witnesses to the ends of the earth. (Alleluia)
Antiphon 2 I appointed you a prophet to the nations. (Alleluia)
Antiphon 3 Go and make disciples of all nations. (Alleluia)

Reading *From the Proper of the Day*

Responsory (Is. 66:18; Mt. 5:6)
I am coming to gather all nations and tongues
   – and they shall see my glory.
Let your light shine before others
   – and they shall see my glory.
Glory to the Father and to the Son and to the Holy Spirit.
I am coming to gather all nations and tongues
   – and they shall see my glory.

Magnificat Antiphon Our Savior Christ Jesus abolished death and brought life and immortality to light through the gospel. (Alleluia)

Litany
Raise up in this and every land evangelists and heralds of your gospel
Lord, have mercy.

Shine in the hearts of all who hear the Word of salvation.
Christ, have mercy.
Bring all the dead into the light of your peace.
Lord, have mercy.

Invitation to the Lord's Prayer
Since in you we live, move and have our being, draw us deeper into your life as we pray with Christ, the One whom you sent into the world.

Collect *From the Proper of the Day*

The Blessing
May the God of our Lord Jesus Christ, the Father of glory, may give us a spirit of wisdom and revelation as we come to know him. **Amen.**

Common of Prophetic Witnesses Morning Prayer

Invitatory Christ proclaims good news to the poor: Come let us worship. (Alleluia)

Hymn When Christ was lifted from the earth *Hymnal 603*

Antiphon 1 Let justice roll down like waters, and righteousness like an ever-flowing stream. (Alleluia)
Antiphon 2 Unarmed truth and unconditional love will have the final word. (Alleluia)
Antiphon 3 Do no wrong or violence to the alien, the orphan, and the widow, or shed innocent blood in this place. (Alleluia)

Reading One *From the Proper of the Day*

Responsory One (Is. 61:6; Jer. 26:12)
The Lord has sent me to bring good news to the oppressed
　　– to proclaim liberty to the captives.
The Lord sent me to prophesy
　　– to proclaim liberty to the captives.
Glory to the Father, and to the Son and to the Holy Spirit
The Lord has sent me to bring good news to the oppressed
　　– to proclaim liberty to the captives.

Canticle – Song of the Servant of Light   *Ego Dominus vocavi*
(Isaiah 42: 6-9)
Antiphon I have given you as a covenant to the people, a light to the nations. (Alleluia)

I am the LORD, I have called you in righteousness, *
    I have taken you by the hand and kept you.

I have given you as a covenant to the people, *
    a light to the nations,

To open the eyes that are blind, *
    to bring out the prisoners from the dungeon,
    from the prison those who sit in darkness.

I am the LORD, that is my name; *
    my glory I give to no other, nor my praise to idols.

See, the former things have come to pass,
and new things I now declare; *
    before they spring forth, I tell you of them.

Antiphon I have given you as a covenant to the people, a light to the nations. (Alleluia)

Reading Two *From the Proper of the Day*

Responsory Two (Lev. 25:10; Is. 32:18)
You shall proclaim liberty throughout the land
    — it shall be a jubilee for you.
My people will abide in peace.
    — it shall be a jubilee for you.
Glory to the Father and **to** the Son and to the Holy Spirit.
You shall proclaim liberty throughout the land
    — it shall be a jubilee for you.

Benedictus Antiphon The Spirit of the Lord is upon me, because he has anointed me to bring good news to the poor. (Alleluia)

Litany
Your servants were lights of justice in a dark world, make us heralds of right relations this day.
Lord, have mercy.
Your witnesses spoke a word of liberty to those who were held captive; let us work with you to free people confined in prisons of thought and prejudice.
Christ, have mercy.
Your prophets were anointed by the Spirit; strengthen us to be prophets in our communities.
Lord, have mercy.

Invitation to the Lord's Prayer
Your reign will dawn on us with justice and mercy so we implore you to shine your light in the world.

Collect *From the Proper of the Day*

The Blessing
May the very Lord of peace give you peace at all times in all ways.
Amen.

Common of Prophetic Witnesses Noonday Prayer

Hymn O Jesus Christ, may grateful hymns be rising *Hymnal 590*

Antiphon Justice, and only justice, you shall pursue, so that you may live and occupy the land that the Lord your God is giving you. (Alleluia)

Reading Isaiah 58: 6-8
Is not this the fast that I choose: to loose the bonds of injustice, to undo the thongs of the yoke, to let the oppressed go free, and to break every yoke? Is it not to share your bread with the hungry, and bring the homeless poor into your house; when you see the naked, to cover them, and not to hide yourself from your own kin? Then your light shall break forth like the dawn, and your healing shall spring up quickly; your vindicator shall go before you, the glory of the Lord shall be your rear guard.

Verse and Response
For freedom Christ has set us free. (Alleluia)
Stand firm, therefore, and do not submit again to a yoke of slavery. (Alleluia)

Collect *From the Proper of the Day or the following*
Almighty God, whose prophets taught us righteousness in the care of your poor: By the guidance of your Holy Spirit, grant that we may do justice, love mercy, and walk humbly in your sight; through Jesus Christ, our Judge and Redeemer, who lives and reigns with you and the same Spirit, one God, now and for ever. Amen.

Common of Prophetic Witnesses Evening Prayer

Hymn Judge eternal clothed in splendor *Hymnal 596*

Antiphon 1 You will know the truth, and the truth will make you free. (Alleluia)
Antiphon 2 Maintain justice, and do what is right, for soon my salvation will come. (Alleluia)

Antiphon 3 You shall proclaim liberty throughout the land to all its inhabitants. (Alleluia)

Reading *From the Proper of the Day*

Responsory (Is. 52:7; Is 33: 5)
Your messenger announces peace
 — **brings good news and announces salvation.**
The Lord fills Zion with justice
 — **brings good news and announces salvation.**
Glory to the Father and to the Son and to the Holy Spirit.
Your messenger announces peace
 — **brings good news and announces salvation.**

Magnificat Antiphon What does the Lord require of you but to do justice, and to love kindness, and to walk humbly with your God. (Alleluia)

Litany
At the close of the day, forgive us for our lack of courage to witness to your justice and strengthen our resolve to relieve the needs of the poor.
Lord, have mercy.
In every age you have called brave souls to proclaim righteousness for the transformation of the
world; may all people welcome the coming of your holy reign.
Christ, have mercy.
You fill us with hope for a world where mercy will embrace all people; welcome the dead into your loving arms.
Lord, have mercy.

Invitation to the Lord's Prayer
Yours is a rule of justice and peace so we pray with all who yearn for righteousness and pray for you to hasten the coming of your kingdom.

Collect *From the Proper of the Day*

The Blessing
May the God of peace himself sanctify you entirely; and may your spirit and soul and body be kept sound and blameless at the coming of our Lord Jesus Christ. **Amen.**

Common of Monastics Morning Prayer

Invitatory Christ became obedient unto death: Come let us worship. (Alleluia)

Hymn O What Their Joy and Their Glory Must Be *Hymnal 623*

Antiphon 1 I saw a great multitude from every nation standing before the throne and before the Lamb. (Alleluia)
Antiphon 2 Clothed in white garments, they follow the Lamb wherever he goes. (Alleluia)
Antiphon 3 The Lord is righteous. The just shall see his face. (Alleluia)
Reading One *From the Proper of the Day*

Responsory One (Ps. 62:1)
For God alone
  – **my soul in silence waits.**
My hope is in God
  – **my soul in silence waits.**
Glory to the Father and to the Son and to the Holy Spirit.
For God alone
  – **my soul in silence waits.**

Canticle – Song of Betrothal *Ecce ego lactabo eam*
(Hosea 2: 14, 16, 18-19, 23)

Antiphon I will betroth you to me in righteousness and in justice, in steadfast love, and in mercy. (Alleluia)

I will allure her, and bring her into the wilderness, *
  and speak tenderly to her.

"And in that day", says the LORD, *
  "you will call me, 'My beloved.'"

And I will make for you *
  a covenant on that day.

With the beasts of the field, the birds of the air, *
  and the creeping things of the ground.

I will abolish the bow, the sword, and war from the land; *
  and I will make you lie down in safety.

I will betroth you to me for ever; *
  I will betroth you to me in righteousness and in justice,
  in steadfast love, and in mercy.

I will betroth you to me in faithfulness; *
   and you shall know the LORD.

You will be my people, *
   and I will be your God.

Antiphon I will betroth you to me in righteousness and in justice, in steadfast love, and in mercy. (Alleluia)

Reading Two *From the Proper of the Day*

Responsory Two (Ps. 119:116; Ps. 63:1)
Sustain me according to your promise, that I may live
   — **abandon me not in my hope.**
My soul thirsts for you
   — **abandon me not in my hope.**
Glory to the Father and to the Son and to the Holy Spirit.
Sustain me according to your promise, that I may live
   — **abandon me not in my hope.**

Benedictus Antiphon Those who love me will keep my word, and my Father will love them, and we will come to them and make our home with them. (Alleluia)

Litany
You call your holy ones to forsake everything and follow you; strengthen all who commit themselves to you in the monastic life.
Lord, have mercy.
You lead your holy ones to encounter you in prayer and sacred reading; open our minds and hearts to meet you in worship and contemplation.
Christ, have mercy.
You set your holy ones as lights in their time; make us witnesses to you in our generation.
Lord, have mercy.

Invitation to the Lord's Prayer
In fellowship with monks, nuns and oblates from centuries past and yet to come, let us approach the throne of grace and pray with Christ.

Collect *From the Proper of the Day*

The Blessing
May we prefer nothing whatever to Christ, and may he bring us all together to everlasting life. **Amen.**

Common of Monastics Noonday Prayer

Hymn Blest are the pure in heart *Hymnal 656*

Antiphon If you earnestly desire to be rich, then love true riches. (Alleluia)

Reading Proverbs 4: 1-6
Listen, children, to a father's instruction, and be attentive, that you may gain insight; for I give you good precepts: do not forsake my teaching. When I was a son with my father, tender, and my mother's favorite, he taught me, and said to me, "Let your heart hold fast my words; keep my commandments, and live. Get wisdom; get insight: do not forget, nor turn away from the words of my mouth. Do not forsake her, and she will keep you; love her, and she will guard you.

Verse and Response
We shall run in the paths of God's commandments. (Alleluia.)
Our hearts overflowing with the inexpressible delight of love. (Alleluia.)

Collect *From the Proper of the Day or one of the following*
O God, whose blessed Son became poor that we through his poverty might be rich: Deliver us from an inordinate love of this world, that we, inspired by the devotion of your servant N., may serve you with singleness of heart, and attain to the riches of the age to come; through Jesus Christ our Lord, who lives and reigns with you, in the unity of the Holy Spirit, one God, now and for ever. Amen.

or this
O God, by whose grace your servant N., kindled with the flame of your love, became a burning and a shining light in your Church: Grant that we also may be aflame with the spirit of love and discipline, and walk before you as children of light; through Jesus Christ our Lord, who lives and reigns with you, in the unity of the Holy Spirit, one God, now and for ever. Amen.

Common of Monastics Evening Prayer

Hymn Jerusalem My Happy Home *Hymnal 620*

Antiphon 1 The just will shine like the sun in the kingdom of their Father. (Alleluia)
Antiphon 2 The saints rejoice forever in heaven. They followed in Christ's footsteps and exult with Christ forever. (Alleluia)

Antiphon 3 How glorious is that kingdom where all the saints rejoice with Christ. (Alleluia)

Reading *From the Proper of the Day*

Responsory (Ps. 68:3)
Let the righteous be glad
     − and rejoice before God.
Let them be merry and joyful
     − and rejoice before God.
Glory to the Father and to the Son and to the Holy Spirit.
Let the righteous be glad
     − and rejoice before God.

Magnificat Antiphon
For Nuns Come, spouse of Christ, receive the crown prepared for you from all eternity. (Alleluia)
For Monks You have died, and your life is hidden with Christ in God. When Christ who is your life is revealed, then you also will be revealed with him in glory. (Alleluia)
For Oblates Let them prefer nothing whatever to Christ, and my he bring us all together to everlasting life. (Alleluia)

Litany
Strengthen your monks, nuns and oblates, the soldiers of Christ, to take up obedience in the service of Christ the King.
Lord, have mercy.
Clothed with faith and good works, show us, in your love, the hidden way that leads to life.
Christ, have mercy.
Faithful to Christ's teaching until death, may we, with all the departed, deserve to share in Christ's kingdom.
Lord, have mercy.

Invitation to the Lord's Prayer
Faithful to the pledge we make of mutual forgiveness, let us ask God to cleanse our hearts as we pray with Christ.

Collect *From the Proper of the Day*

The Blessing
May we run in the path of God's commandments, our hearts overflowing with the inexpressible delight of love. **Amen.**

Common of Professed Religious Morning Prayer

Invitatory The Lord is glorious in his saints: Come, let us worship. (Alleluia)

Hymn Rejoice, ye pure in heart *Hymnal 556*

Antiphon 1 If you would be perfect, go, sell what you possess and give to the poor, and you will have treasure in heaven; and come, follow me. (Alleluia)
Antiphon 2 There are eunuchs who have made themselves eunuchs for the sake of the kingdom of heaven. Whoever is able to receive this, let them receive it. (Alleluia)
Antiphon 3 My food is to do the will of him who sent me, and to accomplish his work. (Alleluia)

Reading One *From the Proper of the Day*

Responsory One (Ps. 63:1; Rev. 21:6)
You are my God
 — **my soul thirsts for you.**
I will give them drink from the fountain of the water of life
 — **my soul thirsts for you.**
Glory to the Father and to the Son and to the Holy Spirit.
You are my God
 — **my soul thirsts for you.**

Canticle of Communion and Mission *Pater sanctifica eos*
(John 17: 17-26)

Antiphon Go, sell what you own, and give the money to the poor, and you will have treasure in heaven; then come, follow me. (Alleluia)

Father, sanctify them in the truth; *
 your word is truth.

As you have sent me into the world, *
 so I have sent them into the world.

For their sakes I sanctify myself, *
 so that they also may be sanctified in truth.

I ask not only on behalf of these,*
 but also on behalf of those who will believe in me
 through their word.

May they all be one,
as you, Father, are in me and I am in you, *
> may they also be in us,
> so that the world may believe that you have sent me.

The glory that you have given me I have given them, *
> so that they may be one, as we are one,
> I in them and you in me.

May they become completely one, *
> so that the world may know that you have sent me
> and have loved them even as you have loved me.

Father, I desire that those also, whom you have given me, *
> may be with me where I am, to see my glory.

You have given me this glory *
> because you loved me before the foundation of the world.

Righteous Father, the world does not know you, *
> but I know you; and these know that you have sent me.

I made your name known to them, *
> and I will make it known.

So that the love with which you have loved me may be in them, *
> and I in them.

Antiphon Go, sell what you own, and give the money to the poor, and you will have treasure in heaven; then come, follow me. (Alleluia)

Reading Two *From the Proper of the Day*

Responsory Two (Ps. 116:18; Ps. 27:6)
I will offer my vows to the Lord
> **− in the presence of all his people.**

I will offer in his tent sacrifices with shouts of joy
> **− in the presence of all his people.**

Glory to the Father and to the Son and to the Holy Spirit.
I will offer my vows to the Lord
> **− in the presence of all his people.**

Benedictus Antiphon The Lord sanctified them by their faith and meekness. God manifested to them his glory. (Alleluia)

Litany
Your holy ones left everything to follow Christ; lead us to live as the poor in spirit.
Lord, have mercy.
Your holy ones follow the Lamb wherever he goes; open our souls to purity of heart.
Christ, have mercy.
Your holy ones obeyed the voice of Christ; teach us obedience to your commands.
Lord, have mercy.

Introduction to the Lord's Prayer
In the company of faithful religious whose consecrated life prefigures the new life of God's reign let us pray that God may hasten the day of its fulfillment.

Collect *From the Proper of the Day*

The Blessing
May all who have freely vowed themselves in the religious live to the Lord diligently and faithfully conform themselves to the life they have promised. **Amen.**

Common of Professed Religious Noonday Prayer
Hymn Jerusalem the golden *Hymnal 624*

Antiphon You, O God, have heard my vows; you have granted me the heritage of those who fear your Name. (Alleluia)

Reading Philippians 3: 8-10
I regard everything as loss because of the surpassing value of knowing Christ Jesus my Lord. For his sake I have suffered the loss of all things, and I regard them as rubbish, in order that I may gain Christ and be found in him, not having a righteousness of my own that comes from the law, but one that comes through faith in Christ, the righteousness from God based on faith. I want to know Christ and the power of his resurrection and the sharing of his sufferings by becoming like him in his death.

Verse and Response
My soul clings to you. (Alleluia)
Your right hand holds me fast. (Alleluia)

Collect *From the Proper of the Day or the following*
O God, whose blessed Son became poor that we through his poverty might be rich: Deliver us from an inordinate love of this world, that we,

inspired by the devotion of your servant N., may serve you with singleness of heart, and attain to the riches of the age to come; through Jesus Christ our Lord, who lives and reigns with you, in the unity of the Holy Spirit, one God, now and for ever. Amen.

Common of Professed Religious Evening Prayer

Hymn Sing alleluia forth in duteous praise *Hymnal 619*

Antiphon 1 Jesus called them; and they left their family and followed him. (Alleluia)
Antiphon 2 I count everything as loss because of the surpassing worth of knowing Christ Jesus my Lord. (Alleluia)
Antiphon 3 Every one who has left houses or brothers or sisters or father or mother or children or lands, for my name's sake, will receive a hundredfold, and inherit eternal life. (Alleluia)

Reading *From the Proper of the Day*

Responsory (Ps. 116:14; Ps. 65:1)
I will fulfill my vows to the Lord
– **in the presence of all God's people.**
To you shall vows be performed in Jerusalem
– **in the presence of all God's people.**
Glory to the Father and to the Son and to the Holy Spirit.
I will fulfill my vows to the Lord
– **in the presence of all God's people.**

Magnificat Antiphon The Lord will espouse them forever in fidelity and mercy. (Alleluia)

Litany
In response to your call, faithful men and women surrendered all things to serve your people, strengthen us in our care for the neglected among us.
Lord, have mercy.
In imitation of the apostolic church, they shared a common life of fellowship; open your church to receive people from different ways of life .
Christ, have mercy.
In anticipation of the resurrection, they lived for your alone; bring all the departed into the life you prepare for us.
Lord, have mercy.

Introduction to the Lord's Prayer
Faithful to the Spirit, who consecrates us in Baptism and deepens that holiness in Religious Profession, let us pray that the Spirit may draw us in the holy life of God.

Collect *From the Proper of the Day*

The Blessing
With the voice of thanksgiving may all professed religious sacrifice to you what they have vowed and be a sign of your presence in the church. **Amen.**

Common of Holy Persons Morning Prayer

Invitatory The Lord is glorious in the saints: Come let us adore him. (Alleluia)

Hymn Blest are the pure in heart *Hymnal 656*

Antiphon 1 You shall be for me a priestly kingdom and a holy nation. (Alleluia)

Antiphon 2 The Lord set his heart in love on your ancestors alone and chose you, their descendants after them, out of all the peoples. (Alleluia)

Antiphon 3 I have redeemed you; I have called you by name, you are mine. (Alleluia.)

Reading One *From the Proper of the Day*

Responsory (Ps. 32: 12; Ps. 100:1)
Be glad, you righteous
    – and rejoice in the Lord.
Serve the Lord with gladness
    – and rejoice in the Lord.
Glory to the Father, and to the Son and to the Holy Spirit.
Be glad, you righteous
    – and rejoice in the Lord.

Canticle – Song of the Beatitudes *Beati pauperes spiritu*
(Matthew 5: 3-12)

Antiphon Blessed are the pure in heart, for they will see God. (Alleluia)

Blessed are the poor in spirit, *
    for theirs is the kingdom of heaven.

Blessed are those who mourn, *
    for they will be comforted.

Blessed are the meek, *
  for they will inherit the earth.

Blessed are those who hunger and thirst for righteousness, *
  for they will be filled.

Blessed are the merciful, *
  for they will receive mercy.

Blessed are the pure in heart, *
  for they will see God.

Blessed are the peacemakers, *
  for they will be called children of God.

Blessed are those who are persecuted for righteousness' sake, *
  for theirs is the kingdom of heaven.

Blessed are you when people revile you and persecute you *
  and utter all kinds of evil against you falsely on my account.

Rejoice and be glad, for your reward is great in heaven, *
  for in the same way they persecuted the prophets
  who were before you.

Antiphon Blessed are the pure in heart, for they will see God. (Alleluia)

Reading Two *From the Proper of the Day*

Responsory (Ps. 37:31; Ps. 36: 10)
The law of their God is in their heart
  — their footsteps shall not falter.
You favor those who are true of heart
  — their footsteps shall not falter.
Glory to the Father and **to** the Son and to the Holy Spirit.
The law of their God is in their heart
  — their footsteps shall not falter.

Benedictus Antiphon Blessed are the poor in spirit, for theirs is the kingdom of heaven. Blessed are the pure in heart, for they will see God. (Alleluia)

Litany
You set your holy ones apart as lights in their generation. Make us lights shining in a dark world.
Lord, have mercy.

Your holy ones bore witness to you by their faith and good works. Strengthen all people of faith to model their lives on the faith you have given them.
Christ, have mercy.
Your holy ones served you in their prayer and in their work. Deepen our prayer and sustain our works of service.
Lord, have mercy.

Introduction to the Lord's Prayer
Christ calls us to be a holy people consecrated by the Holy Spirit, so in the Spirit of holiness we pray.

Collect *From the Proper of the Day*

The Blessing
May God give us a spirit of wisdom and revelation as we come to know him, so that, with the eyes of our heart enlightened, we may know what are the riches of his glorious inheritance among the saints. **Amen.**

Common of Holy Persons Noonday Prayer

Hymn O what their joy and the glory must be *Hymnal 623*

Antiphon As God's chosen ones, holy and beloved, clothe yourselves with compassion, kindness, humility, meekness, and patience. (Alleluia)

Reading Romans 8: 28-30
We know that all things work together for good for those who love God, who are called according to his purpose. For those whom he foreknew he also predestined to be conformed to the image of his Son, in order that he might be the firstborn within a large family. And those whom he predestined he also called; and those whom he called he also justified; and those whom he justified he also glorified.

Verse and Response
They shall receive a blessing from the Lord. (Alleluia)
A just reward from the God of their salvation. (Alleluia)

Collect *From the Proper of the Day or one of the following*
Almighty God, you have surrounded us with a great cloud of witnesses: Grant that we, encouraged by the good example of your servant N., may persevere in running the race that is set before us, until at last we may with him attain to your eternal joy; through Jesus Christ, the pioneer and perfecter of our faith, who lives and reigns with you and the Holy Spirit, one God, for ever and ever. Amen.

or this

O God, you have brought us near to an innumerable company of angels, and to the spirits of just men made perfect: Grant us during our earthly pilgrimage to abide in their fellowship, and in our heavenly country to become partakers of their joy; through Jesus Christ our Lord, who lives and reigns with you and the Holy Spirit, one God, now and for ever. Amen.

or this

Almighty God, by your Holy Spirit you have made us one with your saints in heaven and on earth: Grant that in our earthly pilgrimage we may always be supported by this fellowship of love and prayer, and know ourselves to be surrounded by their witness to your power and mercy. We ask this for the sake of Jesus Christ, in whom all our intercessions are acceptable through the Spirit, and who lives and reigns for ever and ever. Amen.

Common of Holy Persons Evening Prayer

Hymn Ye watchers and ye holy ones *Hymnal 618*

Antiphon 1 Well done, good and trustworthy slave; you have been trustworthy in a few things, I will put you in charge of many things; enter into the joy of your master. (Alleluia)
Antiphon 2 Rejoice and be glad, for your reward is great in heaven. (Alleluia)
Antiphon 3 If you have not been faithful with what belongs to another, who will give you what is your own? (Alleluia)

Reading *From the Proper of the Day*

Responsory (Ps. 11:8)
The Lord is righteous
  – **God delights in righteous deeds.**
The just shall see God's face
  – **God delights in righteous deeds.**
Glory to the Father and to the Son and to the Holy Spirit.
The Lord is righteous
  – **God delights in righteous deeds.**

Magnificat Antiphon Come, you that are blessed by my Father, inherit the kingdom prepared for you from the foundation of the world. (Alleluia)

Litany
You call your holy people to represent Christ and the Church; help us to bear witness to Christ wherever we may be.
Lord, have mercy.
You give your holy people gifts to carry on Christ's work of reconciliation in the world. Help them to take their place in the life, worship and governance of the church.
Christ, have mercy.
You call all Christians to follow Christ and to work, pray and give for the spread of your rule; bring the faithful departed and all the dead to the light of your life.
Lord, have mercy.

Introduction to the Lord's Prayer
As we make every effort to live in peace with everyone and to be holy let us ask the Father for that holiness that will open our hearts to see the Lord.

Collect *From the Proper of the Day*

The Blessing
May we agree with one another, live in peace; and the God of love and peace will be with us. **Amen.**

Common of Ember Days Morning Prayer

Invitatory Christ sends disciples to the ends of the earth: Come, all nations, and worship God. (Alleluia)

Hymn God of the prophets, bless the prophets' heirs *Hymnal 359*

Antiphon 1 I will take some of the spirit that is on you and put it on them; and they shall bear the burden of the people along with you. (Alleluia)
Antiphon 2 According to the grace of God given to me, like a skilled master builder I laid a foundation, and someone else is building on it. (Alleluia)
Antiphon 3 I sent you to reap that for which you did not labor. Others have labored, and you have entered into their labor. (Alleluia)

Reading One *From the Proper of the Day*

Responsory One (Ps. 43:4; Heb. 13:15)
I will go to the altar of God
    − to the God of my joy and gladness.

Let us continually offer a sacrifice of praise to God
   — **to the God of my joy and gladness.**
Glory to the Father and to the Son and to the Holy Spirit.
I will go to the altar of God
   — **to the God of my joy and gladness.**

Canticle – Song of the Evangelist *Quam pulchri super montes*
(Isaiah 52: 7–10)

Antiphon The herald of the Gospel brings good news and announces salvation. (Alleluia)

How beautiful upon the mountains *
   are the feet of the messenger who announces peace.

The herald brings good news, *
   announces salvation,
   and says to Zion, "Your God reigns."

Listen! Your sentinels lift up their voices, *
   together they sing for joy.

In plain sight they see *
   the return of the LORD to Zion.

Break forth together into singing, *
   you ruins of Jerusalem.
The LORD has comforted his people, *
   he has redeemed Jerusalem.

The LORD has bared his holy arm *
   before the eyes of all the nations.

All the ends of the earth shall see *
   the salvation of our God.

Antiphon The herald of the Gospel brings good news and announces salvation. (Alleluia)

Reading Two *From the Proper of the Day*

Responsory Two (Ps.132: 9, 17)
Let your priests be clothed with righteousness
   — **let your faithful people sing with joy.**
I will clothe her priests with salvation
   — **let your faithful people sing with joy.**
Glory to the Father and to the Son and to the Holy Spirit.

Let your priests be clothed with righteousness
 — let your faithful people sing with joy.

Benedictus Antiphon Select from among yourselves seven people of good standing, full of the Spirit and of wisdom, whom we may appoint to the ministry. (Alleluia)

Litany
For all members of your Church in their vocation and ministry, that they may serve you in a true and godly life.
Lord, have mercy.
For all called to serve as bishops, priests and deacons in your church that they may faithfully fulfill the duties of their ministry, build up your Church, and glorify your Name.
Christ, have mercy.
For those who do not yet believe, and for those who have lost their faith, that they may receive the light of the Gospel.
Lord, have mercy.

Invitation to the Lord's Prayer
Let us pray that the Father bring the nations into his fold, pour out his Spirit on all flesh, and hasten the coming of his kingdom.

Collect Almighty God, the giver of all good gifts, in your divine providence you have appointed various orders in your Church: Give your grace, we humbly pray, to all who are [now] called to any office and ministry for your people; and so fill them with the truth of your doctrine and clothe them with holiness of life, that they may faithfully serve before you, to the glory of your great Name and for the benefit of your holy Church; through Jesus Christ our Lord, who lives and reigns with you, in the unity of the Holy Spirit, one God, now and for ever. Amen.

The Blessing
May the Lord see that the harvest is plentiful, but the laborers are few; and so send out laborers into his harvest. **Amen.**

Common of Ember Days Noonday Prayer
Hymn Strengthen for service *Hymnal 312*

Antiphon Ask the Lord of the harvest to send out laborers into his harvest. (Alleluia)

Reading Matthew 26: 18-20
Jesus came and said to them, "All authority in heaven and on earth has been given to me. Go therefore and make disciples of all nations,

baptizing them in the name of the Father and of the Son and of the Holy Spirit, and teaching them to obey everything that I have commanded you. And remember, I am with you always, to the end of the age."

Verse and Response
How beautiful upon the mountains. (Alleluia)
Are the feet of the messenger who announces peace. (Alleluia)

Collect O God, you led your holy apostles to ordain ministers in every place: Grant that your Church, under the guidance of the Holy Spirit, may choose suitable persons for the ministry of Word and Sacrament, and may uphold them in their work for the extension of your kingdom; through him who is the Shepherd and Bishop of our souls, Jesus Christ our Lord, who lives and reigns with you and the Holy Spirit, one God, for ever and ever. Amen.

Common of Ember Days Evening Prayer

Hymn Lead us, heavenly Father, lead us *Hymnal 559*

Antiphon 1 You shall be for me a priestly kingdom and a holy nation. (Alleluia)
Antiphon 2 Serve one another with whatever gift each of you has received. (Alleluia)
Antiphon 3 Each of us was given grace according to the measure of Christ's gift. (Alleluia)

Reading *From the Proper of the Day*

Responsory (Is. 6:8; Ez. 3:4)
Whom shall I send, and who will go for us?
  – **Here am I; send me.**
Go to the house of Israel and speak my very words to them
  – **Here am I; send me.**
Glory to the Father and to the Son and to the Holy Spirit.
Whom shall I send, and who will go for us?
  – **Here am I; send me.**

Magnificat Antiphon Follow me and I will make you fish for people. And immediately they left their nets and followed him. (Alleluia)

Litany
For the holy Church of God, that it may be filled with truth and love, and be found without fault at the Day of your Coming.
Lord, have mercy.

For all who fear God and believe in you, Lord Christ, that our divisions may cease and that all may be one as you and the Father are one.
Christ, have mercy.
For all who have died in the communion of your Church, and those whose faith is known to you alone, that, with the Blessed Virgin Mary and all the saints, they may have rest in that place where there is no pain or grief, but life eternal.
Lord, have mercy.

Invitation to the Lord's Prayer
O God of the nations of the earth, remember the multitudes who have been created in your image but have not known the redeeming work of our savior Jesus Christ as we pray.

Collect Almighty and everlasting God, by whose Spirit the whole body of your faithful people is governed and sanctified: Receive our supplications and prayers, which we offer before you for all members of your holy Church, that in their vocation and ministry they may truly and devoutly serve you; through our Lord and Savior Jesus Christ, who lives and reigns with you, in the unity of the Holy Spirit, one God, now and for ever. Amen.

The Blessing
May the Lord send ministers of Christ Jesus to the church in the priestly service of the gospel of God, so that the offering of all people may be acceptable, sanctified by the Holy Spirit. **Amen.**

Common of Rogation Days Morning Prayer

Invitatory God blesses our world with abundant bounty: Come let us worship. Alleluia

Hymn O Jesus crowed with all renown *Hymnal 292*

Antiphon 1 The Lord God will give the rain for your land in its season and you will gather in your grain, your wine, and your oil. Alleluia.
Antiphon 2 Creation waits with eager longing for the revealing of the children of God. Alleluia.
Antiphon 3 You shall eat your fill and bless the Lord your God for the good land that he has given you. Alleluia.

Reading One *From the Proper of the Day*

Responsory One(Job 38: 12, 16)
Have you commanded the morning
      − **and caused the dawn to know its place?**

Have you entered into the springs of the sea
> — and caused the dawn to know its place?

Glory to the Father and to the Son and to the Holy Spirit.
Have you commanded the morning
> **— and caused the dawn to know its place?**

Canticle – Song of the Wilderness *Laetabitur deserta*
(Isaiah 35:1-7,10)

Antiphon The desert shall blossom abundantly, and rejoice with joy and singing. Alleluia.

The wilderness and the dry land shall be glad, *
> the desert shall rejoice and blossom;

It shall blossom abundantly, *
> and rejoice with joy and singing.

They shall see the glory of the LORD, *
> the majesty of our God.

Strengthen the weary hands, *
> and make firm the feeble knees.

Say to the anxious, "Be strong, do not fear! *
> Here is your God, coming with judgment to save you."

Then shall the eyes of the blind be opened, *
> and the ears of the deaf be unstopped.

Then shall the lame leap like a deer, *
> and the tongue of the speechless sing for joy.

For waters shall break forth in the wilderness *
> and streams in the desert;

The burning sand shall become a pool *
> and the thirsty ground, springs of water.

The ransomed of God shall return with singing, *
> with everlasting joy upon their heads.

Joy and gladness shall be theirs, *
> and sorrow and sighing shall flee away.

Antiphon The desert shall blossom abundantly, and rejoice with joy and singing. Alleluia.

Reading Two *From the Proper of the Day*

Responsory Two (Ps 107: 37, 38)
They sowed fields, and planted vineyards
 – and brought in a fruitful harvest.
The Lord blessed them, so that they increased greatly
 – and brought in a fruitful harvest.
Glory to the Father and to the Son and to the Holy Spirit.
They sowed fields, and planted vineyards
 – and brought in a fruitful harvest.

Benedictus Antiphon Consider the lilies of the field, how they grow; they neither toil nor spin, yet I tell you, even Solomon in all his glory was not clothed like one of these. Alleluia.

Litany
Walk with those who till, plant, and care for fields, pastures, gardens and orchards that they may be strengthened by your constant presence in all their labors.
Lord, have mercy.
Give us favorable weather and growing conditions that our farming efforts may not be in vain.
Christ, have mercy.
May the hungry be fed and may we always be mindful of their needs and wants. May governments around the world make good and wise decisions regarding their people and the food they need.
Lord, have mercy.

Invitation to the Lord's Prayer
Asking God's blessing on the work of farmers, industry and commerce, let us trust God to sustain their labor.

Collect Almighty God, Lord of heaven and earth: We humbly pray that your gracious providence may give and preserve to our use the harvests of the land and of the seas, and may prosper all who labor to gather them, that we, who are constantly receiving good things from your hand, may always give you thanks; through Jesus Christ our Lord, who lives and reigns with you and the Holy Spirit, one God, for ever and ever. Amen.

The Blessing
May the Lord command the blessing upon us in our barns and places of industry, and in all that we undertake. May God bless us in the land that the Lord our God is giving us. **Amen.**

Common of Rogation Days Noonday Prayer

Hymn For the beauty of the earth *Hymnal 416*

Antiphon Regard all utensils and goods of the monastery as sacred vessels of the altar. Alleluia.

Reading Sirach 38: 31, 32, 34
All artisans rely on their hands, and all are skillful in their own work. Without them no city can be inhabited, and wherever they live, they will not go hungry. They maintain the fabric of the world, and their concern is for the exercise of their trade.

Verse and Response
They set hearts on finishing their handiwork. Alleluia.
They are careful to complete its decoration. Alleluia.

Collect Almighty God, whose Son Jesus Christ in his earthly life shared our toil and hallowed our labor: Be present with your people where they work; make those who carry on the industries and commerce of this land responsive to your will; and give to us all a pride in what we do, and a just return for our labor; through Jesus Christ our Lord, who lives and reigns with you, in the unity of the Holy Spirit, one God, now and for ever. Amen.

Common of Rogation Days Evening Prayer

Hymn Earth and all stars *Hymnal 412*

Antiphon 1 Each builder must choose with care how to build on the foundation. Alleluia.
Antiphon 2 Those who want to be rich fall into temptation and are trapped by many senseless and harmful desires. Alleluia.
Antiphon 3 Do your work quietly and to earn your own living. Brothers and sisters, do not be weary in doing what is right. Alleluia.

Reading *From the Proper of the Day*

Responsory (Job 34: 29, 28)
From whose womb did the ice come forth
    – and who has given birth to the frost of heaven?
Has the rain a father?
    – and who has given birth to the hoarfrost of heaven?
Glory to the Father and to the Son and to the Holy Spirit.
From whose womb did the ice come forth
    – and who has given birth to the frost of heaven?

Magnificat Antiphon Take care! Be on your guard against all kinds of greed; for one's life does not consist in the abundance of possessions. Alleluia.

Litany
Keep us aware and sensitive to the needs of our farmers and their families. May they have a fair return for their efforts.
Lord, have mercy.
Bless all those who work in related agricultural businesses and those who are involved in the handling and sale of our agricultural products.
Christ, have mercy.
Give peace and strength to those who are bearing painful, heartbreaking burdens, and show us how we might be of assistance to them.
Lord, have mercy.

Invitation to the Lord's Prayer
Asking God's blessing on the work of farmers, industry and commerce, let us trust God to sustain their labor.

Collect O merciful Creator, your hand is open wide to satisfy the needs of every living creature: Make us always thankful for your loving providence; and grant that we, remembering the account that we must one day give, may be faithful stewards of your good gifts; through Jesus Christ our Lord, who with you and the Holy Spirit lives and reigns, one God, for ever and ever. Amen.

The Blessing
May the Almighty God, who provides us with every blessing in abundance, so that by always having enough of everything, we may share abundantly in every good work. **Amen.**

Common of National Holidays Morning Prayer

Invitatory The Lord is a God of justice and peace: Come let us worship. (Alleluia)

Hymn God of our fathers *Hymnal 718*

Antiphon 1 God is not ashamed to be called their God; indeed, he has prepared a city for them. (Alleluia)
Psalms are taken from the appointed day in the Psalter.
Antiphon 2 God is able to provide you with every blessing in abundance, so that by always having enough of everything, you may share abundantly. (Alleluia)

Antiphon 3 Love your enemies and pray for those who persecute you. (Alleluia)

Reading One *From the Proper of the Day*

Responsory One (Ps. 145: 8-9))
The Lord is gracious and full of compassion
    — **slow to anger and of great kindness.**
The Lord is loving to everyone
    — **slow to anger and of great kindness.**
Glory to the Father and to the Son and to the Holy Spirit.
The Lord is gracious and full of compassion
    — **slow to anger and of great kindness.**

Canticle – Song of the Trustful   *Benedictus vir*
(Jeremiah 17: 7-8)

Antiphon Those of steadfast mind you keep in peace— in peace because they trust in you. (Alleluia.)

Blessed are those who trust in the LORD, *
    whose trust is the LORD.

They shall be like a tree planted by water, *
    sending out its roots by the stream.

It shall not fear when heat comes, *
    and its leaves shall stay green.

In the year of drought it is not anxious, *
    and it does not cease to bear fruit.

Antiphon Those of steadfast mind you keep in peace— in peace because they trust in you. (Alleluia.)

Reading Two *From the Proper of the Day*

Responsory Two (Ps 33:5, 1)
The Lord loves righteousness and justice
    — **the loving kindness of the Lord fills the whole earth.**
It is good for the just to sing praises
    — **the loving kindness of the Lord fills the whole earth.**
Glory to the Father and to the Son and to the Holy Spirit.
The Lord loves righteousness and justice
    — **the loving kindness of the Lord fills the whole earth.**

Benedictus Antiphon You have multiplied the nation, you have increased its joy; they rejoice before you as with joy at the harvest. (Alleluia)

Litany
We thank you for the natural majesty and beauty of this land. They restore us, though we often destroy them.
Lord, have mercy.
We thank you for the great resources of this nation. They make us rich, though we often exploit them.
Christ, have mercy.
We thank you for the men and women who have made this country strong. They are models for us, though we often fall short of them.
Lord, have mercy.

Invitation to the Lord's Prayer
Let us pray with the Prince of Peace that we may reverently use our freedom, and that he help us to employ it in the maintenance of justice in our communities and among the nations.

Collect *From the Proper of the Day or the following*
For Social Justice
Almighty God, who created us in your own image: Grant us grace fearlessly to contend against evil and to make no peace with oppression; and, that we may reverently use our freedom, help us to employ it in the maintenance of justice in our communities and among the nations, to the glory of your holy Name; through Jesus Christ our Lord, who lives and reigns with you and the Holy Spirit, one God, now and for ever. Amen.

The Blessing
May we imitate our God who executes justice for the orphan and the widow, and who loves the strangers, providing them with food and clothing. **Amen.**

Common of National Holidays Noonday Prayer

Hymn God bless our native land *Hymnal 716*

Antiphon Proclaim liberty to the captives, and release to the prisoners. (Alleluia)
Psalms are taken from the appointed day in the Psalter.

Reading John 14:27
Peace I leave with you; my peace I give to you. I do not give to you as the world gives. Do not let your hearts be troubled, and do not let them be afraid.

Verse and Response
O Lord, you will ordain peace for us. (Alleluia)
For all that we have done, you have done for us. (Alleluia)

Collect *From the Proper of the Day*

Common of National Holidays Evening Prayer

Hymn O day of peace *Hymnal 597*

Antiphon 1 You judge the peoples with equity and guide the nations upon earth. (Alleluia)
Psalms are taken from the appointed day in the Psalter.
Antiphon 2 The Lord guards the paths of justice and preserves the way of his faithful ones. (Alleluia)
Antiphon 3 Walk in the way of the good, and keep to the paths of the just. (Alleluia)

Reading *From the Proper of the Day*

Responsory (Ps. 33:12, 8)
Blessed is the nation whose God is the Lord
   — blessed the people he has chosen to be his own.
Let all who dwell in the world stand in awe of the Lord
   — blessed the people he has chosen to be his own.
Glory to the Father and to the Son and to the Holy Spirit.
Blessed is the nation whose God is the Lord
   — blessed the people he has chosen to be his own.

Magnificat Antiphon They shall beat their swords into plowshares, and their spears into pruning hooks; nation shall not lift up sword against nation, neither shall they learn war any more. (Alleluia)

Litany
We thank you for the torch of liberty which has been lit in this land. It has drawn people from every nation, though we have often hidden from its light.
Lord, have mercy.

We thank you for the faith we have inherited in all its rich variety. It sustains our life, though we have been faithless again and again.
Christ, have mercy.
We thank you for the lives of generations of people from diverse nations who contributed to this nation, grant them and all the departed a place of peace.
Lord, have mercy.

Invitation to the Lord's Prayer
Let us pray with the Prince of Peace that we may reverently use our freedom, and that he may help us to employ it in the maintenance of justice in our communities and among the nations.

Collect *From the Proper of the Day*

The Blessing
May God strengthen us to do justice, and to love kindness, and to walk humbly with our God. **Amen.**

Common of the Faithful Departed Morning Prayer

Invitatory Come let us worship God, for whom all are alive. (Alleluia)

Hymn All my hope on God is founded *Hymnal 665*

Psalm 51 *Miserere mei, Deus*
Antiphon Make me hear of joy and gladness, that the body you have broken may rejoice. (Alleluia)

1 Have mercy on me, O God,
 according to your loving-kindness; *
  in your great compassion blot out my offenses.

2 Wash me through and through from my wickedness *
  and cleanse me from my sin.

3 For I know my transgressions, *
  and my sin is ever before me..

4 Against you only have I sinned *
  and done what is evil in your sight.

5 And so you are justified when you speak *
  and upright in your judgment.

6 Indeed, I have been wicked from my birth, *
  a sinner from my mother's womb.

7 For behold, you look for truth deep within me, *
    and will make me understand wisdom secretly.

8 Purge me from my sin, and I shall be pure; *
    wash me, and I shall be clean indeed.

9 Make me hear of joy and gladness, *
    that the body you have broken may rejoice.

10 Hide your face from my sins *
    and blot out all my iniquities.

11 Create in me a clean heart, O God, *
    and renew a right spirit within me.

12 Cast me not away from your presence *
    and take not your holy Spirit from me.

13 Give me the joy of your saving help again *
    and sustain me with your bountiful Spirit.

14 I shall teach your ways to the wicked, *
    and sinners shall return to you.

15 Deliver me from death, O God, *
    and my tongue shall sing of your righteousness,
    O God of my salvation.

16 Open my lips, O Lord, *
    and my mouth shall proclaim your praise.

17 Had you desired it, I would have offered sacrifice, *
    but you take no delight in burnt-offerings.

18 The sacrifice of God is a troubled spirit; *
    a broken and contrite heart, O God, you will not despise.

19 Be favorable and gracious to Zion, *
    and rebuild the walls of Jerusalem.

20 Then you will be pleased with the appointed sacrifices,
    with burnt-offerings and oblations; *
        then shall they offer young bullocks upon your altar.

Antiphon Make me hear of joy and gladness, that the body you have broken may rejoice. (Alleluia)

Psalm 65 *Te decet hymnus*

Antiphon To you that hear prayer shall all flesh come, because of their transgressions. (Alleluia)

1 You are to be praised, O God, in Zion; *
    to you shall vows be performed in Jerusalem.

2 To you that hear prayer shall all flesh come, *
    because of their transgressions.

3 Our sins are stronger than we are, *
    but you will blot them out.

4 Blessed are they whom you choose
  and draw to your courts to dwell there! *
    they will be satisfied by the beauty of your house,
    by the holiness of your temple.

5 Awesome things will you show us in your righteousness,
  O God of our salvation, *
    O Hope of all the ends of the earth
    and of the seas that are far away.

6 You make fast the mountains by your power; *
    they are girded about with might.

7 You still the roaring of the seas, *
    the roaring of their waves,
    and the clamor of the peoples.

8 Those who dwell at the ends of the earth
  will tremble at your marvelous signs; *
    you make the dawn and the dusk to sing for joy.

9 You visit the earth and water it abundantly;
  you make it very plenteous; *
    the river of God is full of water.

10 You prepare the grain, *
    for so you provide for the earth.

11 You drench the furrows and smooth out the ridges; *
    with heavy rain you soften the ground and bless its increase.

12 You crown the year with your goodness, *
    and your paths overflow with plenty.

13 May the fields of the wilderness be rich for grazing, *
    and the hills be clothed with joy.

14 May the meadows cover themselves with flocks,
   and the valleys cloak themselves with grain; *
      let them shout for joy and sing.

Antiphon To you that hear prayer shall all flesh come, because of their transgressions. (Alleluia)

Psalm 63 *Deus, Deus meus*

Antiphon My soul clings to you; your right hand holds me fast. (Alleluia)

1 O God, you are my God; eagerly I seek you; *
   my soul thirsts for you, my flesh faints for you,
      as in a barren and dry land where there is no water.

2 Therefore I have gazed upon you in your holy place, *
      that I might behold your power and your glory.

3 For your loving-kindness is better than life itself; *
      my lips shall give you praise.

4 So will I bless you as long as I live *
      and lift up my hands in your Name.

5 My soul is content, as with marrow and fatness, *
      and my mouth praises you with joyful lips,

6 When I remember you upon my bed, *
      and meditate on you in the night watches.

7 For you have been my helper, *
      and under the shadow of your wings I will rejoice.

8 My soul clings to you; *
      your right hand holds me fast.

9 May those who seek my life to destroy it *
      go down into the depths of the earth;

10 Let them fall upon the edge of the sword, *
      and let them be food for jackals.

11 But the king will rejoice in God;
   all those who swear by him will be glad; *
      for the mouth of those who speak lies shall be stopped.

Antiphon My soul clings to you; your right hand holds me fast. (Alleluia)

Reading One Isaiah 25: 6-9

Responsory One (Job 19:25-26)
I know that my Redeemer lives
   − In my body, I shall see God.
I myself shall see and my eyes behold him.
   − In my body, I shall see God.
Glory to the Father, and to the Son and to the Holy Spirit.
I know that my Redeemer lives
   − In my body, I shall see God.

Canticle − Song of The Resurrection *Nemo enim*
(Romans 14: 7-10)

Antiphon I am Resurrection and I am Life. (Alleluia.)

We do not live to ourselves, *
   and we do not die to ourselves.

If we live, we live to the Lord, *
   and if we die, we die to the Lord.

So then, whether we live or whether we die, *
   we are the Lord's.

For to this end Christ died and lived again, *
   so that he might be Lord of both the dead and the living.

Antiphon I am Resurrection and I am Life. (Alleluia.)

Reading Two John 11: 21-27

Responsory Two
You who raised Lazarus, already corrupted, from the grave
   − grant them rest, O Lord, and a place of forgiveness.
You shall come to judge the living and the dead and the world by fire
   − grant them rest, O Lord, and a place of forgiveness.
Glory to the Father, and to the Son and to the Holy Spirit.
You who raised Lazarus, already corrupted, from the grave
   − grant them rest, O Lord, and a place of forgiveness.

Benedictus Antiphon I am the resurrection and the life. Those who believe in me, even though they die, will live, and everyone who lives and believes in me will never die. (Alleluia)

Litany
God of all light, at break of day, we rejoice in the resurrection of Christ; bring all the departed into the light of Christ's risen life.
Lord, have mercy.
Lord Christ, you wept at the tomb of your friend Lazarus; comfort all who mourn.
Christ have mercy.
You raised the dead to life; give eternal life to all the departed.
Lord, have mercy.

Invitation to the Lord's Prayer We pray with Christ, the Resurrection and the Life, to bring all the dead to behold the Father's face.

Collect O God, the Maker and Redeemer of all believers: Grant to the faithful departed the unsearchable benefits of the passion of your Son; that on the day of his appearing they may be manifested as your children; through Jesus Christ our Lord, who lives and reigns with you and the Holy Spirit, one God, now and for ever. Amen.

The Blessing
May the God of peace, who brought back from the dead our Lord Jesus, the great shepherd of the sheep, by the blood of the eternal covenant, make us perfect in everything good so that we may do his will, working among us that which is pleasing in his sight. **Amen.**

Common of the Faithful Departed Noonday Prayer

Hymn From glory to glory advancing *Hymnal 326*

Psalm 70 *Deus, in adjutorium*
Antiphon I am poor and needy; come to me speedily, O God. (Alleluia)

1 Be pleased, O God, to deliver me; *
 O LORD, make haste to help me.

2 Let those who seek my life be ashamed
 and altogether dismayed; *
  let those who take pleasure in my misfortune
  draw back and be disgraced.

3 Let those who say to me "Aha!" and gloat over me turn back, *
  because they are ashamed.

4 Let all who seek you rejoice and be glad in you; *
  let those who love your salvation say for ever,
  "Great is the LORD!"

5 But as for me, I am poor and needy; *
    come to me speedily, O God.

6 You are my helper and my deliverer; *
    O Lord, do not tarry.

Psalm 85 *Benedixisti, Domine*

1 You have been gracious to your land, O Lord, *
    you have restored the good fortune of Jacob.

2 You have forgiven the iniquity of your people *
    and blotted out all their sins.

3 You have withdrawn all your fury *
    and turned yourself from your wrathful indignation.

4 Restore us then, O God our Savior; *
    let your anger depart from us.

5 Will you be displeased with us for ever? *
    will you prolong your anger from age to age?

6 Will you not give us life again, *
    that your people may rejoice in you?

7 Show us your mercy, O Lord, *
    and grant us your salvation.

8 I will listen to what the Lord God is saying, *
    for he is speaking peace to his faithful people
    and to those who turn their hearts to him.

9 Truly, his salvation is very near to those who fear him, *
    that his glory may dwell in our land.

10 Mercy and truth have met together; *
    righteousness and peace have kissed each other.

11 Truth shall spring up from the earth, *
    and righteousness shall look down from heaven.

12 The Lord will indeed grant prosperity, *
    and our land will yield its increase.

13 Righteousness shall go before him, *
    and peace shall be a pathway for his feet.

Psalm 86 *Inclina, Domine*

1 Bow down your ear, O LORD, and answer me, *
    for I am poor and in misery.

2 Keep watch over my life, for I am faithful; *
    save your servant who puts his trust in you.

3 Be merciful to me, O LORD, for you are my God; *
    I call upon you all the day long.

4 Gladden the soul of your servant, *
    for to you, O LORD, I lift up my soul.

5 For you, O LORD, are good and forgiving, *
    and great is your love toward all who call upon you.

6 Give ear, O LORD, to my prayer, *
    and attend to the voice of my supplications.

7 In the time of my trouble I will call upon you, *
    for you will answer me.

8 Among the gods there is none like you, O LORD, *
    nor anything like your works.

9 All nations you have made will come
  and worship you, O LORD, *
    and glorify your Name.

10 For you are great;
   you do wondrous things; *
    and you alone are God.

11 Teach me your way, O LORD,
   and I will walk in your truth; *
    knit my heart to you that I may fear your Name.

12 I will thank you, O LORD my God, with all my heart, *
    and glorify your Name for evermore.

13 For great is your love toward me; *
    you have delivered me from the nethermost Pit.

14 The arrogant rise up against me, O God,
   and a band of violent men seeks my life; *
    they have not set you before their eyes.

15 But you, O LORD, are gracious and full of compassion, *
    slow to anger, and full of kindness and truth.

16 Turn to me and have mercy upon me; *
      give your strength to your servant;
      and save the child of your handmaid.

17 Show me a sign of your favor,
      so that those who hate me may see it and be ashamed; *
      because you, O LORD, have helped me and comforted me.

Antiphon I am poor and needy; come to me speedily, O God. (Alleluia)

Reading 1 John 3: 1-2
See what love the Father has given us, that we should be called children of God; and that is what we are. The reason the world does not know us is that it did not know him. Beloved, we are God's children now; what we will be has not yet been revealed. What we do know is this: when he is revealed, we will be like him, for we will see him as he is.

Verse and Response
I believe that I shall see the goodness of the Lord. (Alleluia)
In the land of the living. (Alleluia)

Collect Lord Jesus Christ, by your death you took away the sting of death: Grant to us your servants so to follow in faith where you have led the way, that we may at length fall asleep peacefully in you and wake up in your likeness; for your tender mercies' sake. Amen.

Common of the Faithful Departed Evening Prayer

Hymn Christ the Victorious, give to your servants *Hymnal 358*

Psalm 116 *Dilexi, quoniam*

Antiphon I will walk in the presence of the Lord in the land of the living. (Alleluia)

1 I love the LORD, because he has heard
    the voice of my supplication, *
      because he has inclined his ear to me
      whenever I called upon him.

2 The cords of death entangled me;
    the grip of the grave took hold of me; *
      I came to grief and sorrow.

3 Then I called upon the Name of the LORD: *
      "O LORD, I pray you, save my life."

4 Gracious is the LORD and righteous; *
     our God is full of compassion.

5 The LORD watches over the innocent; *
     I was brought very low, and he helped me.

6 Turn again to your rest, O my soul, *
     for the LORD has treated you well.

7 For you have rescued my life from death, *
     my eyes from tears, and my feet from stumbling.

8 I will walk in the presence of the LORD *
     in the land of the living.

9 I believed, even when I said,
   "I have been brought very low." *
     In my distress I said, "No one can be trusted."

10 How shall I repay the LORD *
     for all the good things he has done for me?

11 I will lift up the cup of salvation *
     and call upon the Name of the LORD.

12 I will fulfill my vows to the LORD *
     in the presence of all his people.

13 Precious in the sight of the LORD *
     is the death of his servants.

14 O LORD, I am your servant; *
     I am your servant and the child of your handmaid;
     you have freed me from my bonds.

15 I will offer you the sacrifice of thanksgiving *
     and call upon the Name of the LORD.

16 I will fulfill my vows to the LORD *
     in the presence of all his people,

17 In the courts of the LORD'S house, *
     in the midst of you, O Jerusalem.
     Hallelujah!

Antiphon I will walk in the presence of the Lord in the land of the living. (Alleluia)

Psalm 121 *Levavi oculos*

Antiphon The Lord shall preserve you from all evil; it is he who shall keep you safe. (Alleluia)

1 I lift up my eyes to the hills; *
 from where is my help to come?

2 My help comes from the LORD, *
 the maker of heaven and earth.

3 He will not let your foot be moved *
 and he who watches over you will not fall asleep.

4 Behold, he who keeps watch over Israel *
 shall neither slumber nor sleep;

5 The LORD himself watches over you; *
 the LORD is your shade at your right hand,

6 So that the sun shall not strike you by day, *
 nor the moon by night.

7 The LORD shall preserve you from all evil; *
 it is he who shall keep you safe.

8 The LORD shall watch over your going out
 and your coming in, *
 from this time forth for evermore.

Antiphon The Lord shall preserve you from all evil; it is he who shall keep you safe. (Alleluia)

Psalm 130 *De profundis*

Antiphon If you, Lord, were to note what is done amiss, O LORD, who could stand? (Alleluia)

1 Out of the depths have I called to you, O LORD;
 LORD, hear my voice; *
 let your ears consider well the voice of my supplication.

2 If you, LORD, were to note what is done amiss, *
 O LORD, who could stand?

3 For there is forgiveness with you; *
 therefore you shall be feared.

4 I wait for the LORD; my soul waits for him; *
 in his word is my hope.

5 My soul waits for the LORD,
   more than watchmen for the morning, *
      more than watchmen for the morning.

6 O Israel, wait for the LORD, *
      for with the LORD there is mercy;

7 With him there is plenteous redemption, *
      and he shall redeem Israel from all their sins.

Antiphon If you, Lord, were to note what is done amiss, O LORD, who could stand? (Alleluia)

Reading Revelation 7: 9-17

Responsory
Lord where shall I hide myself from you face?
   — **For in my life I have greatly sinned.**
I am afraid because of my transgressions.
   — **For in my life I have greatly sinned.**
Glory to the Father, and to the Son and to the Holy Spirit.
Lord where shall I hide myself from you face?
   — **For in my life I have greatly sinned.**

Magnificat Antiphon Blessed are the dead who from now on die in the Lord. They will rest from their labors, for their deeds follow them. (Alleluia)

Litany
In the midst of life we are in death; from whom can we seek help?
From you alone, O Lord, who by our sins are justly angered.
Lord, have mercy.
Lord, you know the secrets of our hearts; shut not your ears to our prayers but spare us O Lord.
Christ, have mercy.
O worthy and eternal Judge, do not let the pains of death turn us away from you at our last hour.
Lord, have mercy.

Invitation to the Lord's Prayer We pray with Christ, the Resurrection and the Life, to bring all the dead to behold the Father's face.

Collect Lord Jesus Christ, Son of the living God, we pray you to set your passion, cross, and death between your judgment and our souls, now and in the hour of our death. Give mercy and grace to the living; pardon and rest to the dead; to your holy Church peace and concord; and to us sinners everlasting life and glory; for with the Father and the Holy Spirit you live and reign, one God, now and for ever. Amen.

The Blessing
May God, who is rich in mercy, out of the great love with which he loved us even when we were dead through our trespasses, make us alive together with Christ. **Amen.**

Lectionary for the Daily Office

Concerning the Daily Office Lectionary

The Daily Office Lectionary is arranged in a two-year cycle. Year One begins on the First Sunday of Advent preceding odd-numbered years, and Year Two begins on the First Sunday of Advent preceding even-numbered years. (Thus, on the First Sunday of Advent, 1976, the Lectionary for Year One is begun.) Three Readings are provided for each Sunday and weekday in each of the two years. Two of the Readings may be used in the morning and one in the evening; or, if the Office is read only once in the day, all three Readings may be used. When the Office is read twice in the day, it is suggested that the Gospel Reading be used in the evening in Year One, and in the morning in Year Two. If two Readings are desired at both Offices, the Old Testament Reading for the alternate year is used as the First Reading at Evening Prayer. When more than one Reading is used at an Office, the first is always from the Old Testament (or the Apocrypha). When a Major Feast interrupts the sequence of Readings, they may be re-ordered by lengthening, combining, or omitting some of them, to secure continuity or avoid repetition. Any Reading may be lengthened at discretion. Suggested lengthenings are shown in parentheses. In this Lectionary (except in the weeks from 4 Advent to 1 Epiphany, and Palm Sunday to 2 Easter), the Psalms are arranged in a seven-week pattern which recurs throughout the year, except for appropriate variations in Lent and Easter Season. In the citation of the Psalms, those for the morning are given first, and then those for the evening. At the discretion of the officiant, however, any of the Psalms appointed for a given day may be used in the morning or in the evening. Likewise, Psalms appointed for any day may be used on any other day in the same week, except on major Holy Days.

Year One

The Season of Lent
Ash Wednesday 95 *For the Invitatory* & 32, 143 | | 102, 130
Jonah 3:1—4:11 Heb. 12:1-14 Luke 18:9-14
Thursday 37:1-18 | | 37:19-42
Deut. 7:6-11 Titus 1:1-16 John 1:29-34
Friday 95 *For the Invitatory* & 31 | | 35
Deut. 7:12-16 Titus 2:1-15 John 1:35-42
Saturday 30, 32 | | 42, 43
Deut. 7:17-26 Titus 3:1-15 John 1:43-51

Week of 1 Lent
Sunday 63:1-8(9-11), 98 | | 103
Deut. 8:1-10 1 Cor. 1:17-31 Mark 2:18-22
Monday 41, 52 | | 44
Deut. 8:11-20 Heb. 2:11-18 John 2:1-12
Tuesday 45 | | 47, 48
Deut. 9:4-12 Heb. 3:1-11 John 2:13-22
Wednesday 119:49-72 | | 49, [53]
Deut. 9:13-21 Heb. 3:12-19 John 2:23—3:15
Thursday 50 | | [59, 60] or 19, 46
Deut. 9:23—10:5 Heb. 4:1-10 John 3:16-21
Friday 95* For the Invitatory & 40, 54 | | 51
Deut. 10:12-22 Heb. 4:11-16 John 3:22-36
Saturday 55 | | 138, 139:1-17(18-23)
Deut. 11:18-28 Heb. 5:1-10 John 4:1-26

Week of 2 Lent
Sunday 24, 29 | | 8, 84
Jer. 1:1-10 1 Cor. 3:11-23 Mark 3:31—4:9
Monday 56, 57, [58] | | 64, 65
Jer. 1:11-19 Rom. 1:1-15 John 4:27-42
Tuesday 61, 62 | | 68:1-20(21-23)24-36
Jer. 2:1-13 Rom. 1:16-25 John 4:43-54
Wednesday 72 | | 119:73-96
Jer. 3:6-18 Rom. 1:28—2:11 John 5:1-18
Thursday [70], 71 | | 74
Jer. 4:9-10, 19-28 Rom. 2:12-24 John 5:19-29
Friday 95 *For the Invitatory* & 69:1-23(24-30)31-38 | | 73
Jer. 5:1-9 Rom. 2:25—3:18 John 5:30-47
Saturday 75, 76 | | 23, 27
Jer. 5:20-31 Rom. 3:19-31 John 7:1-13

Week of 3 Lent
Sunday 93, 96 | 34
Jer. 6:9-15 1 Cor. 6:12-20 Mark 5:1-20
Monday 80 | 77, [79]
Jer. 7:1-15 Rom. 4:1-12 John 7:14-36
Tuesday 78:1-39 | 78:40-72
Jer. 7:21-34 Rom. 4:13-25 John 7:37-52
Wednesday 119:97-120 | 81, 82
Jer. 8:18—9:6 Rom. 5:1-11 John 8:12-20
Thursday [83] or 42, 43 | 85, 86
Jer. 10:11-24 Rom. 5:12-21 John 8:21-32
Friday 95* *For the Invitatory* & 88 | 91, 92
Jer. 11:1-8,14-20 Rom. 6:1-11 John 8:33-47
Saturday 87, 90 | 136
Jer. 13:1-11 Rom. 6:12-23 John 8:47-59

Week of 4 Lent
Sunday 66, 67 | 19, 46
Jer. 14:1-9,17-22 Gal. 4:21—5:1 Mark 8:11-21
Monday 89:1-18 | 89:19-52
Jer. 16:10-21 Rom. 7:1-12 John 6:1-15
Tuesday 97, 99, [100] | 94, [95]
Jer. 17:19-27 Rom. 7:13-25 John 6:16-27
Wednesday 101, 109:1-4(5-19)20-30 | 119:121-144
Jer. 18:1-11 Rom. 8:1-11 John 6:27-40
Thursday 69:1-23(24-30)31-38 | 73
Jer. 22:13-23 Rom. 8:12-27 John 6:41-51
Friday 95* *For the Invitatory* & 102 | 107:1-32
Jer. 23:1-8 Rom. 8:28-39 John 6:52-59
Saturday 107:33-43, 108:1-6(7-13) | 33
Jer. 23:9-15 Rom. 9:1-18 John 6:60-71

Week of 5 Lent
Sunday 118 | 145
Jer. 23:16-32 1 Cor. 9:19-27 Mark 8:31—9:1
Monday 31 | 35
Jer. 24:1-10 Rom. 9:19-23 John 9:1-17
Tuesday [120], 121, 122, 123 | 124, 125, 126, [127]
Jer. 25:8-17 Rom. 10:1-13 John 9:18-41
Wednesday 119:145-176 | 128, 129, 130
Jer. 25:30-38 Rom. 10:14-21 John 10:1-18
Thursday 131, 132, [133] | 140, 142
Jer. 26:1-16 Rom. 11:1-12 John 10:19-42
Friday 95* *For the Invitatory* & 22 | 141, 143:1-11(12)
Jer. 29:1,4-13 Rom. 11:13-24 John 11:1-27, or 12:1-10
Saturday 137:1-6(7-9), 144 | 42, 43
Jer. 31:27-34 Rom. 11:25-36 John 11:28-44, or 12:37-50

Holy Week *(See notes on readings)*
Palm Sunday 24, 29 □ 103
Zech. 9:9-12** 1 Tim. 6:12-16**
Zech. 12:9-11; 13:1,7-9*** Matt. 21:12-17***
Monday 51:1-18(19-20) □ 69:1-23
Jer. 12:1-16 Phil. 3:1-14 John 12:9-19
Tuesday 6, 12 □ 94
Jer. 15:10-21 Phil. 3:15-21 John 12:20-26
Wednesday 55 □ 74
Jer. 17:5-10, 14-17 Phil. 4:1-13 John 12:27-26
Maundy Thursday 102 □ 142, 143
Jer. 20:7-11 1 Cor. 10:14-17; 11:27-32 John 17:1-11(12-26)
Good Friday 95* *For the Invitatory* & 22 □ 40:1-14(15-19),54
Wisdom 1:16—2:1,12-22 1 Peter 1:10-20 John 13:36-38**
or Gen. 22:1-14 John 19:38-42***
Holy Saturday 95* *For the Invitatory* * & 88 □ 27
Job 19:21-27a Heb. 4:1-16** Rom. 8:1-11***
**Intended for use in the morning   ***Intended for use in the evening*

Easter Week *(See notes on readings)*
Easter Day 148, 149, 150 □ 113, 114, or 118
Exod. 12:1-14** ——— John 1:1-18**
Isa. 51:9-11*** Luke 24:13-35, or John 20:19-23***
Monday 93, 98 □ 66
Jonah 2:1-9 Acts 2:14,22-32* John 14:1-14
Tuesday 103 □ 111, 114
Isa. 30:18-21 Acts 2:36-41(42-47)* John 14:15-31
Wednesday 97, 99 □ 115
Micah 7:7-15 Acts 3:1-10* John 15:1-11
Thursday 146, 147 □ 148, 149
Ezek. 37:1-14 Acts 3:11-26* John 15:12-27
Friday 136 □ 118
Dan. 12:1-4,13 Acts 4:1-12* John 16:1-15
Saturday 145 □ 104
Isa. 25:1-9 Acts 4:13-21(22-31)* John 16:16-33
* *Duplicates the First Lesson at the Eucharist. Readings from Year Two may be substituted.*
** *Intended for use in the morning* *** *Intended for use in the evening*

Week of 2 Easter
Sunday 146, 147 □ 111, 112, 113
Isa. 43:8-13 1 Pet. 2:2-10 John 14:1-7
Monday 1, 2, 3 □ 4, 7
Dan. 1:1-21 1 John 1:1-10 John 17:1-11
Tuesday 5, 6 □ 10, 11
Dan. 2:1-16 1 John 2:1-11 John 17:12-19
Wednesday 119:1-24 □ 12, 13, 14
Dan. 2:17-30 1 John 2:12-17 John 17:20-26
Thursday 18:1-20 □ 18:21-50
Dan. 2:31-49 1 John 2:18-29 Luke 3:1-14
Friday 16, 17 □ 134, 135
Dan. 3:1-18 1 John 3:1-10 Luke 3:15-22
Saturday 20, 21:1-7(8-14) □ 110:1-5(6-7), 116, 117
Dan. 3:19-30 1 John 3:11-18 Luke 4:1-13

Week of 3 Easter
Sunday 148, 149, 150 | 114, 115
Dan. 4:1-18 1 Pet. 4:7-11 John 21:15-25
Monday 25 | 9, 15
Dan. 4:19-27 1 John 3:19—4:6 Luke 4:14-30
Tuesday 26, 28 | 36, 39
Dan. 4:28-37 1 John 4:7-21 Luke 4:31-37
Wednesday 38 | 119:25-48
Dan. 5:1-12 1 John 5:1-12 Luke 4:38-44
Thursday 37:1-18 | 37:19-42
Dan. 5:13-30 1 John 5:13-20(21) Luke 5:1-11
Friday 105:1-22 | 105:23-45
Dan. 6:1-15 2 John 1-13 Luke 5:12-26
Saturday 30, 32 | 42, 43
Dan. 6:16-28 3 John 1-15 Luke 5:27-39

Week of 4 Easter
Sunday 63:1-8(9-11), 98 | 103
Wisdom 1:1-15 1 Pet. 5:1-11 Matt. 7:15-29
Monday 41, 52 | 44
Wisdom 1:16—2:11, 21-24 Col. 1:1-14 Luke 6:1-11
Tuesday 45 | 47, 48
Wisdom 3:1-9 Col. 1:15-23 Luke 6:12-26
Wednesday 119:49-72 | 49, [53]
Wisdom 4:16—5:8 Col. 1:24—2:7 Luke 6:27-38
Thursday 50 | [59, 60] or 114, 115
Wisdom 5:9-23 Col. 2:8-23 Luke 6:39-49
Friday 40, 54 | 51
Wisdom 6:12-23 Col. 3:1-11 Luke 7:1-17
Saturday 55 | 138, 139:1-17(18-23)
Wisdom 7:1-14 Col. 3:12-17 Luke 7:18-28(29-30)31-35

Week of 5 Easter
Sunday 24, 29 | 8, 84
Wisdom 7:22—8:1 2 Thess. 2:13-17 Matt. 7:7-14
Monday 56, 57, [58] | 64, 65
Wisdom 9:1, 7-18 Col. (3:18—4:1)2-18 Luke 7:36-50
Tuesday 61, 62 | 68:1-20(21-23)24-36
Wisdom 10:1-4(5-12)13-21 Rom. 12:1-21 Luke 8:1-15
Wednesday 72 | 119:73-96
Wisdom 13:1-9 Rom. 13:1-14 Luke 8:16-25
Thursday [70], 71 | 74
Wisdom 14:27—15:3 Rom. 14:1-12 Luke 8:26-39
Friday 106:1-18 | 106:19-48
Wisdom 16:15—17:1 Rom. 14:13-23 Luke 8:40-56
Saturday 75, 76 | 23, 27
Wisdom 19:1-8, 18-22 Rom. 15:1-13 Luke 9:1-17

Week of 6 Easter
Sunday 93, 96 ¦ 34
Ecclus. 43:1-12, 27-32 1 Tim. 3:14—4:5 Matt. 13:24-34a
Monday 80 ¦ 77, [79]
Deut. 8:1-10 James 1:1-15 Luke 9:18-27
Tuesday 78:1-39 ¦ 78:40-72
 Deut. 8:11-20 James 1:16-27 Luke 11:1-13
Wednesday 119:97-120 ¦ ——
Baruch 3:24-37 James 5:13-18 Luke 12:22-31
Eve of Ascension —— ¦ 68:1-20
2 Kings 2:1-15 Rev. 5:1-14
Ascension Day 8, 47 ¦ 24, 96
Ezek. 1:1-14, 24-28b Heb. 2:5-18 Matt. 28:16-20
Friday 85, 86 ¦ 91, 92
Ezek. 1:28—3:3 Heb. 4:14—5:6 Luke 9:28-36
Saturday 87, 90 ¦ 136
Ezek. 3:4-17 Heb. 5:7-14 Luke 9:37-50
Week of 7 Easter
Sunday 66, 67 ¦ 19, 46
Ezek. 3:16-27 Eph. 2:1-10 Matt. 10:24-33,40-42
Monday 89:1-18 ¦ 89:19-52
Ezek. 4:1-17 Heb. 6:1-12 Luke 9:51-62
Tuesday 97, 99, [100] ¦ 94, [95]
Ezek. 7:10-15,23b-27 Heb. 6:13-20 Luke 10:1-17
Wednesday 101, 109:1-4(5-19)20-30 ¦ 119:121-144
Ezek. 11:14-25 Heb. 7:1-17 Luke 10:17-24
Thursday 105:1-22 ¦ 105:23-45
Ezek. 18:1-4,19-32 Heb. 7:18-28 Luke 10:25-37
Friday 102 ¦ 107:1-32
Ezek. 34:17-31 Heb. 8:1-13 Luke 10:38-42
Saturday 107:33-43, 108:1-6(7-13) ¦ ——
Ezek. 43:1-12 Heb. 9:1-14 Luke 11:14-23
Eve of Pentecost —— ¦ 33
Exod. 19:3-8a,16-20 1 Pet. 2:4-10
The Day of Pentecost 118 ¦ 145
Isa. 11:1-9 1 Cor. 2:1-13 John 14:21-29

Year Two

The Season of Lent
Ash Wednesday 95 *For the Invitatory* & 32, 143 | | 102, 130
Amos 5:6-15 Heb. 12:1-14 Luke 18:9-14
Thursday 37:1-18 | | 37:19-42
Hab. 3:1-10(11-15)16-18 Phil. 3:12-21 John 17:1-8
Friday 95 *For the Invitatory* & 31 | | 35
Ezek. 18:1-4,25-32 Phil. 4:1-9 John 17:9-19
Saturday 30, 32 | | 42, 43
Ezek. 39:21-29 Phil. 4:10-20 John 17:20-26

Week of 1 Lent
Sunday 63:1-8(9-11), 98 | | 103
Dan. 9:3-10 Heb. 2:10-18 John 12:44-50
Monday 41, 52 | | 44
Gen. 37:1-11 1 Cor. 1:1-19 Mark 1:1-13
Tuesday 45 | | 47, 48
Gen. 37:12-24 1 Cor. 1:20-31 Mark 1:14-28
Wednesday 119:49-72 | | 49, [53]
Gen. 37:25-36 1 Cor. 2:1-13 Mark 1:29-45
Thursday 50 | | [59, 60] or 19, 46
Gen. 39:1-23 1 Cor. 2:14—3:15 Mark 2:1-12
Friday 95 *For the Invitatory* & 40, 54 | | 51
Gen. 40:1-23 1 Cor. 3:16-23 Mark 2:13-22
Saturday 55 | | 138, 139:1-17(18-23)
Gen. 41:1-13 1 Cor. 4:1-7 Mark 2:23—3:6

Week of 2 Lent
Sunday 24, 29 | | 8, 84
Gen. 41:14-45 Rom. 6:3-14 John 5:19-24
Monday 56, 57, [58] | | 64, 65
Gen. 41:46-57 1 Cor. 4:8-20(21) Mark 3:7-19a
Tuesday 61, 62 | | 68:1-20(21-23)24-36
Gen. 42:1-17 1 Cor. 5:1-8 Mark 3:19b-35
Wednesday 72 | | 119:73-96
Gen. 42:18-28 1 Cor. 5:9—6:8 Mark 4:1-20
Thursday [70], 71 | | 74
Gen. 42:29-38 1 Cor. 6:12-20 Mark 4:21-34
Friday 95 *For the Invitatory* & 69:1-23(24-30)31-38 | | 73
Gen. 43:1-15 1 Cor. 7:1-9 Mark 4:35-41
Saturday 75, 76 | | 23, 27
Gen. 43:16-34 1 Cor. 7:10-24 Mark 5:1-20

Week of 3 Lent
Sunday 93, 96 ❘ 34
Gen. 44:1-17 Rom. 8:1-10 John 5:25-29
Monday 80 ❘ 77, [79]
Gen. 44:18-34 1 Cor. 7:25-31 Mark 5:21-43
Tuesday 78:1-39 ❘ 78:40-72
Gen. 45:1-15 1 Cor. 7:32-40 Mark 6:1-13
Wednesday 119:97-120 ❘ 81, 82
Gen. 45:16-28 1 Cor. 8:1-13 Mark 6:13-29
Thursday [83] or 42,43 ❘ 85, 86
Gen. 46:1-7,28-34 1 Cor. 9:1-15 Mark 6:30-46
Friday 95 *For the Invitatory* & 88 ❘ 91, 92
Gen. 47:1-26 1 Cor. 9:16-27 Mark 6:47-56
Saturday 87, 90 ❘ 136
Gen. 47:27—48:7 1 Cor. 10:1-13 Mark 7:1-23

Week of 4 Lent
Sunday 66, 67 ❘ 19, 46
Gen. 48:8-22 Rom. 8:11-25 John 6:27-40
Monday 89:1-18 ❘ 89:19-52
Gen. 49:1-28 1 Cor. 10:14—11:1 Mark 7:24-37
Tuesday 97, 99, [100] ❘ 94, [95]
Gen. 49:29—50:14 1 Cor. 11:17-34 Mark 8:1-10
Wednesday 101, 109:1-4(5-19)20-30 ❘ 119:121-144
Gen. 50:15-26 1 Cor. 12:1-11 Mark 8:11-26
Thursday 69:1-23(24-30)31-38 ❘ 73
Exod. 1:6-22 1 Cor. 12:12-26 Mark 8:27—9:1
Friday 95 *For the Invitatory* & 102 ❘ 107:1-32
Exod. 2:1-22 1 Cor. 12:27—13:3 Mark 9:2-13
Saturday 107:33-43, 108:1-6(7-13) ❘ 33
Exod. 2:23—3:15 1 Cor. 13:1-13 Mark 9:14-29

Week of 5 Lent
Sunday 118 ❘ 145
Exod. 3:16—4:12 Rom. 12:1-21 John 8:46-59
Monday 31 ❘ 35
Exod. 4:10-20(21-26)27-31 1 Cor. 14:1-19 Mark 9:30-41
Tuesday [120], 121, 122, 123 ❘ 124, 125, 126, [127]
Exod. 5:1—6:1 1 Cor. 14:20-33a,39-40 Mark 9:42-50
Wednesday 119:145-176 ❘ 128, 129, 130
Exod. 7:8-24 2 Cor. 2:14—3:6 Mark 10:1-16
Thursday 131, 132, [133] ❘ 140, 142
Exod. 7:25—8:19 2 Cor. 3:7-18 Mark 10:17-31
Friday 95 *For the Invitatory* & 22 ❘ 141, 143:1-11(12)
Exod. 9:13-35 2 Cor. 4:1-12 Mark 10:32-45
Saturday 137:1-6(7-9), 144 ❘ 42, 43
Exod. 10:21—11:8 2 Cor. 4:13-18 Mark 10:46-52

Holy Week
Palm Sunday 24, 29 | 103
Zech. 9:9-12** 1 Tim. 6:12-16**
Zech. 12:9-11,13:1,7-9*** Luke 19:41-48***
Monday 51:1-18(19-20) | 69:1-23
Lam. 1:1-2,6-12 2 Cor. 1:1-7 Mark 11:12-25
Tuesday 6, 12 | 94
Lam. 1:17-22 2 Cor. 1:8-22 Mark 11:27-33
Wednesday 55 | 74
Lam. 2:1-9 2 Cor. 1:23—2:11 Mark 12:1-11
Maundy Thursday 102 | 142, 143
Lam. 2:10-18 1 Cor. 10:14-17; 11:27-32 Mark 14:12-25
Good Friday 95 *For the Invitatory* & 22 | 40:1-14(15-19),54
Lam. 3:1-9, 19-33 1 Pet. 1:10-20 John 13:36-38**
John 19:38-42***
Holy Saturday 95** & 88 | 27
Lam. 3:37-58 Heb. 4:1-16** Rom. 8:1-11***
**Intended for use in the morning ***Intended for use in the evening*

Easter Week
Easter Day 148, 149, 150 | 113, 114, or 118
Exod. 12:1-14** ——— John 1:1-18**
Isa. 51:9-11*** Luke 24:13-35, or John 20:19-23***
Monday 93, 98 | 66
Exod. 12:14-27 1 Cor. 15:1-11 Mark 16:1-8
Tuesday 103 | 111, 114
Exod. 12:28-39 1 Cor. 15:12-28 Mark 16:9-20
Wednesday 97, 99 | 115
Exod. 12:40-51 1 Cor. 15:(29)30-41 Matt. 28:1-16
Thursday 146, 147 | 148, 149
Exod. 13:3-10 1 Cor. 15:41-50 Matt. 28:16-20
Friday 136 | 118
Exod. 13:1-2, 11-16 1 Cor. 15:51-58 Luke 24:1-12
Saturday 145 | 104
Exod. 13:17—14:4 2 Cor. 4:16—5:10 Mark 12:18-27
*** Intended for use in the morning *** Intended for use in the evening*

Week of 2 Easter
Sunday 146, 147 | 111, 112, 113
Exod. 14:5-22 1 John 1:1-7 John 14:1-7
Monday 1, 2, 3 | 4, 7
Exod. 14:21-31 1 Pet. 1:1-12 John 14:(1-7)8-17
Tuesday 5, 6 | 10, 11
Exod. 15:1-21 1 Pet. 1:13-25 John 14:18-31
Wednesday 119:1-24 | 12, 13, 14
Exod. 15:22—16:10 1 Pet. 2:1-10 John 15:1-11
Thursday 18:1-20 | 18:21-50
Exod. 16:10-22 1 Pet. 2:11-25 John 15:12-27
Friday 16, 17 | 134, 135
Exod. 16:23-36 1 Pet. 3:13—4:6 John 16:1-15
Saturday 20, 21:1-7(8-14) | 110:1-5(6-7), 116, 117
Exod. 17:1-16 1 Pet. 4:7-19 John 16:16-33

Week of 3 Easter
Sunday 148, 149, 150 ❏ 114, 115
Exod. 18:1-12 1 John 2:7-17 Mark 16:9-20
Monday 25 ❏ 9, 15
Exod. 18:13-27 1 Pet. 5:1-14 Matt. (1:1-17),3:1-6
Tuesday 26, 28 ❏ 36, 39
Exod. 19:1-16 Col. 1:1-14 Matt. 3:7-12
Wednesday 38 ❏ 119:25-48
Exod. 19:16-25 Col. 1:15-23 Matt. 3:13-17
Thursday 37:1-18 ❏ 37:19-42
Exod. 20:1-21 Col. 1:24—2:7 Matt. 4:1-11
Friday 105:1-22 ❏ 105:23-45
Exod. 24:1-18 Col. 2:8-23 Matt. 4:12-17
Saturday 30, 32 ❏ 42, 43
Exod. 25:1-22 Col. 3:1-17 Matt. 4:18-25

Week of 4 Easter
Sunday 63:1-8(9-11),98 ❏ 103
Exod. 28:1-4,30-38 1 John 2:18-29 Mark 6:30-44
Monday 41,52 ❏ 44
Exod. 32:1-20 Col 3:18—4:6(7-18) Matt. 5:1-10
Tuesday 45 ❏ 47,48
Exod. 32:21-34 1 Thess. 1:1-10 Matt. 5:11-16
Wednesday 119:49-72 ❏ 49,[53]
Exod. 33:1-23 1 Thess. 2:1-12 Matt. 5:17-20
Thursday 50 ❏ [59,60] or 114, 115
Exod. 34:1-17 1 Thess. 2:13-20 Matt. 5:21-26
Friday 40,54 ❏ 51
Exod. 34:18-35 1 Thess. 3:1-13 Matt. 5:27-37
Saturday 55 ❏ 138,139:1-17(18-23)
Exod. 40:18-38 1 Thess. 4:1-12 Matt. 5:38-48

Week of 5 Easter
Sunday 24, 29 ❏ 8, 84
Lev. 8:1-13,30-36 Heb. 12:1-14 Luke 4:16-30
Monday 56, 57, [58] ❏ 64, 65
Lev. 16:1-19 1 Thess. 4:13-18 Matt. 6:1-6,16-18
Tuesday 61, 62 ❏ 68:1-20(21-23)24-36
Lev. 16:20-34 1 Thess. 5:1-11 Matt. 6:7-15
Wednesday 72 ❏ 119:73-96
Lev. 19:1-18 1 Thess. 5:12-28 Matt. 6:19-24
Thursday [70], 71 ❏ 74
Lev. 19:26-37 2 Thess. 1:1-12 Matt. 6:25-34
Friday 106:1-18 ❏ 106:19-48
Lev. 23:1-22 2 Thess. 2:1-17 Matt. 7:1-12
Saturday 75, 76 ❏ 23, 27
Lev. 23:23-44 2 Thess. 3:1-18 Matt. 7:13-21

Week of 6 Easter
Sunday 93, 96 | 34
Lev. 25:1-17 James 1:2-8,16-18 Luke 12:13-21
Monday 80 | 77, [79]
Lev. 25:35-55 Col. 1:9-14 Matt. 13:1-16
Tuesday 78:1-39 | 78:40-72
Lev. 26:1-20 1 Tim. 2:1-6 Matt. 13:18-23
Wednesday 119:97-120 | ———
Lev. 26:27-42 Eph. 1:1-10 Matt. 22:41-46
Eve of Ascension ——— | 68:1-20
2 Kings 2:1-15 Rev. 5:1-14
Ascension Day 8, 47 | 24, 96
Dan. 7:9-14 Heb. 2:5-18 Matt. 28:16-20
Friday 85, 86 | 91, 92
1 Sam. 2:1-10 Eph. 2:1-10 Matt. 7:22-27
Saturday 87, 90 | 136
Num. 11:16-17,24-29 Eph. 2:11-22 Matt. 7:28—8:4
Week of 7 Easter
Sunday 66, 67 | 19, 46
Exod. 3:1-12 Heb. 12:18-29 Matt. Luke 10:17-24
Monday 89:1-18 | 89:19-52
Joshua 1:1-9 Eph. 3:1-13 Matt. 8:5-17
Tuesday 97, 99, [100] | 94, [95]
1 Sam. 16:1-13a Eph. 3:14-21 Matt. 8:18-27
Wednesday 101, 109:1-4(5-19)20-30 | 119:121-144
Isa. 4:2-6 Eph. 4:1-16 Matt. 8:28-34
Thursday 105:1-22 | 105:23-45
Zech. 4:1-14 Eph.4:17-32 Matt. 9:1-8
Friday 102 | 107:1-32
Jer. 31:27-34 Eph. 5:1-20 Matt. 9:9-17
Saturday 107:33-43, 108:1-6(7-13) | ———
Ezek. 36:22-27 Eph. 6:10-24 Matt. 9:18-26
Eve of Pentecost ——— | 33
Exod. 19:3-8a,16-20 1 Pet. 2:4-10
The Day of Pentecost 118 | 145
Deut. 16:9-12 Acts 4:18-21,23-33 John 4:19-26

Holy Days

	Morning Prayer	Evening Prayer
St. Matthias February 24	80 1 Samuel 16:1-13 1 John 2:18-25	33 1 Samuel 12:1-5 Acts 20:17-35
St. Joseph March 19	132 Isaiah 63:7-16 Matthew 1:18-25	34 2 Chronicles 6:12-17 Ephesians 3:14-21
Eve of the Annunciation		8, 138 Genesis 3:1-15 Romans 5:12-21 or Galatians 4:1-7
The Annunciation March 25	85, 87 Isaiah 52:7-12 Hebrews 2:5-10	110:1-5(6-7),132 Wisdom 9:1-12 John 1:9-14
St. Mark April 25	145 Ecclesiasticus 2:1-11 Acts 12:25—13:3	67, 96 Isaiah 62:6-12 2 Timothy 4:1-11
SS. Philip & James May 1	119:137-160 Job 23:1-12 John 1:43-51	139 Proverbs 4:7-18 John 12:20-26
Eve of the Visitation		132 Isaiah 11:1-10 Hebrews 2:11-18
The Visitation May 31	72 1 Samuel 1:1-20 Hebrews 3:1-6	146,147 Zechariah 2:10-13 John 3:25-30
St. Barnabas June 11	15, 67 Ecclesiasticus 31:3-11 Acts 4:32-37	19, 146 Job 29:1-16 Acts 9:26-31
Special Occasions **Eve of the Dedication**		48,122 Haggai 2:1-9 1 Corinthians 3:9-17
Anniversary of the Dedication of a Church	132 1 Kings 8:1-13 John 10:22-30	29, 46 1 Kings 8:54-62 Hebrews 10:19-25

	Morning Prayer	Evening Prayer
Eve of the Patronal Feast		27, or 116,117 Isaiah 49:1-13 or Ecclesiasticus 51:6b-12 Ephesians 4:1-13 or Revelation 7:9-17 or Luke 10:38-42
The Patronal Feast	92,93, or 148, 149 Isaiah 52:7-10 or Job 5:8-21 Acts 4:5-13 or Luke 12:1-12	96,97 or 111,112 Jeremiah 31:10-14 or Ecclesiasticus 2:7-18 Romans 12:1-21 or Luke 21:10-19
Eves of Apostles and Evangelists		48, 122, or 84, 150 Isaiah 43:10-15* or Isaiah 52:7-10** Revelation 21:1-4,9-14 or Matthew 9:35—10:4

Devotional Prayers

The Angelus
The Angel of the Lord announced to Mary
And she conceived by the Holy Spirit.
Hail Mary, full of grace, the Lord is with you. Blessed are you among women, and blessed is the fruit of your womb, Jesus
Holy Mary, Mother of God, pray for us sinners, now and at the hour of our death. Amen.

Behold the handmaid of the Lord
Be it unto me according to your word
Hail Mary, full of grace, the Lord is with you. Blessed are you among women, and blessed is the fruit of your womb, Jesus
Holy Mary, Mother of God, pray for us sinners, now and at the hour of our death. Amen.

And the Word was made flesh.
And dwelled among us.
Hail Mary, full of grace, the Lord is with you. Blessed are you among women, and blessed is the fruit of your womb, Jesus
Holy Mary, Mother of God, pray for us sinners, now and at the hour of our death. Amen.

V: Pray for us, O holy Mother of God.
R: *That we may be made worthy of the promises of Christ.*
Let us pray:
Pour your grace into our hearts, O Lord, that we who have known the incarnation of your Son Jesus Christ, announced by an angel to the Virgin Mary, may by his cross and passion be brought to the glory of his resurrection; through Jesus Christ our Lord. *Amen.*

Regina Coeli
O Queen of heaven, rejoice, alleluia.
The Son whom you carried, alleluia,
Has risen according to his word, alleluia.
Pray for us to God, alleluia.

Rejoice and be glad, O Virgin Mary, alleluia!
— For the Lord is risen indeed, alleluia.
Let us pray:
O God, you gave joy to the world through the resurrection of your Son, our Lord Jesus Christ. With the prayers of the Virgin Mary, his Mother, we may obtain the joys of everlasting life, through Jesus Christ our

Lord, who lives and reigns with you, in the unity of the Holy Spirit, one God, now and for ever. Amen.

The General Thanksgiving
Almighty God, Father of all mercies,
we your unworthy servants give you humble thanks
for all your goodness and loving-kindness
to us and to all whom you have made.
We bless you for our creation, preservation,
and all the blessings of this life;
but above all for your immeasurable love
in the redemption of the world by our Lord Jesus Christ;
for the means of grace, and for the hope of glory.
And, we pray, give us such an awareness of your mercies,
that with truly thankful hearts we may show forth your praise,
not only with our lips, but in our lives,
by giving up our selves to your service,
and by walking before you
in holiness and righteousness all our days;
through Jesus Christ our Lord,
to whom, with you and the Holy Spirit,
be honor and glory throughout all ages. Amen.

A Prayer of St. Chrysostom
Almighty God, you have given us grace at this time with one accord to make our common supplication to you; and you have promised through your well-beloved Son that when two or three are gathered together in his Name you will be in the midst of them: Fulfill now, O Lord, our desires and petitions as may be best for us; granting us in this world knowledge of your truth, and in the age to come life everlasting. Amen.

A General Thanksgiving

Accept, O Lord, our thanks and praise for all that you have done for us.
We thank you for the splendor of the whole creation, for the beauty of this world, for the wonder of life, and for the mystery of love.
We thank you for the blessing of family and friends, and for the loving care which surrounds us on every side.
We thank you for setting us at tasks which demand our best efforts, and for leading us to accomplishments which satisfy and delight us.
We thank you also for those disappointments and failures that lead us to acknowledge our dependence on you alone.

Above all, we thank you for your Son Jesus Christ; for the truth of his Word and the example of his life; for his steadfast obedience, by which he overcame temptation; for his dying, through which he overcame death; and for his rising to life again, in which we are raised to the life of your kingdom.

Grant us the gift of your Spirit, that we may know him and make him known; and through him, at all times and in all places, may give thanks to you in all things. Amen.

Acknowledgements

Litany
The Rogation Day litanies from The Diocese of Saskatoon of the Anglican Church of Canada.

Collects
Benedictine Sanctoral
March 21 Transitus of our Holy Father St. Benedict
July 11 Our Holy Father Saint Benedict of Nursia
November 14 All Souls of the Benedictine Order

Monastery of the Glorious Cross, Branfort, Ct.
February 10 Scholastica Evening Prayer I, Morning Prayer,

Scholastica Project of the Monastic Liturgy Forum
February 10 Scholastica Evening Prayer II

Trappist Sanctoral
April 30 The Holy Abbots of Cluny:
May 15 Pachomius
November 13 All Saints of the Benedictine Order
November 19 Mechtild

Original Compositions
August 16 Roger Schutz
August 26 Raimon Panikkar

Canticles for Daily or Weekly Use

Canticle You are God   *Te Deum laudamus*

You are God: we praise you;
You are the Lord: we acclaim you;
You are the eternal Father:
All creation worships you.
To you all angels, all the powers of heaven,
Cherubim and Seraphim, sing in endless praise:
   Holy, holy, holy Lord, God of power and might,
   heaven and earth are full of your glory.
The glorious company of apostles praise you.
The noble fellowship of prophets praise you.
The white-robed army of martyrs praise you.
Throughout the world the holy Church acclaims you;
   Father, of majesty unbounded,
   your true and only Son, worthy of all worship,
   and the Holy Spirit, advocate and guide.
You, Christ, are the king of glory,
the eternal Son of the Father.
When you became man to set us free
you did not shun the Virgin's womb.
You overcame the sting of death
and opened the kingdom of heaven to all believers.
You are seated at God's right hand in glory.
We believe that you will come and be our judge.
   Come then, Lord, and help your people,
   bought with the price of your own blood,
   and bring us with your saints
   to glory everlasting.

The First Book of Common Prayer suggested that during Lent the Te Deum be substituted with the Benedicite. Following that practice, the Benedicite is offered as an alternative Canticle to the Te Deum during Lent.

A Song of Creation *Benedicite omnia opera Domini*

(Song of the Three Young Men, 35-65)
One or more sections of this Canticle may be used. Whatever the selection, it begins with the Invocation and concludes with the Doxology. The Doxology replaces the Gloria for the Canticle

Antiphon The creation itself will be set free from its bondage to decay and will obtain the freedom of the glory of the children of God.

Invocation
Glorify the Lord, all you works of the Lord, *
  praise him and highly exalt him for ever.
In the firmament of his power, glorify the Lord, *
  praise him and highly exalt him for ever.

I *The Cosmic Order*
Glorify the Lord, you angels and all powers of the Lord, *
  O heavens and all waters above the heavens.
Sun and moon and stars of the sky, glorify the Lord, *
  praise him and highly exalt him for ever.

Glorify the Lord, every shower of rain and fall of dew, *
  all winds and fire and heat.
Winter and summer, glorify the Lord, *
 praise him and highly exalt him for ever.

Glorify the Lord, O chill and cold, *
  drops of dew and flakes of snow.
Frost and cold, ice and sleet, glorify the Lord, *
  praise him and highly exalt him for ever.

Glorify the Lord, O nights and days, *
  O shining light and enfolding dark.
Storm clouds and thunderbolts, glorify the Lord, *
  praise him and highly exalt him for ever.

II *The Earth and its Creatures*
Let the earth glorify the Lord, *
  praise him and highly exalt him for ever.

Glorify the Lord, O mountains and hills,
and all that grows upon the earth, *
    praise him and highly exalt him for ever.

Glorify the Lord, O springs of water, seas, and streams, *
    O whales and all that move in the waters.
All birds of the air, glorify the Lord, *
    praise him and highly exalt him for ever.

Glorify the Lord, O beasts of the wild, *
    and all you flocks and herds.
O men and women everywhere, glorify the Lord, *
    praise him and highly exalt him for ever.

III The People of God
Let the people of God glorify the Lord, *
    praise him and highly exalt him for ever.
Glorify the Lord, O priests and servants of the Lord, *
    praise him and highly exalt him for ever.

Glorify the Lord, O spirits and souls of the righteous, *
    praise him and highly exalt him for ever.
You that are holy and humble of heart, glorify the Lord, *
    praise him and highly exalt him for ever.

Doxology
Let us glorify the Lord: Father, Son, and Holy Spirit; *
    praise him and highly exalt him for ever.
In the firmament of his power, glorify the Lord, *
    praise him and highly exalt him for ever.

Antiphon The creation itself will be set free from its bondage to decay and will obtain the freedom of the glory of the children of God.

The Song of Zechariah *Benedictus Dominus Deus*

Luke 1: 68-79

Blessed be the Lord, the God of Israel; *
    he has come to his people and set them free.
He has raised up for us a mighty savior, *
    born of the house of his servant David.
Through his holy prophets he promised of old,
    that he would save us from our enemies, *
    from the hands of all who hate us.
He promised to show mercy to our fathers *
    and to remember his holy covenant.
This was the oath he swore to our father Abraham, *
    to set us free from the hands of our enemies,
Free to worship him without fear, *
    holy and righteous in his sight
    all the days of our life.
You, my child, shall be called the prophet of the Most High, *
    for you will go before the Lord to prepare his way,
To give his people knowledge of salvation *
    by the forgiveness of their sins.
In the tender compassion of our God *
    the dawn from on high shall break upon us,
To shine on those who dwell in darkness
and the shadow of death, *
    and to guide our feet into the way of peace.
Glory to the Father, and to the Son, and to the Holy Spirit: *
    as it was in the beginning, is now, and will be for ever. Amen.

The Song of Mary *Magnificat*

Luke 1:46-55

My soul proclaims the greatness of the Lord,
my spirit rejoices in God my Savior; *
    for he has looked with favor on his lowly servant.
From this day all generations will call me blessed: *
    the Almighty has done great things for me,
    and holy is his Name.
He has mercy on those who fear him *
    in every generation.
He has shown the strength of his arm, *
    he has scattered the proud in their conceit.
He has cast down the mighty from their thrones, *
    and has lifted up the lowly.
He has filled the hungry with good things, *
    and the rich he has sent away empty.
He has come to the help of his servant Israel, *
    for he has remembered his promise of mercy,
The promise he made to our fathers, *
    to Abraham and his children for ever.
Glory to the Father, and to the Son, and to the Holy Spirit: *
    as it was in the beginning, is now, and will be for ever. Amen.

Made in the USA
Las Vegas, NV
03 March 2025